FORTRAN 77
Programming

INTERNATIONAL COMPUTER SCIENCE SERIES

Consulting editors   **A D McGettrick**   University of Strathclyde

                J van Leeuwen   University of Utrecht

SELECTED TITLES IN THE SERIES

An Introduction to Numerical Methods with Pascal   *L V Atkinson and P J Harley*

Comparative Programming Languages   *L B Wilson and R G Clark*

Distributed Systems: Concepts and Design   *G Coulouris and J Dollimore*

Software Prototyping, Formal Methods and VDM   *S Hekmatpour and D Ince*

Numerical Methods in Practice: Using the NAG Library   *T Hopkins and C Phillips*

C Programming in a UNIX Environment   *J Kay and R Kummerfeld*

An Introduction to Functional Programming through Lambda Calculus   *G Michaelson*

Numerical Methods with FORTRAN 77: A Practical Introduction   *L V Atkinson, P J Harley and J D Hudson*

Software Engineering (3rd edn)   *I Sommerville*

High-Level Languages and their Compilers   *D Watson*

Programming in Ada (3rd edn)   *J G P Barnes*

Elements of Functional Programming   *C Reade*

Interactive Computer Graphics: Functional, Procedural and Device-Level Methods   *P Burger and D Gillies*

Software Development with Modula-2   *D Budgen*

Common Lisp Programming for Artificial Intelligence   *T Hasemer and J Domingue*

Program Derivation: The Development of Programs from Specifications   *R G Dromey*

Program Design with Modula-2   *S Eisenbach and C Sadler*

Object-Oriented Programming with Simula   *B Kirkerud*

Parallel Processing: Principles and Practice   *E V Krishnamurthy*

Real-Time Systems and Their Programming Languages   *A Burns and A Wellings*

Programming for Artificial Intelligence: Methods, Tools and Applications   *W Kreutzer and B J McKenzie*

The Programming Process: An introduction using VDM and Pascal   *J T Latham, V J Bush and I D Cottam*

SECOND EDITION

FORTRAN 77
Programming

With an Introduction to the Fortran 90 Standard

T. M. R. ELLIS

Computing Teaching Centre
University of Oxford

ADDISON-WESLEY
PUBLISHING
COMPANY

Wokingham, England · Reading, Massachusetts · Menlo Park, California
New York · Don Mills, Ontario · Amsterdam · Bonn
Sydney · Singapore · Tokyo · Madrid · San Juan

The programs in this book have been included for their instructional value. They have been tested with care but are not guaranteed for any particular purpose. The publisher does not offer any warranties or representations, nor does it accept any liabilities with respect to the programs.

Many of the designations used by manufacturers and sellers to distinguish their products are claimed as trademarks. Addison-Wesley has made every attempt to supply trademark information about manufacturers and their products mentioned in this book. A list of the trademark designations and their owners appears on p. xxii.

Cover designed by Crayon Design of Henley-on-Thames using an illustration of the Forth Bridges reproduced with permission © Scottish Tourist Board and printed by The Riverside Printing Co. (Reading) Ltd.
Typeset by DMD.
Printed and bound in Great Britain by The Bath Press, Avon.

First printed 1990.

British Library Cataloguing in Publication Data
Ellis, T.M.R. (T Miles R)
  Fortran 77 programming: with an introduction to the Fortran 90 standard – 2nd ed. – (International computer science series).
  I. Title   II. Ellis, T.M.R. (T Miles R). Structured approach to Fortran 77 programming   III. Series
  005.13'3

  ISBN 0–201–41638–7

Library of Congress Cataloging in Publication Data
Ellis, T. M. R.
  FORTRAN 77 programming : with an introduction to the Fortran 90 standard / T.M.R. Ellis.
    p.   cm. – (International computer science series)
  Rev. ed. of: A structured approach to FORTRAN 77 programming.
  Includes bibliographical references.
  ISBN 0–201–41638–7
  1. FORTRAN 77 (Computer programming language)   I. Ellis, T.M.R., Structured approach to FORTRAN 77 programming.   II. Title.
III. Series.
QA76.73.F25E43   1990
005.28'2–dc20   89–28993
                                                        CIP

To Maggie
(Őnélküle nem csinálhatom)

Preface

To the teacher

Since the first edition of this book was completed the rate of change in all matters related to computing has grown ever faster, and the computing facilities available to today's students were scarcely even dreamed of then. This second edition has, therefore, been extensively revised and extended to meet the needs of the 1990s.

The most obvious change from the first edition is in the order in which the various features of Fortran are presented, and a few words of explanation are appropriate concerning this.

Order of introduction of Fortran features

The Computing Teaching Centre (CTC) at the University of Oxford, of which I have the privilege to be the first Director, is a central (service) department that teaches courses about all aspects of computing to students of all disciplines, both on a vocational basis and through courses organized in conjunction with their own (academic) departments. This gives the teaching staff of the CTC a unique perspective on the problems encountered by widely differing types of student on different types of courses, and we have spent a great deal of time developing new approaches to teaching in order to obtain the best results. In particular we have found that there are very few textbooks for *any* language that introduce the features of the language in what we have now established to be the best order. This revision of an already widely used textbook has used this experience to create what may be seen by many as a radically new approach, but which is in reality simply a formalization of the methods already developed at the CTC.

The most obvious aspect of this change is that procedures are introduced in Chapter 4, after a discussion of arithmetic and assignment, but before meeting any control structures. This means that procedures are treated as a natural basic programming block and that students learn to develop programs in a modular fashion from the outset. Our experience at the CTC has been that students have far less trouble with procedures if they are introduced at this early stage than if they are left until most of the other features of the language have been met and the students' own programming styles have begun to form.

Another major change from the first edition is that arrays are discussed very much earlier – in Chapter 6, immediately after the introduction of DO loops and before meeting IF statements. Once again, this is a natural place to introduce arrays, since the majority of loops are actually used in conjunction with arrays, and the array (at least in its one-dimensional version) is a very simple concept for most students to understand.

The availability of both arrays and procedures at this relatively early stage means that the examples and exercises can be more realistic than is usually the case in introductory programming texts.

Probably the greatest change in the way in which computers are used since the publication of the first edition has been in the use of files. At that time most student programs were submitted on cards, and the use of files was normally left until towards the end of a programming course. Nowadays cards have disappeared, and programs are normally typed at a keyboard using some form of editor and then input from there. One result of this has been that the provision of data in a file, and the output of results to one, have become the normal procedures for students rather than the exceptions. The third major change in ordering from the first edition, therefore, is that the discussion of sequential files has been brought forward to the end of Part I, immediately after the introduction of formatted input and output. (In keeping with the philosophy of the first edition, and after several more years of experience, I see no point in cluttering up the early stages of learning to program with the full Fortran input/output facilities; list-directed input/output is extremely easy to use and provides all that the student needs for these crucial early stages.)

Numerical methods

Another major change is the introduction of two chapters devoted to a discussion of numerical methods. The first of these, Chapter 11, opens Part II of the book and is concerned with a fairly detailed discussion of the problems of precision and round-off errors in calculations and some of the ways in which these can be minimized. This chapter first introduces the concept of DOUBLE PRECISION variables, and includes worked examples of two common numerical procedures: the fitting of a straight line to a set of data points using a least-squares approximation; and an iterative solution of non-linear equations, using the bisection method. The final section of this chapter introduces COMPLEX variables and illustrates their use by means of a program for use in designing a band-pass electronic filter.

Chapter 18 is also devoted to numerical methods, and contains descriptions of a number of useful techniques for solving common problems such as the solution of non-linear equations, the solution of sets of simultaneous linear equations, the fitting of cubic splines and similar curves to a set of data points, and the integration of a function. All these techniques are accompanied by fully worked examples, which, together with those in Chapter 11, provide a useful basic numerical analysis library.

These two chapters and the last section of Chapter 14, which describes how to carry out the normal vector and matrix arithmetic operations using Fortran arrays, can be omitted by students who do not have a mathematical or scientific bias, as they are self-contained and the rest of the book does not use any of the matters discussed within them. This book is, therefore, equally valid for those other groups of students, such as social scientists, who also wish to learn Fortran.

Fortran 90

The final major change from the first edition is related to the evolution of the Fortran language. At the time of writing, the ANSI X3J3 committee, of which I am a member, has completed the final draft of the next ANSI Standard Fortran, while the ISO–IEC JTC1/SC22/WG5 committee, of which I am also a member, has approved the same document as the next ISO Standard Fortran. This latest version of Fortran, which will be known as Fortran 90, will contain a large number of very substantial extensions to Fortran 77, some of which will have a radical effect upon the way in which Fortran programs will be written in the mid 1990s and beyond. Part III of this book gives an outline of this new Fortran, although it is possible that the final version may differ very slightly from that shown there. Furthermore, throughout the book those areas of Fortran 77 where programming practices may change as a result of the introduction of Fortran 90 are identified by a special **F90** symbol in the margin, identical to the one adjacent to this sentence. It is important to appreciate that *all* of Fortran 77 is included in Fortran 90, so nothing *has* to change; however, the availability of better and more flexible features undoubtedly means that programming styles *will* change in due course as teachers and programmers get to grips with the new features. The F90 logo is simply to draw the reader's attention to areas where change may be appropriate in due course.

F90

Obsolescence in Fortran

A language cannot grow without also changing and, just as there are words and expressions in any natural language that were widely used a hundred years ago but are now completely forgotten, so it is with programming languages. The X3J3 committee has identified a small number of features that are obsolete and should probably be removed from the formal definition of the language at the next revision (or the one after!). Some of these, such as the ASSIGN statement, are not discussed at all in this book, while the others are briefly discussed in Chapter 19, together with a small number of other features, such as the use of real DO loop control variables, which, although not on X3J3's list, should not, in my opinion, be used in modern programs.

Examples and exercises

Programming is an engineering discipline (information engineering), and as such draws on both art and science. As with any other branch of engineering it involves both the learning of the theory and the incorporation of that theory into practical work. In particular, it is impossible to learn to write good programs without plenty of practical experience, and it is also impossible to learn to write *good* programs without the opportunity to see and examine other people's programs.

This book uses the concept of an English-language **structure plan** as an aid to program design, and from its first introduction in Chapter 4 structure plans are developed for all the worked examples. There are 44 such worked examples and over 150 complete programs and subprograms in this book, of which 89 are in the main text and the remainder are included as example solutions to some of the programming exercises. *All of these have been fully tested using the Prospero PC Fortran compiler on a Research Machines Nimbus AX computer.* Since many of these programs, subroutines and functions may be of more general use, there is a special index to them at the end of the book.

Each chapter contains two types of exercise for the student. There is at least one set of **self-test exercises**, which do not require the writing of complete programs and are designed to enable the student to verify his/her understanding of the material covered in the chapter. Answers, with explanations where appropriate, to all of these exercises are included at the end of the book. In addition, at the end of each chapter there are a number of **programming exercises** for the student to write *and test on a computer*. Example solutions to some of these are also included at the end of the book.

Because students from many different subject areas need to learn Fortran, great care has been taken to avoid any bias towards particular scientific or engineering concepts in the worked examples. The purpose of these examples is to help the student to understand how to use particular programming concepts and how to develop well-structured programs using these concepts. Many of these worked examples are, therefore, intended to solve quite general and non-scientific problems that will be understood by students of any background.

The 264 programming exercises, on the other hand, are mainly drawn from a range of different scientific and engineering disciplines, although there are a few more general ones that do not assume any particular prior scientific knowledge. In this way teachers can direct their students to those programming exercises that are most appropriate for their specific background, while ensuring that students with a different background can attempt a different set of exercises.

Instructor's Guide

An Instructor's Guide is also available from the publishers. This contains a short summary of the major points involved in each chapter, with a note of any particular areas where experience shows that students may have problems. The Instructor's Guide also contains example solutions to over 130 of the programming exercises, in addition to those included in this book.

To the student

This book has been written for those with little or no previous computing experience and endeavours to teach you how to plan and write good, well-structured programs using the current version of the Fortran language, commonly referred to as Fortran 77. The book is particularly suitable for undergraduate programming courses in the pure and applied sciences, as well as in many social sciences, and will also be found appropriate for anyone who is interested in learning how to write computer programs for scientific, technical, or other primarily numerical applications.

The impetus for the first edition of this book came primarily from the production, in 1980, of a Fortran 77 videotape teaching course, which has met with considerable success in Great Britain and other countries. The first edition of this book followed broadly the same structure as that course, although it was not directly based on it. This edition, however, approaches the language in a quite different way, based upon 10 years' experience in teaching Fortran 77 and on the changes in attitudes in programming generally. The approach used is pedagogic in nature, and the various features of Fortran 77 are introduced at appropriate stages of the development of your programming skills. A comprehensive index enables the book to be used as a source of reference after you have learned the essential features of the language.

The book consists of two main parts, which cover the whole of the Fortran 77 language, together with a third part consisting of a single chapter that gives an overview of what is to come in Fortran 90 when compilers for that greatly extended version of Fortran become available in the early 1990s. Throughout the first two parts of the book those topics that

F90

will be affected in some way when Fortran 90 becomes available are identified by a special **F90** symbol in the margin, like the one here. This is simply an indication to you that the availability of Fortran 90 may change the way in which that topic will, ideally, be dealt with. It is, however, important to emphasize that *all of Fortran 77 is included in Fortran 90*, and therefore any changes made with the advent of Fortran 90 will be purely voluntary. For example, Fortran 90 includes several extensions to the syntax available for loops, including the addition of an EXIT statement that does *exactly* what I recommend in Section 8.4 when introducing the concept of a conditional DO loop. In that case, therefore, the **F90** symbol indicates that a better way will be available in Fortran 90 – a way, incidentally, that will remove the one major use for the GOTO statement. On the other hand, the **F90** symbols against the title and most of the section headings for Chapter 15 are there because of the inclusion in Fortran 90 of a completely new, and potentially more flexible, approach to global data, in the form of a **module**. This will complement COMMON, *but will not replace it*, but you should be aware of a new approach on the horizon.

Of the two main parts of the book, Part I introduces the fundamental principles of programming and good program design. Chapters 2 and 3 cover the basic structure of a Fortran program and the principles of arithmetic and assignment, before the Chapter 4 introduces the fundamental programming concept of **procedures**. This chapter also introduces the idea of an English-language **structure plan** as an aid to good program design. The next two chapters cover loops and arrays, as a natural development of what has been covered thus far, before Chapter 7 introduces the concept of decision-making. Chapter 8 then shows how this concept can be used to create different types of loop. The final chapters in Part I then examine how the Fortran input/output system works, including an introduction to sequential files.

After a short 'Intermission', during which the development and testing of programs is discussed, the second part of the book examines in depth those more advanced or complicated features of Fortran that are so important in the production of *real* programs. One feature of this part of the book is the inclusion of two chapters (11 and 18) devoted to **numerical methods**. This is an extremely important area for many Fortran programmers, but of no concern at all to others. Those who fall in the latter group, mainly non-scientists, can safely omit these two chapters and possibly the last section of Chapter 14, which discusses vector and matrix manipulation, since none of the matters discussed is referred to elsewhere. After the first of these special chapters, Part II continues with an investigation of the rather complicated area of character handling, followed by a short look at the remaining Fortran data types. The next two chapters continue the investigation of data handling with, first, a further look at arrays, especially those with more than one dimension, and then an examination of the whole area of global data storage. This is followed by a further look at procedures, and an examination of the more abstruse aspects of input/output formatting, before a discussion of the remaining file-handling facilities, including the use of direct-access files.

Chapter 18 is the second chapter devoted to numerical methods, and is followed by the final chapter of Part II, which contains a short description of a number of features of Fortran 77 that have largely fallen into disuse, or that *should* fall into disuse! Because of its longevity, a number of features of earlier versions of Fortran have long been superseded by newer, better features. Nevertheless, they remain part of the language and are briefly discussed in this chapter. As a general rule, none of them should be used in new programs, but they will frequently be found in programs written some years ago.

The book contains a considerable number of examples; nevertheless, one of the most important factors in learning how to write computer programs is practice. In order to help you to develop your skills and to eliminate your faults there are two types of exercise throughout the book:

- At the end of each chapter, and sometimes in the middle of the chapter as well, there is a short **self-test**. This is intended to check your understanding of the material presented in that chapter, or part of a chapter. The answers to *all* the test questions will be found at the end of the book, together with some explanation where this seems appropriate, and you should check your answers with those provided. If they are not (almost) all correct then you should read the chapter, or part of it, again until you are sure that you understand the points that had been missed.

- In addition to the tests, there are a number of **programming problems** at the end of each chapter. These are drawn from a number of different disciplines and there will be a number that are particularly relevant to your own personal background and field of study. *It is essential that you should both write as many as possible of these programs and test them on a computer.* If necessary (and it usually will be!) they should then be corrected and tested again, until such time as they work correctly. At the end of the book are sample solutions for a number of these problems, but I strongly recommend that you do not look at these until *after* you have obtained your own working solution.

Acknowledgements

This book has developed from my experience in teaching and using various dialects of Fortran over the past 25 years, during which time I have received advice, assistance and encouragement from a great many people. I cannot attempt to identify them all, but I do wish to acknowledge a particular debt of gratitude to two people who in very different ways have had a profound influence upon what success I may have had. The first of these is Art Pfeiffer of the Illinois Institute of Technology Research Institute in Chicago, from whom I learned a great deal about good programming practice during a four-month secondment in 1966. The second is the late Herbert Deas, whose words of praise and encouragement after my first lecture course at the University of Sheffield gave me the confidence that every new lecturer needs. To them both I offer my grateful thanks.

The writing of this extensively revised edition was made very much easier by my being granted study leave by the University of Oxford, and I am very grateful for this assistance. That I was able to use this leave to write much of this book at home is due to the generosity of my college, Christ Church, in giving me a grant for the purchase of word-processing equipment, and to Mike Fischer, Managing Director of Research Machines, for enabling me to purchase a Nimbus AX computer identical to the one I use at work for substantially less than the already low educational price.

I must also thank the anonymous reviewers whose comments on an initial draft of this edition have been encouraging and helpful in fine-tuning the manner and the order in which various topics are introduced. I should also like to thank my colleague in the Computing Teaching Centre, Nicola Timbrell, for her very useful comments on a later draft, and also Adam Chambers, Dean Johnson, Stephen Lee and John Woods for their assistance in preparing most of the programming exercises.

The text of the first edition of this book was typed by Sandra Bissatt, and I shall always be grateful for the many long hours she spent alone with her typewriter and my almost illegible handwritten manuscript. In order to create this revised edition the whole book had first to be retyped into a modern word-processing package (WordPerfect) from a copy of the first edition, and I am very grateful to Lynn Burroughs and Emma Collen for doing this so quickly and efficiently. All the subsequent revisions and new material were then easily typed by myself. The programming examples have all been tested on a Nimbus AX, using the Prospero PC Fortran compiler, before being incorporated into the text.

I must also pay tribute to those members of Addison-Wesley who have put so much time and effort into the production of this book, especially Simon Plumtree, Stephen Bishop and, above all, Lynne Balfe, who had to bear the brunt of my frustration when things went wrong, and did so with unfailing good humour and understanding.

Finally I must thank my wife, Margaret, and my children, David, Sarah and Richard, for putting up with my late hours, and for their patience and forbearance yet again during the many evenings and week-ends while this book was being written.

On a lighter note, I feel that I should say a few words about the cover of this book. The cover of the first edition was based on a suggestion made by my wife, and showed the famous bridge that gives its name to Ironbridge in Shropshire – the first in the world to be entirely built using cast iron. As I said in the preface to that edition: 'You can read whatever you like into this – building bridges, developing structures, elegance, style, permanence, etc. – but at least it makes a change from abstract patterns and punched cards!' At the suggestion of some of my colleagues on the ANSI X3J3 Fortran committee this edition also has a bridge on the cover, but this time of a quite different sort – in fact, two bridges. The old Forth railway bridge in the foreground symbolizes old 'brute force' technology that has stood the test of time, while the more recent Forth road bridge in the distance symbolizes newer, more elegant technology and the fact that this complements but does not supersede its predecessor. For those who would prefer a more whimsical reason, the railway bridge will celebrate its centenary in the year that this book is published (1990), while the road bridge was opened only a few days before I wrote my first Fortran program in 1964! I wonder which bridge we shall use for Fortran 90?

T. M. R. Ellis

Oxford
March 1990

Contents

Introduction

1

All computers consist of essentially the same principal components, which allow them to perform calculations and comparisons, to store information for later use, and to communicate with the outside world. For a computer to carry out a particular sequence of operations it must be given detailed **instructions** in a form that it can understand. Because these **machine language** instructions are difficult for humans to understand, and because they are restricted to a particular type of computer, we write **programs** in an English-like **high-level language**, which is then translated into a form that the computer can understand by another program called a **compiler**.

Fortran was the first such programming language, and is still the most widely used for scientific and technological purposes. It is over 10 years since the current version of Fortran, known as **Fortran 77**, was standardized, and a new, greatly extended, version of the language, to be known as **Fortran 90**, is expected to be internationally standardized in late 1990 or early 1991. Fortran 90, which is summarized in Chapter 20, includes all of Fortran 77, and programs written in Fortran 77 will therefore be fully usable well into the 21st century.

1.1 Computers, programs and high-level languages

What is a computer? This is a question frequently asked by those who come into contact with computers and computing, and yet it is a question that is extremely difficult to answer. To an electronics engineer a computer may be just a collection of transistors, resistors, capacitors, integrated circuits and many other basic elements of electronic hardware. On the other hand, to a computer scientist it may be an electromechanical realization of a complex logical design; to a businessman it may be a 'black box' that provides him with accurate details of his business and projections into the future for different hypothetical scenarios; and to a child it may be a magic box that provides him with an almost infinite variety of electronic games. All of these, and many more, are perfectly valid answers to the question posed above, for a computer is an extremely powerful tool, which, chameleon-like, can appear in almost any guise that its users require.

Nevertheless, at heart a computer is merely an inanimate collection of electronic circuits and devices with, usually, a considerable amount of electromechanical equipment attached to it. What sets a computer apart from other machines that may be built from similar (or even identical) component parts is its ability to *remember* a sequence of instructions and to *obey* these instructions at a predetermined point in time. Such a sequence of instructions is called a **program**, and what we usually refer to as a computer is more correctly called a **stored-program computer**. How we write a program to instruct the computer to perform the task(s) that we require of it is the subject of this book.

The first stored-program computer was designed by Charles Babbage in England in the 19th century; however, the complexity of its construction and the extreme accuracy required in its many hundreds of gear-wheels meant that it was not practicable to build a computer of the size necessary for most real-life calculations. One (the Difference Engine) was built and can be seen in the Science Museum in London, but its more sophisticated successor (the Analytical Engine) proved too complex to build. It was not until the early 1940s that the ideas were to be once more taken up, but this time using thermionic valves and other electrical devices as the basic components.

The programming of these early machines (that is, the writing of the instructions that would form the program for the solution of a particular problem) was a highly complex task, since the instructions were represented by strings of 0s and 1s known as **machine code** and were unique to a particular type of computer.

It was not long, therefore, before a more compact form of code was devised in which each group of three **binary digits** (or **bits**) was replaced by a single number in the range 0–7 (the **octal** equivalent of the 3-bit binary number). Thus the binary sequence

```
010100011 010 000 010111
```

would be replaced by the sequence

```
243 2 0 27
```

This was still a matter for a specialist, although, as there were only a handful of computers in the world, that in itself was of no great importance. Even for a specialist it was difficult to remember which code number represented which operation, and where each data value was kept in the computer's memory. The next development was the creation of a mnemonic form for the instructions, and the use of names to identify memory locations. For example

```
LDA 2 X
```

meant *load a special location (register 2) with the contents of location X*. This is known as **assembly-language** programming, and the principles have survived almost unchanged to the present day.

Note that this method of programming requires a detailed understanding of the computer's instructions and their effects, and each type of computer has its own, quite distinct, form of assembly language. During the early and mid 1950s a great deal of effort was expended in finding a method of formulating the program in the *user's* terms and not in those of the computer. The approach adopted by most of the workers in this field was to use an algebraic method of expressing formulae and a 'pidgin English' method of describing the other (non-mathematical) operations. The resulting program was said to use a **high-level language**, since the method enabled a programmer to write programs without needing to know much about the details of the computer itself. One of the earliest of these languages was Fortran.

Since that time the concept has been considerably refined, and today virtually all programs are now written in some form of high-level language (Ada, Pascal, PL/I, COBOL and so on). All such languages have several common features and these must be established before we proceed further. First, almost invariably, English-like expressions are used to define what operations are to be carried out. The problem is expressed in a way that does not demand that the programmer be familiar with the internal working of the computer. Second, the organization of the storage of both program and data is almost completely outside the control of the programmer, who merely chooses a name for abstract storage locations and these are automatically related (through the computer's own operational software) to some real location within the computer's memory. Most importantly, the same program may usually be submitted to many different types of computer without the need for any significant changes.

As was mentioned earlier, the computer can understand only its own machine code and, therefore, before a high-level program can be obeyed by the computer it must be **translated** into the appropriate machine code. A special program (the **compiler**) is used to translate the high-level language program into a machine-code program for a particular computer in such a way that the machine code may be kept for use on subsequent occasions. Since the compiler can only translate correct high-level program statements, an important part of its task is to check the syntax of each statement and to produce **diagnostic** information to help the programmer to correct any errors. Thus the statement

```
A=B+C
```

(which means that the location called A is to have placed in it the sum of the values currently stored in the locations called B and C) might be compiled into the three instructions

```
0110000000000011001010000 (LDX 3 B)
0110000001000011001010010 (ADX 3 C)
0110001000000011001001110 (STO 3 A)
```

On a different type of computer, however, the same statement would be translated into a totally different set of instructions, for example

```
110000010010101111 (B)
110000010010110000 (C)
010001             (+)
110001010010101110 (=A)
```

Thus the same high-level program can be run on two completely different types of computers simply by using two compilers that take the same input but produce quite different outputs. It was the development of this concept that enabled the use of computers to spread from the research laboratory into industry, commerce, government, education and (more recently) even into the home. A high-level program can, therefore, be transported from one place to another, be developed by programmers who neither know nor care about the computer(s) on which it is to run, and outlive the relatively short life of the computer itself in a period of rapid technological change.

1.2   What is a computer?

We can now return to the question posed earlier and define a model of a computer that will enable us to understand more easily exactly what we are doing when we write a program. We have already referred to the computer's **memory** – a set of electronic or magnetic devices in which information may be stored. That information may be either program – instructions that the computer is to obey – or data – values (numbers, words and so on) that the computer is to process in a way defined by a program.

This processing is carried out by the **central processing unit (CPU)**, which consists of (at least) two quite separate parts: a **control unit** that fetches instructions, decodes them, and initiates appropriate action; and an **arithmetic unit**, which carries out arithmetic and other types of operation on items of data.

These two parts – the CPU and the memory – could be said to constitute the computer, but there are other essential parts of the system still to be discussed. To be of any practical use a computer must be able to communicate its results to the outside world, and this calls for some form of **output device**, such as a display screen, a printer or a graph plotter. Similarly, there must be some way of getting both the program and any variable data it requires into the computer and therefore an **input device** is needed, such as a keyboard or, on some older computers, a card reader or a paper tape reader.

Finally there is the question of large and/or long-term data storage. The devices used to form the memory of a computer are normally transient devices – when the power is switched off they lose the information stored in them and are thus of no use for storage of information other than during the running of a program. In addition, if the computer is to be able to access the information in the memory rapidly, the latter can only be of a relatively small size (typically of the order of a few million characters). A memory of more than this size would place unacceptable burdens on both power requirements and physical space. Magnetic media, however, such as discs or tapes coated with a fine magnetic oxide (similar to that used on tapes for domestic cassette or videotape recorders) can be used to store very large amounts of information easily and economically, although at the cost of slower access time. Virtually all computers use magnetic media as a **backing store**, enabling programs and data to be stored in a permanent fashion within the overall computer system. A single unit of program or data is called a **file**.

Thus a computer can be represented by a simple diagram such as that shown in Figure 1.1. The memory and central processor are usually electronic; however, the input, output and backing-store devices also contain mechanical components, with the result that the speed of transfer

Figure 1.1
An idealized computer.

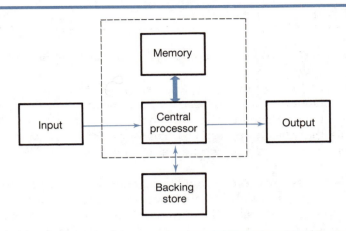

of information between them and the central processor is many times slower than that between the memory and the central processor. Because of this disparity in speed, most computers arrange for transfers between the central processor and the input, output and backing-store devices to proceed semi-autonomously. In many cases the central processor can be bypassed and information is transferred directly to or from the memory. As a result of this, and because they are usually physically separated from the CPU, these types of device are referred to as **peripheral devices** – a distinction that has been emphasized in Figure 1.1 by enclosing the memory and central processor in a 'box'.

This idealized structure applies to all computers, but in recent years the development of the **microcomputer** has changed many people's perception of computers. Whereas large computers, such as a Cray X-MP supercomputer or a Digital Equipment VAX 11/780, can easily be seen to consist of a number of discrete parts, microcomputers, such as an IBM PS/2 or an Apple Macintosh, take up only a few square inches of desk space and appear to consist of little more than a television monitor, a keyboard and a small box. Nevertheless the keyboard is the main input device, the monitor is the main output device, and the small box contains a faster CPU, more memory and more backing store than all but a handful of the most powerful computers of 10 years ago.

Let us now return to the memory and consider its mode of operation. Conceptually we can use an analogy with a large number of glass boxes, each containing a single ball on which is written a number, or a word, or any other single item that we may wish to store. To distinguish one box from another each has a label attached with an identifying name (see Figure 1.2).

Clearly we can find out what is in any of the boxes simply by looking at it, as long as we have the name of the box. Equally clearly, if we

Figure 1.2
A storage model.

wish to put another value in a box we shall first have to remove (or otherwise get rid of) the ball which is already there so as to leave room for the new one. This is exactly the way the computer's memory works – if we wish to find out what is stored in a particular location the process does not affect what is stored there, whereas if we store a new value in some location then whatever was stored there is destroyed and lost.

Now consider the names on the boxes – A, X and P in Figure 1.2. It is quite clear that these are the names of the *boxes* and not their contents, for if we were to store a new ball with the value 6 in box A we would not alter its name, and if we now looked at box A we would find that it contained the value 6 (Figure 1.3). We shall come back to this when we start to write programs, but it is important to realize from the outset that the names that are used to refer to storage locations in the memory always identify the *location* and not the value that is stored there.

The boxes have, by implication, been open so that the current value may be removed and a new one inserted. To complete the analogy with the computer's memory we must have a rule that says that a box is never left empty; every box must contain a ball, even if it is blank or has the value 0. Because such boxes, or rather the corresponding storage locations in the memory, can have their contents changed at will, they are referred to as variable storage locations, or **variables**. Boxes that are identical with these except that they have a sealed lid can have their contents looked at, but it is not possible to replace the contents by a new value. Such storage locations are called constant storage locations, or **constants**.

Figure 1.3
An altered storage model.

1.3 What is Fortran?

Towards the end of 1953 John Backus proposed to his employers, the International Business Machines Corporation (IBM), that it would be beneficial if a small research group were to be set up to develop a more efficient and economical method of programming their 704 computer than the assembly language used at that time. The proposal was accepted and the group started work almost at once. By mid 1954 an initial specification had been produced for a programming language of considerable power and flexibility. This language was to be called the IBM Mathematical FORmula TRANslation System, FORTRAN. The project was initially intended purely for use by IBM on a single computer; however, soon after the preliminary report of the language was produced word got out to some of IBM's customers, with the result that the decision was made to make it available to anyone purchasing a 704 computer.

The first *Programmer's Reference Manual* for the FORTRAN language was released in October 1956 and the compiler was finally delivered to customers in April 1957. This was followed 12 months later by FORTRAN II, an improved version of the system with a considerably enhanced diagnostic capability and a number of significant extensions to the language. Despite initial resistance on the grounds that the compiled programs were not as efficient as hand-coded ones, the language soon caught on, and by 1960 IBM had released versions of FORTRAN for their 709, 650, 1620 and 7070 computers. The most important development, however, was that other manufacturers started to write compilers for FORTRAN, and by 1963 there were over 40 different FORTRAN compilers in existence.

One problem, though, was that the 704 FORTRAN (and FORTRAN II) had used certain specific features of the instruction set of the 704 computer and therefore the other FORTRAN compilers tended to do likewise. In addition, the advantages to be gained by having a standard language had not been fully appreciated and there were incompatibilities between different compilers, even between those written by the same manufacturer. As a result of pressure from their users as early as 1961, IBM set about developing a still further improved FORTRAN that did away with the machine-dependent features of FORTRAN II. This new system, FORTRAN IV, was released for the IBM 7030 (Stretch) computer in 1962, and later for the IBM 7090/7094 machines.

The most significant development of all, however, was the decision of the American Standards Association (ASA – now the American National Standards Institute, ANSI) in May 1962 to set up a committee to develop an American Standard FORTRAN. This committee defined two languages: FORTRAN, based largely on FORTRAN IV, and Basic FORTRAN, which was based on FORTRAN II but without the machine-dependent features. These standards were ratified in March 1966.

The existence of an officially defined standard (ANSI, 1966) (which was also effectively an international standard) meant that further development of the language had a firm and well-defined base from which to work. The 1960s and early 1970s saw computers become established in all areas of society, and this dramatic growth led, among other things, to a proliferation of different programming languages. Many of these were oriented towards specific application areas, but a substantial proportion were intended to be **general-purpose languages**. Most noteworthy among these were ALGOL 60, ALGOL 68, BASIC, COBOL, Pascal and PL/I.

In the midst of all this language research and development FORTRAN did not remain static. Computer manufacturers wrote compilers that accepted considerable extensions to the Standard FORTRAN, while in 1969 the ANSI set up a working committee to revise the 1966 standard. Partly because of the many changes in the philosophy and practice of programming during this period, a draft standard did not appear until some seven years had elapsed. During 1977 this draft was the subject of worldwide discussion and comment before a revised version was approved as the new standard (ANSI, 1978).

The new (1977) Standard FORTRAN replaced both the older (1966) FORTRAN and Basic FORTRAN. In order to distinguish the new standard language from the old one, the Standard suggested that the new language should be called FORTRAN 77. (By this time the origin of the name FORTRAN as an acronym had largely been forgotten, and the practice of using capitals to write the name began to die out. The language is therefore referred to as Fortran throughout the remainder of this book.)

Although the Standard was issued in 1978, and was subsequently ratified as an International Standard in 1980, it was several years before compilers for this new and improved version of Fortran became widely available, and it was not until the mid 1980s that it could truly be thought of as the 'universal' Fortran. In the meantime, however, the computing world had not stood still and many new programming concepts were being developed. A new ANSI committee was therefore set up in 1980 to develop the *next* Fortran Standard under authority delegated from the International Standards Organization. This committee (of which the author is a member) had hoped to produce a new Standard by 1988 but was delayed by various technical and procedural difficulties. Nevertheless, the final form of this language (informally referred to as Fortran 90) was agreed in March 1990 and it seems likely that this will be ratified as an International Standard in late 1990 or early 1991. Chapter 20 gives an indication of what this latest version of Fortran will contain in addition to the whole of Fortran 77.

1.4 Why learn Fortran 77?

As we have seen, there are a great many languages available throughout the world, some widely, some not so widely, and some only in one place.

However, two languages stand head and shoulders above the others in terms of their total usage. These languages are COBOL (first released in 1960) and Fortran (first released in 1957).

Fortran was originally designed with scientific and engineering users in mind, and during its first 30 years it has completely dominated this area of programming. For example, most of the body structure of a Boeing 747 airliner or a NASA lunar capsule is manufactured using machine tools whose movements are controlled by means of a Fortran program. The dies used in pressing the body shells of virtually all mass-produced cars are also made by machines controlled by Fortran programs. The control of experiments investigating the subatomic particles that constitute the matter of our universe and the analysis of the results of these experiments are mainly carried out by Fortran programs. The structural analysis of bridges or skyscrapers, the calculation of stresses in chemical plant piping systems, the design of electric generators and the analysis of the flow of molten glass are all usually carried out using computer programs written in Fortran.

Fortran has also been the dominant language in academic circles and has been widely used in other, less obvious, areas. One of the most widely used programs in both British and American universities is SPSS (Statistical Package for the Social Sciences) (Ralston and Rabinowitz, 1978) which enables social scientists to analyse survey or other research data; SPSS is written in Fortran. Indeed, because of the extremely widespread use of Fortran in higher education and industry, many standard **libraries** have been written in Fortran to enable programmers to utilize the experience and expertise of others when writing their own Fortran programs. A notable example is the NAG library (Hopkins and Phillips, 1988; NAG, 1988) a large and extremely comprehensive collection of **subprograms** for numerical analysis applications, which we shall refer to in Chapters 11 and 18 when discussing numerical methods in Fortran programs. Thus, because of the widespread use of Fortran over a period of more than 30 years, a vast body of experience is available in the form of existing Fortran programs. Fortran 77 allows access to all this experience, while adding new and more powerful facilities to the Fortran language.

Unlike Fortran, COBOL is designed primarily for business data-processing use and does not purport to be suitable for scientific or technical programming; Fortran, on the other hand, until the advent of Fortran 77, was notoriously weak on character handling and is still not the most appropriate language for business data-processing. Other high-level languages in widespread use, such as Ada, BASIC, C, LISP, Modula-2, Pascal, PL/I and PROLOG, all have both advantages and disadvantages for their particular fields of use.

This book introduces the Fortran 77 language in a way that will encourage the embryo programmer to develop a good style of programming and a sound approach to the design of programs. It must, however, be emphasized that programming is a practical skill, and to develop this skill it is essential that as many programs as possible are written and tested on a computer. The exercises at the end of each chapter will help here, but it should always be realized that to write fluent, precise and well-structured programs requires both planning and experience. Fortran has evolved over a quarter of a century in what has often been a pragmatic fashion, but always with the emphasis on efficiency and ease of use. Fortran 77 provides a number of powerful features that were not available in earlier versions; these enable Fortran programmers to write more elegant and well-structured programs and to carry out activities (such as character manipulation) that were previously difficult or impossible. As already mentioned, the next Standard version of Fortran is expected around 1990 and will incorporate *all* of Fortran 77. Thus programs written in Fortran 77 will have life well into the 21st century.

Fundamental Principles

PART I

A simple program

2

Fortran programs are typed in lines of up to 72 characters, with the first six columns of each line being reserved for special purposes. The first statement of the program must be a PROGRAM statement, and the last must be an END statement. List-directed input is carried out by a READ statement, and list-directed output by a PRINT statement.

Fortran uses two types of number: **real** numbers and **integers**. Integers are whole numbers within a relatively limited range and are held exactly in the computer's memory, whereas real numbers may have fractional parts and are held as **floating-point** approximations to an accuracy of, typically, seven or eight digits of precision within a vastly wider range than integers. An assignment statement is used to store the value of an arithmetic expression in a named **variable** location.

The various functions of a computer system are controlled by a special program called the **operating system**. Although this aspect of using a computer is not considered in the remainder of this book, it is necessary for a programmer to be familiar with at least a minimal set of commands for the operating system being used in order to control the typing, compiling, executing and correction of programs. In this connection, it is important to realize that the existence of errors in programs is almost inevitable, but there is an important distinction to be made between **syntactic errors**, which are relatively easy to correct, and **semantic errors**, which are much more difficult to identify.

2.1 The program

Figure 2.1 shows a complete Fortran 77 program. It appears to use a number of English words in a fairly understandable way to read two numbers, add them together and print them with their sum and some text. There are a lot of important principles to be learned from this simple program, so each line will be examined in turn to establish exactly what it means and how it is used.

The format in which a Fortran program must be typed is very important. Remember that Fortran was developed in the mid 1950s for internal use (initially) on an IBM 704 computer. The only form of input to that computer was by punched card – that is, a card marked with 80 columns and 12 rows that can have small rectangular holes punched in any of the 960 resulting positions. Each column represented one character (a letter, a digit, a space, or one of several special characters such as +, . *), which was punched as a coded combination of one, two or three holes. Thus a single card could contain 80 characters. The first Fortran system therefore limited the length of a line to 80 characters.

However, the influence of the card went further, for the designers of the first Fortran system decided that, in order to speed up processing, they would use certain parts of the card for specific purposes. To this day, a Fortran statement has to follow certain rules of layout even if, as is very likely, it is being typed directly into the computer from a keyboard without any cards being involved at all. All these rules will not be introduced at this point but two major and two minor ones will be mentioned.

F90

The first rule is that the last eight columns (73–80) are not used at all! To be more accurate, they are not treated as part of the program but can be used for other, identifying purposes. When large programs were punched on cards and submitted to the computer many times, it was a sensible precaution to punch sequence numbers on the cards in case they should be dropped or otherwise become out of order. Nowadays programs are almost invariably either typed directly into the computer or punched on cards that are then read *once* by the computer and stored in a file on backing store. In practice, therefore, columns 73–80 are rarely, if ever, used.

Figure 2.1
A Fortran program.

```
      PROGRAM FIRST
C This is our first program
      PRINT *,'Type two numbers separated by a comma:
      READ *,A,B
      SUM = A+B
      PRINT *,'The sum of',A,' and',B,' is',SUM
      STOP
      END
```

The second rule is that the first six columns are used for special purposes and that as a result the Fortran statements always begin at (or after) column 7.

One of the special purposes for which the first six columns may be used is shown in this first program. If the first column contains a c or an asterisk (*) then the whole line is treated as a **comment** and is ignored when the program is compiled into machine code. It will, however, be listed with all the other lines and is used to add explanatory comments so that the program is easy to understand.

Thus our simple program contains seven lines, of which six start in column 7, while the second line has a c in column 1 and is therefore a comment line whose format is of no concern.

A second, special, use of the first six columns is to specify a **continuation line**. If column 6 of a line contains any character other than a space or a zero then the line is treated as a continuation of the previous line. In this case columns 1–5 of the continuation line must be blank, and column 7 is treated as though it came immediately after column 72 of the previous line. There can be up to 19 continuation lines following any initial line, although it is unusual to need more than one or two.

Nowadays cards are rarely used to input information to a computer, but the constraints originally imposed by cards are likely to remain with us for many more decades, if not for ever. However, it will be assumed in this book that you are typing your program directly into the computer, and *lines* will be referred to rather than cards, although the use of the word *column* is still useful in identifying the position within a line.

One other effect of the original use of cards concerns the **case** of letters. In the early days of card input only the upper-case letters (capitals) could be coded, and so the Fortran language was restricted to the use of upper-case only. This restriction still applies even though all present computers will happily accept both upper- and lower-case letters.

Most Fortran processors will accept lower-case letters as an alternative to upper-case in programs, even though this is, strictly, non-standard. Lower-case will not be used in this book except in two specific circumstances which *are* permitted by the Standard.

The first of these is when writing comments in our programs, where the use of lower-case improves their readability, and since such comments are ignored when the program is being compiled, apart from being listed, this use conforms to the Standard. The other occasion where lower-case will be used is when printing text. Here the Fortran Standard recognizes that the computer may be able to process characters other than the (limited) Fortran character set, and allows any character that can be represented by the processor to appear in a string of text to be output by the program.

We can now return to the program and examine the first few lines.

```
PROGRAM FIRST
```

This line gives a name to the program and consists of the word PROGRAM followed by a name that we can choose. This must satisfy the basic rules for Fortran names and must:

F90

- start with a letter
- contain only letters and digits
- be at most six characters long

In practice many computer systems will allow more than six characters in a name, but their treatment of the seventh and subsequent characters varies considerably. In particular, some will accept all characters up to a much higher limit (typically 31) as meaningful, while others will accept up to 31 but will only consider the first six as meaningful; in such a system MYNAME1 and MYNAME2 will be treated as the same. The Standard specifies a maximum of six and so it is advisable to observe this limit. This will be done throughout the book.

Thus our program is called FIRST, which satisfies the above rules. One point to note is that spaces have no significance in general and may be used, as in ordinary English, to improve the layout. Thus we could equally well have written

```
PROGRAMFIRST
```

which is not very clear to the human reader, although perfectly acceptable to the Fortran compiler, or

```
P R O G R A M   F I R S T
```

or even

```
PRO GRA MFI RST
```

However, since it makes no difference to the computer it is sensible to make the layout easy for the human reader to follow by including spaces in the natural places, between words and/or numbers:

```
PROGRAM FIRST
```

We may choose any name we like for the program (as long as it is a valid Fortran name), but having once chosen a name we cannot use the same name for another purpose (for example, a storage location) in the same program. If we were to do so, it would be confusing for us and the computer and this is something that must always be avoided.

If we do not want to give our program a name at all then the PROGRAM

Us	Computer
123	00000000000000000000000001111011
123.0	00000111111101100000000000000000
0.123	01111101111110111110011101101100
−1.23	10000001011000101000111101011101
−123	11111111111111111111111110000101
$1.058\,254 \times 10^{-15}$	01010000010011000100000101011001
1 347 174 745	01010000010011000100000101011001
PLAY	01010000010011000100000101011001

Figure 2.2
How we and the computer see data items.

statement can be omitted altogether. There is no particular advantage to be gained by so doing, and some compilers may insist on it being present, so it is strongly recommended that every program should start properly with a PROGRAM statement.

The next line

```
C This is our first program
```

is a comment and merely confirms what we already know, namely that this is our first program. It will be listed and otherwise ignored by the compiler.

The third line of the program is where things really start to happen:

```
PRINT *,'Type two numbers separated by a comma: '
```

This statement will probably cause the text shown between apostrophes to be displayed on the screen of your computer or terminal, but is actually much more complex than it appears. We shall examine it in more detail when we look at the similar PRINT statement that appears later in the program. For the moment we shall proceed to the next line:

```
READ *,A,B
```

This apparently simple statement disguises a very complex situation. The input of data (and the output of results) is always the most complicated part of any programming language, and Fortran is no exception. The problem is that we see numbers, words or anything else in quite a different manner from that in which they are stored within the computer.

For example, Figure 2.2 shows how a hypothetical computer might store several numbers and names: it can easily be seen how two apparently similar numbers (123 and 123.0) are stored totally differently, while three very different items (0.000 000 000 000 001 058 254, 1 347 174 745 and the word PLAY) are stored identically. However, even this disguises the true magnitude of the problem, because what we write cannot be read directly by the computer (as a general rule) and must be typed in at a keyboard, or coded in some other way for the computer. In addition there is the question of layout. For example, what does the following line represent?

```
123456789
```

It could be the number 123 456 789, or it could be the nine numbers 1, 2, 3, 4, 5, 6, 7, 8, 9 typed without any intervening spaces, or it could even be the number 12345.6789 with the convention that the decimal point is not typed but is assumed to fall between the fifth and sixth digits. All of these are perfectly valid interpretations of the contents of the line.

We shall see in Chapter 9 how to resolve most of these problems; fortunately Fortran 77 comes to our aid with a special simplified form of input/output that avoids the necessity for any consideration of most of the problems, although at the cost of a slight loss of flexibility. This special type of input/output is called **list-directed input/output**. For the input of data this takes the form

```
READ *, input-list
```

where *input-list* is a list of one or more **variable names** (specifying where the data is to be stored in memory) separated by commas. Thus the statement

```
READ *,A,B
```

tells the computer that it is to read (or input) two data items and store them in the locations A and B respectively. But what are these data items? The answer is that unless otherwise instructed (as we shall see in Chapters 12 and 13) all data is assumed to be numeric. Furthermore, if the first letter of the name of a storage location begins with one of the letters I, J, K, L, M or N the number will be stored as an **integer** (or whole number), while if it begins with one of the remaining 20 letters (A–H, O–Z) the number will be stored as a **real** number (with a decimal part).

The above statement therefore indicates to the computer that the two data items are real numbers and must be stored as such. However, there still remains the question of how the data is to be typed – in other words, what **format** it is in – and from where it is to be read (keyboard, file or elsewhere). The format is defined largely as a result of the input-list – this is the meaning of 'list-directed' – and quite simply means that the first number starts with the first non-blank character and then continues until either a comma, or a blank, or a blank (or blanks) followed by a comma, or the end of a line is reached. The second number (if any) then starts with the next non-blank character, and so on. Notice that this means that the number is not allowed to contain any blank characters. The data for the above READ statement could, therefore, be typed in any of the following ways:

(1)   123.45,67.89

(2)   123.45 67.89

(3)   123.45 , 67.89

(4)   123.45
    67.89

(5)   123.45,
    67.89

If the name of the variable (location) in which the data is to be stored is a real name (that is, it starts with one of the letters A–H or O–Z) then the number may have a decimal point and/or sign as required and, for example, 123 will be treated as 123.0. However, if the name is an integer name then the data must be a whole number, optionally preceded by a sign, and may not contain a decimal point.

When using the simple form of input statement described above, the READ statement will take its data from the **standard input unit**. This will be defined for the computer system being used and will typically be the keyboard in an interactive system or on a microcomputer. In a batch system, where jobs are submitted to be run at some subsequent time without any direct interaction with the user, it will normally be the peripheral device (for example, disc or tape drive) holding the **file** that contains the user's data. A READ statement will input as many lines of data as are necessary to obtain values for all the variable names in the input-list, but a new READ statement will *always* start a new line of data. If a / character is input it is treated as a terminator for the current number (like a space or a comma) *and also for the whole statement*; any variables in the input-list that have not yet had values input and stored will be left unchanged.

Thus our input statement reads two real numbers from the standard input unit and stores them in the variables A and B.

The next statement is easier:

```
SUM=A+B
```

This is called an **assignment statement** because it assigns a value for storage in a variable. The equals sign (=) is misleading because what the statement means is 'take the values stored in A and B, add them together, and store the result in a variable called SUM'. There is, therefore, a sense of direction about the statement and a form such as

```
SUM ← A+B
```

would be rather clearer. It is very important to understand this and not to confuse an assignment statement with an algebraic equation that might look the same. Thus the two statements

```
B=C
```

and

```
C=B
```

are totally different. The first takes the contents of C and stores this value in B; the second stores the value of B in C. If, initially, B contains 1.0 and C contains 2.0 then the first statement leaves B and C both containing the value 2.0, while the second one would leave them both containing the value 1.0.

The next statement

```
PRINT *,'The sum of',A,' and',B,' is',SUM
```

is a list-directed output statement, as was the earlier statement

```
PRINT *,'Type two numbers separated by a comma: '
```

of which discussion has been deferred until now. The list-directed output statement is very similar to the list-directed input statement discussed earlier and takes the form

```
PRINT *, output-list
```

It causes the items in *output-list* to be sent to the **standard output unit** in a format determined by the output-list itself. The standard output unit will usually be the screen on a microcomputer or on a terminal for an interactive system, or the computer's printer for a batch system. The output-list and the output formats are, however, rather more complicated than for input.

The most obvious difference between the output-list and the input-list of a READ statement is that the output-list is not restricted to variable names, but may also contain constants or expressions (expressions are dealt with in Chapter 3). If a name of a variable appears in the output-list the value stored in the location with that name is output in a format that depends on the type of the variable (real, integer, or one of the other types that we shall meet later). If a constant appears in the output-list then it is output in a format that depends upon the type of the constant.

There are three types of constant that concern us at present – real, integer and character:

- A **real** constant is a number that contains a decimal point, and which may (optionally) be preceded by a sign:

  ```
  4.7  -0.01  +3.14159  17.  -.1
  ```

  Another way of expressing a real constant is in **exponent form**. In this form a number, with or without a decimal point, is followed by the letter E and a second number, without a decimal point. It represents a real number in which the first number, the **mantissa**, is multiplied by 10 the number of times specified by the second number, the **exponent**. Thus the five numbers above could also be written:

  ```
  47E-1  -1E-2  3.14159E0  0.17E2  -1E-1
  ```

  This is a particularly useful way of expressing very large or very small constants:

  ```
  1E-6  2.5E10
  ```

- An **integer** constant is a number that does not contain any decimal point, and which may (optionally) be preceded by a sign:

  ```
  4  -1  +275
  ```

- A **character** constant is a sequence of characters enclosed in single quotes (or apostrophes), and is often referred to as a string:

  ```
  'Miles Ellis'  'H2SO4'
  ```

  If it is required to include an apostrophe in a string , two consecutive apostrophes are written; only a single apostrophe is stored within the computer:

  ```
  'Today''s lucky number'
  ```

  The apostrophes that enclose the string are not part of the string, and are not stored in the computer.

The format that is used to output the required values is a 'reasonable' one according to the defining Standard. This means that integers will be printed preceded by one or more spaces, that real numbers (unless they are very large or very small) will be preceded by one or more spaces and limited to a certain number of decimal places (typically four or five), and that characters will be printed exactly as they are stored in the computer's memory. Each PRINT statement will start to print on a new line and continue over as many lines as are necessary.

Thus the first PRINT statement in our program sends a line of output to the standard output unit consisting of the character constant

```
Type two numbers separated by a comma:
```

The second one is more complex, and sends the words The sum of, followed by the value of A, the word and, the value of B, the word is and finally the value stored in SUM (which has, of course, already been assigned the value of A+B). If A were 7.0 and B were 12.0 it would therefore take the following form (or something like it):

```
The sum of    7.0000 and    12.0000 is    19.0000
```

The layout here could do with some improvement, but that will need to wait until the full Fortran input/output capability is discussed in Chapter 9. It will be noted, however, that whereas each number is preceded by several spaces it is only followed by one. This is because a character constant is not preceded by spaces during output and, in fact, the space before and and the one before is are part of the string. If the program had read

```
    PRINT *,'The sum of',A,'and',B,'is',SUM
```

then the result would have been

```
The sum of    7.0000and    12.0000is    19.0000
```

We can also see that because A and B are real numbers the output format is appropriate for such numbers, and has caused the numbers to be printed with four decimal places (all zero!).

The next statement:

```
    STOP
```

has a fairly obvious meaning – it tells the computer to stop. This is where the difference between the logic of a computer and that of a human is once again apparent. *We* know that we have finished (it's obvious) but the computer doesn't know anything – it has to be told. The STOP statement therefore instructs the computer to finish obeying (or **executing**) this program, and to return to the state it is normally in when not obeying such a program.

There is, however, one final statement:

```
    END
```

This indicates that there are no more lines of program to come and marks, therefore, the physical end of the program (or rather, as we shall see in Chapter 4, of this program unit). In Fortran 77 (although not in earlier versions of Fortran) this also has the effect of terminating the execution of the program if it is obeyed and therefore the STOP statement could be omitted. This is not good practice, as the purpose of the two statements is quite different: STOP marks the *logical* end of the program (which, as we shall see later, need not be at the last line) while END merely signifies its *physical* end, and is therefore primarily an instruction to the compiler, informing it that it may now proceed with translating (or compiling) the Fortran program into machine code prior to its execution.

2.2   A word about numbers

The differences between the two types of numbers, real and integer, will now be examined in some detail before any further discussion about their use.

An integer is a whole number and is therefore stored in the computer's memory without any decimal (or fractional) part. However, because of the way in which information is stored there are limits to its size. These limits vary from one computer to another and depend upon the physical design of the computer's memory. This can be illustrated by considering a hypothetical computer that (for ease of comprehension!) stores its data in decimal form instead of the binary (base-2) system used by all normal computers. This means that a single digit will be recorded by means of some device that has 10 states (corresponding to the 10 digits) instead of one with two states (on and off), as required for binary numbers. Each location in the memory used for storing integers will consist of a fixed number of these devices, say eight, which will impose a limit on the size of the number – in this case up to 99 999 999. There remains the question of the sign of the numbers.

Suppose that the device that stored the integer was an electronic equivalent of a milometer (odometer), such as that fitted to a car (see Figure 2.3). If the reading is 00 000 000 and the car moves forward two miles (that is, adds 2) the milometer will read 00 000 002. However, if the car now reverses for three miles (that is, subtracts 3) the reading will successively go to 00 000 001, 00 000 000 and finally 99 999 999. Thus the same reading is obtained for a value of −1 as for +999 999 999, and adding 1 to 99 999 999 will give 0. We could therefore adopt a convention that readings from 1 to

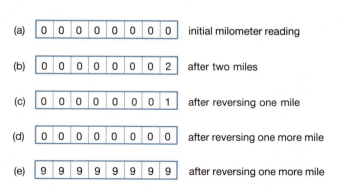

(a) | 0 | 0 | 0 | 0 | 0 | 0 | 0 | 0 | initial milometer reading

(b) | 0 | 0 | 0 | 0 | 0 | 0 | 0 | 2 | after two miles

(c) | 0 | 0 | 0 | 0 | 0 | 0 | 0 | 1 | after reversing one mile

(d) | 0 | 0 | 0 | 0 | 0 | 0 | 0 | 0 | after reversing one more mile

(e) | 9 | 9 | 9 | 9 | 9 | 9 | 9 | 9 | after reversing one more mile

Figure 2.3
Milometer readings during travel.

Figure 2.4
Storage of 8-digit
integers.

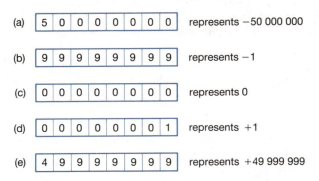

(a) | 5 | 0 | 0 | 0 | 0 | 0 | 0 | 0 | represents −50 000 000

(b) | 9 | 9 | 9 | 9 | 9 | 9 | 9 | 9 | represents −1

(c) | 0 | 0 | 0 | 0 | 0 | 0 | 0 | 0 | represents 0

(d) | 0 | 0 | 0 | 0 | 0 | 0 | 0 | 1 | represents +1

(e) | 4 | 9 | 9 | 9 | 9 | 9 | 9 | 9 | represents +49 999 999

49 999 999 will be considered to be positive, whereas 50 000 000 to 99 999 999 will be considered to be negative, and equivalent to −50 000 000 to −1 respectively. Almost all computers work like this, although when using the binary system the effect is that if the first binary digit (or **bit**) is a 1 the number is negative, while if it is 0 the number is positive.

Using the convention just described our eight-digit memory location can hold a whole number in the range −50 000 000 to +49 999 999, as shown in Figure 2.4.

Now let us consider real numbers. These have a fractional part, and clearly one way would be to assume that, for example, the first four digits come before the decimal point and the second four after it. However, this would mean that the numbers could only lie between −5000.0 and +4999.9999 and that all numbers would be stored with exactly four decimal places. Clearly this is ridiculously restrictive and another way must be found. One solution might be to allow more digits, but the problem with this approach is that a large number of them will be wasted on many occasions. For example, suppose 16 digits were allowed, so as to give the same range as for integers but with eight places of decimals; on the one hand a number such as 100 000 000.0 could not be stored because it needs nine digits before the decimal place, even though none of those after it are needed; on the other a number such as 0.000 000 004 would have to be treated as 0 because it needs nine decimal places, even though none of the eight before the decimal point are needed.

The solution is to consider a real number as a fraction lying between 0.1 and 1.0 that is multiplied or divided by 10 a certain number of times. Thus 100 000 000.0 is the same as 0.1×10^9, and 0.000 000 004 is the same as $0.4/10^8$ or 0.4×10^{-8}.

A method of storage can therefore be defined in which the last six digits represent a fraction to six decimal places (with the first being non-zero), while the first two represent the number of times that the fraction is to be multiplied or divided by 10. Figure 2.5 illustrates this method, which is known as **floating-point** storage.

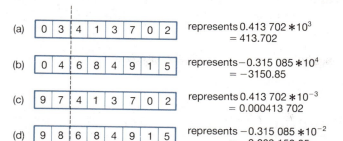

(a) and the remaining boxes: 0 3 | 4 1 3 7 0 2 represents $0.413\,702 * 10^3$
= 413.702

(b) 0 4 | 6 8 4 9 1 5 represents $-0.315\,085 * 10^4$
= −3150.85

(c) 9 7 | 4 1 3 7 0 2 represents $0.413\,702 * 10^{-3}$
= 0.000413 702

(d) 9 8 | 6 8 4 9 1 5 represents $-0.315\,085 * 10^{-2}$
= −0.003 150 85

Figure 2.5
Floating-point numbers.

This method of storage has two main implications. The first is that all numbers, whatever their size, are held to the same degree of accuracy. In the example being used they will all be stored to an accuracy of six significant digits. Thus the problem of wasted digits does not arise. The second implication is that the limits for the size of the numbers are very much greater than was the case for integers. In our hypothetical computer, for example, real numbers can lie anywhere in the range from -5×10^{48} to $+4.999\,99 \times 10^{48}$, and at the same time the smallest number that can be differentiated from 0 is 0.1×10^{-50} (that is, 10^{-51}).

In our hypothetical computer, therefore, the number 03413702 represents the real value 413.702 or the integer value 3 413 702, depending upon which storage method is being used. It is clearly of vital importance that both we and the computer know which of the two possibilities is required.

In a real computer exactly the same situation arises and it is essential that the two methods of storage are clearly defined. Chapter 3 shows how to instruct the computer which method to use, but for the present the default method will be used in which the first letter of the name determines the type of storage required. As has already been mentioned, if the name of a variable starts with one of the letters I, J, K, L, M or N it refers to an integer and the computer therefore uses the integer storage method. If the name starts with one of the other letters then it refers to a real value and the computer uses the floating-point storage method.

It is extremely important that the difference between an integer and a real number is thoroughly appreciated:

- An integer is a whole number, is always held exactly in the computer's memory, and has a (relatively) limited range (for example, between about -2×10^9 and $+2 \times 10^9$ on a typical 32-bit computer).

- A real number, on the other hand, is stored as a floating-point number, is held as an approximation to a fixed number of significant digits and has a very large range (for example, between about -10^{38} and $+10^{38}$ to seven or eight significant digits on the same 32-bit computer).

Where necessary, numbers are converted from one system to the other, as we shall see in Chapter 3.

2.3   Running Fortran programs on a computer

Up to now we have considered the Fortran program in isolation, with little reference to the method whereby the program is input to the computer, compiled and executed, and the results returned to the user. This omission is deliberate and is due to the fact that, whereas the Fortran language is standardized, the computer **operating system** is not. We shall digress slightly and look at the broad principles of the overall computer system.

In the early days of computing the programmer had to do everything himself. He would load his program (probably written in an assembly language or even machine code) and press the appropriate buttons on the machine to get it to work. When the program required data he would either type it in or, more probably, load some data cards. When the program wanted to print results he would ensure that the printer (or other output device) was ready. Before long computers developed in two directions: first, magnetic tapes (and later disks) were added to provide backing store; and second, high-level languages such as Fortran became available. Now he had to load the compiler first and get it to input his program as data. The compiled program (possibly on binary punched cards produced by the compiler) would then be input as before. In addition, if any backing storage was required he had to load the correct tapes. In some cases a full-time operator was employed to carry out all these tasks, but this of course meant that detailed instructions were required to ensure that the job was processed correctly, and so many programmers still preferred to run their programs themselves.

A major change was heralded by the development at Manchester University of the **multiprogramming** system for the Atlas computer. This took advantage of the high speed of a computer's arithmetic and logical functions compared with its input/output functions to process several programs apparently simultaneously. The effect is similar to that experienced by 'amateur' chess-players when facing a chess master in a simultaneous match, where the master plays against a number of opponents at the same time. In fact, of course, he moves from one board to another, but because of his much greater ability and speed in assessing the positions of the pieces he appears to each of his opponents to be devoting most of his time to them. The Atlas system took advantage of the (relatively) long delays during input or output of even a single number to leave that program (whose input/output could proceed autonomously) and start to process another.

The next major development took place more or less at the same time at both Dartmouth College and the Massachusetts Institute of Technology and led to the concept of **time-sharing**, which placed the user at a terminal through which most input/output took place, with each user having a small slice of time in turn. The much slower speed of a terminal allowed more programs to run at once, but because the user was communicating directly with the computer his work was processed much more quickly in this new **interactive** mode of operation than was possible with **batch** working.

However, the advent first of multiprogramming and then of time-sharing meant that it was no longer possible for the programmer, or even a full-time operator, to carry out all the routine tasks associated with loading and executing a program; too many things were happening in different jobs at the same time. Since the computer was now doing several things at once it was natural that it should be given the additional task of organizing its own work. Special programs were therefore written, called **operating systems**, that enabled the programmer to define what he wanted to be done and caused the computer to carry out these instructions. What gradually emerged were new languages (**job control languages**, JCLs) with which the programmer instructed the computer how to run his jobs.

Unfortunately, job control languages are a very long way from being standardized, and in order to run a Fortran program on a particular computer it is almost always necessary to learn something about the JCL for that computer. Throughout the rest of this book this aspect of running programs will be ignored, and the programs themselves will be the area of interest. However, before any programs are actually compiled and executed it will be necessary for the reader to establish the essential features of the JCL that he will be using on his particular computer.

2.4   Errors in programs

It is an unfortunate fact that programs often (one might even say usually) contain errors. These fall into two distinct groups – syntactic (or grammatical) errors and semantic (or logical) errors. An example of the first type of error would be the omission of the asterisk in the READ statement of our first program

```
READ A,B
```

When the compiler is translating this statement it finds that it does not match with any of the valid forms of READ statement (there are several more, as will be seen in Chapters 9, 10 and 17), and the appropriate machine code cannot be generated. It will therefore produce an error message such as

```
***   Syntax error
```

or possibly a more helpful one such as

```
***   READ not followed by asterisk, format reference or left parenthesis
```

Since the program may contain more than one error the compiler will usually continue to check the rest of the program (although in some cases other apparent errors may be found that will disappear when the first one is corrected). However, no machine code will be produced and no loading or execution will take place (if these would have been automatically initiated). An editor will then normally be used to correct the program before it is resubmitted to the compiler.

Errors detected by the compiler (called **compilation errors**) are no great problem. That they are there indicates a degree of carelessness on the part of the programmer, but they can easily be corrected and the program recompiled. Far more serious is an error in the logic of the program. Occasionally this may lead to a compilation error, but usually it will lead either to an error during the execution of the program leading to an abnormal end (such as would occur if a number were accidentally divided by 0, leading to a theoretical answer of infinity, which is too big for any computer!), or leading to incorrect answers. For example, if the fourth line of our program had inadvertently been written as

```
    SUM=A-B
```

then its execution would have led to the result:

```
The sum of    7.0000 and   12.0000 is   -5.0000
```

This is a type of error with which the computer can give no help, since the program is syntactically correct and runs without causing a failure. It produces an incorrect answer because the logic was incorrect and only the programmer or some other thinking human being can correct it.

Because errors in the logic of a program are often quite difficult to find (the trivial error in a very simple program shown above is hardly typical!), it is very important that programs are planned carefully in advance and not rushed. This discussion of errors underlines the importance of a planned structure to programs and programming, and a useful approach to good program design will be developed in the next chapter.

SUMMARY

- A Fortran program is written using a maximum of 72 characters per line.

- Each statement uses only columns 7–72, with columns 1–6 being reserved for special purposes.

- c or * in column 1 causes the remainder of the line to be treated as a comment.

- Any character other than a space or 0 in column 6 causes columns 7–72 to be treated as a continuation of the previous line.

- Fortran names for programs and/or variables are defined as consisting of up to six letters and/or digits, of which the first must be a letter.

- Variables can be named so that their initial letters define their type (A–H and O–Z mean real, I–N means integer).

- Every program should begin with a PROGRAM statement.

- Every program must end with an END statement.

- List-directed READ and PRINT statements are used for simple input of data from the standard input unit and output of results to the standard output unit.

- The arithmetic assignment statement is a means of evaluating an arithmetic expression and storing it in a user-defined variable.

- Fortran 77 statements introduced in Chapter 2:

Initial statement	PROGRAM *name*
List-directed input and output	READ *, *list of names* PRINT *, *list of names and/or values*
Assignment statement	*name* = *expression*
STOP statement	STOP
END statement	END

SELF-TEST EXERCISES 2.1

Attempt all the following tests and then check your answers with the solutions at the end of the book. If you do not get them correct, and you are not sure why your answer is wrong, you should re-read the chapter before proceeding.

1   What are the following – real constants, integer constants, character constants or none of these?

```
17        17.0       '17.0'      -124       -'124'
A         A17        'A17'       2.413      24.196
14+23     +93.715    SEVEN       12         0.0001
3A1       3E1        9.4 3       1  2       "David"
2.3E-5    2.3E-5.0   'David's'   'Mike''s'  'Mike' 's'
```

2   Which of the following are valid Fortran names?

```
FRED     Fred     JACOB    F17A       P119H2R
ALPHA    6F19A    SIXTH    SEVENTH    EIGHTH
R17-4    R17.4    R17 4    $N         N$
```

3   What will be printed by the following program if it reads the data shown below it?

```
      PROGRAM TEST13
C  Read data
      READ *,A,B,C
      READ *,P,Q,R
      READ *,X,Y,Z
      READ *,A,B,C
      READ *,X,Y,Z
C  Print final values stored
      PRINT *,P,Q,R,X,Y,Z,A,B,C
      STOP
      END
```

```
(Data)
1.23 4.56 7
0.9,8
76 54
1    ,    2
345.6
9.8/
1.23/4.56/7.89
```

4   What is the difference between a floating-point number and an integer? What is a real number?

5   Express the following real constants in another form:

```
1.23E5  1.23E-5  1E7  1E-9
```

6   How many errors can you find in the following program?

```
      PROGRAM TEST 116
C  This program will fail to compile!
      PRINT *, 'Please type numbers in response to the following prompts'
      PRINT *, 'A = '
      READ *, A
      PRlNT *, 'B = '
      READ*,B
      PRINT *,'C = '
      READ *,C
      APLUSB = A+B
      PRINT *,'The sum of ',A,' and ',B,' is ',APLUSB
      AMINUSB = A-B
      PRINT *,'The difference between ',A,' and ',B,' is ',AMINUSB
      SUM=A + B + C
      PRINT *,'Your turn now!!  What's the sum of your three numbers?'
      READ *,ANSWER
      PRINT *,'The correct answer is ',SUM
     *        'Your answer was ',ANSWER
      STOP
      END
```

PROGRAMMING EXERCISES

Exercises whose numbers are preceded by an asterisk (such as 2.6 and 2.9) have sample solutions at the end of this book.

2.1   Find out how to use the editor on your computer to type and correct a Fortran program. Also find out how to submit your program for compiling and execution.

2.2   The following simple program contains a number of errors. Identify them and produce a corrected version.

```
      PRINT *,' This is an example program'
      PROGRAM EXAM1
      READ *,'I'
      PRINT ' Thank you, your number was ' I
      PRINT *, Goodbye for now
      END
      STOP
```

Run the corrected program on your computer to check that it does indeed work.

2.3 Enter the following program exactly as shown:

```
PROGRAM TEST
PRINT *,ENTER ONE NUMBER
READ * A
PRINT *,'THE VALUE OF A IS',A
STOP
END
```

The program contains two errors, only one of which will probably be detected by the compiler. Can you find them? Now run the program and correct only those errors detected by the compiler, and run it again. Was the answer printed correct? If not, why not?

2.4 Enter the following Fortran program exactly as shown, and run it.

```
PROGRAM EXAM2
N=2
PRINT *,' 2 x 2 =',NxN
STOP
END
```

Produce a corrected version!

2.5 Write a program that expects three numbers to be entered, but only uses one READ statement, and then prints them out so that you can check that they have been input correctly.

When typing in the numbers at the keyboard try typing them all on one line:

(a) separated by spaces;
(b) separated by commas;
(c) separated by semi-colons.

Also, try typing each of the three numbers in turn followed by RETURN (or ENTER).

This exercise should help you to appreciate how a Fortran program expects input to a list of variables.

*2.6 Write and run a program that will read 10 numbers and find their sum. Test the program with several sets of data, including the following

1, 5, 17.3, 9, -23.7142, 12.9647, 0.0005, -2974, 3951.448 99, -1000

Were the answers what you expected?

2.7 The following program is intended to swap the values of A and B.

```
PROGRAM SWAP
A = 2.5
B = 3.6
B = A
A = B
PRINT *,A,B
STOP
END
```

Correct it so that it works properly. (*Hint*: you may need to use another variable.)

2.8 Modify the program in Exercise 2.7 so that you can enter the two numbers from the keyboard.

*2.9 Write and run a program to read four integers and print the difference between the sum of the first two and the sum of the last two.

2.10 Modify the program you wrote for Exercise 2.7 so that it cyclically permutes values between three variables; that is, so that A takes the value of B, B takes the value of C, and C takes the value of A, with C set initially to 1.4.

2.11 Write a program that reads two numbers greater than 100 000 000 and then prints out their sum and difference. Test it with various pairs of numbers, including the following:

123456789 and 123456788
123456789 and 123456790
1.23456789E8 and 1.2345679E8
1.23456789E13 and 1.2345679E13

Do you notice anything surprising about the results?

2.12 Write a program that prompts the user to enter four decimal numbers (numbers which contain a decimal point) and then reads the numbers into the variables A, B, C and D. The program should keep a running total as each number is entered, printing out the total to date after each new addition.

Try running your program with several sets of data, including the four numbers 17.3, 6.2, 4.2 and 8.8.

Now change the program so that it reads the numbers into four variables called IA, IB, IC and ID, and run it again with the same data. Can you explain why the results are different?

Arithmetic, expressions and assignment

3

Fortran was originally designed for solving mathematical problems, and this is still its major strength. The assignment statement is the main method by which numerical values are calculated and saved for subsequent use, since the **expression** to the right of an = sign is evaluated and **assigned** to the memory location specified by the variable name on the left. Appropriate conversions are carried out between integer and real values as necessary.

Although variable names have an **implicit type**, determined by their initial letter, this can be overridden by an explicit **variable declaration**. It is recommended that all variables should be explicitly declared.

As well as storing values in specific variables by means of an assignment, it is also possible to arrange for variables to be given specified values when the program is first loaded into the computer by means of a DATA statement. It is also possible to declare **named constants**, such as PI, as a clearer and simpler way of including such constant values in a program.

3.1   The assignment statement

The assignment statement

    SUM=A+B

means 'take the values stored in the real variables A and B, add them together, and store the result in a real variable called SUM'. The assignment statement is an extremely important type of statement since it is the most common way in which a value is stored in a particular storage location. It takes the general form

    name = expression

where the name on the left of the equals sign is the name of the storage location to which will be **assigned** the value of the expression on the right of the equals sign. Figure 3.1 illustrates this by reference to the storage model used in Chapter 1.

There are three types of assignment statement corresponding to the three major types of storage location, namely arithmetic assignment, logical assignment and character assignment. The most widely used is the arithmetic assignment statement, and only this type will be considered for the present; the other two types will be discussed in Chapters 12 and 13.

Figure 3.1
Assignment in the
storage model.

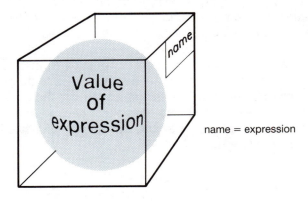

name = expression

3.2   Arithmetic expressions

An arithmetic **expression** is used to express a numeric computation, and evaluation of an arithmetic expression produces a numeric value. Thus A+B is an arithmetic expression whose evaluation leads to the value of the sum of the two numbers (or values) stored in the real variables A and B.

The simplest form of an arithmetic expression is an unsigned constant (for example, 25) or a variable name (for example, A). More complex expressions can be formed by use of arithmetic operators, of which there are five, shown in Figure 3.2.

We have already seen that the expression

    A+B

represents 'A plus B' and is evaluated to give the sum of the real values stored in A and B. In a similar way

    X−Y
    P∗Q
    D/E
    U∗∗V

represent subtraction, multiplication, division and exponentiation, respectively.

The above operators have all been defined in a **dyadic** sense – that is, they have been used between two operands. The + and - operators can also be used as **monadic** operators with only one operand. Thus

    −G

represents the negated value stored in G, while

    +T

has the same value as T.

Operator	Meaning
+	addition
−	subtraction
∗	multiplication
/	division
∗∗	exponentiation

Figure 3.2
Arithmetic operators.

The above examples have all used variable names, but constants can, of course, be used as well:

```
A+5
6.7-X
Q*1.42
S/3
12.5**D
-4.7
+0.13
```

Of course more complex expressions than these are frequently required and this principle can therefore be extended to include as many operators as are necessary. Thus we may write expressions such as

```
A+B/C-12*D**E
```

However, the question that then arises concerns the order of evaluation. For example, what is the value of the following expression?

```
4.0+6.0*2.0
```

There are two possibilities, 20.0 and 16.0. The first is obtained by working from left to right and the second from right to left.

Similarly, consider the following expression:

```
3.0+4.0**2.0-8.0/4.0+2.0
```

The rules in Fortran are the same as the normal arithmetic priority rules, as shown in Figure 3.3, with the proviso that within any one priority level evaluation is carried out from left to right.

Thus in the expression above the exponentiation will be carried out first, causing the expression to reduce to

```
3.0+16.0-8.0/4.0+2.0
```

and then any multiplication or division, leading to

```
3.0+16.0-2.0+2.0
```

Figure 3.3
Arithmetic operator priorities.

Operator	Priority
**	High
* and /	Medium
+ and -	Low

Finally the additions and subtraction are carried out, leading to a value of 19.0.

There is one more aspect of an arithmetic expression left to consider, namely, the use of parentheses (or round brackets). Consider, for example, the algebraic expression

$$\frac{A\ +\ B}{C}$$

Clearly, in order to evaluate this correctly the sub-expression A + B must be evaluated first, and the resulting sum must then be divided by C. This is written in Fortran as

    (A+B)/C

and all is well, because *any expression enclosed in parentheses is evaluated first*. Once again, this is the same as normal arithmetic or algebraic practice. If one pair of parentheses is enclosed within another pair then the inner pair is evaluated first. Thus in the following expression

    A*((B+C)**D-E)

the order of evaluation is as follows:

(1)   Calculate B+C, because this is enclosed in an inner pair of parentheses.
(2)   Evaluate the contents of the outer parentheses in the usual order: first calculate (B+C) raised to the power of D, and then subtract E.
(3)   Finally, multiply A by the result of the above evaluation (at step 2).

If we replace A, B, C, D and E by the numbers 2.0, 3.0, 4.0, 5.0 and 6.0 we can follow this through:

    2.0*((3.0+4.0)**5.0-6.0)

becomes

    2.0*(7.0**5.0-6.0)

then

    2.0*(16807.0-6.0)

then

```
2.0*16801.0
```

and then

```
33602.0
```

There is one important exception to the above rules, which concerns exponentiation. The mathematical expression a^{b^c} is interpreted by mathematicians as $a^{(b^c)}$ and so Fortran follows the same convention. The expression

```
A**B**C
```

is therefore evaluated *from right to left* instead of from left to right as in all other cases, and is equivalent to

```
A**(B**C)
```

We can now use our present knowledge of arithmetic expressions (and assignment statements) to solve some simple examples.

EXAMPLE 3.1

Write a program to read a Celsius temperature and convert it to Fahrenheit, using the formula

$$F = \frac{9C}{5} + 32$$

This is a simple program and can probably be written down without much thought

```
      PROGRAM CONVRT
C
C  A program to convert a Celsius temperature to Fahrenheit
C
      PRINT *,'What is the Celsius temperature? '
      READ *,TEMPC
      TEMPF = 9.0*TEMPC/5.0+32.0
      PRINT *,TEMPC,'C =',TEMPF,'F'
      STOP
      END
```

Notice that the program name (CONVRT) and the names of the two variables used (TEMPC and TEMPF) have been chosen to give an indication of their purpose within the limit of six characters for a name.

The names used for variables (and program names) are purely for the writer's convenience – they have no special meaning to the compiler. Thus instead of TEMPC and TEMPF we could have written C and F, or X and Y, or A17 and B49! However, in order to make the program understandable to the reader (who will often, though not always, be the writer) meaningful names should be used wherever possible. Note that the names used in the above program (and the alternatives just discussed) are all names of real variables. Since we shall be carrying out a division it would not be sensible to use only whole numbers (or integers), and indeed variables used for any form of calculation are almost invariably real variables. Section 3.4 discusses the use of integer variables and expressions in detail.

Since we are using *real* variables to calculate a *real* expression we have written the expression in the third line of the above program using *real* constants:

```
TEMPF = 9.0*TEMPC/5.0+32.0
```

This is not strictly necessary, as one of the rules concerned with evaluating arithmetic expressions states that when evaluating an expression of the form

operand operator operand

both operands must be of the same type (other than in expressions of the form X**2). If one is an integer and the other is real then the integer operand will be converted to its real equivalent before the evaluation takes place. The result of the evaluation will be of the same type as the operands.

This means that if the expression is written in the form

```
9*TEMPC/5
```

then, when it is evaluated, the rules of evaluation will cause the following steps to take place:

(1)   As there are no exponentiations (or parentheses), evaluate multiplications and divisions from left to right.

(2)   Evaluate 9*TEMPC. This is a **mixed-mode expression** (that is, 9 is integer, TEMPC is real); therefore first convert 9 to real (which we shall write as 9.0). Now evaluate 9.0*TEMPC to give a real result.

(3)   Evaluate (9.0*TEMPC)/5. Again this is a mixed-mode expression since the result of the previous step, (9.0*TEMPC), is real and 5 is

integer. Before the evaluation of (9.0*TEMPC)/5.0 is carried out, 5 is therefore converted to real.

(4)   All multiplication and division is now complete, so evaluate additions and subtractions (9.0*TEMPC/5.0)+32. Once again the same thing happens and 32 is converted to real before the final evaluation takes place.

(5)   The real result is now available for storing in a suitable location.

One minor point concerning this expression is that since the order of multiplication and division is immaterial we could have written

```
9.0/5.0*TEMPC+32.0
```

which will clearly be the same as

```
1.8*TEMPC+32.0
```

This is one of those cases where personal style enters into things. This last form of the expression avoids the unnecessary extra division, but at the cost of a loss of clarity in the program. A compromise might be to add a comment line

```
C   Use the formula F=9C/5+32 (=1.8C+32)
      TEMPF=1.8*TEMPC+32.0
```

Finally, notice that the PRINT statement has identified the meaning of the results. If we had written

```
PRINT *,TEMPF,TEMPC
```

it is not obvious from the results printed (just two numbers) what they mean.

EXAMPLE 3.2

Write a program to calculate the nett pay of a British worker who pays 6% of his gross pay towards his superannuation and 25% of what is left as income tax, and also has fixed deductions, for example for health insurance, amounting to £14.40 per week. Print a payslip showing gross pay, nett pay and all deductions.

This is a fairly straightforward program and introduces no new problems:

```
      PROGRAM PAY
C
C  A program to calculate the nett pay of a British worker
C
C  Read gross pay
      PRINT *,'Type gross pay before deductions: '
      READ *,GROSS
C  Superannuation is 6% of gross pay
      SUPER = 0.06*GROSS
C  Tax is 25% of pay, excluding superannuation contributions
      TAXABL = GROSS-SUPER
      TAX = 0.25*TAXABL
C  Fixed weekly deductions of £14—40
      PAYNET = TAXABL-TAX-14.4
C  Print details
      PRINT *,'Gross pay: ',GROSS
      PRINT *,'Superannuation: ',SUPER
      PRINT *,'Tax: ',TAX
      PRINT *,'Insurance: ',14.4
      PRINT *,' '
      PRINT *,'Nett Pay: ',PAYNET
      STOP
      END
```

Because several calculations are carried out in this program whose purpose may not be immediately obvious several comments have been included in the program. It is important to include comments in a program – but they should *explain*, not duplicate, what is going on in terms that can be readily understood at a later date, or by someone else.

Notice that in line 14 the nett pay has been stored in a variable called PAYNET, because NETPAY (the obvious name) would have been integer. Notice also that lines 19 and 20 print only constants. Line 19 prints the insurance details (which are a constant deduction of £14.40), while line 20 prints a single space as a way of printing a blank line. The results might therefore look as shown in Figure 3.4.

The layout of these results leaves a lot to be desired and could be improved by the inclusion of additional spaces in the character constants, for example

```
      PRINT *,'Gross pay:     ',GROSS
```

```
Gross pay:   173.5000
Superannuation:    10.4100
Tax:    40.7725
Insurance:    14.5000

Nett Pay:   107.8175
```

Figure 3.4
Results produced by
Example 3.2.

However the list-directed PRINT statement is essentially a simple form of output statement and is not intended for use where the detailed layout of results is important. For that we need the full power of Fortran formatting, which will be discussed later in Chapter 9.

3.3 REAL and INTEGER declarations

In Example 3.2 we had to use the variable name PAYNET to ensure that it was a real variable. In order to avoid the use of such unnatural names we may always **declare** variable names in a **type specification** statement. This takes the form:

> F90

REAL *name1*, *name2*, ...

or

> F90

INTEGER *name3*, *name4*, ...

and must appear after the initial PROGRAM statement but *before* any of the other (executable) statements that we have met so far. Other specification statements will be discussed in later chapters.

For real and integer variables it is not, of course, necessary to declare their names in this way as the initial letter of their names can be used for this purpose. However, since the other variable types that will be introduced in later chapters must always be declared, many programmers prefer for consistency to declare *all* their variables. Furthermore, many compilers have a facility for reporting the use of any undeclared variables, which provides a useful check against mistyping a name. Figure 3.5 shows how the program written in Example 3.2 would look if all variables were declared.

Many Fortran programmers always use **implicit typing** of real and integer variables by means of the initial letter of their names, and this certainly does ensure that the type of a variable is instantly recognizable. However, many others believe that it is a good discipline to declare all the variables that are used in a program. This practice will be followed in this book and henceforth *all variables will always be declared in complete programs*. In short extracts, on the other hand, the default types will be assumed unless otherwise stated.

```
      PROGRAM PAY
C
C  A program to calculate the nett pay of a British worker
C
      REAL GROSS,SUPER,TAXABL,TAX,NETT
C  Read gross pay
      PRINT *,'Type gross pay before deductions: '
      READ *,GROSS
C  Superannuation is 6% of gross pay
      SUPER = 0.06*GROSS
C  Tax is 25% of pay, excluding superannuation contributions
      TAXABL = GROSS-SUPER
      TAX = 0.25*TAXABL
C  Fixed weekly deductions of £14-40
      NETT = TAXABL-TAX-14.4
      PRINT *,'Gross pay: ',GROSS
      PRINT *,'Superannuation: ',SUPER
      PRINT *,'Tax: ',TAX
      PRINT *,'Insurance: ',14.4
      PRINT *,' '
      PRINT *,'Nett Pay: ',NETT
      STOP
      END
```

Figure 3.5
An example of variable declaration.

3.4   Integer expressions

The discussion of arithmetic expressions in Section 3.2 assumed that all the operands were either real or were converted to a real value before evaluation. However, what about the situation where both operands are integer?

The syntax is quite straightforward, as the five arithmetic operators already met in real expressions can all be used with integers (Figure 3.6).

There is, however, one problem. As long as the operator is +, -, * or ** the evaluation of the expression proceeds without any difficulty, but division is another matter. For example, in the fourth line of Figure 3.6, what is the value of the expression if M has the value 3?

```
I+J
N-6
K*L
4/M
N**4
J*(K/(N+4)-L)**(N-M)
```

Figure 3.6
Integer expressions.

Figure 3.7
Examples of integer
division.

Expression	Value	
17/5	3	
99/100	0	
-12/7	-1	
4/(5-8)	-1	(4/(-3))
17/4*4	16	(4*4)
17/4*4/17	0	(16/17)
17*4/4/17	1	(68/4/17 => 17/17)

The expression reduces to 4/3 which is 1.3333...; but the rule introduced in Example 3.1 stated that the result of the evaluation will be of the same type as the operands. In this case, therefore, the result will be an integer and thus cannot have any fractional part! The solution is to ignore the fractional part of the result and to treat it as equal to 1; thus 4/3 is evaluated to give 1. Similarly, if M was 5 the result would be 0.

The rule is that when integer division is carried out the result is obtained by ignoring any fractional part that would exist had the evaluation been mathematically accurate. Figure 3.7 shows the results obtained by evaluating several integer expressions that contain integer divisions.

The last three examples in Figure 3.7 show how, owing to the loss of fractional parts, the order of multiplication and division is important when using integers. Integer division is, therefore, used only for certain specific purposes, and is not used at all in most programs. It can, however, be a cause of errors in programs if care is not taken. Consider, for example, the program written in Example 3.1 to convert a Celsius temperature to Fahrenheit.

This used the formula

$$F = \frac{9C}{5} + 32$$

which appeared in the original program as

```
TEMPF = 9.0*TEMPC/5.0+32.0
```

or, more succinctly, as we saw later

```
TEMPF = 9*TEMPC/5+32
```

Now consider what might have happened if the formula had been written (equally correctly) as

$$F = \frac{9C}{5} + 32$$

If the programmer had followed this and written

```
TEMPF = 9/5*TEMPC+32
```

the wrong results would have been obtained! This is because when the expression is evaluated the process works from left to right. Thus the first sub-expression to be evaluated is 9/5. Here both operands are integer and so an integer division is carried out, leading to a value of 1.

The next step is to evaluate (9/5)*C, that is 1*C. This is a mixed-mode expression and so 1 is converted to its real equivalent – but it is clearly too late. The expression has effectively been reduced to TEMPC+32.

The ideal solution is never to write mixed-mode expressions, and then there will be no chance of this error occurring. In practice, however, mixed-mode expressions are no problem as long as care is taken to ensure that no integer division takes place where it is not intended.

EXAMPLE 3.3

Work out what will be printed by the following program:

```
PROGRAM EX33
REAL X1,X2,X3,A1,A2,A3
INTEGER N1,N2,N3,M1,M2,M3
X1 = 5
N1 = 5
X2 = -9
N2 = -9
X3 = 4
N3 = 4
A1 = X1*X2/X3
M1 = N1*N2/N3
A2 = X2/X3*X1
M2 = N2/N3*N1
A3 = X1/X3*X2
M3 = N1/N3*N2
PRINT *,A1,A2,A3
PRINT *,M1,M2,M3
STOP
END
```

A glance at the program shows that each pair of lines is the same except that X1, X2, X3, A1, A2 and A3 are replaced by N1, N2, N3, M1, M2 and M3 respectively. Thus the calculation of A1 in line 10 leads to the value -11.25 ($5.0*(-9.0)/4.0$), while in a similar manner line 12 leads to a value of -11.25 for A2 ($-9.0/4.0*5.0$), and line 14 stores -11.25 ($5.0/4.0*(-9.0)$) in A3.

The first integer calculation in line 11 causes the value −11 (5*(−9)/4 → −45/4) to be stored in M1. However line 13 sets M2 to the value −10 (−9/4*5 → −2*5), while line 15 stores −9 in M3 (5/4*(−9) → 1*(−9))!

The results are therefore

```
-11.25   -11.25   -11.25
 -11      -10       -9
```

Thus we see that although the order of evaluation of multiplication and division makes no difference when using real operands, it can make a significant difference when using integers.

EXAMPLE 3.4

Write a program that reads the number of apples that can be packed in a carton and the number of apples that need to be packed. Print the number of cartons that the apples will fill and the number that will be left over.

This problem is an example of the use of integer division to find a whole-number quotient and remainder.

```
      PROGRAM APPLES
C
C  A program to calculate the number of apple cartons required
C
      INTEGER BOXFUL,APPLES,FULL,LEFT
C  Read number per box and total number of apples
      PRINT *,'How many apples can be packed into a box? '
      READ *,BOXFUL
      PRINT *,'How many apples are there? '
      READ *,APPLES
C  Calculate number of full boxes and number of apples left over
      FULL = APPLES/BOXFUL
      LEFT = APPLES-FULL*BOXFUL
C  Print results
      PRINT *,'There will be ',FULL,' full cartons'
      PRINT *,'and ',LEFT,' apples left over'
      STOP
      END
```

In this program the integer division in line 12 will set FULL to the largest integer that is not greater than the (mathematical) number of boxes. Thus if each box would take 72 apples and there were 450 apples in all, the value of FULL would be 6 (since 450/72 is 6.25). Line 13 then finds the remainder by multiplying this by the divisor (the number per box) and subtracting the result from the total number of apples. Thus with the figures just used the remainder would be 18.

If the number left over (the remainder) had alone been required it could have been calculated in a single expression:

```
LEFT = APPLES-APPLES/BOXFUL*BOXFUL
```

3.5   Arithmetic assignment

Any implications that the different types of expressions, real, integer and mixed-mode, may have for the rest of the assignment statement have not yet been considered.

The result of the evaluation of an arithmetic expression will be integer if *all* the operands are integer and will be real if *any* of the operands are real. (Since a mixed-mode expression has the integer operand converted to real and has a real result, it follows that if any operand in an expression is real then either all the operands are real, in which case the result is obviously real, or there will be a mixed-mode expression at some point in the evaluation and all subsequent sub-expressions will be mixed-mode, leading to a real result.) In all the examples used so far we have ensured that a real result is stored in a real variable, and an integer result is stored in an integer variable. But what will happen in the following cases?

```
X=I*J-K*L
N=P*Q/R
M=I+4*J/K-A
```

In the first case the expression to the right of the equals sign is integer, whereas the variable on the left is real. Here there is no problem and the real equivalent of the integer value is assigned to X. Thus if I, J, K and L have the values 3, 5, 6 and 2 respectively, the value of the expression is 3 (3*5-6*2) and so the *real* representation of 3 (which we shall write as 3.0) is stored in X.

In the second case all the items in the expression are real and so a real result is obtained, which is to be assigned to the integer variable N. In this case the real value is converted to integer and, in a similar way to integer division, the fractional part (if any) is lost. Thus if P, Q and R have the values 6.0, 7.0 and 9.0, the value of the expression is 4.6666... and so the value 4 is assigned to N. Notice in particular that the real value is **truncated** and not rounded. This can lead to problems if care is not taken. For example, if P, Q and R have values 2.0, 3.0 and 6.0 then the expression reduces to 6.0/6.0, which clearly should cause N to take the value 1; however, the calculation might lead to a value (before truncation) of 0.9999..., which although close enough to 1.0 for most purposes will lead to N taking the value of 0! The solution to this difficulty is to add a small value before truncation, for example N=P*Q/R+0.001.

The third case shows an expression that is integer except for one operand. If I, J and K are assumed to have the same values as before (3, 5 and 6) and A is 4.1 then the evaluation of the expression proceeds as follows:

(1) I+4*5/K-A → I+20/K-A
(2) I+20/6-A → I+3-A
(3) 3+3-A → 6-A
(4) 6-4.1 → 6.0-4.1 → 1.9

Finally the value 1.9 must be assigned to M, which therefore takes the value 1, owing to truncation.

EXAMPLE 3.5

During a journey a driver stops to fill up with fuel several times. Each time he stops he always puts in exactly eight gallons. At the end of the journey he fills up the tank until it is full (as it was at the start) and notes the amount needed and also the total distance travelled in miles (the milometer does not show fractions of a mile). Write a program to read the number of miles travelled, the number of stops for fuel and the amount put in at the end of the journey, and then to print the average fuel consumption in miles per gallon *to the nearest whole number*. (Round up for 0.5 upwards, round down for less than 0.5.)

This is a fairly straightforward exercise apart from the question of rounding:

```
      PROGRAM FUEL
C
C  A program to calculate average fuel consumption
C
      INTEGER MILES,STOPS,MPG
      REAL TOPUP
      PRINT *,'How far did you travel (in miles)? '
      READ *,MILES
      PRINT *,'How many times did you fill up with fuel? '
      READ *,STOPS
      PRINT *,'How much fuel did you put in at the end? '
      READ *,TOPUP
      MPG = MILES/(8.0*STOPS+TOPUP)+0.5
      PRINT *,'Average mpg was',MPG
      STOP
      END
```

Calculated mpg	+0.5	Value stored in MPG
34.0	34.5	34
34.49	34.99	34
34.5	35.0	35
34.99	35.49	35

Figure 3.8
The effect of rounding in Example 3.5.

Let us examine the assignment statement in line 13 more closely. The first step will be to evaluate the expression in parentheses, which will calculate the amount of fuel used. Notice that this is a mixed-mode expression and will cause the result to be real. The number of miles travelled is then divided by this figure in another mixed-mode expression, thus leading to a real result for the miles per gallon. However if this were then assigned to the integer variable MPG it would be truncated and, for example, 35.9 would be stored as 35, which is not what is required. The constant 0.5 is therefore added to the calculated MPG before it is assigned. Figure 3.8 shows the effect of this in some specific instances and it can easily be seen that it causes rounding to take place exactly as required.

3.6   Defining initial values

Quite often when we are writing programs there is a need for some of the variables used to be assigned an initial value before the program really starts to do anything. When a program is loaded into the computer after it has been compiled, a substantial part of the memory it occupies is thereby set to some value (namely the machine-code instructions). On many systems all the variable space will also be set to a predefined value (sometimes 0, sometimes an 'impossible' value that will cause an error if accessed before the program has given the variable a value).

In Fortran it is possible to instruct the compiler to arrange that, when the compiled program is loaded, certain defined variables are loaded with specific initial values. This is achieved with a DATA statement, which takes the form

DATA *nlist1/clist1/, nlist2/clist2/, . . .*

F90

or

DATA *nlist1/clist1/nlist2/clist2/ . . .*

F90

where each *nlist* is a list of variable names and each *clist* is a list of constants. There must be exactly the same number of items in a *clist* as in the corresponding *nlist*. The effect of the statement is to ensure that each variable in *nlist* is given the initial value specified by the corresponding constant in *clist*. Thus

```
DATA A,B,N/1.0,2.0,17/,CODE/8667/
```

will give the real variables A and B initial values of 1.0 and 2.0, the integer variable N an initial value of 17, and the real variable CODE an initial value of 8667.

The normal rules of arithmetic assignment apply and the constant will be converted to the appropriate type if necessary.

It frequently happens that several variables are to be given the same initial value, in which case it is possible to precede the constant with the number of repetitions required and an asterisk. Thus a DATA statement setting the six variables I-N to zero could be written as follows:

```
DATA I,J,K,L,M,N/6*0/
```

A DATA statement must appear after any specification statements. It is usual practice to place DATA statements at the beginning of the executable portion of the program, but this is not necessary. (They could equally well be placed immediately before the END statement, although this does make their purpose, which is to provide initial values, slightly less apparent!) Wherever a DATA statement is placed it will cause initialization to be carried out when the program is loaded, that is, just before the start of execution.

3.7 Giving names to constants

As well as giving initial values to variables, a DATA statement can be used to give a value to a variable that is never changed:

```
DATA PI/3.1415926536/
```

This variable can then be used in place of the constant both to save writing (as here) and to improve the clarity of the program. However, we are using a variable in place of a constant, which is not a desirable course of action for several reasons: on aesthetic (or stylistic) grounds, because of practical considerations such as efficiency; and, most importantly, because of the possibility of the variable being (erroneously) assigned another value.

The PARAMETER statement allows us to give a name to a constant, and takes the form

```
PARAMETER (name1=const1,name2=const2,...)
```

F90

where *const1* and so on, are constants or constant expressions and *name1* and so on, are the names to be associated with them. Notice that the part of the statement that defines the name and value looks exactly like an assignment statement, except that the expression on the right of the equals sign is composed only of constants. Thus a better way of giving a value to PI is to write

```
PARAMETER (PI=3.1415926536)
```

which defines PI as a constant with the required value. On every occasion in the program that PI is referred to, the compiled program will use the value 3.1415926536.

A constant expression can be used to define constants that can be defined more accurately as an expression – for example:

```
PARAMETER (THIRD=1.0/3.0)
```

or where the value is expressed more clearly by an expression, such as

```
PARAMETER (PI3BY4=3.0*PI/4.0)
```

When an expression is used in this way there are two restrictions:

- Only the operators +, -, * and / may be used, except that ** may be used as long as the exponent is integer; parentheses may be used in the normal way.
- If a named (or **symbolic**) constant appears in a constant expression it must have been defined in an earlier PARAMETER statement, or in an earlier part of this statement.

The latter rule means that the following is allowed:

```
PARAMETER (PI=3.1415926536,PI3BY4=3.0*PI/4.0)
```

If the implied type of the constant name is not suitable then it must appear in a type statement to define the correct type. Such a type statement must come *before* the PARAMETER statement in the program. Apart from this a PARAMETER statement may appear anywhere after the initial (PROGRAM) statement and before the first DATA or executable statement.

The normal rules for mixed-mode expressions and assignments apply, and therefore the statement

```
PARAMETER (ICON=3.0/4*5,CON=3/4*5.0)
```

will result in the constant ICON having a value of 3 (3.0/4*5 → 3.0/4.0*5 → 0.75*5 → 3.75 → 3), while CON will have a value of 0.0 (3/4*5.0 → 0*5.0 → 0.0).

A named constant that has been defined in a PARAMETER statement may appear in any subsequent statement as part of an arithmetic expression, or may appear as a value in a DATA statement.

3.8   Expressions in output lists

In Chapter 2 we mentioned that the output list for a PRINT statement can consist of variables, constants and expressions. Arithmetic expressions have now been examined in some detail and it can be seen how an expression could be used directly in a PRINT statement. There are, however, two points to beware of. The first of these is that if an expression appears in an output list then clearly the value of that expression cannot be preserved for future use. For example, Figure 3.9 shows an alternative solution to Example 3.4 that uses no assignment statements. However, as a result of this the expression APPLES/BOXFUL appears, and is evaluated twice, on consecutive lines.

The second point concerns type conversion, specifically the truncation that takes place when a real quantity is stored in an integer variable. For instance, in Example 3.5 the variable MPG is only used to store an

---

Figure 3.9
An alternative solution to
Example 3.4.

```
      PROGRAM APPLES
C
C  A program to calculate the number of apple cartons required
C
      INTEGER BOXFUL,APPLES
C  Read number per box and total number of apples
      PRINT *,'How many apples can be packed into a box? '
      READ *,BOXFUL
      PRINT *,'How many apples are there? '
      READ *,APPLES
C  Calculate and print number of full boxes and number of apples left
      PRINT *,'There will be ',APPLES/BOXFUL,' full cartons'
      PRINT *,'and ',APPLES-(APPLES/BOXFUL)*BOXFUL,' apples left over'
      STOP
      END
```

integer value prior to its being printed. However, if the assignment to MPG were eliminated and the arithmetic expression included in the PRINT statement, no conversion to integer would take place. A solution to this problem will be seen in the next chapter.

SUMMARY

- The order of evaluation of an arithmetic expression is: ** first, then *
  and /, and finally + and –. Expressions in parentheses are evaluated
  first.

- Integer division involves truncation of the result.

- Real values are truncated before being assigned to integer variables.

- Integer values are automatically converted to real in a mixed-mode
  expression.

- The DATA statement provides initial values for variables.

- The PARAMETER statement is used to give a name to a constant.

- Expressions can be used in the output list of a PRINT statement as an
  alternative to first assigning the value of the expression to a variable.

- Fortran 77 statements introduced in Chapter 3:

Type declaration	REAL *list of names* INTEGER *list of names*
Assignment statement	*name = expression* for example, X = A+B 　　　　　　　　N = I–J 　　　　　　　　P = Q*R 　　　　　　　　W = D/E 　　　　　　　　L = K**M 　　　　　　　　H = I+3.0*X**(B–J)
Initial value specification	DATA *list of names/list of values/*
Constant declaration	PARAMETER (*name=constant_expression*)

SELF-TEST EXERCISES 3.1

1   What are the values of the following Fortran expressions?

```
17-12*4          45/4*4            9.5+23/2         9.5+2.3/.2
4-6+18.0/3/3     4-(6+18.0/3/3)    19-7-9           19-(7-9)
3**2**3          4.0**16.0**0.5
```

2   If the statements

```
REAL A,B,C
INTEGER I,J,K
READ *,A,B,C,I,J,K
```

are used to read the following data

```
19,26,-12
19,26,-12
```

what will be the values printed by the following statements?

```
PRINT *,A+C+B/K
PRINT *,I+K+J/C
PRINT *,A+C+J/K
PRINT *,A+(C+J)/K
```

3   What will be printed by the following program if it is given the data listed below it?

```
PROGRAM TEST33
REAL A,B,C,D,E,F
INTEGER I,J,K,L,M,N
DATA A,B,C,D,E,F/1.0,2.0,3.0,4.0,5.0,6.0/
DATA I,J,K,L,M,N/1,2,3,4,5,6/
READ *,A,B,C
READ *,I,J,K
D=D+A*B**K
E=D+C
F=E+F+C*I**J
L=L+D
M=M+E
N=N+F
PRINT *,'The results are as follows:'
PRINT *,'A=',A,' B=',B,' C=',C
PRINT *,'D=',D,' E=',E,' F=',F
PRINT *,'I=',I,' J=',J,' K=',K
PRINT *,'L=',L,' M=',M,' N=',N
STOP
END
```

(data)
```
3/4/5
3,4,5
```

PROGRAMMING EXERCISES

3.1   Write a program to input a number x and print the values of $x - 1$, $x + 2$ and $x^2 + x - 2$.

3.2   Write a program that inputs a number x and prints the value of $(1 + 1/x)^x$.

3.3   Write a program that initializes the variables D, E and F to the values 1.2, 3.4 and 5.9 and then computes and prints the two values

```
RES1 = D*E**F
RES2 = (D*E)**F
```

Why are the two values different?

3.4   Modify the program written for Exercise 3.3 so that the two variables RES1 and RES2 are not needed.

*3.5   Write and test a program that will read up to 20 examination marks, and calculate their average. (*Hint*: you will need to read the number of marks first, and then utilize one of the special features of list-directed input.)

3.6   Write a program that will input an amount in pounds and print the corresponding amount in dollars, assuming an exchange rate of £1 = \$1.62.

3.7   The reduced mass of a diatomic molecule is given by the expression

$$\mu = \frac{m_a m_b}{m_a + m_b}$$

Write a program that calculates μ where you enter m_a and m_b from the keyboard.

3.8   Write a program that evaluates b, where b is given by

$$b = \frac{x + y^2}{z} - a$$

using each of the following statements in turn in your program.

```
B = (((X+Y)/Z)**2)-A
B = X+Y/Z**2-A
B = (X+Y/Z**2)-A
B = ((X+Y)/Z**2)-A
```

Can you explain the results you get?

3.9   Write a program that reads two integer numbers from the keyboard, where the first number read is to be smaller than the second. Try the following exercises and explain the results you get.

  (a)   Assign the two numbers to real variables. Divide the smaller number by the larger and assign the result to a real variable. Print out the result.
  (b)   Assign the first number to a real variable and the second to an integer. Divide the smaller number by the larger and assign the result to a real variable. Print out the result.
  (c)   Assign the first number to an integer variable and the second to a real. Divide the smaller number by the larger and assign the result to a real variable. Print out the result.
  (d)   Assign the two numbers to integer variables. Divide the smaller number by the larger and assign the result to a real variable. Print out the result.

3.10   Four people pick 285 apples. The owner of the orchard keeps 40% of these, the pickers share the rest evenly and any remainder is made into a pie. Write a program to calculate how many apples the owner, each picker and the pie receive.

3.11   When visitors come to dinner Mr Smith always makes them Danish Apple Cake. For four people this requires the following ingredients:

  675 g   of apples
   75 g   of butter
  150 g   of sugar
  100 g   of breadcrumbs
  150 ml of cream

Write a program that inputs the number of people coming to dinner, and then prints the amount of each ingredient required.

3.12   A man wishes to build a brick wall 4 ft high along one side of his garden. The bricks are 9 in long, $4\frac{1}{2}$ in wide, and 3 in high, and there should be $\frac{1}{2}$ in of mortar between bricks. Write a program to calculate how many bricks he will need if the wall is to be 23 ft 6 in long, and then use this program to calculate the number of bricks needed for walls of different heights and lengths.

*3.13   A small business wishes to use a computer program to calculate how to make up the pay packets for its employees. The program should read the total amount to be paid, and print the number of £20, £10 and £5 notes and £1, 50p, 20p, 10p, 5p, 2p and 1p coins needed. (There are 100p in £1.) It is a union requirement that every pay packet should contain at least 40p in coins, and at least one £5 note. Subject to this restriction, the pay packet should contain as few coins and notes as possible.

Write a program to provide the required information, and test it with a wide variety of cases, including examples of a total pay of £125.39 and £65.40.

3.14   A sheet-metal-stamping company buys its metal in rectangular sheets of various sizes – 2, 5 or 10 m long by 2, 4 or 6 m wide. It has an order for a number of circular discs of a given diameter (less than 1 m) and wishes to waste as little metal as possible.

Write a program that reads the number and diameter of discs required and the size of the sheet, and then calculates the number of sheets of this size required and the percentage of the metal wasted.

Then modify your program so that it cycles through all the available sheet sizes automatically and prints the required information for each sheet size so that the user can decide which sheet size will produce least wastage.

3.15   The frequency, ν, and wavelength, λ, of a light wave are related by the expression:

$$\nu = c/\lambda$$

where c (the speed of light) has the value $2.9979 \times 10^8 \, ms^{-1}$.

Write a program that asks the user for a wavelength (in metres) and uses the above formula to convert it to a frequency (in Hertz). Use a PARAMETER declaration for the speed of light.

3.16   A body that experiences a uniform acceleration moves a distance s in a time t, where s is given by the formula

$$s = \tfrac{1}{2}at^2 + ut$$

where a is the acceleration in metres per second squared (ms^{-2}), and u is the initial velocity in metres per second (ms^{-1}).

A body falling freely under gravity is in such a situation, with $a = g = 9.81 \, ms^{-2}$.

Write a program that sets up the acceleration due to gravity as a parameter, and asks the user for the body's initial velocity (in ms^{-1}) and time of flight (in seconds). The program should then calculate and print the height from which the body fell.

3.17   Calculate the Coulomb potential at a distance r from a particle with a charge of z. The required formula is

$$\phi(r) = \frac{ze}{4\pi\epsilon r}$$

where $e = 1.6 \times 10^{-19}\,\text{C}$, $\epsilon = 8.86 \times 10^{-12}\,\text{Fm}^{-1}$, and $\pi = 3.1416$. r is specified in metres (m) and z is an integer number. Use DATA and PARAMETER statements appropriately to initialize your variables and constants.

Procedures and structure plans

4

The procedure is the fundamental building block of a Fortran program, and Fortran contains two types: subroutines and functions. Both types of procedures are examples of Fortran subprograms. A complete Fortran program consists of a main program unit and any number of subprogram program units.

Fortran contains a library of intrinsic functions, which provide many of the most commonly used mathematical functions (trigonometric, logarithmic and so on) as well as a number of other useful functions. They all take a value provided as an argument and return some other value calculated from that argument. The Fortran programmer can also write his own functions to supplement or replace those provided as part of the language.

A **subroutine** is a more flexible form of procedure that allows the programmer to break the program into small parts, each performing a single task, which communicate with each other by means of their arguments.

It is essential that the overall structure of a program is planned before starting to write any code. A method known as a **structure plan** is introduced as a means of developing the structure of the program and its procedures by successively refining each step until it is easy to code. This concept of 'modular' program development is the key to good program design and the minimization of errors.

4.1 Procedures, subprograms and functions

All the programs written so far have consisted of a number of lines of instructions such that if they are all obeyed in sequence the required actions will take place. However, this is not always the way we do things in real life. For example, look at Figure 4.1. This is the kind of note that the author's wife might leave to tell him how to cook a meal. It is a sequence of instructions but with one important feature – *not all the instructions are there*. The main part of the preparation is covered in one of her cookery books, so instead of writing it all down she simply referred him to the appropriate page of the book. There was no point in her either copying it out or describing what to do in her own words; it was much easier to make use of what had already been written by the author of the book.

In a rather different vein, Figure 4.2 shows an extract from a car maintenance manual. In this case there is a lot of cross-referencing to other sections of the manual, which describe how to carry out certain basic procedures. This is done to avoid duplication and to keep the structure of the manual fairly simple and logical. For example, any electrical work required is dealt with by a reference to the appropriate part of Chapter 9 (see steps 5.2 and 5.3).

Figure 4.1
An example of the use of a standard cooking procedure.

Miles

Can you make the Hot Pot ? I'll be back around 1.30.

Peel half-a-dozen potatoes and cut them into slices. Do the same with an onion.

The lamb is in the fridge – chop it into smallish chunks (about 1½ inches !)

Details are in Mary Berry's Cookbook, but ignore the bit about kidneys and mushrooms.

Put it on at 11.00 – DON'T FORGET.

Love
Maggie

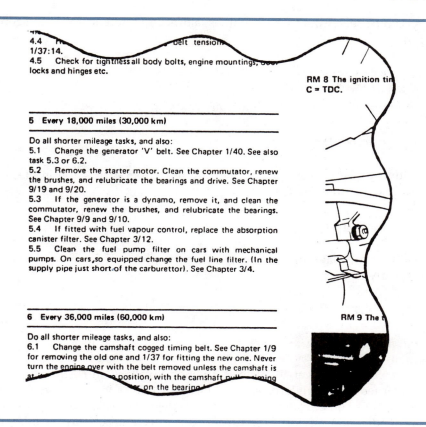

4.4 ... belt tension ...
1/37:14.
4.5   Check for tightness all body bolts, engine mountings, door locks and hinges etc.

RM 8 The ignition tir
C = TDC.

---

5   Every 18,000 miles (30,000 km)

Do all shorter mileage tasks, and also:
5.1   Change the generator 'V' belt. See Chapter 1/40. See also task 5.3 or 6.2.
5.2   Remove the starter motor. Clean the commutator, renew the brushes, and relubricate the bearings and drive. See Chapter 9/19 and 9/20.
5.3   If the generator is a dynamo, remove it, and clean the commutator, renew the brushes, and relubricate the bearings. See Chapter 9/9 and 9/10.
5.4   If fitted with fuel vapour control, replace the absorption canister filter. See Chapter 3/12.
5.5   Clean the fuel pump filter on cars with mechanical pumps. On cars so equipped change the fuel line filter. (In the supply pipe just short of the carburettor). See Chapter 3/4.

---

6   Every 36,000 miles (60,000 km)

Do all shorter mileage tasks, and also:
6.1   Change the camshaft cogged timing belt. See Chapter 1/9 for removing the old one and 1/37 for fitting the new one. Never turn the engine over with the belt removed unless the camshaft is at ... a position, with the camshaft pul ... iming ... on the bearing ...

RM 9 The t

Figure 4.2
Using cross-referencing to avoid duplication (Reproduced with permission from *Fiat 128 Owner's Workshop Manual*, published by J. H. Haynes & Co. Ltd, 1974).

Both of these techniques (use of standard procedures and avoidance of duplication with consequent structural improvements) are needed in programming as well. In Fortran a special section of program that is in some way referred to whenever required is known as a **procedure**, and is one type of **subprogram**.

Procedures (or subprograms) fall into two broad categories, namely those written by the programmer (or by some other person who then allows the programmer to use them) and those that are part of the Fortran language. There is a further categorization, based upon their mode of use, into what are called **subroutines** and **functions**.

All the procedures that are part of the Fortran language are functions and are referred to as **intrinsic functions**. The purpose of a function is to take one or more values (or **arguments**) and create a single result. Thus:

SIN(X)   produces the value of $\sin x$ (where X is in radians)
LOG(X)   produces the value of $\log_e x$
SQRT(X) produces the value of $\sqrt{x}$

As can be seen from these examples, a function reference takes the general form

name(argument)

or, where there are two or more arguments,

name(arg1,arg2, ...)

A function is used simply by referring to it in an expression in place of a variable or constant. Thus

```
A+B*LOG(C)
```

will first calculate $\log_e C$, then calculate $B*\log_e C$, and finally add A to this. Similarly

```
-B+SQRT(4*A*C)
```

will first calculate 4*A*C, then use the function to find its square root, and finally add this to -B.

There are over 40 intrinsic functions available in Fortran 77, mainly concerned with standard mathematical functions such as those illustrated above, but some dealing with other matters. A full list will be found in Appendix A. Many of these functions can have arguments of more than one type, in which case the type of the result will usually (though not always) be of the same type as the arguments. Thus

```
REAL X
   .
   .
ABS(X)
```

will produce the absolute value of the real variable X (that is, the value ignoring the sign) as a real quantity, whereas

```
INTEGER N
   .
   .
ABS(N)
```

will produce the absolute value of the integer variable N as an integer quantity.

The functions that exhibit this quality are referred to as **generic**

```
      PROGRAM FUEL
C
C  A program to calculate average fuel consumption
C
      INTEGER MILES,STOPS
      REAL TOPUP
      PRINT *,'How far did you travel (in miles)? '
      READ *,MILES
      PRINT *,'How many times did you fill up with fuel? '
      READ *,STOPS
      PRINT *,'How much fuel did you put in at the end? '
      READ *,TOPUP
C  Use INT function to ensure that an integer value is printed
      PRINT *,'Average mpg was',INT(MILES/(8.0*STOPS+TOPUP)+0.5)
      STOP
      END
```

Figure 4.3
An alternative solution for Example 3.5.

functions since the name really refers to a group of functions, of which the appropriate one will be selected by the compiler, depending upon the type of the arguments. It is also possible to refer directly to the actual function instead of using its generic name (for example, IABS(N)), although this is only to provide compatibility with earlier versions of Fortran that had no generic capability, and is not normally recommended.

A particularly important set of generic functions are those concerned with converting a value from one type to another (for example, from real to integer). Figure 4.3 shows how the INT function can be used to solve the problem that was raised at the end of the last chapter concerning the conversion of a mixed-mode expression to an integer value without first assigning it to an integer variable.

EXAMPLE 4.1

A farmer has a triangular field that he wishes to sow with wheat. Write a program that reads the lengths of the three sides of the field (in metres), and the sowing density (in grams per square metre). Print the number of 10 kg bags of wheat he must purchase in order to sow the whole field.

The crux here is the equation

$$\text{area} = \sqrt{s(s-a)(s-b)(s-c)}$$

for the area of a triangle whose sides have lengths a, b and c, where $2s=a+b+c$.

```
      PROGRAM WHEAT
C
C  A program to calculate the quantity of wheat needed to sow a field
C
      REAL A,B,C,S,AREA,DENSTY,QTY
      INTEGER NBAGS
C  Read the lengths of the sides of the field and the sowing density
      PRINT *,'Type the lengths of the three sides of the field (m): '
      READ *,A,B,C
      PRINT *,'What is the sowing density (g/sq m)? '
      READ *,DENSTY
C  Calculate area of field
      S = 0.5*(A+B+C)
      AREA = SQRT(S*(S-A)*(S-B)*(S-C))
C  Calculate quantity of wheat in kilograms and number of bags
      QTY = DENSTY*AREA*0.001
      NBAGS = (QTY+9.0)/10.0
C  Print results
      PRINT *,'Area of field is ',AREA,' sq m'
      PRINT *,NBAGS,' 10 kg bags will be required'
      STOP
      END
```

The program uses the SQRT function to calculate the area of the field, and then calculates the number of kilograms of wheat that are required. The expression (QTY+9.0)/10.0 is used to calculate the number of 10 kg bags required. If QTY is an exact multiple of 10.0 the addition of 9.0 will have no effect, owing to the subsequent truncation. However, if there would have been a remainder of 1 or more after dividing QTY by 10.0 (that is, 1 kg or more of wheat) then the addition of 9.0 will cause an extra bag to be specified, from which the extra amount can be taken.

4.2   External functions

The intrinsic functions available as part of the Fortran 77 language cover many of the major mathematical functions, but there are a great many other functions that are not included. In this case we need to write our own **function subprograms**, normally referred to as **external functions** to distinguish them from the intrinsic functions.

An external function takes a very similar form to the programs written so far, except that the first statement of the function is not a PROGRAM statement but a special FUNCTION statement, which takes the form

FUNCTION *name*(*d1*,*d2*, . . .)

where *d1*, *d2*, ... are **dummy arguments** that represent the **actual arguments** that will be used when the function is used (or **referenced**). For example, a function to calculate the average of five numbers could be written as follows:

```
      FUNCTION AVRAGE(X1,X2,X3,X4,X5)
C
C  This function returns the average of its five arguments
C
      REAL X1,X2,X3,X4,X5,SUM
      SUM=X1+X2+X3+X4+X5
      AVRAGE=SUM/5.0
      RETURN
      END
```

There are, however, two very important points to notice about this function.

The first is that, although the five dummy arguments and the variable SUM have been declared, there is one further variable, called AVRAGE, that has not been declared. Furthermore, this variable has the same name as the function, in direct contradiction of the rule established in Chapter 2 for the name of the program.

In fact this is a special variable, and is the means by which a function returns its value. Every function *must* contain a variable having the same name as the function, and this variable *must* be assigned, or otherwise given, a value to return as the value of the function before an exit is made from the function.

Of course, since this special **return variable** will be assigned a value, it must have a type (for example, REAL or INTEGER), and in this example that type will be REAL because the name begins with the letter A. However, the type of this name cannot be declared in the usual way because it is also the name of the function. If we wish to give it an explicit type, therefore, the word FUNCTION is preceded with the type:

```
      REAL FUNCTION AVRAGE(X1,X2,X3,X4,X5)
```

The other important feature of this function concerns the RETURN statement, which is analogous to the STOP statement, except that it does not terminate all execution but simply that of the function, returning to the place where the function was referenced to continue execution.

Before leaving this function let us briefly consider the situation in which we wish to write a function that has no arguments. In this unusual situation we must still include the parentheses around the non-existent argument when using the function to indicate that the function name (FUN, for example) is not a variable name:

```
      RESULT=FUN( )
```

Figure 4.4
A main program unit.

```
PROGRAM name
       .
       .
Specification statements, ...
       .
       .
Executable statements
       .
       .
END
```

4.3   Programs and program units

Up to this point subprograms have not been of much concern and programs have been considered to consist of a sequence of statements starting with an optional PROGRAM statement and finishing with an END statement, as shown in Figure 4.4. More correctly, this should now be defined as the **main program unit**. There can also be subprogram program units of various types. An **external function program unit** (see Figure 4.5) begins with a FUNCTION statement, as we have already seen, but otherwise has the same structure as a main program unit.

A **subroutine program unit** (see Figure 4.6) also has the same overall structure except that the first statement is a SUBROUTINE statement (see Section 4.5).

A **block data program unit** (see Figure 4.7) is also essentially the same, except that it does not contain any executable statements (and is described in Section 15.5).

A program can, therefore, consist of a number of different program units, of which exactly one must be a main program unit. Execution of the program will start at the beginning of the main program unit.

There may be any number of subprogram units in a complete program, and one of the most important concepts of Fortran is that *one*

Figure 4.5
An external function
program unit.

```
FUNCTION name(arg, ...)
       .
       .
Specification statements, ...
       .
       .
Executable statements
       .
       .
END
```

```
      SUBROUTINE name(arg, ...)
              .
              .
```

Specification statements, ...

```
              .
              .
```

Executable statements

```
              .
              .
      END
```

Figure 4.6
A subroutine program
unit.

program unit is never aware of any other program unit. The only link between a
calling program and a subprogram is through the name of the subprogram
and the arguments and/or function value, and this link is completed (after
compilation has finished) only when the full program is loaded ready for
execution. This very important principle means that it is possible to write
subprograms totally independently of the main program, and so opens up
the way for **libraries** of subprograms.

A main program unit, or simply a main program, can therefore be
written to demonstrate the use of our function. This might be as follows:

```
      PROGRAM DEMO
C
C  This program uses the external function AVRAGE
C
      REAL A1,A2,A3,A4,A5,AV,AVRAGE
C  Read data
      PRINT *,'Type five numbers: '
      READ *,A1,A2,A3,A4,A5
C  Calculate average and print it
      AV = AVRAGE(A1,A2,A3,A4,A5)
      PRINT *,'The average of the following numbers'
      PRINT *,A1
      PRINT *,A2
      PRINT *,A3
      PRINT *,A4
      PRINT *,A5
      PRINT *,'is ',AV
      STOP
      END
```

```
      BLOCK DATA name
              .
              .
```

Specification statements, ...

```
              .
              .
      END
```

Figure 4.7
A block data program
unit.

Figure 4.8
The effect of not declaring the function MEAN to be REAL.

Result of function MEAN, which represents 413.702 ($= 0.413\,702 * 10^3$)

0	3	4	1	3	7	0	2

Main program interprets this as an integer: 3 413 702

0	3	4	1	3	7	0	2

Main program converts this value to its real equivalent ($= 0.341\,370 * 10^7$)

0	7	3	4	1	3	7	0

'Result' is incorrect by a factor of 8257.58.

Notice that AVRAGE has been declared to be real. In this particular case this declaration is not strictly necessary since AVRAGE would have an implicit real type, but we have decided to declare all variables, and so for consistency this should include the names of all external functions. To see why this is often essential, let us assume that instead of AVRAGE we had called the function MEAN.

In the function subprogram the statement

```
REAL FUNCTION MEAN(X1,X2,X3,X4,X5)
```

would have ensured that all calculations were carried out using real arithmetic, and that the result of the function was real. However, if no other action were taken, the statement

```
AV = MEAN(A1,A2,A3,A4,A5)
```

in the main program would be treated by the compiler as a reference to a function called MEAN that returns an integer result (because its name begins with M), even though it actually produces a real result. It would therefore attempt to convert this (real) result to a real number in order to assign the value to the real variable AV. The effect would be to produce a result that would be quite different from the correct answer. Figure 4.8 shows the effect of this in a particular case, using the 'milometer' storage system of Chapter 2 (see also Figures 2.4 and 2.5).

More will be said about this later, but for the moment it should simply be stressed that the external function is treated as being completely independent from the main program. The only links are the arguments and the name of the function.

4.4 Structure plans

The overall logic and structure of our programs so far have been quite straightforward and it has been easy to write the programs without any additional planning. In general, this will not be the case and some form of additional planning or **analysis** is essential. This is particularly true once we start to instruct the computer how to take decisions and to repeat parts of the program a number of times. One traditional way of planning programs is by use of flowcharts; however these, by their nature, tend to encourage badly structured programs and modern programming practice frowns on their use.

Probably the best approach to program design is first to list the major objectives and then to expand each of these objectives to a (slightly) greater level of detail. Further expansions lead to more detailed objectives, and so on. Eventually a level of detail is reached which can easily be converted to a program directly. Exactly what this final level of detail is will depend upon the problem and the skill and experience of the programmer. This broad approach is called **top-down analysis** and the method of developing a final design is called **stepwise refinement**.

Exactly how the various levels of the design plan are written is a matter of personal preference and may be influenced partly by the language in which the final program will be written. The approach evolved by the author is particularly well suited to Fortran programs and is called a **structure plan**.

The approach can best be illustrated by developing a structure plan for the last example, which was concerned with calculating the number of bags of wheat required to sow a triangular field. The first plan might be simply a statement of the problem:

> 1 Read lengths of sides of field and sowing density
>
> 2 Calculate and print number of bags needed

Notice that each line has been numbered. This is not strictly necessary at this stage but will be very useful later.

Now the first step is fairly straightforward but the second needs elaboration, so we can go to a greater level of detail:

> 2.1 Calculate area of field
> 2.2 Calculate weight of seed required
> 2.3 Calculate the number of bags, including any partly used one
> 2.4 Print number of bags

If we wished we could put more information in these steps, such as the formulae to be used:

> **2.1** Calculate area of field ($= \sqrt{s(s-a)(s-b)(s-c)}$)
> **2.2** Calculate weight of seed required (= area × density)
> **2.3** Calculate number of bags (=(wt + 9)/10 to allow for a partly used bag)
> **2.4** Print results

There are no hard and fast rules about structure plans (or any other design aid) as they are intended to assist in the development of a particular individual's programs and will therefore reflect his or her particular skills (and weaknesses). The important point is that the development of the structure plan should enable the programmer to get the logic of the program clear and well defined before bothering with detailed coding. At the same time the final plan should contain enough detail for the coding to be carried out directly without any further analysis. The top-down approach means that the details are brought in only after the overall structure for (part of) the program has been thought out, and the two, slightly conflicting, aspects of program design are kept apart as far as possible.

It is essential, when writing most programs, to plan the structure before starting to write the code – otherwise errors in the logic are almost inevitable.

EXAMPLE 4.2

Five groups of students are each asked to carry out a series of experiments to determine the tensile strength of a piece of metal. There are five different experiments, each of which should produce the same answer. Write a program to produce the mean tensile strength calculated by each group and the standard deviation of their results, and also the mean and standard deviation of the different student group results.

Start by developing a structure plan.

> **1** Read five sets of five results
>
> **2** For each set calculate and print the mean and standard deviation
>
> **3** Calculate and print the mean and standard deviation of the group results

Before refining the plan notice that step 2 is really five steps, each of which calculates and prints the mean and standard deviation of five results. If we use the five means already calculated then step 3 reduces to the same problem – calculating the mean and standard deviation of five results.

We can now refine step 2:

> **2** For each set
> **2.1** Calculate the mean of five results
> **2.2** Calculate the standard deviation of these five results
> **2.3** Print the mean and standard deviation

while step 3 becomes

> **3**
> **3.1** Calculate the mean of five means from step 2
> **3.2** Calculate the standard deviation of these five means
> **3.3** Print the mean and standard deviation

Now in Section 4.2 we wrote a function to calculate the mean of five values, so we can use this in our new program, as it can be seen that the same operation will have to be carried out on five sets of data.

Similarly, we can write a function to calculate the standard deviation. The final program could look like this:

```
      PROGRAM METAL
C
C  This program summarizes experimental results
C
      REAL A1,A2,A3,A4,A5,B1,B2,B3,B4,B5,C1,C2,C3,C4,C5,
     *     D1,D2,D3,D4,D5,E1,E2,E3,E4,E5,AMEAN,ASTDEV,
     *     BMEAN,BSTDEV,CMEAN,CSTDEV,DMEAN,DSTDEV,
     *     EMEAN,ESTDEV,XMEAN,XSTDEV,AVRAGE,STDEV
C  Input data by groups
      PRINT *,'Type the five results for each group in turn'
      PRINT *,'Group A: '
      READ *,A1,A2,A3,A4,A5
      PRINT *,'Group B: '
      READ *,B1,B2,B3,B4,B5
      PRINT *,'Group C: '
      READ *,C1,C2,C3,C4,C5
      PRINT *,'Group D: '
      READ *,D1,D2,D3,D4,D5
      PRINT *,'Group E: '
      READ *,E1,E2,E3,E4,E5
```

```
C  Calculate mean and standard deviation for each group
      AMEAN = AVRAGE(A1,A2,A3,A4,A5)
      ASTDEV = STDEV(A1,A2,A3,A4,A5,AMEAN)
      PRINT *,'Group A mean is ',AMEAN,' with a standard deviation of ',
     *        ASTDEV
      BMEAN = AVRAGE(B1,B2,B3,B4,B5)
      BSTDEV = STDEV(B1,B2,B3,B4,B5,BMEAN)
      PRINT *,'Group B mean is ',BMEAN,' with a standard deviation of ',
     *        BSTDEV
      CMEAN = AVRAGE(C1,C2,C3,C4,C5)
      CSTDEV = STDEV(C1,C2,C3,C4,C5,CMEAN)
      PRINT *,'Group C mean is ',CMEAN,' with a standard deviation of ',
     *        CSTDEV
      DMEAN = AVRAGE(D1,D2,D3,D4,D5)
      DSTDEV = STDEV(D1,D2,D3,D4,D5,DMEAN)
      PRINT *,'Group D mean is ',DMEAN,' with a standard deviation of ',
     *        DSTDEV
      EMEAN = AVRAGE(E1,E2,E3,E4,E5)
      ESTDEV = STDEV(E1,E2,E3,E4,E5,EMEAN)
      PRINT *,'Group E mean is ',EMEAN,' with a standard deviation of ',
     *        ESTDEV
C  Now calculate overall group totals
      XMEAN = AVRAGE(AMEAN,BMEAN,CMEAN,DMEAN,EMEAN)
      XSTDEV = STDEV(AMEAN,BMEAN,CMEAN,DMEAN,EMEAN,XMEAN)
      PRINT *,'Overall mean is ',XMEAN,' with a standard deviation of ',
     *        XSTDEV,' between groups'
      STOP
      END

      REAL FUNCTION AVRAGE(X1,X2,X3,X4,X5)
C
C  Calculates the mean of its five arguments
C
      REAL X1,X2,X3,X4,X5,SUM
      SUM = X1+X2+X3+X4+X5
      AVRAGE = SUM/5.0
      RETURN
      END

      REAL FUNCTION STDEV(X1,X2,X3,X4,X5,XMEAN)
C
C  Calculates the standard deviation of the first five arguments,
C  whose mean is supplied as the sixth argument
C
      REAL X1,X2,X3,X4,X5,XMEAN
     *     T1,T2,T3,T4,T5
C
C  STDEV = SQRT(SIGMA((X(I)-XMEAN)**2)/N)
C
      T1 = (X1-XMEAN)**2
      T2 = (X2-XMEAN)**2
      T3 = (X3-XMEAN)**2
      T4 = (X4-XMEAN)**2
      T5 = (X5-XMEAN)**2
      STDEV = SQRT((T1+T2+T3+T4+T5)/5.0)
      RETURN
      END
```

This program works correctly and will therefore solve our problem. It is also the best that we can do at present. But it looks very long-winded and repetitive. The next two chapters will show how it can be dramatically shortened, and at the same time made considerably more flexible.

4.5   Subroutines

In Section 4.1 two types of procedures in Fortran were mentioned – functions and subroutines. It is now time to examine how a subroutine differs from a function. Essentially the difference lies in how they are referenced and how their results are returned.

A function, as we have seen, is referenced in the same way as a variable: simply by writing its name, followed by any arguments it may have enclosed in parentheses. It causes a **transfer of control** so that instead of continuing to process the current statement the computer obeys the statements contained within the function. The execution of the function utilizes the values provided as arguments to calculate a value (the **function value**) which is available as the value of the function reference, just as writing the name of a variable provides a value – the value stored in a particular memory location. A function reference, therefore, is not a complete statement but is part of an expression, and may appear anywhere that an expression may appear (for example, on the right-hand side of an assignment statement, in an output list, as an argument in a function reference, and so on). A number of intrinsic functions, which are defined within the Fortran language, and external functions, which we wrote ourselves, have already been used, but both types are referenced in the same way, for example:

```
var = fun(arg1,arg2, …)
PRINT *,fun1(arg1,arg2, …)
var = fun2(fun1(arg1,arg2, …),a2,a3, …)
```

A subroutine, on the other hand, is accessed by means of a CALL statement, which gives the name of the subroutine and a list of **arguments** which will be used to transmit information between the (main) program and the subroutine:

```
CALL name(arg1,arg2, …)
```

The CALL statement causes a transfer of control so that, instead of obeying the next statement in the program, the computer obeys the statements contained within the subroutine *name*. When the subroutine has completed its task it returns to the calling program, ready to obey the next statement.

Some of the arguments may be used to return 'results', where this is appropriate.

If a subroutine has no arguments then the subroutine name is simply given in the CALL statement

    CALL *sub*

We can see how this works by rewriting the function AVRAGE used in the last section as a subroutine:

```
      SUBROUTINE AVRAGE(X1,X2,X3,X4,X5,AV)
C
C  This subroutine returns the average of its first five arguments in AV
C
      REAL X1,X2,X3,X4,X5,AV,SUM
      SUM = X1+X2+X3+X4+X5
      AV = SUM/5.0
      RETURN
      END
```

Note that in this case the result of the subroutine is assigned to a variable (AV) that is itself a dummy argument. In the main program the corresponding actual argument will contain the result on return from the subroutine:

```
      PROGRAM DEMO2
C
C  This program uses the subroutine AVRAGE
C
      REAL A1,A2,A3,A4,A5,MEAN
C  Read data
      PRINT *,'Type five numbers: '
      READ *,A1,A2,A3,A4,A5
C  Calculate average and print it
      CALL AVRAGE(A1,A2,A3,A4,A5,MEAN)
      PRINT *,'The average of the 5 numbers is ',MEAN
      STOP
      END
```

Notice that the name of the subroutine (AVRAGE in this case) is simply a means of identification; it does not have any type, and it cannot appear in a type specification statement.

4.6 Actual arguments, dummy arguments, and local variables

We have seen that when a function or subroutine is referenced, information is passed to it through its arguments; in the case of a subroutine information may also be returned to the calling program unit through its

Figure 4.9
A storage model.

arguments. The relationship between the **actual arguments** in the calling program unit and the **dummy arguments** in the subroutine or function is of vital importance in this process.

The actual mechanism used is unimportant, and may vary from one computer system to another, but a model that will serve to illustrate the process can be easily created. The important thing to realize is that the dummy arguments do not actually exist – they are a means of identifying actual locations in memory that will be used as actual arguments by the calling program.

Chapter 1 introduced a model in which variables were represented by glass boxes, and their values by balls stored in the boxes (Figure 4.9). We may represent dummy arguments by a notice-board, with a section for each dummy argument. When the procedure (function or subroutine) is called from some other program unit a message is pinned up for each dummy argument identifying the corresponding actual argument, as shown in Figures 4.10 and 4.11. Whenever a reference is made to one of these dummy arguments in the procedure the notice-board will be used to show to which *actual* location in the memory (one of the actual arguments) is being referred.

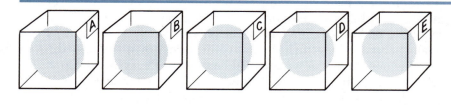
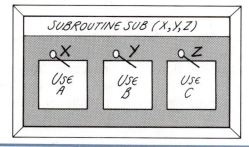

Figure 4.10
A representation of
`CALL SUB(A,C,D)`.

Figure 4.11
A representation of
CALL SUB(B,E,B).

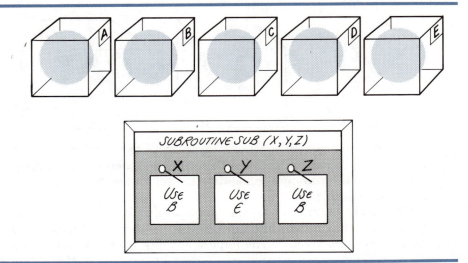

It follows from this model that, whereas an actual argument may be a variable (an open box) or a constant (a closed and sealed box), a dummy argument is a pseudo-variable, in the sense that the corresponding area of the notice-board may have different notices pinned on it, and can be used just like a variable in the procedure even though it never really exists.

However, a procedure will usually also require additional variables, and here we discover another very important principle: the **locality of variables**. Each program unit is aware only of its own **local variables** and the pseudo-variables known as dummy arguments. It is unaware of, and cannot access, any of the variables used in other program units.

This is extremely important because it means that when writing a subprogram, or a main program, we need not be concerned that names might clash with those used in another program unit. This is exactly analogous to names within a family: the Jenkins family in Figure 4.12 had no qualms about calling their children Kimberley, Sian and David, even though the Jones family down the road have called theirs David, Sarah and Kimberley. Mrs Jenkins and Mrs Jones can both refer to Kimberley or David without any possibility of confusion. Kimberley Jenkins is *local* to the Jenkins family, while Kimberley Jones is not part of the Jenkins family (she is 'unknown' to them) but is *local* to the Jones family.

The importance of local variables combined with arguments cannot be over-emphasized, as it is the reason why it is possible to write libraries of useful subroutines and functions that can subsequently be used in other people's programs. There is a way to get round this dependence on arguments to pass information between program units, as we shall

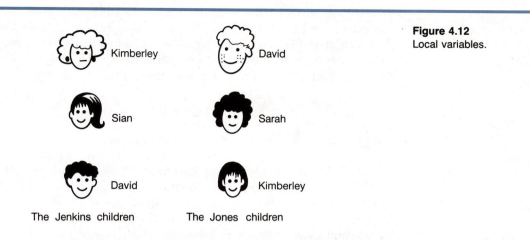

Figure 4.12
Local variables.

Kimberley   David

Sian   Sarah

David   Kimberley

The Jenkins children   The Jones children

discover in Chapter 15, but for most purposes this locality of variables is absolute.

4.7   The SAVE statement

Each subprogram is, as we have seen, an independent program unit: its variables are local to it and may be accessed by another program unit only if they are used as actual arguments in a call to a subroutine or function. Once a RETURN has been obeyed from a subroutine or function to the program unit that called it, then all the local variables in that subroutine or function become inaccessible until it is called once more. In Fortran 77 these local variables are said to become **undefined** when this happens, and the corresponding memory location becomes available for use by other program units. If the subprogram is entered again its local variables will once more be available for use by that subprogram.

The important effect of this is that when a subprogram is re-entered its local variables will have undefined values, even if they had been assigned particular values on the previous entry. There are, however, a number of occasions when it is highly desirable for the value of one or more items to be preserved between calls. This can be achieved by use of the SAVE statement, which takes the form

    SAVE *name1*,*name2*,...

where each *name* is the name of a local variable. This is a specification statement, and must therefore appear before any executable statements. As its name implies, it causes all those items in the list to be saved on exit from the subprogram so that on a subsequent entry they have the value that they had before. If a SAVE statement has no names following it:

```
SAVE
```

then it will cause the saving of *all* variables that can be saved.

In practice this statement is not normally required, since most Fortran 77 compilers perform an automatic SAVE of all variables on exit from a subroutine or function. You should be aware, however, that this need not necessarily be the case and you should use the SAVE statement if it is important that a local variable has the same value on entry to the subroutine or function that it had on the last exit from the procedure, especially if the program is likely to be run on several different computers.

4.8 Procedures as an aid to program structure

One of the great advantages of subprograms is that they enable us to break a program design into several smaller, more manageable sections, and then to write and test each of these independently of the rest of the program. This paves the way for an approach known as **modular program development**.

This approach breaks the problem down into its major functions, each of which can then be developed independently of the others. In a large project these functions, or **modules**, may be developed by different people. If necessary a module itself may be subdivided into further modules. All that is necessary is that the **interface** between a module and the rest of the program be well defined.

This interface consists of two parts. The first, the interface proper, is the list of arguments supplied to the module (or rather to the subprogram that is, in effect, the main program unit of the module). The second is the specification of the action of the module.

A structure plan gives very great assistance in modular development, as it identifies in a natural way the major functions of the program. Rather than expanding these functions within a single structure plan, as we have been doing up to now, each of these major functions can be treated as a separate module to be developed independently. Once developed they can be integrated to form the complete program according to the top-level structure plan. This idea will be developed further in later chapters, but for the present the concept of a structure plan will be combined with that of a modular program structure.

For example, the structure plan developed for Example 4.2 can be very slightly modified to show the procedures in the following manner:

1 Read five sets of five results

2 For each set
  2.1 Calculate the mean of five results – AVRAGE
  2.2 Calculate the standard deviation of these five results – STDEV
  2.3 Print the mean and standard deviation

3
  3.1 Calculate the mean of five means from step 2 – AVRAGE
  3.2 Calculate the standard deviation of these five means – STDEV
  3.3 Print the mean and standard deviation

Further structure plans could then be developed for the procedures AVRAGE and STDEV:

AVRAGE(X1,X2,X3,X4,X5)

1 Calculate sum of arguments

2 Calculate and return average

STDEV(X1,X2,X3,X4,X5,XMEAN)

1 Calculate squares of differences between X1, and so on, and their mean, XMEAN

2 Calculate square root of the average of the squares

3 Return standard deviation

Notice that we have specified the interface at the head of the structure plan for each procedure.

Of course, in this example we are working back-to-front since we have already written the program, but it illustrates the technique that will be used henceforth when necessary.

SUMMARY

- Intrinsic functions are a special class of 'built-in' procedures.

- Generic functions enable the same intrinsic functions to be used with different types of arguments.

- Fortran programs consist of a main program unit and optionally any number of subprogram units.

- Subprograms may be subroutines or functions.

- Every external function has a type, which may be declared in the initial FUNCTION statement.

- Every function must contain a return variable, having the same name as the function, which is used to return the function value.

- Communication between program units is achieved by arguments.

- Every program unit has its own set of local variables.

- Local variables become undefined when a RETURN is made from the program unit, unless they appear in a SAVE statement.

- An English-language structure plan provides a means for top-down analysis of the problem and step-wise refinement to a level of detail that can easily be coded.

- Subroutines provide the means for modular program development.

- Fortran 77 statements introduced in Chapter 4:

Initial statements	SUBROUTINE *name*(*list of dummy arguments*)
	SUBROUTINE *name*
	FUNCTION *name*(*list of dummy arguments*)
	FUNCTION *name*( )
	type FUNCTION *name*(*list of dummy arguments*)
	type FUNCTION *name*( )
RETURN statement	RETURN
Function reference	*function_name* (*list of actual argument*)
	for example X = SIN(Y)
	A = B+SQRT(ABS(C*D))
	function_name( )
Subroutine call	CALL *subroutine_name*(*list of actual arguments*)
	CALL *subroutine_name*
Saving local variables	SAVE *list of variable names*
	SAVE

SELF-TEST EXERCISES 4.1

1   What will be printed by the following program?

```
PROGRAM TEST41
INTEGER N1,N2,N3,N4,N5
DATA N1,N2,N3,N4,N5/1,2,3,4,5/
CALL PRNT(N1,N2)
CALL PRNT(N1,N3)
CALL PRNT(N1,N4)
CALL PRNT(N1,N5)
STOP
END

SUBROUTINE PRNT(N,M)
INTEGER N,M,X
SAVE X
DATA X/50/
X=N*(X/M)
N=N+M
PRINT *,X
RETURN
END
```

2   What will be printed by the following program?

```
PROGRAM TEST42
INTEGER N1,N2,N3,N4,N5
DATA N1,N2,N3,N4,N5/1,2,3,4,5/
PRINT *,UPDATE(N1,N2)
PRINT *,UPDATE(N1,N3)
PRINT *,UPDATE(N1,N4)
PRINT *,UPDATE(N1,N5)
STOP
END

INTEGER FUNCTION UPDATE(N,M)
INTEGER N,M,X
SAVE X
DATA X/50/
X=N*(X/M)
UPDATE=N+M
RETURN
END
```

3   Write the initial statement and the declarations for any dummy
arguments for subprograms designed to carry out the following tasks.
(Don't worry that you couldn't actually write the subprogram yet; you
can specify its interface with a calling program unit without knowing
how to write it.)

(a) Print an error message based on an error code that may be −1 or an integer in the range 1 to 10.

(b) Calculate and return the cube root of a number.

(c) Find the roots (if any) of a quadratic equation of the form

$$ax^2 + bx + c = 0.$$

(d) Establish whether a whole number is prime. (A number is prime if it is divisible only by itself and by 1.)

(e) Calculate and return the square root of a number.

(f) Read whatever is typed at the standard input unit until a whole number greater than 0 is typed, and return that number.

PROGRAMMING EXERCISES

Many larger programs are structured in such a way that each of the major functions (input of data, calculation of each type of analysis, printing of results) is handled by a different subroutine, or group of subroutines, which can be written and tested independently. In the following exercises you should write your solutions in this way, even though it may not be strictly necessary. Write a structure plan for the program before you start coding.

4.1   Write a subroutine which, when supplied with the coordinates of two points (x_1,y_1) and (x_2,y_2), calculates the distance of each point from the origin and the distance between the points.

Note that the distance d_1 of point 1 from the origin is given by the formula

$$d_1 = \sqrt{x_1^2 + y_1^2}$$

while the distance d between the two points is given by

$$d = \sqrt{(x_2-x_1)^2 + (y_2-y_1)^2}$$

Test your subroutine in a short program to check that it works correctly with several different sets of data.

4.2   Write a function which, when supplied with the coordinates of two points (x_1,y_1) and (x_2,y_2), calculates the distance between the points. Test your function to make sure that it works correctly.

Now modify the subroutine that you wrote for Exercise 4.1 so that it uses this function to carry out all the necessary calculations.

4.3   Write a program that uses the intrinsic function TAN to evaluate the value of tan x for x having the values 0, $\pi/8$, $\pi/6$, $\pi/4$ and $\pi/2$. Don't be surprised if the last calculation gives a strange answer. (If you don't

understand the reason for this, look up a graph of $\tan x$ in a
mathematics text!)

4.4 Write a function to give the logarithm of a number to base b. (Use
the equation $\log_b x = \log_{10} x / \log_{10} b$.)

*4.5 A credit card company produces monthly statements for its
customers. Each statement shows the following information:

- the amount outstanding from last month;
- the interest due on that amount for the month;
- any payment received since the last statement;
- the total spent with the card since the last statement;
- the total amount now outstanding.

The customer can then pay any amount as long as it is at least 5% of
the outstanding amount.
   Write a program which reads the amount outstanding, details of
payments made and total spending, and the current interest rate, and
then produces an appropriate statement.

4.6 A physicist has carried out a number of experiments using
Callendar and Barnes' apparatus to determine the specific heat capacity
of a liquid. The specific heat capacity is calculated by the formula

$$c = \frac{IVt}{m(\theta_2 - \theta_1)}$$

where I is the current through the heating coil; V is the potential
difference across its terminals; t is the time between the start of the
experiment and the end; m is the mass of liquid that flows through the
apparatus during this time; θ_1 is the temperature of the liquid entering
the apparatus and θ_2 the temperature of the liquid leaving it.
   Write a program to read the results of these experiments, and to
print the mean value calculated for the specific heat capacity of the
liquid and the standard deviation of these values.

*4.7 A builder, possibly the same one as in Exercise 3.12, wishes to
calculate the relative costs of building a wall using different sizes of
bricks and different types of mortar. The thickness of the wall will
always be one brick's depth. Regardless of the size of brick and the type
of mortar, the thickness of the mortar will always be $\frac{1}{2}$ in. Write a
program to help him.
   The program should read the size of the bricks and their cost, the
cost of the mortar per cubic inch, and the height and length of the wall.
It should calculate how many bricks will be required and their cost, how

much mortar is required and its cost, and the total cost (excluding labour!).

*4.8   Repeat Exercise 3.13, but using a subprogram to calculate how many coins (or notes) are required of a particular denomination.

4.9   Repeat the last part of Exercise 3.14, but using a subprogram for the main calculation to simplify the structure and the size of the whole program.

4.10   Write a program to convert a number of seconds to hours, minutes and seconds.

4.11   Write a subroutine that calculates the position, velocity and acceleration of a body undergoing simple harmonic motion using the equations given below:

$$\text{position} = a\sin(nt + \epsilon)$$
$$\text{velocity} = na\cos(nt + \epsilon)$$
$$\text{acceleration} = -an^2\sin(nt + \epsilon)$$

Use as starting values $n = 3.14159265$, $\epsilon = 0$, $a = 2.5$. Specify your own value for t.

4.12   Write an integer function that rounds a real number to its nearest integer value. Compare the answer you get with that of the intrinsic function NINT.

4.13   Modify your solution for Exercise 3.17 so that the Coulomb potential is calculated using a function. What happens if you pass your constants to the function as arguments?

4.14   The escape velocity from the surface of a planet (the velocity that a spacecraft must reach to escape from the gravitational field of the planet and travel off into space) is given by the expression:

$$v_{esc} = \sqrt{\frac{2GM}{R}}$$

where G is the gravitational constant (6.67×10^{-11} N m^2 kg^{-2}), M is the mass of the planet (in kg) and R is the planet's radius (in metres).
   Write a function that accepts the planetary mass and radius as its input and returns the escape velocity. Use your function to compare the escape velocities from the Earth, Jupiter and the Moon using the

following data:

Planet	Mass (kg)	Radius (m)
Earth	6.0E24	6.4E6
Moon	7.4E22	1.7E6
Jupiter	1.9E27	7.1E7

4.15 Write a program to convert the ecliptic latitude β and longitude λ of an astronomical object into right ascension α and declination δ using the formulae

$$\alpha = \tan^{-1}\frac{\sin(\lambda)\cos(\epsilon)-\tan(\beta)\sin(\epsilon)}{\cos(\lambda)}$$

$$\delta = \sin^{-1}(\sin(\beta)\cos(\epsilon)+\cos(\beta)\sin(\epsilon)\sin(\lambda))$$

where $\epsilon=0.4091$. Assume that all quantities are in radians. (Note: use the ATAN2 intrinsic function for the first expression.)

4.16 The right ascension of an astronomical object is generally given in units of time, where 24 hours equals 360 degrees, while the declination is usually given in degrees. Write a subroutine to convert the two quantities from radians into these units, and incorporate it into your solution for Exercise 4.15.

4.17 In Einstein's famous equation $E=mc^2$, the energy E is in joules if the mass m is in kilograms and c is the speed of light in metres per second ($=2.9979\times10^8\,\mathrm{ms}^{-1}$). Write a function to calculate the energy equivalent of a given mass. Roughly how much energy is equivalent to the mass of a sugar cube (approximately 1E−3 kg)?

4.18 The gravitational force F between two bodies of masses m_1 and m_2 is given by the formula

$$F = \frac{Gm_1m_2}{r^2}$$

where $G = 6.672E-11\ \mathrm{N\,m^2\,kg^{-2}}$; r is the distance between the bodies (in metres); and the masses m_1 and m_2 are measured in kilograms.

Write a program that uses a REAL function to evaluate the gravitational force between two bodies given their masses and separation. Define G as a parameter (and think about where it should be specified).

4.19 A sequence of 'pseudo-random' numbers (numbers that appear to be purely random for most purposes, although they are actually derived from a mathematical formula) can be produced by the following expression:

$$X_{n+1} = \text{Frac}((X_n + A)**B)$$

where the function Frac(x) means 'take the fractional part of x', X_n means the nth random number (which is a real number between 0.0(inclusive) and 1.0(exclusive)), A is a real constant and B is (usually) an integer constant. Write a function to implement this random number generator. You should initialize the value of X_0 using a DATA statement in the function, and ensure the value returned as the most recent pseudo-random number is kept using SAVE. A and B should be fixed; take A = 1.234 56 and B = 8 as an example. (This is not a particularly good random number generator. Aficionados may wish to research in more detail the art of generating pseudo-random numbers.)

4.20 Write functions that use the random number generator produced for Exercise 4.19 to simulate:

(a) the throw of a dice;
(b) the total of three dice;
(c) the toss of a coin.

Loops

5

The DO **statement** is a means of repeating a section of code a given number of times, thus creating a form of program 'loop' known as a DO **loop**.

A DO loop may contain any Fortran statements, including another (**nested**) DO statement, but there are some restrictions on the *last* statement of the loop. To avoid any problems it is recommended that the CONTINUE statement, which does nothing, be the last statement of a DO loop.

5.1   Program repetition

So far most of our programs have taken rather longer to write than it would have taken to solve the problem by hand! This is because they have consisted of a series of instructions that are obeyed in sequence *once only*. In many cases the programs would be much more useful if they could be repeated with different sets of data. For instance, Example 3.1 converted a single Celsius temperature to Fahrenheit and Example 3.2 calculated one worker's pay. They would be much more useful if they could convert 50 temperatures or calculate 100 workers' pay details.

Before we see how we can do this in Fortran let us look at a structure plan. The structure plan for Example 3.1 would look like this:

> **1**   Read Celsius temperature
>
> **2**   Calculate Fahrenheit equivalent
>
> **3**   Print both temperatures

We could alter this in two ways to allow a larger number of conversions. The first and most obvious way is to write

> **1**   Repeat the following 50 times
> **1.1** Read Celsius temperature
> **1.2** Calculate Fahrenheit equivalent
> **1.3** Print both temperatures

which quite clearly states that we wish to repeat the whole process 50 times. Thus a total of 50 Celsius temperatures must be supplied as data and a total of 50 conversions will be carried out and printed.

This is perfectly acceptable and is clearly the sort of requirement that will appear frequently. However, if a large number of temperatures were to be converted, a more useful way might be as follows:

> **1**   Repeat the following for each Celsius temperature from 0 to 100 in steps of 5
> **1.1** Calculate Fahrenheit equivalent
> **1.2** Print both temperatures

Clearly this will produce a table of equivalent temperatures at 5° intervals from 0 °C to 100 °C without the need for any data to be prepared at all.

We could rewrite step 1 of the earlier version in this same style by introducing a 'counter':

> **1** Repeat the following for each value of a 'counter' from 1 to 50 (in steps of 1)

The counter in this case is a variable whose only purpose is to record how many times the statements have been repeated.

5.2   DO **loops**

The repetition of a number of statements a predetermined number of times is so important that Fortran contains a special statement with exactly the features that are required. It is called a DO **statement** and takes the form

DO *label*, *var=e1*,*e2*,*e3*

F90

The statement starts with the word DO, which, like PROGRAM, READ, PRINT, STOP and END, is a word with a special meaning in Fortran. The rest of the statement consists of two parts separated by a comma (although this comma can be omitted for compatibility with earlier versions of Fortran).

The first part is a **statement label**. This identifies the last statement in the group that is to be repeated and consists of a whole number in the range 1 to 99 999.

The second part consists of the name of a variable (*var*) followed by an equals sign and then either two or three arithmetic expressions separated by commas:

var=e1,*e2* or *var=e1*,*e2*,*e3*

The variable is usually an integer variable, although Chapter 19 will show that there are situations when this need not be the case. It is called the DO **variable**. The two or three expressions define the number of times that the statements are to be obeyed.

Note that if we follow each of the steps in one of the structure plans introduced above we find ourselves back at the beginning (see Figure 5.1). It can be clearly seen that a loop will be traced during this process. For this reason this type of program structure is called a **program loop**, or simply a **loop**, and a loop that is controlled by a DO statement is called a DO **loop**.

Figure 5.1
A loop.

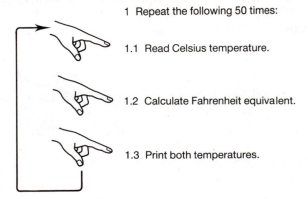

1 Repeat the following 50 times:

   1.1 Read Celsius temperature.

   1.2 Calculate Fahrenheit equivalent.

   1.3 Print both temperatures.

When a DO statement is first encountered the three expressions $e1$, $e2$ and $e3$ are evaluated to give three values $m1$, $m2$ and $m3$ of the same type as the variable, var. Informally we can consider these three values to be the initial value of the variable var ($m1$), the amount it is to be incremented by each time the loop is repeated ($m3$), and the final value ($m2$) – although the last will not always be the case.

The number of times the loop is to be obeyed (the **trip count**) is calculated using the following formula:

$$\text{MAX}\left(0,\text{INT}\left(\frac{m2-m1+m3}{m3}\right)\right)$$

Thus the statement

```
DO 100,I=0,100,5
```

leads to a trip count of 21, that is, $(100-0+5)/5$. On the other hand the statement

```
DO 50,J=0,100,9
```

leads to a trip count of 12, that is, $\text{INT}\left(\frac{100-0+9}{9}\right)$, while the statement

```
DO 999,K=100,0,10
```

leads to a trip count of 0, that is, $\text{MAX}\left(0,\ \text{INT}\left(\frac{0-100+10}{10}\right)\right)$.

If the trip count is 0 then the statements in the loop will be ignored. However, if it is greater than 0 (it cannot be less) the DO variable is set to the

DO statement	Trip count	DO variable values	Figure 5.2
			DO statement evaluation.
DO 10, I=1,10,1	10	1,2,3,4,5,6,7,8,9,10	
DO 25, J=20,50,5	7	20,25,30,35,40,45,50	
DO 99, L=7,19,4	4	7,11,15,19	
DO 1, K=4,17,5	3	4,9,14	
DO 5, I=−20,20,6	7	−20,−14,−8,−2,4,10,16	
DO 30, N=25,0,−5	6	25,20,15,10,5,0	
DO 100, M=20,−20,−6	7	20,14,8,2,−4,−10,−16	

value $m1$ and the statements in the loop obeyed. When the last statement in the loop has been obeyed the DO variable is incremented by $m3$ and the loop obeyed again if the trip count is greater than 1. The process is repeated until the loop has been obeyed the required number of times.

This may sound complicated, but in practice it is really very simple. For example, in Figure 5.2 it can be seen that where an integer variable is used with a positive increment the three expressions can be thought of as initial value, final (or maximum) value and increment. The loop will continue to be obeyed until another pass through the loop would cause the DO variable to become greater than the value of the second expression ($m2$). If the increment is negative then $m2$ represents a minimum value.

In a great many cases the DO variable is only being used as a counter so that a loop of the type 'repeat the following n times' can be set up. In this case the increment ($m3$) will be 1, and if desired may be omitted altogether. Thus the statements

> DO *label, var=e1,e2*

and

> DO *label, var=e1,e2,*1

are identical in their effect.

However, one aspect of the DO statement is still unresolved. We have seen how a C in column 1 indicates that the line is a comment, but have made no other use of the first six columns. A further use is to identify a particular line by means of a **label**.

A label is a whole number written in columns 1–5. It follows, therefore, that the number must lie in the range 1–99 999. One of the reasons for labelling a line is to identify the last statement of a DO loop. The number chosen can be any whole number in the specified range as long as it is unique – that is, used once only.

There are some restrictions on the statements that may appear as the last line of a DO loop. For obvious reasons the following are not permitted:

- PROGRAM: since this is the first statement it is clearly not possible in any case.
- STOP: as this would prevent any looping.
- END: as this would prevent any looping.

Several other forbidden terminating statements will be dealt with in the next chapter.

In order to avoid any problems many programmers finish DO loops with a special statement

```
CONTINUE
```

This does absolutely nothing! It can, however, be labelled and it can appear as the last statement in a DO loop.

EXAMPLE 5.1

Write a program to read 100 exam marks and calculate the average mark.

This problem requires us to use a loop to read the marks and accumulate their sum. Remember to set the sum to 0 before starting. The structure plan is:

> 1 Initialize sum (to 0)
>
> 2 Repeat 100 times
> 2.1 Read a mark
> 2.2 Add it to the cumulative sum
>
> 3 Calculate and print average mark

Indenting the steps in the loop helps to emphasize the structure: this will be done in the program also.

```
      PROGRAM MARKS
C
C  This program finds the average of 100 marks
C
      INTEGER I,MARK,MKSUM
      MKSUM = 0
      PRINT *,'Type 100 marks: '
```

```
      DO 10, I=1,100
         READ *,MARK
         MKSUM = MKSUM+MARK
   10 CONTINUE
      PRINT *,'Average mark is' ,MKSUM/100.0
      STOP
      END
```

Notice that the average is calculated using the *real* constant 100.0, thus causing real division to be used to give a real value for the average.

EXAMPLE 5.2

Write a program that first reads the number of people sitting an exam, then reads their marks, and prints the highest and lowest, followed by the average mark.

This is a variation of Example 5.1, which uses a variable to control the number of times the loop is repeated. It also will need the use of the MAX and MIN intrinsic functions – see Appendix A.

1 Initialize sum and maximum mark to 0, minimum mark to a large value

2 Read number of examinees

3 Repeat N times
   3.1 Read a mark
   3.2 Add it to cumulative sum
   3.3 Set maximum to maximum mark so far
   3.4 Set minimum to minimum mark so far

4 Calculate average

5 Print maximum, minimum and average marks

Initialization of variables must always be handled carefully. In this case the cumulative sum must obviously start at 0, but what about the maximum and minimum marks? What we shall do (at steps 3.3 and 3.4) is to compare each mark with the highest (or lowest) read previously and store the higher (or lower) as the new maximum (or minimum). It follows therefore that initially the maximum must be set to a lower value than any marks are likely to take, and the minimum must be set to a higher value than is likely to occur. If marks are to lie in the range 0–100 then the two extremes could be used. As there are only three variables to be initialized assignment statements could be used, but as a general rule it is preferable to use a DATA statement for initialization, as this causes the initial values to be stored when the program is first loaded.

The program then follows easily:

```
      PROGRAM EXAMS
C
C  This program prints statistics about a set of exam results
C
      INTEGER I,N,MARK,MKSUM,MAXMK,MINMK
      REAL AV
C  Set initial values
      DATA MKSUM/0/,MAXMK/0/,MINMK/100/
C  Read number of marks, and then the marks
      PRINT *,'How many marks are there? '
      READ *,N
      PRINT *,'Type ',N,' marks: '
      DO 10, I=1,N
         READ *,MARK
C  On each pass, update sum, maximum and minimum
         MKSUM = MKSUM+MARK
         MAXMK = MAX(MAXMK,MARK)
         MINMK = MIN(MINMK,MARK)
   10 CONTINUE
C  Calculate average mark and output results
      AV = REAL(MKSUM)/N
      PRINT *,'Highest mark is',MAXMK
      PRINT *,'Lowest mark is',MINMK
      PRINT *,'Average mark is',AV
      STOP
      END
```

Notice particularly the line after the end of the loop in which the average is calculated. Since both MKSUM and N are integer the expression MKSUM/N would cause integer division to take place. The intrinsic function REAL converts an integer to its real equivalent, thus forcing a real division to take place.

5.3   Restrictions on DO loops

Unlike most other statements in Fortran a DO statement affects one or more following statements, and the whole **range** of the loop (from the DO statement to the terminal statement of the loop) is necessarily governed by certain rules. These rules do not in any way restrict what would normally be carried out in the loop.

A brief consideration of the mechanism necessary for a DO loop to

Program		Action	
DO label, var $= e1,e2,e3$	1	Calculate trip count	
	2	Set var to initial value ($m1$)	
	3	Leave loop if trip count $= 0$ (go to step $n + 4$)	
First statement	4	*First statement*	
.			
.			
.			
label *Terminal statement*	n	*Terminal statement*	
	$n + 1$	Add $m3$ to var	
	$n + 2$	Subtract 1 from trip count	
	$n + 3$	Go back to step 3	
Next statement	$n + 4$	*Next statement*	

Figure 5.3
Actions taken during
DO loop processing.

operate will show the reasons for the few restrictions that do exist. Figure 5.3 shows the processes that are required at the start of the loop to calculate the trip count and initialize the DO variable, and at the end to increment the DO variable and decide whether another pass through the loop is required. There are two key points to note. The first is that the DO variable is set to its initial value *before* the decision is made whether to obey the loop at all. The second is that *after* the last (terminal) statement of the loop some extra instructions will be inserted by the compiler to increment the DO variable, decrement the trip count and return to the start of the loop to decide whether another pass is required.

It is clear, therefore, that there are three situations that could conflict with this structure, namely: altering the DO variable within the body of the loop; obeying statements within the loop (and hence the 'housekeeping' at the end) without first obeying the DO statement that sets up various values and variables; and having as the terminal statement of the loop some statement that affects the following statement(s) and that will be disrupted by the extra housekeeping statements. (Since the trip count is stored in a location known only to the compiler it is not possible for the Fortran program to access it directly, and it therefore cannot be changed other than by the DO loop housekeeping statements.)

These three possible conflict situations are covered by the three restrictions on DO loops:

- The DO variable must not be altered within the DO loop, although its value may be used in an expression.

- It is not permitted to enter the range of a DO loop except by obeying the initial DO statement.

● The terminal statement of a DO loop must be one that is complete in itself and will always allow processing to continue at the next statement. Of the statements met so far this rules out PROGRAM, STOP, END and DO. If you are in any doubt you can always finish the loop with a CONTINUE statement.

5.4 Nested DO loops

Apart from the restrictions mentioned above concerning the last statement of a DO loop, there are no restrictions concerning the type of statements that can appear within the body of such a loop. In particular there may be another DO statement as long as the range of this DO loop is totally within the first one. Figure 5.4 illustrates examples of valid and invalid structures.

A few moments' thought will confirm that the invalid structure cannot be correct since the end of the first loop (at label 1) will cause a return to the start of the second loop during the next pass, even though it was never completed, while, once the first loop is completed, the end of the second loop will cause an (illegal) return to the middle of the first loop (that is, the start of the second one). If the loops are indented as shown it is obvious what is legal and what is not without any further thought.

The one point to remember about nested loops is that, since the DO variable may not be altered during the loop, the inner loop must use a different DO variable from that used by the outer one.

There are innumerable examples of the usefulness of nested

Figure 5.4
Valid and invalid DO loop nesting.

	Permitted	Not permitted
	DO 1, ...	DO 1, ...
	.	.
	.	.
	DO 2, ...	DO 2, ...
	.	.
	.	.
	2 CONTINUE	1 CONTINUE
	.	.
	.	.
	1 CONTINUE	2 CONTINUE

DO loops, based on structure plans such as the following:

> Repeat for each street
>   Repeat for each house
>   Repeat for each occupant
>   Process personal details

or

> Repeat for each experiment
>   Repeat for each reading
>   Process experimental reading

Many of these examples are most appropriate when used in conjunction with **arrays** of values, as the next chapter will show; however, a good example of the power of DO loops when used together is given in Example 5.3.

Finally, there is no limit to the number of loops that may be nested within each other, although it is not easy to imagine a situation requiring more than two or three levels. Since the number of times the innermost loop is obeyed increases alarmingly with each extra level of nesting, it is not normally sensible to try to do very much at once, on the grounds of time and cost.

EXAMPLE 5.3

Write a program to print a set of multiplication tables from 2 times up to 12 times.

We can see from the structure plan that this will be a short, yet powerful, program.

> **1**   Repeat for I from 2 to 12
>   **1.1** Print heading
>   **1.2** Repeat for J from 1 to 12
>   **1.2.1** Print 'I times J is I*J'

Figure 5.5
A program to print
multiplication tables.

```
      PROGRAM TABLES
C
C  A program to print multiplication tables from 2 to 12 times
C
      INTEGER I,J
      DO 10, I=2,12
        PRINT *,' '
        PRINT *,I,' times table'
        DO 10, J=1,12
10        PRINT *,I,' times',J,' is',I*J
      STOP
      END
```

The program is equally simple:

```
      PROGRAM TABLES
C
C  A program to print multiplication tables from 2 to 12 times
C
      INTEGER I,J
      DO 10, I=2,12
        PRINT *,' '
        PRINT *,I,' times table'
        DO 20, J=1,12
20        PRINT *,I,' times',J,' is',I*J
10 CONTINUE
      STOP
      END
```

In this instance the inner loop is finished with a PRINT statement instead of
a CONTINUE; however, as there is nothing else to do in the outer loop a
CONTINUE has been used as the terminal statement so that it can be labelled.
This is not strictly necessary, as Fortran allows two loops to be terminated
by the same statement. Since the rule is that an inner loop must be totally
within an outer one there is no confusion, and the compiler generates the
code in such a way that the inner loop is finished before any attempt is
made to return for another pass through the outer loop. The program can
therefore be modified to take account of this. Figure 5.5 shows the
modified program and Figure 5.6 shows part of the results produced by
running it.

```
       .            .            .
       .            .            .
       .            .            .
3 times         9 is        27
3 times        10 is        30
3 times        11 is        33
3 times        12 is        36

4 times table
4 times         1 is         4
4 times         2 is         8
4 times         3 is        12
4 times         4 is        16
4 times         5 is        20
4 times         6 is        24
4 times         7 is        28
4 times         8 is        32
4 times         9 is        36
4 times        10 is        40
       .            .            .
       .            .            .
       .            .            .
```

Figure 5.6
Part of the results
produced by the TABLES
program.

5.5   The DO variable on exit from the loop

One problem area concerns the value of the DO variable after leaving the loop. There are two situations here and both can easily be resolved by considering the sequence of operations, as shown in Figure 5.3. This shows that:

(1)   The DO variable is set to its initial value *before* any decision is made as to whether to obey the loop.

(2)   The DO variable is updated at the end of each pass through the loop, but *before* a decision is made about another pass.

(3)   The DO variable is not altered anywhere else.

It follows that if an exit is made from the loop before it has been completed (as we shall see in Chapter 8) then the DO variable has the value that it had during the last pass (that is, its 'current' value). On the other hand, if the loop has been completed the DO variable is incremented before the decision is made and will thus have the value it would have had on the next pass. An example will illustrate this.

EXAMPLE 5.4

What is printed by the following program?

```
PROGRAM EX45
INTEGER I,J,K,L
DO 1, I=1,10
  DO 1, J=I,I**2
    DO 1, K=J+1,I*10
1       L = I+J+K
PRINT *,I,J,K,L
STOP
END
```

Initially I is set to 1 and then the second DO statement has initial and terminal values of 1 and 1. This gives a trip count of 1 so the next DO statement is obeyed for values of K from J+1 (that is, 2) to 10. On the last pass K is 10 and L is set to 12. K is then increased to 11 prior to the completion of the innermost loop. J is then incremented to 2 and the middle loop is almost complete. Finally I is increased to 2 and the process is repeated.

On the last pass through the outer loop I is 10 and the middle loop is obeyed with J taking values from 10 to 100. On the last but one pass J is 99 and the inner loop is to be obeyed with K taking values from J+1 (that is, 100) to I*10 (100). K therefore becomes 100 and L is set to 209 (10+99+100).

K is now incremented to 101 at the completion of the loop and incremented to 100 for another pass through the middle loop. This leads to the inner DO statement stipulating that K is to run from 101 to 100. K is therefore set to 101 but the trip count calculated is 0 and therefore the loop is not obeyed. It is therefore the end of the inner loop and so J is increased to 101. This is, however, the end of the middle loop, so I is incremented to 11. This is now the end of the outer loop, and so the values printed are

11 101 101 209

SUMMARY

- The DO loop is a means of repeating a block of statements a given number of times (the trip count).

- A trip count of 0 means that the loop is *not* obeyed at all.

- A statement label is a whole number in the range 1–99 999 written in columns 1–5.

- Some statements, such as PROGRAM, STOP, END and DO, cannot appear as the terminal statement of a DO loop.

- The CONTINUE statement (which does nothing, but can be labelled) can be used to terminate a DO loop.

- Nested DO loops may share the same terminal statement.

- After normal completion of a DO loop, the DO variable has the value it would have had on the next pass through the loop.

- Fortran 77 statements introduced in Chapter 5:

DO statement	DO *label*, *int_var=expr1*, *expr2*, *expr3*
CONTINUE statement	CONTINUE
DO loop structure	DO *label*, *int_var=expr1*, *expr2*

.

Fortran statements

.

label CONTINUE

SELF-TEST EXERCISES 5.1

1 How many times will the loops controlled by the following DO statements be obeyed?

    (a) DO 10, I=-5,5
    (b) DO 20, J=1,12,2
    (c) DO 30, K=17,15,-1
    (d) DO 40, L=17,15
    (e) DO 50, J=100,350,15
    (f) DO 60, K=10,10,10

2 What will be printed by the following program?

```
PROGRAM TEST2
INTEGER I,J,K,L,M,N
DATA I,J,K,L,M,N/1,2,4,8,2*0/
DO 40, I=J,K,L
  K=I
  DO 30, J=L,M,K
    N=J
    DO 20,K=L,N
      DO 10,L=I,K
        M=K*L
10      CONTINUE
20    CONTINUE
30  CONTINUE
40 CONTINUE
PRINT *,I,J,K,L,M,N
STOP
END
```

3 What will be printed by the following program?

```
PROGRAM TEST3
INTEGER I,J,K,L,M,N
DATA I,J,K,L,M,N/1,2,4,8,2*0/
DO 40, I=J,K,L
  K=-I
  DO 30, J=L,M,K
    N=J
    DO 20,K=L,N
      DO 10,L=I,K
        M=K*L
10      CONTINUE
20    CONTINUE
30  CONTINUE
40 CONTINUE
PRINT *,I,J,K,L,M,N
STOP
END
```

PROGRAMMING EXERCISES

Write your programs in a modular fashion, and produce a structure plan for each program before you start coding it.

*5.1   Write a program to print a table of squares, cubes, square roots and cube roots of whole numbers from 1 to 100 inclusive.

5.2   Write a program to display the 42 times table. (42×1 up to 42×12).

5.3   Write a program to generate and display the first 20 even numbers. Then modify the program to generate and display the first 20 odd numbers.

5.4   The students in a class each take several examinations (not more than six). Write a program that reads the number of students, the number of examinations, and all the marks, and then prints the average mark obtained by each student, the average mark for each examination, and the overall average mark for the class. (*Hint*: you will need to utilize one of the features of list-directed input to deal with the unknown number of examinations.)

5.5   The small business referred to in Exercise 3.13 identifies its employees by numbers running consecutively from 101 upwards. Write a new program that reads the number of employees, calculates the cash requirements for each employee (in order) in the same way as before, prints each employee's number together with the cash breakdown for his/her pay packet, and finally prints the total number of each denomination of coin and note required.

5.6   Write a program to print out the values of the first 20 terms of the series

$$1+1/2, \ 1+1/(1+1/2), \ 1+1/(1+1/(1+1/2)), \ \ldots$$

5.7   The derivative of $\sin x$ can be approximated by

$$\frac{\sin(x+h) - \sin(x-h)}{2h}$$

where h is small. Tabulate the values of $\sin x$, the approximate derivative, and the true derivative $\cos x$, for values of x between 0 and 1.5 radians in steps of 0.1, using a value of 0.05 for h.

5.8   Write a program that uses exactly two DO loops to print out the following list of numbers in the order given:

1, 2, 3, 4, 5, 6, 7, 8, 9, 10, 11, 13, 15, 17, 19, 21, 23, 25, 27, 29, 31, 34, 37, 40, 43, 46, 49, 52, 55, 58, 61

5.9   The international standard paper sizes, such as A4, are given by the formula

$$2^{1/4-n/2} \times 2^{-1/4-n/2} \text{ metres}$$

where n is the number following the letter A. Write a program to print the international paper sizes in centimetres from A0 down to A6.

*5.10   A cricketer's batting average is calculated by dividing the total number of runs he has scored by the number of times he has been out. A 'not out' score is therefore added to his total runs without affecting the number of times he has been out.

Write a program that first reads the number of players in a cricket club and then, for each player, reads the number of innings followed by the scores in each innings. A 'not out' score will be preceded by a minus sign to distinguish it from the other scores. The program should calculate the average for each player and his highest score, and then print the batting statistics in the following form:

Player	Innings	Not Out	Highest Score	Total Runs	Average
1	n1	no1	hs1	t1	av1
2	n2	no2	hs2	t2	av2
.	.	.	.	.	.
.	.	.	.	.	.
n	nn	non	hsn	tn	avn

5.11   A lever is the simplest machine known to man, and provides a means of lifting loads that would otherwise be too heavy.

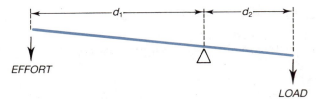

In the above diagram, the relationship between the human *EFFORT* and the actual *LOAD* is given by the equation

$$EFFORT \times d_1 = LOAD \times d_2$$

Write a program that will produce a table of the effort required to raise a load of 2000 kg when the distance of the load from the fulcrum (d_2) is fixed at 2 m. The program should print out the effort required for levers of lengths differing in steps of 2 m between two limits (minimum and maximum), which should be input from the keyboard.

Use the results produced by the program to determine the shortest lever that could be used to raise the load if the maximum effort is equivalent to 25 kg.

5.12 The length L of a bar of metal at a temperature T is given by the equation

$$L = L_0 + ETL_0$$

where the temperature is measured in degrees Celsius (°C), L_0 is the length of the bar at 0 °C, and E is the coefficient of expansion.

Write a program that will produce a set of tables showing the lengths of various bars of metal at various temperatures, assuming that each bar is exactly 1 m long at 20 °C. For each type of metal, the program should read the coefficient of expansion and the range of temperatures to be covered.

5.13 Modify your answer to Exercise 4.11 to produce a table of 10 values of the position, velocity and acceleration of the simple harmonic oscillator over 1 period of the oscillation. Produce the results in the form of a table.

5.14 Halley's comet appears approximately every 76 years, and its last appearance was in 1986. Write a program to display the dates of the comet's next 10 appearances.

5.15 The exponentiation operator ** is generally slower than repeated multiplication when a whole number power is required – for example, (A**2) takes longer to evaluate than (A*A). With this in mind, write a program to evaluate a quartic polynomial expression of the form:

$$Y = a0 + a1*X + a2*X^2 + a3*X^3 + a4*X^4$$

without using the exponentiation operator.

The program should first ask for the value of X, then each of the coefficients $a0$ to $a4$ in order.

5.16 The Fibonacci sequence of numbers is one in which each number is the sum of the previous two. It starts

1, 1, 2, 3, 5, 8, ... and so on

Write a program to generate the first 36 members of the sequence.

5.17   Write a computer program to simulate marching. Ask the user how many people are marching, and how many steps they are going to take. For each step, each marcher takes a left stride (write 'LEFT' on the screen) and then each marcher takes a right stride (write '♦♦♦♦♦♦RIGHT', where ♦ represents a space). So two people marching three steps should produce:

```
LEFT
LEFT
        RIGHT
        RIGHT
LEFT
LEFT
        RIGHT
        RIGHT
LEFT
LEFT
        RIGHT
        RIGHT
```

Arrays F90

6

6.1 Arrays of variables
6.2 Array declarations
6.3 Using arrays and array elements

6.4 Arrays as arguments to procedures
6.5 Giving initial values to an array
6.6 Input and output of arrays

It is often convenient to refer to a group of related items of the same type by giving them the same group name and identifying the individual items by their position in the set. In Fortran an **array** is used for this purpose. Each item within an array is referred to as an **array element**, and is identified by means of an integer **subscript**, which follows the array name in parentheses.

An array must always be declared in an extended type declaration statement, which also contains a specification of the range of possible subscripts and hence the size of the array.

Array elements may be used in all situations in which a variable name can be used, but are particularly useful in conjunction with a DO loop whose control variable can be used as an array subscript, thus enabling each pass through the loop to use a different array element.

The name of an array is normally only used with a subscript as part of an array element name, but can appear on its own in three situations: when an array is being used as an argument to a procedure; when a whole array is being given initial values in a DATA statement; and for input or output of the whole array. A special **implied** DO **list** can be used to give initial values to part of an array, or to input or output part of an array.

6.1 Arrays of variables

So far, in all the programs written one name has been used to refer to one location in the computer's memory. Sometimes, as in Example 4.2, this has meant that the same sequence of statements has been repeated several times but with different names for the variables. There are a great many situations when we should like to repeat a sequence of statements (for example, in a loop) but instead of always using the same set of variables we should like to use a different set, and then another, and so on.

One way to do this would be to use a group or **array** of locations in the memory, all of which are identified by the same name, but with an index, or **subscript**, to identify individual locations. Figure 6.1 illustrates this concept, using the same types of boxes as were used in Chapter 1 to explain the concept of named memory locations.

Thus the whole set of n boxes is called A, but within the set we can identify individual boxes by their position within the set. Mathematicians are familiar with this concept and would refer to a set like this as the *vector* A, and to the individual elements as $A_1, A_2, \ldots A_n$.

In Fortran we cannot adopt the mathematical concept of a subscript to identify these elements (although we do borrow the name); instead the name of the array is followed by an identifying integer value enclosed in parentheses: `A(1), A(2), ... A(n)`.

More precisely, an **array element** is defined by writing the name of the array followed by a subscript, where the subscript consists of an integer expression (known as the **subscript expression**) enclosed in parentheses. Thus, if A, B and C are arrays, the following are all valid ways of writing an array element:

```
A(10)
B(I+4)
C(3*I+MAX(I,J,K))
A(INT(B(I)*C(J)+A(K)))
```

Notice that function references are allowed as part of the subscript expression, as are array elements (including elements of the same array).

Figure 6.1
An array of memory locations.

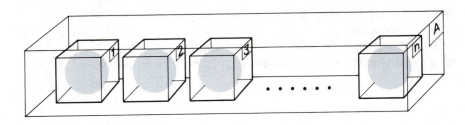

6.2   Array declarations

When a variable is referred to for the first time, either in a specification statement, a DATA statement, or an executable statement, the compiler will allocate an appropriate storage unit (or units in the case of some other types of variables, as we shall see in Chapters 11 and 13). It is not always possible to tell from these statements how many storage units to allocate for an array, and never from the first one alone. Since the compiler needs to know how many storage units are required so that it can allocate a contiguous area of the memory for the array, it is necessary to declare the size of the array at the start of the program.

The easiest way to do this is to follow the name of the array in an appropriate type declaration by the number of array elements enclosed in parentheses:

```
REAL A(20),TABLE(35)
INTEGER AGE(100),NUMBER(25)
```

In this form of declaration the subscripts will run upwards from 1 to the size of the array, and thus the integer array AGE may have subscripts running from 1 to 100, inclusive.

If we wish to have subscripts that do not start at 1 we can use an extended form of declaration consisting of the minimum and maximum values of the subscript, separated by a colon, with the complete subscript specification being enclosed in parentheses:

```
REAL KEY(0:20)
INTEGER ERROR(-10:10)
```

In this case the real array KEY can have subscripts in the range from 0 to 20, and therefore has a size of 21, while the integer array ERROR also has a size of 21, but has subscripts running from −10 up to +10.

It can be seen that the simple form of array declaration is the same as the more comprehensive one with a minimum subscript value of 1:

```
INTEGER AGE(1:100),NUMBER(1:25)
```

There is another way of declaring an array, although it is included in Fortran 77 mainly for historical reasons and is not normally used. This is by use of a DIMENSION statement:

```
DIMENSION KEY(0:20),ERROR(-10:10),AGE(100)
```

This performs exactly the same array declaration function as do the REAL, INTEGER and other type specification statements shown above, but does not

Figure 6.2
Array and function
references.

```
PROGRAM FIG62
REAL TOM
      .
      .
      .
A=TOM(I)
B=ABS(J)
C=FRED(K)
      .
      .
      .
END
```

specify any type. If the type of the array is not that implied by its initial
letter then a separate type statement is required

```
INTEGER AGE,ERROR
REAL KEY
DIMENSION KEY(0:20),ERROR(-10:10),AGE(100)
```

Since the dimensions could have been included in the type statements
there is little point in having a separate DIMENSION statement. If a DIMENSION
statement *is* used then it must come with the other specification statements
before any DATA or executable statements.

The specification of the maximum, and possibly minimum, subscript is called the **dimension declarator** and must be a *constant*. The array
name followed by a dimension declarator in parentheses is called an **array
declarator**.

The primary reason for declaring an array is to enable the compiler
to allocate sufficient storage space. Another important reason was hinted
at in Chapter 4 when subroutines and functions were discussed. Figure 6.2
shows a short extract from a program that does nothing in particular;
however, look at the three assignment statements. The first one is clearly
intended to assign the Ith element of the array TOM to A; TOM appears in an
array declaration at the start of the program. The second one has exactly
the same structure, but this time it requires that the intrinsic function ABS be
used to find the absolute value of J before assigning this value to B (after
converting it to real). The third assignment statement also takes exactly the
same form. However, there is no array declaration and FRED is not the name
of an intrinsic function. In this case, therefore, the compiler *assumes* that
FRED is an external function subprogram that is being provided by the user
and generates the necessary subprogram code to call the function. The
value of the function will then be assigned to C.

Thus there are three different ways in which an expression of the
form

name(expression)

can be interpreted. An intrinsic function is recognized by the compiler, but the distinction between an array element and a function reference can be made only because *the array must already have been declared before any reference is made to it*.

6.3   Using arrays and array elements

F90

An array element can be used anywhere that a variable can be used. In exactly the same way as a variable, it identifies a unique location in the memory to which a value can be assigned or input, and whose value may be used, for example, in an expression or output list. The great advantage is that by altering the value of the subscript it can be made to refer to a different location.

The use of array variables within a loop therefore greatly increases the power and flexibility of a program. This can be seen in Figure 6.3, where a short loop enables up to 100 sets of survey data to be input *and stored* for subsequent analysis in a way that is not otherwise possible. This program also illustrates how useful the PARAMETER statement can be when dealing with large numbers of arrays.

In the program each array has a maximum subscript of 100 and thus the program is suitable for up to 100 sets of data. The maximum value of the control variable for the conditional DO loop is, therefore, also 100. There may be other uses of this same maximum value of 100 elsewhere in the program. If we wish to change this value, either during testing or because there is more data than anticipated, there will be a number of statements to change, which is both time-consuming and a potential source of errors. Of course, a maximum value could be read for the DO loop control variable, but the array dimension declarators must be constants or constant expressions, *not* variables. Figure 6.4, however, shows the same program but using a named constant MAXSIZ to specify the size of the arrays.

```
PROGRAM SURVEY
INTEGER SEX(100),AGE(100)
REAL HEIGHT(100),WEIGHT(100)
DO 10, I=1,100
   READ *,SEX(I),AGE(I),HEIGHT(I),WEIGHT(I)
   IF (SEX(I).EQ.9) GOTO 11
10 CONTINUE
11     .
       .
       .
   END
```

Figure 6.3
Inputting data to an array.

Figure 6.4
Using a PARAMETER with
arrays.

```
PROGRAM SURVEY
INTEGER MAXSIZ
PARAMETER (MAXSIZ=100)
INTEGER SEX(MAXSIZ),AGE(MAXSIZ)
REAL HEIGHT(MAXSIZ),WEIGHT(MAXSIZ)
DO 10, I=1,MAXSIZ
   READ *,SEX(I),AGE(I),HEIGHT(I),WEIGHT(I)
   IF (SEX(I).EQ.9) GOTO 11
10 CONTINUE
11      .
        .
        .

END
```

In this case it is clear that by changing the single PARAMETER statement we can effect the required change throughout the program. There is no possibility of either forgetting to change one occurrence, or altering an occurrence of the constant 100 that has a different meaning and, therefore, should not be changed.

An array name, unlike an array element, can only be used in a limited number of situations. This is because the array name refers, in some sense, to the *whole* array, and therefore cannot be used in the same situations as can a variable or an array element. We have already seen that the array name can appear in a type-statement and in an array declarator. It can also be used as an argument to a subroutine or function:

```
PROGRAM ARGS
REAL A(100),B(50),C
CALL GETARR(A,B,C)
   .
   .
   .
```

Other situations in which an array name can appear without any subscript are in a DATA statement, and in an input/output statement; others will be described in later chapters.

SELF-TEST EXERCISES 6.1

1   **(a)** What is an array? and what is an array element?
      (b) How is a dimension declarator written? and what is the difference between a dimension declarator and an array declarator?
      (c) What (if any) are the constraints on a subscript expression?

2   Write declarations for suitable arrays in which to store the following sets of data:

(a)   The information collected in an (anonymous) survey of people attending a meeting of Gamblers Anonymous. Each person is asked how much (s)he earns each week, how many times (s)he goes gambling each week, how much (s)he loses on average each week gambling, what is the largest single win, what is the largest single loss, and how many weeks (s)he has been a gambling addict.

(b)   The measurements made in an experiment in which a sample piece of metal (or other material) is fixed in a device and then hit repeatedly by a mass of variable weight (but fixed for each experiment) dropped from a specified height until it fractures. The mass, height, and number of blows are recorded.

(c)   The heights above a base plane at various points on the surface of a three-dimensional model.

(d)   The temperature at 6 a.m., noon, 6 p.m. and midnight on each day of a year, and the number of days on which the noon temperature was below, respectively, $-10°$, $-9°$, $-8°$, ... $+30°$, and on which it was over $30°C$.

3   How many errors can you find in the following program fragment, and how would you correct them?

```
PROGRAM TEST2
REAL A(50),B(1:100),C(-20:20)
INTEGER I,J,K1(20),K2(10:50)
DO 10, I=1,20
   READ *,A(I),B(I),C(I)
   K1(I) = A(I)*D(I)
   K2(I) = A(I)*B(I)
   PRINT *,A(I),B(I),C(I),D(I)
10 CONTINUE
   DO 20, I=-20,20
      K2(I+30) = C(I)-A(I+20)
      K3(I+30) = B(I)-A(I+30)
20 CONTINUE
   DO 30, I=10,50
      PRINT *,A(I),B(I),K2(I),K3(I)
30 CONTINUE
   STOP
   END
```

6.4   Arrays as arguments to procedures

Chapter 4 showed how arguments are used to pass information between a subroutine or function and the calling program unit. In the case of scalar variables this is a straightforward process, but with arrays certain complications arise. Consider, for example, the following subroutine:

```
      SUBROUTINE AVRAGE(X,N,AV)
C
C This subroutine calculates the average of the N values stored in the
C array X, and returns it in AV
C
      REAL X(100),AV,SUM
      INTEGER I,N
C Sum the elements in a loop
      SUM=0.0
      DO 10, I=1,N
10    SUM=SUM+X(I)
C Calculate the average and return
      AV=SUM/N
      RETURN
      END
```

This is a variation on the subroutine written in Section 4.5, but instead of calculating the average of exactly five values it can deal with up to 100 values (or even more, as we shall see).

We have already established in Chapter 4 the conceptual mechanism used to relate the dummy arguments N and AV with the actual arguments used in the call to the subroutine, but what about the dummy array X? This does not actually require any space to be reserved in the computer's memory because, just as in the case of scalar variables, the *actual* space used is that allocated to the actual argument. However, as we saw in Section 6.2, an array declaration is also required in order that the compiler can distinguish between a reference to an array element and a reference to a function. The problem is that the subroutine may not know how large the actual array argument is.

In fact this does not normally matter, since the statement

```
REAL X(100)
```

tells the compiler that X is an array, and the value of 100 will not actually be used as no memory space needs to be allocated. Sometimes, however, a compiler will incorporate checks on the value of the subscripts to ensure that they do not go outside the declared range, and in that case there could be problems. Also, it is aesthetically, and maybe practically, displeasing to have a dimension given in an array declaration that is unnecessary and may have the wrong value. Fortran therefore provides two alternative solutions.

In the case of a dummy array argument it is permitted to have a variable as the dimension of the array, as long as the variable name also appears as a dummy argument of the same subprogram (or appears in a COMMON block in the same subprogram – see Chapter 15). If the array declaration includes both minimum and maximum subscript values then either or both of these may be variable names, with the same restriction.

Thus in the above subroutine the array declaration could be

altered to

```
REAL X(N)
```

which makes it absolutely clear what is going on. A declaration of this type is called an **adjustable array declaration**, because it allows the size of the array to be adjusted each time the subroutine is called.

It is also permitted to replace the dimension, or the upper bound (or maximum subscript value) by an asterisk, which indicates that this is an array that is assumed to be large enough for any operations carried out on it. This type of array declaration is therefore called an **assumed-size array declaration**. It will be seen later that there are some restrictions on the use of assumed-size arrays, but they can, nevertheless, be a useful feature in certain circumstances. Since there can be no checking of the array bounds, however, it is the programmer's responsibility to ensure that the actual array argument is always large enough. Using an assumed-size dummy array, the declaration in the subroutine AVRAGE would become

```
REAL X(*)
```

The subject of arrays as arguments will be discussed in more depth in Chapter 14, when we learn more about arrays and their use in procedures.

EXAMPLE 6.1

In Example 4.2 we developed a very long and repetitive program to produce some simple statistics relating to a set of experiments. Rewrite this program using arrays.

We shall start by reminding ourselves of our original structure plan:

1 Read five sets of five results

2 For each set
   2.1 Calculate the mean of five results – AVRAGE
   2.2 Calculate the standard deviation of these five results – STDEV
   2.3 Print the mean and standard deviation

3
   3.1 Calculate the mean of five means from step 2 – AVRAGE
   3.2 Calculate the standard deviation of these five means – STDEV
   3.3 Print the group mean and standard deviation

Since we shall be using arrays, the structure plans for the two functions will be slightly modified:

> AVRAGE(X(N),N)
>
> **1** Sum the N elements of the array X
>
> **2** Calculate and return the average

> STDEV(X(N),N,XMEAN)
>
> **1** Calculate the sum of the squares of differences between the N elements of the array X and their mean, XMEAN
>
> **2** Calculate the square root of the average of the squares
>
> **3** Return the standard deviation

Notice that the heading for these structure plans indicates that X is an array with a dimension of N. Remember that the structure plan is a guide – it does not have to use Fortran syntax!

The final program will then follow readily:

```
      PROGRAM METAL
C
C  This program summarizes experimental results
C
      REAL A(5),B(5),C(5),D(5),E(5),GMEAN(5),GSTDEV(5),
     *     XMEAN,XSTDEV,AVRAGE,STDEV
C  Input data by groups
      PRINT *,'Type five results for group A, followed by five for',
     *        'group B, etc.'
      READ *,A,B,C,D,E
C  Calculate mean and standard deviation for each group
      GMEAN(1) = AVRAGE(A,5)
      GSTDEV(1) = STDEV(A,5,GMEAN(1))
      PRINT *,'Group A mean is ',GMEAN(1),
     *        ' with a standard deviation of ',GSTDEV(1)
      GMEAN(2) = AVRAGE(B,5)
      GSTDEV(2) = STDEV(B,5,GMEAN(2))
      PRINT *,'Group B mean is ',GMEAN(2),
     *        ' with a standard deviation of ',GSTDEV(2)
      GMEAN(3) = AVRAGE(C,5)
      GSTDEV(3) = STDEV(C,5,GMEAN(3))
      PRINT *,'Group C mean is ',GMEAN(3),
     *        ' with a standard deviation of ',GSTDEV(3)
```

```
      GMEAN(4) = AVRAGE(D,5)
      GSTDEV(4) = STDEV(D,5,GMEAN(4))
      PRINT *,'Group D mean is ',GMEAN(4),
     *          ' with a standard deviation of ',GSTDEV(4)
      GMEAN(5) = AVRAGE(E,5)
      GSTDEV(5) = STDEV(E,5,GMEAN(5))
      PRINT *,'Group E mean is ',GMEAN(5),
     *          ' with a standard deviation of ',GSTDEV(5)
C  Now calculate overall totals
      XMEAN = AVRAGE(GMEAN,5)
      XSTDEV = STDEV(GMEAN,5,XMEAN)
      PRINT *,'Overall mean is ',XMEAN,' with a standard deviation of ',
     *          XSTDEV
      STOP
      END

      REAL FUNCTION AVRAGE(X,N)
C
C Calculates the mean of the N elements of X
C
      REAL X(N),SUM
      INTEGER I,N
      SUM = 0.0
      DO 10, I=1,N
10    SUM=SUM+X(I)
      AVRAGE = SUM/N
      RETURN
      END

      REAL FUNCTION STDEV(X,N,XMEAN)
C
C Calculates the standard deviation of the N elements of X,
C whose mean is supplied as the third argument
C
      REAL X(N),XMEAN,SUM
      INTEGER I,N
C
C STDEV = SQRT(SIGMA((X(I)-XMEAN)**2)/N)
C
      SUM=0.0
      DO 10, I=1,N
10    SUM=SUM+(X(I)-XMEAN)**2
      STDEV = SQRT(SUM/N)
      RETURN
      END
```

This program is very much simpler than the original one and, in addition, the two functions AVRAGE and STDEV will work correctly for *any* number of values supplied in the array X. Notice also how the input has been radically simplified by the use of array names. The data items will be read in the order A(1), A(2), A(3), A(4), A(5), B(1), B(2), ... which is exactly the same order as in our earlier version.

However, the main program still contains a series of repeated sets of three statements, which look as though they should be capable of further simplification. Such a simplification is indeed possible, but it is not quite so straightforward as it appears. This problem will be revisited in Chapter 14, when we shall have all the necessary tools at our disposal.

6.5   Giving initial values to an array

The elements of an array may be given initial values in three different ways. The first of these uses a form of DATA statement exactly the same as that introduced in Section 3.6, except that array elements are included in the list of names. Thus the following statements will set the first four elements of the array A to zero, and the last one to −1.0. The other elements of A (A(5) to A(19)) are not given any initial value and are therefore initially undefined.

```
PROGRAM INIT1
REAL A(20)
DATA A(1),A(2),A(3),A(4)/4*0.0/,A(20)/-1.0/
   .
   .
   .
```

If more than a few elements of an array are to be initialized, it is not necessary to write out the names of all the individual array elements; instead we may use an **implied** DO **list**. This takes the form:

$(dlist, int=m1, m2, m3)$

or simply

$(dlist, int=m1, m2)$

where *dlist* is a list of array element names and the expression *int=m1, m2, m3* or *int=m1, m2* is similar to the corresponding expression in a DO loop, except that *int* (the **implied** DO **variable**) must be an integer variable, *m1*, *m2* and *m3* must be constants or constant expressions, and *m3* must be positive. The implied DO variable exists only for the purposes of the DATA statement and does not affect the value of any other variable having the same name.

The effect of the implied DO list is to repeat the list of array element names for each value of the implied DO variable. Thus the statements

```
PROGRAM INIT2
REAL A(20)
DATA (A(I),I=1,4)/4*0.0/,A(20)/-1.0/
        .
        .
        .
```

have exactly the same effect as those in the previous example, in which
A(1), A(2), A(3) and A(4) were all listed individually. The following
statements show a more sophisticated use in which A(1), A(2), A(4), A(5),
A(7), ... are set to zero, while every third array element (A(3), A(6), ...) is set
to 1:

```
PROGRAM INIT3
REAL A(20)
DATA (A(I),A(I+1),I=1,19,3)/14*0.0/,
*       (A(I),I=3,18,3)/6*1.0/
        .
        .
        .
```

The third and last way of initializing an array is to write the name of the
array (without any subscripts) in the list of items to be initialized, and
exactly the right number of values in the value list:

```
PROGRAM INIT4
REAL A(20)
DATA A/20*0.0/
        .
        .
        .
```

In this case, therefore, the array name represents a list of *all* its elements, in
order, and requires the corresponding number of values.

6.6   Input and output of arrays

The situation with regard to the input and output of arrays is very similar
to that which exists for DATA statements. Thus individual array elements
may appear in an input or output list in the same way as variable names.
An implied DO list may appear in order to define a sequence of array
elements, and an array name may appear (unsubscripted) in order to
specify *all* the elements of the array. The major difference is that the
restrictions on the implied DO list in a DATA statement do not apply in an

Figure 6.5
Input using an implied
DO list.

```
PROGRAM ARINPT
REAL A(20)
READ *,N,(A(I),I=1,N)
       .
       .
       .
END
```

Figure 6.5
Input using an implied
DO list.

input/output statement and the rules are exactly the same as those that apply to a DO statement. In particular, since the defining expressions for the implied DO may be variables or variable expressions they may be dependent upon values input by the same statement (see Figure 6.5).

This form of input statement must, however, be used with care, for it opens the door to a frequent cause of errors. Consider, for example, what would happen if there were more than 20 data items, say 25. The READ statement would read this number and then, under the control of the implied DO list, would read sufficient data to occupy the array elements of A(1) to A(25). However, A was declared with a maximum subscript of only 20. Unfortunately, checking that the subscript value is within the defined bounds is a time-consuming task. Many compilers will only insert the code for such checking into the compiled program upon request, for example during testing. If such checking is absent or inactive the program will store the 25 values in 25 consecutive storage units starting at A(1). The last five of these are, however, not part of the array A and may be other variables, constant values or even, in some situations, part of the program!

The fact that these memory locations have been overwritten may not be immediately apparent, and the subsequent incorrect results and/or program failure can be very difficult to find. To guard against this possibility it is often preferable first to read the number of values, then to check that this is acceptable, and only then to read the full set of data. Figure 6.6 shows a modified version of the program from Figure 6.5.

Figure 6.6
Improved use of an
implied DO list for input.

```
PROGRAM ARINPT
REAL A(20)
READ *,N
IF (N.GE.1 .AND. N.LE.20) THEN
   READ *,(A(I),I=1,N)
ELSE
   PRINT *,'Invalid number: ',N
END IF
       .
       .
       .
END
```

SUMMARY

● An array is an ordered set of array elements stored in consecutive memory locations.

● An array and the range of its subscripts must be declared.

● Array elements are used in the same way as variables.

● An implied DO in both DATA statements and input/output lists is used to specify several consecutive array elements.

● An unsubscripted array name in a DATA statement or input/output list represents a list of all the elements of the array.

● Fortran 77 statements introduced in Chapter 6:

Array declarations	*type name (declarator),* ...
	for example, REAL A(100),B(10:50),C(-10:10)
	DIMENSION *name(declarator),* ...
Initializing arrays	DATA *array_name/list of values/*
	DATA *list of array_elements/list of values/*
	DATA (*name(int),int=e1,e2,e3)/list of values/*
Input and output of arrays	READ *,*array_name*
	PRINT *,(*array_name(int),int=e1,e2,e3*)

SELF-TEST EXERCISES 6.2

1 What is the difference between an adjustable array declaration and an assumed-size array declaration? Give an example of each.

2 What are the values of the integer variables I and J at the conclusion of the following statements?

```
      PROGRAM TEST2
      REAL A(50),B(50)
      INTEGER I,J,K
      DATA I,J,K/3*0/
      DO 10, I=1,10
        READ *,A(I)
   10 CONTINUE
      READ *,(B(J),J=1,20)
```

3 Write the necessary declaration and DATA statements to create an array called MONTH such that MONTH(1) contains the number of days in the month of January, and so on.

4 Write the necessary declaration and DATA statements to create an array called LEAP such that LEAP(*yr*) is 1 if the subscript *yr* has the value of a leap year (1988, 1992, etc.) and is 0 otherwise.

5 Write the necessary declaration and input statements to allow you to input and store for subsequent processing:

(a) the batting record of a member of a cricket team, consisting of the number of innings and the scores for each innings;

(b) the readings from three strain gauges during an experiment in which an electric current is passed through a fixed rod and the expansion or contraction measured at (approximately) regular intervals.

PROGRAMMING EXERCISES

6.1 Write a program that will read up to 20 integer numbers and print them out in the reverse order to that in which they were typed.

6.2 Write a program that prompts the user to type 10 numbers in ascending order (that is, each number typed is greater than the previous one), and stores them in an integer array COUNT. The data should be stored in such a way that a statement in the program of the form

```
      PRINT *, COUNT
```

will print the numbers in *descending* order.

6.3 Write a program that reads and stores two distinct lists of integer numbers and then finds and prints their union. (The union is the collection of all items that are in at least one of the lists.)

6.4 Modify the program you wrote for Exercise 5.16 so as to store the first 36 Fibonacci numbers in an array, and then print them out four to a line at the end.

6.5 Write a program that converts an 8-digit binary number to its decimal equivalent. You can store the binary number in an 8-element integer array, in which each array element contains either a 1 or 0. Use a data statement to initialize your array.

6.6 Fill up an integer array with the numbers 1 through to 8. Write your program such that it prints out the array elements

    (a) in a column;
    (b) two to a line;
    (c) four to a line.

6.7 The normal probability function ϕ is defined as:

$$\phi(x) = \frac{1}{\sqrt{2\pi}} e^{-x^2/2}$$

Write a program to evaluate $\phi(x)$ for values of x from -3.0 to $+3.0$ in steps of 0.2, and store these in an array. Display the results in a table, with five values to a line.

6.8 The number of pupils at each of five schools are 229, 441, 382, 545 and 316 respectively. Write a program to print the total number of pupils, the average number per school, and the percentage of the pupils at each of the schools.

*6.9 In Ellistown all goods sold in shops, other than food, attract a 5% sales tax. In addition, all goods other than printed materials (such as books and newspapers) attract a State tax of 3% intended to subsidize the State Printing House.
    Write a program that takes as its input the details about a number of purchases, each consisting of the price and a sales code (1=food, 2=books, 3=newspapers, 4=other printed material, 9=other items), and prints the total cost of the goods, the total City Tax and the total State Tax.

6.10 The dot product of two three-dimensional vectors $(A1,A2,A3)$ and $(B1,B2,B3)$ is defined as:

$$A \cdot B = (A1*B1)+(A2*B2)+(A3*B3)$$

Write a function to calculate the dot product of two such vectors.

How would you generalize your function to cope with vectors with more than three dimensions?

6.11 The vector product of two three-dimensional vectors $(A1,A2,A3)$ and $(B1,B2,B3)$ is defined as:

$$(C1,C2,C3) = (A1,A2,A3) \times (B1,B2,B3)$$

where $C1=A2*B3-A3*B2$, $C2=A3*B1-A1*B3$, and $C3=A1*B2-A2*B1$)

Write a function to calculate the vector product of two such vectors.

How would you generalize your function to cope with vectors with more than three dimensions?

6.12 Use your solutions to Exercises 6.10 and 6.11 to write a routine to evaluate the scalar triple product of three vectors A, B, C (where $A=(A1,A2,A3)$, and so on) which is defined as $[ABC]=A.(B \times C)$ and confirm that $[ABC]$ is also equal to $B.(C \times A)$ and $C.(A \times B)$.

6.13 Exercise 5.10 involved writing a program to calculate the batting averages of the members of a cricket club. Modify that program so that the relevant details are stored in arrays, and then print out only the details for the three players with the highest averages. (*Hint*: you can use the MAX intrinsic function to achieve this.)

6.14 An array is to contain the following values, representing the amounts of money that people have invested with a bank:

12.25, 19.00, −10.25, −17.60, 200.40

The bank has a policy that every year people have 10% added to or subtracted from their bank balance depending on whether they are in credit or debit.

Write a program that passes the array as an argument to a subroutine where this calculation is performed. Print out the array in the main part of the program. How do the accounts change over the next five years assuming that nobody makes any withdrawals or deposits?

6.15 Write a function DIST2(X,Y) that calculates the distance between two points in space, using the formula

$$distance = \sqrt{\sum_{i=1}^{3}(X(i)-Y(i))^2}$$

If P, Q and R are the three points (1,2,3), (3,1,0) and (2,5,−1) check that the sum of the distances between any two pairs of points is greater than, or equal to, the distance between the third pair of points.

*6.16 In a psychology experiment volunteers are asked to carry out 10 simple tests, and a record is kept of which tests they pass and which they fail. This record consists of a 1 for a pass, and a 0 for a fail.

Write a program which inputs the test results of a set of volunteers and prints the percentage of the volunteers who passed each test. (*Hint*: use an array of size 10 in which to accumulate the passes.)

Decisions

As well as arithmetic expressions Fortran contains the facility for writing **logical expressions**, which have the value *true* or *false*. Such expressions may be formed by use of **relational operators**, which compare the relationship between two arithmetic values, or by **logical operators**, which are used to combine two or more logical values.

Logical expressions are used by the **block IF statement** and the **logical IF statement** to enable a program to take decisions, and to execute different parts of the program depending upon the results of those decisions.

Figure 7.1
An example of decisions
in English.

Q: How do I get to Budapest from Vienna?

A: It depends how you want to travel.
      If you are in a hurry *then*
          you should fly from Schwechat airport in Vienna to Ferihegy
          airport in Budapest;
      but if you are a romantic or like trains *then*
          you should take the Orient Express from the Sudbanhof to
          Budapest's Keleti palyudvar;
      but if you have plenty of time *then*
          you can travel on one of the boats that ply along the Danube;
      otherwise
          you can always go by road.

7.1   Choice and decision-making

In everyday life we frequently come up against a situation that involves several possible alternative courses of action, requiring us to choose one of them according to some decision-making criterion. Figure 7.1 shows a hypothetical discussion about how to get from Vienna to Budapest. Clearly there are several answers, depending on the preferred method of travel and the time available. If we eliminate the details of the answer we see that it has a definite structure, as shown in Figure 7.2.

Each of the various alternative forms of transport (or 'actions') is preceded by a condition or test of the form '*if* some criterion holds, *then* ...', apart from the last form (travel by road), which is included as a final alternative should none of the others be suitable and is preceded by the word *otherwise*.

Fortran 77 has a very similar construction, shown in Figure 7.3,

Figure 7.2
English-language
alternatives.

If criterion *then*
    action
but if criterion *then*
    action
but if criterion *then*
    action
otherwise
    action

```
IF (criterion) THEN
   action
ELSE IF (criterion) THEN
   action
ELSE IF (criterion) THEN
   action
ELSE
   action
END IF
```

Figure 7.3
Fortran 77 alternatives.

which uses the words IF and THEN exactly as they were used in the English language example, the words ELSE IF where the English used *but if*, and the word ELSE instead of *otherwise*. In addition, so that there is no doubt about the end of the final 'action', the words END IF are placed at the very end. The only other difference is that the criterion on which the decision will be based is enclosed in parentheses. This structure is known as a **block IF structure** and the initial IF ... THEN is called a **block IF statement**.

The way a block IF works is that each decision criterion is examined in turn. If it is true then the following action, or 'block' of Fortran statements, is obeyed. If it is not true then the next criterion (if any) is examined. If none of the criteria is found to be true then the block of statements following the ELSE (if there is one) is obeyed; if there is no ELSE statement, as in Figure 7.4, then no action is taken and the computer moves on to the next statement, that is, the one following the END IF statement. There must always be an IF statement (with a corresponding block of statements) and an END IF statement, but ELSE IF and ELSE statements are optional.

Before this facility can be used for taking one of several alternative courses of action the criteria on which the decisions will be based must be defined. These all consist of a new type of expression – a **logical expression**.

```
IF (criterion) THEN
   action
END IF
```

Figure 7.4
A minimal block IF.

7.2   Logical expressions

In the English-language discussion about how to get from Vienna to Budapest the decision depended upon the truth or otherwise of certain assertions. Thus '*if* you are in a hurry *then* travel by plane' could be expressed (rather quaintly) as '*if* it is true that you are in a hurry *then* travel

Figure 7.5
Relational operators and expressions.

A.LT.B is *true* if A<B
P.LE.Q is *true* if P≤Q
X.GT.Y is *true* if X>Y
I.GE.J is *true* if I≥J
S.EQ.T is *true* if S=T
U.NE.V is *true* if U≠V

by plane', and similarly for the other decision criteria. It can be seen that each decision depends upon whether some assertion is true or false.

The Fortran decision criterion is also an assertion that is true or false. Because this is a new concept, and not to be confused with numbers or character strings, the values *true* and *false* are called **logical values**, and an assertion (or expression) that can take one of these two values is called a **logical expression**. The simplest forms of logical expression are those expressing relationships between two numeric values; thus

```
A.GT.B
```

is true if the value of A is greater than the value of B, and

```
I.EQ.J
```

is true if the value of I is equal to the value of J.

Notice that in these two cases the names A and B, and I and J, are separated by a composite item consisting in each case of two letters enclosed by full stops. This is because when Fortran was first defined it was not possible to punch such signs as < or >. All **logical operators** therefore consist of two, three or four letters enclosed between full stops.

The two expressions shown above, which express a relationship between two values, are a special form of logical expression called a **relational expression** and the operators are called **relational operators**. Figure 7.5 shows the six relational operators that exist in Fortran, and a few moments' thought will show that they define all possible relationships between two arithmetic values.

Indeed there is a certain amount of redundancy, which leads to the possibility of expressing the same condition in several different ways; for example, the following four relational expressions are identical in their effect and will always give the same results.

```
B**2.GE.4.0*A*C
B**2-4.0*A*C.GE.0
4.0*A*C.LE.B**2
4.0*A*C-B**2.LE.0
```

F90

The mathematically oriented reader will recognize them as expressing the condition for a quadratic equation to have two real roots.

This variety means that each programmer is free to choose his or her own way of expressing such conditions. For example, the author would always use the first one above, as it is the way in which he always thinks of the condition (that is, $b^2 \geqslant 4ac$).

Notice that in these examples the values being compared are not necessarily expressed as variables or constants but as arithmetic expressions. All arithmetic operators have a higher priority than any logical operator and arithmetic expressions are therefore evaluated *before* any comparisons take place. The formal definition of a relational expression is thus

> *expression*   *relational_operator*   *expression*

EXAMPLE 7.1

In Example 4.1 the number of bags of wheat required to sow a triangular field was calculated. Modify this program to deal with the situation in which an exact number of full bags is required, in a more aesthetically pleasing manner (and one that is easier to follow).

In Example 4.1 we added 9 to the quantity of seed required before dividing by 10. This uses the truncation mechanism to specify an extra bag (which will only be partially used) if the true quantity is not an exact multiple of 10. A much better way would be to use a block IF. A revised structure plan could then read:

1   Read lengths of sides of field and sowing density

2   Calculate area of field and weight of seeds

3   Calculate number of full bags needed

4   If any more seed needed then
   4.1 Add 1 to number of bags

5   Print size of field and number of bags

We can find out if any more is needed by testing whether the amount required is greater than the amount in the bags.

```
      PROGRAM WHEAT
C
C  A program to calculate the quantity of wheat needed to sow a field
C
      REAL A,B,C,S,AREA,DENSTY,QTY
      INTEGER NBAGS
C  Read the lengths of the sides of the field and the sowing density
      PRINT *,'Type the lengths of the three sides of the field (m): '
      READ *,A,B,C
      PRINT *,'What is the sowing density (g/sq m)? '
      READ *,DENSTY
C  Calculate area of field
      S = 0.5*(A+B+C)
      AREA = SQRT(S*(S-A)*(S-B)*(S-C))
C  Calculate quantity of wheat in kilograms and number of bags
      QTY = DENSTY*AREA*0.001
      NBAGS = QTY/10.0
C  Check to see if any more seed required
      IF (QTY.GT.10*NBAGS) THEN
         NBAGS=NBAGS+1
      END IF
C  Print results
      PRINT *,'Area of field is ',AREA,' sq m'
      PRINT *,NBAGS,' 10 kg bags will be required'
      STOP
      END
```

There are two important points to note here. The first is that the relational expression is comparing a real value (QTY) with an integer one (10*NBAGS). In this case the expression is evaluated by comparing the difference between the two arguments and 0; thus the expression

```
      QTY.GT.10*NBAGS
```

is evaluated as

```
      (QTY-10*NBAGS).GT.0.0
```

It is thus clear that 10*NBAGS will be converted to its real equivalent and a real subtraction then performed.

The second point concerns the accuracy of real arithmetic. Real numbers are stored in the computer as an approximation to a defined degree of accuracy and therefore when such numbers are used in arithmetic expressions the least significant digits may get lost. Figure 7.6 illustrates this in the context of hand calculation to six digits of accuracy, where the product of two four-digit numbers requires seven digits to be accurate; the answer is therefore expressed as a six-digit number after rounding the sixth digit. The normal rule is that if the first digit to be omitted (that is, the seventh digit in this case) is in the range 0–4 then it (and any subsequent

Multiply 25.39 by 17.25 to six significant figures

$$
\begin{array}{r}
25.39 \times \\
17.25 \\
\hline
2539 \\
17773 \\
5078 \\
12695 \\
\hline
4379775
\end{array}
$$

Answer is 437.978

Figure 7.6
An example of rounding errors in hand calculations.

ones) are simply dropped, but if it is in the range 5–9 (as in this example) then the last significant digit is increased by one (from 7 to 8 in this case) before the remainder are dropped.

A computer operates in exactly the same way and therefore any real arithmetic operation, especially multiplication or division, is liable to introduce such a rounding error. Usually this is of no consequence as the computer is working to a greater accuracy than required for the problem. However, there are three cases where it *does* matter. One of these is where a great deal of numerical calculation is being carried out; in this case the accuracy can be increased, as we shall see in Chapter 11. The second case is where the calculated real number is to be truncated before being stored as an integer. The third case is where we wish to compare or subtract two real numbers that are almost exactly the same. The last two situations may be illustrated with an example.

Let us suppose that the sides of the field are 130 m, 100 m and 130 m, and that the sowing density is 25 g/m². A few moments' calculation shows that the area of the field is 6000 m², and hence that 150 kg of seed are required. NBAGS should therefore be 15 and the test should find that these contain exactly enough seed. In practice, though, it probably won't be like that. For example, the calculation of the area could lead to a value such as 5999.999 999 (to 10 significant figures) or to 6000.000 001. The subsequent calculation of the quantity of seed will give further possible rounding errors leading to a (real) value for QTY/10.0 of perhaps 14.999 999 99 or 15.000 000 01.

Although for all practical purposes these two values are the same as the true value of 15, when they are truncated to calculate NBAGS they will lead to integer values of 14 and 15 respectively. In the first case QTY will clearly be greater than 10*NBAGS and so the situation will be compensated for. In the second case, however, it is possible that QTY is fractionally more than 150.0 (for example 150.000 000 1) and that the relational expression will be true, leading to a calculation of 16 bags.

We can deal with this by *never* testing whether two real values are equal (which is essentially what we are doing here in the borderline case) but rather by testing whether their difference is acceptably small. In this case, therefore, we could say that, since the numbers being compared are of the order of 100 (actually 150 in this example), then, since any errors in calculation will be much less than 1%, we could alter the test to read

```
IF (QTY.GT.10*NBAGS+1) THEN
   NBAGS=NBAGS+1
END IF
```

A better way would be to relate it directly to the value of NBAGS and write

```
IF (QTY.GT.10.01*NBAGS) THEN
   NBAGS=NBAGS+1
END IF
```

EXAMPLE 7.2

Write a program to read the coefficients of a quadratic equation and print its roots.

This program will use the formula

$$x = \frac{-b \pm \sqrt{b^2 - 4ac}}{2a}$$

where

$$ax^2 + bx + c = 0 \quad \text{and} \quad a \neq 0$$

There are several potential problems, so we start with a structure plan:

1 Read coefficients

2 If $b^2 > 4ac$ then
   2.1 Calculate the two roots
   but if $b^2 = 4ac$ then
   2.2 Calculate two equal roots
   otherwise
   2.3 There are no roots

3 Print results

There are three possible cases, namely two (unequal) roots, two identical roots, and no (real) roots, which correspond to $b^2>4ac$, $b^2=4ac$ and $b^2<4ac$ respectively. However, before starting to write the program we should have a more detailed look at this plan.

First we notice that there are two tests comparing b^2 and $4ac$ and, in addition, that the value of b^2-4ac will be required at step 2.1. A lot of unnecessary calculation can therefore be avoided if we calculate the value of b^2-4ac once only, before carrying out any tests.

The second point concerns mathematical rounding, as discussed above. The problem here is particularly acute because if, for example, b^2-4ac is calculated to be $0.000\,000\,000\,1$ (instead of 0) an unnecessarily complicated calculation will ensue, while if it should be calculated to be $-0.000\,000\,000\,1$ the program will assume that there are no real roots when there are, in fact, two equal ones. This is dealt with by comparing b^2-4ac with a very small number, but one which is large enough to be larger than any likely rounding error – for example, 10 times the smallest positive real number that can be stored on the computer.

The third point is that step 2.3 has a different effect from steps 2.1 and 2.2 in that it does not produce any results for step 3 to print. It would be easier, therefore, to print the roots in steps 2.1 and 2.2 and a message in step 2.3. Our structure plan is now as follows:

---

1 Set e to a very small value

2 Read coefficients

3 Calculate b^2-4ac

4 If $b^2-4ac>e$ then
   4.1 Calculate and print two roots
   but if $b^2-4ac>-e$ then
   4.2 Calculate and print two equal roots
   otherwise
   4.3 Print message 'no roots'

Notice the way the test now works. First we test whether b^2-4ac is greater than a very small value (e). If it is not then it is zero (for our purpose) or negative. We now test whether it is greater than a very small negative value ($-e$). If it is, then since it is also less than or equal to a very small positive value, it can be considered to be 0. We can now write the program – a trivial task now that it has been properly thought out and planned.

```
      PROGRAM QUAD
C
C  This program solves a quadratic equation
C
      REAL A,B,C,D,ROOTD,E,X,X1,X2
C  E is a very small number, but greater than likely rounding errors
      PARAMETER (E=1E-9)
C  Read coefficients
      PRINT *,'Type coefficients: '
      READ *,A,B,C
C  Calculate main expression
      D=B**2 - 4*A*C
C  Check possibilities
      IF (D.GT.E) THEN
C  b**2>4ac - so two real roots
        ROOTD=SQRT(D)
        X1=(-B+ROOTD)/(A+A)
        X2=(-B-ROOTD)/(A+A)
        PRINT *,'Roots are',X1,X2
      ELSE IF (D.GT.-E) THEN
C  b**2=4ac (within + or - 1E9) - so two equal roots
        X=-B/(A+A)
        PRINT *,'Roots are',X,X
      ELSE
C  b**2<4ac - so no real roots
        PRINT *,'There are no real roots'
      END IF
      STOP
      END
```

If the program is to be run from a terminal, this is all that is needed. However, if it is to be run in any form of batch system, with the results being output on a printer, it is highly desirable to include an extra statement to print the data – the three coefficients in this case. The following statement, just after the READ statement, is all that is required.

```
      PRINT *,'The coefficients of the equation are',A,B,C
```

7.3   The block IF structure

Examples 7.1 and 7.2 have shown the block IF structure in operation, and it is now appropriate to define formally the way it works. Figure 7.7 shows in diagrammatic form the basic structure, and it can be seen that it starts with a block IF statement and ends with an END IF.

Between these statements there may be one or more blocks of Fortran statements. Each such block is preceded by an IF (in the case of the first one), ELSE IF or ELSE statement, and is followed by an ELSE IF or (in the

```
IF (logical expression) THEN
   block of Fortran statements
ELSE IF (logical expression) THEN
   block of Fortran statements
ELSE IF (logical expression) THEN
         .
         .
         .
ELSE
   block of Fortran statements
END IF
```

Figure 7.7
The block IF structure.

case of the last one) END IF statement. There may be any number of ELSE IF statements or none at all, and there may be one ELSE statement or none at all. If there is an ELSE statement then it must, of course, immediately precede the last block of statements.

There are no restrictions concerning the statements that constitute a block other than the obvious one that any DO or block IF statements must have all their controlled statements within the same block. (Any other course would clearly be nonsense.) Thus the final statement of a DO loop must be in the same block as the initial DO statement, and the END IF statement of a block IF must be in the same block as its initial block IF statement. In the latter case the **nested block IF structure** is said to be at a lower level – see Figure 7.8. In order to clarify the structure each level is

```
IF (logical expression) THEN
   block of Fortran statements
ELSE IF (logical expression) THEN
   Fortran statements
   IF (logical expression) THEN
      block of Fortran statements
            .
            .
            .
   END IF
   Fortran statements
ELSE IF (logical expression) THEN
         .
         .
         .
END IF
```

Figure 7.8
Nested block IF structure.

shown indented, in a similar way to the indenting of DO loops in Chapter 5.

The block IF is a very powerful structure as it reflects the way in which real-life decisions usually arise. It also has the added advantage that its use encourages the development of a well-formulated structure for the program. Fortran 77, however, contains a number of other types of statement that can be used to cause the computer to take decisions and/or to alter the normal sequential execution of program statements. These exist in Fortran 77 mainly for historical reasons and to retain compatibility with earlier versions of the language. One of these can be useful in certain situations, as described in the next section, but the others are not recommended, other than in a particular construction that is described in Chapter 8. They are described briefly in Chapter 19, which is concerned with various obsolete features of Fortran 77.

F90

7.4   The logical IF statement

Until the advent of Fortran 77, the most powerful decision-making statement in Fortran took the form

    IF (logical expression) Fortran statement

This is exactly equivalent to the minimal block IF with a block consisting of a single statement

    IF (logical expression) THEN
       Fortran statement
    END IF

Because the second part of the logical IF statement is only a single statement, however, there are some restrictions that must be observed. Thus it is not permissible to have a DO statement or a block IF statement following the logical expression (or, of course, an ELSE IF, ELSE or END IF statement), nor is it permissible to have another logical IF statement there.

On its own, therefore, the logical IF statement has limited usefulness. Essentially it is a means of making the execution of a single statement conditional upon the value of a logical expression. Although it is the chronological ancestor of the block IF it should be considered as merely a 'shorthand' version of the minimal block IF with a single-statement block. Nevertheless, because it is more compact, it can be used in a number of situations without any loss of clarity or efficiency.

EXAMPLE 7.3

Write a program that reads 100 sets of data, each consisting of two coordinates and a code. Using a plotter attached to your computer, plot an X at every point and surround it with a circle if the code is negative.

The first question is: how do we plot a series of points on a graph plotter? This is, in fact, a specific example of a general problem – namely, how do we carry out complex actions that are common to large numbers of computer users? (Examples are statistical analysis, numerical analysis and graphics, as well as a number of more application-oriented activities.) In Chapter 4 the whole concept of subprograms, both functions and subroutines, was discussed in some detail, and clearly it would be sensible to confine the control of a graph plotter, or other graphical device, to one or more subroutines. In practice, however, we would not normally write these subroutines ourselves.

One of the great virtues of Fortran is that the complete independence of subprograms, apart from the specification of their **interfaces** (or calling sequences), makes it very easy for such subprograms to be written by different people at different times in different places, and to be brought together only when the program is loaded into the computer. This concept of **independent compilation** leads naturally to the creation of **libraries** of useful procedures, usually subroutines. For example, a graphical library might contain a subroutine called BOX, which draws a rectangular box whose sides are defined by coordinates supplied as arguments. Anyone could then use this without having to bother about the details of using the graph plotter or other graphic devices (and those details can be extremely complex). Similarly, a subroutine called GAUSS might solve a set of simultaneous linear equations using the Gaussian elimination method, without requiring the programmer even to understand the method used. (For those who are interested in numerical methods, Section 18.4 does, in fact, discuss how to write such a subroutine and includes a fully tested example.)

Such libraries range from major (commercial) international libraries, such as the NAG library of numerical analysis procedures (NAG Ltd, 1988) or the SPSS library of statistical and survey analysis procedures (SPSS Inc., 1988), to purely local libraries of useful procedures developed by a particular organization, department, or individual programmer. The availability of such libraries is one of the great strengths of Fortran, for it ensures that hard-won experience is not lost, and is one of the major reasons for the language's continuing success.

For this example the existence of a library of graphical procedures that contains, among other things, the four subroutines specified in Figure 7.9 will be assumed. We can now develop a structure plan for our problem, and write the corresponding program.

Figure 7.9
Four procedures from a
hypothetical graphics
library.

PSTART	initializes plotting
PCROSS(X,Y,W)	draws a cross whose centre is at the point (X,Y) and whose width (the length of its arms) is W
PCIRCL(X,Y,R)	draws a circle of radius R whose centre is at the point (X,Y)
PEND	terminates plotting

1   Initialize plotting

2   Repeat the following 100 times
    2.1 Read a set of data
    2.2 Draw a cross
    2.3 If the code is negative then
        2.3.1 Draw a circle

3   Terminate plotting

```
      PROGRAM POINTS
C
C This program plots a cross at each of 100 data points, and surrounds
C negatively coded ones with a circle
C
      INTEGER I,N
      REAL X,Y,WIDTH,RADIUS
C WIDTH is the width of each cross
C RADIUS is the radius of the surrounding circle
      PARAMETER (WIDTH=0.25,RADIUS=0.5*WIDTH)
C Initialize plotting
      CALL PSTART
C Plot data points
      DO 10, I=1,100
         READ '*,X,Y,N
         CALL PCROSS(X,Y,WIDTH)
         IF (N.LT.0) CALL PCIRCL(X,Y,RADIUS)
10    CONTINUE
C Terminate plotting and end
      CALL PEND
      STOP
      END
```

Notice that because the subroutines PCROSS and PCIRCL both require three
arguments, the last of which defines the size of the cross or circle, we have
used a named constant to give a cross of width 0.25 in and a circle of the
same diameter (so as to exactly surround it).

A logical IF statement has been used since it is much neater than the block IF alternative:

```
IF (N.LT.0) THEN
   CALL PCIRCL(X,Y,RADIUS)
END IF
```

The DO loop ends on a CONTINUE because, as might be expected, an IF statement (or an END IF) cannot be the last statement of a DO loop.

7.5   More about logical expressions

We have seen how the block IF and logical IF use the value of a logical expression to determine their course of action, and the six relational operators have been used to create such a logical expression. However, this is often not enough. For example, in Figure 7.1, which discussed the alternative ways of travelling from Vienna to Budapest, the second decision took the following form:

but if you are a romantic *or* like trains *then*

Here we have not one decision criterion but two criteria, only one of which needs to be satisfied for the appropriate action to be taken:

you should take the Orient Express from the Sudbanhof to Budapest's Keleti palyudvar.

A similar double criterion could have been used to cater for the fact that some people are afraid of flying:

If you are in a hurry *and* you are not afraid of flying *then* you should fly from Schwechat airport in Vienna to Ferihegy airport in Budapest.

In this case the use of the word *and* indicates that *both* the criteria must be satisfied for the specified action to be carried out.

In Fortran the same two words are used to form composite logical expressions, but written as .OR. and .AND. in a similar way to that used for the relational operators .GT., .EQ., and so on. These, too, are logical operators, used to combine two logical expressions:

logical_expression logical_operator logical_expression

L1	L2	L1.OR.L2	L1.AND.L2
true	true	true	true
true	false	true	false
false	true	true	false
false	false	false	false

Thus we could write

```
(A.LT.B).OR.(C.LT.D)
```

or

```
(X.LE.Y).AND.(Y.LE.Z)
```

In fact the parentheses shown in these examples are not strictly necessary because the relational expressions will always be evaluated first, but to human eyes expressions such as

```
A.LT.B.OR.C.LT.D
```

and

```
X.LE.Y.AND.Y.LE.Z
```

are not immediately clear and can cause some confusion. The effect of the .OR. and .AND. operators is as one would expect. .OR. gives a result that is true if *either* of its operands is true, whereas .AND. gives a true result only if *both* are true. Figure 7.10 illustrates this.

Two other logical operators exist that do not have an exact equivalent in normal English usage, namely .EQV. and .NEQV. The first of these gives a true result if both its operands have the same value (that is, both are true or both are false), while the other (.NEQV.) is the opposite and gives a true result if they have opposite values. Figure 7.11 illustrates this.

Essentially these operators are used in complex logical expressions to simplify their structure. Thus the following two expressions are equi-

L1	L2	L1.EQV.L2	L1.NEQV.L2
true	true	true	false
true	false	false	true
false	true	false	true
false	false	true	false

Operator	Priority
.NOT.	highest
.AND.	.
.OR.	.
.EQV. and .NEQV.	lowest

Figure 7.12
Logical operator
priorities.

valent in their effect:

```
(A.LT.B.AND.X.LT.Y).OR.(A.GE.B.AND.X.GE.Y)
A.LT.B.EQV.X.LT.Y
```

There is one further logical operator, .NOT. Unlike all the other relational and logical operators this has only a single operand, whose value it inverts. Thus if the logical expression L is true then .NOT.L is false, and vice versa. As with relational operators, the effect of the .NOT. operator on an expression can always be obtained in some other way; for example the following expressions are equivalent in their effect:

```
.NOT.(A.LT.B.AND.B.LT.C)
A.GE.B.OR.B.GE.C
```

and, of course

```
.NOT.(A.LT.B.EQV.X.LT.Y)
A.LT.B.NEQV.X.LT.Y
```

However, in some circumstances (especially when logical values are stored in special variables, as we shall see in Chapter 13) the .NOT. operator can make a logical expression clearer.

If logical operators are used to build up a complicated logical expression it is clearly important that the priority rules used in its evaluation are understood (just as in an arithmetic expression where * and / have a higher priority than + or –). Figure 7.12 shows the priority order, and it should be noted that, as with arithmetic operators, parentheses can be used to change this order. It should also be noted that any arithmetic operators or relational operators (*in that order*) have a higher priority than any logical operators.

EXAMPLE 7.4

A set of survey data contains the age and weight of the respondents together with a code to indicate their sex (0=female, 1=male). Write a program that reads the number of people in the survey and then calculates the average weight of the men between the ages of 21 and 35 (inclusive).

This is a common type of problem and should not cause us much difficulty. Our structure plan will be as follows:

---

1   Initialize the sums of weights and people to zero

2   Read the number of people (N)

3   Repeat N times
   3.1 Read age, weight and sex code
   3.2 If male *and* aged between 21 and 35 then
      3.2.1 Add weight to sum of weights
      3.2.2 Add one to sum of people

4   Calculate and print average weight

Note that in order to calculate the average weight we shall need to calculate the sum of the weights of the people concerned (step 3.2.1) and also to count them (3.2.2), and that we must therefore ensure that they are both set to 0 at the start (step 1). The program is now straightforward.

```
      PROGRAM AVWT
C
C  This program produces the average weight of some of the respondents
C  to a health survey
C
      INTEGER I,N,AGE,SEX,NUM
      REAL WT,SUMWT
C  Read number of respondents
      PRINT *,'How many sets of data? '
      READ *,N
C  Read data and accumulate sums
      PRINT *,'For each person type age and weight'
      PRINT *,'followed by 0 if female, or 1 if male'
      DO 10, I=1,N
        READ *,AGE,WT,SEX
        IF (SEX.EQ.1 .AND. 21.LE.AGE .AND. AGE.LE.35) THEN
          SUMWT=SUMWT+WT
          NUM=NUM+1
        END IF
   10 CONTINUE
C  Calculate and print average weight
      IF (NUM.GT.0) THEN
        PRINT *,'There were',NUM,' men aged between 21 and 35'
        PRINT *,'Their average weight was',SUMWT/NUM
      ELSE
        PRINT *,'There were no men aged between 21 and 35'
      END IF
      STOP
      END
```

Notice the block IF at the end of the program. Just because the problem asks for the average weight of males between 21 and 35 it does not mean that there will necessarily be any such people in the survey data. If there were none, and the program always calculated the average, then it would fail because it would try to divide by 0 – an impossible action and one that on a computer will cause a failure known as **overflow**, owing to its efforts to calculate an infinitely large number. The block IF at the end of the program detects this situation and prints a suitable message.

EXAMPLE 7.5

Using the same set of data as in Example 7.4, write a program that prints a table showing the number of women, and their average weight, in each of the age bands 20 or under, 21–35, 36–49, 50–64, 65 or over, followed by a similar table for the men.

This problem could be tackled in a similar way to the last one, but it would involve keeping 10 pairs of sums, and carrying out a rather complicated set of tests to establish which pair was to be used. A far better way, and one with much more general applicability, would be to store the data in an array and then to use a procedure with appropriate arguments to produce each set of statistics.

One problem with this approach, and a problem that is very common, is that we must set a maximum size for the array, and hence for the number of respondents. A figure must be chosen that is neither absurdly large, which would waste memory space, nor absurdly small, which would lead to problems with larger sets of data.

Our structure plan could be as follows:

1 Read number of respondents

2 If the number is too large then
   2.1 Print error message and stop

3 Read data

4 Print 'Women's statistics' (heading)

5 For each age range
   5.1 Calculate number and average – STATS
   5.2 Print next line of table

6 Print 'Men's statistics' (heading)

7 For each age range
   7.1 Calculate number and average – STATS
   7.2 Print next line of table

> STATS(AGE(N),WT(N),SEX(N),N,SEXRQD,MINAGE,MAXAGE,
> NUMBER,AVWT)
>
> **1** Initialize NUMBER and SUMWT
>
> **2** For each respondent
> **2.1** If SEX(I)=SEXRQD *and* MINAGE⩽AGE(I)⩽MAXAGE then
> **2.1.1** Add WT(I) to SUMWT and 1 to NUMBER
>
> **3** Calculate average weight in AVWT

Notice that the subroutine STATS has nine arguments: four are required to pass the survey data (AGE, WT, SEX and N), three to provide the selection criteria (SEXRQD, MINAGE and MAXAGE), and two to return the results (NUMBER and AVWT). This is quite a large number, although by no means unusual. Chapter 12 shows how this could be reduced to five, or even to zero.

The program can now be written easily.

```
      PROGRAM AVWT
C
C  This program produces tables of age/weight statistics
C  from a health survey
C
      INTEGER MAXSIZ,FEMALE,MALE
      PARAMETER (MAXSIZ=100,FEMALE=0,MALE=1)
      INTEGER I,N,NUMBER,AGE(MAXSIZ),SEX(MAXSIZ),MINAGE(5),MAXAGE(5)
      REAL WT(MAXSIZ),AVWT
      DATA MINAGE/0,21,36,50,65/,MAXAGE/20,35,49,64,1000/
C  Read number of respondents and check validity
      PRINT *,'How many sets of data? '
      READ *,N
      IF (N.GT.MAXSIZ) THEN
        PRINT *,'Too many data sets.  Only ',MAXSIZ,' allowed.'
        STOP
      END IF
C  Read data
      PRINT *,'For each person type age and weight'
      PRINT *,'followed by 0 if female, or 1 if male'
      READ *,(AGE(I),WT(I),SEX(I),I=1,N)
C  Print heading for women
      PRINT *,'Statistics for female respondents to health survey'
C  Calculate and print required values for each age range
      DO 10,I=1,5
        CALL STATS(AGE,WT,SEX,N,FEMALE,MINAGE(I),MAXAGE(I),NUMBER,AVWT)
        PRINT *,NUMBER,' women aged between',MINAGE(I),' and',MAXAGE(I),
     *          ' with an average weight of',AVWT
   10 CONTINUE
C  Print heading for men
      PRINT *,' '
      PRINT *,'Statistics for male respondents to health survey'
```

```
C  Calculate and print required values for each age range
      DO 20,I=1,5
         CALL STATS(AGE,WT,SEX,N,MALE,MINAGE(I),MAXAGE(I),NUMBER,AVWT)
         PRINT *,NUMBER,' men aged between',MINAGE(I),' and',MAXAGE(I),
     *             ' with an average weight of',AVWT
  20  CONTINUE
      STOP
      END

      SUBROUTINE STATS(AGE,WT,SEX,N,SEXRQD,MINAGE,MAXAGE,NUMBER,AVWT)
C
C  This subroutine calculates the number and average weight of those
C  respondents with a specified sex and age-range
C
      INTEGER AGE(N),SEX(N),N,SEXRQD,MINAGE,MAXAGE,NUMBER
      REAL WT(N),AVWT
C  Local variables
      INTEGER I
      REAL SUMWT
C  Initialize sums
      NUMBER=0
      SUMWT=0.0
C  Calculate sums
      DO 10,I=1,N
         IF (SEX(I).EQ.SEXRQD .AND.
     *       MINAGE.LE.AGE(I) .AND. AGE(I).LE.MAXAGE) THEN
            NUMBER=NUMBER+1
            SUMWT=SUMWT+WT(I)
         END IF
  10  CONTINUE
C  Calculate average weight and then return
      IF (NUMBER.GT.0) THEN
         AVWT=SUMWT/NUMBER
      ELSE
         AVWT=0.0
      END IF
      RETURN
      END
```

Notice that the main program has been considerably simplified by storing the details of the age ranges in two arrays. In order to deal with the over-65 age group the maximum age for the last group has been set ridiculously high (1000). A minor refinement would be to detect this case before printing and to print a different message. Also, notice that if there are no people in a particular category then the subroutine STATS sets the average weight to 0. Again, a refinement would be to detect this and omit the average weight from that line of the table.

   Finally, note that the use of a PARAMETER statement to create integer constants FEMALE and MALE makes the use of the codes 0 and 1 for male and female much easier to read in the program.

SUMMARY

- Relational operators allow comparisons to be made.

- Logical operators allow multiple comparisons to be made.

- The block IF statement is the major method of introducing the concept of choice and decision-making into a program.

- The logical IF statement is used where only a single statement is to be the subject of a logical decision.

- Independent compilation is one of Fortran's great strengths and has led to the creation of many libraries of subroutines (and functions).

- Fortran 77 statements introduced in Chapter 7:

Relational expressions	*expression relational_operator expression* for example A.LT.B I.EQ.(J+K
Logical expressions	*expression logical_operator expression* for example A.LT.B .AND. C.GE.D I.NE.J .OR. (X.LE.Y .AND. M.GT.N)

Block IF structure	IF (*logical_expression*) THEN
	    Block of Fortran statements
	ELSE IF (*logical_expression*) THEN
	    Block of Fortran statements
	ELSE IF (*logical_expression*) THEN
	
	ELSE
	    Block of Fortran statements
	END IF

Logical IF statement	IF (*logical_expression*) *Fortran statement*

SELF-TEST EXERCISES 7.1

1 What is the difference between a logical operator and a relational operator?

2 What are the values of the following expressions?

    (a) `1.GT.2`
    (b) `(1+3).GE.4`
    (c) `(1+3).LE.4`
    (d) `(0.1+0.3).LE.0.4`
    (e) `2.GT.1 .AND. 3.LT.4`
    (f) `3.GT.2 .AND. (1+2).LT.3 .OR. 4.LE.3`
    (g) `3.GT.2 .OR. (1+2).LT.3 .AND. 4.LE.3`
    (h) `3.GT.2 .AND. (1+2).LT.3 .EQV. 4.LE.3`

3 What will be printed by the following program?

```
      PROGRAM TEST3
      INTEGER I
      DO 10, I=1,25
C The intrinsic function MOD returns the remainder after dividing
C its first argument by its second
      IF (MOD(I,2).EQ.0) THEN
        PRINT *,I,' is even'
      ELSE IF (MOD(I,3).EQ.0) THEN
        PRINT *,I,' is divisible by 3'
      ELSE IF (MOD(I,5).EQ.0) THEN
        PRINT *,I,' is divisible by 5'
      END IF
   10 CONTINUE
      STOP
      END
```

4 What will be printed by the following program?

```
      PROGRAM TEST4
      INTEGER I
      DO 10, I=1,25
C The intrinsic function MOD returns the remainder after dividing
C its first argument by its second
      IF (MOD(I,2).EQ.0) PRINT *,I,' is even'
      IF (MOD(I,3).EQ.0) PRINT *,I,' is divisible by 3'
      IF (MOD(I,5).EQ.0) PRINT *,I,' is divisible by 5'
   10 CONTINUE
      STOP
      END
```

PROGRAMMING EXERCISES

*7.1   Write a program that will request a number to be typed at the keyboard and will then inform the user whether the number is positive, negative or zero.

7.2   Write a function *that does not use any intrinsic functions* and will determine the larger of two numbers.

7.3   Write a program that accepts a positive integer as its input and informs the user of whether:

(a)   the number is odd or even;
(b)   it is divisible by seven;
(c)   it is a perfect square (its square root is a whole number).

Modify your program to find the first even number that is divisible by 7 and is a perfect square.

7.4   Write a program that reads a number from the keyboard, and prints 'Happy' that number of times, then reads another number and prints 'Sad' that number of times, and repeats this process until the number zero is typed.

7.5   Write a program that reads a number between 1 and 6 from the keyboard and prints out the corresponding word, that is, 'one', 'two', and so on.

7.6   A Pythagorean triple is a set of three positive integers (A,B,C) such that:

$$A**2 = B**2 + C**2$$

Write a program to display all such triples where both B and C are less than 15. Avoid displaying the same triple twice!

*7.7   A simple method of determining whether an integer is a prime number is to try dividing it by all integers less than or equal to its square root, and checking to see whether there is any remainder.

Write a program to determine whether a number is a prime using this method, printing at least one of its factors if it is not.

7.8   Write a program that will determine how much income tax a person pays, given the following basis for taxation:

Income	Tax rate
£0–5000	0%
£5001–20000	25%
£20001+	32%

7.9   A bicycle wheel has a diameter of 70 cm. Write a program that will accept the time for each successive rotation, and after each entry will print out the total time, the total distance travelled, the average speed and the maximum speed in kilometres per hour.

7.10   In an examination a student is awarded a distinction if he or she has obtained more than 30% above the average obtained by the whole class. To ensure fair marking, the students are identified only by a unique number in the range 1000 to 1999.

Write a program that will input the marks obtained by the members of the class, then print out the average mark and the identifying numbers of any students obtaining distinction, together with their marks.

7.11   The current I drawn by an electrical appliance of power P watts from a supply voltage V volts is:

$$I = P / V$$

where I is in amperes (A). A particular mains cable can safely carry 5 A. Write a program that asks the user for the power and supply voltage of an appliance, and displays a warning if the appliance cannot be safely used with this cable.

7.12   A meteorologist makes daily rainfall measurements for one week, obtaining the values in mm. Write a program that calculates the mean, maximum and minimum rainfall for the week, and check it with the following data:

Mon	Tues	Wed	Thurs	Fri	Sat	Sun
2.6	1.0	0.0	0.5	0.25	0.1	1.5

7.13 The number of entries in a cycle race is so large that it is decided to divide them into two separate races, based upon their times in an initial time trial.

Write a program which reads the total number of riders and then, for each rider, his number and time in the trial. All those whose time is less than the mean time of all the riders will be in race A, with the remainder being in race B. The program should print a list, showing each rider's number and the race (A or B) to which he has been allocated.

7.14 In a ladies' gymnastics competition each competitor is awarded a mark in the range 0 to 6, in increments of 0.1, by each of six judges. The highest and lowest marks are ignored, and the other four are averaged to give the final mark. Write a program to read the six marks for each gymnast, and print her final mark.

It is subsequently claimed that judge number 5 has been consistently giving too high marks to the leading gymnasts, and it is agreed that all his marks between 5.7 and 6.0 should be reduced by 0.1, and his marks between 5.0 and 5.6 should be reduced by 0.05. His other marks are left unaltered. Modify your program to read the original marks and then to make this adjustment before calculating the final marks.

7.15 A company produces digital watches and sells them for $15 each. However, it gives a discount for multiple orders as follows:

2–4	5%	5–9	10%	10–29	15%
30–99	20%	100–299	25%	300+	30%

Write a program to input the number of watches required and to print the gross cost, the discount (if any) and the nett cost.

7.16 The brightness of a binary star varies as follows. At time $t = 0$ days its magnitude is 2.5, and it stays at this level until $t = 0.9$ days. Its magnitude is then determined by the formula

$$3.355 - \log_e(1.352 + \cos(\pi(t - 0.9)/0.7))$$

until $t = 2.3$ days. Its magnitude is then 2.5 until $t = 4.4$ days, and it is then determined by the formula

$$3.598 - \log_e(1.998 + \cos(\pi(t - 4.4)/0.4))$$

until $t = 5.2$ days. It then remains at 2.5 until $t = 6.4$ days, after which the cycle repeats with a period of 6.4 days.

Write a program which will input the value of the time t and print the brightness of the star at that time.

7.17   The following polynomial is intended to approximate the function e^x for $0 < x < 1$

$$1 + 1.0118*x + 0.4274*x^2 + 0.2791*x^3$$

Tabulate this polynomial, EXP(x), and the difference between the two for x from 0 to 1 in steps of 0.005, and print the maximum deviation from the true value.

   Repeat this exercise using the polynomial

$$1 + x + \frac{x^2}{2} + \frac{x^3}{6}$$

obtained from the Taylor expansion of e^x.

7.18   The roots of an equation $y = f(x)$ are those values of x for which y is zero. Thus the roots of the equation shown graphically below are $x = 1$ and $x = 2$.

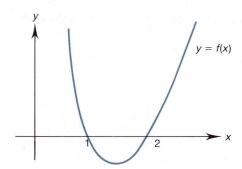

Many problems in physics and engineering require the solution of such an equation. This subject is discussed in some detail in Chapters 11 and 18, but Newton's method of solution (often known as the Newton–Raphson method) will be summarized briefly here.

   Essentially, this method uses one estimate of a root as the basis for calculating a better estimate, and repeats this process until the estimates converge to a single value. Thus, if x_1 is the first estimate, then the second estimate x_2 is given by the equation

$$x_2 = x_1 - \frac{f(x_1)}{f'(x_1)}$$

where $f(x_1)$ is the value of the function $y = f(x)$ at $x = x_1$, and $f'(x_1)$ is the value of the first derivative of $f(x)$ at $x = x_1$.

Generalizing this to the *n*th estimate, the (*n*+1)th estimate is given by

$$x_{n+1} = x_n - \frac{f(x_n)}{f'(x_n)}$$

Write a program to use this relationship, which is often referred to as Newton's iteration, to find the roots of the equation

$$y = x^2 - 3x + 2$$

(where $f(x) = x^2 - 3x + 2$, and $f'(x) = 2x - 3$)

Your program should use a subroutine to return the values of $f(x_n)$ and $f'(x_n)$ given the value of x_n. Obviously Newton's iteration must be used several times to obtain successively improved estimates. Your program should read the required accuracy for the final estimate from the keyboard.

Note that for more complex or less well-behaved functions the Newton–Raphson method may never converge to a solution of the required accuracy. This problem, and how to deal with it, is discussed in Chapter 18. Furthermore, some functions may have no roots; Exercise 11.12 will illustrate one way of dealing with this situation.

Other types of loop

8

The only form of loop construct in Fortran is the DO loop. For some purposes, however, it is desirable to create a loop that is not dependent upon a counting operation to determine when it should be terminated. The **DO ... WHILE loop** and the **REPEAT ... UNTIL loop** are the two best known forms of such loops, and both can be readily simulated by use of a logical IF statement and a GOTO statement.

In some circumstances, however, such loops can lead to **infinite loops** and a better approach is to combine the DO loop with the logical IF and GOTO statements to create a **conditional** DO **loop**.

8.1 DO ... WHILE and REPEAT ... UNTIL loops

All the loops used so far have been controlled by a DO statement and have, therefore, been of the form

> Repeat the following *n* times:
>   Block of statements

Such loops are often referred to as **counting loops**, since they are controlled by counting how many times the loop has been obeyed. However, there are frequently occasions when we wish to control looping by some means other than counting. Such loops are controlled by observing the state of some logical expression. Two of the most common forms of such **conditional loops** are as follows:

- Repeat the following *while* some condition is true
    Block of statements
- Repeat the following *until* some condition is true
    Block of statements

Some languages have special statements for these types of loops, but Fortran does not, although some implementations of Fortran 77 do provide such constructs (particularly for the DO ... WHILE case) as extensions to the language. However, with the addition of one further control statement such loops can be easily created in standard Fortran if required.

8.2 The GOTO statement

This new statement is the **unconditional** GOTO statement, and takes the form

> GOTO *label*

where *label* is a statement label on an executable statement somewhere in the same program unit. *The GOTO statement is, potentially, an extremely dangerous statement and, if used at all, should be used with very great care.*

The reason why it is dangerous is that it can cause a transfer of control to almost anywhere in the program unit, thus losing all sense of structure and logic, and leading to what are often referred to as 'spaghetti programs' because of their convoluted structure.

The only situation in which a GOTO statement should normally be used is to create special forms of loop, as described in the next section.

```
label1 IF (.NOT. condition) GOTO label2
       block of Fortran statements
       GOTO label1
label2 next statement
```

Figure 8.1
The repeat ... while loop
structure.

8.3 IF controlled loops

Although Fortran contains only one form of loop control structure, a logical
IF statement can be used together with one or two GOTO statements to
simulate the two additional forms of loop referred to above, as shown in
Figures 8.1 and 8.2.

In the first case the loop is to be repeated as long as some condition
is true. The loop is started with an IF statement that will GOTO the statement
immediately after the end of the loop if the condition is not true, and the
loop is terminated with an unconditional GOTO that returns to the start of the
loop. As long as the condition is true, therefore, the block of statements in
the loop is obeyed and control is then returned to the beginning; once it
becomes false the first GOTO is obeyed and control is passed to the statement
immediately after the end of the loop.

The second case is even simpler. Here the first statement of the
block that is to be repeated is labelled and a logical IF is added at the end of
the loop, which causes a return to the beginning if the condition is false.
Once it becomes true then the IF statement does not obey the GOTO and
execution continues from the statement following the loop.

One potential danger with both of these types of loop is that if the
terminal condition never occurs there will be no exit from the loop,
resulting in a condition known as an **infinite loop**.

The major difference between these two types of loop is that
'repeat ... while' need not be obeyed at all (in the case where the condition
is initially false), whereas 'repeat ... until' will always be obeyed at least
once. This is quite obvious when we look at Figures 8.1 and 8.2, where the
placing of the IF statement means that the 'repeat ... while' form need not
be obeyed since the initial test takes place before the start of the loop, while
the only test for the 'repeat ... until' form of loop comes at the end. We can
see how both of these can be used by modifying Examples 7.3 and 7.2.

```
label1 first statement
       block of Fortran statements
       IF (.NOT. condition) GOTO label1
       next statement
```

Figure 8.2
The repeat ... until loop
structure.

EXAMPLE 8.1

Write a program that reads a series of sets of data, each consisting of two coordinates and a code. Using a plotter attached to your computer, plot an X at every point and surround it with a circle if the code is negative. A zero code means that this is the last point.

This is the same problem as Example 7.3 except that, instead of having a fixed number of points, the number is determined by a special (zero) code for the last one. The structure plan is therefore only a minor variation on the one we used earlier.

> **1** Initialize plotting
>
> **2** Repeat until a zero code is read
> **2.1** Read a set of data
> **2.2** Draw a cross
> **2.3** If the code is negative then
> **2.3.1** Draw a circle
>
> **3** Terminate plotting

Notice that to draw a cross for every point, including the last one, the loop must be obeyed at least once, and so the second type of loop (repeat … until) is appropriate. The program then follows.

```
      PROGRAM POINTS
C
C This program plots a cross at each of a set of data points,
C and surrounds negatively coded ones with a circle.
C The data is terminated by a point with a zero code.
C
      INTEGER N
      REAL X,Y,WIDTH,RADIUS
C WIDTH is the width of each cross
C RADIUS is the radius of the surrounding circle
      PARAMETER (WIDTH=0.25,RADIUS=0.5*WIDTH)
C Initialize plotting
      CALL PSTART
C
C Start of loop
C
C Read next set of data
    1 READ *,X,Y,N
C Plot point
      CALL PCROSS(X,Y,WIDTH)
```

```
      IF (N.LT.0) CALL PCIRCL(X,Y,RADIUS)
C  Return to start of loop if this is not the terminating point
      IF (N.NE.0) GOTO 1
C  Terminate plotting and end
      CALL PEND
      STOP
      END
```

Here it can be seen that, since the condition for ending the loop was `N.EQ.0`, the condition to be used in the `IF` statement should be `.NOT.N.EQ.0` or, more succinctly, `N.NE.0`.

EXAMPLE 8.2

Write a program to read a series of sets of coefficients of quadratic equations and to print their roots. The data is terminated by a zero set ($a=b=c=0$).

This is an extension of Example 7.2, which solves a number of equations instead of just one. Unlike the situation in Example 8.1, however, the final data set is not part of the data but is purely a terminator. If we attempted to solve the equation using the formula $x = (-b \pm \sqrt{b^2-4ac})/2a$, when a, b and c were all 0 we would cause a program failure by attempting to evaluate 0/0. In this case, therefore, the 'repeat...while' structure is appropriate, and our structure plan will be:

1   Set e to a very small value

2   Read the first set of coefficients

3   Repeat while a, b and c are non-zero
   3.1 Calculate b^2-4ac
   3.2 If $b^2-4ac>e$ then
      3.2.1 Calculate and print two roots
      but if $b^2-4ac>-e$ then
      3.2.2 Calculate and print two equal roots
      otherwise
      3.2.3 Print message 'no roots'
   3.3 Read next set of coefficients

Notice that we need to read the first set of coefficients before we enter the loop, and then always to read the next set after we have solved the equation. This is because the form of the condition requires that we have the coefficients at the very start of the loop. Once again the program is quite straightforward.

```
      PROGRAM QUAD2
C
C  This program solves a set of quadratic equations
C
      REAL A,B,C,D,ROOTD,E,X,X1,X2
C  E is a very small number, but greater than likely rounding errors
      PARAMETER (E=1E-6)
C  Read first set of coefficients
      PRINT *,'Type the coefficients of a quadratic equation: '
      READ *,A,B,C
C
C  Start of loop
C
C  Test for terminating condition (a=b=c=0)
    1 IF (A.EQ.0.0 .AND. B.EQ.0.0 .AND. C.EQ.0.0) GOTO 2
C  Calculate main expression
      D=B**2 - 4*A*C
C  Check possibilities
      IF (D.GT.E) THEN
C  b**2>4ac - so two real roots
         ROOTD=SQRT(D)
         X1=(-B+ROOTD)/(A+A)
         X2=(-B-ROOTD)/(A+A)
         PRINT *,A,'x**2 +',B,'x +',C,' = 0 has roots',X1,' and',X2
      ELSE IF (D.GT.-E) THEN
C  b**2=4ac (within + or - 1E9) - so two equal roots
         X=-B/(A+A)
         PRINT *,A,'x**2 +',B,'x +',C,' = 0 has roots',X,' and',X
      ELSE
C  b**2<4ac - so no real roots
         PRINT *,A,'x**2 +',B,'x +',C,' = 0 has no real roots'
      END IF
C  Read next set and return to start of the loop
      PRINT *,'Type the coefficients of a quadratic equation: '
      READ *,A,B,C
      GOTO 1
C  Exit from loop
    2 STOP
      END
```

The initial test could probably have been abbreviated to a test for A alone, because if A.EQ.0 then the equation is not a quadratic and the division by A+A will cause an error. It would seem reasonable, therefore, to assume that if A.EQ.0 this is the special terminator. However, the order of evaluation means that if A.NE.0 then the whole condition is false and so the comparisons of B and C with zero will not take place; the only time they will be checked is when A *is* zero, that is, for the terminating data set.

8.4 Conditional DO loops

F90

The one great danger in the forms of loop described above is the situation that can result if the condition for ending the loop never arises. In the two examples just discussed this would mean that the programs would attempt to read more data, and in its absence would probably fail. However, consider the common situation in which no data is being read in the loop, but in which successive calculations are being made until further iterations produce no significant change in the result. Examples, in the form of structure plans, might be:

> Repeat while the error factor is greater than a very small value
>   Calculate the next value
>   Calculate the error factor between this and the last value

> Repeat until the error factor is less than a very small value
>   Calculate the next value
>   Calculate the error factor between this and the last value

It is well known to mathematicians that some types of series approximations will converge rapidly to a point where further terms in the series have a negligible effect, that others will do so more slowly, and that others will never do so but will oscillate around the 'true' value. If an attempt were made to evaluate a series approximation of the third type, using either of the types of loop above, then it would never terminate and there would be an **infinite loop**.

An infinite loop is just one of the dangers implicit in the use of any form of GOTO statement. It is often more advisable to use a combination of DO loop and logical IF to create other types of loop, in order that a **fail-safe structure** is created. We can express these in the following ways:

> Repeat the following up to *n* times while some condition is true
>   Block of statements

> Repeat the following *n* times or until some condition is true
>   Block of statements

Figure 8.3
The improved
repeat ... while loop
structure.

```
DO label1, var=1,n
    IF (.NOT. condition) GOTO label2
    block of Fortran statements
label1 CONTINUE
label2 next statement
```

The Fortran implementations of these two loop structures are shown in Figures 8.3 and 8.4.

It can be seen that both of them now have a very similar structure, with a single *forward* GOTO controlled by a logical IF statement. The absence of any *backward* GOTOs means that there is no danger of creating an infinite loop and also restores a well-defined structure to the program. In fact these two structures can be generalized to form what will henceforth be called a **conditional** DO **loop**.

This is, quite simply, a DO loop that contains one or more conditions upon which an exit is made from the loop:

> Repeat the following *n* times
>   If some condition is true then exit to *exit point*
>   Block of statements
>   If some condition is true then exit to *exit point*
>   Block of statements
>   .
>   .
>   .
>   If some condition is true then exit to *exit point*
> *exit point* Next statement

Figure 8.5 shows the Fortran implementation of this structure. The most important thing to notice about it is that, regardless of the number of

Figure 8.4
The improved
repeat ... until loop
structure.

```
DO label1, var=1,n
    block of Fortran statements
    IF (condition) GOTO label2
label1 CONTINUE
label2 next statement
```

```
DO label1, var=1,n
    IF (condition1) GOTO label2
    block of Fortran statements
    IF (condition2) GOTO label2
    block of Fortran statements
```

        .

        .

        .

```
    IF (conditionm) GOTO label2
label1 CONTINUE
label2 next statement
```

Figure 8.5
The general form of a
conditional DO loop.

tests within the body of the loop, *they should all exit to the same place*. Only in this way can the development of an unstructured and potentially dangerous situation be avoided.

    It will be seen that the three types of loops used earlier are all special cases of this general form:

F90

- A DO loop is a conditional DO loop with *no* tests.

- A repeat ... while loop is a conditional DO loop with a single test at the beginning.

- A repeat ... until loop is a conditional DO loop with a single test at the end.

EXAMPLE 8.3

A set of exam marks is provided together with a code (0 = female, 1 = male) to indicate the sex of the examinee. The data is terminated by a record containing a negative code. It is required to calculate the average mark for the class, and also the average mark for the boys and girls separately.

    The program for this problem needs to produce a sum of all the marks and to count the examinees in order to calculate the class average, and also needs to do the same for the boys and the girls separately. With the total figures and those for the boys we can easily calculate the girls' figures without the need to accumulate them. The structure plan is therefore as follows:

> **1**   Initialize sums for marks and pupils
>
> **2**   Repeat the following
>   **2.1** Read a mark and code
>   **2.2** If code is negative then exit
>   **2.3** Update sum of marks
>   **2.4** If code is male (=1) then
>   **2.4.1** Update sum of boys' marks
>   **2.4.2** Add 1 to count of boys
>
> **3**   Calculate number of girls and their total mark
>
> **4**   Calculate and print required averages

Remember that a conditional DO loop counts how many times it is obeyed. This value is available after exit from the loop, thus avoiding the need to count the total number of pupils. The program can now be written from the structure plan, although we must first decide on the maximum number of times we shall allow the loop to be repeated. Since the problem refers to a class a maximum of 100 should be more than sufficient.

```
      PROGRAM EXAMS
C
C This program calculates some simple examination statistics
C
      INTEGER FEMALE,MALE,MAXSIZ
      PARAMETER (FEMALE=0,MALE=1,MAXSIZ=100)
      INTEGER I,MARK,SEX,BOYS,GIRLS,TOTAL,BMARKS,GMARKS,TMARKS
      DATA BOYS,GIRLS,TOTAL,BMARKS,GMARKS,TMARKS/6*0/
C Repeat at most MAXSIZ times
      PRINT *,'Type up to ',MAXSIZ,' marks.'
      PRINT *,'Each mark must be followed by 0 for a female student'
      PRINT *,'or by 1 for a male student.'
      PRINT *,'Data should be ended by a dummy mark, followed by -1'
      DO 10, I=1,MAXSIZ
C Read next mark and sex code
         READ *,MARK,SEX
C Exit from loop if sex code is negative
         IF (SEX.LT.0) GOTO 20
C Accumulate total marks, and boys' statistics if necessary
         TMARKS=TMARKS+MARK
         IF (SEX.EQ.MALE) THEN
           BMARKS=BMARKS+MARK
           BOYS=BOYS+1
         END IF
   10 CONTINUE
C Exit from loop - store total number, and calculate figures for girls
```

```
   20 TOTAL=I-1
      GIRLS=TOTAL-BOYS
      GMARKS=TMARKS-BMARKS
C Calculate and print numbers and averages
      IF (TOTAL.GT.0) THEN
        PRINT *,'There are',TOTAL,' pupils.  Their average mark is',
     *          REAL(TMARKS)/TOTAL
        IF (GIRLS.GT.0) THEN
          PRINT *,'There are',GIRLS,' girls.  Their average mark is',
     *             REAL(GMARKS)/GIRLS
        ELSE
          PRINT *,'There are no girls in the class'
        END IF
        IF (BOYS.GT.0) THEN
          PRINT *,'There are',BOYS,' boys.  Their average mark is',
     *             REAL(BMARKS)/BOYS
        ELSE
          PRINT *,'There are no boys in the class'
        END IF
      ELSE
        PRINT *,'There are no marks!'
      END IF
      STOP
      END
```

Notice that at the exit from the loop we set TOTAL to the value I-1. There are two cases – either the special terminator data is read, or the maximum number (100) of sets of marks are read with no terminator. Let us look at each of these cases separately.

Assume that the class has 35 pupils. On the first pass through the loop I is 1 and the first pupil's mark is read. On the next pass I is 2 and the second pupil's mark is read. On the 35th pass I is 35 and the 35th, and last, pupil's mark is read. On the next pass I is therefore 36 and the terminator data is read. On exit from the loop I is thus 1 more than the number of pupils.

If no terminator is read, then after 100 pupils' marks have been read the loop will finish. In Chapter 5 we saw that if a DO loop completes its defined number of passes then the DO variable will have the value *it would have had on the next pass*. In our case this will be 101 – one more than the number of pupils whose marks were read.

In both cases, therefore, the number of pupils is I-1, although it might be desirable to include an extra statement between those labelled 10 and 20:

```
      PRINT *,'*** No terminator - only',MAXSIZ,' marks read ***'
```

This will draw attention to the omission of some marks if the 'fail-safe' action of the DO loop came into effect too soon.

There are two points to note about the calculation and printing of the averages. The first is that a test is made to see if there are any pupils in each category (so as to avoid dividing by zero) and a suitable message printed if there are not. The second concerns the calculation of the average. The program has assumed that the marks are integers, and of course the number of pupils is an integer. The expression TMARKS/TOTAL would therefore lead to an integer division being carried out and the average given in integer form (truncated, not even rounded!). This is not suitable and so steps must be taken to force a real division.

One approach would be for the sums of marks to be kept in real variables. The ensuing expressions would be mixed-mode and would therefore be evaluated using real arithmetic. Alternatively, the sums can be converted to real form once they have been calculated. The easiest way to do this is to use the intrinsic function REAL, which simply produces as its result the real equivalent of its argument, thus once again leading to a mixed-mode expression.

SUMMARY

- Repeat ... while and repeat ... until loops can be simulated using a logical IF and an unconditional GOTO statement.

- The combination of logical IF statements and a DO loop can be used to create a powerful, general-purpose conditional DO loop.

- Fortran 77 statements introduced in Chapter 8:

Unconditional GOTO statement	GOTO *label*

DO ... WHILE loop structure	*label1* IF (.NOT. *condition*) GOTO *label2*
	        Block of Fortran statements
	        GOTO *label1*
	label2 *next statement*

REPEAT ... UNTIL loop structure	*label1* *first statement*
	        Block of Fortran statements
	        IF (.NOT. *condition*) GOTO *label1*
	next statement

Conditional DO loop structure	DO *label1*, *var*=1,*n*
	
	        .
	
	    IF (*logical_expression*) GOTO *label2*
	
	        .
	
	    IF (*logical_expression*) GOTO *label2*
	
	        .
	
	label1 CONTINUE
	label2 *next statement*

SELF-TEST EXERCISES 8.1

1   What is the major difference between a DO ... WHILE loop and a REPEAT ... UNTIL loop?

2   Give three situations in which a GOTO statement is necessary.

3   What sort of loop should be used in the following situations? Give a brief Fortran example in each case.

(**a**) The input of a fixed number of sets of values into a corresponding set of arrays.
(**b**) The input of a variable number of sets of values into a corresponding set of arrays, where the number of sets to be input is part of the data.
(**c**) The input of a variable number of sets of values into a corresponding set of arrays, where the data is terminated by a special, unique data set.

4   A particular iterative process operates by calculating successive terms of a mathematical series until the value of the last term is less than a predefined tolerance value. Write an outline structure plan for this process.

PROGRAMMING EXERCISES

8.1   Write a program using the DO ... WHILE loop structure that counts down to zero from a value typed in at the keyboard.

8.2   Write a program that prints values of x and y, where $y = \log(x)$ and $x = 9.0, 8.0, 7.0,...$ Use the REPEAT ... UNTIL loop structure to prevent the computer from attempting to calculate $\log(0)$. Why is this necessary?

8.3   Write a program that keeps printing x and x^2 for input values of x as long as x is positive.

8.4   Write a program to compute the logarithms of the numbers 1, 2, 3, and so on, until the result is greater than 2.5.
     Now modify your program so that it will print the largest integer whose logarithm is less than a value input from the keyboard.

8.5   Write a program that produces the sine, cosine and tangent of an angle typed in at the keyboard.

Modify the program so that the user can try more than one angle without having to rerun the program, but can stop the program from executing when desired.

8.6   Using the method described in Exercise 7.7, write a program that will list all the prime numbers less than 32768.

8.7   The value of $\sin x$ (where x is in radians) can be expressed by the infinite series

$$\sin x = x - \frac{x^3}{3!} + \frac{x^5}{5!} - \frac{x^7}{7!} + \frac{x^9}{9!} - \ldots$$

where $n! = n*(n-1)*(n-2)*\ldots*2*1$.

Write a program that reads a value of x and uses the above series to calculate $\sin x$ to an accuracy that is also input from the keyboard. (*Hint*: $\sin(x + 2\pi) = \sin x$ and a value of x that lies between $-\pi$ and $+\pi$ may therefore be used to reduce the size of the terms of the expression. Once this has been done every term after the second is smaller than its predecessor, and so it is easy to know when to stop the calculation.)

*8.8   Modify the program written as Exercise 8.7 so that it produces a table showing the value of $\sin x$ for x taking values from $0°$ to $90°$ in steps of $1°$, where $360° = 2\pi$ radians. Each line should show the angle (in degrees), the value of $\sin x$ calculated by the program, and the value of $\sin x$ calculated by use of the intrinsic function SIN.

8.9   A gambling game is proposed, based on the repeated tossing of a coin until it comes up tails. You stake 2 cents. If the coin comes up tails on the first toss then you win one cent, if it comes up tails on the second toss then you win two cents, if on the third then three cents, and so on.

Write a program to simulate this, and find the expected winnings (or loss!) per game by simulating a large number of games. Repeat the problem for a game in which the payout goes 1, 2, 4, 8, ... instead of 1, 2, 3, 4, ...

*8.10   Students in an examination are awarded a pass if they average over 50% for the three papers, and a distinction if they average more than 75%. Each student is identified only by a number in the range 101 to 199. Write a program to read the three marks for each student and to print his or her result (distinction, pass, or fail). The data is terminated by a 'dummy' student having a student number of 999. Finally, the program should print the average mark for all students, and the average for each group (that is, those with distinctions, those with passes, and those who failed).

8.11   The current I drawn by an electrical appliance of power P is related to the supply voltage V by:

$$I = P/V$$

where I is measured in amperes (A).

A company has five types of electrical cable available, with specifications as shown:

Cable no.	Cost/metre	Max.current (A)	Max.voltage (V)
1	5	5	120
2	8	4	240
3	14	13	240
4	20	30	120
5	35	15	1000

Write a program to display the cheapest suitable flex (if any) for a device of given power and voltage ratings.

8.12   In a simple simulation of a lunar lander, the downward speed V at time $T + 1$ seconds is related to the speed at time T by the expression:

$$V(T + 1) = V(T) + 5 - F$$

where the number 5 allows for the acceleration due to gravity, and F is the number of units of fuel burnt in that second. The height H of the lander above the moon's surface changes according to the equation

$$H(T + 1) = H(T) - V(T)$$

Write a program to implement this simple simulation. The lander starts at a height of 200 units, and the user may choose every second how much fuel to burn (between 0 and 10 units). The user should try to achieve a soft landing (that is, have a speed of less than 10 units when H first drops below zero) using the minimum total quantity of fuel.

8.13   The Fibonacci sequence was introduced in Exercise 5.16, and the ratio of consecutive numbers in the series (1/1, 1/2, 2/3, 3/5, ...) tends to the Golden Ratio

$$\frac{\sqrt{5} - 1}{2}$$

Write a program to determine how far along the sequence you have to go until the difference between the Golden Ratio and that of consecutive numbers is less than 10^{-6}.

8.14 Write a program to solve Kepler's equation ($E - e\sin E = M$) for E, with eccentricity $e = 0.05$, using the following method.
Start with $E = M$. Then successively set E to

$$E - \frac{E - e\sin E - M}{1 - e\cos E}$$

until the change between successive estimates is less than 10^{-6}.

8.15 The pressure inside a bottle of lemonade is given by the expression

$$0.00105*T^2 + 0.0042*T + 1.352$$

in atmospheres (atm), where T°C is the temperature of the lemonade. When the pressure exceeds 3.2 atm the bottle will explode.
Write a program to print the pressure inside the bottle for the temperature rising in one degree steps from 15°C until the bottle explodes.

8.16 The yield of a chemical reaction after time t seconds at a temperature of T°C is given by $1 - e^{-kt}$, where $k = \text{EXP}(-2000/(T+273.16))$.
Write a program that allows the user to enter the temperature, and then prints out the yield for each minute until it reaches 95%.

Simple input/output facilities

9

The list-formatted input/output used up to this point is very convenient, especially for input, but allows the programmer very little control over the layout of his data and, especially, his results. The full Fortran input/output capability allows complete control over both the layout of data and results and the **peripheral device** (keyboard, screen, printer, disc) from which the data is to be read or to which the results are to be sent.

The concept of a separate format allows the layout of the data or results to be specified in a FORMAT statement, or by an **embedded format**, which is then used by a READ, WRITE or PRINT statement to convert the data from its external representation into the computer's internal form, or vice versa.

A particular case is concerned with the output of results to a printer, where the Fortran input/output system uses an extra **printer control** character at the start of each line to control the vertical movement of the paper, thus allowing overprinting, double spacing or printing at the top of the next page.

9.1   The interface with the computer

The computer can now be instructed to manipulate information, repeat sequences of instructions and take alternative courses of action, depending upon decisions that are made during the execution of the program. Compared with the sophistication of which we are capable in these areas, our control over the interpretation of data and the presentation of results has so far been woefully primitive. The problem arises because it is in this area that the world of the computer (where everything is stored as an electric or magnetic signal in one of only two states) comes face-to-face with the world of the human computer user (where there are an almost infinite number of ways of storing or presenting information). It is the interface between these two worlds that must now be examined.

A graphic example of this problem can be seen in the line of data shown in Figure 9.1, which has the digits 1 to 9 typed in the first nine columns. What does this represent? It could be:

- the number 123 456 789;
- or the nine numbers 1, 2, 3, 4, 5, 6, 7, 8 and 9;
- or the three numbers 123, 456, 789;
- or even the number 12 345.678 9;
- or the four numbers 1.23, 0.45, 67 and 8900;
- or it could be one of hundreds of other valid interpretations.

The output of results presents even greater difficulties. If, for example, we wished to print the character string `The answers are` followed by the values stored in the two real variables `x` and `y` we should have a vast choice of ways in which to arrange our results. They could all be on one line like this:

```
The answers are 12.34 -7.89
```

or they could be on three lines:

```
The answers are

12.34    -7.89
```

Figure 9.1
A line of input data.

```
123456789
```

or

```
The answers are
   12.34
  -7.89
```

or a number of other variations. They could also be printed immediately below the last item, or separated from it by one or more blank lines, or at the top of a new page, or in the middle of one. The number might be printed with two decimal places, or with five, or with any other number. The possibilities are enormous.

There is a further problem concerned with where the data comes from and where the results are to go. Is the data typed directly at a keyboard, or is it perhaps kept on backing store – and if so, where? Are the results to be displayed on a screen, printed on a printer, or sent to backing store? And in any of these cases is the peripheral device a 'local' one (that is, one that is more or less directly attached to the computer), or is it at some remote site, possibly many miles away?

So far we have used two simple **list-directed** statements for input and output. For input we write

```
READ *, input-list
```

and for output

```
PRINT *, output-list
```

If we consider the READ statement first, we find that the source of the data is dealt with by a neat piece of sleight-of-hand. Input is taken, it was said in Chapter 2, from the **standard input unit**, which is defined by the particular computer system being used; typically, it will be the keyboard. The interpretation of the data is dealt with primarily by treating a space or a comma (or a /) as a separator between items of data.

In a similar way, the PRINT statement sends its results to the **standard output unit**, which is also processor dependent, but which will usually be the terminal screen or the computer's printer. The layout of the results is less satisfactory, since each PRINT statement starts at the beginning of the next line and prints the various items in a 'reasonable' format. This varies according to the type (and size) of the values to be output, and is defined by the writer of the Fortran compiler and not by the standard. In effect, the results will always be clearly printed, but the programmer has virtually no control over their layout.

These two list-directed input/output statements are thus severely restricted in their ability to define both the format of the information and its source or destination; nevertheless, as we have seen, they can be extremely useful, especially for input, in a great many cases.

The remainder of this chapter will examine how we can provide the flexibility needed in many cases for both input and output. We shall restrict ourselves to the input of numbers and the output of numbers and constant character strings for the present. In Part II of this book new types of variables (such as characters) will be introduced, and the input/output facilities will be extended as and when necessary.

9.2 The FORMAT concept

An input statement must contain (at least) three types of information: where the data is to be found, where it is to be stored, and how it is to be interpreted. Similarly, an output statement must define where the results are to be found, where they are to be sent, and in what form they are to be displayed. These three types of information are not all dealt with in the same way.

In English language terms a READ instruction says: 'read some information from unit n (for example, a keyboard or a file on backing store) and store it in the variables X, Y and Z'. This cannot (usually) be fully achieved without defining the layout of the data and so some supplementary information is usually supplied. Figure 9.2 shows a variation of the

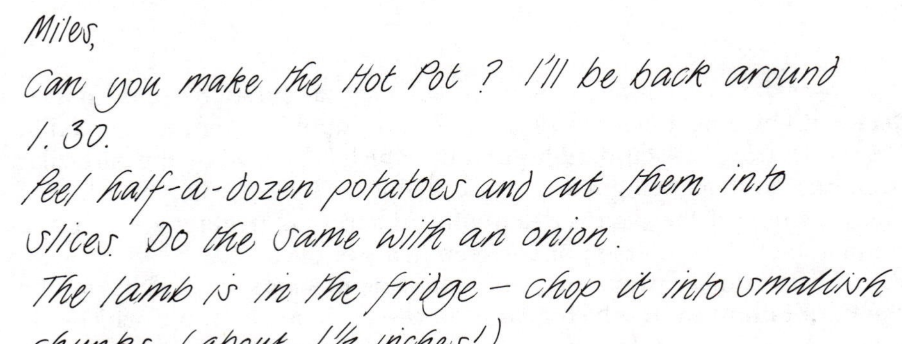

Figure 9.2
More cooking instructions.

Miles,

Can you make the Hot Pot? I'll be back around 1.30.

Peel half-a-dozen potatoes and cut them into slices. Do the same with an onion.

The lamb is in the fridge — chop it into smallish chunks (about 1½ inches!)

Follow the instructions in the book,* but ignore the bit about kidneys and mushrooms

Put it on at 11.00 — DON'T FORGET

Love Maggie

* Mary Berry's Cookbook, page 78. It's in the top drawer.

instructions for cooking lunch that were used earlier (see Figure 4.1): it can be seen that a footnote refers to the cookery book to be used and the page on which to find the recipe. The body of the instructions is thus of the form 'do this ...', while the footnote provides extra information that is necessary if the instructions are to be obeyed satisfactorily.

The Fortran input/output statements operate in a similar way, and indeed we have been using exactly the same convention without realizing it in all the programs we have written. When we wrote

```
READ  *,X,Y,Z
```

or

```
PRINT *,'Result is',FRED
```

the asterisk (*) was actually referring to a **format** for the data or results. This format, supplied by the system, is called a **list-directed format**, and is defined by reference to the input or output list. If we wished we could define our own format and refer to it by writing

READ *label*, input-list

or

PRINT *label*, output-list

where *label* is the number of a **statement label** that will appear elsewhere in the same program unit, attached to a special FORMAT statement that will define the layout of the data or results, as appropriate. Thus our input statement could take either of the forms

```
READ *, input-list
READ label, input-list
```

and our output statements could do likewise:

```
PRINT *, output-list
PRINT label, output-list
```

The facilities available in Fortran 77 for defining the format of data and results are extremely powerful and provide enormous flexibility to the programmer. Before considering them, however, the basic input/output statements must be examined in more detail. Once we have seen the variations that are possible we shall return to examine the FORMAT statement and to see how it is used in conjunction with both input and output statements.

9.3 The READ statement

The two variants of the READ statement already encountered take their input from the standard input unit. In order to vary this, and to allow the possibility of monitoring the success or otherwise of the reading process, a more general form of READ statement must be used. This takes the form

    READ (*cilist*) input-list

where *cilist* represents a **control information list**, consisting of one or more items known as **specifiers**, separated by commas. Figure 9.3 shows a list of these specifiers, all of which take the same basic form

    keyword = value

although in two cases the keyword may, in certain circumstances, be omitted. These specifiers, or rather those that are used in a particular case, may appear in any order as long as the full form (with keyword) is used.
     There must always be a **unit specifier** in the control information list, which takes the form

    UNIT = *u*

where *u* is the peripheral unit from which input is to be taken (or the name of an 'internal file' – see Chapter 17). It takes the form of an integer expression whose value is zero or positive, or it may be an asterisk to indicate that the standard input unit is to be used. The way in which the unit number is related to a particular peripheral device is, to a large extent, dependent upon the computer system being used. Normally several units will be **preconnected** and will automatically be available to all programs. The standard input unit and the standard output unit will be preconnected in this way, but a particular Fortran 77 implementation may well have other preconnected units. Any other peripheral devices or files that are required must be given a unit number by the program and connected to that program by an OPEN statement (see Section 10.4).

Figure 9.3
Control information list
specifiers.

UNIT	= *u*	(or *u*)
FMT	= *f*	(or *f*)
REC	= *rn*	
ERR	= *s*	
END	= *s*	
IOSTAT	= *ios*	

The standard input unit will usually be preconnected either as unit 1 or as unit 5. (This is purely for historical reasons. While many early Fortran systems used unit 1 to denote the card reader and unit 2 the printer, IBM and several other manufacturers called these devices units 5 and 6. A great many programs written in earlier versions thus expect their input from unit 1 or 5 and send their results to unit 2 or 6, depending upon the type of computer being used. For compatibility, a Fortran 77 system is likely to preserve the convention previously in use at a particular site.) We shall assume that the standard input unit is unit 1, but it must be emphasized that *this is only an assumption*; a particular implementation may use any positive number or zero for the standard input unit.

With this assumption we may write

```
UNIT = 1
```

or

```
UNIT = *
```

to identify the standard input unit. If, and only if, the unit specifier is the first item in the control information list we may omit the keyword and = sign, and simply write

```
1
```

or

```
*
```

Normally the input will need to be converted from some *external* form, such as signals sent by a keyboard, to an *internal* form suitable for storing in the computer's memory, although in some circumstances (see Chapter 17) this is not necessary. To carry out this conversion a FORMAT statement is needed, and this is identified by a **format specifier**, which takes the form

```
FMT = f
```

where f is the statement label of the appropriate FORMAT statement, or an asterisk to indicate list-directed formatting, or an embedded format (see Section 9.8). If the format specifier is the second item in the control information list and the first item is a unit specifier without any keyword (that is, u) then the keyword and = sign may also be omitted from the format specifier. Thus the following are all acceptable alternatives:

```
READ (UNIT=1,FMT=100) X,Y,Z
READ (FMT=100,UNIT=1) X,Y,Z
READ (1,FMT=100) X,Y,Z
READ (1,100) X,Y,Z
```

We can also see that the statement

```
READ (*,*) A,B,C
```

is identical to the earlier list-directed input statement

```
READ *,A,B,C
```

as is the statement

```
READ (1,*) A,B,C
```

if, and only if, unit 1 is also the standard input unit.

The next input specifier (REC = *rn*) does not concern us at this stage. It is used for direct access input and is discussed in detail in Chapter 17.

The remaining three specifiers are concerned with monitoring the reading process. The first of them

```
ERR = s
```

takes special action if an error should occur. This might be one of several types, such as misreading of data or running out of data. Normally if this happens execution of the program is terminated; however, if an error specifier is included in the control information list of the READ statement that caused the error, processing will continue from a statement in the program that has a statement label *s*. Thus if an error occurs during the statement

```
READ (UNIT=1,FMT=100,ERR=999) A,B,C
```

the program will continue from the statement with label 999. In this event, the items in the input list become **undefined** – in other words, it is not known what value they contain – as does the position in the input data. In most cases, therefore, it is impossible to continue, but the program can take such action as the programmer may deem appropriate (such as printing intermediate results) before it finishes.

A special type of error concerns the situation in which a program tries to read more data than is available. There are actually two situations here. One concerns the use of files, in which a special marker called an **end-of-file record** (see Section 10.3), may come after all the data; and the other concerns simple input such as we are considering. In the former case, and *in some implementations* when dealing with simple input, we can take special notice of running out of data by use of the end-of-file specifier

    END = s

This is similar to the error specifier and causes processing to continue from the statement labelled s if the READ statement encounters an end-of-file marker or otherwise sets an **end-of-file condition** (see Section 10.3). If a particular Fortran 77 implementation sets an end-of-file condition, and not an error, when it runs out of data, this can be used as an easy way of detecting the end of the data for a program.

The final specifier enables more information to be made available to the program in the event of an error, and takes the form

    IOSTAT = ios

where *ios* is an integer variable. It will be discussed in Chapter 17.

9.4   The WRITE and PRINT statements

Output is essentially the reverse of input, so far as the transfer of information is concerned, and as one would expect, the facilities available are essentially the same. The most obvious difference is that for input the word READ is used in all cases, but for output there are two words. We have used the PRINT statement for list-directed output and the same form of statement could be used for user-formatted output to the standard output unit. To take advantage of the full range of facilities, however, we use a different word, WRITE, in a form of statement that is almost identical to that used for input:

    WRITE (*cilist*) output-list

Exactly the same specifiers are available as for the READ statement, although it will not normally be possible to encounter an end-of-file condition during output. The only other difference is the obvious one that an asterisk as a unit identifier refers to the standard *output* unit. Thus the following statements have an identical effect:

```
WRITE (UNIT=*,FMT=*) P,Q,R
WRITE (FMT=*,UNIT=*) P,Q,R
WRITE (*,FMT=*) P,Q,R
WRITE (*,*) P,Q,R
PRINT *,P,Q,R
```

The choice of a unit number for the standard output unit is dependent upon the particular implementation. It will usually be 2 (when 1 is used for input) or 6 (when 5 is used for input), although some interactive systems may use the same number for both the keyboard and the screen of a terminal. In this book *it will be assumed that the standard output unit is 2* and that, therefore, the following statements are equivalent:

```
WRITE (2,75) D,E,F
WRITE (*,75) D,E,F
```

9.5 The FORMAT statement

In the above variations of READ, WRITE and PRINT statements the format of the data or results has been defined by a format specifier of the form

FMT = *f*

where *f* is either a statement label or an asterisk (to indicate list-directed formatting), or simply by writing

READ *f*, input-list
PRINT *f*, output-list

where *f* is defined in the same way. We are now ready to examine the FORMAT statement.

This takes the form

label FORMAT (*ed1*,*ed2*, . . . *edn*)

where *ed1*,...*edn* are **edit descriptors**. These will be used to convert (or edit) the data in one form (for example, as holes in a card or values in a memory location) into another form (for example, values in a memory location or characters on a printed sheet). Notice that a FORMAT statement will *always* have a statement label because it is not the same as the other statements, but is more like a footnote (see Section 9.2). In computer terminology it is **non-executable** and is always used by another statement, which identifies it by its label.

Figure 9.4 shows some of the edit descriptors used for input, and these will be examined in turn. Other edit descriptors will be introduced later. The first three shown are concerned with reading numeric characters and converting them into either integer or real numbers, while the remainder are concerned with altering the order in which these characters are read.

Descriptor	Meaning
I*w*	Read the next *w* characters as an integer
F*w*.*d*	Read the next *w* characters as a real number with *d* digits after the decimal place if no decimal point is present
E*w*.*d*	
*n*X	Ignore the next *n* characters
T*c*	Next character to be read is at position *c*
TL*n*	Next character to be read is *n* characters before (TL) or after (TR) the current position
TR*n*	

Figure 9.4
Some edit descriptors for input.

The first, and simplest, edit descriptor is used for inputting whole numbers that are to be stored in an *integer* variable, and consists of the letter I followed by a number *w*. This indicates that the next *w* characters are to be read and interpreted as an integer. Thus if we wished to read the line shown in Figure 9.1 (which had the digits 1 to 9 typed in columns 1 to 9) as a single integer we could write

```
     READ 101,N
 101 FORMAT (I9)
```

although the resulting number (123 456 789) would be too large to hold as an integer on most computers and would probably lead to an error. The READ statement could also be written in one of several other ways – for example:

```
     READ (UNIT=1,FMT=101) N
     READ (FMT=101,UNIT=*) N
     READ (1,101) N
     READ (*,101) N
```

In future examples only one of the various alternatives will be used without any further comment.

If we wished to read the same line as nine separate integers (1, 2, 3, … 9) then we could write

```
     READ (1,102) N1,N2,N3,N4,N5,N6,N7,N8,N9
 102 FORMAT (I1,I1,I1,I1,I1,I1,I1,I1,I1)
```

This format interacts with the READ statement in the following way.

First the READ statement recognizes that it requires an integer to store in N1; the FORMAT statement indicates that the first item to be read is an integer occupying one column (I1). The character '1' is therefore read and converted to the internal form of an integer before being stored in N1. The READ statement then requires another integer and the FORMAT indicates that this is to come from the *next* column (I1). And so the process is repeated until the ninth column is read and the value 9 stored in N9. The READ statement is now satisfied and so input of this line of data is complete.

Notice that there is an implied concept of a *pointer* that is always indicating which is the next character of the input record to be read. Normally this pointer is moved through the record as characters are read; however, the X and T edit specifiers allow the pointer to be moved without any characters being read.

The X edit descriptor takes the form of a whole number *n* followed by an X and causes the pointer to be moved forward across *n* characters. The next character to be read will be *n* positions to the right of the current position and the effect is to ignore the next *n* characters. Thus, using the same data line, the statements

```
      READ (*,103) K
  103 FORMAT (4X,I5)
```

will ignore the first four columns and then read the next five as an integer; the value 56 789 will therefore be stored in K. Similarly

```
      READ (1,104) I,J
  104 FORMAT (I2,3X,I3)
```

will cause the value 12 to be stored in I and 678 in J. Notice that in this case the 9 typed in column 9 is not read because the format specifies the first eight columns.

The T (for 'Tab') edit descriptor comes in three variations. The first consists of the letter T followed by a whole number *c* and causes a tab to character position *c*; in other words the next character to be read will be from position *c*. Thus the statements

```
      READ (UNIT=1,FMT=105) I,J,K
  105 FORMAT (T4,I2,T8,I2,T2,I4)
```

will first move the pointer to position 4 and read the number 45 into I, then move it to position 8 before reading 89 into J, and then move it to position 2 before reading the number 2345 into K. The T edit descriptor thus provides a means not only of skipping over unwanted characters but also of going back in the record and reading it (or parts of it) again.

The T edit descriptor moves to a character position that is defined *absolutely* by its position in the record. The TL and TR edit descriptors, on the other hand, specify a *relative* tab – that is, a move to a character position defined relative to the current position. The letters TR followed by a number *n* indicate that the next character is to be *n* positions to the right of the current position; it is thus identical in its effect to *n*x. The letters TL followed by a number *n* specify a tab to the left, and cause the next character to be *n* positions to the left of (or before) the current position. If TL*n* would cause the next position to be before the first character of the record then the pointer is positioned at the start of the record; TL followed by a large number can therefore always be used to return to the beginning of the record (as can T1).

EXAMPLE 9.1

If an input record (for example, a line of type or a row of holes in a card) consists of the ten digits 1, 2, 3, 4, 5, 6, 7, 8, 9, 0 repeated five times, what is stored in the variables I, J, K, L, M and N after the following statements?

```
110 FORMAT(T5,I4,21X,I3,TL7,I2,TR13,I3,TL45,TR7,I5,TL5,I5)
    READ 110,I,J,K,L,M,N
```

The READ statement requires six integers and will use the FORMAT labelled 110 to obtain them. The T5 descriptor causes the following I4 descriptor to start at position 5 and to read 5678 into I, leaving the pointer at position 9. The 21X descriptor moves the pointer 21 positions to the right and the following I3 descriptor thus starts at position 30 and reads the characters 012, that is 12, leaving the pointer at position 33.

TL7 then moves the pointer back 7 positions to position 26 and the number 67 is read and stored in K. The pointer is then moved 13 positions to the right, to position 41, and the number 123 is read into the variable L, leaving the pointer at position 44.

The next edit descriptor is TL45, which will attempt to move the pointer 45 characters to the left; however, as this would move it to before the start of the record, it is positioned at the first character position. The following TR7 therefore moves the pointer to position 8 and the value 89 012 is read into M, as a result of the I5 descriptor.

The last two edit descriptors cause the pointer to be moved back five characters and then five characters to be read as an integer. This causes the same characters to be read for N as for M. The final state of the six variables is therefore:

I 5678	J 12	K 67
L 123	M 89 012	N 89 012

Finally the F edit descriptor (or the E edit descriptor, which is identical on input) is used for reading real values. It consists of the letter F or E followed by a number w, a decimal point, and a second number d, and can be used in two rather different ways, depending upon the format of the data.

Figure 9.5
Another line of data.

```
.23.56.8
```

If the data is typed with a decimal point in the appropriate position then the edit descriptor causes the next w characters to be read and converted into a real number. The value of d is irrelevant (although it must be included in the format).

On the other hand, if the w columns that are to be read as a real number do not contain any decimal point then the d indicates where one may be assumed to have been omitted, by specifying that the number has d decimal places. Thus (assuming our usual input record, as shown in Figure 9.1) the statements

```
      READ 121,X
  121 FORMAT (F9.4)
```

will cause the first nine characters to be read as a real number with four decimal places. The variable X will therefore have the number 12345.6789 stored in it. In a similar way

```
      READ 122,A,B,C,D
  122 FORMAT (F3.1,F2.2,F3.0,TL6,F4.2)
```

will cause the value 12.3 to be stored in A, 0.45 in B, 678.0 in C, and 34.56 in D.

Consider now the same program statements used to read a line typed as shown in Figure 9.5. The first edit descriptor requires three columns to be read, and since these (.23) contain a decimal point the second part of the edit descriptor is ignored and the value 0.23 is stored in A. In a similar way the F2.2 descriptor causes the characters .5 to be read, and B is therefore given the value 0.5. The F3.0 edit descriptor also has its second part overridden by the decimal point in 6.8 and so this is the value stored in C. Finally TL6,F4.0 causes the characters 3.56 to be read, and so this value is stored in D. Figure 9.6 summarizes the result of reading these two lines of data.

Figure 9.6
The effect of the F edit descriptor during input.

```
      READ 123,A,B,C,D
  123 FORMAT (F3.1,F2.2,F3.0,TL6,F4.2)
```

Data:	123456789	.23.56.8
A contains	12.3	0.23
B contains	0.45	0.5
C contains	678.0	6.8
D contains	34.56	3.56

As a general rule, data which is to be stored in the form of real values will be presented to the computer with the decimal points in their correct places. However, sometimes, especially when the data has been collected independently from the programmer, it is presented in the form of whole numbers that need to be processed by the computer as real numbers.

EXAMPLE 9.2

A survey consisting of a maximum of 1000 respondents has recorded the name, age, sex, marital status, height and weight of a number of people. The information has been recorded as follows:

Name   in columns 1–20
Sex   coded in column 23
                     0=female
                     1=male
Marital status coded in column 25
                     0=single
                     1=married
                     2=widowed
                     3=divorced
                     4=cohabiting
                     9=unknown
Age (years)   in columns 27, 28
Height (cm)   in columns 31–33
Weight (kg)   in columns 36–42 in the form *kkk.ggg*

The data is terminated by a line that has 99 typed in columns 21 and 22.

Write and test a procedure to read the data and store it, apart from the names, in a form suitable for subsequent analysis. Such analysis will require the heights to be stored in metres.

When developing a large program it is often a good idea to write and thoroughly test an input procedure first. When developing the rest of the program we can then be confident that the data is being correctly input, and can concentrate on the other parts of the program.

A structure plan for this program will be very simple:

1 Read data INPUT

2 Repeat *n* times (where *n* is the number of sets of data read)
   2.1 Print data set number, sex, marital status, age, height and weight

INPUT(SEX(N),STATUS(N),AGE(N),HT(N),WT(N),N,NUMBER)

1 Repeat up to *N* times
1.1 Read next record
1.2 If terminator found then exit

2 Return number of data sets read

The program is also quite straightforward, since the only difficult part is working out the correct format in which to describe the data.

```
      PROGRAM TEST
C
C  This program is a "driver" to test the subroutine INPUT
C
      INTEGER MAXSIZ
      PARAMETER (MAXSIZ=1000)
      INTEGER I,NUMBER,SEX(MAXSIZ),STATUS(MAXSIZ),AGE(MAXSIZ)
      REAL HT(MAXSIZ),WT(MAXSIZ)
C  Call INPUT to read the data
      PRINT *,'Type data as follows:'
      PRINT *,'Columns  1-20  Name'
      PRINT *,'Column      23  Sex (0=female, 1=male)'
      PRINT *,'Column      25  Marital status (0=single, 1=married,'
      PRINT *,'                2=widowed, 3=divorced, 4=cohabiting,'
      PRINT *,'                9=unknown)'
      PRINT *,'Columns 27,28  Age (in years)'
      PRINT *,'Columns 31-33  Height (in cm)'
      PRINT *,'Columns 36-42  Weight (in kg in the form kkk.ggg)'
      PRINT *,' '
      PRINT *,'Data should be terminated by the number 99 typed'
      PRINT *,'in columns 21 and 22'
      PRINT *,' '
      CALL INPUT(SEX,STATUS,AGE,HT,WT,MAXSIZ,NUMBER)
C  Print data
      PRINT *,NUMBER,' sets of data read:'
      PRINT *,' '
      DO 10, I=1,NUMBER
         PRINT *,I,': ',SEX(I),STATUS(I),AGE(I),' yrs',HT(I),' m',
     *           WT(I),' kg'
   10 CONTINUE
      STOP
      END

      SUBROUTINE INPUT(SEX,STATUS,AGE,HT,WT,N,NUM)
C
C  This subroutine reads a set of personal data laid out as follows:
C          Columns  1-20  Name
C          Column      23  Sex (0 or 1)
C          Column      25  Marital status (0, 1, 2, 3, 4 or 9)
C          Columns 27,28  Age (in years)
```

```
C            Columns 31-33  Height (in cm)
C            Columns 36-42  Weight (in kg in the form kkk.ggg)
C
C  The number 99 typed in columns 21,22 terminates input
C
       INTEGER I,N,CODE,SEX(N),STATUS(N),AGE(N)
       REAL HT(N),WT(N)
C  Loop to read data
       DO 10, I=1,N
          READ 100,CODE,SEX(I),STATUS(I),AGE(I),HT(I),WT(I)
C  Check if this is the terminator record
          IF (CODE.EQ.99) GOTO 11
    10 CONTINUE
       PRINT *,N,' records read with no terminator'
C  Set number of data sets read and return
    11 NUM=I-1
       RETURN
   100 FORMAT(20X,I2,I1,1X,I1,1X,I2,2X,F3.2,2X,F7.0)
       END
```

Notice that the FORMAT statement does not need to be placed next to the READ statement. Many programmers place all their FORMATs together at the end of the program (before the END of course) as has been done here, as this enables them to be easily found and checked when necessary. In this case we see that T20,I2 will cause the first item read to be an integer taken from columns 21 and 22; this is where the terminator code is typed on the last line. I1,1X,I1 will then cause the single digit codes for sex and marital status to be read from columns 23 and 25, before 1X,I2 causes the age to be read as an integer from columns 27 and 28.

The height is typed in columns 31–33 in centimetres; however, it is required that it be stored internally as a real value in metres. The edit descriptors 2X,F3.2 will cause columns 31–33 to be read as a real number with two decimal places; thus if the data was typed as 172 (that is, 172 cm) it will be stored in the variable HT as 1.72 (1.72 m = 172 cm). The edit descriptor therefore automatically converts an integer height in centimetres to a real height in metres.

The final item to be read is the weight, and this is typed in columns 36–42 as a real number in kilograms and grams. The edit descriptors 2X,F7.0 will deal with this; the decimal point in the data will mean that the second part of the F edit descriptor (0) is ignored.

The program uses a conditional DO loop to ensure that too many records are not read, and prints an error message if appropriate.

We now come to the use of the FORMAT statement for output. Figure 9.7 shows some of the edit descriptors used for this purpose, most of which are similar to those used for input.

	Descriptor	Meaning
Figure 9.7 Some edit descriptors for output.	Iw	Output an integer in the next w character positions
	$Fw.d$	Output a real number in the next w character positions with d decimal places
	$Ew.d$	Output a real number in the next w character positions using a scientific format with d decimal places in the mantissa and four characters for the exponent
	nX	Ignore the next n character positions
	Tc	Output the next item starting at character position c
	TLn TRn	Output the next item starting n character positions before (TL) or after (TR) the current position
	$'c_1c_2c_3...c_n'$	Output the string of characters $c_1c_2c_3...c_n$ starting at the next character position
	$nHc_1c_2c_3...c_n$	Output the n characters following the H in the next n character positions

The I edit descriptor (Iw) causes an integer to be output in such a way as to utilize the next w character positions. These w positions will consist of (if necessary) one or more spaces, followed by a minus sign if the number is negative, followed by the value of the number. Thus the statements

```
    I=23
    J=715
    K=-12
    PRINT 201,I,J,K
201 FORMAT (I5,I5,I5)
```

will produce a line of output as follows (where the symbol ♦ represents a space):

♦♦♦23♦♦715♦♦-12

If the output is to go to the computer's printer then the results that actually appear will probably be very slightly different; this is discussed in Section 9.6. If it is sent to a display screen, or most other peripheral devices, the layout should be exactly as defined.

The F edit descriptor operates in a similar way: $Fw.d$ indicates that a real number is to be output occupying w characters, of which the last d are to follow the decimal point. The real value is *rounded* (not truncated) to d places of decimals before being output. Rounding is carried out in the usual arithmetic way. Thus the statements

```
    X=3.14159
    Y=-275.3024
    Z=12.9999
    PRINT 202,X,Y,Z
202 FORMAT (F10.3,F10.3,F10.3)
```

will produce the following line of output:

♦♦♦♦♦3.142♦♦-275.302♦♦♦♦13.000

Notice that, because the edit descriptor specifies only three places of decimals, the value of X is printed as 3.142 (rounded up), the value of Y as -275.302 (rounded down), and the value of Z as 13.000 (rounded up).

The E edit descriptor is also used for outputting real numbers, but using a scientific form of notation. Before discussing it, however, we must extend our understanding of the format of real numbers.

We have seen already (Section 2.1) that a real constant may be written followed by an exponent (for example, 1.5E-6) and a similar extension is allowed in the format of numbers being input. In this case the exponent may take one of three forms:

- a signed integer constant;
- E followed by an optionally signed constant;
- D followed by an optionally signed constant.

In the latter two cases the letter (D or E) may be followed by one or more spaces.

Thus the number 361.764 may be presented in any of the following ways:

```
361.764
3.61764+2
361764-3
36.1764E1
3617.64D-1
3.61764E +2
```

For output, however, there are significant differences. As we have already seen, such data may be input using either the $Fw.d$ or $Ew.d$ edit descriptors. As discussed above, $Fw.d$ will output a real number rounded to d decimal places with an external field of width w.

The E edit descriptor, however, produces a representation of a real number consisting of a decimal fraction in the range 0.1 to 0.9999... with d digits of precision, followed by a four-character exponent, the complete number occupying a field width of w characters. It is therefore much more flexible, and will cater more easily than the F edit descriptor with very large

Figure 9.8
An example of tabular
printing.

```
      PROGRAM FIG98
      INTEGER I
      REAL X,THIRD
      PARAMETER (THIRD=1.0/3.0)
C  Loop to print x, square root of x, and cube root of x, for x=1,10
      DO 10, I=1,10
         X=I
  10    PRINT 201,X,SQRT(X),X**THIRD
      STOP
 201  FORMAT(F10.4,F10.4,F10.4)
      END
```

```
      1.0000      1.0000      1.0000
      2.0000      1.4142      1.2599
      3.0000      1.7321      1.4422
      4.0000      2.0000      1.5874
      5.0000      2.2361      1.7100
      6.0000      2.4495      1.8171
      7.0000      2.6458      1.9129
      8.0000      2.8284      2.0000
      9.0000      3.0000      2.0801
     10.0000      3.1623      2.1544
```

or very small numbers. The number 0.000 036 176 4, for instance, will be output as shown below with various edit descriptors:

```
     F10.4        0.0000
     F12.6        0.000036
     F14.8        0.00003618
     E10.4     0.3618E-04
     E12.6     0.361764E-04
     E14.8     0.36176400E-04
```

In some implementations the exponent may consist of a + or – sign followed by three digits:

```
     E11.3     0.362-004
```

It is important to realize that, for *all* numeric edit descriptors, if the number does not require the full field width w it will be preceded by one or more spaces. By allowing more room than is necessary, several numbers may be spaced across the page and the printing of tables becomes very easy, as can be seen in Figure 9.8. In this case the FORMAT statement specifies that the three items to be printed ($x, \sqrt{x}, \sqrt[3]{x}$) are all to use an edit descriptor of F10.4. The three numbers are therefore spread evenly across the page, with the next three directly below them, and so on.

In the example shown in Figure 9.8, as in several other programs in this section, the same edit descriptor has been repeated several times. A number, called a **repeat count**, may be placed *before* the I, F or E edit descriptors to indicate how many times they are to be repeated. Thus

```
201  FORMAT (3I5,4F6.2)
```

is identical to

```
201 FORMAT (I5,I5,I5,F6.2,F6.2,F6.2,F6.2)
```

The first version, using a repeat count, is both easier to write and, more importantly, easier to read than the full version. A repeat count may be used in formats for both input and output to cause repetition of an edit descriptor used in conjunction with an input or output list item; it cannot be used to repeat the other edit descriptors.

The X edit descriptor is used on output to ignore, or skip over, the next n character positions. If no output has yet been sent to these positions the effect is to insert n spaces; if some output has already been sent to these positions, however, the X edit descriptor merely moves the pointer. The effect of nX is best appreciated by assuming that an output record always consists of spaces before the start of a WRITE or PRINT statement, and that nX moves the pointer n character positions to the right.

The T, TL and TC edit descriptors also operate in the same way as for input, assuming the output record initially consists of spaces, and enables items to be positioned in an exact place in the record (or line).

There are two additional edit descriptors that can be used only for output; both of these cause a (constant) string of characters to be output, starting at the next character position. The first of these is known as the **apostrophe edit descriptor** and consists of a string of characters enclosed between apostrophes. This is of exactly the same form as the character strings that we have used in PRINT statements to identify the meaning of our results. Thus, if we write

```
     I=74
     J=149
     WRITE (*,202) I,J,I+J
 202 FORMAT ('The sum of',I4,' and',I4,' is',I5)
```

we shall obtain the results printed as follows:

```
The sum of  74 and 149 is  223
```

Notice that the last two apostrophe edit descriptors start with a space to separate the string from the preceding number.

The second edit descriptor is older and is not recommended (except for one situation described in Section 9.6). It does exactly the same as the apostrophe descriptor, but in a more clumsy and error-prone manner. This is the H **edit descriptor** and consists of a number n followed by H and then n characters. The n characters will be output starting at the next character position. Thus the FORMAT shown above could also be written

```
202 FORMAT (10HThe sum of,I4,4H and,I4,3H is,I5)
```

This edit descriptor is included in Fortran 77 only for compatibility with earlier versions of Fortran.

EXAMPLE 9.3

A piece of experimental apparatus is monitoring the radioactive decay of a specimen. At approximately regular intervals it records the time since the start of the experiment (in hundredths of a second), the number of α-particles, the number of β-particles and the amount of γ-radiation emitted during the interval. These are output as an eight-digit number (for the time) and three six-digit numbers. There are five spaces between each number.

Write a program to read this data and to print a table containing the following information: a sequence number for each interval, the length of the interval, the three readings obtained and the average emission of α-particles, β-particles and γ-rays (per second) during the interval. After 1000 time intervals print the time interval that had the highest rate of emission of γ-radiation.

As usual start with a structure plan:

1 Initialize maximum radiation and interval

2 Print column headings

3 Repeat 1000 times
    3.1 Read next set of data
    3.2 Calculate length of interval and average emissions
    3.3 Print details
    3.4 If γ-radiation > max. γ-radiation then
        3.4.1 Save maximum γ-radiation and interval number

4 Print details of maximum γ-radiation

This is fairly straightforward except for step 2. We shall be printing a table with eight columns and it is sensible to identify these by headings. We can do this by means of a WRITE statement that has no output list, but which uses a FORMAT consisting solely of apostrophe edit descriptors together with any necessary positioning descriptors.

We also need to consider the formats for both input and output. As is often the case, the format of the data is already defined and our FORMAT statement must therefore reflect it. In this case it is quite simple:

```
101 FORMAT (F8.2,5X,I6,5X,I6,5X,I6)
```

The time is provided in hundredths of a second, so the easiest approach is to read it as a real number in seconds with an implied decimal point before the last two digits. The other items are all integers. Notice that on this occasion we have a repeated sequence (5X,I6). We can shorten the FORMAT in two ways: by enclosing this sequence in parentheses and preceding it by a repeat count; or by including the leading spaces as part of the numeric field (but see Section 17.3):

```
101 FORMAT (F8.2,3(5X,I6))
```

or

```
101 FORMAT (F8.2,3I11)
```

Notice in the first case that the X edit descriptor can be repeated when it is part of a repeated sequence that contains at least one repeatable edit descriptor.

Output is rather different because usually, though not always, we have complete control over its format. In this case we have a table of eight items: a sequence number, a time interval (to one hundredth of a second), three integer values and three averages. A suitable format might be:

```
202 FORMAT (I6,F8.2,3I8,3F8.2)
```

Here all the edit descriptors have a field width greater than is necessary, in order to space the columns across the page and leave room for column titles. We can now write the program:

```
      PROGRAM DECAY
C
C  This program processes experimental data relating to
C  radioactive decay
C
      INTEGER I,ALPHA,BETA,GAMMA,MAXINT,MAXDAT,IN,OUT
C  MAXDAT is the number of readings to be processed
      PARAMETER (MAXDAT=1000)
```

```
C  IN and OUT are the standard input and output unit numbers
       PARAMETER (IN=1,OUT=2)
       REAL TIME,PERIOD,MAXG,TLAST,AVA,AVB,AVG
       DATA MAXG,TLAST/2*0.0/,MAXINT/0/
C  Print headings
       WRITE (OUT,201)
C  Process MAXDAT sets of data
       DO 10, I=1,MAXDAT
          READ (IN,101) TIME,ALPHA,BETA,GAMMA
C  Calculate interval since last readings
          PERIOD=TIME-TLAST
          TLAST=TIME
C  Calculate average rates of emission
          AVA=ALPHA/PERIOD
          AVB=BETA/PERIOD
          AVG=GAMMA/PERIOD
C  Print statistics for this interval
          WRITE (OUT,202) I,PERIOD,ALPHA,BETA,GAMMA,AVA,AVB,AVG
C  Check for maximum gamma radiation
          IF (AVG.GT.MAXG) THEN
             MAXG=AVG
             MAXINT=I
          END IF
   10 CONTINUE
C  Print details of interval with maximum gamma radiation
       WRITE (OUT,203) MAXG,MAXINT
       STOP
  101 FORMAT (F8.2,3(5X,I6))
  201 FORMAT (T5,'Interval',T16,'Time',T23,'Alpha',T32,'Beta',T39,
     *         'Gamma',T47,'Av. A',T55,'Av. B',T63,'Av. G')
  202 FORMAT (I11,F8.2,3I8,3F8.2)
  203 FORMAT (T5,'Maximum average gamma radiation was',F7.2,
     *         ' in interval',I5)
       END
```

Notice the use of the named constants IN and OUT for the unit numbers in the input and output statements. This is a particularly useful approach since it means that, if the program should be moved to another computer that uses different unit numbers for the input and output units, the change needs to be made in only one place – the PARAMETER statement.

An example of part of the results produced by this program can be seen in Figure 9.9.

This example is typical of the class of problems for which the E edit descriptor may be better than the F edit descriptor, since the size and range of the results may be unknown when it is written and may vary quite widely between different experiments. Thus, while the average values for α-particles shown in Figure 9.9 are all printed to four significant digits, the averages for β-particles vary between three and four and the average γ-radiation always has five significant digits. And yet all data was collected at the same time with, presumably, the same intrinsic level of accuracy.

Interval	Time	Alpha	Beta	Gamma	Av. A	Av. B	Av. G
·	·	·	·	·	·	·	·
·	·	·	·	·	·	·	·
·	·	·	·	·	·	·	·
990	2.56	175	23	401	68.36	8.98	156.64
991	2.59	168	22	395	64.86	8.49	152.51
992	2.48	181	27	412	72.98	10.89	166.13
993	2.51	177	25	410	70.52	9.96	163.35
994	2.48	166	29	391	66.94	11.69	157.66
995	2.54	181	25	397	71.26	9.84	156.30
996	2.51	169	28	407	67.33	11.16	162.15
997	2.58	159	23	388	61.63	8.91	150.39
998	2.51	177	26	401	70.52	10.36	159.76
999	2.47	173	24	398	70.04	9.72	161.13
1000	2.52	183	28	403	72.62	11.11	159.92

Maximum average gamma radiation was 174.28 in interval   741

Figure 9.9
Results produced by the DECAY program.

Using an E edit descriptor for these three values will enable them all to be shown to the same level of accuracy.

Do not, however, fall into the trap of believing that just because the results are printed to d digits of precision they are necessarily accurate to that degree. More will be said about this in Chapter 11.

Figure 9.10 shows the result of running a slightly modified version of the same program with the same data as before. The only change is to the three format statements 201, 202 and 203, to allow all averages to be printed to five digits of precision.

Interval	Time	Alpha	Beta	Gamma	Av. A	Av. B	Av. G
·	·	·	·	·	·	·	·
·	·	·	·	·	·	·	·
·	·	·	·	·	·	·	·
990	2.56	175	23	401	0.68359E+02	0.89844E+01	0.15664E+03
991	2.59	168	22	395	0.64865E+02	0.84942E+01	0.15251E+03
992	2.48	181	27	412	0.72984E+02	0.10887E+02	0.16613E+03
993	2.51	177	25	410	0.70518E+02	0.99602E+01	0.16335E+03
994	2.48	166	29	391	0.66935E+02	0.11694E+02	0.15766E+03
995	2.54	181	25	397	0.71260E+02	0.98425E+01	0.15630E+03
996	2.51	169	28	407	0.67331E+02	0.11155E+02	0.16215E+03
997	2.58	159	23	388	0.61628E+02	0.89147E+01	0.15039E+03
998	2.51	177	26	401	0.70518E+02	0.10359E+02	0.15976E+03
999	2.47	173	24	398	0.70040E+02	0.97166E+01	0.16113E+03
1000	2.52	183	28	403	0.72619E+02	0.11111E+02	0.15992E+03

Maximum average gamma radiation was 0.17428E+03 in interval   741

Figure 9.10
Results produced by the modified DECAY program.

SELF-TEST EXERCISES 9.1

1   Find out which are the standard input and output units for the computer that you are using, and also if any other units are preconnected.

2   If the user responds to the following program fragment by typing the nine digits 1 to 9 without any intervening characters, what will be printed? (All variables are assumed to have default type.)

```
      READ (*,101) M,N,P,Q
      PRINT 200,M,N,M-N,P,Q,P-Q
  101 FORMAT(T6,I4,TL6,I4,TL6,F4.1,TL6,F4.2)
  200 FORMAT(5X,I4,' minus',I5,' is',I5,TR4,F6.2,' minus',F6.2,
     *          ' is',F8.3)
```

3   Write formats and associated input or output statements to read or print the dimensions of a box as follows:

   (a)   Read the dimensions in metric form, where each side is less than 10 m and the data is typed in the form

   m.*cc* by *m*.*cc* by *m*.*cc*

   (b)   Read the dimensions in feet and inches, where each side is less than 30 ft and the data is typed in the form

   ff'ii" by *ff'ii"* by *ff'ii"*

   (c)   Print the dimensions and the volume of the box in the form

   a * *b* * *c* (*v* cubic feet)

9.6   Printer control characters

It has been shown how a FORMAT statement can be used to define the layout of data or results. However, when the results are being output on a printer there is one further level of control possible, namely a (limited) control of the vertical spacing of the printed output.

When a line of output is sent to the *printer* the first character of the line is removed and treated as a **printer control character**, which determines how much the paper is to be moved up before the remainder of the line is printed. There are four characters that have a particular significance in this regard, as shown in Figure 9.11. If the first character is not one of these four then the effect on the printer is undefined; in practice, however,

Character	Vertical spacing before printing
♦ (space)	one line
0 (zero)	two lines
1 (one)	first line of next page
+ (plus)	no paper advance (overprint)

Figure 9.11
Printer control
characters.

any other character will usually have the same effect as does a space – that is, printing will take place on the *next* line.

Because the first character is removed and not printed it is important to insert an extra (control) character at the start of each record that is to be output to the printer; Figure 9.12 shows what can happen if this is not done.

Because the edit descriptor in format 200 (F5.2) allowed room for only two digits before the decimal point, and format 201 allowed room for only one, the records produced were as follows:

```
♦3.00
♦4.00
12.00
0.750
```

The printer, however, needs the first character. In the first two lines this merely means that the leading space, shown as ♦, is removed, causing the correct number to be printed on the next line. The third line, however,

```
      PROGRAM DEMO
      REAL X,Y
      X=3.0
      Y=4.0
      WRITE (*,200) X
      WRITE (*,200) Y
      WRITE (*,200) X*Y
      WRITE (*,201) X/Y
      STOP
  200 FORMAT (F5.2)
  201 FORMAT (F5.3)
      END
```

Figure 9.12
An example of printer
control errors.

(output)
```
3.00
4.00
```
-------------------------------- *Page break* --------------------------------
```
2.00

.750
```

starts with a one. This is removed and the remainder of the record (2.00) is printed at the top of the *next page*, as defined by the (apparent) control character (1). A similar thing happens with the next line, where the leading zero causes double spacing (that is, a blank line before printing).

There are several ways in which a control character can be inserted at the start of a line, especially if it is a space (as is usually the case). The author always uses the H edit descriptor for this purpose, *and for no other*, so that it stands out as not being part of the format proper. The two formats shown in Figure 9.12 could be rewritten as:

```
200 FORMAT (1H ,F5.2)
201 FORMAT (1H ,F5.3)
```

Note that this applies only to the *printer*; other output devices, including those that produce printed output, such as some types of terminal, do not need a control character and will print the complete record. Note also that the PRINT statement automatically inserts a (space) control character at the start of each line if the standard output unit is the printer.

9.7   More sophisticated FORMAT statements

The foregoing has provided the means whereby a program may define formats of considerable complexity for both input and output. However, a number of other facilities are available to enable still more aspects of input and output to be defined. Probably the most important of these concern multi-record formats and the repetition of formats.

Let us consider a hypothetical program that wishes to read 12 real numbers into an array A, typed four to a line. With our present knowledge we could write:

```
    READ 100,(A(I),I=1,4)
    READ 100,(A(I),I=5,8)
    READ 100,(A(I),I=9,12)
100 FORMAT (4F12.3)
```

However, consider what would happen if we wrote

```
    READ 100,A
100 FORMAT (4F12.3)
```

After the READ statement has used the FORMAT to input four real numbers (which are placed in the first four elements of A) it finds that the input list is not yet exhausted, and that another real number is required. The format *is* completed, however, and it follows that this input record contains no more useful information. There is only one sensible thing to do at this stage – read a new record and interpret its contents using the same FORMAT. This is exactly what happens.

Whenever a FORMAT is fully used up and there are still items in the input (or output) list awaiting processing, the FORMAT will be repeated. The rules governing the point from which it will be repeated are quite straightforward:

- If there are no nested parentheses then the format is repeated from the beginning.
- If the format contains any nested parentheses then it is repeated from the left parenthesis corresponding to the rightmost nested parenthesis.
- If the left parenthesis defined above is preceded by a repeat count then the format is repeated including the repeat count.

The following examples should make this clear; an arrow (↑) is shown below the point from which repetition (if any) will take place.

```
1 FORMAT (I6,10X,I5,3F10.2)
         ↑

2 FORMAT (I6,10X,I5,(3F10.2))
                    ↑

3 FORMAT (I6,(10X,I5),3F10.2)
             ↑

4 FORMAT (F6.2,(2F4.1,2X,I4,4(I7,F7.2)))
               ↑

5 FORMAT (F6.2,2(2F4.1,2X,I4),4(I7,F7.2))
                              ↑

6 FORMAT (F6.2,(2(2F4.2,2X,I4),4(I7,F7.2)))
               ↑

7 FORMAT ((F6.2,2(2F4.2,2X,I4),4(I7,F7.2)))
          ↑
```

The repetition of a format can be extremely useful; however, in many cases it is desirable to be able to define a format that consists of two or more separate lines, or (more accurately) **records**. This is achieved by the / **edit descriptor** (which need not be separated from any preceding or succeeding descriptor by a comma). This indicates the end of the current record.

On input a / causes the rest of the current record to be ignored and the next input item to be the first item of the *next* record. On output a / terminates the current record and starts a new one. Thus the statements

```
      READ (1,101) A,B,C,I,J,K
  101 FORMAT (2F10.2,F12.3/I6,2I10)
```

will read three real numbers from the first record and three integers from a second. Similarly, the statements

```
      WRITE (2,201) A,B,A+B,A*B
  201 FORMAT (1H1,T10,'Multi-record example'/
     *         1H0,'The sum of',F5.2,' and',F5.2,' is',F6.2/
     *         1H ,'Their product is',F8.2)
```

will cause a title to be placed at the top of a new page, the sum of A and B to be printed after leaving a blank line, and their product to be printed on the next line.

Several / descriptors in succession cause several input records to be skipped or several null (blank) records to be output. Thus

```
      READ (1,102) A,B,C,I,J,K
  102 FORMAT (2F10.2,F12.3//I6,2I10)
```

will cause the real numbers to be read from the *first* record and the integers from the *third*. The second record will be skipped and not read.

Multiple / descriptors are particularly useful on output, as we can see below:

```
      WRITE (2,202) A,B,A+B,A*B
  202 FORMAT (1H1////T10,'Multi-record example'///
     *         1H ,'The sum of',F5.2,' and',F5.2,' is',F6.2//
     *         1H ,'Their product is',F8.2////)
```

This will print four blank lines at the top of a new page before the title, two blank lines before the first line of results, a further blank line before the second, and three blank lines after the last line (thus separating it from any results printed later in the program).

Finally, it should be pointed out that the combination of a / edit descriptor and a repeated format can provide a very high degree of flexibility; thus the following format:

```
  110 FORMAT (I6/(I4,3F12.2))
```

specifies that the first record consists of a single integer and the following ones of an integer followed by three real numbers, since the format will be repeated as many times as necessary from the left parenthesis before the I4 descriptor.

9.8   Embedded formats

A format has been considered thus far as a *footnote*, appearing in a labelled FORMAT statement that is referenced as and when required by an input or output statement. This is normally the most convenient method, since the format defines the layout (or format) of the data or results on some external medium. It may then be referred to, if necessary, by READ or WRITE statements in several places in a program.

Sometimes, however, a format is referred to only once, and it may seem more appropriate to include the format with the input/output statement. This is called an **embedded format**, and may be constant or may vary. Chapter 12 discusses the handling of variable character data, and Section 12.6 describes how a variable format may be created and embedded in an input or output statement. Only constant formats will therefore be considered at this stage.

In any READ, WRITE or PRINT statement we may include an embedded format by replacing the FORMAT label in that statement with a character constant that consists of a **format specification** (as used in a FORMAT statement after the word FORMAT). The format specification therefore begins with a left parenthesis and ends with a right parenthesis, and we may write

```
      READ (1,'(2F8.6,I3)') X,Y,N
```

as an alternative to

```
      READ (1,123) X,Y,N
  123 FORMAT (2F8.6,I3)
```

Naturally all the variations that have already been discussed are also allowed, for example:

```
      READ (FMT='(2F8.6,I3)',UNIT=*) X,Y,N
      READ '(2F8.6,I3)',X,Y,N
```

One important point to note here concerns a format that contains an apostrophe edit descriptor; for example:

```
  201 FORMAT (1H1,'Results of primary analysis'////)
```

Since the apostrophe edit descriptor takes the form of a character constant it cannot be included directly within another character constant because the multiple apostrophes would create errors. *Remember that an apostrophe is included within a character constant by representing it by two consecutive apostrophes.* If the above format were to be embedded in a WRITE statement it would, therefore, take the following form:

```
      WRITE (2,'(1H1,''Results of primary analysis''////)')
```

Figure 9.13
Embedded formats
containing apostrophes.

Title required: Dumkopf's results

(a) FORMAT statement: `WRITE (2,200)`
                        `200 FORMAT (1H1,'Dumkopf''s results')`

(b) Embedded format: `WRITE (2,'(1H1,''Dumkopf''''s results'')')`

An even worse case is where the title itself includes an apostrophe, as shown in Figure 9.13. It can be seen that the apostrophe in the title is represented by no less than four consecutive apostrophes!

SUMMARY

- A unit number is used to identify a particular input or output unit.

- Every Fortran 77 implementation has preconnected standard input and output units.

- List-directed READ and PRINT statements use the standard input and output units.

- Extended READ and WRITE statements use a control information list to define units, formats and exception action.

- FORMAT statements define the layout of data or results.

- A format may be embedded in an input or output statement.

- A printer control character is required to control vertical paper movement for output to the printer.

- Fortran 77 statements introduced in Chapter 9:

Input and output statements	READ *, *input list*
	READ *label*, *input list*
	READ *format*, *input list*
	READ (*control information list*) *input list*
	PRINT *, *input list*
	PRINT *label*, *input list*
	PRINT *format*, *input list*
	WRITE (*control information list*) *input list*
FORMAT statement	FORMAT(*list of edit descriptors*)
Embedded format	'(*list of edit descriptors*)'

SELF-TEST EXERCISES 9.2

1   Find out what peripheral device, if any, your computer system treats as the printer for the purpose of interpreting printer control characters.

2   Write a FORMAT statement that can be used with a single WRITE statement to produce the following heading (where the items in italic are variable information):

```
         ANNUAL REPORT OF HACKIT & DEBUG INC.

            Year ending 15th March 1990


     Total income from sales           $    972.46
     Total income from fraud           $3174000.00

     Total income for year             $3174972.46


     Software development expenses      $  45375.00
     Software purchase costs            $     99.95
     Lawyer's fee                       $ 250000.00
     Fines imposed by various courts    $2500000.00

     Total expenses for year            $2795474.95

     NETT OPERATING PROFIT FOR YEAR     $ 379497.51
```

3   What will be printed by the following statements?

```
    I = 4
    J = 9
    X = 4.0/9.0
    PI = 3.14159
    WRITE (*,200) I,J,I*J,X,PI,I,PI*I*I
200 FORMAT (5X,'I has the value',I4/5X,'J has the value,I4/
   *        5X,'Their product is',I3//
   *        5X,'I divided by J is',F7.4//
   *        T10,'The value of pi is ',F7.4/T10,'and the area'
   *        ' of a circle of radius',I2,' is',F8.4)
```

4   **(a)** What will be printed by the following statements if unit 2 is not a printer?

```
        .
        .
    REAL X(50)
        .
        .
```

```
      DO 10, I=1,50
        X(I)=I/9.0
  10    CONTINUE
      WRITE (2,'(1H ,3F6.2,/F7.3,2(F7.3,2F4.1))'), (X(I),I=1,25)
```

(b) What is printed if unit 2 is a printer?

PROGRAMMING EXERCISES

9.1   Find out the standard input and output units for the computer
that you are using. Also find out if any other units are preconnected. If
In represents the standard input unit, and *Out* represents the standard
output unit find out what happens if you refer to * and either *In* or *Out*
in the same program.

   When you have established the answers to the questions run the
following programs to see if they behave as you expect.

(a)
```
      PROGRAM UTEST1
      INTEGER IN,OUT,Num1,Num2
C  In and Out should be replaced by the appropriate unit numbers
C  for the computer you are using
      PARAMETER (IN=In, OUT=Out)
      WRITE (*,*) 'Please type a 4 digit integer '
      READ (*,*) Num1
      WRITE (OUT,*) 'Please type a 3 digit integer '
      READ (IN,*) Num2
      WRITE (OUT,*) 'The numbers you typed were as follows'
      PRINT 10,Num1,Num2
  10 FORMAT (1H ,I4,' and',I4)
      STOP
      END
```

(b)
```
      PROGRAM UTEST2
      INTEGER IN,OUT,Num1,Num2
C  In and Out should be replaced by the appropriate unit numbers
C  for the computer you are using
      PARAMETER (IN=In, OUT=Out)
      WRITE (OUT,*) 'Please type a 4 digit integer '
      READ (IN,*) Num1
      WRITE (*,*) 'Please type a 3 digit integer '
      READ (*,*) Num2
      PRINT *,'The numbers you typed were as follows'
      WRITE (OUT,10) Num1,Num2
  10 FORMAT (1H ,I4,' and',I4)
      STOP
      END
```

9.2   The actual implementation of printer control characters, especially
+ (to produce output on the same line as the previous record) and 1 (to

start a new page) can vary – especially when the output device is a display screen. Run the following program to establish what happens on your computer system.

```
      PROGRAM PTEST
C  This program tests the effect of printer control characters
      INTEGER DSPLAY,PRNTER,N
C  Display should be replaced by the unit number of the display
C  on your computer, and Printer by the unit number of the
C  printer (if one is available).
      PARAMETER (DSPLAY=Display, PRNTER=Printer)
      WRITE (DSPLAY,100)
      WRITE (PRNTER,100)
  100 FORMAT (1H1,'This line should be at the top of a new page'/
     *        1H ,'This should be on the next line'/
     *        1H0,'This line should be after a blank line'/
     *        1H ,'This line should be'/
     *        1H+,'                 on the next line'/
     *        1H0,23X,'after a blank line'/
     *        1H+,'And this one should be')
C  Wait until you have checked the output to the display
      WRITE (DSPLAY,*) 'Check the display and then type an integer'
      READ *,N
C  Repeat, especially to see what happens to the display
      WRITE (DSPLAY,100)
      WRITE (PRNTER,100)
      STOP
      END
```

*9.3   Write a program to display a 'multiplication square'. The numbers 1–12 should run across the top of the table and down the side, with the entries holding the relevant product. Thus the first few lines would be:

		1	2	3	4	5	6	7	8	9	10	11	12
X													
1		1	2	3	4	5	6	7	8	9	10	11	12
2		2	4	6	8	10	12	14	16	18	20	22	24
3		3	6	9	12	.	.	.					

9.4   Write a program that will input a date and convert it to the number of days since 1st January 1900.

9.5   Obtain a printed 4-figure logarithm table. Write a program to print a similar table.

9.6   Write a program that finds the positive difference between two 3-digit integer numbers and produces the result of the calculation in the form:

```
The positive difference between n1 and n2 is n3
```

Use formatted read and print statements in your program.

9.7 Write a program that inputs today's date and will print out the next day's date.

9.8 Write a program that allows the user to convert a monetary value in dollars, pounds, francs or marks into its equivalent in any of the other currencies. Assume exchange rates of £1 = \$1.62 = 10.1 francs = 3.02 marks.

9.9 Store twelve 5-digit telephone numbers in an array. Purely by changing the output format, print the numbers as

(a) a single column of numbers;
(b) four rows of three numbers;
(c) a single line of numbers.

*9.10 In Exercise 5.10 you were asked to produce a table of cricket statistics. Using only list-directed output your table will not have been as well laid-out as you might have wished. Modify your program (or write a new one) so that the format of the table is exactly as shown below (where ♦ represents a single space)

```
    Player♦♦Innings♦♦Not♦Out♦♦♦Highest♦♦♦Total♦♦♦♦♦Average
                               Score       Runs

♦♦♦n♦♦♦♦♦♦♦♦nn♦♦♦♦♦♦♦♦nn♦♦♦♦♦♦♦♦nnn♦♦♦♦♦nnnn♦♦♦♦♦nnn.dd
    n          nn          nn          nnn       nnnn      nnn.dd
    .           .           .           .          .         .
    .           .           .           .          .         .
    .           .           .           .          .         .
```

9.11 Write a program to print a bank statement. The user should be asked for the opening balance and the amount of each of a number of transactions, which may be debits or credits. Once all transactions have been entered, the program should calculate the final balance and generate a printout of the form:

```
Opening balance:  123.45
Transactions:
Debit   Credit     Total
1.23               122.22
5.00               117.22
        25.00      142.22

Closing balance:  142.22
```

Is the REAL data type suitable for such financial calculations?

9.12 The expression

$$\sin A \sin B - \frac{(\cos(A - B) - \cos(A + B))}{2}$$

should be zero for all values of A and B. Write a program that will produce a square table showing the calculated values of the function for values of A and B between 0 and 3 in steps of 0.25.

9.13 A railway timetable has to be produced in the following form:

Station no.	Arrival	Departure
1	–	1.20
2	2.05	2.15
3	2.35	2.45
4	3.20	3.30
5	3.40	–

Write a program that prints out the timetable on the screen as given above.

9.14 Angles are often expressed in degrees, minutes and seconds, where there are 360 degrees in a full circle, 60 minutes in a degree, and 60 seconds in a minute. Write a program that reads an angle as three integer values, representing the degrees, minutes and seconds, and then computes its value as a decimal number of degrees, and also its value in radians (where there are 2π radians in a circle, and π may be taken as 3.141 592 36). The program should display the angle in all three forms, using four decimal places for the value in decimal degrees, and an appropriate number of decimal places for the value in radians.

9.15 A chemist makes five measurements of the rates of three different reactions. The data collected is shown below:

Reaction A	Reaction B	Reaction C
20.6	16.9	90.6
31.2	20.2	100.2
10.9	30.7	98.7
15.4	30.2	117.2
12.1	30.0	88.6

Write a program that calculates the mean rate and standard deviation for each reaction. The standard deviation is given by the formula

$$\sigma = \sqrt{\sum_i (x_i - \mu)^2}$$

where μ is the mean and x_i is the ith measurement for each reaction. Use formatted output to reproduce a table consisting of three columns for the experimental data followed by the mean and standard deviation for each reaction.

9.16   Following an earthquake it is required to print out the seismic measurements recorded at a number of different centres around the world. Write a program that reads several sets of data from the keyboard, each consisting of the longitude and latitude of the recording instrument (as two pairs of integer numbers) and the strength measured on the Richter scale (as a real number).

Latitudes to the west of the Greenwich meridian are recorded as negative values (for example, 23°48′ W is recorded as −23,48), and those to the east as positive values. Similarly, longitudes north of the equator are recorded as positive, and those to the south as negative.

Your program should print the measurements as a table in the following form:

```
Seismic measurements recorded after Milesville earthquake
◆◆◆◆◆Recording Station◆◆◆◆◆◆◆◆◆◆◆◆Richter
◆◆◆◆◆Longitude◆◆◆◆◆Latitude◆◆◆◆◆Strength
◆◆◆◆◆◆◆nn°nn'◆N◆◆◆◆nnn°nn'◆W◆◆◆◆◆◆◆◆nn.nn
       nn°nn' S    nnn°nn' E        nn.nn
         .           .                .
         .           .                .
```

Keeping data in files

10

One of the most important aspects of computing is a program's ability to save the data that it has been using for subsequent use, either by itself or by another program. This involves the output of the data to a **file**, usually on some magnetic medium, for input at some later time.

Data is output to, and input from, a file by use of the same READ and WRITE statements that are used for simple input and output, but using an input/output unit that is **connected** to a specified file. The data in a file may be converted from its internal representation to a form similar to that used on a screen or printer, known as **formatted** data, or it may be left in its internal representation as **unformatted** data. In either case, the data within a file is split up into a number of **records** of a predefined size.

Formatted files are normally used for data that is to be transferred to another computer; unformatted files are normally used for data that is to be read by a program running on the same computer or an identical one elsewhere.

10.1   Files and records

The input/output facilities met so far will allow us to carry out many of the things that we are likely to want to do, with one major exception. All our programming to date has been based on the assumption that when the program is run it reads some data from the keyboard (or other standard input unit), processes it, produces some results that are displayed on the screen or sent to a printer, and finishes. Once the program has finished nothing is left within the computer system. This ignores two very important situations.

The first arises when there are more than a few lines of data: it is usually far more appropriate to type the data into a **file**, possibly using the same editor that is used to type and edit the program, and for the program then to read the data directly from the file. Similarly, where there are more than a few lines of results to be displayed it is often more convenient to send them to a file that can subsequently be displayed in sections or sent to a printer, as appropriate.

The second situation is a related one, in which results produced by one program are required as data for another program or another run of the same program. Examples of this type of application range from data processing activities such as payroll calculation or financial accounting, where past records are essential, to analysis of scientific experiments over a period of time, control of airline reservations, scheduling of production, or any other activity that requires knowledge of some past events of the same or similar type.

The backing store or **file store** of the computer system is used for this purpose. This consists of special input/output units, usually, though not always, based on magnetic tape and/or rapidly rotating magnetic disks. Information may be transferred to and from these units by using READ and WRITE statements in a manner similar to that of data and results transferred via the standard input and output units. However, before this is examined in more detail, two important concepts must be defined: a **record** and a **file**.

Records have been referred to informally, when discussing input and output, to refer to a sequence of characters such as a line of typing or a printed line of results. However, a record does not necessarily correspond in this way to some physical entity: it refers to some defined sequence of characters *or of values*. There are three types of record in Fortran 77 – formatted, unformatted and endfile records – and these will be discussed in some detail in the next two sections.

A sequence of records forms a **file** of which there are two types – internal files (see Section 17.4) and external files.

An **external file** is an identifiable sequence of records that is stored on some external medium. Thus a sheet of printed results is a file.

Regardless of this strict definition, however, when we refer to a file we normally mean one that is kept on backing store. There are two main types of backing store (magnetic tape and magnetic disk) and they have one very important difference.

A magnetic tape is essentially a **sequential** storage medium: each record on such a tape will normally be written immediately following the previously written record. The normal way of reading the records is in the order in which they were written. A typical magnetic tape is over 2000 ft long (or almost 0.75 km) and may contain as many as 50 million characters or their equivalent. It would be extremely time-consuming to search for individual records in a random order. A magnetic disk, on the other hand, not only contains a considerably larger amount of information (perhaps as many as 500 million characters) but can access any of it in a fraction of a second since, at worst, the read head needs to travel only a few inches to position itself on the required part of the disk. Such a storage unit can therefore be used for **direct access** of information, as well as sequential access. Because the information anywhere on a magnetic disk (or other similar device) can be accessed so rapidly, and because a disk can hold so much information, a single disk will usually store a large number of separate files of information, frequently belonging to a number of different users of the computer. It is the job of the computer's operating system to keep a catalogue of all the files so that they can be made available to a program when required.

Because of the problems of sequential access, a magnetic tape often consists of a single file, but the computer's operating system will catalogue this so that a record is kept of which file is stored on which tape. Thus the operating system will, usually, be able to request that the appropriate tape be loaded whenever a program wishes to use a file stored on that tape.

For most purposes the differences between the various types of backing store unit may be ignored and only their mode of access (sequential or direct) considered. However, before we start to use either type of file the three types of record that may make up a file must be investigated in more detail.

10.2 Formatted and unformatted records

The first type is called a **formatted record**. It consists of a sequence of characters selected from those that can be represented by the processor being used – that is, the 49 characters in the Fortran character set plus any other special characters that may be permitted. A formatted record is written by the same type of formatted output statement introduced in Chapter 9:

```
    WRITE (3,200) A,B,N,M
```

or by an output statement that uses list-directed formatting:

```
    WRITE (4,*) P,Q,X,Y
```

It may also be created by some means other than a Fortran program; for example, it may be typed at a keyboard.

A formatted record is read by a formatted input statement, including one that uses list-directed formatting.

An aspect of input or output records with which we have not concerned ourselves until now is their *length*. This is important in some situations, especially when using direct-access files (see Section 17.5), and for a formatted record is measured in characters. Thus if the first statement above has an associated format

```
 200 FORMAT (2F10.3,2I6)
```

then the length of the record(s) produced will be 32 characters.

The second, list-directed, output statement is more awkward, since an understanding of the formats used (which may depend upon the size of the numbers and/or strings) is necessary before the length of the record produced can be determined. However, list-directed formatting will not normally be used in situations where the length of the record(s) needs to be known. The length of a record may also depend upon the processor and the external medium (for example, consider what happens with printer control characters when output is sent to the printer) and may be zero in some circumstances.

A formatted record is formatted so that it can be represented in a form that human beings (or another different type of computer) can understand. The work involved in converting values from their internal (binary) representation into character form, or vice versa, imposes a considerable overhead. If the information is being written to a file so that the same program, or another one on the same computer, can subsequently read it back there is clearly no need to convert it to character form. (Indeed, where real numbers are concerned, the process of converting to character form and then converting back to internal form will probably introduce errors, owing to the difference in precision of the internal and character representations.) For this purpose there exists in Fortran 77 a second type of record – an **unformatted record**.

An unformatted record consists of a sequence of values (in a processor-dependent form) and is, essentially, a copy of some part, or parts, of the memory. An unformatted record can be produced only by an unformatted output statement, which is the same as a formatted WRITE statement but without any format specifier:

```
WRITE (6) A,B,N,M
WRITE (UNIT=5,ERR=99) X,Y,Z
```

Similarly, an unformatted record can be read only by an unformatted input statement:

```
READ (6) A,B,N,M
READ (UNIT=5,END=98,ERR=99) X,Y,Z
```

The length of an unformatted record is measured in computer-dependent terms, and will depend primarily upon the output list used when it was written. The two most common units of measurement are **bytes** and **words** (see Appendix D for a definition of these). It is essential that, where the length is important, the programmer is aware of the units used on his computer, and of the relationship between these units and the various types of information. For example, a computer system that uses bytes as a unit of measurement will typically use one byte for a character storage unit and four bytes for a numeric storage unit, whereas one that uses words as a unit of measurement might use one word for a character storage unit and two for a numeric one, or even one word for both types of storage unit.

One important difference between the input/output of formatted records and that of unformatted ones is that, whereas a formatted input or output statement may read or write more than one record by use of a suitable format, such as

```
   WRITE (5,500) N,M,(A(I),I=1,100)
500 FORMAT (2I8/(4F12.4))
```

an unformatted input or output statement will always read or write exactly *one* record. The length of the input list in an unformatted READ statement must therefore be the same length as the output list that wrote it, or less (in which case the last few items will remain unread).

10.3   Endfile records

As well as formatted and unformatted records there is a third type of record, which is particularly important for files that are to be accessed sequentially; this is the **endfile record**. It can occur only as the last record of a file and is written by a special statement:

Figure 10.1
Specifiers for use with
ENDFILE.

```
UNIT   = u     (or u)
ERR    = s
IOSTAT = ios
```

ENDFILE u

or

ENDFILE($auxlist$)

In the first case u is the unit number to which an endfile record is to be written, while in the second case $auxlist$ may contain any of the specifiers shown in Figure 10.1, which are the same as the corresponding specifiers already introduced for use with a WRITE statement.

The ENDFILE statement writes a special endfile record to the specified file and leaves the file positioned after that record. It is not possible to write to, or read from, that file subsequently without first repositioning it, using a REWIND or BACKSPACE statement (see Section 10.5).

An endfile record has no defined length, but if it is read by an input statement it will cause an **end-of-file condition** that can be detected by an END or IOSTAT specifier in a READ statement. If it is not specifically detected in this way an error will occur and the program will fail.

It is good practice to place an endfile record at the end of all sequential files. In this way a program that subsequently reads the file can detect the end of the file very easily without the need for any other special records or counts. It also acts as a safeguard against an error that might cause the program not to detect the end of the information in the file.

10.4   Connecting an external file to your program

There is one further important difference between input/output using files and the input/output that we have been concerned with up to now, and that concerns the identification of the input/output unit that is to be used. Before any input/output unit can be used it has to be **connected** to the program, although certain peripheral units (such as the standard input unit and the standard output unit) will always be **preconnected**. How to connect a particular file to our program and the implications of this process will now be examined.

Every computer system normally has a very large number of files that in some sense *belong* to that computer. Some, such as a printer listing, do not belong to it for very long, while others, such as files on backing

```
UNIT    = u      (or u)
FILE    = fn
STATUS  = st
ACCESS  = acc
FORM    = fm
ERR     = s
IOSTAT  = ios
```

Figure 10.2
Some of the specifiers
for use with OPEN.

store, may belong to it for a considerable period. These files have been
created by the various users of the computer, or by those who are
responsible for its operation, or even by the computer's own operating
system, and have various levels of accessibility. For example, a file
containing a library of widely used subroutines, or a Fortran 77 compiler,
will probably be available to all users of the computer; a file created by a
user to contain his own private research data, on the other hand, will
almost certainly be accessible only by the user. At any given time,
therefore, a particular program will be allowed to access only a certain
number of the files held by the computer; only these files are said to **exist**
for that program.

Before a file can exist it must be **created**. Notice that this does not
necessarily have any effect on the total number of files known to the whole
computer system – the act of creating a file simply means that the file exists
for the program that creates it. For example, a program may wish to access
a file belonging to another user; the act of creating the file in this case
merely means granting access to it, whereupon it will exist for this
program. In a similar way, **deleting** a file means terminating its existence; it
does not *necessarily* mean that the file is removed from the computer
system. One effect of this is that a file may exist and yet not contain any
records – for example, when it has just been created but not yet written to.

For any information to be transferred between a file and a program
the file must be connected to a unit; in other words, a logical connection (or
relationship) must be established between the file and a unit number (as
used in a READ or WRITE statement). In some cases a physical connection
must also be established (for example, a particular magnetic tape must be
loaded on a tape deck, or a floppy disk loaded into a personal computer).
Some units will be preconnected to a program, but all others must be
specifically connected, before being used, by means of an OPEN statement.
This takes the form

OPEN (*olist*)

where *olist* is a list of **open specifiers**, as shown in Figure 10.2. The first of
these, UNIT, must be present, while the others are all optional.

The UNIT specifier takes the same form as in the READ, WRITE and ENDFILE statements and, as in those cases, 'UNIT=' may be omitted if this is the first specifier.

If we are concerned with files on backing store they will normally have a name by which they are known to the computer system. This name is specified by the FILE specifier,

FILE=*fn*

where *fn* is a **character expression** that, after the removal of any trailing blanks, takes the form of a file name for the particular computer system. Use of character variables has not yet been discussed and so for the present we shall consider this in its simplest form, namely a constant character string. Thus if a file name is MILES–ELLIS, we could connect the file of that name to our program with the following statement:

OPEN (9,FILE='MILES–ELLIS')

This will connect unit 9 to the specified file, and thereafter any input or output using unit 9 will read from or write to that file.

We sometimes wish to define certain restrictions on our use of the file; for example we may wish to ensure that we do not overwrite an existing file by accident. We may use the STATUS specifier for this purpose by writing

STATUS=*st*

where *st*, after removing any trailing blanks, is either OLD, NEW, SCRATCH or UNKNOWN. Note that *st* is a character *expression* or *string* and therefore we actually write

STATUS='OLD'
STATUS='NEW'

and so on.

If *st* is OLD then the file *must already exist*, whereas if it is NEW then it *must not already exist*. If a file whose status is specified as NEW is successfully opened, its status is changed to OLD and any subsequent attempt to OPEN the file as NEW will fail.

If *st* is SCRATCH then a special unnamed file is created for use by the program; when the program ceases execution the file will be deleted and will cease to exist. Such a file can therefore be used as a temporary file for the duration of execution only. It is not permitted, for obvious reasons, to specify that the status of a named file (that is, one with a FILE specifier) is SCRATCH.

Finally, if *st* is UNKNOWN, or if no STATUS specifier is included, the status of the file is dependent upon the particular implementation. In most cases if the file exists it will be treated as OLD, if it does not exist it will be treated as NEW. Some implementations have different UNKNOWN conditions and so no assumptions should be made without checking on the exact situation for the computer being used.

The next two specifiers define what type of file we require, in terms of its mode of access and whether or not it is formatted. The first of these

```
ACCESS=acc
```

specifies the mode of access that is to be used; ignoring any trailing blanks, *acc* is either of the character expressions, or strings, SEQUENTIAL or DIRECT. If this specifier is omitted, SEQUENTIAL is assumed; in general, therefore, an ACCESS specifier is used only to define DIRECT access. Direct-access input/output will be examined in Chapter 17, but until then we can ignore the ACCESS specifier.

Because of the different ways in which they are written and read, the records in a file must either all be formatted or all be unformatted, and the specifier

```
FORM=fm
```

is used to specify which is required. The character expression *fm* must take one of the two values FORMATTED or UNFORMATTED, after the removal of any trailing blanks. If this specifier is omitted then the file is assumed to be formatted if it is connected for sequential access, but unformatted if it is connected for direct access. Thus

```
OPEN (9,FILE='DATAFILE')
```

will connect the file DATAFILE to unit 9 as a formatted, sequential access file. On the other hand

```
OPEN (7,STATUS='SCRATCH',FORM='UNFORMATTED')
```

will create a temporary scratch file and connect it to unit 7 as an unformatted, sequential access file.

The last two specifiers are concerned with recognizing when an error occurs during the connection process (for example, if the named file does not exist or is of the wrong type). In the event of an error the execution of the program will be terminated unless either an ERR or IOSTAT specifier is present (or both); these are similar in effect to those used with READ, WRITE and ENDFILE. If the specifier

```
ERR=s
```

Figure 10.3
Specifiers for use with
CLOSE.

```
UNIT   = u      (or u)
STATUS = st
ERR    = s
IOSTAT = ios
```

is present and an error occurs, processing will continue from the statement with label *s*. The IOSTAT specifier is discussed in Chapter 17.

In certain circumstances it is permitted to obey an OPEN statement that refers to a unit already connected to a file. There are essentially three cases, although only one will be mentioned here; the other two will be discussed in Chapter 17 when the remaining, more sophisticated, aspects of Fortran file-handling are examined. The one situation that is relevant now is where the file in the OPEN statement is not the same as that currently connected to the specified unit. In this case the currently connected file is disconnected (see the description of CLOSE below) and the specified new file is connected.

It is never permitted to attempt to connect a unit to a file if that file is already connected to a different unit.

Sometimes it is useful to be able to **disconnect** a file, even though this will be done automatically when the program's execution is finished. This can be achieved by use of the statement

```
CLOSE (auxlist)
```

where *auxlist* is a list of one or more of the specifiers shown in Figure 10.3.

There *must* be a UNIT specifier, and the ERR and IOSTAT specifiers take the usual form. The STATUS specifier, however, is used to define what is to happen to the file after it has been disconnected. If the character expression *st* has the value KEEP, after the removal of any trailing blanks, then the file will continue to exist; however, if it has the value DELETE, the file will cease to exist and cannot be accessed again by the program. If no STATUS specifier is given then KEEP is assumed, unless the file was opened with a STATUS='SCRATCH' specifier, in which case DELETE is assumed.

10.5   File positioning statements

As well as opening and closing a file, writing records to it or reading records from it, there are two further statements that enable us to *position*

UNIT = *u* (or *u*)	**Figure 10.4**
ERR = *s*	Specifiers for use with
IOSTAT = *ios*	BACKSPACE and REWIND.

the file. The first of these takes the form

        BACKSPACE *u*

or

        BACKSPACE (*auxlist*)

It causes the file to be positioned just before the *preceding* record (that is, it enables the program to read the last record again). *auxlist* is a list of UNIT, ERR or IOSTAT specifiers, as shown in Figure 10.4.

The other file positioning statement is

        REWIND *u*

or

        REWIND (*auxlist*)

which causes the file to be positioned just before the *first* record so that a subsequent input statement will start reading the file from the beginning.

These two statements are particularly important when dealing with endfile records, because if a program has read or written an endfile record it cannot read or write any more records until a BACKSPACE or REWIND statement has positioned the file before the endfile record (Section 10.3).

One further important point about the positioning of a file particularly concerns the writing of information to a file in a sequential manner. The rule in Fortran is that *writing a record to a sequential file destroys all information in the file after that record*. This is, in part, a reminder of the days when all sequential files were on magnetic tape and the physical characteristics of a magnetic tape unit had exactly this effect.

Thus it is not possible to use BACKSPACE and/or REWIND to position a file so that a particular record can be overwritten by a new one, but only so that the rest of the file can be overwritten or a particular record or records can be read. (Selective overwriting of individual records is possible with direct access files – see Section 17.5).

A common use of BACKSPACE in conjunction with ENDFILE is to add information at the end of a previously written file; for example:

```
             .
             .
             .
  C   Read up to end-of-file
     20 READ (8,END=21)
           GOTO 20
     21 BACKSPACE 8
  C   Now add new information
           WRITE (8) ...
             .
             .
             .
  C   Terminate file with an end-of-file ready for next time
           ENDFILE 8
             .
             .
             .
```

EXAMPLE 10.1

A survey has been carried out to obtain statistics concerning the occupation of people in a certain area. The results of the survey are available for input to the computer in the following format:

Columns 1–20	Name
Column 23	Sex = 0 if female
	= 1 if male
Column 25	Job status = 1 if in full-time education
	= 2 if in full-time employment
	= 3 if in part-time employment
	= 4 if temporarily unemployed
	= 5 if not working or seeking a job

This is followed by one or more items, depending on the job status of the respondent:

Job status = 1 columns 28,29 Age

= 2 columns 28–31 Monthly salary (£)

= 3 columns 28–31 Monthly salary (£)
columns 34–37 Other monthly income (£)

= 4 columns 28,29 Age
columns 32–34 No. of months unemployed

= 5 columns 28,29 Age
column 31   Code
= 1 if looking after children
= 2 if looking after other relatives
= 3 for any other reason

The data is terminated by a record that is blank apart from a 9 in column 23 (sex).

Write a program to read the data and print the percentage of each sex in full-time education who are 18 or over, the average length of unemployment for those under 18 and those over 45, and the percentage of men who are not in full-time education who stay at home to look after the children.

The major problem here is the variable format of the data. We shall see in Chapter 17, how an 'internal' file can be used to simplify this, but we can tackle it with what we know by reading parts of the record more than once. On examining the data format in detail we see that there are two possibilities:

(1)   columns 28,29 age
        column 31   blank or a special code
        columns 32–34 blank or the number of months unemployed
(2)   columns 28–31 monthly salary
        columns 34–37 other monthly income or blank

Since all these items are integer quantities it will be easy to define a format to convert the data into these values and then use the job status code to determine which are meaningful. We cannot wait until we have read the job status code and then read the rest of the record because that would start a new record! A suitable format specification is

```
(T23,I1,1X,I1,2X,I2,1X,I1,I3,T28,I4,2X,I4)
```

One final decision needs to be made. The problem, as specified, can be solved without the need to store all the data. However, in principle it is better to design the program in a way that will make it easy to extend it at a later date if necessary. We shall write our program, therefore, with a separate input procedure that will store the data in a series of arrays for subsequent analysis. Since none of the data will be negative, we can set the unused elements to a negative value, which can easily be distinguished from the actual data.

We can now write a structure plan.

1   Initialize totals
2   Read the data – INPUT

> **3** Repeat *n* times (where *n* is the number of data sets)
>   **3.1** If job=education then
>   **3.1.1** Increment total (male or female)
>   **3.1.2** If age≥18 then increment 'old total' (male or female) otherwise
>   **3.1.3** If sex=male then
>   **3.1.3.1** Increment males not in full-time education
>   **3.1.3.2** If job=looking after children then
>   **3.1.3.2.1** Increment no. of full-time fathers
>   **3.1.4** If job=unemployed then
>   **3.1.4.1** If age<18 then
>   **3.1.4.1.1** Update unemployment nos. and times
>   **3.1.4.2** If age>45 then
>   **3.1.4.2.1** Update unemployment nos. and times
>
> **4** Calculate and print averages and percentages

Notice the logic in step 3.1. First we see if the person is in full-time education: if so, we increment appropriate totals. If the person is not in full-time education there are two possibilities in which we are interested: however, these are not exclusive and so they will form nested IF blocks, not a single one.

> INPUT(SEX(N),STATUS(N),AGE(N),CODE(N),PERIOD(N),
>   MONSAL(N),MONINC(N),N,PEOPLE)
>
> **1** Repeat up to N times
>   **1.1** Read next record
>   **1.2** If SEX(I) is 9 then exit from input loop
>   **1.3** If STATUS(I) is 2 or 3 then set AGE(I) negative
>   **1.4** If STATUS(I) is 1, 2, 3 or 4 then set CODE(I) negative
>   **1.5** If STATUS(I) is 1, 2, 3 or 5 then set PERIOD(I) negative
>   **1.6** If STATUS(I) is 1, 4 or 5 then set MONSAL(I) negative
>   **1.7** If STATUS(I) is 1, 2, 4 or 5 then set MONINC(I) negative
>
> **2** Return number of data sets read in PEOPLE

We can write the program from this structure plan quite easily:

```
      PROGRAM JOBS
C
C  This program produces various statistics about employment
```

```
C
C  Up to MAXDAT data records are processed
C
C  Each record contains some of the following information about
C  respondents to a survey:
C  Sex, age, job status code, monthly salary, other monthly income,
C  how long unemployed, other information code
C
C  MAXDAT is the maximum number of data records that can be processed
       INTEGER MAXDAT
       PARAMETER (MAXDAT=1000)
C  Input data variables
       INTEGER SEX(MAXDAT),STATUS(MAXDAT),AGE(MAXDAT),CODE(MAXDAT),
      *         PERIOD(MAXDAT),MONSAL(MAXDAT),MONINC(MAXDAT)
C  Data codings
       INTEGER FEMALE,MALE,FULLED,FULLJB,PARTJB,JOBLES,ATHOME,
      *         CHILD,RELTIV,OTHER,UNUSED
       PARAMETER (FEMALE=0,MALE=1,FULLED=1,FULLJB=2,PARTJB=3,JOBLES=4,
      *            ATHOME=5,CHILD=1,RELTIV=2,OTHER=3,UNUSED=-1)
C  Data counting variables
       INTEGER NEDM,NEDF,NEDM18,NEDF18,MNOTED,NDADS,YNOJOB,YTIME,
      *         ONOJOB,OTIME
C  Miscellaneous variables
       INTEGER I,PEOPLE
       REAL EDM18,EDF18,YAVTIM,OAVTIM,FTDADS
C  Initialize counting variables
       DATA NEDM,NEDF,NEDM18,NEDF18,MNOTED,NDADS,YNOJOB,YTIME,ONOJOB,
      *      OTIME/10*0/
C
C  Start of main program - read data
C
       CALL INPUT(SEX,STATUS,AGE,CODE,PERIOD,MONSAL,MONINC,MAXDAT,PEOPLE)


C
C  Process data
C
       DO 10, I=1,PEOPLE
          IF (STATUS(I).EQ.FULLED) THEN
C  Respondent is in full-time education
             IF (SEX(I).EQ.FEMALE) THEN
                NEDF=NEDF+1
                IF (AGE(I).GE.18) NEDF18=NEDF18+1
             ELSE
                NEDM=NEDM+1
                IF (AGE(I).GE.18) NEDM18=NEDM18+1
             END IF
          ELSE
             IF (SEX(I).EQ.MALE) THEN
C  Respondent is male and not in full-time education
                MNOTED=MNOTED+1
                IF (STATUS(I).EQ.ATHOME .AND. CODE(I).EQ.CHILD)
      *              NDADS=NDADS+1
             END IF
             IF (STATUS(I).EQ.JOBLES) THEN
```

```
C   Respondent is unemployed
              IF (AGE(I).LT.18) THEN
                YNOJOB=YNOJOB+1
                YTIME=YTIME+PERIOD(I)
              ELSE IF (AGE(I).GT.45) THEN
                ONOJOB=ONOJOB+1
                OTIME=OTIME+PERIOD(I)
              END IF
            END IF
          END IF
   10 CONTINUE
C   Print main title and number of records read
        WRITE (*,'(1H1,20X,''Results of employment survey''///
     *          1H ,20X,I4,'' records read''//)') PEOPLE
C   Calculate percentage of those in full-time education aged 18 or over
        EDF18=100.0*NEDF18/NEDF
        EDM18=100.0*NEDM18/NEDM
        WRITE (*,201) EDF18,EDM18
C   Calculate average lengths of unemployment
        YAVTIM=REAL(YTIME)/YNOJOB
        OAVTIM=REAL(OTIME)/ONOJOB
        WRITE (*,202) YAVTIM,OAVTIM
C   Calculate percentage of men looking after children
        IF (NDADS.EQ.0) THEN
          WRITE (*,'(1H0,20X,''There are no men, not in full-time '',
     *          ''education,''/1H ,20X,''who stay at home to look '',
     *          ''after children'')')
        ELSE
          FTDADS=100.0*NDADS/MNOTED
          WRITE (*,203) FTDADS
        END IF
        STOP
  201 FORMAT (1H0,20X,F5.1,'% of girls, and'/
     *          1H ,20X,F5.1,'% of boys'/
     *          1H ,20X,'in full-time education are aged 18 or over.')
  202 FORMAT (1H0,20X,'Average length of unemployment is:'/
     *          1H ,20X,F5.1,' months for those under 18'/
     *          1H ,20X,F5.1,' months for those over 45')
  203 FORMAT (1H0,20X,F5.1,'% of men who are not in full-time ',
     *          'education'/1H ,20X,'stay at home with their children')
        END


        SUBROUTINE INPUT(SEX,STATUS,AGE,CODE,PERIOD,MONSAL,MONINC,
     *                  N,PEOPLE)
C
C   This subroutine reads up to N data records prepared as follows,
C   returning the number read in PEOPLE
C
C   Columns 1-20  Name
C            23   Sex (0 or 1) or terminator (9)
C            25   Job status (1-5)
C          28,29  Age - for status 1, 4 or 5
C          28-31  Monthly salary - for status 2 and 3
C          32-34  Other monthly income - for status 3
```

```
C           32-34  Months unemployed - for status 4
C              31  Special code (1-3) - for status 5
C
C  Input data variables (arguments)
         INTEGER SEX(N),STATUS(N),AGE(N),CODE(N),PERIOD(N),
     *           MONSAL(N),MONINC(N),N,PEOPLE
C  Data codings
         INTEGER FEMALE,MALE,ENDATA,FULLED,FULLJB,PARTJB,JOBLES,ATHOME,
     *           CHILD,RELTIV,OTHER,UNUSED
       PARAMETER (FEMALE=0,MALE=1,ENDATA=9,
     *            FULLED=1,FULLJB=2,PARTJB=3,JOBLES=4,ATHOME=5,
     *            CHILD=1,RELTIV=2,OTHER=3,UNUSED=-1)
C  Miscellaneous variables
         INTEGER I
C
C  Loop to read data
C
         DO 10, I=1,N
C  Read next set of data
           READ 100,SEX(I),STATUS(I),AGE(I),CODE(I),PERIOD(I),
     *             MONSAL(I),MONINC(I)
C  Check for end of data
         IF (SEX(I).EQ.ENDATA) GOTO 11
C  Set unused array elements to UNUSED (-1)
         IF (STATUS(I).EQ.FULLJB .OR. STATUS(I).EQ.PARTJB) THEN
           AGE(I)=UNUSED
         ELSE
           MONSAL(I)=UNUSED
         END IF
         IF (STATUS(I).NE.ATHOME) CODE(I)=UNUSED
         IF (STATUS(I).NE.JOBLES) PERIOD(I)=UNUSED
         IF (STATUS(I).NE.PARTJB) MONINC(I)=UNUSED
   10 CONTINUE
C  N records read with no terminator·
         PRINT *,'Warning. ',N,' records read with no terminator'
   11 PEOPLE=I-1
         RETURN
  100 FORMAT (T23,I1,1X,I1,2X,I2,1X,I1,I3,T28,I4,2X,I4)
         END
```

Notice that the part of the main loop that deals with over-18s in education has a slightly different structure from that in the plan (3.1.1 and 3.1.2). The use of a logical IF clarifies the structure in this case. Also notice that it is not enough to test (for the males) whether CODE is 1 (CHILD). If STATUS was not 5 (ATHOME) the value of CODE might be anything, so STATUS must be checked as well.

Notice, also, a slight simplification of the tests in INPUT concerned with the method of setting certain array elements to *unused*: because the two cases where the age is not provided are the only two in which the monthly salary *is* provided, and the other items were not provided in four cases, it is more succinct to invert the tests.

```
Results of employment survey


    23 records read

  33.3% of girls, and
  57.1% of boys
in full-time education are aged 18 or over.

Average length of unemployment is:
  2.3 months for those under 18
  12.5 months for those over 45

There are no men, not in full-time education,
who stay at home to look after children
```

Finally it should be pointed out that, apart from the case of full-time fathers, the program has not checked to see if there were no respondents in a particular category. This is purely to shorten an already lengthy example. In real life the program should include checks of the form

```
IF (NEDM.GT.0) THEN ...
```

Figure 10.5 shows the results obtained by running the program on a sample set of data.

SUMMARY

- A record is a formatted sequence of characters or an unformatted sequence of values.

- A file is a sequence of records.

- Files may be sequential or direct-access.

- The OPEN statement connects a file to a specified input or output unit.

- The ENDFILE statement places a special end-of-file marker on a sequential file.

- The REWIND and BACKSPACE statements are used for positioning a sequential file.

- Fortran 77 statements introduced in Chapter 10:

Input/output statements	*read/write* (*unformatted cilist*) *input list*
	for example READ (7,END=99) A,B,C
	WRITE (8) X,Y,Z
File termination statement	ENDFILE *unit_number*
	ENDFILE (*auxiliary information list*)
File connection statement	OPEN (*auxiliary information list*)
File disconnection statement	CLOSE (*auxiliary information list*)
File positioning statements	BACKSPACE *unit_number*
	BACKSPACE (*auxiliary information list*)
	REWIND *unit_number*
	REWIND (*auxiliary information list*)

SELF-TEST EXERCISES 10.1

1   Find out the operating system requirements regarding file names on your computer system, and any local conventions if appropriate (for example, on a shared computer system). Also establish whether your Fortran system provides any extensions to the OPEN statement (for example, to the STATUS specifier) to accord with the particular operating system facilities.

2   What is the difference between an unformatted record and a formatted record? When should you use unformatted input/output, and when should you use formatted?

3   Which of the following two output statements will produce the longer record?

```
WRITE (3,'(10I5)') (K(I),I=1,10)
WRITE (3) (K(I),I=1,10)
```

4   What will be printed by the following program fragment?

```
      N=1
      DO 10,I=1,10
        DO 5,J=1,5
          WRITE (3) N
          N=N+1
    5   CONTINUE
        BACKSPACE 3
   10 CONTINUE
      REWIND 3
      DO 20,I=1,10
        READ (3) N
   20 CONTINUE
      DO 30,I=1,10
        READ (3) N,N
        PRINT *,N
   30 CONTINUE
```

PROGRAMMING EXERCISES

Most of the exercises in this chapter involve the writing of a program to read data from a file. Data can be put in a file either by another program or by typing it into the file using your computer's editor - normally the same one that you use when typing your program.

10.1   Establish how to type data into a file on your computer, and any conventions and/or requirements imposed on you with regard to the names that you may give to your files.

To ensure that you have the details correct, use your editor to create a file containing three lines (or records) each containing four numbers (in any form you wish). Then write a program that reads these 12 numbers into a 12-element array, prints the 12 numbers in any form you wish, and writes them as four rows of three to a second file. Finally, print the contents of this second file by whatever means is most appropriate on your computer.

*10.2 A file contains a list of 10 integers stored one per line. Write a program to read this list and write it to another file with the order of the numbers reversed.

10.3 Modify your solution to Exercise 10.2 so that it can cope with a file with a variable number of integers, up to a maximum of, say, 100. (*Hint*: you will need to use END=... in your READ statement).

Can you think of a way of writing the program so it can deal with an arbitrary, and possibly very large, number of integers (so large that they can't all be held in an array)?

10.4 Write a program that allows a user to type a series of real numbers into a file. Your program should enable the user to check that the data written to the file has been correctly entered (by use of the BACKSPACE command).

10.5 Rewrite the currency conversion program written as Exercise 9.8 so that it reads the exchange rates from a file.

10.6 Type the following data into a file:

```
12.36   0.004   1.3536E12   2320.326
13.24   0.008   2.4293E15   5111.116
15.01   0.103   9.9879E11   3062.329
11.83   0.051   6.3195E13   8375.145
14.00   0.001   8.0369E14   1283.782
```

(Note that this file will be used again for Exercise 17.6.)

By constructing an appropriate formatted input statement, read each line of data from the file into four variables, and determine the number of numbers, n, in the file and the absolute value of the largest number, m (that is, the largest number ignoring its sign). Do *not* presume in your program that you know how many lines of data are in the file.

Now read the data again, but this time store each number in an array as its input value divided by the largest value, m. This process is known as *normalizing* the data. Print the values of the normalized array four to a line.

10.7 Write a program to read in the following data from a file:

```
12.25♦♦12.00
13.26  14.00
14.00  10.00
56.21  50.00
17.20  17.00
```

where ♦ represents a blank, or space, character.

The figures in the two columns represent actual and estimated costs of office equipment for a university department. Calculate the error of each estimate as a percentage of the estimate, and write a new file consisting of three columns, the first two being those in the original file and the third column containing the percentage error in the estimate.

10.8 Modify your answer to Exercise 10.7 so that the output data overwrites the original data in the input without closing and reopening the file. (*Hint*: use REWIND.)

10.9 Type the following data into a file:

```
21♦♦♦32.642♦♦♦♦0.103E6
48    41.001    0.792E7
62    12.608    0.465E5
```

where ♦ indicates a space.

Write a program to read this data from the file using an appropriate format statement, and display it on the screen in exactly the same format.

10.10 A file contains a list of integers, one per line. The total number of integers is unknown and may be very large. Write a program to display all numbers in the file that are more than three standard deviations from the mean, together with the line number on which they occur.

*10.11 A bank wishes to write a simple program to produce statements from a file containing details of the transactions that have taken place during a given period. Each record of the file is laid out as follows:

aaaaaaaa♦♦♦*dd*♦*mm*♦*yy*♦♦♦*cccccc*♦♦♦*nnnnnnn.nn*

where *aaaaaaaa* is the 8-digit account number,
  dd♦*mm*♦*yy* is the date of the transaction,
  cccccc is the 6-digit cheque number for a debit, and is blank for a credit, and
  nnnnnnn.nn is the (positive) amount of the credit or debit.

A second file contains details of the balances on the various accounts at the beginning of the period, with each record taking the form:

aaaaaaaa♦♦♦±*nnnnnnn.nn*

where *aaaaaaaa* is the 8-digit account number, and

> *nnnnnnn.nn* is the balance at the end of the last statement period (positive or negative).

The program should read an account number from the keyboard, find the existing balance (if any), and print a statement showing all the transactions which have taken place on that account in the form

```
Statement for Account aaaaaaaa
                      Previous balance    ±nnnnnnn.nn

dd/mm/yy    ccccc    Debit    −nnnnnnn.nn   ±nnnnnnn.nn
dd/mm/yy    ccccc    Debit    −nnnnnnn.nn   ±nnnnnnn.nn
dd/mm/yy             Credit    nnnnnnn.nn   ±nnnnnnn.nn
   .          .        .          .            .
   .          .        .          .            .
dd/mm/yy      .        .          .         ±nnnnnnn.nn

                      Current balance     ±nnnnnnn.nn
```

The program should also produce an updated file containing the current balances of all account holders. (Don't forget about any accounts where there has been neither a credit nor a debit during the period.)

10.12 The 'mode' of a set of numbers is the number that occurs most frequently. Write a program to find the mode of a set of up to 100 integers stored in a file, where all of the integers are between 0 and 100 (they are exam results, say). If more than one number is equally common, your program should say so and display all such numbers.

Now modify your program so it can cope with a situation in which the integers are not necessarily between 0 and 100.

10.13 Write a program to calculate $\cosh^2 x$ and $\sinh^2 x$ for x taking values between 0 and 10 in steps of 0.5, and to write these calculated values to a file. Your program should then call a subroutine that will read these pairs of values from the file and print their differences.

10.14 Modify the program you wrote for Exercise 9.16 so that the seismic data is read from a file in which the data from each seismic recording centre is stored as follows:

$$ccc \blacklozenge \blacklozenge ll,mm \blacklozenge \blacklozenge \pm LL,MM \blacklozenge \blacklozenge rr.rr$$

where *ccc* is the centre's identifying number; *ll,mm* are the degrees and minutes of latitude of the centre (with negative degrees representing west of Greenwich and positive representing east of Greenwich); *LL,MM* are the degrees and minutes of longitude of the centre (with negative degrees representing north of the equator and positive representing south of the equator); and *rr.rr* is the strength of the shock on the Richter scale.

10.15 A psychologist studying alcoholism has conducted a survey on drinking habits and has stored the data collected from each respondent in a file in the following format:

Col 1	Sex (0=female, 1=male)
Cols 3–5	Age (in years)
Cols 9,10	Social class (A, B, C1, C2, D or E)
Col 14	Normal drink (1=beer, 2=wine, 3=whisky, 4=gin, 5=other spirits, 6=sherry, 7=cider, 8=soft drinks, 9=other)
Col 17	Normal place of drinking (1=at home, 2=in a bar, 3=elsewhere)

For those who mainly drink at home

Col 19	0=only drink when with guests, 1=otherwise
Cols 23,24	Average number of drinks when with guests
Cols 27,28	Average number of drinks otherwise

For those who mainly drink in a bar

Col 19	Average number of evenings per week spent in a bar
Cols 23,24	Average number of drinks per visit

For those who mainly drink elsewhere

Col 19	Usual drinking place (1=while staying at a hotel, 2=while travelling, 3=at a friend's home, 4=elsewhere)
Cols 23,24	Average number of drinks per week

Write a program that reads this data from the file into an appropriate number of arrays and uses the information to produce the following statistics:

(a) the percentage of the respondents (by sex) who normally visit a bar more than three times a week;

(b) the most popular drink for each sex in a bar, at home, at someone else's home, and while travelling;

(c) the average beer consumption per night amongst men who drink their beer mainly in a bar;

(d) the average number of whiskies consumed (by sex) in a bar, at home (both with and without guests) and in a hotel at which the drinker is staying.

10.16 The heliocentric coordinates L, R, ψ of a planet can be calculated from its elements $M0$, tp, e, i, Ω, a, ω as follows.

Take D to be the number of days since 1st January 1990. M can then be calculated using the formula

$$M = 2\pi(D/tp - \text{INT}(D/tp)) + M0$$

Now solve Kepler's equation ($E - e\sin E = M$) for E using the method described for Exercise 8.14. (If you have the program you wrote for Exercise 8.14 it should be easy to convert it into a suitable subroutine for use in this program.)

Then

$$\nu = 2\tan^{-1}\left(\left(\frac{1+e}{1-e}\right)^{\frac{1}{2}} \tan\frac{E}{2}\right)$$

$$L1 = \nu + \omega$$

$$R1 = \frac{a(1-e^2)}{(1+e\cos\nu)}$$

$$\psi = \sin^{-1}(\sin(L1)\sin i)$$

$$L = \tan^{-1}(\tan(L1)\cos i)$$

$$R = R1\cos\psi$$

Given the following elements for the Earth and Jupiter

Planet	$M0$	tp	e	i	Ω	a	ω
Earth	6.2435	365.2564	0.01672	0	0	1.0000	1.7906
Jupiter	3.9028	4332.287	0.04808	0.02277	1.7535	5.2026	4.8027

write a program which reads a date and calculates the heliocentric coordinates of the Earth and Jupiter, and also calculates the ecliptic coordinates of Jupiter from the formulae

$$\lambda = \tan^{-1}\left(\frac{R_E\sin(L_J-L_E)}{R_J-R_E\cos(L_J-L_E)}\right) + L_J$$

$$\beta = \tan^{-1}\left(\frac{R_J\tan\psi_J\sin(\lambda-L_J)}{R_E\sin(L_J-L_E)}\right)$$

Finally your program should convert these coordinates to right ascension α and declination δ using the formulae

$$\alpha = \tan^{-1}\frac{\sin(\lambda)\cos(\epsilon)-\tan(\beta)\sin(\epsilon)}{\cos(\lambda)}$$
$$\delta = \sin^{-1}(\sin(\beta)\cos(\epsilon)+\cos(\beta)\sin(\epsilon)\sin(\lambda))$$

(where $\epsilon = 0.4091$), as was carried out in Exercise 4.15.

10.17 Modify the program written for Exercise 10.16 so that it reads a date from the keyboard and writes the predicted weekly positions of Jupiter for the following 12 months to a file (which can subsequently be inspected and/or listed).

Intermission –
Developing and testing
programs

The first part of this book has covered the fundamental principles of programming and of most of the major concepts of Fortran 77. The second part will develop from this basic framework until the full power of the language is available to solve even the most complex problems. It is appropriate at this stage, however, to pause and consider the way in which we actually develop and test our programs.

Anyone who has ever been involved with helping others to get their programs to work correctly has come across the *last bug syndrome*. A **bug** is the programmer's expression for an error in a program and it appears that almost every program 'is working perfectly except for one *last* bug'. The trouble is that when you have found and corrected it there always seems to be *another* last bug! Many of the errors that cause this problem could have been eliminated by better program design, and still more could be eliminated by a planned approach to testing.

This book is about programming in Fortran 77, and as such it naturally concentrates on the design of well-structured programs and the coding techniques that are used to implement that design. However, we should never lose sight of the fact that the object of writing a program is to instruct a computer to carry out some action or to solve some problem; *the program is not an end in itself*. Our job is not finished, therefore, until the program works correctly and deals in an appropriate manner with any reasonable (or even unreasonable) 'exception situations'. Indeed, it is usually the exceptions that cause the most trouble. For example, it is relatively easy to write a compiler that will process an absolutely correct Fortran 77 program and produce a correct machine-code program. It is, however, far more difficult to make that compiler deal in a sensible way with any of the myriad syntactic or other errors made when writing a Fortran 77 program, however unlikely or far-fetched they may be. The logical complexity of most programs means that it is unlikely that any method will ever be devised to *prove* them to be totally correct. We must therefore rely on good design to minimize the likelihood of errors, together with well-structured and comprehensive testing to search out any that *have* managed to slip into our programs.

Program testing is both a negative and a destructive process. Its purpose is to use data similar to the real data on which the program is designed to execute in order to discover any errors or omissions in the program. This means that, although program testing can establish the presence of errors in a program, it cannot prove their absence. It is thus an essentially negative process.

The destructive aspect of program testing arises because it attempts to cause the program to fail or to produce incorrect results. It is psychologically difficult to attempt to destroy what one has just created, and it is therefore highly desirable that the testing should be carried out, largely or at least partially, by someone other than the programmer.

The *testing* of a program should never be confused with the **debugging** of that program. The former is the systematic execution of the program with specially prepared data with the intention of establishing the presence of any errors that may exist. The debugging of the program, on the other hand, is the process of establishing the cause of these errors and then correcting the program so as to eliminate them. Although these two processes are closely related it is important to realize that they are quite distinct, and must be approached from rather different viewpoints.

It is appropriate here to outline some of the most important aspects of testing in the context of an actual example. The best methods of debugging will depend upon the computer system being used, as most systems will contain facilities for producing **dumps** of variables and other stored values, for stopping at predefined **breakpoints** to investigate the current state of any required aspect of the program and its data, for **single stepping** through the program statement by statement, and so on. In addition, the inclusion of extra PRINT statements at key places can often provide the information needed for debugging.

To illustrate the main principles of planned program testing Example 10.1, which was concerned with the analysis of a set of survey data detailing the job(s) or other activities of the respondents, will be considered.

Probably the single most important rule about program testing is to progress in stages in an **incremental** fashion. A program of any significant size will, almost inevitably, contain a number of errors when it is first written. (This may appear to be an admission of failure, but it is a fact of life and must not be ignored.) If the complete program is written before any testing takes place then it can be extremely difficult to debug the program because the testing will show the presence of errors but it will not usually be apparent in which part of the program the trouble lies. We therefore *always* adopt a stage-by-stage, or incremental, approach to program development and testing.

We have already seen how we can split a program into its major constituent elements and write each of these as a separate procedure. We can then test each of these procedures individually before linking them to form the complete program. This process is known as **bottom-up** development and testing, and contrasts with the **top-down** design process that we have been using. Occasionally it may be appropriate to carry out a form of top-down testing, but this is usually more cumbersome and is relevant only in rather specialized situations.

Returning to Example 10.1, we find that a simplified structure plan for the main program is as follows:

1   Initialize totals

2   Read the data – INPUT

3   Repeat for each record
  3.1 If Job = education then
      3.1.1 Update appropriate totals
      otherwise
      3.1.2 If sex = male then
            3.1.2.1 Update appropriate totals
      3.1.3 If job = unemployed then
            3.1.3.1 Update appropriate totals

4   Calculate and print results

The first part of the program to be written is, logically, that part which deals with the input of the data and the recognition of the end of the data. In order to check this part it would seem sensible to print the data as it is read. We can therefore modify the structure plan for the INPUT subroutine to include the printing of both the raw data *and* the data that is stored as a result of processing this data:

INPUT

1   Repeat the following
  1.1 Read the next record
  1.2 Print record as read
  1.3 If sex = 9 then exit from loop
  1.4 Process record and update data arrays

2   Print total number of data records read (N)

3   Repeat N times, that is, once for each record read
  3.1 Print contents of next element of all data arrays

A subprogram can then be written according to the above plan and tested with suitable test data.

One important point to note is that it is often desirable to reduce various program limits during testing. For example, in the sample solution to Example 10.1 a maximum of 1000 sets of data was assumed. It is sensible to reduce this to a more manageable number (for example 20) during testing, since this will be enough to test the various different paths through the program and also the effect of exceeding the maximum permitted amount of data. The use of a PARAMETER for this limit makes this type of change particularly easy.

When preparing test data it is essential to make particularly thorough tests on, or close to, the borderline between different cases. The following list shows what is required in order to test thoroughly this simple input loop:

(1)   valid data, including at least one of each category for which printed results are required, less than maximum total number of records, data correctly terminated;

(2)   valid data, including at least one of each category for which printed results are required, exactly the maximum total number of records, data correctly terminated;

(3)   valid data, including at least one of each category for which printed results are required, more than the maximum total number of records, data correctly terminated;

(4)   no data other than the terminator;

(5)   as (1), but with no terminator;

(6)   as (2), but with no terminator;

(7)   as (3), but with no terminator;

(8)   no data.

Thus cases (1–4) test what happens with different amounts of otherwise valid data, while cases (5–8) repeat these tests for data without the special terminating record. The INPUT subroutine should deal with all these cases in a sensible and predictable fashion. Note that the sample solution in Chapter 10 could be improved to check for the presence of a terminator in cases (2) and (6) by reading one more record after the maximum number have been read and testing to see if it is the terminator; as written, the program will fail in cases (5) and (8).

Once these eight cases have been dealt with successfully, further tests can be carried out to ensure that all valid combinations of data items are read correctly, and that invalid data is recognised and processed appropriately. Invalid data falls into two distinct groups – correctly formatted but meaningless data, and incorrectly formatted data. Examples of the former are a sex code other than 0,1 or 9 (terminator), job status outside the range 1–5, etc. How many checks are inserted in the program for these types of errors depends very much on the source of the data; for example, if it was computer-generated or has already been checked by some other program then it can normally be assumed to be correct in this respect. (The sample solution in Chapter 10 omits all such checks – mainly for reasons of economy of space in this book, but also to improve the clarity of the program.)

Incorrectly formatted data (for example, characters where numbers are expected) will usually cause a catastrophic failure, and there is relatively little that can be done about this other than using an ERR= specifier to enable a warning to be printed, ignoring the input record, and continuing execution. In practice, however, this rarely provides any improvement over simply allowing the program to fail!

Once this program has been fully tested we should be confident that the data will be read correctly. This is always a very important step because until we know that the data is being input in the way we intended, any testing of later stages of the program is difficult and potentially error-prone.

The next stage in building up the complete program might be to analyse those aged over 18 who are still in full-time education:

---

1   Initialize totals

2   Read the data - INPUT

3   Print data read by INPUT

4   Repeat for each record
    4.1 If job = education then
        4.1.1 Increment total (male or female)
        4.1.2 If age > 18 then increment 'old total' (m/f)

5   Print totals and percentages

Since we have already written and tested steps 2 and 3 we need only supply data that will test the new parts of the program. This does not mean that only data in which *job status* is *full-time education* should be supplied, but means that each data set can lie within the maximum data limits and be properly terminated, since we have already tested the behaviour of the INPUT subroutine in the other (invalid data) situations. Examples of suitable test data sets are:

(1)   one record, job status = full-time education;

(2)   one record, job status ≠ full-time education;

(3)   more than one record, job status = full-time education in all records;

(4)   more than one record, job status = full-time education in some records;

(5)   more than one record, job status ≠ full-time education in all records.

In cases (1), (3) and (4) appropriate combinations of sex (all male, all female, mixed sexes) and age (all under 18, all exactly 18, all over 18) should be included.

One point that is often overlooked is that when testing a program we must always ensure that we know *exactly* what the answers should be. It is quite easy for a program to contain some (minor) error that leads to the answer calculated being similar to the correct answer, and yet not exactly the same. If the programmer has not worked out in advance exactly what results he or she is expecting then this type of error may slip through unnoticed.

The process of gradually extending the program can then be continued until eventually the full program is working correctly. Because at each step we add only a relatively small amount of extra code we do not have far to look if errors do occur, and there is much less chance of any mistakes being missed.

Finally, never make the mistake of thinking that some section of the program 'is bound to work and doesn't need testing'. It is a chastening experience to realize how easy it is to miss even the most obvious error in one's own programs.

The features and concepts that we shall be discovering during the second part of this book will enable and encourage us to develop larger and more sophisticated programs than were appropriate in the first part. It is, therefore, a matter of increasing importance that programs are not only well designed, but also developed and tested in a planned and well-structured manner.

Towards Real Programs

PART
II

An introduction to numerical methods in Fortran 77 programs

This chapter can be omitted by those with no interest in numerical applications.

The floating-point representation of real numbers is a compromise between accuracy and flexibility and will almost always lead to **round-off errors** in calculations of any complexity. One method of minimizing such errors is to use **double precision**, which uses two storage locations for each real value instead of one, thus allowing greatly increased precision. It is also important that the programmer is aware of the **stability** and **conditioning** of any numerical process used.

Two examples of widely used numerical methods are given. The first explains how to use the **method of least squares** to calculate the equation of the straight line having the best fit to a set of data points, and demonstrates its use in a program to calculate Young's modulus from a set of experimental measurements on a wire under stress. The second explains how to use the **bisection method** to find the roots of a polynomial equation, and illustrates it by the development of a subroutine to find the roots of any equation of the form $f(x)=0$.

Because Fortran was developed from the beginning as a language for scientists and technologists it has always had the capability of carrying out complex arithmetic. All the usual mathematical operations can be carried out with complex numbers, and the (generic) mathematical intrinsic functions also operate correctly with complex arguments. The use of complex numbers is illustrated by the development of a program to calculate the characteristics of a simple electronic band-pass filter.

11.1   Numerical calculations, precision, and rounding errors

The Fortran language was originally designed to help in the solution of numerical problems, and this is still by far the largest class of problems for which Fortran programs are used. However, it is extremely important that the writer *and the user* of such programs should be aware of the intrinsic limitations of a computer in this area, and of the steps that may be taken to improve matters.

The two main types of numbers used in Fortran programs (REAL and INTEGER) have already been introduced, but it is appropriate at this stage to review their characteristics briefly.

INTEGER numbers are stored in an exact form, without any fractional part, and all calculations performed upon them, other than division, lead to a result that is mathematically accurate. In the case of division any fractional part in the (mathematical) result is discarded. Typically, INTEGER numbers can be in the range -10^9 to $+10^9$. INTEGER numbers are normally used for counting and similar operations; they are not normally appropriate for numerical calculation.

REAL numbers, on the other hand, are stored as an *approximation* to the mathematical value using a floating-point representation, which allows a wide range of values to be stored with approximately the same degree of precision. Typically, a REAL number will be stored in a computer to about 7 or 8 digits of precision, with a range of around -10^{38} to $+10^{38}$. Numerical calculations normally use REAL numbers, although in certain circumstances two other types of number may also be used. These will be discussed later in this chapter. Unless otherwise stated, the following discussion of numerical methods will assume that all numbers are REAL numbers.

Having established that the numbers used in numerical calculations are approximations, held to a specified degree of precision, we must analyse what effect this may have on the results of such calculations. This was discussed briefly in Chapter 7, when we referred to the manner in which we deal with precision when carrying out manual calculations, but we must now examine the problem in slightly more depth.

For this purpose assume the existence of a computer that stores its numbers in a **normalized decimal floating-point form** – that is, in a decimal equivalent of the way in which (binary) floating-point numbers are stored in a normal computer. Assume further that these numbers are stored with four digits of precision. Finally, assume that the exponent must lie in the range -9 to $+9$. Figure 11.1 shows some examples of the way numbers will be stored in this computer.

Notice that two of the numbers shown in Figure 11.1 cannot be represented on our decimal computer. The first of these, 9 876 543 210.123 4, would require an exponent of 10, which is more than

External value	Internal representation
37.5	$0.3750*10^2$
123.456	$0.1235*10^3$
123 456 789.123 45	$0.1235*10^9$
9 876 543 210.123 4	cannot be represented – exponent is 10
0.000 001 234 567 8	$0.1235*10^{-6}$
0.999 999 999 999 9	$0.1000*10^1$
0.000 000 000 037 5	cannot be represented – exponent is −10

Figure 11.1
Number storage in the decimal floating-point computer.

the computer will allow. Any attempt to store a number whose exponent is too large, as here, will create a condition known as **overflow**, and will normally cause an error at this stage of the processing. Obviously, once a calculation has overflowed then all subsequent calculations using this result will also be incorrect.

A similar situation arose with the final number shown in Figure 11.1, 0.000 000 000 037 5, which would have required an exponent of −10, which is less than the computer will allow. This situation, which is known as **underflow**, is less serious than overflow, since the effect is that the number is too close to 0 to be distinguished from it. Many computers will not report this form of error, and will store the number as 0; in some numerical calculations, however, it is important to know when underflow has occurred and so some computer systems do report its occurrence as a non-fatal error.

We can now look at how our decimal computer will carry out simple arithmetic calculations. Before progressing further, however, note that most computers carry out arithmetic in a special set of **registers** that allow more digits of precision than does the main memory; we shall, therefore, assume that our computer has arithmetic registers capable of storing numbers to eight digits of precision – that is, twice the memory's precision.

Consider first the sum of the two fractions $\frac{11}{9}$ and $\frac{1}{3}$. The first number will be stored as $0.1222*10^1$ on our computer, while the second, $\frac{1}{3}$, will be stored as $0.3333*10^0$. However, before these two numbers can be added together they must be converted so that they both have the same exponent. (Digits following a space in the numbers below represent the extra digits available in the arithmetic registers.)

$$0.1222*10^1 + 0.0333\ 3*10^1 \rightarrow 0.1555\ 3*10^1$$
$$\rightarrow 0.1555*10^1$$

Now the correct internal representation of $(\frac{11}{9} + \frac{1}{3})$, namely $\frac{14}{9}$, is $0.1556*10^1$, so even this simple calculation has introduced an error in the fourth significant figure, owing to round-off.

Consider now the result of a slightly longer calculation in which the five numbers 4, 0.0004, 0.0004, 0.0004 and 0.0004 are added together. Since arithmetic on computers always involves only two operands at each stage, the steps are as follows:

(1) $0.4000*10^1 + 0.0000\,4*10^1 \rightarrow 0.4000\,4*10^1$
$$\rightarrow 0.4000*10^1$$

(2) $0.4000*10^1 + 0.0000\,4*10^1 \rightarrow 0.4000\,4*10^1$
$$\rightarrow 0.4000*10^1$$

and so on.

The result will be $0.4000*10^1$, that is, 4.0, whereas we can easily see that it should be 4.002 when rounded to four significant digits.

Now consider what would have happened if the addition had been carried out in the reverse order:

(1) $0.4000*10^{-3} + 0.4000*10^{-3} \quad \rightarrow 0.8000*10^{-3}$

(2) $0.8000*10^{-3} + 0.4000*10^{-3} \quad \rightarrow 1.2000*10^{-3}$
$$\rightarrow 0.1200\,0*10^{-2}$$
$$\rightarrow 0.1200*10^{-2}$$

(3) $0.1200*10^{-2} + 0.0400\,0*10^{-2} \rightarrow 0.1600*10^{-2}$

(4) $0.1600*10^{-2} + 0.0400\,0*10^{-2} \rightarrow 0.2000*10^{-2}$

(5) $0.0002\,000*10^1 + 0.4000*10^1 \quad \rightarrow 0.4002\,000*10^1$
$$\rightarrow 0.4002*10^1$$

Thus in this case the result will be 4.002, which is the correct answer.

This example shows that, whenever possible, it is preferable to add numbers in order of increasing value in order to minimize errors due to round-off.

A much more serious example of this type of problem comes when we subtract two numbers. Consider, for example, the effect of subtracting $\frac{12}{41}$ from $\frac{5}{17}$. The latter is represented as $0.2941*10^0$ and $\frac{12}{41}$ as $0.2927*10^0$ in our decimal computer and so the subtraction proceeds as follows:

$$0.2941*10^0 - 0.2927*10^0 \rightarrow 0.0014*10^0$$
$$\rightarrow 0.1400*10^{-2}$$

However, $\frac{5}{17} - \frac{12}{41}$ is equal to $\frac{1}{697}$, or $0.1435*10^{-2}$. The error in the calculation is, therefore, equivalent to over 2.4 per cent, which is hardly the accuracy we might expect from a computer!

This example illustrates that great care must always be exercised when subtracting numbers that may be almost equal, as the loss of precision resulting from the calculation can seriously affect the result of the calculation.

It is not intended to continue this discussion here, since the question of arithmetic precision is quite complicated, especially when we turn to multiplication and division. It is enough at this stage to draw attention to the problem. There are several excellent books on this topic if the problems are particularly important for a particular class of work; some of them are listed in the bibliography at the end of this book (Atkinson *et al.*, 1989; Hopkins and Phillips, 1988; Ralston and Rabinowitz, 1978).

However, one approach to dealing with this problem that is often sufficient is to use a different type of numeric variable for those parts of a calculation where loss of precision may be serious. This is described in the next section.

11.2   DOUBLE PRECISION **variables**

As we have seen, a real value is an *approximation* that represents a numeric value to a specified precision using a floating-point representation. The accuracy of this approximation is determined by the form of the floating-point number, which is allocated a fixed number of bits for the mantissa (thus defining the *precision*), and a fixed number for the exponent (thus defining the *range* of the numbers). For some types of calculation the accuracy of arithmetic using real values may not be enough, and so a second form of number is available with a larger number of significant digits. This uses two consecutive numeric storage units and is called **double precision** (although it does not necessarily hold numbers to exactly twice as many significant digits of precision). Double precision variables must be declared in a type specification statement that takes the form

```
DOUBLE PRECISION name1,name2,...
```

F90

The input and output of double precision values is performed by F or E edit descriptors in exactly the same way as for real values.

Double precision constants are written in the exponent and mantissa form, but with a D to separate the two parts, instead of an E as with real constants (see Section 2.1), thus:

1D–7	is double precision 0.000 000 1
14713D–3	is double precision 14.713
12.7192D0	is double precision 12.7192
9.413D5	is double precision 941 300.0

When double precision values are used in a mixed-mode arithmetic expression a process occurs similar to that with which we are already familiar. The expression is evaluated in stages using the normal priority rules: if one operand is double precision and the other is real or integer,

Figure 11.2
A comparison of real
and double precision
arithmetic.

	Double precision arithmetic		Real arithmetic	
N	Value	Time (μs)	Value	Time (μs)
1	1.000 000 000 000 000	121	1.000 000 00	80
2	0.999 999 999 999 993	134	0.999 998 45	121
3	0.999 999 999 999 972	188	0.999 977 59	161
4	0.999 999 999 999 986	215	0.999 982 36	175
5	0.999 999 999 999 886	256	0.999 669 31	202
10	0.999 999 999 999 957	445	0.999 354 96	323
25	0.999 999 999 994 621	998	0.997 840 17	742
50	0.999 999 999 877 943	1875	0.995 070 58	1403
75	0.999 999 999 797 680	2699	0.992 040 40	2105
100	0.999 999 999 742 911	3603	0.989 615 56	2766

the latter is converted to double precision before the operation is carried out, to give a double precision result.

For many purposes real arithmetic is quite accurate enough, especially if care is taken over the way in which calculations are carried out. If it is not sufficient then double precision variables can be used, either in critical areas or throughout the program as appropriate.

One of the great advantages of the Fortran 77 intrinsic functions is that most of them have **generic** names (see Appendix A). This means that if, for example, SIN is called with a real argument then it is evaluated using real arithmetic to give a real result; if it is called with a double precision argument then it is evaluated using double precision arithmetic to give a double precision result. The same applies, of course, to operators (+, −, *, / and **), and so if all the real variables are declared as double precision this is normally all that is required to ensure that all operations are carried out in double precision rather than real (single precision). When transferring a program from one computer to another with inherently less precision this can be extremely useful.

The use of double precision variables usually imposes a very significant overhead on the program, however, causing it to take considerably longer to run. Figure 11.2 shows an example of some of the results produced by a program that evaluates the following expression for various values of N:

$$\left(\sqrt{\frac{N}{N-1} \times \frac{N-2}{N-3} \times \cdots \times 1}\right)^2 \times \frac{N-1}{N} \times \frac{N-3}{N-2} \times \cdots \times 1$$

This expression is, of course, equal to 1 for any value of N. But in a calculation of this nature it is impossible to eliminate the effect of rounding errors, which will tend to have an increasingly large effect as N increases.

The program was run on a 16-bit minicomputer, and it can be seen that even when $N=100$ the double precision calculation is extremely accurate and the result would be printed as 1.0 if nine or fewer decimal places were specified. However, when using ordinary real calculation, the result with $N=2$ is accurate to only five places; with $N=100$ the error comes in the second decimal place!

It must be emphasized that this is a totally artificial example, but it does show that if a great deal of calculation is required (especially including multiplication and/or division) the use of double precision arithmetic may be highly desirable.

Figure 11.2 also gives an indication of the time overhead involved in using double precision. Even for $N=1$ (which is essentially the calculation of $(\sqrt{1.0})^2$) the double precision version took 121 µs, compared with only 80 µs for the real or single precision one, while for $N=100$ the times were 3603 µs and 2766 µs respectively. (1 µs is 0.000001 seconds.)

11.3 Conditioning and stability

The previous two sections have shown how important it is for the programmer to be aware of the effect of round-off errors in computer calculations, and has indicated some of the approaches that can be used to contain the problem. However, it is also important that the programmer is aware of the likelihood of a particular calculation being seriously affected by such problems. Two factors that are important in assessing this are the **stability** of a numerical process, and its **conditioning**.

A **well-conditioned process** is one that is relatively insensitive to changes in the values of its parameters, so that small changes in these parameters produce only small changes in the behaviour of the process. An **ill-conditioned process**, on the other hand, is one that is highly sensitive to changes in its parameters, and where small changes in these parameters produce large changes in the behaviour of the process.

An example of an ill-conditioned problem might be the pair of simultaneous equations

$$x + y = 10$$
$$1.002x + y = 0$$

the solution of which is clearly

$$x = -5000$$
$$y = 5010$$

However, if some round-off (for example on the four-digit decimal machine referred to in Section 11.1) had led to the second equation being expressed as

$$1.001x + y = 0$$

then the solution would have been

$$x = -10000$$
$$y = 10010$$

which is very different from the correct solution; while if the round-off error had led the coefficient of x in the second equation to be 1.000 (to four significant digits) then the problem would have been insoluble!

Clearly the reason for this extremely ill-conditioned behaviour is that in this case the two equations represent lines that are almost parallel, and therefore a very small change in the gradient of one will cause a very large movement of their point of intersection. A computer program that generated these equations and then solved them would stand a high chance of being so inaccurate as to be completely useless.

On the other hand, the two equations

$$x + y = 10$$
$$1.002x - y = 0$$

which have the solution

$$x = 4.995$$
$$y = 5.005$$

are clearly well conditioned. A change of the coefficient of x in the second equation to 1.001 or 1.000 would lead to solutions of

$$x = 4.998 \quad \text{or} \quad x = 5.0$$
$$y = 5.002 \qquad\quad y = 5.0$$

respectively. This is because in this case the two lines are almost perpendicular to each other.

There are techniques that will detect whether, for example, a system of simultaneous equations is ill conditioned, but a discussion of these is beyond the scope of this book. An excellent description of these and other related problems can be found in Atkinson *et al.* (1989).

Related to the conditioning of a numerical process is its **stability**. A numerical process is said to be *stable* if small changes in its data, *including round-off errors,* lead to only small changes in its solution; it is said to be *unstable* if such small changes lead to large changes in the solution.

It is important to note, however, that a key element of the stability of a numerical process on a computer is the method used by the computer hardware and the compiler library routines to carry out arithmetic and intrinsic functions. For example, the results shown in Figure 11.2 were

	Real arithmetic		Double precision arithmetic	
N	1982 Mini	1989 Micro	1982 Mini	1989 Micro
2	0.999 998 45	0.999 999 94	0.999 999 999 999 993	1.000 000 000 000 000
5	0.999 669 31	1.000 000 01	0.999 999 999 999 886	1.000 000 000 000 000
10	0.999 354 96	0.999 999 98	0.999 999 999 999 957	1.000 000 000 000 000
25	0.997 840 17	0.999 999 82	0.999 999 999 994 621	1.000 000 000 000 000
50	0.995 070 58	1.000 000 01	0.999 999 999 877 943	1.000 000 000 000 000
100	0.989 615 56	0.999 999 94	0.999 999 999 742 911	1.000 000 000 000 001
250		0.999 999 40		1.000 000 000 000 000
500		1.000 000 83		1.000 000 000 000 001
1 000		1.000 001 20		1.000 000 000 000 000
2 000		1.000 000 23		1.000 000 000 000 003
5 000		1.000 000 61		0.999 999 999 999 997
10 000		1.000 000 23		0.999 999 999 999 981

Figure 11.3
A comparison of arithmetic accuracy and stability.

produced on a very popular 16-bit minicomputer in 1982. The same program was run in 1989 on a 16-bit microcomputer (a Research Machines Nimbus AX/286 using the Prospero PC Fortran compiler) with dramatically improved results, as shown in Figure 11.3. In particular, it is worth noting that the Nimbus single-precision result for all the values of N that were tried up to 10 000 were more accurate than *any* of the earlier calculations for N greater than 1! Furthermore, in contrast to the earlier situation, it is clear that on the Nimbus there is no advantage in using double-precision arithmetic for this calculation, since there is no significant loss of precision through the use of single-precision arithmetic.

SELF-TEST EXERCISES 11.1

1   Define overflow and underflow. Which is the more important?

2   In each of the following cases two possible orders of calculation are shown that are mathematically equivalent. Which is the better to use on a computer, and why?

    (a) $a \times a - b \times b$ or $(a+b) \times (a-b)$
    (b) $(a-b)/c$ or $a/c - b/c$
    (c) $(a+b)/c$ or $a/c + b/c$
    (d) $a+b+c+d+e$ or $e+d+c+b+a$ where $0<a<b<c<d<e$
    (e) $a/b - c/d$ or $((a \times d) - (b \times c))/(b \times d)$

3   Define a stable numerical process, and an unstable one. What is the effect of round-off errors on the stability of a numerical process?

4   Define a well-conditioned numerical process, and an ill-conditioned one. What is the effect of round-off errors on the conditioning of a numerical process?

5   What is the difference between a REAL variable and a DOUBLE PRECISION variable?

6   Which of the following two programs will give the more accurate results?

```
      PROGRAM TEST6A
      REAL X,Y,Z
      READ 100,X,Y
      Z = X-Y
      PRINT 200,X,Y,Z
      STOP
  100 FORMAT (2F10.4)
  200 FORMAT (5X,'The difference between',F14.8,' and',F14.8,
     *                ' is',F14.8)
      END
```

```
      PROGRAM TEST6B
      DOUBLE PRECISION X,Y,Z
      READ 100,X,Y
      Z = X-Y
      PRINT 200,X,Y,Z
      STOP
  100 FORMAT (2F10.4)
  200 FORMAT (5X,'The difference between',F14.8,' and',F14.8,
     *                ' is',F14.8)
      END
```

11.4   Data fitting by least-squares approximation

A frequent situation in the experimental sciences is that data have been collected that, it is believed, will satisfy a linear relationship of the form

$$y = ax + b$$

However, owing to experimental error, sets of data collected at different times will rarely exhibit exactly the same relationship: they can typically be represented graphically as in Figure 11.4. Fitting a straight line through the data in such a way as to obtain the fit that most closely reflects the true relationship is, therefore, a widespread need. One well-established technique is known as the **method of least squares**.

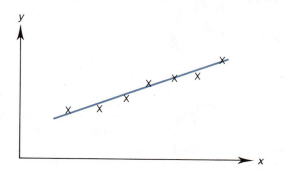

Figure 11.4
Experimental data that
exhibits a linear
relationship.

This method can be applied to any polynomial, but for the present only the linear case will be considered. If we assume that the equation

$$y = ax + b$$

is a possible best fit, we can test its accuracy by calculating the predicted values of y for the actual data values of x and comparing them with the corresponding data values. The difference between the calculated value y' and the experimental value y is called the **residual**, and the method of least squares attempts to minimize the sum of the squares of the residuals for all the data points. Figure 11.5 shows the residuals for the data in Figure 11.4 in graphical form, and it can easily be seen that using the square of the residuals eliminates the problem caused by some predicted values being too large and others being too small.

Simple differential calculus leads to the conclusion that the sum of the squares of the residuals is minimized when the two coefficients a and b

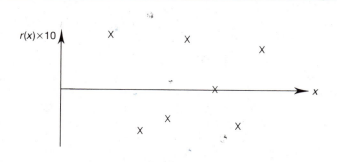

Figure 11.5
Residuals for the data
from Figure 11.4.

are defined as follows:

$$a = \frac{(\Sigma x_i)(\Sigma y_i) - n(\Sigma x_i y_i)}{(\Sigma x)^2 - n(\Sigma x_i^2)}$$

$$b = \frac{\Sigma y - a(\Sigma x)}{n}$$

It is worth noting that it is quite common for one item (or sometimes more) of a set of experimental data to be less accurate than the rest. Clearly this can lead to an erroneous result, and it is therefore sometimes appropriate to ignore one item of a data set and attempt to fit a straight line through the remaining items.

The value of the sum of the squares of the residuals, often referred to simply as the **residual sum**, can be a good guide as to how closely the equation fits the data. If it is a perfect fit then all data points will lie on the line and the residual sum will be zero. If it is required to compare the **goodness of fit** of two or more equations, then the one with the lowest residual sum can be taken to be the best fit. It would clearly be possible to repeat the fitting process first using all data points, and then leaving each data point in turn out of the calculation. The solution chosen would be the one with the lowest residual sum.

EXAMPLE 11.1

Figure 11.6 shows the results obtained from an experiment to calculate the Young's modulus of the material used to make a piece of wire. Write a program to calculate the value of Young's modulus for this material and the natural (unstretched) length of the wire.

Figure 11.6
Experimental data from
Young's modulus
experiment.

Weight on wire (lb)	Measured length (in)
10	39.967
12	39.971
15	39.979
17	39.986
20	39.993
22	40.000
25	40.007
28	40.016
30	40.022

Average of five measurements of the diameter was 0.0125 in.

In this experiment the extensions produced in the wire by suspending various weights from it were measured very accurately. Young's modulus is defined by the equation

$$E = \frac{\text{stress}}{\text{strain}}$$

which can be expressed as

$$E = \frac{f/A}{e/L} \quad \text{or} \quad E = \frac{fL}{Ae}$$

where f is the applied force (the weight), A is the cross-sectional area of the wire (measured at several points and averaged), e is the extension, and L is the unstressed length of the wire.

In this case, in order to eliminate the effect of any curl or kinking in the wire, no measurements were taken in a completely unstressed condition but the length of the wire was measured instead under an initial load and then under various heavier loads, as indicated in Figure 11.6.

From the above definition of Young's modulus we can derive the equation

$$e = kf$$

where

$$k = \frac{L}{AE}$$

However, we do not have the value of e, but rather the value of l, where

$$e = l - L$$

We therefore need to fit the equation

$$l = kf + L$$

to the experimental data. We shall then be able to calculate the value of E. A structure plan for this program is as follows:

1   Read data – N sets into arrays LEN and WT, plus cross-sectional area of wire

2   Find equation of line with WT as x-coordinate and LEN as y-coordinate – LSTSQR

3   Calculate Young's modulus

> LSTSQR(X,Y,N,A,B)
>
> **1**   Calculate sums of X(I), Y(I), X(I)*Y(I), and Y(I)^2
>
> **2**   Calculate coefficients of equation Y = AX + B, which provides a least-squares fit to the data
>
> **3**   Return coefficients

A suitable program is:

```
      PROGRAM YOUNG
C
C This program calculates Young's modulus for a piece of wire
C from experimental data, and also the unstretched length of the wire.
C
      PARAMETER (PI=3.1415926536,G=386.0)
C Local variable declarations
      PARAMETER (MAXDAT=100)
      REAL D,K,L,E,LEN(MAXDAT),WT(MAXDAT)
      REAL LSUM,WSUM,LWSUM,W2SUM
      INTEGER I,N
C
      PRINT *,'How many sets of data? '
      READ *,N
C Check that there is not too much data
      IF (N.GT.MAXDAT) THEN
         PRINT *,'Too much data.  Maximum number of sets is ',MAXDAT
         STOP
      END IF
C Read data
      PRINT *,'Type data in pairs: WEIGHT (lbs), LENGTH (ins)'
      DO 10, I=1,N
         PRINT 100,I
  100 FORMAT(I4,': ')
         READ *,WT(I),LEN(I)
C Convert mass to weight
         WT(I)=G*WT(I)
   10 CONTINUE
      PRINT *,'What is the diameter of the wire (ins)?'
      READ *,D
C Call LSTSQR to fit a straight line through the data using a least
C squares fit
      CALL LSTSQR(WT,LEN,N,K,L)
C Calculate E (Young's modulus) = L/AK = L/(0.25*PI*D*D*K)
      E=L/(0.25*PI*D*D*K)
C Print results
      PRINT 200,L,E
  200 FORMAT(/5X,'The unstressed length of the wire is ',F7.3,' in'/
     *        5X,'Its Young''s modulus is ',E10.4,' lb.in⁻¹.sec⁻²')
      STOP
      END
```

```
      SUBROUTINE LSTSQR(X,Y,N,A,B)
C
C  Calculates the coefficients of the equation Y=AX+B that best fits
C  the data supplied in the arrays X and Y, using a least squares fit
C
C  Arguments
      INTEGER N
      REAL X(N),Y(N),A,B
C  Local variables
      INTEGER I
      REAL XSUM,YSUM,XYSUM,X2SUM
C  Initialize summation variables
      XSUM=0.0
      YSUM=0.0
      XYSUM=0.0
      X2SUM=0.0
C  Calculate sums
      DO 10, I=1,N
         XSUM=XSUM+X(I)
         YSUM=YSUM+Y(I)
         XYSUM=XYSUM+X(I)*Y(I)
         X2SUM=X2SUM+X(I)**2
   10 CONTINUE
C  Calculate coefficients
      A=(XSUM*YSUM-N*XYSUM)/(XSUM**2-N*X2SUM)
      B=(YSUM-A*XSUM)/N
      RETURN
      END
```

Figure 11.7 shows the result of running this program with the data provided in Figure 11.6.

```
How many sets of data? 9
Type data in pairs: WEIGHT (lbs), LENGTH (ins)
1: 10,39.967
2: 12,39.971
3: 15,39.979
4: 17,39.986
5: 20,39.993
6: 22,40
7: 25,40.007
8: 28,40.016
9: 30,40.022
What is the diameter of the wire (ins)? 0.025

    The unstressed length of the wire is  39.938 ins
    Its Young's modulus is 0.1131E+11 lb.in⁻¹.sec⁻²
```

Figure 11.7
The results produced by
YOUNG using data from
Figure 11.6.

11.5 Iterative solution of non-linear algebraic equations

The previous section was concerned with fitting a straight line as an approximation to a set of data points. However, many real-life situations will not result in a straight-line fit but in some non-linear relationship of the form

$$y = f(x)$$

Ways of fitting non-linear functions (or *polynomials*) to experimental data will be investigated in Chapter 18, but at this stage it is appropriate to discuss one approach to solving such an equation.

If $f(x)$ is a quadratic function then we can solve the resulting equation

$$ax^2 + bx + c = 0$$

without any difficulty, as we did in Example 7.2. In general, however, the equation will be more complex than this and some other method is required to solve it. Such methods are usually based on calculating an approximation to the true value of a root of the equation

$$f(x) = 0$$

and then successively refining this approximation until further refining would achieve no useful purpose.

Figure 11.8 shows the graphical representation of a function $y = f(x)$, and it is clear that the roots of the equation

$$f(x) = 0$$

Figure 11.8
$y = f(x)$ and the roots of the equation $f(x) = 0$.

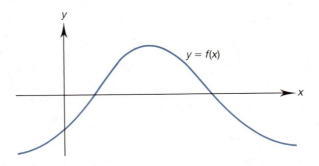

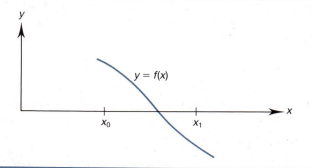

Figure 11.9
Finding an initial interval
that contains a root of
$f(x) = 0$.

are the values of x at which the curve intersects the x-axis. This leads us to a simple, yet powerful, approach to calculating these roots:

> If $f(x_i) < 0$ and $f(x_j) > 0$ then there must be a root in the interval $x_i < x < x_j$

The **bisection method** uses this fact by evaluating the value of $f(x)$ at the point mid-way between x_i and x_j and then repeating the process until the value of x is sufficiently close to the true value of the root. As in all **iterative methods** the problem is in deciding when it is time to stop – what the **convergence criteria** are for the problem.

Essentially, there are three possible criteria that we might use to terminate an iterative search for a root of the equation, all of which depend upon some value becoming less than some extremely small number e:

(1) that the magnitude of the function, $|f(x_i)|$, should be less than e;

(2) that the error $|x_i - x_r|$, where x_r is the true value of the root, should be less than e;

(3) that the difference between successive approximations, $|x_i - x_{i-1}|$, should be less than e.

Different methods will use different criteria to terminate the iteration. In the case of the bisection method it is clear that at each step the interval that surrounds the true value of the root is halved. For example, if the two initial values $f(x_0)$ and $f(x_1)$ have opposite signs, then the root must lie between them (see Figure 11.9), and the value of $f(x_2)$ is calculated, where

$$x_2 = \frac{x_1 + x_0}{2}$$

If the sign of $f(x_2)$ is the same as that of $f(x_0)$ then the root must lie in the interval $x_2 < x < x_1$, while if it is opposite then the root must lie in the interval $x_0 < x < x_2$. In either case the new interval is half the size of the first one (which is, of course, the reason for the name of this method).

After n iterations the interval will, therefore, be of size t, where

$$t = \frac{x_1 - x_0}{2^n}$$

The true root must, therefore, differ from any point within this interval by no more than t and, in particular, must differ from the mid-point of this interval by no more than $t/2$. Therefore, even though we do not know the value of the true root we can, rather surprisingly, use criterion 2 to stop the iteration when we are within a predetermined tolerance of the true value.

The observant reader will have noticed one problem with the procedure outlined above, namely the assumption that we have two initial values x_0 and x_1 between which the root lies. How do we find these two initial values? And how do we ensure that there is only *one* root between x_0 and x_1? For the moment we shall ignore this problem and assume that we have already determined, possibly by graphical means, an initial rough approximation to the root, which allows us to choose suitable values for x_0 and x_1; in Chapter 18 this topic will arise again.

EXAMPLE 11.2

Write a program to find the root of the equation $f(x) = 0$ that lies in a specified interval. The program should use an external function to define the equation, and the user should input the details of the interval in which the root lies and the accuracy required.

Our initial structure plan might be as follows:

> 1   Read range (X0 and X1) and tolerance (T)
>
> 2   Set interval boundaries (XL,XR) to X0 and X1
>
> 3   Call subroutine to find a root in this interval – BISECT
>
> 4   If root found then
>   4.1 Print root;
>   otherwise
>   4.2 Print error message

> BISECT(XL,XR,T,ROOT,COUNT)
>
> 1   If XL and XR do not bracket a root then
>   1.1 Set COUNT to −1 and return

2   Repeat MAX times
    2.1 Calculate mid-point (XM) of interval
    2.2 If (XM-XL)<T then exit with ROOT=XM and COUNT=0
        to indicate success
    2.3 Determine which half-interval the root lies in and set XL
        and XR appropriately

3   No root found, so set COUNT to number of iterations to
indicate failure to converge quickly enough

The only slightly tricky step is 1.3, where we determine in which of the two half-intervals the root lies. We can expand this step as follows:

    1.3.1 Calculate FL and FM, the values of F(XL) and F(XM)
    1.3.2 If FL*FM is less than 0 then
        1.3.2.1 FL and FM have opposite signs, so set XR to
            XM
    otherwise
        1.3.2.2 FL and FM have the same sign, so set XL to
            XM

Step 1 will test for the initial condition in a similar way.

Notice that, although the intrinsic SIGN function will deliver the sign of one of its arguments, the easiest way to determine if two values have opposite signs is to multiply them together and test whether their product is negative.

It will also be noted that we appear to have overlooked the situation in which FM is equal to 0 – that is, XM is the true root. *This is not actually the case, however, for we must be careful not to mix up different convergence criteria.* We already know that since real numbers are approximations we should never compare two real numbers for equality during this type of process, but should rather compare their difference with a very small number. However, the basis of the bisection method is that we successively halve the size of the bracketing interval until it becomes less than a specified tolerance. We must not interject another tolerance into the problem without very careful consideration of its meaning.

The comparison of FM with 0 is an application of the first of our convergence criteria; but, as we can see from Figure 11.10, the fact that $f(x_k)$ is within a specified tolerance e of 0 does *not* mean that x_k is within e of the true root. In the case of this example the user of the program will supply the tolerance for x, and it is not possible to deduce the tolerance for $f(x)$ without further information.

Figure 11.10
A comparison of convergence criteria 1 and 2.

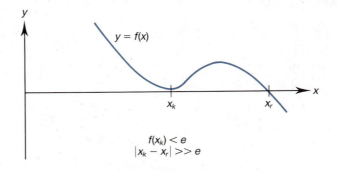

$$f(x_k) < e$$
$$|x_k - x_r| >> e$$

The program can now be written.

```
      PROGRAM ROOT
C
C  This program calculates a root of the equation F(X)=0 in a specified
C  interval to within a specified tolerance of X from the true root, by
C  use of the bisection method
C
C  The function F(X) is supplied as an external function
C
C  Local variables
      REAL X0,X1,XLEFT,XRIGHT,TOLER,ROOT
      INTEGER COUNT
C
C  Read range and tolerance
      PRINT *,'Type two values for X that bracket the required root: '
      READ *,X0,X1
      PRINT *,'Type required tolerance for X: '
      READ *,TOLER
C  Set up initial interval boundaries
      IF (X0.LT.X1) THEN
         XLEFT=X0
         XRIGHT=X1
      ELSE
         XLEFT=X1
         XRIGHT=X0
      END IF
C  Call BISECT to find a root
      CALL BISECT(XLEFT,XRIGHT,TOLER,ROOT,COUNT)
C  Check to see if a root was found
      IF (COUNT.EQ.0) THEN
C  Yes.  Print it
      PRINT 100,ROOT,TOLER
C  No root was found.  Establish why, and print error message
      ELSE IF (COUNT.LT.0) THEN
C  Both initial points on same side of x-axis
         PRINT 101,XLEFT,XRIGHT
      ELSE
```

```
C  Iteration did not converge
          PRINT 102,COUNT,XLEFT,XRIGHT
       END IF
       STOP
  100 FORMAT('A root was found at X =',F10.5,' to a tolerance of ',E7.1)
  101 FORMAT('The values of F at the initial values of X (',F10.5,
     *         ' and ',F10.5,')'/'both lie on the same side of the axis ',
     *         'and bisection is not possible')
  102 FORMAT(I5,' iterations have been carried out without reaching an'/
     *         'acceptably small interval.  The next interval would have'/
     *         'been bounded by X =',F10.5,' and X =',F10.5)
       END


       SUBROUTINE BISECT(XL,XR,T,ROOT,COUNT)
C
C  This subroutine attempts to find a root of the equation Y=F(X)
C  that lies between X=XL and X=XR to within a tolerance in X of T
C
C  The function F is supplied as an external function;  F(XL) and F(XR)
C  must have opposite signs
C
C  Dummy arguments
       REAL XL,XR,T,ROOT
       INTEGER COUNT
C  Parameter to control non-convergence due to poor initial data
       INTEGER MAX
       PARAMETER (MAX=100)
C  Local variables
       REAL XM
       INTEGER I
C  External function
       REAL F
C
C  Check that initial points bracket a root
       IF ((F(XL)*F(XR)).GT.0.0) THEN
C  FL and FR have the same sign.  Return with error set
          COUNT=-1
          RETURN
       END IF
C  Loop until root found
       DO 10, I=1,MAX
          XM=0.5*(XL+XR)
C  ** While testing print current estimate
          PRINT *,XM
C  Is this value close enough?
          IF ((XM-XL).LE.T) GOTO 11
C  No.  Find the next interval.  If F(XL) and F(XM) have opposite signs
C  then a root lies between XL and XM, otherwise it is between XM and XR
          IF ((F(XL)*F(XM)).LT.0.0) THEN
             XR=XM
          ELSE
             XL=XM
          END IF
   10 CONTINUE
```

```
C  MAX iterations without convergence - return error code
        COUNT=MAX
        RETURN
C  Root found - return success code
   11 COUNT=0
        ROOT=XM
        RETURN
        END
```

Note that we have included an extra PRINT statement in BISECT to print the value of XM (the current estimate) at each iteration. Once the program has been tested this statement would normally be removed. Figure 11.11 shows the result of running this program using the following function subprogram to define the equation to be solved:

```
REAL FUNCTION F(X)
REAL X
F=X+EXP(X)
RETURN
END
```

Figure 11.11
The solution of
$x + e^x = 0$ using BISECT.

```
Type two values for X that bracket the required root: -10,0
Type required tolerance for X: 1E-5
 -5.000000
 -2.500000
-1.2500000
-6.2500000E-01
-3.1250000E-01
-4.6875000E-01
-5.4687500E-01
-5.8593750E-01
-5.6640625E-01
-5.7617187E-01
-5.7128906E-01
-5.6884765E-01
-5.6762695E-01
-5.6701660E-01
-5.6732177E-01
-5.6716918E-01
-5.6709289E-01
-5.6713104E-01
-5.6715011E-01
-5.6714057E-01
A root was found at X=  -0.56714 to a tolerance of 0.1E-04
```

11.6   COMPLEX **variables**

There is still one more type of numeric variable, although it is somewhat esoteric and is mainly used for certain specialist applications, such as the calculations frequently carried out by electrical engineers. This type of variable is called **complex** and consists of two parts, a **real part** and an **imaginary part**. In Fortran such a number is stored in two consecutive numeric storage units as two separate real numbers, the first representing the real part and the second the imaginary part. A complex variable is declared in a type specification statement of the form

```
COMPLEX name1,name2,...
```

F90

A complex constant is written as a pair of real numbers, separated by a comma and enclosed in parentheses:

```
(1.5, 7.3)
(1.59E4, -12E-1)
```

In mathematical terms the complex number (X,Y) is written $X + iY$, where $i^2 = -1$. Electrical engineers, however, usually use the letter j rather than i; we shall do so in the following discussion. This definition of a complex number leads to the rules for complex arithmetic that are shown in Figure 11.12.

In Fortran real or integer numbers may be combined with complex numbers to form a mixed-mode expression, but *double precision numbers may not be*.

F90

The evaluation of such a mixed-mode expression is achieved by first converting the real or integer number to a complex number with a zero imaginary part. Thus if Z1 is the complex number (X1, Y1), and R is a real number, then

```
R*Z1
```

If	Z1	$= (X1,Y1)$
and	Z2	$= (X2,Y2)$

then
$Z1+Z2 = (X1+X2,Y1+Y2)$
$Z1-Z2 = (X1-X2,Y1-Y2)$
$Z1*Z2 = (X1*X2-Y1*Y2,X1*Y2+X2*Y1)$
$Z1/Z2 = \left(\dfrac{X1*X2+Y1*Y2}{X2^2+Y2^2}, \dfrac{X2*Y1-X1*Y2}{X2^2+Y2^2} \right)$

Figure 11.12
Complex arithmetic.

Figure 11.13
An example of complex
arithmetic.

```
      PROGRAM COMPLX
      COMPLEX A,B,C
C  Read two complex numbers
      READ (1,'(2F10.3)') A,B
      C=A*B
C  Print data items and their product
      WRITE (2,200) A,B,C
      STOP
  200 FORMAT (1H0,'  A = (',F10.3,',',F10.3,')'/
     1         1H0,'  B = (',F10.3,',',F10.3,')'/
     2         1H0,'A*B = (',F10.3,',',F10.3,')')
      END
```

(output)

```
  A = (    12.500,     8.400)
  B = (     6.500,     9.600)
A*B = (     0.610,   174.600)
```

is converted to

$$(R,0)*(X1,Y1)$$

which is evaluated as

$$(R*X1,R*Y1)$$

Similarly, if I is an integer, then

$$I+Z1$$

is evaluated as

$$(REAL(I)+X1,Y1)$$

Several special functions are available for use with complex numbers. For example, AIMAG(Z) obtains the imaginary part of Z and CONJG(Z) obtains the *complex conjugate* (X,-Y).

Many of the generic functions, such as SIN, LOG, and so on, can also be used with complex arguments. Full details of intrinsic functions that can be used with complex numbers can be found in Appendix A.

Finally it should be mentioned that the input and output of complex numbers are achieved by reading or writing two real numbers, corresponding to the real and imaginary parts, using any appropriate edit descriptor. Figure 11.13 shows an example of complex input and output.

EXAMPLE 11.3

When an alternating voltage is applied to an electrical circuit both its phase and its amplitude are affected by the characteristics of the circuit. In order to simplify calculations relating to such situations, electrical engineers calculate a *transfer function* for the circuit. If the value of the transfer function at a frequency w is $H(w)$, then the amplitude of the output voltage is simply the amplitude of the input voltage multiplied by the magnitude of $H(w)$, while the phase of the output voltage is the phase of the transfer function added to the phase of the input voltage. (The magnitude of the transfer function is its absolute value; its phase is the arctangent of the imaginary part divided by the real part.)

A very common type of circuit in electronic equipment is a *filter circuit* such as that shown in Figure 11.14, which consists of a capacitor and an inductor in series, with a resistor in parallel. By varying the sizes of the three components it is possible to produce: a *high-pass filter*, which passes high frequencies with little attenuation but substantially reduces the amplitude of low-frequency signals; a *low-pass filter*, which does the reverse; or a *band-pass filter*, which reduces both high- and low-frequency signals, allowing only frequencies within an intermediate band to pass without attenuation.

Write a program to produce a table showing the phase and amplitude of the output signal from the circuit shown in Figure 11.14, for different input frequencies and for different values of the components.

We can use Kirchhoff's laws to derive the transfer function for this system, which is

$$H(f) = \frac{R}{1/2\pi jfC + 2\pi jfL + R}$$

or

$$H(f) = \frac{2\pi jfRC}{1 - (2\pi f)^2 LC + 2\pi jfRC}$$

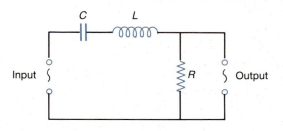

Figure 11.14
A simple electronic filter.

where f is the frequency of the signal in hertz (cycles/second).

A structure plan for the program is quite simple.

> **1** Repeat as long as necessary
> **1.1** Read values of R and C
> **1.2** Read range of frequencies F1 to F2 and step size FINC
> **1.3** Repeat for F from F1 to F2 in steps of FINC
>   **1.3.1** Calculate transfer function
>   **1.3.2** Calculate magnitude and phase shift
>   **1.3.3** Print frequency, magnitude and phase shifts
> **1.4** Ask if another case required
> **1.5** If no more cases then STOP

The program is also quite straightforward. The only problem concerns step 1.4. In Chapter 12 we shall see how to input (and output) variable character strings, and will then be able to control a program such as this by causing the program to print something like

```
Any more cases?
```

and requiring the user to reply by typing Yes or No. However, for the present we can only input numbers, and so we shall deal with this situation as in earlier examples by assuming that if the input values of R, L and C are all 0 then there is no more data.

```
      PROGRAM FILTER
C
C This program calculates the transfer function for a simple electronic
C filter, consisting of a capacitor and an inductor in series, with a
C resistor in parallel, and then prints the voltage amplification and
C phase shift that it produces on input signals in a specified range
C of frequencies
C
      PARAMETER (PI=3.1415926536,TWOPI=2.0*PI,MAX=1000)
C Local variables
      INTEGER F1,F2,FINC,F,I
      REAL R,C,L,AMP,PHASE
      COMPLEX H
C
C Start of loop - read circuit data
      DO 30,I=1,MAX
         PRINT *,'What is the value of the capacitance (microfarads)? '
         READ *,C
         PRINT *,'What is the value of the inductance (millihenries)? '
         READ *,L
         PRINT *,'What is the value of the resistance (kilo-ohms)? '
         READ *,R
```

```
C  Test to see if this is the terminator
         IF (C.EQ.0.0 .AND. L.EQ.0.0 .AND. R.EQ.0.0) GOTO 31
C  Read frequency data
   10    PRINT *,'Give initial and final frequencies, and increment (Hz)'
         READ *,F1,F2,FINC
C  Check for validity
         IF (F1.GT.F2 .OR. FINC.LE.0 .OR. FINC.GT.(F2-F1)) THEN
           PRINT *,'Data is inconsistent.  Please try again'
           GOTO 10
         END IF
C  Data is OK - Print title for this circuit, and column headers
         PRINT 100,F1,F2,C,L,R
  100 FORMAT(1H1,'Frequency response between ',I5,' Hz and ',I5,' Hz'
     * /1H ,'for a filter with a series capacitance of ',F7.3,
     * ' microfarads'/1H ,'and a series inductance of ',F7.3,
     * ' millihenries'/1H ,'in parallel with a resistance of ',F7.3,
     * ' kilo-ohms is:'//
     * 1H ,'Frequency',T15,'Voltage',T30,'Phase'/
     * 1H ,'  (Hz)',    T15,'amplification',T30,'shift'/)
C  Convert capacitance to farads, inductance to henries,
C  and resistance to ohms
         C=C*1.0E-6
         L=L*1.0E-3
         R=R*1.0E3
C  Loop for required frequencies
         DO 20, F=F1,F2,FINC
C  Calculate transfer function
         H=CMPLX(R,0.0)/CMPLX(R,TWOPI*F*L-1.0/(TWOPI*F*C))
         H=CMPLX(0.0,TWOPI*F*R*C)/
     *       CMPLX(1.0-TWOPI*TWOPI*F*F*L*C,TWOPI*F*R*C)
C  Amplification factor is absolute value of H
         AMP=ABS(H)
C  Phase shift is arctangent of imaginary part divided by real part
         PHASE=ATAN2(AIMAG(H),REAL(H))
         PHASE=180.0*PHASE/PI
C  Print results for this frequency
         PRINT 101,F,AMP,PHASE
  101 FORMAT(1H ,I6,T15,F9.3,T30,F5.1)
   20    CONTINUE
   30    CONTINUE
C  1000 cases processed without a terminator!
         PRINT *,'The maximum number of cases (1000!) has now been ',
     * 'processed'
         PRINT *,'If you require still more you must re-run the program'
C  Terminator read - stop processing
   31 STOP
      END
```

Note that when calculating the transfer function H we used the first form
shown in the earlier discussion, namely

$$H(f) = \frac{R}{1/2\pi jfC + 2\pi jfL + R}$$

Figure 11.15
An extract from the
results obtained from
FILTER.

Frequency response between 1000 Hz and 20000 Hz
for a filter with a series capacitance of 0.022 microfarads
and a series inductance of 72.000 millihenries
in parallel with a resistance of 4.700 kilo-ohms is:

Frequency (Hz)	Voltage amplification	Phase shift
1000	0.570	55.3
2000	0.866	30.0
3000	0.976	12.6
4000	1.000	0.0
5000	0.985	-9.8
6000	0.952	-17.8
7000	0.911	-24.4
8000	0.866	-30.0
9000	0.821	-34.8
10000	0.778	-39.0
11000	0.736	-42.6
12000	0.698	-45.8
13000	0.662	-48.6
14000	0.628	-51.1
15000	0.598	-53.3
16000	0.569	-55.3
17000	0.543	-57.1
18000	0.519	-58.7
19000	0.497	-60.2
20000	0.476	-61.6

which was coded in Fortran as

```
H=CMPLX(R,0.0)/CMPLX(R,TWOPI*F*L-1.0/(TWOPI*F*C))
```

where the expression $1/2\pi jfC$ was converted to $-j/2\pi fC$ by multiplying top
and bottom by j, remembering that $j^2=-1$. We could, alternatively, have
used the second form of the relationship,

$$H(f) = \frac{2\pi jfRC}{1-(2\pi f)^2LC+2\pi jfRC}$$

which was derived as a result of multiplying both top and bottom of the
first form by $2\pi jfC$. In that case the Fortran expression would have been

```
      H=CMPLX(0.0,TWOPI*F*R*C)/
     *    CMPLX(1.0-TWOPI*TWOPI*F*F*L*C,TWOPI*F*R*C)
```

Figure 11.15 shows the result of running this program for a particular
circuit. Notice that at 4000 Hz there is no attenuation at all, and that there is

only a relatively slight attenuation between 2 kHz and 8 kHz. This circuit is therefore a band-pass filter that substantially attenuates frequencies below 1 kHz and above 15 kHz; it is thus suitable for use in audio equipment, since this is the frequency band of most relevance in this type of application. (In practice, since the circuit contains only passive elements, it is unlikely that such a primitive filter would actually be used in high-fidelity equipment – but we are not concerned here with the finer points of electronic circuit design!)

SUMMARY

- REAL values are held in a computer as floating-point approximations to the true mathematical values.

- The programmer must always be aware of the effects of round-off during calculation.

- Overflow will occur if a calculation would result in an exponent that is larger than the maximum possible exponent value. It is a fatal condition.

- Underflow will occur if a calculation would result in an exponent that is smaller than the minimum possible exponent value. It normally results in the value being set to zero.

- DOUBLE PRECISION variables use two consecutive numeric storage locations to provide a larger mantissa, and hence greater precision.

- Ill-conditioned numerical processes are very sensitive to small changes in their parameters. It is important that the programmer is aware whether any numerical methods he is using are well-conditioned or ill-conditioned.

- The stability of a numerical process is a measure of its conditioning, including the effect of round-off errors.

- The method of least-squares approximation is a simple and effective method of fitting a straight line through a set of data points.

- The residual sum gives an indication of the goodness of fit of a least-squares approximation, and can be used to eliminate maverick data points.

- Iterative methods are usually used to solve non-linear (or polynomial) equations.

- The bisection method is a simple iterative method for solving non-linear equations that uses the error from the true root as the convergence criterion.

- COMPLEX variables use two consecutive numeric storage locations to represent a complex number as two real numbers, corresponding to the real and imaginary parts.

- Fortran 77 statements introduced in Chapter 11:

  Type declarations   DOUBLE PRECISION *list of names*
                                 COMPLEX *list of names*

SELF-TEST EXERCISES 11.2

1   What are the three main types of convergence criteria for an iterative process?

2   In the method of data fitting by least-squares approximation, what are the residuals and the residual sum?

3   How is the residual sum used as a measure of goodness of fit in a least-squares approximation?

4   Name two potential problems with the bisection method for finding the roots of a polynomial.

5   What will be printed by the following program?

```
PROGRAM TEST5
REAL Z
COMPLEX A,B
A = (1.0,2.0)
B = (3.0,4.0)
Z = 5.0
PRINT *,A,B,Z
PRINT *,A+B,A-B,A+Z
PRINT *,A*B,Z*B,A/B
PRINT *,A/Z,Z/A,CONJG(Z/A)
STOP
END
```

PROGRAMMING EXERCISES

11.1   Write a program that calculates π using first REAL and then DOUBLE PRECISION variables. Print out the answers to as many decimal places as your machine will allow and compare the result with a tabulated value.

11.2   Tabulate the values of $1 - \cos x$ to four decimal places for x between 0 and 10^{-4} in steps of 10^{-5}, using a REAL variable for x. Repeat using a DOUBLE PRECISION variable for x.

Finally, repeat both the above using the fact that

$$1 - \cos x = 2 \sin^2 \frac{x}{2}$$

11.3   Write a program to evaluate the factorial of 200. (*Hint*: use logs.) Compare your result with Stirling's approximation for large n:

$$\log_e(n!) = (n+0.5)\log_e n - n + \frac{\log_e(2\pi)}{2}$$

(Note that these are all logs to base e.)

11.4   The polynomial

$$63x^3 - 183x^2 + 97x + 55$$

has three real roots between -10 and $+10$. Write a program to find them, using the bisection method.

   (*Hint*: you must first find intervals in which the roots lie; this can be achieved by tabulating the value of the polynomial for various values of x.)

*11.5   Use the program you wrote for Exercise 11.4 to find those roots of the following equations which lie in the range $-10 \leqslant x \leqslant 10$.

   (a) $10x^3 - x^2 - 39x + 72$
   (b) $20x^3 - 52x^2 - 17x + 24$
   (c) $5x^3 - x^2 - 8x + 16$
   (d) $10x^4 + 13x^3 - 19x^2 + 8x + 48$
   (e) $x^4 + 2x^3 - 23x^2 - 24x + 144$
   (f) $9x^4 - 42x^3 - 1040x^2 + 5082x - 5929$

11.6   The Taylor series is a method of calculating an approximation to a particular function. For example, the Taylor series for the function sin(x) is:

$$\sin(x) = x - \frac{x^3}{3!} + \frac{x^5}{5!} - \frac{x^7}{7!} + \frac{x^9}{9!} - \dots$$

where x is an angle in radians, and $n!$ is the factorial function of n, that is, $n \times (n-1) \times (n-2) \times \dots \times 2 \times 1$.

   Write a program to evaluate the first five terms of the above series, and compare the accuracy achieved with the intrinsic function SIN (which almost certainly uses the same technique). Now modify your program so that it uses a variable number of terms in the series, and keeps adding terms until they become sufficiently small. Note that an efficient program should calculate each term in the series from the previous one. Compare the accuracy obtainable with REAL and DOUBLE PRECISION variables.

11.7   Write a program that reads the values of two complex numbers w and z from the keyboard as two pairs of real numbers, and calculates the following values:

$$w+z$$
$$\bar{z}$$
$$\bar{w}$$
$$z^2$$
$$z.\bar{z}$$

where $\bar{z}$ is the complex conjugate of z.

Test your program with several sets of data, including the following:

   (i) $w = 2 + 1j$, $z = 4 + 3j$
   (ii) $w = 8 + 3j$, $z = 5 + 2j$

11.8   The polar form of the complex number z $(=x+jy)$ is written as (R,θ), where $R=|z|$ (the absolute value of z, which is equal to $\sqrt{(x^2+y^2)}$ and $\theta = \tan(y/x)$.

Write a subroutine to convert a complex number to its polar form.

If $z=1+j$ and $w=1+3j$, write a program that uses your subroutine to print the values of the following expressions in polar form, with θ given in degrees:

$$z$$
$$w$$
$$z^*w$$
$$z/w$$
$$z+w$$
$$z-w$$
$$2^*z$$
$$z^2$$
$$\sqrt{z}$$

11.9   The roots of the quadratic equation

$$az^2 + bz + c = 0$$

are given by the formula

$$z = \frac{-b \pm \sqrt{b^2 - 4ac}}{2a}$$

Allowing for the fact that the expression $b^2 - 4ac$ may be negative (by using COMPLEX variables), write a program that calculates the roots of such an equation, and use it to find the roots of the following equations:

$$z^2 - 1 = 0$$
$$z^2 + 1 = 0$$
$$z^2 - 3z + 4 = 0$$
$$z^2 - 3z - 4 = 0$$

11.10 Given a complex number c $(= x + iy)$, write a program that iteratively carries out the process

$$z = z^2 + c$$

where z is COMPLEX and is initially zero. Choose your own value for c with both x and y between -1 and $+1$, and repeat the process until $z \geqslant 100$. Print out how many iterations it took. The Mandlebrot fractal pictures that you may have seen in science magazines or on television are produced using this algorithm.

11.11 The following set of experimental data is to be fitted to a curve of the form $y = e^{ax}$

x	0.0	0.1	0.2	0.3	0.4	0.5	0.6	0.7	0.8	0.9	1.0
y	1.07	1.40	1.56	2.30	2.92	3.52	4.57	6.00	7.33	9.69	12.04

This can be done as follows. The sum of the squares of the residuals is given by

$$\sum_{i=0}^{10} (y_i - \exp(ax_i))^2$$

and this must be minimized with respect to a. Simple differentiation therefore tells us that the following equation needs to be solved for a

$$\sum_{i=0}^{10} x_i(y_i - \exp(ax_i))\exp(ax_i) = 0$$

Write a program to solve this using the bisection method and hence find the estimated value of a.

11.12 In Exercise 7.18 you wrote a program to find the roots of the equation

$$y = x^2 - 3x + 2$$

using the Newton–Raphson Method. However, if we applied the same method to the equation

$$y = x^2 - 3x + 5$$

we should find that there are no roots for this equation. Modify the program you wrote for Exercise 7.18 to use this equation to confirm that the iteration does not converge.

Now modify the program so that all the variables are complex and run it again, making sure that the initial estimate has a non-zero imaginary part. You should obtain two complex roots for the equation.

*11.13 Exercise 7.18 referred to Newton's iteration, as a means of finding the roots of a polynomial by Newton's method, and defined it by the equation

$$x_{n+1} = x_n - \frac{f(x_n)}{f'(x_n)}$$

This leads us to a method of calculating the first derivative $f'(x)$ of a function $f(x)$, using the Newton quotient:

$$f'(x) = \frac{f(x+h) - f(x)}{h}$$

where h is small. Write a program to compute the Newton quotient for the function

$$f(x) = x^2 - 3x + 2$$

at the point $x = 2$ (where we can readily calculate that the exact answer is 1). Your program should print a table showing the value of h and the calculated value of $f'(x)$, for values of h starting at 1 and decreasing by a factor of 10 on each repetition. You will find that when h becomes too small the calculation loses all semblance of accuracy due to rounding errors.

Modify your program to use a new set of values for h in the region that showed the greatest accuracy. What is the best value for h for this function, when $x = 2$?

11.14 Exercise 11.13 showed how rounding errors affected the calculation of the first derivative of a function by means of the Newton quotient. Repeat the exercise, but carrying out all the calculations in double precision arithmetic.

Now repeat the same process, using both real and double precision arithmetic, for the following functions at the points specified:

(a) $x^2 - 3x + 2$ at $x = 1.5$ (exact value is 0)
(b) $x^3 - 6x^2 + 12x - 5$ at $x = 1$ (exact value is 3)
(c) $x^3 - 6x^2 + 12x - 5$ at $x = 2$ (exact value is 0)
(d) $x^3 - 6x^2 + 12x - 5$ at $x = 3$ (exact value is 12)

What does this tell you about choosing the value for h?

Character handling

12

Whereas numbers of all types are stored in **numeric storage units**, character data is stored in **character storage units**, each of which can store exactly one character in a coded form. A character variable consists of one or more character storage units and must be declared in a type declaration statement that includes the length of each variable being declared.

Because a character variable always has a fixed length, character data of a different length will be truncated from the right or extended with blanks on the right before assignment. A special concatenation operator allows two character strings to be combined to form a single character string. It is also possible to define a **substring** of a character variable, which can then be used in the same way as a character variable, apart from one restriction relating to assignment.

Character data can be input and output in a similar way to numbers; however, if an input data string is too long for the variable to which it is being input, it will be truncated from the left (for compatibility with the addition of extra blanks on the left during output, if this is necessary to fill the specified field width).

Character strings can be compared using the normal relational operators, in which case the ordering is processor dependent in some aspects. Alternatively, intrinsic procedures are available that compare two character strings using the ordering specified in the ASCII character code.

12.1   Characters and character storage units

So far all our variables have been either integer or real. We can now consider the storage of characters in variables. There is, however, one very great difference between the storage of numbers and the storage of characters. A typical modern computer might use 32 bits (0s or 1s) to store a real or integer number in what is formally called a **numeric storage unit**. Such a numeric storage unit might be able to hold integers in the range from about -2×10^9 to $+2 \times 10^9$, or real numbers in the range -10^{38} to $+10^{38}$, with an accuracy of about seven significant figures. However, the same storage unit would probably hold only *four* characters in coded form. This is because each character normally requires either six or eight bits (depending on the code being used). Characters are therefore dealt with in a rather different way.

F90

A **character storage unit** is a location in the memory that will hold exactly *one* character (or rather the code for one character), and a **character variable** will consist of one or more character storage units. There is no assumption about the relationship, if any, between numeric and character storage units, although in practice most computers will use the same physical memory devices for both types, so that, for example, four 8-bit character storage units may be kept together in what would otherwise be a single 32-bit numeric storage unit.

F90

Programs in the Fortran language are written using only 49 different characters, which are known as the **Fortran character set** and are shown in Figure 12.1.

However, any particular implementation will almost certainly have codes for other characters, since a 6-bit code gives 64 different codes and an 8-bit code gives 256. Appendix D gives two examples of widely used coding systems, although the actual codes should not normally be of any concern to the programmer (but see Section 12.4). Any character that can be coded by a particular processor can be stored as part of a character constant or character variable.

F90

Figure 12.1
The Fortran character set.

```
A B C D E F G H I J K L M N O P Q R S T U V W X Y Z
0 1 2 3 4 5 6 7 8 9
♦ = + - * / ( ) , . $ ' :
```

where ♦ represents the space character

12.2 CHARACTER **variables and expressions**

Before we can store characters in a variable we must declare the variable to be of CHARACTER type, in much the same way that we have been declaring INTEGER and REAL variables. The declaration statement for a character variable takes one of several, closely related, forms:

```
CHARACTER name1,name2,...
CHARACTER*len name1,name2,...
CHARACTER name1*len1,name2*len2,...
CHARACTER*len name1*len1,name2*len2,...
```

F90

The first form states that the variables called *name1*, *name2*, and so on, are to be CHARACTER variables, and that each such variable is to consist of *one* character storage unit – that is, each will contain exactly one character.

The second form states that each of the variables is to consist of *len* character storage units, and that each will therefore contain exactly *len* characters.

The third form specifies a (different) **length** for each variable; thus *name1* contains *len1* characters, *name2* contains *len2* characters, and so on. If any name is not followed by a length (*len*) then it is given a single character storage unit, that is, a length of 1.

Finally, the fourth variation states that unless otherwise specified each variable has a length of *len*; thus

```
CHARACTER*4 A,B*6,C
```

gives A and C four character storage units each, and B six storage units.

The length (*len*) may be specified either as a positive integer constant or as an integer constant *expression* enclosed in parentheses. Thus the following three sets of declarations have an identical effect:

```
CHARACTER*6 A,B,C

PARAMETER (LEN=6)
CHARACTER*LEN A,B,C

PARAMETER (LEN=9)
CHARACTER*(LEN-3) A,B,C
```

Once we have declared a character variable we can, of course, use it in character expressions and assignment statements in a similar way to numeric variables. There are, however, a number of very important differences, of which the most obvious concerns the length of a character variable or expression. We can see these most readily by means of an example:

```
PROGRAM CHAREX
CHARACTER*4 A*3,B,C
A='END'
B=A
C='FINAL'
STOP
END
```

Here three character variables are declared, two of length 4 and one (A) of length 3. The first assignment statement assigns the character constant 'END' to A. We can readily see that the value to be assigned (the constant) has a length of 3 and so it exactly occupies the three storage units that constitute the variable A, and all is well.

The next assignment statement (B=A) is, however, more of a problem. A has a length of 3 and contains the three characters END; B, however, has a length of 4, so what will be stored in the four storage units?

The answer is that if a character string has a shorter length than the variable to which it is to be assigned then *it is extended to the right with blank (or space) characters* until it is the correct length. In this case, therefore, it will have a single blank character added after the letter D, thus making its length 4.

The third assignment statement poses the opposite problem. Here the character constant to be assigned has a length of 5, whereas the variable, C, has a length of 4. In this case the string is **truncated** from the right to the correct length before assignment.

At the end of this program, therefore, the three variables A, B and C contain the character strings 'END', 'END◆' and 'FINA', respectively, where ◆ represents a blank, or space, character.

The importance of this extension and truncation makes it desirable that we restate these rules more formally:

When assigning a character string to a character variable whose length is not the same as that of the string, the string is extended on the right with blanks, or truncated from the right, to make its length the same as that of the character variable to which it is being assigned.

However, the ability to assign a character constant, or the string stored in a character variable, does not in itself take us very far. Just as we have had arithmetic expressions and logical expressions, we can also create character expressions. The major difference between character expression and the other types of expression is that there are very few things we can actually do with strings of characters.

One thing that we can do, though, is combine two strings to form a

```
PROGRAM CHARS
CHARACTER*5 A*8,B,C
A='ALPHABET'
B=A(:5)
C=A(6:)//A(5:5)
STOP
END
```

Figure 12.2
Character expressions.

third, composite, string. This process is called **concatenation** and is carried out by means of a **concatenation operator** (//):

```
'Fred'//'die'
```

The composite string will, of course, have a length equal to the sum of the lengths of the two strings that were concatenated to form it.

There are no other meaningful things that we can do with two strings in order to produce a third string. One further operation is possible on a single character string, however: the identification and extraction of a *part* of the string. A part of a string that is identified in this way is called a **substring** and is defined by following the string, or the name of the variable containing the string, by either one or two integer expressions separated by a colon and enclosed in parentheses:

```
'rhubarb'(2:4)
ALPHA(5:7)
BETA(4:)
GAMMA(:6)
DELTA(I:J+K)
```

The first of the two integer expressions defines the position in the string of the *first* character of the substring, while the second defines the position of the *last* character of the substring. The positions within a character string are numbered from 1 up to the length of the string, and it follows, therefore, that the values of both integer expressions must lie in this range, and that the first must be less than or equal to the second. If the first expression is omitted then the substring starts at the beginning of the string; if the second is omitted then it continues to the end.

Figure 12.2 illustrates this. A substring consisting of the first five characters of A ('ALPHA') is assigned to B, and the concatenation of two substrings ('BET' and 'A') causes the string 'BETA' to be assigned to C. Notice that the two substrings have lengths of 3 and 1, resulting in a length of 4 for the composite string; this is extended to a length of 5 before it is assigned to C.

It is also possible to assign a value to a substring without altering the rest of the variable. Thus if we added an extra statement

```
A(4:)='INE'
```

after the assignment to C in the program shown in Figure 12.2, the string stored in A would become 'ALPINE '. It is instructive to examine this in detail.

The substring A(4:) is the substring from character 4 to the end of A – a total of five characters. The string 'INE' only has a length of 3 so it is extended by adding two blank characters before being assigned to A(4:). The assignment means that the old substring value ('HABET') is replaced by the new value ('INE '), leaving the rest of A unchanged. The final result, therefore, is that A contains 'ALPINE '.

F90

There is one very important restriction concerning the assignment of character expressions. *None of the character positions to which a value is being assigned may appear in the character expression on the right-hand side of the equals sign.* The assignment of a character string may, with certain processors, take place in several steps, and not all at once as is the case with numbers; if this rule did not exist, part of the string might be altered before it had been assigned. Thus the expression

```
A(4:6)=A(2:4)
```

is *not* allowed, while the expression

```
A(4:6)=A(1:3)
```

is allowed, since none of the character positions on the left-hand side also appears on the right-hand side.

EXAMPLE 12.1

Write a program that, with apologies to Neil Armstrong, uses 'a kindly giant' to convert 'A small step for a man' into 'A giant leap for mankind' without using any other character constants.

This program will be purely concerned with character manipulation and, as it consists solely of assignment statements of a somewhat artificial nature, does not need a structure plan.

```
      PROGRAM MOON
C
C  This program is an example of character substring manipulation
C
      CHARACTER*24 A,B,C
```

```
C  Initialize base strings
      DATA A/'a kindly giant'/,B/'A small step for a man'/
C  Print first phrase
      PRINT *,B
C  Create 'lean' in C
      C=B(6:6)//B(11:11)//B(21:)
C  Change 'small ste' to 'giant lea'
      B(3:11)=A(10:15)//C
C  Change 'a man' to 'mankind'
      C=B(20:)
      B(18:)=C(:3)//A(3:6)
C  Print second phrase
      PRINT *,B
      STOP
      END
```

Notice the use of a DATA statement to initialize the two character variables A and B with the two strings 'a kindly giant' and 'A small step for a man'. The DATA statement can be used with characters in much the same way as we have been using it with real and integer variables. In particular, the same rules operate regarding the length of the initial strings as with assignment, leading to the specified string being truncated if it is too long for the specified variable or extended to the right with blanks if it is too short.

Figure 12.3 illustrates the steps in this program. The first assignment statement extracts the letters l, e and an from the string stored in B and combines them to form the string 'lean' in C. The substring 'small ste' in B is then replaced by the string 'giant lea' (formed by concatenating a substring of A and C to form the string 'giant lean', which is itself truncated before assignment). Once this has been done, the last few characters of B are stored in C before being replaced in B two places to the left (to avoid breaking the rule about having the same character position on both sides of the equals sign) after being concatenated with a substring taken from A.

```
PROGRAM MOON
CHARACTER*24 A,B,C
DATA A/'a kindly giant'/,B/'A small step for a man'/
                         A: 'a kindly giant          '
                         B: 'A small step for a man  '
                         C: '                        '
PRINT *,B
C=B(6:6)//B(11:11)//B(21:)
                         C: 'lean                    '
B(3:11)=A(10:15)//C
                         B: 'A giant leap for a man   '
C=B(20:)
                         C: 'man                     '
B(18:)=C(:3)//A(3:6)
                         B: 'A giant leap for mankind'
PRINT *,B
STOP
END
```

Figure 12.3
The progress of MOON.

This removes the sequence `'a '` before `'man'`, allowing the string `'mankind'` to replace `' a man'`. The variable B now contains the required string `'A giant leap for mankind'`.

12.3   Input and output of character variables

Now that we have seen how to declare and manipulate character variables, it is clearly desirable that we establish how to read characters into such variables and write characters from them. To do this we need a new edit descriptor – the A **edit descriptor** – as shown in Figures 12.4 and 12.5.

The A edit descriptor can be used in two ways – with or without a field width w. To understand fully the way in which it operates we need to consider input and output separately.

On input, the edit descriptor Aw refers to the next w characters (much as Iw and F$w.d$ refer to w characters). However, a character variable has a defined length and any string that is to be stored in it must be made to have the same length. Let us assume that the length of the input list item is *len*.

- If w is less than *len* extra blank characters will be added at the end to extend the length of the input character string to *len*. This is similar to the procedure with assignment.

- If w is greater than *len*, however, the *rightmost len* characters of the input character string will be stored in the input list item. This is the *opposite* of what happens with assignment.

The reason for this difference – that on input the rightmost *len* characters are stored while during assignment the leftmost *len* characters are assigned – can be understood if we consider the output of characters. In this case, Aw will cause characters to be output to the next w character positions of the

Figure 12.4
Edit descriptors for inputting characters.

Descriptor	Meaning
Aw	Read the next w characters as characters
A	Read sufficient characters to fill the input list item, stored as characters

Descriptor	Meaning
A*w*	Output the output list item as a string of characters in the next *w* character positions
A	Output the output list item as a string of characters with no leading or trailing blanks item, stored as characters

Figure 12.5
Edit descriptors for
outputting characters.

output record; once again we need to establish exactly what happens if the length of the output list item is not *w*.

- If *w* is greater than *len* the character string will be right-justified within the output field (that is, positioned as far as possible to the right), and will be preceded by one or more blanks. This is similar to the procedure with the I and F edit descriptors.
- If *w* is less than *len* then the leftmost *w* characters will be output.

A comparison of the two sets of rules shows that they are compatible with each other. Thus if characters are written using a particular format and if the results produced could be subsequently read using an identical format, then the values stored would be the same as those originally output – see Figure 12.6.

```
      PROGRAM CHEX1
      CHARACTER*4 A,B
      A='DAFT'
      B='DOG'
      WRITE (2,201) A,B
  201 FORMAT(1H ,A6,3X,A3)
      STOP
      END
```

Figure 12.6
Input and output of
characters.

(output)
```
 DAFT    DOG
```

```
      PROGRAM CHEX2
      CHARACTER*4 A,B
      READ (1,101) A,B
  101 FORMAT(A6,3X,A3)
      STOP
      END
```

A contains 'DAFT' and B contains 'DOG '

Figure 12.7
Character input and
assignment.

```
        PROGRAM CHEX3
        CHARACTER*4 A,B,C*6
C  Data read is typed as 'ABCDEFABCDEF'
        READ (1,101) A,C
    101 FORMAT(2A6)
        B=C
        WRITE (2,201) A,B,C
    201 FORMAT (1H ,'A:''',A4,''', B:''',A4,''', C:''',A6,'''')
        STOP
        END
```

(output)
A:'CDEF', B:'ABCD', C:'ABCDEF'

A few moments' thought shows that, if during output blanks were added at the beginning, as they logically must be for $w > len$, while input strings were truncated at the right, then there *would* be a major incompatibility. The rules elaborated above are, therefore, the only ones that make sense.

Figure 12.7 demonstrates this difference. Both A and C are read using an A edit descriptor. In the first case, therefore, only the rightmost four characters are stored. C is now assigned to B, and in this case the leftmost four characters are stored. The printed result confirms this difference between direct input to A and indirect input to B via C (whose length is the same as the field width).

For both input and output the field width need not be specified, in which case a field width is used that is equal to the length of the input/ output list item. This can be particularly useful on output, since it can enable the same basic format to be used with character variables of different lengths, but on input it should be used with extreme caution. When characters are read they should normally either occupy a known field width, in which case Aw can be used, or be read in such a way that the *data* controls the input.

There is one further way of reading and writing character information, namely the use of list-directed formatting. This can be useful for output (subject to the limitations of list-directed formatting regarding overall layout), but is of less use for input.

If a character variable or expression appears in the output list of a WRITE or PRINT statement that is using list-directed formatting, the effect is the same as if an A edit descriptor had been used – that is, the full character string is output, using as many character positions as are necessary. We have used this form of output in most of our earlier programs when writing statements such as:

```
PRINT *,'This is a string of characters!'
```

The only item in the output list here is a character constant, which is, after all, a very simple form of character expression. We could equally well have written

```
STRING='This is a string of characters!'
PRINT *,STRING
```

where STRING is a character variable of length 31.

Input is, however, rather different. We have seen in connection with numbers that a data item for list-directed input is terminated by a space, a comma, a slash (/), or the end of a record. Since spaces (in particular) often occur in character data there would clearly be a problem if character data was not identified in some other way.

In Fortran 77 any character data that is read by a list-directed READ statement must be enclosed between apostrophes (as for a character constant). Thus if a character variable appears in the input list of a READ statement that is using list-directed formatting, the corresponding data item must consist of a string of one or more characters enclosed between apostrophes. If the data contains an apostrophe then this must be represented by two consecutive apostrophes. A character string input in this way may be continued onto a second or subsequent record. However, it is not usually convenient to provide character data in this form, and so list-directed formatting is of less use with character data than with numeric data.

F90

EXAMPLE 12.2

The four-round scores in a golf tournament are typed into the computer in the following way:

columns	1–20	player's name
	22,23	
	25,26	
	28,29	player's scores
	31,32	

The data is terminated by typing END OF DATA in columns 1–11. Assuming that the total scores for all the players are different, write a program to print the names of the winner and the runner-up, together with their scores for each round. (Note for non-golfers: the player with the lowest total score is the winner.)

There is one slight problem here concerning the recognition of the terminator; however, as we shall see in the next section, the six relational operators introduced in Chapter 7 can be used to compare characters as well as numbers. In this case we are comparing only for equality, and we need only state here that if the two strings being compared are of unequal length then the shorter one is extended on the right with spaces before the two strings are compared.

We can now produce a structure plan:

> **1**   Initialize details for first two places
>
> **2**   Repeat the following
> **2.1** Read name and scores
> **2.2** If name = 'END OF DATA' then exit
> **2.3** Calculate total score
> **2.4** If total < current leader then
>   **2.4.1** Move current leader to second place
>   **2.4.2** Insert this player as new leader
>   but if total < current second player then
>   **2.4.3** Insert this player as new second player
>
> **3**   Print details of first two players

Note here the logic for checking the player's score against the best so far and for moving the details down the list. We can now write the program.

```
      PROGRAM GOLF
C
C  This program prints the details of the first two players
C  in a golf tournament
C
C  Maximum number of players
      INTEGER MAX
      PARAMETER (MAX=100)
C  First two players' names, round scores and totals
      CHARACTER*20 LEADER,RUNUP
      INTEGER SCORE1(4),TOTAL1,SCORE2(4),TOTAL2
C  Data name, round and total scores
      CHARACTER*20 PLAYER
      INTEGER SCORE(4),TOTAL
C  Miscellaneous variables
      INTEGER I
C  Initialize first two players' scores to very high values
C  and their names to empty strings
      DATA LEADER,RUNUP/2*' '/,
     *      SCORE1,SCORE2,TOTAL1,TOTAL2/8*500,2*2000/
C  Main loop to process all players' scores
      PRINT *,'Type scores as follows:'
      PRINT *,'--------Name--------- R1 R2 R3 R4'
      PRINT *,'A name typed as ''END OF DATA'' terminates data input'
```

```
          DO 10, I=1,MAX
             PRINT *,'Next player: '
             READ '(A20,4(1X,I2))',PLAYER,SCORE
C  Check for end of data
             IF (PLAYER.EQ.'END OF DATA') GOTO 11
C  Calculate total score and compare it with leaders
             TOTAL=SCORE(1)+SCORE(2)+SCORE(3)+SCORE(4)
             IF (TOTAL.LT.TOTAL1) THEN
C  Move leader to runner-up, and this player to leader
                CALL MOVE(LEADER,TOTAL1,SCORE1,RUNUP,TOTAL2,SCORE2)
                CALL MOVE(PLAYER,TOTAL,SCORE,LEADER,TOTAL1,SCORE1)
             ELSE IF (TOTAL.LT.TOTAL2) THEN
C  Move this player to runner-up
                CALL MOVE(PLAYER,TOTAL,SCORE,RUNUP,TOTAL2,SCORE2)
             END IF
      10    CONTINUE
          PRINT 201,MAX
      11 PRINT 202,LEADER,TOTAL1,SCORE1,RUNUP,TOTAL2,SCORE2
          STOP
     201 FORMAT (1H0,'No terminator found.  Only first',I4,
         *              ' players processed')
     202 FORMAT (1H1,'Fortran 77 Golf Tournament'///
         1          1H ,'The Winner and Runner-up were:'//
         2          (1H ,A20,2X,'Total:',I4,' (',3(I2,','),I2,')'))
          END


          SUBROUTINE MOVE(PLAYR1,TOTAL1,SCORE1,PLAYR2,TOTAL2,SCORE2)
C
C  This subroutine moves the name and scores for PLAYR1 into those
C  for PLAYR2
C
          CHARACTER*20 PLAYR1,PLAYR2
          INTEGER TOTAL1,SCORE1(4),TOTAL2,SCORE2(4),I
C
          PLAYR2=PLAYR1
          TOTAL2=TOTAL1
          DO 10, I=1,4
      10    SCORE2(I)=SCORE1(I)
          RETURN
          END
```

When we exchange players' names and scores we must take care about the order in which we do it. If we were to put the new player's details in first position before moving the previous leader's details to second position we should find that we had destroyed values that we wished to keep. Since there are three such sets of exchanges to be carried out a (very) simple subroutine has been written to perform the move. This also has the effect of making the main program easier to follow.

Another point concerns the formats for the input of the data and the printing of the results. The input format is the easier so we shall examine this first. It consists of an A20 edit descriptor, followed by 1X, I2, repeated four times. This corresponds to character data in columns 1–20 and four

Figure 12.8
Results produced by the
GOLF program.

```
Fortran 77 Golf Tournament'


The Winner and Runner-up were:

Faldo, Nick             Total: 277 (71,69,68,69)
Lyle, Sandy             Total: 278 (69,69,72,68)
```

integers in columns 22–23, 25–26, 28–29 and 31–32, which is exactly how the data was specified.

The output format is much more interesting. The first two lines start a new page, print an overall title and then print a heading for the actual results. The last line of the format is complicated: we note that it consists of a nested format expression,

```
(1H ,A20,2X,'Total:',I4,' (',3(I2,','),I2,')'))
```

If any repetition of the format occurs it will start from the beginning of this nested expression. This outputs a printer control character followed by a 20-character value (which will be a player's name). After two spaces `Total:` is printed, followed by an integer occupying four characters. A look at the `PRINT` statement shows us that the total score is output after the name, and since this cannot require more than three digits (because it is the sum of four 2-digit scores) there will be a space after the colon, before the score.

This is followed by a space and a left parenthesis enclosed in apostrophes, and then a three-times-repeated sequence (I2,',') which will output three 2-digit integers followed by commas. Finally another two-digit integer is output, followed by a right parenthesis. The complete sequence when printed would therefore look like this:

```
Miles Ellis             Total: 309 (81,77,82,69)
```

(Those who have seen the first edition of this book will notice an improvement in the author's golf!)

If we now examine the `PRINT` statement we see that the names and scores of both the winner and the runner-up are included in the same output list. When the winner's details have been printed, therefore, the format will be exhausted and will repeat from the beginning of the nested expression, thus printing the second player's results in the same format. Figure 12.8 shows the results of running the program.

12.4   Comparing character strings

In the last example we used a character string as a terminator for the data and checked for it with the statement

```
IF (PLAYER.EQ.'END OF DATA') GOTO 11
```

As might be expected, we can use all six relational operators (.GT., .GE., .EQ., .NE., .LE. and .LT.) to compare character strings; what is not so obvious, however, is how we define the relationship between two strings.

   The key to this is the **collating sequence** of letters, digits and other characters. Fortran 77 lays down four rules for this, covering letters, digits and the space or blank character.

(1)   The 26 upper-case letters are collated in the following order:
      A B C D E F G H I J K L M N O P Q R S T U V W X Y Z

(2)   The 10 digits are collated in the following order:
      0 1 2 3 4 5 6 7 8 9

(3)   Digits are either all collated before the letter A, or all after the letter Z.

(4)   A space (or blank) is collated before both letters and digits.

The other 12 special characters, and any others that may be available on a particular computer system, do not have any defined position in the collating sequence. In practice they will usually be ordered according to the internal code used by the computer as long as this code satisfies the above rules. Appendix D shows two of the more widely used internal codes.

   When two character operands are being compared there are three distinct stages in the process:

(1)   If the two operands are not the same length, the shorter one is extended on the right with blanks until it is the same length as the other.

(2)   The two operands are compared character by character, starting with the leftmost character, until a difference is found or the end of the operands is reached.

(3)   If a difference is found, then the relationship between these two different characters defines the relationship between the two operands.

The result of this process is that the relational expression always has the value we would instinctively expect it to have. Thus

```
'ADAM'.GT.'EVE' is false
```

because 'A' comes before 'E' and therefore 'A'.GT.'E' is *false*.

> 'ADAM'.LT.'ADAMANT' is *true*

because after 'ADAM' has been extended the relationship reduces to
' '.LE.A' after the first four characters have been found to be the same.
Since a blank comes before a letter, this is *true*.

> '120'.LT.'1201' is *true*

because the first difference in the strings leads to an evaluation of
' '.LT.'1', which is *true* since a blank also comes before a digit.

Notice, however, that the values of the expressions

> 'XA'.LT.'X4'

and

> 'VAR-1'.GT.'VAR.1'

are not defined. In the first case the standard does not define whether
letters are to be before or after digits and so the value of 'A'.LT.'4' will
depend upon the particular computer system being used. In the second
case the special characters are not defined at all, so that the value of
'-'.GT.'.' depends upon the computer system.

One further point should be mentioned here, namely the effect of
lower-case letters. The Fortran collating sequence refers only to upper-case
letters, and so the values of the following expressions are all undefined:

> 'adam'.GT.'eve'
> 'Adam'.LT.'Adamant'
> 'TOM'.GT.'Tom'

In practice, however, the codes used for lower-case letters are invariably in
the normal alphabetic order, and almost invariably *follow* the upper-case
letters. On most, if not all, computers, therefore:

> 'adam'.GT.'eve' is *false*
> 'Adam'.LT.'Adamant' is *true*
> 'TOM'.GT.'Tom' is *false*

It must be emphasized, however, that this is not part of the Standard, and
it is conceivable, though unlikely, that this ordering does not hold on some
Fortran 77 implementations.

These undefined areas are not, in practice, any problem. It is
unlikely that any normal application would expect to compare character

LGE(C1,C2) is the same as C1.GE.C2 using ASCII character ordering

LGT(C1,C2) is the same as C1.GT.C2 using ASCII character ordering

LLE(C1,C2) is the same as C1.LE.C2 using ASCII character ordering

LLT(C1,C2) is the same as C1.LT.C2 using ASCII character ordering

Figure 12.9
Intrinsic functions for
lexical comparison.

strings (other than for equality) in which the order was to be determined by characters other than letters, digits or blanks. The concepts of alphabetic or numeric ordering are natural ones, as is the concept of shorter strings coming before longer ones that start with the shorter one (that is, *John* comes before *Johnson*, *alpha* before *alphabet*, and so on). The only practical area of doubt concerns the question of whether digits come before or after letters.

If, for reasons of portability, it is required to define the ordering of *all* characters, another way of comparing them is available. This uses one of the four intrinsic functions shown in Figure 12.9. These functions return the value *true* or *false* after a comparison that uses the ordering of characters defined in the American National Standard Code for Information Interchange (ANSI X3.4 1977), which is usually referred to as **ASCII**. This code, which is widely used as an internal code, is shown in Appendix D.1.

Since the four lexical comparison functions return a logical value they can be used in logical expressions in the same way as a relational or logical expression. For example, the following block IF structure will obey the block of statements only if the characters in the variable NAME start with one of the characters <, = or > (see Appendix D.1).

```
IF (LGE(NAME,'<') .AND. LLT(NAME,'?')) THEN
   block of statements
END IF
```

EXAMPLE 12.3

A hospital has a library of subprograms used to update various medical records, arrange appointments and provide statistics. In particular, the subroutine ADMIT is used to plan admittances for surgical operations and requires three character arguments: the patient's name, the surgeon and the type of operation. The proposed date of admission (as an 11-character string, *dd mmm yyyy*) and the expected length of stay in days (as an integer) are returned through two further arguments. In order to avoid any accusations of bias the hospital has decided that the surgeon to operate on a particular patient will be chosen according to the following rules:

(1)   The patient is given a number based on his or her name. If it starts with:

> A–D the number is 1;
> E–J the number is 2;
> K–P the number is 3;
> R–T the number is 4;
> U–Z the number is 5.

(2)   This number is multiplied by the patient's age (in years).

(3)   The resulting number is divided by 17 and the remainder taken.

(4)   If the patient is female, one is added.

(5)   The remainder after dividing by 4 is taken and the patient allocated to:

> Mr Awful   if it is 3;
> Mr Brilliant   if it is 2;
> Mr Careless   if it is 1;
> Mr Dreadful   if it is 0 (that is, there is no remainder).

Write a program that reads a set of patients' details and prints a list showing for each patient his or her name, operation, surgeon, proposed date of admission, and anticipated length of stay in hospital. The data is typed as follows:

> columns 1–20   patient's name;
> column 23   sex (M or F);
> columns 26–28 age (in years);
> columns 31–40 operation required.

The data is terminated by a line that consists solely of the word END in columns 1–3.

As usual we start with a structure plan, although in this case (unless we wish to include the details of determining the surgeon) it is a very simple one.

---

1 Repeat the following
  1.1 Read the next patient's details
  1.2 If name = END then exit
  1.3 Determine surgeon's name
  1.4 Use ADMIT to arrange operation
  1.5 Print details

The determination of the surgeon at step 1.3 could be described in more detail, but since we already have this in the description of the problem there seems little point. We can therefore proceed to the program.

```
      PROGRAM HOSPTL
C
C  This program plans admissions to hospital
C
C  MAX is the maximum number of patients dealt with by the program
      INTEGER MAX
      PARAMETER (MAX=1000)
C  Input data variables
      CHARACTER*20 NAME,SEX*1,OP
      INTEGER AGE
C  Miscellaneous variables
      CHARACTER SRGEON*9,DATE*11
      INTEGER I,N,LENGTH
C  Main loop to read and process patient data
      PRINT *,'Type data as follows: '
      PRINT *,'---Patient''s name---  S  Age  -Operation Required-'
      PRINT *,'(---20 characters---)     (3)  (---20 characters---)'
      PRINT *,'where S is the patient''s sex - M or F'
      DO 10, I=1,MAX
        PRINT *,'Next patient: '
        READ (*,100) NAME,SEX,AGE,OP
C  Check for end of data
      IF (NAME.EQ.'END') GOTO 11
C  Select surgeon
C  Step 1.  Set N to a value based on initial letter of name
      IF (NAME.LT.'E') THEN
        N=1
      ELSE IF (NAME.LT.'K') THEN
        N=2
      ELSE IF (NAME.LT.'R') THEN
        N=3
      ELSE IF (NAME.LT.'U') THEN
        N=4
      ELSE
        N=5
      END IF
C  Steps 2 and 3.  Multiply by age and divide by 17, taking remainder
      N=MOD(N*AGE,17)
C  Step 4.  Add 1 for women
      IF (SEX.EQ.'F') N=N+1
C  Step 5.  Select surgeon
      N=MOD(N,4)
      IF (N.EQ.3) THEN
        SRGEON='Awful'
      ELSE IF (N.EQ.2) THEN
        SRGEON='Brilliant'
      ELSE IF (N.EQ.1) THEN
        SRGEON='Careless'
      ELSE
        SRGEON='Dreadful'
      END IF
```

```
C  Call ADMIT to book patient in, and return date for admission
       CALL ADMIT(NAME,SRGEON,OP,DATE,LENGTH)
C  Print details
   10  PRINT 200,NAME,DATE,OP,SRGEON,LENGTH
C  No terminator
       PRINT *,MAX,' records read with no terminator'
   11 STOP
  100 FORMAT (A20,2X,A1,2X,I3,2X,A20)
  200 FORMAT (1H0,A20,' to enter hospital on ',A11/
     1         1H ,A20,' will be performed by Mr ',A9/
     2         1H ,'Patient''s expected length of stay is',I3,' days')
      END
```

The main points to note about this program are: the way the first block IF successively eliminates groups of names; the use of the MOD function to calculate a remainder; and the call to the subroutine ADMIT, with the three values required stored in the first three arguments and the two results of the subroutine's calculations returned by means of the last two arguments. An example of the results produced by this program can be seen in Figure 12.10.

Figure 12.10
Results produced by the HOSP program.

```
James Sidebotham     to enter hospital on 17 Jun 1989
Brain transplant     will be performed by Mr Careless
Patient's expected length of stay is 84 days

Peter Worrier        to enter hospital on 23 Mar 1989
Toe amputation       will be performed by Mr Careless
Patient's expected length of stay is  5 days

Jane Bossit          to enter hospital on 19 Sep 1989
Appendectomy         will be performed by Mr Dreadful
Patient's expected length of stay is  7 days

Arthur Knowsall      to enter hospital on 12 May 1989
Gallstone removal    will be performed by Mr Awful
Patient's expected length of stay is  5 days

Susan McTavish       to enter hospital on  5 Feb 1990
Facelift             will be performed by Mr Brilliant
Patient's expected length of stay is 12 days
```

SELF-TEST EXERCISES 12.1

1   If A, B, C and D are all character variables of length 6, what will be stored in D after the following statements?

```
A = 'Miles Ellis'
B = 'Fortran 77'
C = 'Tremendous'
```

```
      DO 10, I=2,3
        D=A(I:)
        A=D
        D=C(I:)
        C=D
10    CONTINUE
      D = B(:3)//C(1:1)//A(2:)
```

2   If A, B, C and D are all character variables of length 6, what will be
stored in D after the following statements if the data typed for the READ
statement is as follows?

```
Miles Ellis
Fortran 77
Tremendous
```

```
      READ *,100,A,B,C
      DO 10, I=2,3
        D=A(I:)
        A=D
        D=C(I:)
        C=D
10    CONTINUE
      D = B(:3)//C(1:1)//A(2:)
```

3   What will be printed by the following program?

```
      PROGRAM TEST1
      CHARACTER*25 A*44,B
      A = 'This is an odd example of character handling'
      B = A(:4)//A(31:)
      B(11:) = B(3:10)
      B(13:16) = A(37:)
      A(8:8) = A(19:)
      B(17:) = A(29:30)//A(42:)
      B(3:4) = A(22:)
      B(13:15) = B(4:5)
      B(8:8) = A(24:)
      B(23:) = A(8:)
      WRITE (*,'(1H1,'//B(13:15)//')') B
      STOP
      END
```

4   If the three character variables P, Q and R are all of length 8 and
have been assigned values by the statements

```
      P = 'CASE 12'
      Q = 'Case 12'
      R = 'CASE 12.'
```

what are the values of the following expressions?

 (a) `P.LE.Q`
 (b) `Q.LE.R`
 (c) `P.LE.R`
 (d) `LLE(P,Q)`
 (e) `LLE(Q,R)`
 (f) `LLE(P,R)`

F90　12.5　CHARACTER arrays

Just as we can declare an array of integer or real variables, so we can declare an array of character variables. We must, however, very carefully distinguish between the *elements* of a character array and the *characters* of a character string or substring. A character array declaration takes the form

```
CHARACTER*len name1(dim1)*len1, ...
```

Notice that if a character array name includes a *length specifier*, it comes after the *dimension declarator*. Also, notice that every element of a character array has the same length. Thus the following declarations declare three character arrays, with A having 20 elements, each of length 6, B also having 20 elements but of length 30, and C having 25 elements, also of length 30:

```
CHARACTER*30 A(20)*6,B(20),C(25)
```

It is also important to recognize the difference between an array of single characters and a character string. Thus, in the following declaration CARR and CSTR will both hold 20 characters, but CARR holds them as 20 single-character array elements, while CSTR holds them in a single character variable of length 20:

```
CHARACTER CARR(20),CSTR*20
```

EXAMPLE 12.4

As part of a larger project, it is required to write a program that will input data relating to sales made in a large department store during the previous day. The data has been transcribed from records produced by each cash-till and consists of the following items:

columns 1–4	department code;
columns 11–14	goods code;
columns 21–36	price;
columns 31–36	amount tendered by customer;
columns 41–46	change given.

The last three items all take the same format – LLL.pp, where LLL is the number of pounds and pp is the number of pence.

The departments are in four groups (hardware, electrical, furnishing and clothing), with the first letter of the department code being H, E, F, or C as appropriate.

The data is terminated by a record that consists of the word END in columns 1–3 and is otherwise blank.

The program is to read each input record and check that the figures for price, amount tendered and change given are consistent with each other. If they are, the data is to be passed to a subroutine called FILE, which takes three arguments: the department code, the goods code and the price, in that order. If there is an error then a message should be printed.

When all the data has been input the total sales for each group of departments should be printed, unless there was an error in some of the data for that group.

We shall start, of course, with a structure plan.

---

1 Initialize group totals

2 Repeat the following
    2.1 Read the next set of data
    2.2 If it is 'END' then exit
    2.3 If data is valid then
        2.3.1 Send data to FILE
        2.3.2 Update group total
    otherwise
        2.3.3 Print error message
        2.3.4 Set group error flag

3 Repeat for each department group
    3.1 If no data errors then
        3.1.1 Print total sales
    otherwise
        3.1.2 Print error message

Clearly we need to keep the group totals and error flags in arrays; one other array will also be required to contain the four group names. We can now write the program.

```
      PROGRAM SALES
C
C  This program processes data recorded by cash-tills
C
C  The data is arranged as follows:
C    Cols 1-4    Department code (4 chars)
C         11-14  Goods code (4 chars)
C         21-26  Price (LLL.pp)
C         31-36  Amount tendered (LLL.pp)
C         41-36  Change given (LLL.pp)
C
C  MAX is maximum number of records
C  IN is the unit number for the data, OUT is the standard output unit
      INTEGER MAX,IN,OUT
      PARAMETER (MAX=10000,IN=3,OUT=6)
C  Variables for input of data
      CHARACTER*4 DEPT,GOODS
      REAL PRICE,TENDRD,CHANGE
C  Name of data file
      CHARACTER*20 DATAFL
C  Arrays for storage of cumulative results
      INTEGER STATUS(4),OK,ERROR
      PARAMETER (OK=0,ERROR=-1)
      REAL TOTAL(4)
C  Array for storage of group names
      CHARACTER GROUP(4)*10
C  Miscellaneous variables
      INTEGER I,J
C  Initialization
      DATA TOTAL/4*0.0/,STATUS/4*OK/
      DATA GROUP/'Clothing','Electrical','Furnishing','Hardware'/
C  Get name of data file and open it on unit IN
      PRINT *,'What is the name of the data file? '
      READ '(A)',DATAFL
      OPEN (IN,FILE=DATAFL,STATUS='OLD')
C  Loop to read data
      DO 10, I=1,MAX
        READ (IN,101) DEPT,GOODS,PRICE,TENDRD,CHANGE
C  Check for end of data
        IF (DEPT.EQ.'END') GOTO 11
C  Check figures for consistency
        IF (ABS(TENDRD-PRICE-CHANGE).LT.0.01) THEN
C  Data OK, so pass to FILE and update group total
          CALL FILE(DEPT,GOODS,PRICE)
          DO 5, J=1,4
            IF (DEPT(:1).EQ.GROUP(J)(:1)) TOTAL(J)=TOTAL(J)+PRICE
    5     CONTINUE
        ELSE
C  Data faulty - print warning and set group status to ERROR
          WRITE (OUT,201) DEPT,GOODS,PRICE,TENDRD,CHANGE
          DO 6, J=1,4
            IF (DEPT(:1).EQ.GROUP(J)(:1)) STATUS(J)=ERROR
```

```
      6        CONTINUE
            END IF
     10    CONTINUE
C  No data terminator
            WRITE (OUT,202) MAX
C  Print group totals (or error reports)
     11 DO 15, J=1,4
            IF (STATUS(J).EQ.OK) THEN
               WRITE (OUT,203) GROUP(J),TOTAL(J)
            ELSE
               WRITE (OUT,204) GROUP(J)
            END IF
     15    CONTINUE
            STOP
    101 FORMAT (2(A4,6X),3(F6.2,4X))
    201 FORMAT (1H0,'Data error in following record:'/
      *         1H ,2(A4,6X),3(F6.2,4X))
    202 FORMAT (1H0,'No terminator found in data after',I6,' records')
    203 FORMAT (1H0,A,' sales worth ',F9.2)
    204 FORMAT (1H0,A,' figures contained data error(s)')
            END
```

Notice that it is not possible to have an array of named constants, and so the names of the four groups have been stored as (initialized) variables, in order that they can be searched in the loop. Notice also that it is perfectly acceptable to define a substring of a character array element, as in the two tests of the form

```
        IF (DEPT(:1).EQ.GROUP(J)(:1)) ...
```

This test compares the first character of the departmental code, stored in DEPT, with the first character of each of the four group names, stored in the array GROUP. Since the substring is a substring of an array element, the subscript expression (in parentheses) comes before the substring descriptor (also in parentheses).

An alternative approach to the decisions and actions in the main input loop would be first to set an integer (say J) to one of the values 1, 2, 3 or 4, depending upon the group code, and then to use this as a subscript to the arrays TOTAL and STATUS. The main loop would then take the following form:

```
      DO 10, I=1,MAX
            READ (IN,101) DEPT,GOODS,PRICE,TENDRD,CHANGE
C  Check for end of data
            IF (DEPT.EQ.'END') GOTO 11
C  Establish group number
            DO 5, J=1,4
               IF (DEPT(:1).EQ.GROUP(J)(:1)) GOTO 6
      5     CONTINUE
```

```
C  Check figures for consistency
   6   IF (ABS(TENDRD-PRICE-CHANGE).LT.0.01) THEN
C  Data OK, so pass to FILE and update group total
           CALL FILE(DEPT,GOODS,PRICE)
           TOTAL(J)=TOTAL(J)+PRICE
       ELSE
C  Data faulty - print warning and set group status to ERROR
           WRITE (OUT,201) DEPT,GOODS,PRICE,TENDRD,CHANGE
           STATUS(J)=ERROR
       END IF
  10   CONTINUE
```

12.6   Character expressions as embedded formats

In Section 9.8 we saw that a format could be embedded in an input or output statement by expressing it as a character constant. A character constant is a special case of a character expression, and it should, therefore, come as no surprise to discover that a character expression can appear as an embedded format:

```
READ (1,FORM) A,B,C
WRITE (2,FORM1//FORM2) X,Y,Z
PRINT FORM1(I:J)//FORM2//FORM3, P,Q,R
```

This can be a particularly useful feature in situations where the format of the output may differ depending on the values of the information being output (or some other criterion). A simple example of its use is given below.

EXAMPLE 12.5

Write a program that reads a name (from columns 1–20) followed by the number of boy and girl children the person has (in columns 23 and 25, respectively). Print the name and total number of children in an easily readable fashion.

The logic of this program is so simple that we do not need a structure plan. The only difficulty lies in arranging the output format.

```
      PROGRAM FAMILY
C
C  A demonstration program to illustrate variable formats
C
      INTEGER MAX
      PARAMETER (MAX=100)
      INTEGER I,BOYS,GIRLS,TOTAL
      CHARACTER*35 F,F1,NAME*20
      PARAMETER (F1='(1H0,A20,'' has '',I1,'' children'')')
C  Loop to read data
      PRINT *,'Type data as follows:'
      PRINT *,'---Name (20 chars)---  b g'
      PRINT *,'where b is the number of boys and g the number of girls'
      PRINT *,'Type END to finish'
      DO 10, I=1,MAX
        READ '(A20,T23,I1,1X,I1)',NAME,BOYS,GIRLS
C  Check for end of data
        IF (NAME.EQ.'END') GOTO 11
C  Calculate total number of children
        TOTAL=BOYS+GIRLS
C  Form suitable format for output
        F=F1
        IF (TOTAL.EQ.0) THEN
          F(18:21)=' ''no'
        ELSE IF (TOTAL.EQ.1) THEN
          F(28:)=''')'
        ELSE IF (TOTAL.GE.10) THEN
          F(19:19)='2'
        END IF
        IF (TOTAL.GT.0) THEN
          PRINT F,NAME,TOTAL
        ELSE
          PRINT F,NAME
        END IF
10    CONTINUE
C  No terminator
      PRINT *,MAX,' records read with no terminator'
11  STOP
      END
```

We can see (from the first block IF) that there are four cases:

(1)   If the number of children is 0, then the value of F is altered to

```
'(1H0,A20,'' has '', ''no children'')'
```

(2)   If it is 1, it is altered to

```
'(1H0,A20,'' has '',I1,'' child'')'
```

(3)   If it is 10 or more, it is altered to

```
'(1H0,A20,'' has '',I2,'' children'')'
```

(4)   Otherwise it is left as the original value of F1,

```
'(1H0,A20,'' has '',I1,'' children'')'
```

Notice that when counting characters in a character string the representation of an apostrophe (' ') occupies only *one* character position.

These will allow the results to be well laid out, with none of the bad grammar (such as `1 children`) that is seen far too often in computer-produced tables.

It is also possible to use a character array as an embedded format. In this case, however, the format is considered to be a concatenation of *all* the elements of the array. Thus, the two PRINT statements in the following program will produce identical results.

```
      PROGRAM IOEX
C
C  An example of an embedded format in an array
C
      INTEGER I,J
      REAL X
      CHARACTER*25 F(10)
      I=273
      J=17
      F(1) = '('
      F(2) = '1H1,'
      F(3) = '''The result of dividing'','
      F(4) = 'I4,'
      F(5) = ''' by'','
      F(6) = 'I4,'
      F(7) = ''' is'','
      F(8) = 'F9.3'
      F(9) = ')'
      X = REAL(I)/J
      PRINT 201,I,J,X
  201 FORMAT(1H1,'The result of dividing',I4,' by',I4,' is',F9.3)
      PRINT F,I,J,X
      STOP
      END
```

The use of a complete array to build up a variable format can be useful in some circumstances, especially when, as in the next example, it is required to build up a complex format during the execution of the program from a number of separate elements. The program will therefore be written using an array; the reader may wish to rewrite it using substrings.

EXAMPLE 12.6

A common problem with programs concerned with geometric definition is that of printing the mathematical formulae defining the various surfaces, since these have a very wide range of formats. Write a simplified version of the printing element of such a program that takes its data as a number of items on separate lines and prints their interpretation as defined below.

The data consists of:

(1)   a name of up to six characters;
(2)   an integer code = 1 for a point;
                          = 2 for a line;
                          = 3 for a circle;
(3)   three real numbers, as defined below.

The results should consist of a single printed line in one of the following forms:

> *name* is the point (A,B,C)
> *name* is the line $Ax+By+C = 0$
> *name* is the circle $(x-A)^2 + (y-B)^2 = R^2$

where A, B, C and R are the real numbers read as data. There should be no unnecessary spaces (for example, after names) and no multiple signs (for example, $+-5.0y$). All data values lie in the range -100.0 to $+100.0$ and are accurate to two places of decimals. A name of **** indicates the end of data.

This example is an exercise in formatting, but nevertheless a structure plan will be useful:

1   Repeat the following
1.1 Read *name*
1.2 If *name* is **** then exit
1.3 Read *code*, A, B and C (or R)
1.4 Find length of *name* (say L)
1.5 Print *name* in first L chars, followed by 'is the'
1.6 If *code* = 1 then
    1.6.1 Print 'point (A,B,C)'
    but if *code*=2 then
    1.6.2 Print 'line $Ax + By + C = 0$'
    but if *code* = 3 then
    1.6.3 Print 'circle $(x-A)^2 + (y - B)^2 = R^2$'

We shall need to establish a means of deciding in what format to print the numbers to avoid extra spaces and/or multiple signs.

The extra spaces can be dealt with by determining the size of each number and using an appropriate field width. The multiple signs can be dealt with in a similar manner by not printing a + sign if the number is negative.

We can now proceed with the program.

```
      PROGRAM GEODAT
C
C This program demonstrates how to use a variable format, stored in
C an array, to print geometric data relating to the definition of
C various geometric entities.
C
C Arrays for format elements
      CHARACTER*12 FORM(14),FORMC(11),FNAME(6)*3,FNUM(6)*5
C Input variables
      CHARACTER NAME*8
      INTEGER TYPE
      REAL A(3)
C Miscellaneous variables
      INTEGER I,J,N
      REAL X
C Initialize format elements
C
C                   (1H0,      A6,       'is the ',
      DATA FORM/'   (1H0,', 'A6,', '''is the '',', 11*' '/
C
C                   'circle    ',        '(x',        '',       F7.2,
      DATA FORMC/'' 'circle   '',', '''(x'',', '''''',', 'F7.2,',
C
C          ')**2 + (y',      '',       F7.2,     ')**2  = ',       '',
     1     '''')**2 + (y'',', '''''',', 'F7.2,', '''')**2  = '',', '''''',',
C
C          F7.2,     )
     2     'F7.2,', ')'/
C
      DATA FNAME/'A1,', 'A2,', 'A3,', 'A4,', 'A5,', 'A6,'/
      DATA FNUM/'F4.2,', 'F5.2,', 'F6.2,', 'F7.2,', 'F8.2,', 'F9.2,'/
C Allow for 100 entities
      DO 50, I=1,100
C Read name of next entity
      READ '(A6)',NAME
C Check for end of data
      IF (NAME.EQ.'****') GOTO 55
C Read rest of data
      READ '(I1/(F7.2))',TYPE,A
C Find length of name by searching for two consecutive blanks
      N=INDEX(NAME,'  ')-1
C Store A"N" edit descriptor
      FORM(2)=FNAME(N)
C Copy master format
      DO 10, J=4,14
  10     FORM(J)=FORMC(J-3)
```

```
C  Adjust values of coefficients for circles
         IF (TYPE.EQ.3) THEN
            A(1)=-A(1)
            A(2)=-A(2)
            A(3)=A(3)**2
         END IF
C  Find sizes of numbers and adjust format as necessary
         DO 20, J=1,3
            X=ABS(A(J))
            IF (X.LT.10.0) THEN
              N=1
            ELSE IF (X.LT.100.0) THEN
              N=2
            ELSE IF (X.LT.1000.0) THEN
              N=3
            ELSE IF (X.LT.10000.0) THEN
              N=4
            ELSE
              N=5
            END IF
C  Add 1 to N if minus sign is to be printed
            IF (A(J).LT.0.0) N=N+1
   20    FORM(3*J+4)=FNUM(N)
C  Modify according to type
         IF (TYPE.EQ.1) THEN
C  Point
            FORM(4)='''point '','
            FORM(5)='''(''','
            FORM(8)=''',''','
            FORM(11)=''',''','
            FORM(14)=''')'''')'
         ELSE IF (TYPE.EQ.2) THEN
C  Line
            FORM(4)='''line '','
            FORM(5)=''''''','
            IF (A(1).NE.0.0) THEN
              FORM(8)='''x'''','
              IF (A(2).GT.0.0) FORM(9)='''+'''','
            ELSE
              FORM(7)=''''''','
              FORM(8)=''''''','
            END IF
            IF (A(2).NE.0.0) THEN
              FORM(11)='''y'''','
              IF (A(3).GT.0.0) FORM(12)='''+'''','
            ELSE
              FORM(10)=''''''','
              FORM(11)=''''''','
            END IF
            IF (A(3).EQ.0.0) FORM(13)=''''''','
            FORM(14)=''' = 0''')'
         ELSE
C  Circle
            IF (A(1).GT.0.0) THEN
              FORM(6)='''+'''','
```

```
              ELSE IF (A(1).EQ.0.0) THEN
                 FORM(7)=''''','
              END IF
              IF (A(2).GT.0.0) THEN
                 FORM(9)='''+'','
              ELSE IF (A(2).EQ.0.0) THEN
                 FORM(10)=''''','
              END IF
           END IF
C  Format is now ready - so print the details
     50    PRINT FORM,NAME,A
     55 STOP
        END
```

A careful analysis of the program will show that most of the logic is concerned with identifying the length of the name of the surface and the size and sign of the three numbers, and then creating A and F edit descriptors of the correct field width. The length of the name (maximum 6) is found by storing it in a variable (NAME) of length 8 and then using the intrinsic function INDEX to find the first two consecutive spaces. If the length is 6 then these will be the two extra spaces added to make the length 8; however, if the name read was less than six characters, the first space will come after the last character of the name. It is therefore an easy matter to determine how many characters there are in the name.

The numbers are dealt with more easily since they must lie in the range −100.0 to +100.0 (apart from the constant term for the circle (R^2) which lies in the range 0 to 10000.0). It is a trivial matter, therefore, to determine the number of digits (including a sign) and hence the field width required. Where appropriate, a + sign is inserted before positive numbers. Special attention is also paid to zero values of A, B or C for a line, and A or B for a circle, so as to avoid such awkward expressions as 0.0x, which is replaced by a null string '', or (x-0.0)**2, which is replaced by x**2.

The method used by the program is to base all three formats (for circle, line and point) on that for a circle, and replace appropriate elements. This will leave many extra spaces between edit descriptors, which will be ignored. Essentially, therefore, the program generates a format in one of the following three forms:

```
(1H0, A6, ' is the ', 'point ', '(', '', F7.2, ',', '', F7.2, ',',
*     '', F7.2, ')')

(1H0, A6, ' is the ', 'line ', '', '', F7.2, 'x', '+', F7.2, 'y',
*     '+', F7.2', '= 0')

(1H0, A6, ' is the ', 'circle ', '(x', '+', F7.2, ')**2 + (y',
*     '+', F7.2, ')**2 = ', '', F7.2 )
```

with appropriate field widths for the A and F edit descriptors.

```
ICHAR(C)       gives the integer equivalent of C
CHAR(I)        gives the character equivalent of I
LEN(C)         gives the length of C
INDEX(C1,C2)   gives the starting position of the substring C2 within C1
```

Figure 12.11
Character manipulation functions.

12.7 Intrinsic functions for character manipulation

F90

Fortran 77 contains eight intrinsic functions for use in various types of character operations. We have already met four of these (LGT, LGE, LLE and LLT) and have seen that they are used to compare two character strings using the lexical collating sequence defined in the ASCII coding system. The remaining functions are shown in Figure 12.11.

ICHAR(C) returns as its value an integer, corresponding to the internal code, which represents the *single* character C. This integer number will lie in the range 0 to $n-1$ inclusive (where n is the number of different characters that can be represented by the particular computer being used), and is the position of the character in the collating sequence, where the first character in the sequence has the coded value 0. Thus if ICHAR(C1).LT.ICHAR(C2) is true, then C1 must come before C2 in the collating sequence.

CHAR(I) is the inverse of ICHAR and returns the character corresponding to the number I, where $0 < I < n-1$. Thus

CHAR(ICHAR(C)) is the same as C
ICHAR(CHAR(I)) is the same as I, for $0 < I < n-1$

LEN(C) returns as its value the length of the character variable or expression provided as its argument. It is primarily of use in subprograms where the length of dummy arguments is not known (see Section 12.8).

INDEX(C1,C2) is used to search for the first occurrence of the string C2 in C1. If the *complete* string C2 does exist within C1, the value returned is the starting position of C2 in C1. If it does not, then the value 0 is returned. Example 12.7 shows an interesting use of this function.

EXAMPLE 12.7

Several pages of text have been typed into a file called TEXTDATA, using a maximum of 80 characters per line; none of the words in the text is split between lines. The final line consists of six asterisks in the first six columns. Write a program that counts the number of times the word THE occurs in the text.

We shall start with a structure plan:

> **1** Open data file
>
> **2** Initialize count
>
> **2** Repeat the following
> **2.1** Read a line
> **2.2** If it is the terminator (******) then exit
> **2.3** Repeat the following
> **2.3.1** If the rest of the line does not contain THE then exit
> **2.3.2** Add 1 to the count of THEs
> **2.3.3** Adjust the start of the line
>
> **3** Print result

Notice that we shall need to search through each line in turn, looking for the word THE. This can be done by repeatedly looking at the current line, but starting each time from the position immediately *after* the end of the last THE. A further problem is to avoid treating THEM, THEIR, and so on as correct matches. The easiest way to do this is to search for the five-character sequence '♦THE♦'; the problem of words at the left- and right-hand edges of a line can be dealt with by adding extra spaces.

```
      PROGRAM SEARCH
C
C This program counts the number of times the word THE appears
C in a file
C
      INTEGER COUNT,START,POS,MAXLIN,I,J
      CHARACTER*82 LINE
C MAXLIN is the maximum number of lines accepted
      PARAMETER (MAXLIN=1000)
C Initialize line and count
      DATA COUNT/0/,LINE/' '/
C Open data file as unit 3
      OPEN (3,FILE='TEXTFILE')
C Loop to read and process lines
      DO 10, I=1,MAXLIN
        READ (3,'(A80)') LINE(2:81)
C Check for end of data
        IF (LINE.EQ.' ******') GOTO 11
C Start searching at beginning of line
        START=1
C Loop to search current line - a maximum of 20 matches is possible
        DO 5, J=1,20
          POS=INDEX(LINE(START:),' THE ')
          IF (POS.EQ.0) GOTO 10
```

```
C  THE found - update count and start of next search
         COUNT=COUNT+1
         START=START+POS+3
    5    CONTINUE
   10 CONTINUE
C  No terminator
      PRINT *,MAXLIN,' lines read without a terminator'
   11 PRINT '(''The word THE occurred '',I4,'' times'')', COUNT
      STOP
      END
```

Notice that the 82-character variable LINE can be set to spaces by assigning a single space (which will be extended to 82 spaces). In a similar way, the terminator (' ******' in columns 1–7) will be extended to 82 characters by adding 75 spaces.

The READ statement (using unit 3 with an embedded format) reads the 80 characters from the line into positions 2–81 of LINE, thus leaving a space at the beginning and end of the string. The search can now be made for ' THE ' with safety.

For each new line START is set to 1 and a match is sought in the substring from position START to the end of the line. If a match is made, the intrinsic function INDEX sets POS to the position *within that substring* of the first character of ' ♦THE♦'; this is used to increase START to point to the space immediately after THE and the process is repeated. If no match is made, then POS is set to 0 by INDEX and the next line is read. (Setting START to point to the space after THE avoids any problems when THE is in columns 78–80 of the line. If we set START to the character after the space it would cause an error in this situation unless LINE was given a length of 83.)

The final count is printed by a simple PRINT statement with an embedded format.

Note that it is not necessary to CLOSE the unit (3) that is connected to the input file as this will be done automatically when the program ends.

12.8   CHARACTER arguments to procedures   [F90]

If a procedure (subroutine or function) is to have a CHARACTER variable or array as an argument then we must pay particular attention to the *length* of the dummy argument. This length must be less than or equal to the length of the actual argument; if it is less than the length of the actual argument then only the leftmost *len* characters will be treated as the dummy argument (where *len* is the length of the dummy argument). This can cause

<table>
<tr><td>

Figure 12.12
Finding the length of a
character dummy
argument.

</td><td>

```
      SUBROUTINE SPLIT(C,N)
C
C This subroutine prints the character string C as N substrings
C of equal length (apart, possibly, from the last one)
C
C Dummy arguments
      INTEGER N
      CHARACTER C*(*)
C Local variables
      INTEGER LENC,LENS,START,I
C Get length of C
      LENC=LEN(C)
C Calculate length of substrings
      LENS=LENC/N
C Round up the substring lengths
      IF (N*LENS.LT.LENC) LENS=LENS+1
C Print first N-1 substrings
      DO 10, I=1,N-1
        START=(I-1)*LENS+1
        PRINT '(1H ,A)',C(START:START+LENS-1)
 10     CONTINUE
C Print last substring
      START=(N-1)*LENS+1
      PRINT '(1H ,A)',C(START:)
      RETURN
      END
```

</td></tr>
</table>

problems in a general subroutine and a special form of character declaration is therefore available for dummy arguments, in which the length of the character variable is written as (*); this causes the length of the dummy argument to be defined as being the same as that of the actual argument:

```
      SUBROUTINE SUB(N,C,X)
      CHARACTER C*(*)
         .
         .
         .
```

As a general rule, unless the length of a dummy argument never changes for different calls to the procedure, it is advisable to declare all character dummy arguments in this way to ensure that everything works correctly. If it is required to know the actual length then the intrinsic function LEN may be used. Figure 12.12 shows an example of this.

If the dummy argument is a character array things get more complicated because of the interaction between the array elements. This is best illustrated by considering how a character array is stored in the memory of the computer.

```
 1  2  3  4  5  6  7  8  9  10          53 54 55 56 57 58 59 60
┌──┬──┬──┬──┬──┬──┬──┬──┬──┬──┐     ┌──┬──┬──┬──┬──┬──┬──┬──┐
│  │  │  │  │  │  │  │  │  │  │- - -│  │  │  │  │  │  │  │  │
└──┴──┴──┴──┴──┴──┴──┴──┴──┴──┘     └──┴──┴──┴──┴──┴──┴──┴──┘
```

Figure 12.13
Correspondence between character array arguments.

Actual array
```
┌───────────────┬─ - - - - - ─┬───────────────┐
│     A(1)      │             │     A(10)     │
└───────────────┴─ - - - - - ─┴───────────────┘
```
Dummy array
```
┌───────┬───────┬─ - - - ─┬───────┬───────┐
│  D(1) │  D(2) │         │ D(14) │ D(15) │
└───────┴───────┴─ - - - ─┴───────┴───────┘
```

Figure 12.13 shows part of an actual array argument (A), which consists of 10 elements, each of length 6; the total length of the array is thus 60 characters. It also shows a dummy array (D), which consists of 15 elements, each of length 4. If the array name A is the actual argument then the first *character* of the first element of A is the same as the first character of the first element of D. We can readily see that, although there is a correspondence between characters, there is *no* correspondence between array elements unless both arrays have the same length declared for their elements. If the actual argument is an array element or an array element substring, then the first character of the element or substring corresponds to the first character position of the dummy array. In all cases the dummy argument array must not extend beyond the end of the actual argument array.

If the length of the dummy array is declared as (*) then each element of that array will have the same length as each element of the actual argument array. Notice, though, that even in this case correspondence between array elements is not assured – for example, when the actual argument is a substring of an array element that does not start at the first character of that array element.

12.9 CHARACTER functions

F90

In Chapter 4 we saw that it was possible to write our own *external* real and integer functions. We can also, of course, write **character functions** to return a single character result, but we will normally wish to specify the *length* of the result, and here we face a similar problem to that discussed in the last section relating to dummy arguments. The solution is very similar.

If a length specification is provided it must be a constant or a constant expression, or it may be written as (*); in the latter case, the function assumes a character length the same as that specified in the

Figure 12.14
An example of the use of a character function.

```
PROGRAM MAIN
CHARACTER*10 CFUN,CH
        .
        .
CH=CFUN(X,Y,Z)
        .
        .
END

SUBROUTINE SUB
CHARACTER*6 CFUN,CH
        .
        .
CH=CFUN(A,B,C)
        .
        .
END

CHARACTER*(*) FUNCTION CFUN(A,B,C)
        .
        .
END
```

program unit from which it is referenced. Thus, in the example shown in Figure 12.14, the function CFUN is a character function of length 10 when it is referenced from the main program, but one of length 6 when it is referenced from the subroutine SUB.

EXAMPLE 12.8

Write a function program, and a test program for it, which could be used to code a message (or, to be technically accurate, to *encrypt* it) by replacing each letter in the message by the one following it in the alphabet (z is replaced by A), leaving all other characters unaltered.

A suitable approach would be to define a character function with a single character as its argument that returns the encrypted character as its value. The structure plan for such a function is:

> **1** If CH is in the range A–Y or in the range a–y then
> **1.1** return the next letter
> otherwise if it is Z then
> **1.2** return A
> otherwise if it is z then

> **1.3** return a
> otherwise
> **1.4** return CH unaltered

The only difficulty appears to be how we find the next letter. The use of the intrinsic function ICHAR to obtain an integer representation of a character and CHAR to obtain a character representation of an integer will be satisfactory as long as the 26 letters are represented by 26 consecutive integers. This will usually be the case and we shall assume it is so for this example; some internal codes, however, are not contiguous (see, for example, Appendix D.2) and if such codes are used to provide the integer equivalents with CHAR and ICHAR then the following program will not work.

```
      CHARACTER FUNCTION CODE(CH)
C
C  This function encrypts its argument by returning the next letter
C
      CHARACTER CH
      IF (('A'.LE.CH .AND. CH.LE.'Y') .OR.
     *    ('a'.LE.CH .AND. CH.LE.'y')) THEN
C  Character lies between A and Y or between a and y
C  NOTE:   This algorithm will work only if alphabetic character codes
C           are consecutive
          CODE=CHAR(ICHAR(CH)+1)
C  Z and z must be dealt with individually
      ELSE IF (CH.EQ.'Z') THEN
          CODE='A'
      ELSE IF (CH.EQ.'z') THEN
          CODE='a'
      ELSE
C  Non-alphabetic characters are not encrypted
          CODE=CH
      END IF
      RETURN
      END
```

A suitable test or *driver* program (as these main program units are usually called) is as follows:

```
      PROGRAM CODER
C
C  This program is a driver program for the encryption function CODE
C
      INTEGER I
      CHARACTER MESSGE*50,CHR,CODE
C  Read a test message of up to 50 characters
      PRINT *,'Type a message of up to 50 characters'
      READ '(A)',MESSGE
C  Loop to encrypt the message character by character, storing the
```

```
C   encrypted characters in the original character string
        DO 10, I=1,50
            CHR=CODE(MESSGE(I:I))
10      MESSGE(I:I)=CHR
        PRINT *,'The encrypted message is:'
        PRINT *,MESSGE
        STOP
        END
```

Notice that the input message is limited to 50 characters; this should be quite enough to test the function. Also note that the function is called repeatedly with a one-character substring and that the encrypted version is stored in a one-character variable CHR before being stored in the original message. It would be illegal to write

```
        MESSGE(I:I)=CODE(MESSGE(I:I))
```

because of the restriction on characters that forbids any character position appearing on both sides of the equals sign in an assignment statement.

SUMMARY

- CHARACTER variables must be declared together with their length.

- Character substrings may be referred to in place of character variables.

- Character strings may be combined by use of the concatenation operator (//).

- Character strings are ordered according to a defined collating sequence.

- Character expressions or arrays may be used in embedded formats.

- Fortran 77 statements introduced in Chapter 12:

Type declaration	CHARACTER *list of names*
	CHARACTER**length** *list of names*
	CHARACTER *name1****len1**, *name2****len2**, ...
	CHARACTER**length** *name1****len1**, *name2*, ...
	CHARACTER *name1*(*declarator*)***len1**, ...
Character expressions	*string1*//*string2*
	where *string* is a character variable,
	character array element,
	character constant,
	or character substring
Character substring specification	*name*(*first pos* : *last pos*)
	name(*first pos* :)
	name(: *last pos*)

SELF-TEST EXERCISES 12.2

1   What does the following procedure do?

```
      SUBROUTINE TEST1(C1,C2)
      CHARACTER C1(*),C2*(*)
      INTEGER I,N
      N=LEN(C2)
      DO 5, I=1,N
    5    C1(I)=C2(I:I)
      RETURN
      END
```

2   Can you identify a situation in which the above subroutine might fail? If so, how could this situation be detected and appropriate action taken?

3   What does this procedure do?

```
      CHARACTER*(*) FUNCTION TEST3(C,N)
      CHARACTER C(N)
      INTEGER I,N
      DO 5, I=1,N
    5    TEST3(I:I)=C(I)
      RETURN
      END
```

4   Can you identify a situation in which the above function might fail? If so, how could this situation be detected and appropriate action taken?

5   What is the difference between an embedded format that is stored in a character variable and one that is stored in a character array?

PROGRAMMING EXERCISES

*12.1 Write a program to print a list of the characters in the Fortran character set, followed by their internal representation on your computer.

12.2 Find out how many characters there are in the character set used by your computer; it will probably be 64, 128 or 256. Then write a program to print a list of all the characters in the order of their internal representation (that is, from 0 to 63, 0 to 127, 0 to 255, or some other range, as appropriate).

12.3 Write a program to find the number of occurrences of the letter 'E' in a given sentence.

12.4 Write a program that reverses the character order in the phrase 'TSEB◆SI◆NARTROF' where ◆ denotes a space.

12.5 Write a program that asks the user for a sentence and displays the same sentence with every occurrence of the word 'PINK' changed to 'BLUE'. (Remember there may be more than one substitution.)
Can your program cope instead with changing 'RED' to 'GREEN'?

12.6 Write a program such that the user enters the atomic number of one of the following chemical elements of the periodic table and the program produces the appropriate chemical symbol.

Atomic no.	Chemical symbol
1	H
2	He
3	Li
4	Be
5	B
6	C
7	N
8	O
9	F
10	Ne

12.7 Write a program to sort the following list of character strings assigned to a character array in the following order 'EXPECT', 'IN', 'SCIENTIFIC', 'WORK', 'COMPUTERS', 'BRIGHT', 'FORTRAN' into alphabetical order. The array elements should then be concatenated to produce a sentence.

12.8 Write a program that will read a file of text, truncate each line to 20 characters, and print it in four columns (on a printer, if one is available).

12.9 Type two or three paragraphs from this book into a file. Then write a program to locate the longest word in the file and display it on the screen, together with a count of the number of letters in the word.

12.10 Using the results obtained by running the program written for Exercise 12.9, modify the program so that it extracts the individual words from a file and stores them in an array. The program should print the contents of the array in a suitable format.

12.11 A file contains the text of a business letter – up to 100 lines with no more than 80 characters on a given line. Write a program to count the number of occurrences of the word 'very' in the letter.

Will your program cope with:

(a) 'Every care has been taken …'
(b) 'Very sincerely yours,'
(c) 'We are VERY concerned …'

12.12 Modify the program that you wrote for Exercise 10.15 so that it reads the social class of the respondent (instead of ignoring it), and uses it to produce two additional tables:

(a) the average number of visits to a bar per week for those who drink mainly in a bar, by social class (A, B, C1, C2, D, E) and by sex;
(b) the most popular drink for each sex, by social class.

12.13 A file contains telephone numbers and names as follows:

John Smith 234567
Mary Jones (0999) 123456

.
.
.

Write a program to search the file for a particular name (surname, forename or both) and display the line or lines with the phone number.

*****12.14** A church is creating a list of its members on a computer system, and has a file in which each record, amongst other things, contains the following information about each person:

Columns 1–30	First name and surname (separated by a space)
Column 32	Sex (M or F)
Columns 34–36	Age
Column 38	Marital status (S=single, M=married, W=widowed, D=divorced)

The file is terminated by an end-of-file marker.

Write a program that will read the contents of the file and print it in the following format:

```
0001  Roch, Mike  Married (Male) 33
0002  Prowse, Julie  Single (Female) 31
0003  Gough, Steven  Single (Male) 27
0004  Cope, Tonia  Married (Female) 46
```

12.15 A simple encryption technique for sending coded messages is to substitute one letter of the alphabet for another – for example 'A' might become 'Z', 'B' become 'Y' and so on. Such a code can be broken by counting the frequency of occurrence of the various letters in a sample of coded text, and comparing with the frequencies of the letters in normal English. Thus the most common letter in the code probably translates as 'E', the second most common as 'T' and so on.

Write a program for use in breaking such a code. Your program should accept as its input a file containing several lines of coded text, count the number of times each of the letters A–Z occurs in this sample, and display these results in a table in order of decreasing frequency.

12.16 The major natural satellites of the first five planets from the sun are:

Planet no.	Name	Names of Satellites (in order of increasing orbital radius)
1	Mercury	(none)
2	Venus	(none)
3	Earth	Moon
4	Mars	Phobos, Deimos
5	Jupiter	Io, Europa, Ganymede, Callisto

Write a program that stores the above information in a suitable form, and lists all the satellites (if any) of a planet chosen by the user.

Now modify your program so that it accepts the name of a satellite as its input, and displays the planet and number of that satellite, as follows:

Name of Satellite?
Deimos
Deimos is satellite number 2 of Mars

12.17 Mrs Smith is moving from Cambridge, Massachusetts, to Cambridge, England, and wants to be able to convert her recipes from American measures to British measures using the following conversions:

American	British
1 cup flour	4 oz. flour
1 cup butter	8 oz. butter
1 cup sugar	6 oz. sugar
1 cup confectioner's sugar	4 oz. icing sugar
1 cup milk	8 fl. oz. (= 0.4 pints) milk

Write a program that will read lines of the recipe with the quantity in the first four character positions, followed by the units (which may be ignored), followed by the name of the ingredient. Your program should convert this data into the number of ounces of the ingredient (or the number of pints in the case of milk), and print the revised list of ingredients. Any lines not containing one of the above ingredients should be left unaltered.

12.18 Modify the program you wrote for Exercise 12.17 so that the quantity does not have to occupy the first four columns, but occupies only as many characters as are required. Your data should now contain a space after the quantity and a space after the units, which can be used by the program to identify the required fields.

12.19 A hexadecimal number is a number which is expressed to base sixteen, with the letters A to F representing 10 to 15. Thus the hexadecimal number 3D is the equivalent of the decimal number 61 (3*16 + 13), and the hexadecimal number 1A5 is the equivalent of 421 (256 + 10*16 + 5).

Write a function that will return the hexadecimal equivalent (of type CHARACTER*4) of its non-negative INTEGER argument I, where I < 32768. Test your function in a program that reads a number from the keyboard and prints the hexadecimal equivalent. Your program should continue until a negative number is input.

12.20 The bubble sort is a very simple (and very inefficient) means of sorting an array. It works as follows.

Compare the first and second elements of the array; if they are in the wrong order exchange them, otherwise do nothing. Repeat this process for the second and third elements, then for the third and fourth elements, and so on. At the conclusion of this process the last value in the sorted sequence will have 'bubbled' along to the last element of the array, and will therefore be in the correct place. Now repeat the process, which will result in the next-to-last value being moved to the next-to-last element. Repeat the process until all the values have been moved to their correct places.

(Clearly, improvements can be made by, for example, examining all n elements of the array in the first pass, the first $n-1$ elements in the second pass, and so on, but you should not feel any obligation to refine your program in this way – the simplest approach will be sufficient for now.)

Write a subroutine to sort the contents of a CHARACTER array using a bubble sort and then incorporate it in a modified version of the program written for Exercise 12.10 that will print the words in alphabetic order.

Finally, make a further refinement to your program that will eliminate duplicate words. This final version will, therefore, print an alphabetic list of all the words used in a particular piece of text.

12.21 Write a function (NEXTCH) that returns the next character from a string input from the keyboard. The function should store the string in a suitable location and SAVE it between calls. Each time the function is entered it should check if there are any characters left in the string and request a new string from the keyboard if there are not. If there are characters left, or if a new string has just been read, the function should return the next one and set a pointer to indicate the next character.

Test this function by using it to recreate a string input from the keyboard and display it.

(This type of function is often essential in programs such as compilers and other language processors, which must analyse the input character by character to determine its syntax and meaning.)

Other data types

13

As well as REAL, INTEGER and CHARACTER data types Fortran 77 contains a LOGICAL data type and two further numeric types – DOUBLE PRECISION and COMPLEX.

LOGICAL variables are used to store logical values (*true* or *false*), usually so that they can be used as an **error flag** for later inspection.

DOUBLE PRECISION variables are used to provide greater numerical precision, where the nature of the calculation makes this necessary, while COMPLEX variables enable a program to carry out complex arithmetic. These two data types were described in more detail in Chapter 11.

13.1   The six Fortran data types

Fortran 77 has six intrinsic data types available for use by the programmer. By far the most important, for most purposes, are the two fundamental numeric data types, REAL and INTEGER, which were introduced in Chapter 2, and the CHARACTER data type, which was introduced in the last chapter. However, Fortran 77 also contains three further data types that are used for special purposes.

Two of these, DOUBLE PRECISION and COMPLEX, were discussed in Chapter 11 as part of our initial discussion of numerical methods and techniques. Their purpose is briefly outlined in Section 13.4 for the benefit of readers who have chosen to omit Chapter 11, although those readers will probably have little need for either DOUBLE PRECISION or COMPLEX variables.

The final data type, LOGICAL, was extensively used in programs written before the advent of Fortran 77 (which introduced the CHARACTER data type to Fortran), but is probably of less relevance nowadays. It is discussed in Sections 13.2 and 13.3.

F90

13.2   LOGICAL variables

We have already seen that logical expressions have one of two values – *true* or *false*. We can also store such a logical value in a **logical variable**, which we must, of course, first declare in a type specification statement. This takes the form:

> LOGICAL *name1*, *name2*, . . .

F90

A logical variable is stored in a *numeric* storage unit (as are integer and real variables) even though only two values are possible.

Once we can store a logical value it becomes necessary to be able to define a logical constant and to read or write logical values. The two possible values are written as

> .TRUE. and .FALSE.

and may be used in an assignment statement in the usual way:

```
PROGRAM LOGVAR
LOGICAL ERFLAG
ERFLAG=.FALSE.
```

A logical variable is normally used in three situations:

- To save the results of evaluating a logical expression that would otherwise be evaluated in several different places.
- To enable the value of a logical expression to be saved for use at a later stage when it might no longer be possible to evaluate it.
- To clarify a program by use of a meaningful name.

The first of these can be illustrated by reference to Example 8.4, which produced some rather complicated statistics from a survey of people's occupations. One of the items of data in this example was the age of the respondent. In two places there was a test of the form

```
IF (AGE(I).GE.18)...
```

while in another place it appeared inverted:

```
IF (AGE(I).LT.18)...
```

If at the start of the program we had included the declaration

```
LOGICAL ADULT
```

and had added the statement

```
ADULT = AGE(I).GE.18
```

at the start of the main loop, we could replace the first two tests by statements of the form

```
IF (ADULT)...
```

and the third by

```
IF (.NOT.ADULT)...
```

The assignment statement may look a trifle odd at first, but the right-hand side is simply an assertion, or logical expression, which has the value *true* or *false*, and which can therefore be assigned to the logical variable ADULT.

The evaluation of expression AGE(I).GE.18 is therefore carried out only once on each pass through the loop, regardless of the number of times a decision is to be made on the adulthood of the respondent.

The other main use of a logical variable is to remember a condition for use later. A typical example is a program that reads its data and checks it for validity before proceeding to some analysis of that data. If there is an error in the validity of the data there is no point in carrying out the analysis.

Suppose, for example, that an accounting program is reading details of sales and performing certain operations as a result. As a rough check on the data the account number is checked to lie in the range 1–250 and the total value is checked to be less than £500. A program can be written to input the data in a loop and then carry out some analysis if, and only if, all the data was within the limits specified.

```
      PROGRAM ACCNTS
C
C  This program fragment shows the use of a logical variable
C  as an error flag
C
      LOGICAL DTAERR
      INTEGER ACCNUM,I
      REAL VALUE
C  DTAERR is initialized as false
      DATA DTAERR/.FALSE./
C  Loop to read and process data
      DO 10, I=1,100
         READ *,ACCNUM,VALUE
C  Set DTAERR if data is invalid
         DTAERR=DTAERR
     1           .OR. ACCNUM.LT.1 .OR. ACCNUM.GT.250
     2           .OR. VALUE.GE.500.0
         .
         .
         .
   10 CONTINUE
      IF (.NOT.DTAERR) THEN
         .
         .
         .
      END IF
      STOP
      END
```

Notice here that the logical variable DTAERR is initially set to *false*. Then, after each set of data has been read, it is set to its current value *or* ACCNUM outside its range *or* sales value too large. Thus, if either the account number or the sales value is outside its permitted range then DTAERR is set to *true*. Thereafter it is set to *true* every time through the loop without the need to check the account number or sales value. At the end of the loop it will, therefore, be true if *any* data item was in error, and can be used in a block IF to determine what action (if any) should be taken.

Logical values may be input and output, with certain restrictions, by use of the L edit descriptor (see Figure 13.1). On output the logical values *true* and *false* are represented by T and F, respectively, preceded by an

Descriptor	Meaning	
L*w*	(a) Read the next *w* characters as a representation of a logical value	**Figure 13.1** The L edit descriptor.
	(b) Output *w*−1 blanks followed by T or F to represent a logical value	

appropriate number of spaces. On input there are essentially two possible ways of representing *true* and *false*.

       T*ccc...c*   or   F*ccc...c*
      .T*ccc...c*   or   .F*ccc...c*

where *ccc...c* represents *any* characters. In all cases there may be leading blanks. Thus, for example, all the following will be input by the edit descriptor L10 as true:

```
T
TRUE
True
.T
.T.
.TRUE.
Truthful
Tremendous
      .TRUE.
          T
```

while the following will all be input as false:

```
F
FALSE
False
.F
.F.
.FALSE.
Futile
Fanciful
      .FALSE.
          F
```

If the first non-blank character(s) in an input field are not T, F, .T, or .F an error will occur.

As was mentioned in Section 13.1, the use of LOGICAL variables has become less widespread since the introduction of CHARACTER variables to Fortran as part of Fortran 77. For example, the extract from an accounting program shown above could also be written:

```
      PROGRAM ACCNTS
C
C  This program fragment shows the use of a character variable
C  as an error flag
C
      CHARACTER*5 DTACHK,ERROR,OK
      PARAMETER (ERROR='Error',OK='OK')
      INTEGER ACCNUM,I
      REAL VALUE
C  DTACHK is initialized as OK
      DATA DTACHK/OK/
C  Loop to read and process data
      DO 10, I=1,100
         READ *,ACCNUM,VALUE
C  Set DTACHK to 'Error' if data is invalid
         IF (ACCNUM.LT.1 .OR. ACCNUM.GT.250 .OR. VALUE.GE.500.0)
     *      DTACHK=ERROR
              .
              .
              .
  10     CONTINUE
      IF (DTACHK=OK) THEN
              .
              .
              .
      END IF
      STOP
      END
```

Not only is this use of a CHARACTER variable as an error flag just as easy to follow as the earlier use of a LOGICAL error flag, but it is more flexible and, obviously, does not suffer from the same problems with regard to input and output.

13.3   LOGICAL functions

A rather more valuable use for the LOGICAL data type is as the type of a function, where it is often useful to be able to return a result that simply indicates whether or not some condition is true. This will also usually improve the readability of the program.

For example, in Chapter 12, as part of the solution for Example 12.8, we wrote a function that was to be used in encrypting messages. Part of that function was concerned with establishing whether a character was alphabetic, in which case it was to be encrypted, or non-alphabetic, in which case it was to remain unaltered. This could have been achieved by use of a logical function of the form

```
LOGICAL FUNCTION ALPHA(C)
CHARACTER C
ALPHA=('A'.LE.C .AND. C.LE.'Z' .OR.
*       'a'.LE.C .AND. C.LE.'z')
RETURN
END
```

which could then have been used in the main function simply by writing a statement such as

```
IF ALPHA(CH) THEN ...
```

13.4 DOUBLE PRECISION and COMPLEX variables

The two remaining data types were described in some detail in Sections 11.2 and 11.6. A brief description is included here for readers who have chosen to omit the chapters concerned with numerical methods.

We have stated that a real value is an *approximation*, which represents a numeric value to a specified precision using a **floating-point** representation. The accuracy of this approximation is determined by the form of the floating-point number, which is allocated a fixed number of bits for the mantissa (thus defining the *precision*), and a fixed number for the exponent (thus defining the *range* of the numbers). A **double precision** value uses two consecutive numeric storage units to increase the size of the mantissa, and possibly also the exponent, thus providing greater precision. Double precision variables must be declared in a type specification statement that takes the form

```
DOUBLE PRECISION name1,name2,...
```

F90

The input and output of double precision values are performed by F or E edit descriptors in exactly the same way as for real values.

Double precision constants are written in the exponent and mantissa form, but with a D to separate the two parts instead of an E as with real constants (see Section 2.1), thus:

1D–7	is double precision 0.000 000 1
14713D–3	is double precision 14.713
12.7192D0	is double precision 12.7192
9.413D5	is double precision 941 300.0

When using double precision values in a mixed-mode arithmetic expression a process occurs that is similar to that with which we are already familiar. The expression is evaluated in stages using the normal priority rules; if one operand is double precision and the other is real or integer, the latter is converted to double precision before the operation is carried out, to give a double precision result.

For many purposes real arithmetic is quite accurate enough, especially if care is taken over the way in which calculations are carried out. If it is not sufficient then double precision variables can be used either in critical areas or throughout the program, as appropriate. Before doing so, however, the reader is recommended to read Sections 11.1 and 11.2, which give more information about the effect of arithmetic errors and the use of DOUBLE PRECISION variables to combat it.

The final type of numeric variable is somewhat esoteric and is mainly used for certain specialist applications, such as the calculations frequently carried out by electrical engineers. This type of variable is called **complex** and consists of two parts – a **real part** and an **imaginary part**. In Fortran such a number is stored in two consecutive numeric storage units as two separate real numbers, the first representing the real part and the second the imaginary. A complex variable is declared in a type specification statement of the form

F90

```
COMPLEX name1, name2, ...
```

A complex constant is written as a pair of real numbers, separated by a comma and enclosed in parentheses:

```
(1.5, 7.3)
(1.59E4, - 12E-1)
```

The use of complex variables is described in some detail in Section 11.6 and will not be discussed any further here.

SUMMARY

- LOGICAL variables are used to preserve logical values.

- The L edit descriptor is used to input or output logical values.

- CHARACTER variables provide an alternative method of achieving the results that are possible with LOGICAL variables.

- LOGICAL functions can often improve readability of programs.

- DOUBLE PRECISION variables can be used to provide increased precision.

- COMPLEX variables provide a means of carrying out complex arithmetic.

- Fortran 77 statements introduced in Chapter 13:

  Type declarations   LOGICAL *list of names*
  DOUBLE PRECISION *list of names*
  COMPLEX *list of names*

SELF-TEST EXERCISES 13.1

1 What are the six intrinsic data types in Fortran 77? Give an example of a PARAMETER declaration that establishes a named constant of each type.

2 What does the following function do?

```
LOGICAL FUNCTION TEST2(U,N)
INTEGER U,N,I
REAL X
LOGICAL POS,NEG
READ (U) X
POS = X.GE.0.0
NEG = X.LE.0.0
DO 5, I=1,N-1
  READ (U) X
  POS = POS .AND. X.GE.0.0
  NEG = NEG .AND. X.LE.0.0
5 CONTINUE
TEST2 = POS .OR. NEG
RETURN
END
```

3 Rewrite the function given in TEST2 as a CHARACTER function that uses no LOGICAL variables. Which version do you prefer?

PROGRAMMING EXERCISES

13.1 Write a program to print out the truth tables for .OR., .EQV. and .NEQV. in the same form as the following table for .AND.

A	B	A.AND.B
T	T	T
T	F	F
F	T	F
F	F	F

where the value for the third column is printed as the result of executing a logical expression (and *not* by working out the result and simply printing the table!).

13.2 Write a program that reads three real numbers representing three distances. The program should use these as the arguments to a subroutine that will set three further arguments as follows:

TRI   is set *true* if the three distances could represent the sides of a triangle, that is, no number is greater than the sum of the other two numbers;

ISO   is set *true* if TRI is *true* and at least two of the sides are of equal length, that is, an isosceles triangle;

EQU   is set *true* if TRI is *true* and all three sides are of equal length, that is, an equilateral triangle.

The program should then display an appropriate message.

13.3 Write a program that uses a LOGICAL function to check user-entered character strings for non-alphabetic characters. The program should print a warning if any are found.

13.4 The logical *NAND* operation is the equivalent of performing the .AND. operation, followed by a .NOT. operation. Thus

   NAND(A,B) is the same as .NOT.(A.AND.B)

Write a logical function to perform the *NAND* operation on its two logical arguments.

*13.5 Write a logical function which has two CHARACTER arguments, and which returns the value *true* if the first argument contains the second, and *false* otherwise. Thus, if the function is called WITHIN, then WITHIN('Just testing','test') is *true*, while WITHIN('Just testing','Test') is *false*.

   Test your function with a driver program that inputs pairs of character strings from the keyboard, and uses the result of a function reference to cause one of the following forms of message to be displayed:

(a) `The phrase 'test' is contained within 'Just testing'`
(b) `The phrase 'Test' is not contained within 'Just testing'`

13.6 An 8-bit binary number can be assigned to an 8-element INTEGER array. An 8-element LOGICAL array could be used just as easily. Write a program that adds two 8-bit binary numbers using LOGICAL arrays.

13.7 An (unordered) set **S** of the integers between 1 and 100 can be represented as a logical array A of dimension 100, where n is an element of **S** if A(n) is *true*. Write and test subroutines to give the union and intersection of sets represented in this way.

13.8   Using a logical array with a large number of elements may take up more memory than is available. Devise a way of using an integer array to represent a logical array in such a way that more than one logical value can be stored in one integer value. (*Hint*: remember that integers are stored as binary numbers consisting of a fixed number of bits, each of which can take the value 0 or 1.)

Write a subroutine to put a logical value into any given element of the simulated logical array, and a logical function to obtain the value of any given element. Use these procedures to modify your solution to Exercise 13.7 for sets of integers between 1 and 4000.

13.9   If you use a personal computer, you can tell how long a program takes to run with a stopwatch. If you use a multi-user machine, there is usually some facility that will tell you how much processor time your program has used. Use one or other of these methods, if available, to compare the relative speed of real and double-precision calculations.

Write a 'benchmark' program that will, for example, carry out 10 000 multiplications of two REAL numbers and 10 000 multiplications of DOUBLE PRECISION numbers.

Use a similar procedure to compare the times taken to evaluate $(X*X)$ and $(X**2.0)$.

13.10   The iterative procedure

$$x_{new} = x_{old}r(1 - x_{old})$$
$$x_{old} = x_{new}$$

behaves differently depending on the value of the constant r. In particular, x_{new} converges to a single value for certain values of r.

Taking $r = 1$ and $x_{old} = 0.3$ as starting values write a program using DOUBLE PRECISION variables that prints out x_{new} versus n, where n is the number of iterations. Use a logical variable as a signal to stop the iterations when x has converged to within some user specified accuracy.

The more adventurous might like to experiment to find out what happens to the evolution of x_{new} as r increases gradually from 1 to 4.

More about arrays $\boxed{\text{F90}}$ **14**

The arrays used up to this point have had only a single dimension, and hence only a single subscript. Fortran 77, however, allows an array to have up to seven dimensions. Where an array has more than one dimension the order of storage of the elements is such that the first subscript changes most rapidly, and the last most slowly.

When using arrays as arguments to procedures it is always necessary for the procedure to contain a declaration of the dummy array, but it is not always necessary for the declaration to contain the exact subscript ranges. An adjustable array declaration allows some or all of the dimension declarators to be dummy arguments to the same procedure, or to be in a COMMON block (see Chapter 15) in the same procedure. An assumed size declaration, on the other hand, must only have an asterisk as the last dimension; the other dimensions must all be specified correctly.

An example of a **Straight Selection sorting algorithm** is presented, followed by a worked example in which a pointer array is sorted in order to minimize the data swapping required.

The final section of the chapter shows how a set of procedures may be developed to provide the necessary tools for matrix manipulation. *This section may be omitted by those who have no interest in numerical and/or matrix problems.*

14.1 Multi-dimensional arrays

We have so far considered an array as having a single subscript. This is not sufficient for many purposes where, for example, HT(N,M) could identify the height at grid position (N,M) in a set of geographical data, and Fortran 77 therefore allows us to have up to *seven* subscripts for a single array. The number of subscripts is defined in the array declaration, and thus

```
INTEGER MARK(6,50)
```

defines an array MARK with two subscripts, the first running from 1 to 6, the second from 1 to 50. This array could, for example, be used to store the marks achieved in a series of six examinations by a class of 50 students, where the first subscript identifies the exam and the second the student. This array could also be declared in any of the following ways:

```
INTEGER MARK(1:6,1:50)
INTEGER MARK(6,1:50)
INTEGER MARK(1:6,50)
```

In a similar way the array declaration

```
REAL C(100,100,0:3,0:3)
```

defines a real array with four subscripts, the first two running from 1 to 100, and the second two from 0 to 3. Such an array might be used in a surface-fitting program, in which the surface is split into up to 100 sections in both x and y directions and the equation of the surface in the area that is the Ith in the x direction and the Jth in the y direction is given by

$$\sum_{\substack{N=0,3 \\ M=0,3}} C(I,J,N,M)x^N y^M = 0$$

Note, however, that a multi-subscripted (or multi-dimensional) array can very rapidly use up the available memory and must be used with care. The array C, above, has a size of $100 \times 100 \times 4 \times 4$ requiring 160 000 numeric storage units – rather more than the total memory available on many computers!

An element of a multi-dimensional array must always be written with the correct number of subscripts, and can, of course, be used in exactly the same way as a variable or an element of a single-subscripted array.

We saw in Sections 6.5 and 6.6 how an implied DO may be used to initialize, input or output part of a single-subscripted array. The same is true of a multi-dimensional array.

When we defined an implied DO list as

$$(dlist, int=m1, m2, m3)$$

we said that *dlist* was a list of array element names. We can now extend this definition to state that it is a list of array element names and/or implied DO lists for DATA statements, and a list of *any* input or output list items for input or output statements. Thus we may read data into the array MARK (as declared above) by a statement such as

```
READ 101, ((MARK(I,J),I=1,N),J=I,M)
```

where N is 6 or less and M is no more than 50, in order to keep within the declared bounds of the array.

However, if we wish to use the name of the array without any subscripts in an input/output or DATA statement there is a slight problem. With a single-dimensional array the order in which the array elements are stored is quite obvious, but this is not so with a multi-dimensional array. For example, the array MARK could be stored in the order

```
MARK(1,1) MARK(2,1) ... MARK(6,1) MARK(1,2) ...
```

or it could be stored in the order

```
MARK(1,1) MARK(1,2) ... MARK(1,50) MARK(2,1)...
```

Clearly it is vital that we know which order is used if any data or initial values are to be provided in the correct sequence. The rule used in Fortran is:

A multi-dimensional array is stored in the computer's memory in such a way that the first subscript changes most rapidly, the second next most rapidly, and so on, with the last subscript changing most slowly.

In the case of the array MARK this means that the first of the two alternatives above is the correct one:

```
MARK(1,1) MARK(2,1) ... MARK(6,1) MARK(1,2)...
```

This means that if enough data were supplied to fill the array MARK it would be provided in the same order. With the earlier assumption that the first subscript (in the range 1–6) corresponds to the exam and the second (in the range 1–50) to the student, this would mean that all the marks for one pupil (MARK(1,1) ... MARK(6,1)) would be followed by all the marks for the next pupil. If the data were more readily available with all the marks for one exam followed by all the marks for the next, either the array should be dimensioned

```
INTEGER MARK(50,6)
```

or an implied DO list should be used for input:

```
READ 101, ((MARK(I,J),J=1,50),I=1,6)
```

EXAMPLE 14.1

Students in a particular institution have to sit 12 papers in their final examination, each of which is marked out of 100. They are awarded degrees of varying classes depending upon the following rules:

(1) a student who *averages* at least 75%, and who never gets less than 60% is awarded a First;

(2) a student who does not obtain a First but who averages at least 50% and who never gets less than 30% is awarded a Second;

(3) a student who does not obtain a First or a Second but who averages at least 30% is awarded a Third;

(4) a student who is not classified as First, Second or Third but who averages at least 20%, and achieves at least 35% on three papers, is awarded a Pass.

The results of each paper are provided separately, in alphabetic order of the candidates, all of whom attempt all papers. Write a program to read the results for each paper (name in columns 1–20, mark in columns 23–25) and to print the final class lists with the names in each class being given in alphabetic order. No marks are to be shown, but any student who achieves over 75% in every paper is 'starred' with an asterisk before his/her name. The number of candidates is supplied as the first item of data, and will not exceed 150.

The structure plan for this program will be quite a simple one, the major difficulty being the logic associated with classifying the students. However, it is clear that essentially the same set of tests will be required for each case: to achieve a particular level of pass the candidate must achieve a certain average mark and some number of papers must exceed some other mark. We could tabulate this as shown in Figure 14.1. It should therefore be simple to write a logical function that takes a mark and a set of criteria and returns the value *true* or *false*, as appropriate.

Class	Minimum average mark	Minimum acceptable mark	Number of 'poor' papers allowed
*1	75	75	0
1	75	60	0
2	50	30	0
3	30	–	12
Pass	20	35	9

Figure 14.1
Parameters for degree classification.

One other point that should be apparent is that, although all the classification checks require average marks, the average is not required elsewhere. The logic will work equally well by considering the *total* marks for each candidate, and will avoid the need for much time-consuming and unnecessary division.

We can now proceed to our structure plan:

1 Read number of candidates (N)

2 If N > 150 then fail with an error message

3 Repeat for each exam
   3.1 Repeat for each candidate
      3.1.1 Read next name and mark

4 Repeat for each candidate
   4.1 Calculate total mark
   4.2 Repeat for each class from 0 (= *1) to 4 (= pass)
      4.2.1 If marks achieve this class (CHECK) then
         4.2.1.1 Store class and exit to next candidate

5 Print lists of students in each class

CHECK(TOTAL,MARK(N),N,MINTOT,MINMRK,NUMBER)

1 If TOTAL is less than MINTOT then return *false*

2 Set count of poor papers to 0

3 Repeat for each mark
   3.1 If mark is less than MINMRK then
      3.1.1 Add 1 to count
      3.1.2 If count is greater than NUMBER then return *false*

4 Return *true*

The structure of the data does not show in the structure plan. In this case we shall need four arrays: one for the candidates' names, one (two-dimensional) for their individual marks, one for their total marks, and one for their class.

```
      PROGRAM FINALS
C
C This program produces the classified list of final examination
C candidates based on the marks achieved in 12 papers
C
C MOST is the maximum number of candidates
C EXAMS is the number of exams
      INTEGER MOST,EXAMS
      PARAMETER (MOST=150,EXAMS=12)
C Data arrays
      CHARACTER*20 NAME(MOST)
      INTEGER MARK(EXAMS,MOST),TOTAL(MOST),CLASS(MOST)
C Classification criteria
      INTEGER MINAV(0:4),MINMRK(0:4),NPOOR(0:4)
C Miscellaneous variables
      INTEGER NCANDS,MARKS(EXAMS),I,J
C Function declaration
      LOGICAL CHECK
C Initialization of total marks and classification criteria
      DATA TOTAL/MOST*0/,
     1      (MINAV(I),MINMRK(I),NPOOR(I),I=0,4)/75, 76,  0,
     2                                          75, 60,  0,
     3                                          50, 30,  0,
     4                                          30,  0, 12,
     5                                          20, 35,  9/
C Read number of candidates and check not too big
      PRINT *,'How many candidates are there? '
      READ *,NCANDS
      IF (NCANDS.GT.MOST) THEN
        PRINT 200,MOST,NCANDS
        STOP
      END IF
C Read data
      PRINT *,'Type marks for 1st exam, then for 2nd exam, etc.'
C Read names and marks for first exam
      PRINT *,'Exam number 1:'
      PRINT *,'Type data for each candidate as follows:'
      PRINT *,'--------name-------- mmm   (where mmm is the mark)'
      READ '(A20,2X,I3)',(NAME(I),MARK(1,I),I=1,NCANDS)
C Loop to read remainder of marks
      DO 20, I=2,EXAMS
        PRINT '(1H ,''Exam number '',I2,'':'')',I
        DO 10, J=1,NCANDS
          PRINT '(1H ,A20,2X)',NAME(J)
          READ '(I3)',MARK(I,J)
10      CONTINUE
20    CONTINUE
C Loop to calculate each candidate's class
```

```
         DO 50, I=1,NCANDS
C  Calculate total mark and copy marks to a 1-dimensional array
            DO 30, J=1,EXAMS
               TOTAL(I)=TOTAL(I)+MARK(J,I)
               MARKS(J)=MARK(J,I)
   30       CONTINUE
C  Loop to check each class from the top
            DO 40, J=0,4
               IF (CHECK(TOTAL(I),MARKS,EXAMS,EXAMS*MINAV(J),MINMRK(J),
     *                   NPOOR(J))) THEN
                  CLASS(I)=J
                  GOTO 50
               END IF
   40       CONTINUE
C  Candidate failed!
            CLASS(I)=9
   50    CONTINUE
C  All candidates now processed, so print class lists
         PRINT 201
C  First class honours
         DO 60, I=1,NCANDS
            IF (CLASS(I).LE.1) THEN
               PRINT 210,NAME(I)
C  Check for starred Firsts
               IF (CLASS(I).EQ.0) PRINT 211
            END IF
   60    CONTINUE
         PRINT 202
C  Second class honours
         DO 65, I=1,NCANDS
            IF (CLASS(I).EQ.2) PRINT 210,NAME(I)
   65    CONTINUE
         PRINT 203
C  Third class honours
         DO 70, I=1,NCANDS
            IF (CLASS(I).EQ.3) PRINT 210,NAME(I)
   70    CONTINUE
         PRINT 204
C  Pass
         DO 75, I=1,NCANDS
            IF (CLASS(I).EQ.4) PRINT 210,NAME(I)
   75    CONTINUE
         STOP
  200 FORMAT(1H1,'Error - maximum number of candidates is ',I3/
     *       1H ,'Data specifies ',I3,' candidates'/
     *       1H ,'Processing terminated.')
  201 FORMAT(1H1,'The following are awarded First Class Honours:'//)
  202 FORMAT(1H0,'The following are awarded Second Class Honours:'//)
  203 FORMAT(1H0,'The following are awarded Third Class Honours:'//)
  204 FORMAT(1H0,'The following are awarded Pass Degrees:'//)
  210 FORMAT(1H ,10X,A20)
  211 FORMAT(1H+,9X,'*')
      END
```

```
        LOGICAL FUNCTION CHECK(TOTAL,MARK,N,MINTOT,MINMRK,NUMBER)
C
C  This program returns the value TRUE if
C         (a)  the total mark (TOTAL) is greater than or equal to MINTOT
C         (b)  no more than NUMBER of the marks stored in MARK are less
C              than MINMRK
C  Otherwise it returns FALSE
C
C  Dummy arguments
        INTEGER TOTAL,N,MARK(N),MINTOT,MINMRK,NUMBER
C  Miscellaneous variables
        INTEGER COUNT,I
C  First check total mark
        IF (TOTAL.LT.MINTOT) THEN
          CHECK=.FALSE.
          RETURN
        END IF
C  Avoid individual mark checking if not necessary
        IF (NUMBER.EQ.N) THEN
          CHECK=.TRUE.
          RETURN
        END IF
C  Count poor marks and return appropriate value
        COUNT=0
        DO 10, I=1,N
          IF (MARK(I).LT.MINMRK) THEN
            COUNT=COUNT+1
            IF (COUNT.GT.NUMBER) THEN
              CHECK=.FALSE.
              RETURN
            END IF
          END IF
  10    CONTINUE
        CHECK=.TRUE.
        RETURN
        END
```

Since the data is provided in alphabetic order of candidates, the results for each class will also be in alphabetic order without any extra work on our part. However, since the 'starred' Firsts are to be listed with the other Firsts it is necessary to deal with them in a slightly different way; in the program shown this has been done by using a + printer control character to cause a * to be printed on the same line as that on which the name has already been printed, but one character position to the left of the start of the name. An alternative approach – and one that would have to be used if the output were not to a printer – would be to use different formats for the Firsts and the 'starred' Firsts:

```
        IF (CLASS(I).EQ.0) THEN
C  Starred First
          PRINT 211,NAME(I)
        ELSE IF (CLASS(I).EQ.1) THEN
```

```
C  First
          PRINT 210,NAME(I)
        END IF
              .
              .
  210 FORMAT (1H ,10X,A20)
  211 FORMAT (1H ,9X,'*',A20)
              .
              .
```

Note that the first set of exam marks require the students' names to be typed as well as their marks. For subsequent exams, however, the user is prompted with the name of the student, to ensure that the correct marks are allocated to each student.

We should also note that the reading of the data could be substantially simplified by using a double-nested implied DO, such as the following:

```
READ '(A20,2X,I3)',((NAME(I),MARK(I,J),J=1,NCANDS),I=1,EXAMS)
```

However, this would require considerably more typing, and would not detect any errors in typing until all the data had been input. If, however, the marks had already been input to a file and were being read from there, this would be an ideal form of READ statement.

One other aspect of this program that should be mentioned concerns the copying of each candidate's marks from the array MARK into the smaller, one-dimensional, array MARKS for use as an argument to the function CHECK. An alternative approach would have been to declare the dummy array to be two-dimensional and to pass both dimensions and the value of I (the *candidate* subscript). However, this too is awkward. In the next section we shall meet another solution to this problem.

Finally, it should be noted that in the logical function CHECK an extra test has been inserted. If the total mark (and hence the average) is acceptable, then before counting the number of 'poor' papers a check is made to see if this is actually necessary. For a third class degree only the average matters, and thus all papers can be 'poor' ones. In this case NUMBER will be equal to N, and the loop to check and count can be eliminated.

14.2 Arrays as dummy arguments

We have already seen in Chapter 6 that there are three ways of dealing with the size of a dummy array argument: by declaring the dummy array in the usual way with constant dimensions; by using an adjustable array declaration in which the dimensions of the array (or some of them) are provided as arguments to the same procedure; and by using an assumed-size declaration in which an asterisk (*) is used as one of the dimensions. Thus the following initial statements declare three dummy arrays, one of each type:

```
SUBROUTINE DEMO(A,B,C,N)
REAL A(5),B(N),C(*)
    .
    .
    .
```

In this example all the arrays are one-dimensional, but they can, of course, have up to seven dimensions *with one very important restriction*. In the case of a dummy array with constant dimensions there are no restrictions, but, as we saw in Chapter 6, this is very limiting for use in a subroutine or function, where we normally wish the procedure to work correctly for actual arguments of different sizes. In the case of a dummy array with adjustable dimensions there are again no problems, as long as the dimensions are also dummy arguments to the same procedure or appear in a COMMON block in the same procedure, as described in Chapter 15. But in the case of a dummy array with assumed-size dimensions only the *last* subscript may be represented by an asterisk. We can best understand the reason for this by considering the storage of the array B in the following declaration:

```
REAL B(4,*)
```

Since the first subscript changes fastest, the order of storage is considered to be

```
B(1,1) B(2,1) B(3,1) B(4,1) B(1,2) B(2,2) ...
```

As long as it is only the last subscript whose maximum size is unknown there is no problem, but clearly if the limits for any other subscript were unknown it would be impossible for the compiler to determine the location of any element of the array whose last subscript was greater than 1.

It is also worth reminding ourselves at this point of the other major restriction on the use of assumed-size arrays: we cannot use their names as items in an input/output list (where their unknown size should determine the number of items to be read or written) or as embedded formats (where their unknown number of elements should be concatenated to create the format). These are obviously severe restrictions, and limit the usefulness of assumed-size arrays; nevertheless their use can simplify the calling sequence for many subroutines and functions where it is not necessary to know the exact size of the array at the start of processing.

```
PROGRAM MAIN
REAL X(100),Y(0:5,-10:10)
       .
       .
       .
CALL ARRARG(X)
CALL ARRARG(Y)
CALL ARRARG(X(15))
CALL ARRARG(Y(3,0))
       .
       .
       .
END

SUBROUTINE ARRARG(A)
REAL A(9,6)
       .
       .
       .
END
```

Figure 14.2
Arrays as dummy
arguments.

We must also consider the actual argument that will correspond to a dummy array argument. If a dummy argument is an array (with either constant, adjustable or assumed size), the actual argument need not be an array itself but may also be an array element or an array element substring. If the actual argument is a non-character array name, then as long as it is not larger than the dummy array everything is straightforward and the first element of the dummy array is the same as the first element of the actual array, and so on. This does not, however, mean that the subscripts need to be the same, or even that there need to be the same number of subscripts. Figure 14.2 shows a program extract that contains several calls to the subroutine ARRARG.

The dummy array A has two subscripts, whereas the actual array (X) in the first call has only one and the actual array (Y) in the second has two, but with very different ranges for its subscripts. The following correspondence, therefore, will exist between various elements of these arrays during the first two calls to the subroutine:

A(1,1) and X(1) or Y(0,-10) as appropriate
A(6,1) and X(6) or Y(5,-10) as appropriate
A(7,1) and X(7) or Y(0,-9) as appropriate
A(9,1) and X(9) or Y(2,-9) as appropriate
A(1,2) and X(10) or Y(3,-9) as appropriate
A(5,4) and X(32) or Y(1,-5) as appropriate
A(9,6) and X(54) or Y(5,-2) as appropriate

In Example 14.1 we used a small, one-dimensional array MARK as an actual argument to the logical function CHECK, and repeatedly had to copy the relevant part of the two-dimensional array MARKS to it. We can now see that this was not necessary. If we examine the order in which the elements of MARK are stored we see that they are as follows:

```
MARK(1,1) MARK(2,1) MARK(3,1) ... MARK(n,1) MARK(1,2) ...
```

Since we wish to pass the six array elements

```
MARK(i,1) MARK(i,2) MARK(i,3) MARK(i,4) MARK(i,5) MARK(i,6)
```

to CHECK we must arrange for the array to be stored differently. This is easily achieved by declaring it as

```
INTEGER MARK(EXAMS,MOST)
```

and making the other necessary changes to the references to MARK. We can now remove all reference to the array MARKS and change the reference to the function to read:

```
IF (CHECK(TOTAL(I),MARK(1,I),EXAMS,MINTOT(J),MINMRK(J),
         NPOOR(J)) THEN
```

If the actual argument is a non-character *array element name* then the dummy argument is associated with it in such a way that the first element of the dummy array is the same as the actual (array element) argument. The second two calls to the subroutine ARRARG in Figure 14.2 use this form of actual argument with the following correspondences during the execution of the subroutine:

```
A(1,1) and X(15) or Y(3,0) as appropriate
A(4,1) and X(18) or Y(0,1) as appropriate
A(9,1) and X(23) or Y(5,1) as appropriate
A(1,2) and X(24) or Y(0,2) as appropriate
A(5,4) and X(46) or Y(4,5) as appropriate
A(9,6) and X(68) or Y(2,9) as appropriate
```

If the arrays are character arrays, things can get even more complicated: as we saw in Section 12.8, different *lengths* or the use of a substring as the actual argument can lead to the boundaries between array elements coming at different places in the two procedures. As a general rule, you should not try to be too clever with character array dummy arguments – there is too much scope for error!

EXAMPLE 14.2

In Example 6.1 we developed a program to produce some simple statistics relating to a set of experiments. This program used five one-dimensional arrays in which to store five sets of experimental results. Rewrite this program, using a single two-dimensional array to store the results.

Figure 14.3 shows the main program written in Example 6.1. We are reminded of the repetition of a set of three almost identical statements. If the five arrays A, B, C, D and E are replaced by a single two-dimensional

```
      PROGRAM METAL
C
C  This program summarizes experimental results
C
      REAL A(5),B(5),C(5),D(5),E(5),GMEAN(5),GSTDEV(5),
     *     XMEAN,XSTDEV,AVRAGE,STDEV
C  Input data by groups
      PRINT *,'Type five results for group A, followed by five for',
     *        'group B, etc.'
      READ *,A,B,C,D,E
C  Calculate mean and standard deviation for each group
      GMEAN(1) = AVRAGE(A,5)
      GSTDEV(1) = STDEV(A,5,GMEAN(1))
      PRINT *,'Group A mean is ',GMEAN(1),
     *        ' with a standard deviation of ',GSTDEV(1)
      GMEAN(2) = AVRAGE(B,5)
      GSTDEV(2) = STDEV(B,5,GMEAN(2))
      PRINT *,'Group B mean is ',GMEAN(2),
     *        ' with a standard deviation of ',GSTDEV(2)
      GMEAN(3) = AVRAGE(C,5)
      GSTDEV(3) = STDEV(C,5,GMEAN(3))
      PRINT *,'Group C mean is ',GMEAN(3),
     *        ' with a standard deviation of ',GSTDEV(3)
      GMEAN(4) = AVRAGE(D,5)
      GSTDEV(4) = STDEV(D,5,GMEAN(4))
      PRINT *,'Group D mean is ',GMEAN(4),
     *        ' with a standard deviation of ',GSTDEV(4)
      GMEAN(5) = AVRAGE(E,5)
      GSTDEV(5) = STDEV(E,5,GMEAN(5))
      PRINT *,'Group E mean is ',GMEAN(5),
     *        ' with a standard deviation of ',GSTDEV(5)
C  Now calculate overall totals
      XMEAN = AVRAGE(GMEAN,5)
      XSTDEV = STDEV(GMEAN,5,XMEAN)
      PRINT *,'Overall mean is ',XMEAN,' with a standard deviation of ',
     *        XSTDEV
      STOP
      END
```

Figure 14.3
The main program from Example 6.1.

array R, we can dramatically simplify the program, as follows:

```
      PROGRAM METAL2
C
C  This program summarizes experimental results
C
      INTEGER I
      REAL R(5,5),RMEAN(5),RSTDEV(5),XMEAN,XSTDEV,AVRAGE,STDEV
C  Array to hold group names
      CHARACTER GROUP(5)
      DATA GROUP/'A','B','C','D','E'/
C  Input data by groups
      PRINT *,'Type five results for group A, followed by five for ',
     *        'group B, etc.'
      READ *,R
C  Loop to calculate mean and standard deviation for each group
      DO 10, I=1,5
         RMEAN(I) = AVRAGE(R(1,I),5)
         RSTDEV(I) = STDEV(R(1,I),5,RMEAN(I))
         PRINT 200,GROUP(I),RMEAN(I),RSTDEV(I)
   10 CONTINUE
C  Now calculate overall totals
      XMEAN = AVRAGE(RMEAN,5)
      XSTDEV = STDEV(RMEAN,5,XMEAN)
      PRINT 201,XMEAN,XSTDEV
      STOP
  200 FORMAT (1H ,'Group ',A1,' mean is ',F7.2,
     *        ' with a standard deviation of ',F7.2)
  201 FORMAT (1H0,'Overall mean is ',F7.2,
     *        ' with a standard deviation of ',F7.2)
      END
```

The two functions AVRAGE and STDEV will be identical to those in the earlier program. Notice the use of an array *element* as an actual argument in the references to the two functions, each of which is expecting an *array* as a dummy argument.

14.3 A method of sorting the contents of an array

In Example 14.1 we were asked to provide a list of successful degree candidates in each class in alphabetic order. This did not cause us any difficulty because the data items were already in alphabetic order and our processing did not alter this order. However, that was clearly a somewhat artificial simplification.

Initial order	⑦	①	8	4	6	3	5	2
After first swap	1	⑦	8	4	6	3	5	②
After second swap	1	2	⑧	4	6	③	5	7
After third swap	1	2	3	④	6	8	5	7
After fourth swap	1	2	3	4	⑥	8	⑤	7
After fifth swap	1	2	3	4	5	⑧	⑥	7
After sixth swap	1	2	3	4	5	6	⑧	⑦
After seventh swap	1	2	3	4	5	6	7	8

Figure 14.4
Sorting by straight selection.

The need to sort data into numerical or alphabetic order is a very common one in many computer programs and is easily satisfied with the tools we now have at our disposal. Sorting is a subject into which much research has been carried out over many years; however, for our purposes a simple general-purpose sorting method will suffice. If small amounts of data are to be sorted it is perfectly adequate; but if large amounts are to be sorted one of many specialist sorting methods, such as Quicksort or Pigeon Sort, should be used.

We shall investigate the method of **straight selection** because it is reasonably efficient and easy to understand. Essentially the method involves searching through all the items to be sorted and finding the one that is to go at the head of the unsorted part of the list. This is then *exchanged* with the item currently at the head of that part of the list. The process is then repeated, starting immediately after the item that has just been sorted into its correct place, and so on. Each time, one more item is moved to its correct place. Figure 14.4 shows the progress of such a sort, in which eight numbers are sorted so that the lowest is on the left and the highest is on the right. The two numbers to be exchanged at each stage are circled. (It should be noted that the fourth exchange does not actually take place because the number at the head of the unsorted list is already in the correct place.)

This is quite a simple method to code in Fortran, and we can easily write a subroutine that will sort the data in Example 14.1 into alphabetic order. Our structure plan will be as follows:

SORT(NAME,MARK,NCANDS,EXAMS)

1   Repeat the following for all unsorted names
  1.1 Find 'earliest' remaining name
  1.2 Exchange it with first unsorted name
  1.3 Exchange corresponding sets of marks

The subroutine then follows with little difficulty.

```
      SUBROUTINE SORT(NAME,MARK,NCANDS,EXAMS)
C
C This subroutine sorts the candidates and their marks into
C alphabetic order of their names
C
C Dummy arguments
      CHARACTER*20 NAME(NCANDS)
      INTEGER MARK(EXAMS,NCANDS),NCANDS,EXAMS
C Temporary storage for swapping
      CHARACTER*20 TMPNAM
      INTEGER TMPMRK
C Miscellaneous variables
      CHARACTER*20 FIRST
      INTEGER INDEX,I,J
C Loop to sort NCANDS-1 names into order
      DO 20, I=1,NCANDS-1
C Initialize earliest so far to be the first one in this pass
         FIRST=NAME(I)
         INDEX=I
C Search remaining (unsorted items) for earliest one
         DO 10, J=I+1,NCANDS
            IF (NAME(J).LT.FIRST) THEN
C Earlier one found, so save it and its position
               FIRST=NAME(J)
               INDEX=J
            END IF
   10    CONTINUE
C Exchange names and marks if necessary
         IF (INDEX.NE.I) THEN
            TMPNAM=NAME(I)
            NAME(I)=NAME(INDEX)
            NAME(INDEX)=TMPNAM
            DO 15, J=1,EXAMS
               TMPMRK=MARK(J,I)
               MARK(J,I)=MARK(J,INDEX)
               MARK(J,INDEX)=TMPMRK
   15       CONTINUE
         END IF
   20 CONTINUE
      RETURN
      END
```

All that is now required is to insert the call to the subroutine in the main program immediately after the data has been input, and the order of that data becomes irrelevant as it will be properly sorted before any further processing takes place.

EXAMPLE 14.3

Write a program that prints all the players in the golf tournament described in Example 12.2 in their finishing order (lowest score first, highest score last), together with their position.

Essentially this program merely requires us to sort the data into order of increasing score, in much the same way as we have just done with the examination candidates. However, with six variables for each player, moving these about will take a considerable time. A much better way, therefore, is to leave the player's data where it is and to sort a **pointer** to the data. We can do this by keeping one extra item for each player: his or her position in the original data. We can use this as a subscript to the arrays for names and scores. Our structure plan is therefore as follows:

1 Repeat the following
   1.1 Read name and scores for next player
   1.2 If name = 'END OF DATA' then exit
   1.3 Calculate total score for this player
   1.4 Store player's number

2 Repeat the following for all unsorted places
   2.1 Find lowest remaining score
   2.2 Exchange pointer to it with pointer to first unsorted place

3 Use pointers to print players in their final order

There are no particular problems here and so we can proceed with the program.

```
      PROGRAM GOLF2
C
C  This program prints the details of the players taking part
C  in a golf tournament in the order of their final scores
C
C  Maximum number of players
      INTEGER MAX
      PARAMETER (MAX=100)
C  Players' names, round scores and totals, and pointers
      CHARACTER*20 PLAYER(MAX)
      INTEGER SCORE(MAX,4),TOTAL(MAX),POS(MAX)
C  Miscellaneous variables
      INTEGER NUM,I,J
```

```
C  Read players' names and scores
       PRINT *,'Type scores as follows:'
       PRINT *,'--------Name-------- R1 R2 R3 R4'
       PRINT *,'A name typed as "END OF DATA" terminates data input'
       DO 10, I=1,MAX
         PRINT *,'Next player: '
         READ '(A20,4(1X,I2))',PLAYER(I),(SCORE(I,J),J=1,4)
C  Check for end of data
         IF (PLAYER(I).EQ.'END OF DATA') GOTO 11
C  Calculate total score
         TOTAL(I)=SCORE(I,1)+SCORE(I,2)+SCORE(I,3)+SCORE(I,4)
C  Set up initial pointer
         POS(I)=I
   10 CONTINUE
C  No terminator
       PRINT 201,MAX
C  Store number of players
   11 NUM=I-1
C  Now sort pointer array into order of scores
       CALL SORT(TOTAL,POS,NUM)
C  Pointer array now sorted - so print results of tournament
       PRINT 202,(I,PLAYER(POS(I)),TOTAL(POS(I)),
      *          (SCORE(POS(I),J),J=1,4),I=1,NUM)
       STOP
  201 FORMAT (1H0,'No terminator found.  Only first',I4,
      *          ' players processed')
  202 FORMAT (1H1,'Fortran 77 Golf Tournament'///
     1        1H ,'The final order after four rounds:'//
     2        (1H ,I3,4X,A20,2X,'Total:',I4,' (',3(I2,','),I2,')'))
       END


       SUBROUTINE SORT(SCORE,POS,N)
C
C  This subroutine sorts a pointer array POS into ascending order
C  of the elements of the associated array SCORE
C
C  Dummy arguments
       INTEGER SCORE(N),POS(N)
C  Miscellaneous variables
       INTEGER N,LEAST,INDEX,TMP,I,J
C  Loop to sort N-1 pointers into order
       DO 20, I=1,N-1
C  Initialize lowest so far to be the first one in this pass
         LEAST=SCORE(POS(I))
         INDEX=I
C  Search remaining (unsorted items) for earliest one
         DO 15, J=I+1,N
           IF (SCORE(POS(J)).LT.LEAST) THEN
C  Lower score found, so save it and its position
             LEAST=SCORE(POS(J))
             INDEX=J
           END IF
   15    CONTINUE
```

```
C  Exchange pointers if necessary
         IF (INDEX.NE.I) THEN
            TMP=POS(I)
            POS(I)=POS(INDEX)
            POS(INDEX)=TMP
         END IF
   20 CONTINUE
C  Pointer array now sorted
         RETURN
         END
```

There are several points to note in this program. First, the number of players is checked and a warning printed if more than the maximum allowed for is read without a terminator. The variable NUM is set to the number of players read for use in the sorting phase. The array POS (which is initialized during input) is then sorted into the correct order in a variation of the earlier sorting procedure.

Notice that it is permissible to have an array element as a subscript to an array. INDEX is set to the position of the head of the list of items still to be sorted, and LEAST is set to the total score of the player in that position. A nested loop then looks at all total scores of players after this and if it finds a lower score alters INDEX and LEAST accordingly. When all items have been inspected INDEX will contain the subscript of the element of the array POS that points to the lowest remaining score. If INDEX is the same as I then this is already at the head of the remaining items; if it is not then the pointers are exchanged.

Finally, the results are printed by using POS(I) as a subscript to the players' details in an implied DO list. Notice that the value of the implied DO variable can also be output, thus providing the finishing position. Figure 14.5 shows the beginning of the results produced by this program.

One minor improvement could be made to this program. As can be seen from Figure 14.5, if two or more players have the same score they are

```
Fortran 77 Golf Tournament

The final order after four rounds:

    1    Faldo, Nick           Total: 277 (71,69,68,69)
    2    Lyle, Sandy           Total: 278 (69,69,72,68)
    3    Nicklaus, Jack        Total: 279 (71,70,70,68)
    4    Ballesteros, Seve     Total: 279 (67,72,69,71)
    5    Weiskopf, Tom         Total: 279 (70,69,68,72)
    6    Norman, Greg          Total: 279 (68,69,72,70)
    7    Langer, Bernhard      Total: 280 (70,69,71,70)
```

Figure 14.5
Results produced by the GOLF2 program.

Figure 14.6
Sorted results from the
GOLF2 program.

```
Fortran 77 Golf Tournament

The final order after four rounds:

    1    Faldo, Nick            Total: 277 (71,69,68,69)
    2    Lyle, Sandy            Total: 278 (69,69,72,68)
    3    Ballesteros, Seve      Total: 279 (67,72,69,71)
    4    Nicklaus, Jack         Total: 279 (71,70,70,68)
    5    Norman, Greg           Total: 279 (68,69,72,70)
    6    Weiskopf, Tom          Total: 279 (70,69,68,72)
    7    Langer, Bernhard       Total: 280 (70,69,71,70)
```

listed in an apparently random order. It would be more pleasing, perhaps, if in this situation they were listed in alphabetic order.

Sorting each set of players who have the same total score into alphabetic order would be awkward and inefficient. A better way would be first to sort all the data into alphabetic order, and then to ensure that the relative order of players having the same score is not subsequently altered. Unfortunately, the method we are using to sort the scores does so by exchanging the 'next' player with the one at the head of the unsorted part of the data, thus causing the original ordering to be completely destroyed. However, we can avoid this problem if all the players from the head to the one before the 'next' player are moved down by one position and the 'next' player is inserted into the correct, and now vacant, position.

This method is considerably less efficient than the original one, since it involves many more moves, but it will achieve our desired aim. The initial alphabetic sort can use the more efficient method, and the following code, inserted in place of the block IF that exchanges the pointers in the subroutine SORT will achieve the required result:

```
C  Move pointers if necessary
        IF (INDEX.NE.I) THEN
          TMP=POS(INDEX)
          DO 16, J=INDEX,I+1,-1
   16       POS(J)=POS(J-1)
          POS(I)=TMP
        END IF
```

Figure 14.6 shows the result of running this improved program with the same data as Figure 14.5.

14.4   Vectors and matrices

Up to this point arrays have been considered as convenient ways to process a collection of items of the same type. However, such a concept is widely used in engineering, mathematics, and many scientific applications in an altogether more powerful way. Mathematicians call a one-dimensional array a **vector**, while a two-dimensional array is called a **matrix**, and the use of vector and matrix arithmetic is essential in most serious numerical computation.

Fortran 77 does not contain any intrinsic capability for vector or matrix processing (although Fortran 90 will) and it is therefore necessary to use procedures to carry out the various matrix operations that make much mathematical calculation very much easier. Frequently such procedures will be available as part of a procedure library (such as the NAG library) on the computer system being used, and will enable a very wide range of matrix operations such as triangulation, calculation of determinants and eigenvalues, to be carried out without any difficulty. Since many of these operations involve complex calculations, with the consequent problems of accuracy and rounding, it is normally preferable to use such libraries, which have been written by numerical analysis specialists, rather than attempting to write one's own. However, the simple arithmetic operations do not lead to such numerical problems and Example 14.4 shows how a basic set of matrix procedures could easily be produced.

EXAMPLE 14.4

Write a set of procedures to carry out the following matrix and vector operations:

- sum of two vectors or matrices;
- difference between two vectors or matrices;
- scalar (dot) product of two vectors;
- (cross) product of two vectors, two matrices, a vector and a matrix, or a matrix and a vector.

The first two (sum and difference) are relatively straightforward, as the addition or subtraction is carried out on an element-by-element basis. Thus, if A is a vector of dimension n consisting of the n elements $A_1, A_2, \ldots A_n$ (note, incidentally, the difference in meaning of the word 'dimension' in Fortran and in mathematics) and B is also a vector of dimension n with elements $B_1, B_2, \ldots B_n$, then $A+B$ is the n-dimensional vector C, where $C_i = A_i + B_i$, for $i=1$ to n.

The important thing to notice is that the two vectors must be of the same dimension, and so our procedure should, ideally, check that this is so before proceeding. However, since it is always preferable to use *adjustable* rather than *assumed-size* arrays we can require that the size of both arrays is passed as an argument, thus ensuring that they are specified to be of the same size. A suitable structure plan for vector addition would be as follows:

VADD(A,B,C,N)

1   Repeat for I from 1 to N
    1.1 C(I) = A(I)+B(I)

A structure plan for matrix addition is scarcely more complicated, remembering that in this case both dimensions must match.

MATADD(A,B,C,N,M)

1   Repeat for J from 1 to M
    1.1 Repeat for I from 1 to N
        1.1.1 C(I,J) = A(I,J)+B(I,J)

Note that there are two possible ways of writing this procedure; the other way would have had I as the control variable for the outer loop, and J for the inner one. This is where it is important to remember the order in which the array is stored in memory.

In the form written above the elements of *A* will be accessed in the order $A(1,1)$, $A(2,1)$, ... $A(N,1)$, $A(1,2)$, ... $A(N,M)$, which is the order in which they are stored, with *B* and *C* being accessed similarly. This will enable the computer to process this loop as fast as possible. If we had reversed the order of the loops then the elements of *A* would have been accessed in the order $A(1,1)$, $A(1,2)$, ... $A(1,M)$, $A(2,1)$, ... $A(N,M)$. In the case of large arrays this can lead to very much slower execution of the loop than the first version.

We could now write these two subroutines very easily. However, note that the inner loop of the matrix addition procedure is identical to the vector addition procedure, apart from the presence of a second index, J. Since an $n \times 1$ matrix is effectively the same as an n-dimensional vector we can eliminate the need for a separate vector addition procedure by adopting the convention that a vector is supplied to the matrix addition procedure as a matrix whose second dimension has a size of 1. This is particularly convenient because of the way in which arrays are stored.

Declaration	Storage layout				
REAL P(5)	P(1)	P(2)	P(3)	P(4)	P(5)
REAL Q(5,1)	Q(1,1)	Q(2,1)	Q(3,1)	Q(4,1)	Q(5,1)

Figure 14.7
One- and two-dimensional array storage of a vector.

Consider, for example, a one-dimensional array P of size 5, and a two-dimensional array Q of size 5×1. The storage layout of these two arrays is shown in Figure 14.7, and it can be seen that they are, in fact, identical. Thus it is possible to have an array such as P as the actual argument, while the procedure declares the dummy argument in a form such as Q.

Our procedure can now be written.

```
      SUBROUTINE MATADD(A,B,C,N,M)
C
C  This subroutine adds the two N by M matrices stored in A and B,
C  returning the result in C.  If M is 1, the matrices are vectors.
C
C  Dummy arguments
      INTEGER N,M
      REAL A(N,M),B(N,M),C(N,M)
C  Local variables
      INTEGER I,J
C
      DO 10, J=1,M
        DO 5, I=1,N
          C(I,J)=A(I,J)+B(I,J)
    5   CONTINUE
   10 CONTINUE
      RETURN
      END
```

It should be pointed out that combining the vector and matrix cases in this way will lead to a marginal loss of efficiency in the vector case, since the calculation of the address of a two-dimensional array takes fractionally longer than for a one-dimensional array. This could be eliminated by replacing the two loops in the subroutine by the following:

```
      IF (M.GT.1) THEN
        DO 10, J=1,M
          DO 5, I=1,N
            C(I,J)=A(I,J)+B(I,J)
    5     CONTINUE
   10     CONTINUE
      ELSE
        DO 15, I=1,N
          C(I,1)=A(I,1)+B(I,1)
   15   CONTINUE
      END IF
```

which will enable the compiler to deal with the vector case more efficiently. However, we have now, in effect, recreated two subroutines within a single named subroutine, and it may be felt that it would be better to leave them as separate procedures. This is where personal style takes over.

The procedures for vector and matrix subtraction are the same as those for addition, apart from the replacement of the plus operator by the minus operator, so we shall not concern ourselves with that, but will move on to the two product procedures.

The scalar product of the two vectors A and B is defined as $A_1B_1+A_2B_2+\ldots+A_nB_n$, where A and B are both of dimension n. A suitable structure plan is therefore:

DOTPRD(A,B,AB,N)

1 Set AB to zero.

2 Repeat for I from 1 to N:
2.1 AB=AB+A(I)*B(I)

The procedure is then trivial.

```
      SUBROUTINE DOTPRD(A,B,AB,N)
C
C  This subroutine forms the scalar product of the two vectors A and B,
C  of dimension N, returning the result in AB.
C
C  Dummy arguments
      INTEGER N
      REAL A(N),B(N),AB
C  Local variable
      INTEGER I
C
      AB=0.0
      DO 10, I=1,N
        AB=AB+A(I)*B(I)
   10 CONTINUE
      RETURN
      END
```

Finally we come to the matrix multiplication subroutine. Here there are three cases: vector times matrix, matrix times vector, and matrix times matrix as shown in Figure 14.8.

Once again we can see that the two cases involving vectors are

Vector × matrix A $\times$ X $=$ B

$$[1\ 2\ 3\ -2] \times \begin{bmatrix} 1 & 2 & 1 \\ 2 & 0 & -2 \\ 3 & 1 & -1 \\ 0 & 2 & 1 \end{bmatrix} = [14\ 1\ -8]$$

Figure 14.8
Matrix and vector
multiplication.

Matrix × vector X $\times$ C $=$ D

$$\begin{bmatrix} 1 & 2 & 1 \\ 2 & 0 & -2 \\ 3 & 1 & -1 \\ 0 & 2 & 1 \end{bmatrix} \times \begin{bmatrix} 1 \\ -3 \\ 0 \end{bmatrix} = \begin{bmatrix} -5 \\ 2 \\ 0 \\ -6 \end{bmatrix}$$

Matrix × matrix X $\times$ Y $=$ Z

$$\begin{bmatrix} 1 & 2 & 1 \\ 2 & 0 & -2 \\ 3 & 1 & -1 \\ 0 & 2 & 1 \end{bmatrix} \times \begin{bmatrix} 1 & 0 \\ -3 & -1 \\ 0 & 2 \end{bmatrix} = \begin{bmatrix} -5 & 0 \\ 2 & -4 \\ 0 & -3 \\ -6 & 0 \end{bmatrix}$$

simply special cases of the more general case, in which the vector is considered to be either a $1 \times n$ matrix or an $m \times 1$ matrix, depending upon whether it is on the left or the right of the $n \times m$ matrix.

The mathematical formula for the elements of the matrix Z in the general case is

$$Z_{ij} = \sum_{k=1}^{n} X_{ik} Y_{kj}$$

where X is a $p \times n$ matrix, Y is an $n \times q$ matrix, and their product, Z, is a $p \times q$ matrix.

We can now write a structure plan.

MATMLT(X,Y,Z,P,N,Q)

1 Repeat for I from 1 to P
  1.1 Repeat for J from 1 to Q
     1.1.1 Set Z(I,J) to zero
     1.1.2 Repeat for K from 1 to N
          1.1.2.1 Z(I,J)=Z(I,J)+X(I,K)*B(K,J)

The procedure then follows:

```
      SUBROUTINE MATMLT(X,Y,Z,P,N,Q)
C
C This subroutine forms the matrix product of the two matrices X and Y,
C where X is of dimension P*N and Y of dimension N*Q, returning the
C result in the P*Q matrix Z.
C
C Dummy arguments
      INTEGER P,N,Q
      REAL X(P,N),Y(N,Q),Z(P,Q)
C Local variables
      INTEGER I,J,K
C
      DO 30, I=1,P
        DO 20, J=1,Q
          Z(I,J)=0.0
          DO 10, K=1,N
            Z(I,J)=Z(I,J)+X(I,K)*Y(K,J)
10        CONTINUE
20      CONTINUE
30    CONTINUE
      RETURN
      END
```

Note that the innermost loop has only one executable statement, which adds the product of elements of the arrays X and Y to a cumulative sum that will be an element of the result array Z. This inner loop can be made more efficient by using a variable to accumulate this sum in, say, ZIJ, and then assigning this to the array element outside the inner loop. The inner loop could therefore be replaced by the statements

```
      DO 10, K=1,N
        ZIJ=ZIJ+X(I,K)*Y(K,J)
10    CONTINUE
      Z(I,J)=ZIJ
```

SUMMARY

- Arrays may have up to seven subscripts, and are stored so that the first subscript changes fastest, then the next, and so on.

- Assumed-size arrays may only have their *last* dimension specified by an asterisk.

- The actual argument corresponding to a dummy array argument may be an array name, an array element, or an array element substring.

- The *Straight Selection* sort is a medium-efficiency sorting method that is easy to understand and code.

- When sorting several items at the same time it is more efficient to set up a pointer (or index) array and sort that instead.

- Vectors and matrices can be represented by one-dimensional and two-dimensional arrays respectively.

- Fortran 77 does not contain any intrinsic facilities for matrix manipulation, but suitable procedures are widely available in numerical analysis libraries, such as the NAG library.

- Fortran 77 statements introduced in Chapter 14:

Array declarations   *type name(declarator1,declarator2, ...)*
                          for example REAL MARK(6,50),C(50,50,0:3,0:3)

SELF-TEST EXERCISES 14.1

1   The array TEST1 is declared as follows:

```
REAL TEST1(8,8,4,4)
```

(a)   What is the correct way of referring to the 37th element of this array (for example TEST1(i,j,k,l))?

(b)   What is the correct way of referring to the 653rd element?

(c)   What is the correct way of referring to the 1252nd element?

(d)   How many elements lie between TEST1(4,3,2,1) and TEST1(6,5,4,3)?

2   What restrictions, if any, are there on the use of adjustable dimensions with multi-dimensional dummy array arguments?

3   What restrictions, if any, are there on the use of assumed-size dimensions with multi-dimensional dummy array arguments?

4   The array TEST4 is declared as follows:

```
INTEGER TEST4(15,12)
```

Write suitable statements to print the contents of the array as 12 rows, each having 15 numbers per row. Then write suitable statements to print the contents of the array as 15 rows, each having 12 numbers per row. In both cases you should assume that all 15 elements having the same second subscript should appear in the same column or row, as appropriate.

PROGRAMMING EXERCISES

14.1   Write a program which initializes the array NRAY(2,3) using the following DATA statement:

```
DATA NRAY/1,2,7,8,12,13/
```

The contents of the array should be printed by use of the statement

```
PRINT *,NRAY
```

Now modify the PRINT statement so that the 2 × 3 array is printed first as two rows of three numbers, and then as two columns of three numbers.

You should now be quite clear about the order in which Fortran stores the elements of an array, and of how this is interpreted. So, finally modify the DATA statement in your program to use an implied DO to initialize the array in the opposite order, that is, with rows and columns interchanged.

*14.2 A 4 × 4 character array contains the following information

A	B	C	D
E	F	G	H
I	J	K	L
M	N	O	P

Write a program that fills another array with the following

AP	BO	CN	DM
EL	FK	GJ	HI
IH	JG	KF	LE
MD	NC	OB	PA

using only the original 4 × 4 array as a source for the characters.

14.3   Write a subroutine that contains an arbitrary sized array as one of its arguments containing a set of angles (in radians) at which it is required to evaluate the sine of the angle. The subroutine should print a table of all the values and their sines.
Write a simple program to test your subroutine.

14.4   Write a program to print the matrix products *AB*, *AC*, *BC*, *BA*, *CA* and *CB*, where *A*, *B* and *C* are the matrices

$$\begin{bmatrix} 0 & 1 & 0 \\ -1 & 0 & 0 \\ 0 & 0 & 1 \end{bmatrix} \quad \begin{bmatrix} \sqrt{3}/2 & 1/2 & 0 \\ -1/2 & \sqrt{3}/2 & 0 \\ 0 & 0 & 1 \end{bmatrix} \quad \begin{bmatrix} 1 & 3 & 2 \\ 0 & 4 & 1 \\ 3 & 0 & 2 \end{bmatrix}$$

14.5   Write a program to print the matrices *A*, *A*², *A*³ and *A*⁴, where *A* is the same matrix as in Exercise 14.4.

14.6   Using the same matrices as in Exercise 14.4, write a program to print the values of $(A + B)^2$, $A^2 + 2AB + B^2$, $(A + C)^2$, $A^2 + 2AC + C^2$.

14.7   Write and test a function MABS which calculates $\sum_{I,J=1}^{N} X(I,J)$ for an N × N matrix *X*.

14.8   Write a subroutine which calculates the exponential e^X of a 3 × 3 matrix *X* using the series

$$e^X = 1 + X + \frac{X^2}{2!} + \frac{X^3}{3!} + \frac{X^4}{4!} + \dots$$

The calculation of the value of the series should be terminated when the size of the next term is less than 10^{-6}, where the size is defined as MABS(X), and MABS is the function written in Exercise 14.7.

Use this subroutine in a program which sets three matrices A, B and C to the values shown in Exercise 14.4, and then calculates and displays the values of e^A, e^B, e^C, e^{A+B}, $e^A e^B$, e^{A+C} and $e^A e^C$.

Finally, compare these results with those obtained by a function which takes the exponential of individual elements of a matrix.

14.9 The eigenvalues of a 2×2 array

$$\begin{bmatrix} A & B \\ C & D \end{bmatrix}$$

are the solutions of the quadratic equation

$$(A-x)(D-x) - BC = 0$$

Write a subroutine to calculate the eigenvalues of such an array. (Use the usual formula for the solutions of a generalized quadratic equation.)

Confirm that the eigenvalues of

$$\begin{bmatrix} 5 & -2 \\ 4 & -1 \end{bmatrix}$$

are 1 and 3. Your subroutine should set a logical variable as a warning if no real eigenvalues exist.

14.10 Sales tax (at a rate of 6%) is to be paid on the following items of stationery:

Item	Price before tax
Paper	2.00
Pens	5.00
Folders	1.00
Ring binders	4.50
Paper glue	2.50

Write a program that uses a two-dimensional array to store the basic prices, the amount of sales tax to be paid and the resulting total cost of each item. Print out the result in the form of a table consisting of four columns, the first containing the list of items and the remaining three columns containing the values of the array expressed to two decimal places.

14.11 A bus leaves the terminus on the hour and every half-hour between 7.00 a.m. and 11.00 p.m. on Saturdays, Sundays and Wednesdays. On all other days it runs on the hour and every 20 minutes between 7.00 a.m. and 6.00 p.m., and on the hour and half-hour between 6.00 p.m. and 11.00 p.m.

Write a program that generates the timetable for the whole week, using a 24-hour clock, and stores it in a two-dimensional array. The program should then print the complete timetable using a single PRINT statement.

14.12 A botanist divides a field of dimension 5 m × 10 m into 1 m × 1 m squares. He then searches each square for the number of occurrences of a particular type of wild flower. His results are in the form

```
◆16◆12◆10◆◆3◆◆1◆◆2◆◆0◆◆0◆◆0◆◆0
  11   9   7   4   3   1   1   1   2   1
   6   7   2   2   2   4   7   9  11  17
   3   4  12  13  19  20   6  10   9  13
   7  12  14  17  19  18  22  13  16  16
```

where ◆ denotes a space. Create a data-file containing the data as formatted above. Write a program to read the data into a two-dimensional array and to display the table on the screen. Make the program express the number of flowers found in each square as a percentage of the total number of flowers found. Display a second table of the same type as the first which expresses the results of this calculation to two decimal places.

14.13 A conservation group is investigating the relative populations of badgers, foxes and squirrels in a wooded area on the basis of identifying their 'homes'.

The area under observation has been divided into small 'regions', each 100 m², forming a rectangular area 2 km × 3 km. These regions are identified by a coordinate system in which they are numbered from 0 to 29 west–east, and from 0 to 19 south–north; thus region (12,7) is the region whose south-west corner is 1200 m east of the 'origin' and 700 m north of it (where the 'origin' of the coordinate system is the south-west corner of the larger area being surveyed).

Within each region the number of foxholes, badger sets and squirrel nests has been recorded in the form of the coordinates of the region, followed by three counts of the form

nn Badgers (or Foxes or Squirrels)

Thus a particular record, for region (12,17) might read

```
12 17 3 Badgers 1 Fox 5 Squirrels
```

Unfortunately not all the investigators recorded the animals in the same order!

Write a program to read this data (from a file) and to produce the following initial analyses:

(a) the total population of each type of animal, assuming one animal per hole, set or nest;
(b) the region or regions with the highest population of each type of animal;
(c) the region or regions with the lowest population of each type of animal.

*14.14 A football league consists of 20 teams. After each match three points are awarded for a win and one point for a draw. An unformatted file contains the statistics for the matches played so far with one record for each team. Each record contains the following information:

Name of team
Number of matches played
Number of matches won
Number of matches drawn
Number of matches lost
Number of goals scored ('goals for')
Number of goals conceded ('goals against')
Number of points

Write a program that reads the contents of the file into a suitable set of arrays, and then reads the results of the most recent matches from the keyboard in the form

```
Arsenal 0   Liverpool 8
```

The program should then print the names, number of matches played, and number of points gained for the top three teams and should write the updated details back to the file.

Run your program several times to simulate the first few weeks of a new season.

14.15 Modify the program written for Exercise 14.14 so that a complete league table is displayed in the following format:

	Played	Won	Drawn	Lost	For	Against	Points
Liverpool	6	5	1	0	18	2	16
Arsenal	6	4	1	1	12	10	13
Manchester U	6	4	0	2	13	7	12
Everton	6	3	3	0	12	7	12
.	.	.	.	.	.	.	.
.	.	.	.	.	.	.	.

Teams should be sorted into order with the team having the most points being displayed at the top. If two teams have the same number of points then the order should be based on goal difference (that is, 'goals for' minus 'goals against'), and if these are also equal then they should be displayed in alphabetic order.

Run your program several times to simulate the first few weeks of a new season.

14.16 A file contains a list of words, one per line. Write a program to read the words and write them to another file sorted into alphabetic order.

14.17 A file contains a list of names in the format shown below:

Jones Arthur
Jones Rachel
Andrews Simon

.
.
.

Write a program to read this list and sort it into alphabetic order as the names would appear in a telephone directory (that is, sorted first by surname, with identical surnames appearing in alphabetic order of first name).

14.18 Write a subroutine which sorts an array A with N elements using the following algorithm for the QuickSort method:

(i) start with $I = 1$, $J = N$;
(ii) decrease J until $A(I) > A(J)$, then swap $A(I)$ and $A(J)$;
(iii) increase I until $A(I) > A(J)$, then swap $A(I)$ and $A(J)$;
(iv) repeat the last two actions until I and J are equal, and call this value of I (and J) PIVOT.

A(PIVOT) is now in the correct place and the array has been divided into two sections around PIVOT, each of which can be sorted separately.

If both sections have more than one element then save the start and end positions of the smaller section on a stack, and return to sort the larger section. If only one section has more than one element then return to sort that section. If neither section has more than one element then remove the start and end of a section off the stack and return to sort it. If there is nothing left on the stack then the array is fully sorted.

A stack is a means of storing items such that items can only be removed in the reverse order to that in which they were added to the stack (last in – first out), and is a very useful concept in many algorithms. It can be implemented in Fortran 77 as an array and an integer pointer to the top of the stack. In this case an array of dimension $2 \log_2 N$ will be large enough.

Use your subroutine in a program that reads a list of words from a file and sorts them into alphabetic order.

14.19 Exercise 12.20 introduced the bubble sort, Section 14.3 of this chapter discussed the Straight Selection sort, and Exercise 14.18 explained QuickSort. Write a program that uses a subroutine to sort a large set of numbers into increasing order. If your computer has a procedure for recording the processor time, incorporate it into your program so that you can measure the time taken to complete the sort. If your computer does not possess such a procedure then your program should display a message at the beginning and end of the sorting so that you can record the time with a stop-watch.

Run your program with each of the three sorting procedures, using several different quantities of numbers for each method, and attempt to draw some conclusions about the relative speed of the three methods.

Global data $\boxed{\text{F90}}$ **15**

Large programs frequently require many of their procedures to have access to the same data. As well as the **local storage** used thus far, Fortran 77 has a **global data** capability, using blocks of contiguous storage known as COMMON blocks.

In fact, the name of the COMMON block is the only truly global item; within the block data is identified only by its position. For this reason it is not permitted to have both character storage units and numeric storage units in the same COMMON block.

Because a COMMON block will appear in several different program units, initialization is allowed only in a special form of program unit called a **block data** program unit.

It is also possible to use a similar concept, known as EQUIVALENCE, to share storage within a single program unit.

The use of COMMON (and EQUIVALENCE) is illustrated by an extract from a very large CAD/CAM language processor, APT IV.

15.1   Local storage

Variables and arrays in a program unit are local to that program unit, and are not accessible by any other program units unless they appear as arguments in a 'call' to a subprogram. This has very important implications because it enables a subroutine or function subprogram to be written without any knowledge of the program unit from which it will be called, or indeed of any subprograms that it may itself use. All that is required is that the number and the type of the arguments is known.

The values of any local variables or arrays become undefined when a RETURN is made from a subprogram, unless they appear in a list of names in a SAVE statement or there is a SAVE statement without any list (which saves everything that can be saved).

Frequently, however, situations arise when the desire to develop a program in a modular fashion results in several subprograms having a very large number of arguments in order to access a large number of variables and/or arrays. In these situations the fact that storage is local to a program unit can be a great hindrance, and there is a requirement for a controlled form of **global storage** that can be accessed directly by more than one program unit.

F90   15.2   Global storage

Remember that in Fortran 77 the memory of a computer consists, conceptually, of a (large) number of storage units of two types. The first type is a **numeric storage unit**, and is used to store integers, real numbers, logical values, double precision numbers and complex numbers – the last two each requiring two consecutive storage units. The other type is a **character storage unit**, which is used to store a single character; a character string of length *len* requires *len* consecutive character storage units.

In a program unit we use a *name* to identify a storage unit of an appropriate type or, in the case of an array name or a character name, a block of consecutive storage units. These names, as we have seen, are *local* to the program unit and are for our convenience only. The compiler will refer to storage units by their *addresses* within the memory and will keep a list of names and their corresponding addresses only while it is compiling the program unit. (This is a slight over-simplification, but is sufficient for our present purpose.)

However, some names are preserved and have a *global* significance: for example, the names of any subprograms that are defined or called by another subprogram.

To provide a global storage facility, Fortran allows *blocks* of the memory (consisting of one or more consecutive storage units of the same type) to be identified by a global name, and for the storage units contained within that block to be made available to any program unit that refers to the block by its global name. Such a block of consecutive storage units is called a COMMON **block**.

It is important to realize that the names of the individual storage units are not global names – the whole block is made available, not individual storage units. This means that a program unit may call the items in a COMMON block by any name that it wishes (just as it can use any name for its dummy arguments); the type and order of the items within the block are fixed, not their names.

15.3 **Named** COMMON **blocks**

F90

A named block of storage is defined by a statement of the form

```
COMMON/name/n1,n2,...
```

where *name* is the global name of the COMMON block and *n1,n2,...* is a list of local variable names, array names or array declarators. Thus the statements

```
INTEGER AGE(50)
REAL MARK(50,6)
COMMON/EXAM/NUM,MARK,AV(50),AGE,AVAGE
```

define a COMMON block EXAM, which consists of 402 numeric storage units. In this particular program unit the first of these is an integer NUM, the next 300 a two-dimensional real array MARK, the next 50 a real array AV, the next 50 an integer array AGE, and the last a real number AVAGE.

The COMMON statement is a specification statement and must, therefore, precede any DATA or executable statements. Although not essential, it is good practice to precede it immediately by any type or array declaration statements that refer to items within the COMMON block, as has been done above.

Notice that because the name of a COMMON block is a global name it must be different from the names of any other COMMON blocks *or program units*.

Figure 15.1 illustrates this structure in graphic form, and also shows how the various COMMON blocks may be accessed by different program units.

One consequence of the fact that only the COMMON block name is global is that different program units may refer to the individual storage units within a COMMON block in different ways. For example, the COMMON block EXAM referred to above could be defined in another program unit as

```
COMMON/EXAM/N,TOTAL(50,6),AV(50),NYRS(50),AVYRS
```

Figure 15.1
Local and COMMON
storage.

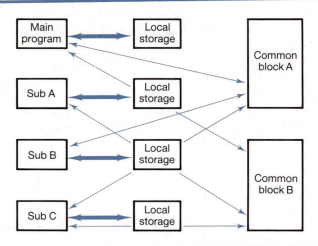

where different names have been used for two of the arrays and for both variables, or even as

```
COMMON/EXAM/N,SCORE(50,7),NAGE(50),AVAGE
```

where the two real arrays have been declared as a single array. The order of storage of array elements (see Section 14.1) means that those elements of SCORE whose second subscript is 7 occupy the last 50 storage units and thus correspond exactly to the array AV in the earlier COMMON block specifications. If the contents of a COMMON block are specified differently in different subprograms, however, it is essential that they should have the same length.

F90

There is one important restriction concerning COMMON blocks. As mentioned in Section 15.2, there are two types of storage unit in Fortran, one for characters and one for everything else. The effect of this is that if a COMMON block contains any character variables or character arrays then it cannot contain any variables or arrays of any other type.

As we would expect, we can declare several COMMON blocks in a single statement; however, because of the format of the statement there are two ways of doing this:

```
COMMON/name1/list1,/name2/list2,...
COMMON/name1/list1/name2/list2/name3/...
```

The second version (without any separating commas) is possible because of the 'slashes' that surround the names of the COMMON blocks. Thus we may write either

```
COMMON/EXAM/N,MARK,AV,AGE,AVAGE,/PUPILS/NAME
```

or

```
COMMON/EXAM/N,MARK,AV,AGE,AVAGE/PUPILS/NAME
```

although the first form is preferred, as its structure is clearer than the second form.

A COMMON block will usually be specified in a single statement. This is not obligatory, and if the same COMMON block name appears in two (or more) COMMON statements in the same program unit then they are treated as though the two (or more) lists were combined into a single list. Thus the statements

```
COMMON/EXAM/NUM
COMMON/PUPILS/NAME,/EXAM/SCORE(50,6),AV(50)
COMMON/EXAM/NAGE(50),AVAGE
```

will have the same effect for the COMMON block EXAM as the statement

```
COMMON/EXAM/NUM,SCORE(50,6),AV(50),NAGE(50),AVAGE
```

The major use of COMMON storage is in large programs, where several subprograms need access to all, or part, of a **database** that consists of a number of arrays and variables. In such situations it would be both inelegant to write subprograms with large numbers of arguments, and also inefficient, since there is always an overhead involved in the processing of the list of arguments on each call to a subroutine or function.

However, the situations in which COMMON blocks are valuable do not lend themselves to act as examples in a book such as this. The last section of this chapter therefore consists of an examination of an extract from a very large computer-aided manufacturing program, which makes very extensive use of COMMON blocks to organize its database.

15.4   **Blank** COMMON

F90

The COMMON statement, as we have seen, allows us to define a block of storage of a fixed size and to identify it by means of a global name. Fortran also allows us to have one further block of storage that is available to any program unit that requires it and that has neither a name nor a fixed size. This is known as **blank** COMMON and is declared in a way similar to that for named COMMON blocks, but without any reference to a COMMON block name:

```
COMMON X,Y,Z(-10:10)
```

Figure 15.2
Blank and named
COMMON.

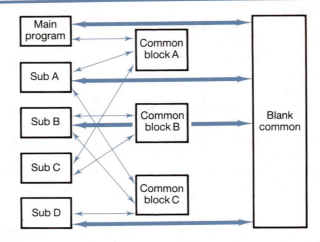

Alternatively, or if the COMMON statement is also declaring a named COMMON block, we can represent the name of blank COMMON by two consecutive slashes:

```
COMMON/PLAYER/NAME,//X,Y,Z(-10:10)
```

There are three main differences between named COMMON blocks and blank COMMON (apart from the absence of a name for blank COMMON). The first is that, unlike a named COMMON block, the size of blank COMMON need not be the same in different program units. Thus, for example, the statement

```
COMMON N,INDEX(500)
```

could appear in a subprogram while the main program unit and the other subroutines could contain

```
INTEGER SCORE(500),INDEX(500)
COMMON N,INDEX,SCORE
```

The other two differences will be discussed in the next two sections of this chapter.

Blank COMMON is usually appropriate where a number of variables and/or arrays are to be made available to all (or nearly all) of the program units in a program, and where they do not include both characters and other types of information. Named blocks are more appropriate where such COMMON storage is required by only a few of the subprograms, or where it is more convenient to split the COMMON storage into several smaller units. Figure 15.2 illustrates this in graphic form.

15.5 Initializing COMMON blocks

F90

We have seen in earlier chapters how DATA statements can be used to give initial values to variables and array elements. These are, of course, *local* variables and the DATA statements therefore provide initial values for storage locations that can be accessed by name only from the program units in which the DATA statements occur.

The situation is potentially rather different with COMMON blocks, since the same storage locations are accessible from several different program units; that, after all, is the purpose of COMMON. This means that if a variable or array element was given an initial value by a DATA statement in one program unit it could also be given a different initial value (presumably by accident) in another – which would lead to confusion and error. It would also cause extra problems for the compiler, which does not really know where the variables, and so on in a COMMON block are situated in the memory, but merely where they are relative to the start of the block; this is satisfactory for most purposes, but not for setting initial values.

To get round these problems, the use of DATA statements to initialize variables and array elements in COMMON blocks is forbidden, except in a special type of subprogram called a **block data program unit**. This was mentioned very briefly in Chapter 4 when discussing the structure of program units. Figure 15.3 shows its overall structure (as already shown in Figure 4.7). Note that it contains *no executable statements*.

A block data subprogram exists for the sole purpose of giving initial values to items contained in COMMON blocks. It cannot be obeyed by means of a CALL or other reference, and any attempt to do so will cause an error. Similarly, the presence of any type of statement other than a specification statement, a DATA statement, or a comment between the initial BLOCK DATA and the final END statements will lead to an error. The name of a block data subprogram is a global name, like that of all other program units; however, there may be one unnamed block data program unit. Since in many programs there is no need for more than one block data program unit the need for a name is frequently absent.

Block data program units also lead us to the second difference between blank COMMON and named COMMON blocks: blank COMMON cannot be

---

BLOCK DATA name

Specification statements,...

END

Figure 15.3
A block data program unit.

initialized and thus cannot appear in a block data program unit. Any COMMON variables or arrays that require initial values must therefore be placed in named COMMON blocks.

F90

15.6 Preserving values in COMMON blocks

In general, when a RETURN is made from a subroutine or function to its calling program unit, the local variables and arrays in that subroutine or function become undefined and do not retain their values for a subsequent entry (see Section 4.7). The SAVE statement enables us to save some, or all, of these values so that they are available for subsequent use.

A similar situation exists with COMMON blocks. A COMMON block enables two or more program units to share a block of memory. It would clearly be nonsense if an exit from a subroutine always caused any COMMON blocks to which it referred to become undefined. However, there is one situation, which is somewhat analogous to the case of local variables in a single subprogram, in which there would be no such conflict. Figure 15.4 illustrates this situation diagrammatically.

The program consists of five program units and three COMMON blocks; furthermore, the subroutines are called in a hierarchical way (for ease of explanation) such that the main program calls SUBA, which calls SUBB, which calls SUBC, which calls SUBD. The diagram also indicates to which COMMON blocks each program unit refers.

If we examine this diagram carefully we see that, as control returns from SUBD back up to the main program, there will at certain stages no

Figure 15.4
Defined and undefined
COMMON blocks.

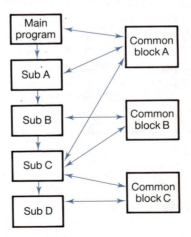

longer be any reference to some of the COMMON blocks. Thus when a RETURN is made to SUBB we find that COMMON block C is no longer accessible, as it is referred to only by SUBC and SUBD. Similarly, COMMON block B is no longer referred to once a RETURN has been made to SUBA. The third COMMON block (A) is referred to in the main program and will, therefore, always be required.

At those stages where a RETURN means that a COMMON block is no longer referred to by either the program unit currently being executed or by any *higher-level* program units, the contents of the COMMON block become undefined in exactly the same way as local variables on exit from a subprogram. If we do not wish this to happen – for example, if we want to keep some or all of the COMMON values for use on the next entry to a subprogram (or group of subprograms) – then we have two options.

The first is to use the SAVE statement. In Section 4.7 this took the form

```
SAVE name1, name2, ...
```

where *name1*, and so on, were the names of local variables or arrays. We can now extend this to include the global names of COMMON blocks (which are declared in the same program unit) enclosed in 'slashes'. Thus the statement

```
SAVE NAME, POS, /CB1/, SCORE
```

will save the three local variables NAME, POS and SCORE and *all* the contents of the COMMON block CB1.

If a COMMON block name appears in a SAVE statement in one subprogram, then it must appear in a SAVE statement in *every* subprogram that refers to that COMMON block.

The second way of preserving the values in a COMMON block (and probably the best way in many cases) is to declare the COMMON block in the main program. It is not necessary to use it there, but simply to include its name in a COMMON statement. As we saw in Figure 15.4, this will mean that there is always a program unit that refers to the COMMON block and it will never become undefined.

In a large program with several named COMMON blocks it is, in any event, good practice to declare *all* the COMMON blocks in the main program unit so that it is possible to see the whole global storage at one time. This will also have the effect of preserving the values of all items in these blocks for the duration of the program.

This leads to the third difference between blank COMMON and COMMON blocks. Blank COMMON *never* becomes undefined; it is truly global and is always preserved throughout the entire execution of the program.

It should be mentioned at this point that, in practice, most Fortran 77 systems always preserve *all* COMMON blocks for the duration of the program's execution. This is analogous to the situation with local variables referred to in Section 4.7. You should be aware, though, that a Fortran 77 processor does not have to preserve COMMON blocks on exit from a subprogram unless its name appears in a SAVE statement in that subprogram or it is referred to by a subprogram at a higher level.

F90   15.7   Sharing storage locations

In the foregoing discussion we have assumed that a COMMON block is being used to enable several program units to access a common set of variables and arrays, in order to provide a common database on which the program units may all operate. However, sometimes we may use a COMMON block for a very different reason – namely, to reduce the amount of storage required, by providing a common storage area used by different subprograms (or groups of subprograms) for completely different purposes. Thus one group of subprograms may contain a declaration such as

```
COMMON/SHARE/TABLE(4,25),MARK(50),N,X,P
```

while another might contain the declaration

```
COMMON/SHARE/A,B,C,AV(9,4,4),D(6)
```

Note that both declarations lead to a size of 153 storage units, although the arrangement and type of value stored in those storage units is totally different.

Presumably the two groups of subroutines will not call each other, as this would destroy the contents of 'their' COMMON block, but will be used in a sequential fashion. It would therefore be possible to have different names for these COMMON blocks and to rely on the processor to release the space used by one block when it becomes undefined. This is not always possible, and in any case many implementations will not reuse the storage space used by a COMMON block that has become undefined.

A more powerful way of sharing storage (or of referring to the same storage unit by two or more names, which comes to the same thing) is by means of the EQUIVALENCE statement. This allows the programmer to instruct the compiler to arrange for two or more variables or array elements to occupy the same storage unit, and takes the form

```
EQUIVALENCE (nlist1),(nlist2),...
```

where each *nlist* is a list of variable names, array element names, array names and character substring names. If one of the names is of type CHARACTER then all the names in that list must also be of type CHARACTER.

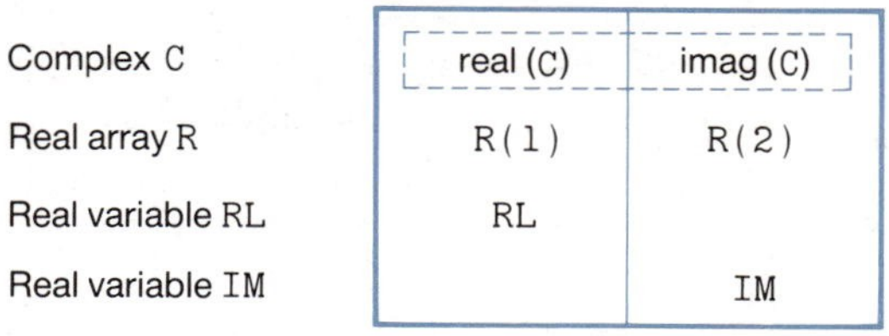

Complex C	real (C)	imag (C)
Real array R	R(1)	R(2)
Real variable RL	RL	
Real variable IM		IM

Figure 15.5
The effect of equivalencing REAL and COMPLEX.

The statement specifies that storage of all the items whose names appear in a list must start at the same storage unit. In this statement *and in no other* an array name is taken to refer to the first element of that array. Apart from the restriction regarding CHARACTER items there are no restrictions on the type of the names in a list and, for example, the statements

```
REAL R(2),RL,IM
COMPLEX C
EQUIVALENCE (R,RL,C),(R(2),IM)
```

will cause the real array R, the real variable RL and the complex variable C all to start at the same place, and will cause the real variable IM to start at the same place as R(2). Figure 15.5 shows that this has the effect of making RL occupy the same storage unit as the real part of C, and IM the same storage unit as the imaginary part of C.

It is not necessary for arrays or character strings to match and it is possible to arrange for them to overlap, as shown in Figures 15.6 and 15.7. In the first of these the array elements X(50) and Y(100) are equivalenced, leading to the relationship shown. This could equally well have been achieved by writing

```
EQUIVALENCE (X,Y(51))
```

or a number of other variations.

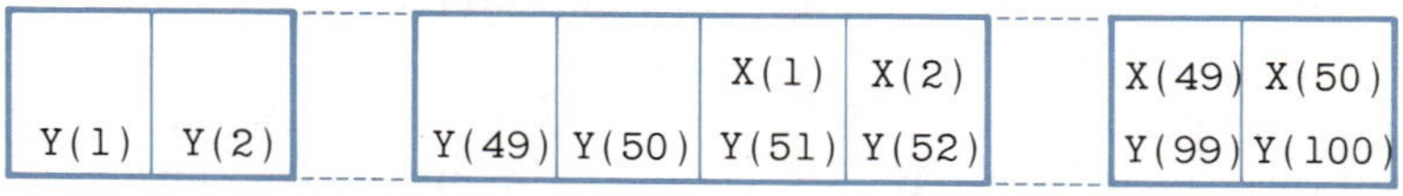

Figure 15.6
Equivalencing arrays.

```
REAL X(50),Y(100)
EQUIVALENCE (X(50),Y(100))
```

Figure 15.7
Equivalencing character
strings.

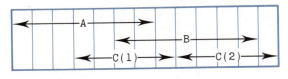

```
CHARACTER*7 A,B,C(2)*5
EQUIVALENCE (A(6:),B),(B(4:),C(2))
```

Figure 15.7 shows a similar situation with characters, where we can refer to substrings as well as variable names, array names and array elements. Once again there are a number of ways of expressing the relationship: for example, the shorter statement

```
EQUIVALENCE (A(6:),B,C(1)(3:))
```

would have done equally well, although reference to a substring of an array element should be avoided where possible, as it is slightly confusing at first sight.

EQUIVALENCE is usually used in large programs in association with COMMON blocks, since it provides an easy way of identifying only those parts of the block that are relevant to a particular subprogram. For example, if a COMMON block contains 10 variables A0 to A9 and ten arrays B0 to B9, each of a different size, such that the total size of the block is 210 storage units, it might be defined as follows:

```
      COMMON/BLK/A0,A1,A2,A3,A4,A5,A6,A7,A8,A9,
     1           B0(5),B1(10),B2(3:9),B3(4,5),B4(8),B5(20),B6(4,6),
     2           B7(-12:12),B8(7,9),B9(6,3)
```

However, if a particular subprogram needed to access only A0, A7 and B4 we could write

```
      COMMON/BLK/BLK(210)
      REAL B4(8)
      EQUIVALENCE(A0,BLK),(A7,BLK(8)),(B4,BLK(53))
```

thereby avoiding the declaration of unnecessary variables and arrays. The next section shows the use of this technique in an extract from a very large real-life program.

In general these techniques are applicable only to large programs, and indeed COMMON is not usually required at all for small or medium-sized programs. In large programs, however, the ability to exercise a substantial degree of control over the layout of storage and its accessibility to different parts of the program can be invaluable.

15.8   An example from real life

The real benefits of COMMON and EQUIVALENCE (especially the latter) cannot easily be demonstrated in a book such as this because they do not become apparent in programs of the size that can be included as examples. This section, therefore, shows a (very) short extract from a real-life program as an illustration of how they can be used in practice.

The program concerned is called APT IV, where APT stands for Automatically Programmed Tools, and was developed under sponsorship from over 100 organizations (including IBM, Boeing, General Motors, Rolls-Royce, English Electric Computers and the US Air Force) at the Illinois Institute of Technology Research Institute in Chicago. The program, in fact, had its origins at MIT in the late 1950s and was under continuous development for over 20 years, first at MIT, then at IITRI, and finally at CAM–I (Computer Aided Manufacturing – International) at Arlington, Texas. The extract shown below dates from the central period of that development and was written in 1968. It predates Fortran 77 by some 10 years and yet, apart from some slight differences of style, is perfectly acceptable more than 20 years later – an eloquent tribute to the longevity of Fortran programs.

APT is a program that processes a high-level language to produce a control tape that drives a numerically controlled machine tool, and has been used in the manufacture of almost all modern airliners, motor cars and spacecraft, and innumerable artifacts that require high-precision machining of some or all of their parts. One part of the program is a library of subroutines used in the analysis of the geometric surfaces defined by the user and in the calculation of the required motion on the machine tool. In 1968, at the time of the first release of APT IV, this library contained 78 geometric definition routines, 92 tool motion routines, and 75 other routines – a total of 245 subroutines! (This was by no means the whole program – merely a part of one of four major phases.)

Owing to the nature of the problem a very considerable number of these subroutines need access to global information and the layout of the storage is of vital importance. There are, in fact, 12 named COMMON blocks, of which one is conceptually divided into 18 different areas, several of which overlap.

Figure 15.8 shows the first 70 or so lines of one subroutine from the library, APT030. Notice that most of the lines are comments. In a large program it is essential to document fully every aspect of the program, and the inclusion of detailed comments and a specification of each subprogram

Figure 15.8
An example of the use
of COMMON and
EQUIVALENCE in APT IV.

```
C
C.....FORTRAN SUBROUTINE            APT030...            3/1/68   GK
C
C                FORTRAN SUBROUTINE APT030
C
C PURPOSE       TO GENERATE THE CANONICAL FORM OF A CIRCLE DEFINED
C               AS TANGENT TO EACH OF TWO GIVEN LINES AND HAVING
C               A GIVEN RADIUS BY THE FOLLOWING APT STATEMENT
C               RESULT = CIRCLE/****, L1, ****, L2, RADIUS, RAD
C               **** = XLARGE, YLARGE, XSMALL, YSMALL
C
C LINKAGE       CALL APT030 (RESULT, M1, L1, M2, L2, RAD)
C
C ARGUMENTS     RESULT   ARRAY TO CONTAIN THE CANONICAL FORM OF
C                        THE RESULTING CIRCLE
C               M1       INTEGER EQUIVALENT OF THE FIRST MODIFIER
C                            1 = XLARGE      2 = YLARGE
C                            4 = XSMALL      5 = YSMALL
C               L1       ARRAY CONTAINING THE CANONICAL FORM OF
C                        THE FIRST INPUT LINE
C               M2       INTEGER EQUIVALENT OF THE SECOND MODIFIER
C                            1 = XLARGE      2 = YLARGE
C                            4 = XSMALL      5 = YSMALL
C               L2       ARRAY CONTAINING THE CANONICAL FORM OF
C                        THE SECOND INPUT LINE
C               RAD      REAL VARIABLE CONTAINING THE VALUE OF THE
C                        DESIRED RADIUS
C
C SUBSIDIARIES TYPE                ENTRY
C               SUBROUTINE         APT003
C               SUBROUTINE         APT020
C               SUBROUTINE         APT078
      SUBROUTINE APT030 (RESULT,M1,L1,M2,L2,RAD)
      REAL L1,L2
      DIMENSION RESULT(7),L1(4),L2(4)
C
C
C
C... 1.MAIN CDE PACKAGE. INCLUDED IN EVERY PROGRAM IN THE SUBROUTINE
C...    LIBRARY.
C
      LOGICAL LDEF
      DIMENSION DEF(75),DSHARE(100),FXCOR(170),HOLRTH(20),SV(442),
     1          ZNUMBR(30),LDEF(15),ISV(379)
      DIMENSION IBRKPT(51),IDEF(20),IFXCOR(60),ISHARE(31),KNUMBR(51)
      COMMON/TOTAL/DEF,DSHARE,FXCOR,HOLRTH,SV,ZNUMBR,LDEF,ISV
      EQUIVALENCE(ISV(30),IBRKPT(1)),(ISV(110),KNUMBR(1)),
     1           (ISV(190),IDEF(1)),(ISV(210),ISHARE(1)),
     2           (ISV(279),IFXCOR(1))
C
C
C
C... 2.DEF BLOCK. REAL VARIABLES USED BY DEF. RED. ROUTINES WHICH MUST
```

```
C...     REMAIN INVIOLATE.
C
       REAL LN1
       DIMENSION       A(12,2),  AHOLD(2,4),     Cl( 8),
      1                LN1( 5),      R(10),   REF(2,4),
C
       EQUIVALENCE (DEF(1),A(1,1)),(DEF(25),AHOLD(1,1)),(DEF(33),C(1)),
      +          (DEF(41),LN1(1)), (DEF(46),R(1)), (DEF(56),REF(1,1))
C
C
C...  3. DSHARE DEF. RED. BLOCK. USED FOR REAL VARIABLES AND SHARED WITH
C...     ARELEM
C
       REAL L
       DIMENSION             C(100),  G(93),  L(83),
      +          P(79), SC(63),  T(47), T1(35),  V(23)
C
       EQUIVALENCE  (DSHARE(100), C(100),  G(93),  L(83),
      +          P(79), SC(63),  T(47), T1(35),  V(23))
C
C...  10. ZNUMBR BLOCK. REAL LITERALS.
C
       EQUIVALENCE (ZNUMBR(1),Z0), (ZNUMBR(2),Z1) , (ZNUMBR( 3),Z2)    ,
      1 (ZNUMBR( 4),Z3)    , (ZNUMBR( 5),Z5)    , (ZNUMBR( 6),Z10)    ,
      2 (ZNUMBR( 7),Z90)   , (ZNUMBR( 8),Z1E6)  , (ZNUMBR( 9),Z1E38)  ,
      3 (ZNUMBR(10),Z5EM1) , (ZNUMBR(11),Z6EM1) , (ZNUMBR(12),Z9EM1)  ,
      4 (ZNUMBR(13),Z11EM1), (ZNUMBR(14),Z12EM1), (ZNUMBR(15),Z1EM2)  ,
      5 (ZNUMBR(16),Z1EM3) , (ZNUMBR(17),Z1EM5) , (ZNUMBR(18),Z5EM6)  ,
      6 (ZNUMBR(19),Z1EM6) , (ZNUMBR(20),Z1EM7) , (ZNUMBR(21),Z1EM9)  ,
      7 (ZNUMBR(22),Z1EM1) , (ZNUMBR(23),ZM1)   , (ZNUMBR(24),DEGRAD) ,
      8 (ZNUMBR(25),PI)
C
             .
             .
             .
```

within that subprogram is a sure way of doing this. This subroutine is used in the definition of a circle, given two tangent lines and its radius.

The subroutine starts with a definition of the COMMON block TOTAL, which is 'included in every program in the subroutine library'. This block consists of eight arrays, each of which will be equivalenced to other variables and/or arrays as appropriate for the particular subroutine.

Block 2 contains a definition of arrays that are equivalenced to the array DEF. Block 3 is a shared block; in other routines blocks 4, 5 and 6 are also equivalenced to the array DSHARE in completely different ways. Thus different groups of subroutines will use this part of the COMMON block TOTAL for their own purposes in a well planned and consistent way.

This subroutine does not use those parts of the COMMON block that correspond to the arrays FXCOR, HOLRTH or SV, and the next set of statements defines block 10, which consists of a set of real variables equivalenced to the array ZNUMBER.

Subsequent blocks in this subroutine also define parts of the array ISV, which is defined in no less than eight ways, not all of which define the whole array. Thus each of the 245 subroutines in the library defines only those parts of the total database that are relevant to its particular needs.

APT is a particularly good example of the use of COMMON and EQUIVALENCE, owing to the combination of its size and complexity with the overall modular structure of the program. However, any large program can probably benefit from an analysis of its global storage requirements, followed by the design of a suitable global database with local entities equivalenced to the appropriate parts.

SUMMARY

- A COMMON block is a contiguous block of memory in which the individual items are identified by their position within the block.

- A COMMON block may have a global name.

- There may be at most one (unnamed) blank COMMON block.

- Initial values can be given to items only in a named COMMON block, and then only in a special, non-executable, BLOCK DATA program unit.

- Named COMMON blocks may become undefined when no currently active program units refer to them, unless referred to in a SAVE statement.

- The EQUIVALENCE statement instructs the compiler to arrange the program's storage so that two or more items share the same location(s).

- Fortran 77 statements introduced in Chapter 15:

COMMON block declaration	COMMON /*name*/ *list of local names* COMMON // *list of local names* COMMON *list of local names*
Initial statement	BLOCK DATA *name* BLOCK DATA
Saving COMMON blocks	SAVE /*common block name*/
Sharing storage	EQUIVALENCE (*name1*,*name2*, ...)

SELF-TEST EXERCISES 15.1

1 ' In subroutine TEST1A there appear the following statements:

```
INTEGER K1(20),K2(20),K3(20)
DOUBLE PRECISION D(15)
COMPLEX Q(5)
COMMON /TEST1/ K1,D,Q,K2,K3
DO 10, I=1,15
   D(I)=I
   K1(I)=I
   K2(I)=2*I
   K3(I)=3*I
10 CONTINUE
DO 20, I=1,5
   Q(I)=(I,-I)
20 CONTINUE
```

In another subroutine, TEST1B, the following statements appear:

```
REAL X(20),Y(2,15),Z(2,10)
INTEGER M1(15),M2(15)
COMMON /TEST1/ X,Y,Z,M1,M2
CALL TEST1A
```

After the call to TEST1A has been executed, what are the values of the array elements X(1), Y(1,1), Y(2,15), Z(1,1), Z(2,5), Z(1,8), M1(1), M1(6), M1(15), M2(1), M2(15)?

2 Write suitable specification statements to create a COMMON data base suitable for:

(a) an accounting program that needs details of customers' names and account numbers, credit limits, outstanding balances, and any other relevant items;

(b) a program to analyse the examination results obtained in a school containing several classes whose pupils are entered in the examinations;

(c) a program to record and analyse data collected at various points on the body of an astronaut undergoing stress experiments – for example, temperature, 'dampness', blood pressure, pulse, rate of breathing, expansion/contraction of muscles, brain activity, time into experiment, and so on.

PROGRAMMING EXERCISES

15.1   Three vectors are given as

$$x = 6i + 7j + 2k$$
$$y = 7i - 2j - 3k$$
$$z = 8i + 5j - 9k$$

where i, j, k are orthogonal unit vectors. Write a program that contains two subroutines, one that adds x to y and one that subtracts z from $x+y$. Neither subroutine should have any dummy arguments. Each vector can be represented by a three-element INTEGER array. Design your program so that the three initial vectors are passed to the appropriate subroutines from the main program unit, where they are initialized. You need pass the result of the first calculation only between the two subroutines. Pass the result of the second calculation to a third subroutine from where it can be output to the screen.

15.2   Modify the program you wrote for Exercise 15.1 so that the three vectors are initialized in DATA statements.

15.3   Rewrite the program extract shown in Figure 15.8 in a style more consistent with Fortran 77.

15.4   In Exercise 4.13 you wrote a function to calculate the Coulomb potential at a given distance from a charged particle. Modify your program so that the function does not use any arguments (that is, they are in a COMMON block).

15.5   Three one-dimensional arrays are declared with the following statements:

```
REAL A(3),B(3),C(3)
EQUIVALENCE (A,B)
```

Write a program containing these declarations which reads three values into each of the arrays A and B, and then stores the sums of corresponding elements of A and B in C. Finally the program should print the three arrays as three columns (A, B and C).
   Were the results what you expected? If not, add extra PRINT statements at various points in your program to obtain intermediate values.

*15.6   A committee investigating housing requirements in a particular township has decided that before developing its future plans it must first obtain a detailed picture of the current housing situation. Accordingly, a survey has been carried out and a file of all people in the township created in which each record contains the following information:

Columns 1–30	First name and surname (separated by a space)
Column 32	Sex (M or F)
Columns 34–36	Age
Column 38	Marital status (S=single, M=married, W=widowed, D=divorced)
Column 40	Form of housing (O=owner–occupier, C=council house tenant, P=private house tenant, R=tenant of part of a house with two or more rooms, B=tenant of part of a house with only one room)
Columns 42–46	Monthly income

The file is terminated by an end-of-file marker.

Create a file with at least 20 records in this format. Then write a subroutine that has no arguments, will read the data into arrays stored in COMMON, and use it in a program that calls the subroutine to read the data and then prints the records in the main program.

15.7 Use a BLOCK DATA subprogram to initialize two arrays NUMB1 and NUMB2 to the following values:

NUMB1(1) = 0	NUMB2(1) = 0
NUMB1(2) = 0	NUMB2(2) = 0
NUMB1(3) = 0	NUMB2(3) = 0
NUMB1(4) = 1	NUMB2(4) = 0
NUMB1(5) = 1	NUMB2(5) = 1
NUMB1(6) = 0	NUMB2(6) = 1
NUMB1(7) = 0	NUMB2(7) = 1
NUMB1(8) = 0	NUMB2(8) = 0

The arrays contain the binary numbers 11000 and 1110. Use a COMMON block to make these arrays available to two subroutines. The first subroutine should perform binary addition of the two numbers, and places the result in NUMB1, while the second should convert the binary number stored in NUMB1 to a decimal value. The result should then be displayed on the screen in the main program.

15.8 **(a)** Write a program to generate all the permutations of the numbers 1 to N, where N is read by the program. (*Hint*: as well as an array P to store the current permutation, it may be useful to generate related arrays, such as W, where $W(P(I))=I$ for $I=1$ to N. Such arrays could be stored in COMMON storage if used in more than one program unit.

(b) The distances by road between five towns A, B, C, D and E are as follows: A–B 7 miles, A–C 7 miles, A–D 6 miles, A–E 10 miles, B–C 11 miles, B–D 3 miles, B–E 4 miles, C–D 12 miles, C–E 9 miles, D–E 6 miles. A salesman has to visit each town once, starting and finishing at A. Write a program to calculate the distances for each possible route, and so find the shortest possible distance.

15.9 For a triangle, any of the following provide sufficient information to determine uniquely all of the sides and angles:

- the three sides;
- two sides and the included angle;
- two angles and the included side.

Write a program that allows the user to choose one of these options, then reads the data and displays the lengths of the three sides and the angles between them. Use a different subroutine for each of the options, with the lengths of the sides, and the angles between them being kept in COMMON storage. Note that if a triangle has three sides of length a, b and c, and opposite angles A, B and C, then the following relations hold:

$$\frac{\sin A}{a} = \frac{\sin B}{b} = \frac{\sin C}{c}$$
$$a^2 = b^2 + c^2 - 2bc\cos A$$

15.10 Using the data file and input subroutine written for Exercise 15.6, write further subroutines to carry out the following operations:

(a) Sort a pointer array to the data so that the data can be printed in alphabetic order of surname. The pointer array should also be stored in COMMON.

(b) Produce an array of pointers (as an argument) that identify all old-age pensioners (male aged 65 or over, female aged 60 or over) living on their own in a type of housing defined by an argument to the subroutine.

(c) Produce an array of pointers (as an argument) that identify all single girls living in bed-sitter accommodation (that is, in a single room in a house).

(d) Print a list of names (surname followed by first name) identified by an array of pointers supplied as an argument.

Finally, write a program that uses the above subroutines to read the data from the file and print lists of old-age pensioners living alone in council houses, single girls living in single rooms, and married owner–occupiers under 40 years old with a monthly income of less than £1000. Each list should be in alphabetic order of surnames, with the sex and age also shown.

More about procedures

16

Procedures have already been shown to be capable of having arguments of many forms, but one that has not yet been discussed is the use of a procedure name as an argument. Any procedure name that is to appear as an actual argument must be declared in an EXTERNAL or INTRINSIC declaration statement, as appropriate. The corresponding dummy argument need not appear in such a declaration unless it is impossible to tell from the context that the dummy argument is the name of a subroutine or function.

A special form of function is one that may be written in a single assignment statement. In this case it may be declared as a **statement function**, with the result that it is available only within the procedure in which it is declared, but is obeyed very much faster, since it is normally incorporated directly into the compiled code by the compiler without the need for external procedure linkages.

$\boxed{\text{F90}}$ # 16.1   A brief review of procedures

Extensive use of procedures has been made throughout this book, since they were first introduced in Chapter 4. From an initial discussion of subroutines and real- or integer-valued functions we have gradually increased their sophistication until there is now little that we cannot do. There are still some further aspects of procedures that have not yet been examined, but before doing so the whole question of *actual arguments* and *dummy arguments* should be briefly re-examined.

The initial SUBROUTINE or FUNCTION statement normally contains a list of dummy arguments, enclosed in parentheses. A CALL to that subroutine, or a reference to that function, contains a list of actual arguments, which must agree, exactly, with the dummy arguments with respect to the number of arguments and their types. During the execution of a CALL statement or a function reference the locations of the actual arguments in the memory will be passed to the procedure in such a way as to enable the dummy arguments to refer to the same memory locations as did the actual arguments.

An actual argument may be any of the following:

(1)   a constant
(2)   a variable name
(3)   an array element name
(4)   a character substring
(5)   an expression
(6)   an array name
(7)   an intrinsic function name
(8)   an external procedure name (subroutine or function)
(9)   a dummy procedure name
(10)   an alternative return specifier

A dummy argument may be any of the following:

- a variable name, for types 1–5 above
- an array name, for types 6 and 3
- a dummy procedure name, for types 7–9
- an asterisk, for type 10

If the dummy argument is a *variable name*, the actual argument may be a constant, a variable name, an array element name, a character substring or an expression, as long as it is of the correct type or delivers a result of the correct type.

If the dummy argument is a *character variable*, its length must be less than or equal to the length of the actual argument; if it is less than the length of the actual argument then only the leftmost *len* characters will be treated as the dummy argument (where *len* is the length of the dummy argument). Alternatively, its length may be declared to be (*), which causes the length of the dummy argument to be defined as equal to that of the actual argument.

If the dummy argument is an *array*, there are three ways of dealing with its dimension. The first is to use an *adjustable array declaration*, in which one or more of the dimensions of the dummy array contains a variable name, provided that any such variable name is also a dummy argument of the same procedure or appears in a COMMON block in the procedure. The second way is to use an *assumed-size array declaration*, in which the *last* subscript is defined by an asterisk; because its size is unknown, an assumed-size dummy array name cannot be used as an item in an input/output list or as an embedded format. The third way is to specify the dimension in the usual manner, although this can restrict the flexibility of the procedure if the compiler inserts array-bound checking.

If a dummy argument is an array (of constant, adjustable or assumed size), the actual argument may be an array, an array element or an array element substring.

- If the actual argument is a non-character array name, then, as long as it is not larger than the dummy array, everything is straightforward and the first element of the dummy array is the same as the first element of the actual array, and so on.

- If the actual argument is a non-character array element name, the dummy argument is associated with it so that the first element of the dummy array is the same as the actual (array element) argument.

- If the dummy argument is a character array, the length of the array elements must also be considered. If the actual argument is an array element or an array element substring, the first character of the element or substring corresponds to the first character position of the dummy array. In all cases the dummy argument array must not extend beyond the end of the actual argument array. If the length of the dummy array is declared as (*), each element of that array will have the same length as each element of the actual argument array.

Most arguments to subroutines fall into one of the two broad categories above, in which the dummy argument is either a variable or an array. However, there are two other possible types of dummy argument that have not yet been discussed: a dummy procedure and an asterisk.

A *dummy procedure* is a means whereby the name of an intrinsic function, a subroutine or an external function may be passed to a subroutine or function as an argument. This has one or two further implications, which are described in Section 16.2 below.

Finally we may use an *asterisk* as a dummy argument in association with a special form of actual argument that allows alternative places for the subroutine to return to. This is not a practice that can be recommended and will not be discussed any further here. It is, however, briefly described in Chapter 19, together with various other obsolete and little-used features of Fortran 77.

16.2 Procedures as arguments

In addition to expressions (including variables, constants and function references) and array names, Fortran 77 allows a calling program to pass the names of procedures to a subroutine by means of its arguments. Before this can be done the subroutine, external function or intrinsic function names must appear in one of two special specification statements that tell the compiler that the names are the names of procedures. The first of these statements declares a list of names to be those of external procedures (subroutines or functions) and takes the form

        EXTERNAL *proc1*,*proc2*, . . .

The second declares a list of names to be intrinsic functions:

        INTRINSIC *fun1*,*fun2*, . . .

The latter declaration is necessary because, as we have seen, it is permissible to have a variable or array of the same name as an intrinsic function. Thus in the absence of an INTRINSIC statement declaring SIGN to be an intrinsic function, the statement

        CALL SUB(A,B,SIGN)

will assume SIGN to be a real variable (unless it is declared to be something else). However, if the declaration

        INTRINSIC SIGN

appears at the start of the program unit then the CALL statement will pass the name of the intrinsic function SIGN to the subroutine SUB. It follows that if a name appears in an INTRINSIC declaration it must not appear in any other specification statement in the same program unit, or be used in any way other than as an intrinsic function in that program unit.

The EXTERNAL statement is similar, and declares that the names given in the statement are those of external procedures. In this case the compiler, as we have already seen, is not otherwise aware of their existence and the reason for the declaration is more obvious. If the name of an intrinsic function appears in an EXTERNAL statement it refers to an external procedure and the intrinsic function of the same name is not available in that program unit. Thus the declaration

```
EXTERNAL LOG
```

will mean that any reference to LOG (as a subroutine or as a function) will refer to an external procedure LOG and that the intrinsic function of the same name cannot be used. Thus if a library of subroutines contains a procedure called LOG it can then be used without any confusion; it also means that the programmer can provide his own LOG function (for example, using a different method of evaluation or to a different base).

If an actual argument is a procedure name (which must appear in an EXTERNAL or INTRINSIC statement), the corresponding dummy argument must be a dummy procedure. A dummy procedure is either a name that will be identified as a subroutine or function name because of its context (that is, it appears after CALL or is followed by a left parenthesis when it has not been declared as an array) or one that appears in an EXTERNAL statement. Thus the name of a procedure may be passed through several subroutines, as can be seen in Figure 16.1.

Notice that, although LOG and SQRT are intrinsic functions and are declared as such in the main program, once a procedure has been passed to another one as an argument, it is a dummy procedure so far as the other is concerned and, if declared, must be declared as EXTERNAL. Thus in Figure 16.1 we see that both SUB and FUN appear in an EXTERNAL statement in a subroutine SUB1. In subroutine SUB2, however, SUB appears in a CALL statement and F appears followed by a left parenthesis (and is not declared as an array); no EXTERNAL declaration is required, therefore, in subroutine SUB2. It is good practice, however, to declare both as EXTERNAL in SUB2.

There is one (small) restriction on the names of intrinsic functions that may appear as actual arguments, namely that the names of intrinsic functions for type conversion (for example, INT, REAL), lexical comparison (LGE, LGT and so on), or maximum and minimum (MAX, MIN and so on) must not be passed to another subroutine in this way. In practice these are not the names one would be likely to want to use in this way, so the restriction is unlikely to cause any difficulty.

There are a number of situations in which it is useful to have procedure names as arguments. One of the most common arises when writing general-purpose subroutines. Such subroutines may be stored in a **library** on the backing store of a computer for general or private use, and are a valuable aid to programming. Frequently large libraries are available

Figure 16.1
An example of
procedures as
arguments.

```
PROGRAM MAIN
EXTERNAL ANALYS
INTRINSIC SQRT,LOG
    .
    .
    .
CALL SUB1(ANALYS,SQRT,A,B)
    .
    .
    .
END

SUBROUTINE SUB1(SUB,FUN,X,Y)
EXTERNAL SUB,FUN
    .
    .
    .
CALL SUB2(N,X,FUN,SUB)
    .
    .
    .
END

SUBROUTINE SUB2(N,A,F,SUB)
    .
    .
CALL SUB(A,N,F(X+2))
    .
    .
    .
END
```

in specialized areas such as numerical analysis or graphics and may be incorporated into any program that requires them. If a subroutine in such a library requires some special action to be carried out that is dependent upon the particular computer and/or program it can call a subroutine whose name has been passed to it as an argument.

EXAMPLE 16.1

The intrinsic functions for trigonometrical functions (SIN, COS, ASIN and so on) operate in radians. Write a general-purpose subroutine that will calculate the sine (or cosine or tangent) of an angle whose value is given in degrees, minutes and seconds of arc and will give the arcsine (or arccos or arctangent) of a real value in the same way. (For non-mathematicians, 2π radians$=360°$, where $\pi=3.141\,592\,653\,6$, and $1°=60$ minutes, 1 minute$=60$ seconds.)

The subroutine will need to be in two parts, one for SIN, COS and TAN, and the other for ASIN, ACOS and ATAN. We can deal with this by adopting a convention that the angle supplied for SIN, COS and TAN will always lie in the range −360° to +360° (which is more than sufficient to cater for all angles), and stating that if the integer number of degrees is outside this range then the arcsine, arccos, or arctangent of the real value is required. The subroutine will have five dummy arguments: three integers for the angle, one real for the sine, cosine, or tangent, and a dummy procedure. The structure plan is quite straightforward:

1 If |degrees|>360 then
  1.1 Calculate 'fun (real value)'
  1.2 Convert angle in radians to one in degrees, and so on
  otherwise
  1.3 Convert angle in degrees, and so on, to radians
  1.4 Calculate 'fun (angle)'

2 Return

The subroutine can then be easily written.

```
      SUBROUTINE TRIG(D,M,S,X,F)
C
C This subroutine is a general trigonometry procedure for
C angles in degrees.
C
C If the absolute value of D is greater than 360 then
C the function F is used to obtain arcF of X, and return the value as
C D degrees, M minutes, S seconds
C
C If the absolute value of D is less than or equal to 360 then
C the function F is used on the angle D degrees, M minutes, S seconds
C with the result returned in X
C
C Dummy arguments
      INTEGER D,M,S
      REAL X
      EXTERNAL F
C Miscellaneous variables
      REAL ANGLE,RLMINS,PI,TWOPI
      PARAMETER (PI=3.1415926536,TWOPI=2.0*PI)
C Establish direction of calculation
      IF (ABS(D).GT.360) THEN
C Arc-function required - calculate and convert to degrees
         ANGLE = F(X)*360.0/TWOPI
C Store degrees in D
         D = ANGLE
C Store minutes in M
         RLMINS = (ANGLE-D)*60.0
         M = RLMINS
```

```
C  Store seconds in S
         S = (RLMINS-M)*60.0+0.5
C  Rounding could set S to 60. Deal with this
         IF (S.EQ.60) THEN
           S = 0
           M = M+1
           IF (M.EQ.60) THEN
             M = 0
             D = D+1
           END IF
         END IF
       ELSE
C  Trig-function required - calculate angle in radians first
         ANGLE = (D+M/60.0+S/3600.0)*TWOPI/360.0
         X = F(ANGLE)
       END IF
       RETURN
       END
```

Figure 16.2
A test program for
subroutine TRIG.

```
       PROGRAM TEST
       INTRINSIC SIN,COS,TAN,ASIN,ACOS,ATAN
       INTEGER I,D,M,S
       REAL X,Y,Z
C  Read up to 50 angles.  A zero angle ends the data
       PRINT *,'Type up to 50 angles.'
       PRINT *,'Each angle should be typed as three whole numbers:'
       PRINT *,'Degrees, minutes, seconds'
       PRINT *,'A zero angle ends the data'
       DO 10, I=1,50
         READ *,D,M,S
         IF (D.EQ.0 .AND. M.EQ.0 .AND. S.EQ.0) GOTO 20
         CALL TRIG(D,M,S,X,SIN)
         PRINT 201,'sin',D,M,S,X
         CALL TRIG(D,M,S,Y,COS)
         PRINT 201,'cos',D,M,S,Y
         CALL TRIG(D,M,S,Z,TAN)
         PRINT 201,'tan',D,M,S,Z
C  Set D to a value >360 to trigger arc-function
         D=1000
         CALL TRIG(D,M,S,X,ASIN)
         PRINT 202,'arcsin',X,D,M,S
         D=1000
         CALL TRIG(D,M,S,Y,ACOS)
         PRINT 202,'arccos',Y,D,M,S
         D=1000
         CALL TRIG(D,M,S,Z,ATAN)
         PRINT 202,'arctan',Z,D,M,S
    10 CONTINUE
    20 STOP
   201 FORMAT (1H0,A,'(',2(I4,','),I4,') is',F10.6)
   202 FORMAT (1H0,A,'(',F10.6,') is',2(I4,','),I4)
       END
```

Figure 16.2 shows an example of a suitable test program for this subroutine.

16.3   Statement functions

An external function is both a procedure and a subprogram; however, another form of function exists that is not a subprogram but is *defined only within one program unit*. Such a function, called a **statement function**, is written in a special way and consists of only a single statement. It takes the form:

> *name(arg1,arg2,....)=expression*

and must be placed *after all specification statements*, but before any executable statements. The expression may include references to: constants; the dummy arguments of the statement function; variables or array elements that are defined within the same program unit (other than any of the same name as one of the dummy arguments); other statement functions, as long as they are defined before this one; intrinsic functions; and external functions (as long as they do not alter the value of any of the statement function's dummy arguments).

For example, in Chapter 13 the concept of a LOGICAL function was introduced and demonstrated by reference to Example 12.8. The function was used by another function (CODE) that was used in encrypting messages, and took the form

```
LOGICAL FUNCTION ALPHA(C)
CHARACTER C
ALPHA=('A'.LE.C .AND. C.LE.'Z' .OR.
*      'a'.LE.C .AND. C.LE.'z')
RETURN
END
```

However, an alternative approach would be to declare it as a statement function within the function CODE as follows:

```
LOGICAL ALPHA
CHARACTER X
ALPHA(X)='A'.LE.X.AND.X.LE.'Z' .OR. 'a'.LE.X.AND.X.LE.'z'
```

The main advantage of a statement function over an external function is speed and efficiency. A statement function is normally dealt with by the compiler, which inserts the appropriate code directly into the statement that is referencing it; it can thus be considered as a form of shorthand for the programmer. An external function reference, on the other hand, involves a transfer of control and of arguments, which imposes a certain overhead.

Typical examples of statement functions are to clarify logical expressions such as ALPHA (above) or the following:

```
LOGICAL ODD
ODD(N)=MOD(N,2).NE.0
```

which returns the value *true* if its integer argument is odd, and *false* if it is even. Another common use is to simplify repeated arithmetic expressions, such as

```
UT(X,Y,T)=-X*SIN(T)+Y*COS(T)
VT(X,Y,Z,T,P)=-(X*COS(T)+Y*SIN(T))*SIN(P)+Z*COS(P)
```

which are used to perform coordinate transformations, and use the intrinsic functions SIN and COS.

SUMMARY

● An actual argument to a subroutine or function may be a constant, a variable name, an array element name, a character substring, an expression, an array name, an intrinsic function name, an external procedure name, a dummy procedure name, or an alternative return specifier.

● A dummy argument may be a variable name, an array name, a dummy procedure name, or an asterisk.

● A procedure name that is to appear as an actual argument name must appear in an EXTERNAL or INTRINSIC statement.

● A statement function is local to the program unit in which it is declared.

● Fortran 77 statements introduced in Chapter 16:

Type declarations	EXTERNAL *procedure name*
	INTRINSIC *intrinsic procedure name*
Statement function definition	*name(list of dummy arguments) = expression*

SELF-TEST EXERCISES 16.1

1   When is an EXTERNAL declaration required?

2   When is an INTRINSIC declaration required?

3   What is the difference between a statement function and an external function? When is the use of a statement function preferable?

PROGRAMMING EXERCISES

16.1   In Exercise 7.18 you wrote a program to find the roots of the polynomial function $x^2 - 3x + 2$. Modify your program so that it uses two external function subprograms F(X) and FPRIME(X) to return the value of the function $f(x)$ and its first derivative $f'(x)$ for a given value of x. Use this program to find the roots of the following equations:

(a) $y = 3x^3 - 6x^2 + 19x - 8$
(b) $y = x^4 + 2x^3 - 23x^2 - 24x + 31$
(c) $y = \sin x + \cos 2x$
(d) $y = \sin (x + \pi/4)$

16.2   The logical function A=>B is defined by the following 'truth table':

A	B	A=>B
False	False	True
False	True	True
True	False	False
True	True	True

Write a statement function LOGICAL IMP(A,B) that implements this function for two logical variables A and B.

***16.3** Write and test statement functions to evaluate the following functions:

(a) The Celsius equivalent of a Fahrenheit temperature $(F = \dfrac{9C}{5} + 32)$.

(b) The metric equivalent of a distance in feet and inches (1 in = 2.54 cm).

(c) The truth or otherwise of the assertion that a real value is an exact whole number (to within a specified tolerance).

(d) The truth or otherwise of the assertion that one real number is an integral factor of another.

16.4 Design a statement function that concatenates three strings into one. Place the statement function in a program where a second function, that can be supplied by the user, performs a particular character manipulation operation, for example, reversing the order of characters in a string before they are concatenated. Write your own function (for example, to reverse the order of characters) and test your program.

16.5 Write a subroutine that accepts as its argument a logical function of two logical variables and generates a printout of its truth table, such as that shown in Exercise 16.2. Test your subroutine by defining several logical statement functions.

16.6 In Exercise 13.9 a simple benchmarking program was developed to compare the speed of execution of REAL and DOUBLE PRECISION arithmetic. In a similar manner the speeds of intrinsic functions will now be compared.

Write a subroutine that will accept an intrinsic function and a number range as its arguments, and evaluate that function over (say) 1000 steps within that range, allowing the user to measure the time taken. Use this to compare the relative times taken to evaluate SIN and SQRT functions.

Now repeat the exercise using DOUBLE PRECISION numbers.

*16.7 Write a program that can be used to encrypt or decrypt a message in the following manner.

A keyword of up to 10 letters is read and used to encrypt the message by allocating each letter in the keyword its numeric position in the alphabet, then replacing each letter of the message by the letter *n* later in the alphabet, where *n* is the value of the next letter of the keyword. The keyword is repeated as often as necessary, and the alphabet is considered to be circular (that is, A follows Z). Numbers are spelled out, digit by digit, and spaces are replaced by the next letter in the keyword. All letters are encrypted to capitals.

The coded message is written in groups of the same length as the keyword, which forms the first group, with extra random letters being added to the end of the last group if necessary. Thus, if the keyword is *Fortran* (6, 15, 18, 20, 18, 1, 14) the message *This exercise is fun* will be encrypted as follows:

$$
\begin{aligned}
T &\to T+6 &&= Z \\
h &\to h+15 &&= W \\
i &\to i+18 &&= A \\
s &\to s+20 &&= M \\
\blacklozenge &\to 18 &&= R \\
e &\to e+1 &&= F \\
x &\to x+14 &&= L \\
e &\to e+6 &&= K \\
r &\to r+15 &&= G \\
\end{aligned}
$$

and so on

leading to the encrypted message

FORTRAN ZWAMRFL KGUCKFN OHRZMOB

Note that the same letter does not normally encrypt to the same encrypted letter, thus eliminating the well-known method of code-breaking based on frequency counts. The decryption part of the program will, of course, use the same procedure in reverse. (*Hint*: first write and test the encryption part of the program; this can then be used to test the decryption part.)

16.8 A racing-tortoise trainer uses a computer to analyse the results of a season's racing. For each race he records in a file the name of the tortoise (Percy, Quentin, Rudolph, Samantha, Tabitha or Ursula), the length of the race (in feet), the time (in hours, minutes and seconds in the form hh.mm.ss) and the tortoise's position in the race.

He wishes to produce a table showing for each tortoise the number of races, and the number of first, second and third places achieved. The details should be sorted on the basis of a scoring system which awards 5 points for a first place, 3 points for second, and 1 point for third.

In addition, for any tortoise that managed an average speed in excess of 1 ft/min in any race, he requires the average speed for that tortoise in all its races.

Write a program to provide the information required, and test it with files created by some other means.

16.9 Angles can be specified in degrees, radians or gradians (where there are 100 gradians to a right angle). Write a program that calculates the height of a tree given the distance from the tree, a, of a point P, and the angle, θ, between P and the top of the tree. Write the program so that it uses a general angle conversion function that can be supplied by any user, such that the user gives the angle θ in any unit he or she chooses and supplies his or her own conversion routine. Write your own conversion routine and test your program for angles given in all three systems.

16.10 The potential energy of a diatomic molecule can be expressed as a function of the distance between two atoms, r, using the expression

$$V = D(1-e^{-\alpha(r-r_e)})^2$$

where D, α and r_e are parameters, for example, $D = 10000$, $\alpha = 0.1$, $r_e = 1.0$. Use a statement function to evaluate V in a program that calculates V for r taking the values 0.5, 1.0, 1.5, 2.0, 2.5, 3.0, 3.5, 4.0, 4.5 and 5.0. Produce the results in the form of a table consisting of two columns.

16.11 The trapezoidal rule for numerically evaluating the integral of a function is

$$\int_l^u f(x)dx = h \ (f_0 + 2f_1 + 2f_2 + \dots + 2f_{n+1} + f_n)$$

where l is the lower limit of the integral (that is, $l = x_{min}$),
u is the upper limit of the integral (that is, $u = x_{max}$),
n is the number of segments into which the range of the integral is divided,
h is the size of each interval $(= \frac{u-l}{n})$, and
f_i is the value of $f(x)$ at $x = l + i*h$.

Write a function that will be provided with the values of l, u, n and the name of an intrinsic function (such as SIN), and will return the value of the integral of the function between the given limits.

Test your function in a program which evaluates $\int_0^\pi \sin x \ dx$. Start with $n = 10$, and then increase n to investigate how it affects the results. Repeat this exercise for $\int_0^\pi \cos x \ dx$.

16.12 The kinetic energy (in joules) given to a body under constant acceleration due to some external force is given by the equation

$$KE = F*d$$

where F is the force and d is the distance over which it acts. When the force changes with position, as with the gravitational attraction between two bodies, the above equation becomes the integral

$$KE = \int_{r_{min}}^{r_{max}} F(r) \ dr$$

where $F(r)$ is the force at a distance r from the source of the force. The value of this integral can be approximated by the equation

$$KE \approx \sum_{i=1}^{n} F(r_i)\delta r$$

where δr is sufficiently small for the force to be considered constant over the distance between r and $r + \delta r$, $n = (r_{max} - r_{min})/\delta r$, and $r_i = r_{min} + i*\delta r$.

In your solution to Exercise 4.18 you wrote a function that returned the force due to gravity between two bodies, given their masses and their separation. (If you have not attempted Exercise 4.18 then you should do it as part of this exercise.) Using this function to calculate the value of $F(r)$, write a program that will calculate the kinetic energy gained by a 20 000 kg asteroid falling on to the Earth from a distance of 100 Earth radii. Assume that the radius of the Earth is 6378.5 km and that the mass of the Earth is 5.976E24 kg.

Note: the force of gravity due to a planet is measured from its centre ($r = 0$) as if all its mass were at one point.

16.13 Exercise 12.20 introduced the bubble sort, Section 14.3 discussed the straight selection sort and Exercise 14.18 explained QuickSort, but all of these sorting subroutines can only sort items of a specific type. Thus a procedure for sorting integers cannot be used to sort characters. However, it can readily be seen that in all methods there are only two situations when the array is referred to:

- when elements I and J of the array are to be compared, and
- when elements I and J of the array are to be exchanged.

Write a sorting subroutine, using whichever method you prefer, that has as two of its arguments a LOGICAL function GREATR and a subroutine SWAP that perform these operations. By calling the sorting subroutine with the names of appropriate procedures as arguments, therefore, an array of any type can be sorted. Use your new subroutine in a program that calls it three times – first to sort a set of integers into ascending order, second to sort a set of words into alphabetic order and third to sort a set of real values into ascending order.

*16.14
```
PXAJQS CMESWR PRIOQI HMHBRF PWPEQP HMUOQY EPAOOX HAJCVS IGYDVX
DXQYZG JXTOMX DXTYQM XYUJZG IRFKUS EDAEJB DEADYX PIFINH HBAPFK
PCOMFW YLHJRG TXEOTH TGOQQX QAIJSE EALJZM PGTJFG BWAEJX TXGYIS
JFFJWB HQUJSE EALJJX CGDYCH DXURVK UYGDVK PRIOQI HCWSFN IXCVFV
AXJCQN ICEJKH PCOMFW UXPBQW UAPNVS JFFJEX NRAYEX PQUYGS

RJXDL APXCA VPFDW APJIZ PTOMZ JBXFZ WGQYA DLQRV GOVKO MJHWN MDPBB
MCEWT MSWLA ETJLP GPSAK ZBRAH OTCTH ELRJM WXQJF QMGJS RAFJV GOMBW
AJYCQ JYMVQ PQBIQ CZNNJ CEZZS VEPXV
```

(*Hint*: see Exercise 16.7.)

More about formats and file-handling

17

The Fortran formatting capability met in earlier chapters provides the means for almost any required form of control over the format of data or results. A number of additional edit descriptors are introduced in this chapter that provide still further control, especially of output layout.

A very useful feature of Fortran 77, in some situations, is the ability to create an **internal file**. This is a character array or variable that can be processed as though it were an external file by the normal Fortran formatted `READ` and `WRITE` statements. In particular, this provides a means for determining the layout of an input record from the first few characters of the record itself.

Another powerful extension of the input/output facilities is the use of **direct access files**. Unlike a conventional **sequential file**, the records of a direct access file can be written and read in any order, thus greatly simplifying the processing of data not provided in a predetermined sequence.

Although the storage of files, and their indexing, is a feature of the operating system and not of the Fortran language, a special `INQUIRE` statement is available that allows the program to enquire of the operating system about certain aspects of any files known to the program. An interesting use of this statement enables a program to cycle automatically through a three-generation (grandfather–father–son) system of files without the need for any external identification of the name of the most recent file.

17.1 A review of Fortran input/output facilities

Up to this point our input/output requirements have been relatively straightforward (as, indeed, they usually are in practice). However, Fortran 77 does provide a number of other, more sophisticated, facilities, which will be examined in this chapter. Before doing so the features that we have already met will be reviewed.

We have seen that input can be carried out by one of the following variations of the READ statement:

```
READ *, input-list
READ label, input-list
READ format, input-list
READ (cilist) input-list
```

and output by one of the following:

```
PRINT *, input-list
PRINT label, input-list
PRINT format, input-list
WRITE (cilist) input-list
```

In the case of the two more complete forms of the READ and WRITE statements, we have met the following specifiers that can appear in the *cilist*:

```
UNIT   = u      (or u)
FMT    = f      (or f)
ERR    = s
END    = s
IOSTAT = ios
```

When discussing these specifiers in Chapter 9 a description of the action of the IOSTAT specifier was omitted, but will be given now. The purpose of this specifier is to enable more information to be made available to the program in the event of an error. It takes the form

```
IOSTAT = ios
```

where *ios* is an integer variable. When a READ or WRITE statement that contains an IOSTAT specifier in its *cilist* is obeyed the variable will be set to a value that indicates the result of the input operation, as shown in Figure 17.1.

ios = 0	if there was no error and no end-of-file	**Figure 17.1**
> 0	if an error occurred	Input/output status values (IOSTAT = *ios*).
< 0	if an end-of-file condition occurred, but no error	

- If no error occurred and there was no end-of-file then the variable is set to 0.
- If there was no error, but an end-of-file condition *did* occur, then it will be set to a negative value. This value is processor-dependent, but the fact that it is negative is really all that matters.
- If there was an error, however, the variable will be set to a positive value. In this case several possible (positive) values will probably be used to indicate different types of error; what these values are and what they mean is, however, dependent upon the particular computer system. In theory this means that the program can decide upon what action to take in the event of different types of error; for example, if running out of data does not set an end-of-file condition it will almost certainly be identifiable by a unique error number. In practice, however, it is usually not possible to take much remedial action after an input/output error and so the extra capability is not actually very useful.

The input/output status specifier can either be used on its own, in which case a test must be included after the READ statement:

```
      .
      .
      READ (*,50,IOSTAT=I) A,B,C
      IF (I.LT.0) THEN
C  End of file
      .
      .
      ELSE IF (I.GT.0) THEN
C  Error
      .
      .
      END IF
C  Continue normal processing
      .
      .
```

Figure 17.2
Some edit descriptors used for formatted input and output.

Descriptor	Meaning for input	Meaning for output
Iw	Read the next w characters as an integer.	Output an integer in the next w character positions.
$Fw.d$	Read the next w characters as a real number, with the last d digits being treated as coming after the decimal point if no decimal point is present.	Output a real number in the next w character positions with d decimal places.
$Ew.d$	Read the next w characters as a real number, with the last d digits being treated as coming after the decimal point if no decimal point is present.	Output a real number in the next w character positions, using a scientific format with d decimal places for the mantissa and four characters for the exponent.
nX	Ignore the next n characters.	Ignore the next n character positions.
Tc	Next character to be read is at position c.	Output the next item starting at character position c.
TLn	Next character to be read is n characters before the current position.	Output the next item starting n character positions before the current position.
TRn	Next character to be read is n characters after the current position.	Output the next item starting n character positions after the current position.
$'c_1c_2c_3...c_n'$	(Not applicable.)	Output the string of characters $c_1c_2c_3...c_n$ starting at the next character position.
$nHc_1c_2c_3...c_n$	(Not applicable.)	Output the n characters following the H in the next n character positions.
$/$	Terminates the reading of the current record.	Terminates the output of the current record.

or it can be used in combination with the error and/or end-of-file specifiers:

```
READ (*,50,IOSTAT=I,ERR=300,END=250) A,B,C
```

in which case these will take care of the branching away from the normal sequence of processing. In both cases the value of I may be inspected to find out the exact cause of the error.

We have also met the OPEN statement and, in particular, have seen how this is used to open a sequential file and *connect* it to a specified unit

number in the program. The following *cilist* specifiers have been used in
OPEN statements:

```
UNIT   = u      (or u)
FILE   = fn
STATUS = st
ACCESS = acc
FORM   = fm
ERR    = s
IOSTAT = ios
```

We have also met, and used, the CLOSE statement and the file positioning
statements ENDFILE, BACKSPACE and REWIND.

When reading or writing *formatted records* we have used the edit
descriptors shown in Figure 17.2.

Finally, we have seen how a format is repeated if there are more
names in the input or output list than there are relevant edit descriptors.

17.2 Some more FORMAT edit descriptors

F90

Figure 17.3 shows most of the remaining edit descriptors, none of which is
used very often. A brief description of each is, however, appropriate.

The : edit descriptor is used to terminate a format if there are no
more list items. This is not usually necessary as the format will terminate in
any case at the next edit descriptor that requires a list item. In an output
format, however, this could cause some unnecessary printing to occur.
Figure 17.4 shows the effect of the : edit descriptor on output.

Descriptor	Meaning
:	Terminate format if there are no more list items.
SP	Print + signs before positive numbers.
SS	Do not print + signs before positive numbers.
S	Processor decides whether to print + signs before positive numbers.
kP	Apply a scale factor of k to numeric input or output.
BN	Ignore blanks in numeric input fields.
BZ	Treat blanks in numeric input fields as zeros.
I$w.m$	Output integer with at least m digits.
E$w.d$Ee	
D$w.d$	Input or output real or double-precision values
G$w.d$	(see text for details).
G$w.d$Ee	

Figure 17.3
Further edit descriptors.

Figure 17.4
An example of : editing.

```
      PROGRAM COLON
      REAL A,B
      A = 3.5
      B = 7.2
      WRITE (2,201) A,B,A+B
      WRITE (2,202) A,B,A+B
      STOP
  201 FORMAT (1H1,'The sum of',F5.2,' and',F5.2,' is',F6.2/
     *        1H ,'Their product is',F8.2)
  202 FORMAT (1H0,'The sum of',F5.2,' and',F5.2,' is',F6.2:/
     *        1H ,'Their product is',F8.2)
      END
```

(output)
The sum of 3.50 and 7.20 is 10.70
Their product is

The sum of 3.50 and 7.20 is 10.70

The SP edit descriptor affects any numbers output by any following edit descriptors in this format, and causes a + sign to be placed before positive numbers (just as a - sign is placed before negative ones). SS has the opposite effect and prevents a + sign being placed before positive numbers. S restores the normal (default) situation, which, for most systems, will be to omit + signs.

The SP edit descriptor would have been useful in Example 12.6, in which variable formats were built up to print details of different types of geometric entities. One of the major difficulties was arranging to eliminate adjacent signs. The use of an SP edit descriptor would have simplified matters because *all* numbers in the particular parts of the equation would have their signs printed. It is left as an exercise for the reader to modify the solution to Example 12.6 to use SP edit descriptors.

BN and BZ are discussed in Section 17.3, while the P edit descriptor is dealt with at the end of this section, after the introduction of the D and G edit descriptors.

Iw.m is an extended form of the I edit descriptor that affects only the output of integers; if used for input it is treated as though it were Iw. On output it specifies the minimum number of digits to be printed, including, if necessary, one or more leading zeros. The value of m must not be greater than that of w, while if it is 0 and the value of the integer is also 0 only blanks are output. Figure 17.5 gives an example of its use.

As well as the F and E edit descriptors there are a number of other ways of inputting and outputting real numbers that provide slight variations on those methods.

```
      PROGRAM IWM
      INTEGER I
      DO 10, I=-10,10,5
         PRINT 220,I,I,I
  10  CONTINUE
 220  FORMAT (I5,I5.2,I5.0)
      END
```

Figure 17.5
An example of Iw.m
editing.

(output)
```
 -10  -10  -10
  -5  -05   -5
   0   00
   5   05    5
  10   10   10
```

For *input* all the following edit descriptors have an identical effect:

> Fw.d
> Ew.d
> Dw.d
> Gw.d
> Ew.dEe
> Gw.dEe

where e may have any value (and is ignored).

For *output*, however, there are significant differences. As we have already seen, Fw.d will output a real number rounded to d decimal places with an external field of width w; Ew.d, on the other hand, will output such a number in an external field of width w using a scientific format, which consists of a decimal fraction of d digits in the range 0.1 to 0.9999..., followed by a four-character exponent.

If the Ew.d is followed by Ee then the exponent consists of e digits. Thus the number 0.000 023 143 6 will be output as shown below with various edit descriptors:

```
    E12.5    0.23144E-04
    E12.6    0.231436E-04
    E12.5E3  0.23144E-004
    E12.6E1  0.231436E-4
```

The D edit descriptor (Dw.d) is the same as the Ew.d descriptor except that the letter E on output may be replaced by a letter D. It exists mainly for compatibility with earlier versions of Fortran. It cannot be used with an Ee suffix.

Finally, the G edit descriptor attempts to provide the best of both

Figure 17.6
A comparison of F, E
and G editing.

Internal value	External representation		
	(F12.5)	(E12.5)	(G12.5)
132651.0	132651.00000	0.13265E+06	0.13265E+06
−132651.0	************	−0.13265E+06	−0.13265E+06
13265.1	13265.10000	0.13265E+05	13256.
−12.43	−12.43000	−0.12430E+02	−12.43
0.10471	0.10471	0.10471E+00	0.10471
0.010471	0.01047	0.10471E−01	0.10471E−01
0.00010471	0.00010	0.10471E−03	0.10471E−03

worlds. On input it is the same as F$w.d$, but on output it uses either the F$w.d$, E$w.d$ or E$w.d$Ee formats depending upon the magnitude of the number being output.

If the magnitude (that is, the absolute value) of the number to be output lies between 0.1 and 10^d (that is, the exponent in E format would lie between 0 and d inclusive) then F format is used; otherwise E formatting takes place. If F formatting is used the field width is reduced by 4 for G$w.d$ and by $e+2$ for G$w.d$Ee, and the number is followed by four spaces or $e+2$ spaces, respectively. In all cases the number is printed, therefore, with d significant digits. Figure 17.6 shows a comparison of F, E and G editing, and the advantage of the G format when a wide range of numbers is possible is readily apparent. Notice in particular that −132 651.0 has proved to be too large for the F format (and has been printed as a row of asterisks), while 0.000 104 71 has lost all semblance of accuracy in the F format.

All three descriptors have their advantages: the layout produced by the F edit descriptor is much clearer to read than that produced by the E edit descriptor; the latter, however, will cover a far wider range of numbers; the G format is used when the programmer is not sure how large or small his results may be, or when they may vary very widely.

The effect of the F, D, E and G edit descriptors can be altered by use of a **scale factor**. This is applied by means of a P edit descriptor (kP), which causes a scale factor of k to be applied to all F, D, E or G edit descriptors following it in a format. Its effect can be somewhat confusing and its use is not, therefore, recommended. It is briefly discussed in Chapter 19, together with other obsolete or little-used features of Fortran 77.

17.3   The inputting of blanks in numbers

We have already seen that data may be read from a number of different sources, one of which will be defined as the *standard input unit*. We have also seen how we can use the OPEN statement to establish a link between our program and any input or output device by a process known as *connecting*. The standard input and output devices, however, are *preconnected* and are automatically available to all programs. This has an important implication when reading numbers.

When a file of information is first connected to a program it is possible to specify that any blanks (or spaces) within a number are to be treated either as blanks (and ignored) or as zeros. Normally, when reading a formatted file that has been connected to the program by means of an OPEN statement, any blank characters that are read as part of a number are ignored. Since, in general, such a file will have been created by another program (or by the same one) any blanks will normally be either leading or trailing and ignoring them is what we would intuitively expect to do. We may, however, specify that blanks are not to be ignored by means of a specifier in the OPEN statement of the form

BLANK=*bl*

where *bl*, ignoring any trailing blanks, is either NULL or ZERO. If it is NULL, or if the specifier is omitted, then any blanks will be ignored in formatted numeric fields; if it is ZERO they will be treated as zeros. A BLANK specifier is not allowed with an unformatted file.

However, in the case of preconnected files (or devices) the situation is slightly different. In earlier versions of Fortran, blank characters in data input from cards (or some other *standard input device*) were normally treated as zeros. This was because, on cards, it was possible to save a lot of time-consuming punching by reading blank columns as zeros. Unfortunately, the committee who drew up the standard definition of Fortran 77 were unable to decide whether it should follow earlier practice with preconnected files or the same pattern as files that are connected by the program.

The Fortran 77 Standard passed this decision back to the compiler writer. At a stroke the whole concept of standardization in an extremely important area was destroyed and there arose a distinct possibility that a program would not transfer correctly to another computer system! (It is worth noting that this omission has been corrected in Fortran 90, which defines the default to be the same for both preconnected and user-connected files.) Fortunately there is a remedy that enables the programmer to override the default used by a particular compiler.

F90

The BZ edit descriptor specifies that blanks are to be treated as zeros for all numeric input edited by I, F, E, D or G edit descriptors in the remainder of the format. Placing BZ at the start of a format ensures that all blanks in numbers are treated as zeros, regardless of the default used by any particular system.

The BN edit descriptor, on the other hand, causes all blanks in numeric input fields to be treated as *null* characters – in other words, they are ignored. BN at the start of an input format ensures that all blanks in numbers are ignored, regardless of the default used by any particular system. However, if *all* the characters in a numeric input field are blank the number is always treated as 0.

This problem was of considerable importance when Fortran 77 was being specified, when much input was still from cards. However, nowadays most data is typed directly into a file from a keyboard, and so it would be unusual not to type all the relevant zeros. There is, therefore, relatively little need for the BZ and BN edit descriptors any more.

The BZ and BN edit descriptors have no effect on any input editing other than that carried out by I, F, E, D or G edit descriptors; they will, however, always override the effect of any BLANK specifier for input using that format. They have no effect at all during output.

17.4　Internal files

An **internal file** is not really a file at all, but behaves like one and can be used to great advantage in particular situations. It is actually a means whereby the power and flexibility of the Fortran 77 formatting process can be used to convert information in the memory from one format to another. Such a file is a character variable, character array element, character array, or character substring.

If an internal file is a character variable, array element or substring it consists of a single record, while if it is a character array it consists of a sequence of records, each of which corresponds to one element of the array. In the latter case the whole file must be input or output by means of a single statement, since a READ or WRITE statement on an internal file *always* starts at the beginning of the file.

An internal file can be read only by a (sequential) formatted READ statement that does not specify list-directed formatting, and it can only be written by a (sequential) formatted WRITE statement that likewise does not specify list-directed formatting; or it can be created by any other appropriate means – for example, by an assignment statement or by input from some other source.

An internal file is specified by using the name of the character variable (or other item) in a READ or WRITE statement in place of the unit identifier. Thus, if LINE is a character variable, we may write

```
WRITE (LINE,201) X,Y,Z
READ (UNIT=LINE,FMT=150) A,B,C
```

and so on.

The following two examples illustrate two typical situations in which an internal file can be useful.

EXAMPLE 17.1

Write a function subprogram that takes a real number (X) and an integer (N) and returns as its value the value of X rounded to N significant digits.

This is an artificial example, since it is difficult to see why we should wish to reduce the accuracy to which numbers are held internally, but it does give a simple illustration of how an internal file can be used. To carry out this function by some other means would involve a complicated sequence of arithmetic operations and tests; however, the E edit descriptor automatically produces a number rounded to a given number of significant digits. All the function needs to do, therefore, is choose an appropriate format, depending on the value of N. We shall assume that N must lie within the range 1–9 (that is, numbers cannot be held to more than nine digits of accuracy) and will treat numbers outside this range as 1 or 9, as appropriate.

```
      REAL FUNCTION ROUND(X,N)
C
C This function returns X rounded to exactly N significant digits
C
C Dummy arguments
      REAL X
      INTEGER N
C FILE will be used as an internal file
      CHARACTER*20 FILE
C Miscellaneous variables
      INTEGER PLACES
      CHARACTER D(9)
C D contains the character representations of 'd' in the edit
C descriptor
      DATA D/'1','2','3','4','5','6','7','8','9'/
C Set PLACES to N, after dealing with out-of-range values
      IF (N.LT.1) THEN
         PLACES=1
      ELSE IF (N.GT.9) THEN
         PLACES=9
      ELSE
         PLACES=N
      END IF
```

```
C  Use a character expression as the format for 'output' to the
C  internal file
      WRITE (FILE,'(E20.'//D(PLACES)//')') X
C  We can now read the rounded value using a simple F format
      READ (FILE,'(F20.0)') ROUND
      RETURN
      END
```

The function first sets PLACES to the number of significant digits and then 'writes' X to the 20-character internal file FILE using a format of E20.d, where d is the character representation of PLACES. This number will occupy a maximum of 16 characters and so a field width of 20 is more than sufficient. The subsequent input is easier since the form of the character representation (including an exponent) means that only the field width is necessary for an F edit descriptor.

EXAMPLE 17.2

A survey has been carried out to obtain statistics concerning the occupation of people in a certain area. The results of the survey are available for input to the computer in the following format:

Columns 1–20	Name	
Column 23	Sex (M/F)	
Column 25	Job status	= 1 if in full-time education
		= 2 if in full-time employment
		= 3 if in part-time employment
		= 4 if temporarily unemployed
		= 5 if not working or seeking a job

This is followed by one or more items, depending on the job status of the respondent:

Job status			
= 1	columns 28, 29	Age	
= 2	columns 28–31	Monthly salary (£)	
= 3	columns 28–31	Monthly salary (£)	
	columns 34–37	Other monthly income (£)	
= 4	columns 28, 29	Age	
	columns 32–34	No. of months unemployed	
= 5	columns 28, 29	Age	
	column 31	Code	
		= 1 if looking after children	
		= 2 if looking after other relatives	
		= 3 for any other reason	

The data is terminated by a record that contains the characters *END* in columns 1–5 and is otherwise blank.

Write an input subprogram that will read a maximum of 1000 records and store the relevant details in suitable arrays for subsequent use by other subprograms.

This data is very similar to that used in Example 10.1. In that case the data was read and re-read by use of T edit descriptors, with unspecified fields being assumed to be blank. A far better way is to read each record into a character variable and then to treat this as an internal file that can be read by an appropriate format.

We shall need the following arrays for the data:

NAME	CHARACTER*20	name of respondent
MALE	LOGICAL	*true* if male, *false* otherwise
STATUS	INTEGER	job status
AGE	INTEGER	age (where appropriate)
SALARY	INTEGER	monthly salary (where appropriate)
EXTRA	INTEGER	other monthly income (where appropriate)
JOBLES	INTEGER	number of months unemployed (where appropriate)
HOME	INTEGER	code for those not working (where appropriate)

Since there are eight of these, and they will be required by other subprograms, we shall place them in two COMMON blocks, one (NAMES) for the CHARACTER array NAME and the other (SURVEY) for the remaining seven arrays. We also notice that, of these eight potential data items, all respondents will have entries in the first three, but none will have entries in more than two of the others. A further examination shows that no respondent is required to give both age and salary, and that no respondent gives more than one of the other three. We may therefore save considerable memory space by use of EQUIVALENCE to enable these two groups to share the same storage.

A structure plan for the subroutine can now be drawn up.

1 Repeat the following up to 1000 times
  1.1 Read next record into an internal file
  1.2 If name is *END* then exit
  1.3 Read name, sex, and job status from file
  1.4 If job status is 1 then
    1.4.1 Read age
    otherwise if job status is 2 then
    1.4.2 Read salary
    .
    .
    .

2 Return with count of people

The subroutine is then quite straightforward

```
      SUBROUTINE INPUT(PEOPLE)
C
C Input routine for occupation survey data
C
C The subroutine reads up to MAX data records prepared as follows,
C returning the number read in PEOPLE
C
C Columns 1-20  Name
C          23  Sex (M or F)
C          25  Job status (1-5)
C       28,29  Age - for status 1, 4 or 5
C       28-31  Monthly salary - for status 2 and 3
C       32-34  Other monthly income - for status 3
C       32-34  Months unemployed - for status 4
C          31  Special code (1-3) - for status 5
C
C The data is terminated by a record containing *END* in cols 1-5
C
C Dummy argument
      INTEGER PEOPLE
C COMMON block declaration
      INTEGER MAX
      PARAMETER (MAX=1000)
      INTEGER STATUS(MAX),AGE(MAX),SALARY(MAX),EXTRA(MAX),JOBLES(MAX),
     *       HOME(MAX)
      LOGICAL MALE(MAX)
      CHARACTER*20 NAME(MAX)
      COMMON /SURVEY/MALE,STATUS,AGE,EXTRA
      EQUIVALENCE (AGE,SALARY),(EXTRA,JOBLES,HOME)
      COMMON /NAMES/NAME
C Miscellaneous variables
      CHARACTER SEX,RECORD*40
      INTEGER I,JSTAT
C Main loop to read data
      DO 10, I=1,MAX
C Read next record into the character variable RECORD
        READ '(A40)',RECORD
C Check if end of data
        IF (RECORD(1:5).EQ.'*END*') GOTO 11
C Now read common data
        READ (RECORD,'(A20,2X,A1,1X,I1)') NAME(I),SEX,JSTAT
C Store sex as a logical value in MALE, and job status in STATUS
        MALE(I)=SEX.EQ.'M'
        STATUS(I)=JSTAT
C Now read remainder of record, depending on status code
        IF (JSTAT.EQ.1) THEN
          READ (RECORD,'(27X,I2)') AGE(I)
        ELSE IF (JSTAT.EQ.2) THEN
          READ (RECORD,'(27X,I4)') SALARY(I)
        ELSE IF (JSTAT.EQ.3) THEN
          READ (RECORD,'(27X,I4,2X,I4)') SALARY(I),EXTRA(I)
```

```
         ELSE IF (JSTAT.EQ.4) THEN
            READ (RECORD,'(27X,I2,2X,I3)') AGE(I),JOBLES(I)
         ELSE IF (JSTAT.EQ.5) THEN
            READ (RECORD,'(27X,I2,1X,I1)') AGE(I),HOME(I)
         END IF
   10 CONTINUE
C  No terminator
      PRINT *,MAX,' records read with no terminator'
C  Return number of records read
   11 PEOPLE=I-1
      RETURN
      END
```

Notice that the original data is read using an A40 edit descriptor, thus creating an all-character representation of the data in the internal file RECORD. This may be dealt with in the usual way as a character variable, or it may be read as an internal file. Thus, for example, the first input from the file and the following statement could be replaced by

```
      NAME(I) = REC(1:20)
      MALE(I) = REC(23:23).EQ.'M'
```

However, the job status code will still need to be converted to integer form and the READ statement is the easiest way to do this. Notice also that the job status has been placed in a variable as well as in the array for ease of writing (and comprehension) in the block IF.

Figure 17.7 shows a driver program suitable for testing this input routine. Once it is fully tested then more complex programs can be written to produce analyses of the data, using this routine to read it.

```
      PROGRAM TEST
C
C  A test program for subroutine INPUT
C  COMMON block declaration
      INTEGER MAX
      PARAMETER (MAX=1000)
      INTEGER STATUS(MAX),AGE(MAX),SALARY(MAX),EXTRA(MAX),JOBLES(MAX),
     *         HOME(MAX)
      LOGICAL MALE(MAX)
      CHARACTER*20 NAME(MAX)
      COMMON /SURVEY/MALE,STATUS,AGE,EXTRA
      EQUIVALENCE (AGE,SALARY),(EXTRA,JOBLES,HOME)
      COMMON /NAMES/NAME
C
      INTEGER NUMBER,I
      CHARACTER SEX
      CALL INPUT(NUMBER)
      DO 10,I=1,NUMBER
```

Figure 17.7
A driver program for use in testing INPUT.

```
          IF (MALE(I)) THEN
            SEX='M'
          ELSE
            SEX='F'
          END IF
          IF (STATUS(I).EQ.1) THEN
            PRINT 201,I,NAME(I),SEX,AGE(I)
          ELSE IF (STATUS(I).EQ.2) THEN
            PRINT 202,I,NAME(I),SEX,SALARY(I)
          ELSE IF (STATUS(I).EQ.3) THEN
            PRINT 203,I,NAME(I),SEX,SALARY(I),EXTRA(I)
          ELSE IF (STATUS(I).EQ.4) THEN
            PRINT 204,I,NAME(I),SEX,AGE(I),JOBLES(I)
          ELSE IF (STATUS(I).EQ.5) THEN
            PRINT 205,I,NAME(I),SEX,AGE(I),HOME(I)
          END IF
   10 CONTINUE
      STOP
  201 FORMAT(1H ,I3,2X,A20,2X,A1,' in education, aged ',I2)
  202 FORMAT(1H ,I3,2X,A20,2X,A1,' employed, earning ',I4)
  203 FORMAT(1H ,I3,2X,A20,2X,A1,' employed part-time, earning ',I4,
      * ' plus ',I4)
  204 FORMAT(1H ,I3,2X,A20,2X,A1,' aged ',I2,' unemployed for ',I3,
      * ' months)
  205 FORMAT(1H ,I3,2X,A20,2X,A1,' aged ',I2,' at home - code ',I1)
      END
```

SELF-TEST EXERCISES 17.1

1   Establish the default treatment of blank characters in numeric fields during input from preconnected files (for example, the standard input unit) on your computer system.

2   *On your computer system*, what will be the effect of reading the record

♦♦123♦56♦♦♦12♦♦♦67♦9

(where ♦ represents a blank character) using the following READ and FORMAT statements?

(a)   READ 100,I,J,K,X,Y
       100 FORMAT (3I3,F6.2,F5.3)

(b)
```
    READ 101,I,J,K,X,Y
101 FORMAT (BZ,3I3,F6.2,F5.3)
```

(c)
```
    READ 102,I,J,K,X,Y
102 FORMAT (BN,3I3,F6.2,F5.3)
```

(d)
```
    READ 110,P,Q
110 FORMAT (2E10.3)
```

(e)
```
    READ 111,P,Q
111 FORMAT (BZ,2E10.3)
```

(f)
```
    READ 112,P,Q
112 FORMAT (BN,2E10.3)
```

3 What is the major difference between an internal file that is a character variable of length 100 and one that is a character array having five elements, each of length 20?

4 What will be printed by the following program?

```
      PROGRAM TEST4
      CHARACTER*5 LINE1(10),LINE2(10)
      INTEGER I
      DATA LINE1/'One','Two','Three','Four','Five','Six','Seven',
     *          'Eight','Nine','Ten'/
      DO 10, I=1,10
        READ (LINE1,100) LINE2(I)
  10  CONTINUE
      PRINT 200,LINE2
      DO 20, I=1,10
        READ (LINE1(I),100) LINE2(I)
  20  CONTINUE
      PRINT 200,LINE2
      READ (LINE1,100) LINE2
      PRINT 200,LINE2
      STOP
 100  FORMAT (A5)
 200  FORMAT (10A6)
      END
```

17.5   Direct access files

One of the problems with magnetic tapes (or any other sequential storage medium) is that it is grossly inefficient to read the information in any order other than sequential, and it is impossible to write information to them other than sequentially. One of the consequences of this is that data processing applications that use this form of backing store spend a large part of their time sorting information into the correct order for the next stage. Many applications, especially those that run in **real time**, such as

Figure 17.8
Single and multiple-disk drives.

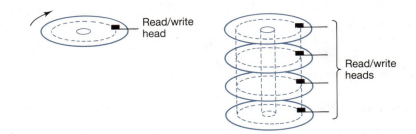

reservation or enquiry systems, are not practicable with this restriction on their access to backing store.

A later form of magnetic storage, which has now largely replaced magnetic tape for all purposes other than archiving, is the magnetic disk. This consists of one or more rapidly rotating disks on which information is written in a series of concentric bands. In systems that have several parallel disks rotating on the same axis (see Figure 17.8), each disk has its own read/write head and information is written on a series of parallel bands (forming a **cylinder**) in order to minimize the movement of the heads. In the case of a personal computer, there is usually only a single disk with two heads, one for each side.

In the worst case, the time it takes to access a particular record on a disk is the time taken to move the read/write head from the outermost to the innermost band (or *track*), or vice versa, plus the time for one complete revolution. This will be only a fraction of a second, and in general the access time is considerably less than this.

A disk unit is known, therefore, as a **direct access** (or sometimes **random access**) device because, for most practical purposes, it can directly access any information stored on it. There are other types of direct access device, but their use is negligible compared with the almost universal use of disks.

The widespread availability of direct access devices was the major factor in the development of sophisticated filing systems on computers. As long as all files were sequential it was impossible to allow large numbers of users to have large numbers of files without the system becoming completely overloaded, with filestore overheads consuming most of the computing power available. A filestore kept on direct access devices, however, does not carry the same overhead.

A file that is kept on a direct access device does not *need* to be accessed in a direct access fashion. Many applications are perfectly suited to sequential access and this is the default form of access to a file in Fortran 77. Direct access files are, however, particularly useful in two related situations. The first of these is when the problem requires the use of direct access in order to read or write the records in the file in a random order; the second is when the problem requires the selective over-writing (or updating) of some individual records in the file. This is not possible with a sequential file since writing a record causes it to become the *last record* in the file (Section 10.5).

If we wish to use a direct access file we must include the specifier

```
ACCESS='DIRECT'
```

in the OPEN statement for the file (see Section 10.4). This is not all that is required, since if a file is to be read and, more especially, written in a random order there are certain 'housekeeping' matters that must be attended to.

The first of these concerns the length of the records in the file. To allow the flexibility of being able to read and write records in any order all the records in the file must have the same length. This is specified in the OPEN statement for the file by the inclusion of the specifier

```
RECL=len
```

where *len* is the length of each record in the file. Formatted record lengths are measured in characters, whereas unformatted record lengths are measured in some unit that depends upon the particular computer system being used (Section 10.2). If a file is connected for direct access it is assumed to be unformatted unless specifically stated to be formatted by means of a FORM specifier (Section 10.4). The nature of direct access devices means that it is rarely possible to transfer a file directly to another type of computer, and it is usually first copied onto a sequential medium such as magnetic tape, or transmitted (sequentially) along a direct connection between the computers. Direct access files are, therefore, usually unformatted and the record length is computer-dependent.

In order to write to, or read from, a direct access file it is necessary to define which record is to be written or read. In Chapter 9 an additional specifier was mentioned:

```
REC=rn
```

which is used for direct access input/output and, indeed, it is the presence (or absence) of this specifier that determines whether a READ or WRITE statement is a direct access input/output statement, or a sequential one; *rn* is the **record number** of the record to be read or written and takes the form of an integer expression with a positive value. Thus the statement

```
WRITE (7,REC=20) A,B,C,D
```

will write the values of A, B, C and D as an unformatted record to record 20 of the direct access file connected to unit 7, and

```
READ (7,REC=I) W,X,Y,Z
```

will read the record number I from the same file.

Although we have stated that every record must have the same length in a direct access file, namely that defined in the OPEN statement, to a large extent Fortran 77 enables us to ignore this restriction. When writing an unformatted record to a direct access file, the length of the record must not exceed the record length specified for the file. If it is less than the specified record length then the rest of the record in the file will be filled with undefined values in order to make it the correct length. As long as we do not attempt to read more than was written, there is therefore no problem.

A similar situation exists with formatted records, except that the record will be filled out with trailing blanks to make it the correct length.

If a format used to write (or read) a direct access file specifies more than one record, then each successive record will be given a number 1 greater than the previous one. Thus the statements

```
    WRITE (8,200,REC=75) (A(I),I=1,100)
200 FORMAT (10F12.2)
```

will cause 10 records to be written, since the format specifies that each record contains 10 real numbers; these records will be numbered from 75 to 84, inclusive.

EXAMPLE 17.3

The employees in an organization have their pay determined in the following way:

(1)   The gross pay consists of N hours at a basic rate of pay plus a higher rate for all subsequent hours. Both rates of pay and the number of basic hours (N) are fixed on an individual basis.

(2)   Tax is a fixed percentage of the gross pay less a tax-free allowance.

(3)   Health insurance is a fixed percentage of that part of the gross pay that falls below a fixed limit.

(4)   The nett pay is the gross pay less tax and health insurance deductions.

A file is kept that contains details of all weekly-paid employees, including their staff numbers, normal hours of work, rates of pay and so on.

Each week, a file of data is prepared containing, for each employee, their staff number and the hours worked (in hours and minutes) during the previous week. This data is collected from various parts of the organization at different times and may, therefore, be considered as being in a random order.

Write a program to update the master file and to produce weekly payslips showing name, staff number, gross pay, deductions and nett pay.

This is a slightly simplified version of one of the classic data processing applications. One of the major problems in this type of application is the matching of new data to that on file. If the data is not to be sorted before input then, clearly, the master file will need to be capable of being accessed in a random fashion. The simplest way to deal with this problem is to use the staff number as the record number and to use it to access directly each employee's cumulative data, update it and produce the payslips.

This problem is a considerable simplification of a real payroll problem: for example, with this approach it is essential to have an input record for every employee, as the absence of an employee would not be recognized. We have also ignored such matters as the addition of new employees and the deletion of those who have left. The simplified problem is nevertheless a realistic one.

We shall assume that the calculation of deductions follows the normal (British) practice and that a change in the rate of tax applies to the whole year, whereas a change in insurance contributions applies only from the date of the change. This means that tax must be calculated by first calculating the tax due on the total gross pay to date in the current year (at the current rate) and subtracting from this the tax already paid.

In addition to the name, staff number, basic weekly hours, basic and overtime rates of pay and weekly tax-free pay, it will be necessary to keep the gross pay earned to date, the gross tax-free pay to date and the tax paid to date. Also, for completeness, it would seem advisable to keep the insurance contributions paid to date and the total nett pay earned to date, although this last can easily be calculated from the other items.

The basic method of operation will be to update each record of the (direct access) master file with new weekly data before producing a payslip. If an employee has not worked during the week then this should normally generate a tax refund because of the increase in the total tax-free pay to date. However, to avoid the additional need to check whether data has been supplied, we shall assume that an employee who has not worked will have a record with 0 hours; a real payroll system would obviously have to keep a careful check on this situation.

The current rates of tax and insurance and the maximum pay on which insurance contributions are based will be read before the employee data.

We are now ready to write a structure plan:

---

1 Open master file

2 Read fixed rates, ...

3 Repeat the following until the end of the employee data
3.1 Read next employee's weekly data record
3.2 Update employee's master record and print payslip –
UPDATE

UPDATE(STFNUM,HOURS)

1 Use STFNUM as key to get employee's master record
1.1 Calculate gross weekly pay
1.2 Calculate deductions
1.3 Calculate nett pay
1.4 Write updated record to new file
1.5 Print payslip

The program now follows from the structure plan.

```
      PROGRAM PAYROL
C
C This program deals with the weekly payroll
C
C Weekly data is input in the following format:
C
C   Staff number:  cols 1-4
C   Hours worked:  hrs in cols 7-9;  mins in cols 11,12
C
C Weekly data is read from a file on unit 5
C Payslips are written to a file called PAYSLIPS on unit 6
C The master file is called WEEKLY-PAYROLL and is on unit 7
C   Note this program assumes 1 unit per character storage unit,
C                             4 units per numeric storage unit
C
C Initial data concerning the name of the weekly data file,
C current tax rates, etc. is requested from the standard input unit
C
C Any error messages are sent to the standard output unit
C
C Maximum number of employees
      INTEGER MAXSTF
      PARAMETER (MAXSTF=5000)
```

```
C  COMMON block declarations
      REAL TAXRTE,INSRTE,INSMAX
      COMMON /TAXINS/TAXRTE,INSRTE,INSMAX
C  Miscellaneous variables
      CHARACTER*20 DATA
      INTEGER STFNUM,I
      REAL HRS,MINS
C
C  Get data file name and open it
      PRINT *,'Name of this week''s data file? '
      READ '(A)',DATA
      OPEN (5,FILE=DATA,STATUS='OLD',ERR=91)
C  Open master file and payslips file
      OPEN (6,FILE='PAYSLIPS',STATUS='NEW',ERR=92)
      OPEN (7,FILE='WEEKLY-PAYROLL',STATUS='OLD',
     *       ACCESS='DIRECT',RECL=56,ERR=93)
C  Read tax rates, etc.
      PRINT *,'Current rate of tax (%)? '
      READ *,TAXRTE
      PRINT *,'Current insurance deduction rate (%)? '
      READ *,INSRTE
      PRINT *,'Maximum gross pay for insurance? '
      READ *,INSMAX
C  Convert percentages to fractions
      TAXRTE=0.01*TAXRTE
      INSRTE=0.01*INSRTE
C  Main loop to update payroll data
      DO 10, I=1,MAXSTF
         READ (5,'(I4,2X,F3.0,1X,F2.0)') STFNUM,HRS,MINS
C  Check for end of data
         IF (STFNUM.EQ.0) GOTO 11
C  Update file and print payslip
         CALL UPDATE(STFNUM,HRS+MINS/60.0)
   10 CONTINUE
C  No terminator
      PRINT 294,MAXSTF
   11 STOP
C  Error during file opening
   91 PRINT 291,DATA
      STOP
   92 PRINT 292
      STOP
   93 PRINT 293
      STOP
  291 FORMAT(1H1,'**** Error during opening of weekly data file ',
     *       A20/1H0,'Processing terminated')
  292 FORMAT(1H1,'**** Error during opening of payslips file PAYSLIPS'/
     *       1H0,'Processing terminated')
  293 FORMAT(1H1,'**** Error during opening of master file ',
     *       'WEEKLY-PAYROLL'/1H0,'Processing terminated')
  294 FORMAT(1H1,'**** Error in weekly data'/1H ,'Maximum permitted ',
     *       'number of records (',I5,') read with no terminator'/
     *       1H0,'Some employees may not have been paid!')
      END
```

```
              SUBROUTINE UPDATE(NUMBER,HOURS)
C
C  This subroutine updates an employee's master record
C  and prints his payslip
C
C  Dummy arguments
        INTEGER NUMBER
        REAL HOURS
C  COMMON block declarations
        REAL TAXRTE,INSRTE,INSMAX
        COMMON /TAXINS/TAXRTE,INSRTE,INSMAX
C  Employee master file record
        CHARACTER*20 NAME
        REAL STDHRS,HRATE,ORATE,ALLOW,CUMGRS,CUMALL,CUMTAX,CUMINS,CUMNET
C  Miscellaneous variables
        REAL GROSS,TAX,WKTAX,WKINS,PAY
C  Get employee's record
        READ (7,REC=NUMBER) NAME,STDHRS,HRATE,ORATE,ALLOW,CUMGRS,
     *       CUMALL,CUMTAX,CUMINS,CUMNET
C  Calculate gross pay
        IF (HOURS.GT.STDHRS) THEN
          GROSS=HRATE*STDHRS+ORATE*(HOURS-STDHRS)
        ELSE
          GROSS=HRATE*HOURS
        END IF
C  Calculate tax due
        CUMGRS=CUMGRS+GROSS
        CUMALL=CUMALL+ALLOW
        TAX=TAXRTE*(CUMGRS-CUMALL)
        WKTAX=TAX-CUMTAX
C  Calculate insurance deduction
        IF (GROSS.GT.INSMAX) THEN
          WKINS=INSRTE*INSMAX
        ELSE
          WKINS=INSRTE*GROSS
        END IF
C  Calculate nett pay
        PAY=GROSS-(WKTAX+WKINS)
C  Print payslip
        WRITE (6,200) NAME,NUMBER,GROSS,WKTAX,WKINS,PAY
  200 FORMAT (1H1,A20,4X,I6/1H0,F8.2,2(5X,F8.2)/1H0,10X,F8.2)
C  Update master file
        WRITE (7,REC=NUMBER) NAME,STDHRS,HRATE,ORATE,ALLOW,CUMGRS,
     *       CUMALL,TAX,CUMINS+WKINS,CUMNET+PAY
        RETURN
        END
```

The main points to notice in this program are that the subroutine UPDATE reads the employee's record and that a record length of 56 has been defined for the master file. Each record consists of the 20-character name and nine real items; a comment at the start of the program states that the units of length are *assumed* to be 1 and 4 for the two types of storage unit.

Thus NAME requires 20 units and each of the other nine items requires 4 units, giving a total of 56.

The other point is that we need a terminator for the data; the program assumes a staff number of 0, which can be provided by a blank terminator record.

This program works correctly but it does have two deficiencies, one major and the other minor. The first is that the same file is used throughout and is updated record by record. If an error should occur (for example, owing to a data error or a machine breakdown) the file will be left in a partially updated state. This is not good practice, and it is always advisable to keep the original version of the file unaltered. This implies copying the file, which will lead us into problems if there are any employees who did not work and for whom no (null) record was submitted, as their records would not be copied and they would disappear from the master file! The solution is either to keep an index of all employees on file and to read each employee who is paid, and then to copy any unpaid employees' records at the end, or to copy the complete file at the start of the program and update this copy.

The second deficiency concerns the record numbers. The standard merely states that these must be positive integers; however, many implementations assume that they will run upwards from 1 to a 'reasonable' number. If this is the case, then a system based on arbitrary numbers may cause problems and we shall need to use a different value for the record number – based, presumably, on the staff number, since this is the only identifying item in the weekly input data.

There are a number of ways of doing this but all will essentially involve producing a table containing staff numbers and corresponding record numbers. The most efficient way is to use a **hashing** technique to create a **hash table**. This is a means whereby an identifier is converted into an integer in a given range (the size of the table). The algorithm used to carry out this conversion will vary depending upon the type of problem, but for our purposes a simple algorithm will serve to demonstrate the principle.

We shall define a table of size MAXSTF and use the *remainder* after dividing the staff number by MAXSTF as a subscript to the table. If this element is already occupied we shall increase the subscript by one and try again. The process is repeated until a vacant element is found; if the end of the table is reached then the search continues from the beginning. A hash table is ideally suited for both the insertion and retrieval of information, but not for its deletion since the appearance of blank elements could upset any subsequent use of the table unless it is completely recreated. In our case the insertion (and if necessary any deletion and reconstruction) will be done by whatever program is used to add employees to the file, and the table will be used in this program only to obtain the record number for a particular employee.

Our table will contain a zero for every element that is unoccupied and the staff number for every element that is occupied. By negating the value of the staff number when the employee's record is updated we can also use the same table at the end of the program to deal with any employees who were not paid because no details of their hours worked were submitted. The table will, of course, be stored in a file and read from there at the start of processing.

The revised program is as follows:

```
      PROGRAM PAYRL2
C
C  This program deals with the weekly payroll
C
C  Weekly data is input in the following format:
C
C     Staff number:  cols 1-4
C     Hours worked:  hrs in cols 7-9;  mins in cols 11,12
C
C  Weekly data is read from a file on unit 5
C  Payslips are written to a file called PAYSLIPS on unit 6
C  The master file is on unit 7
C  The new master file is on unit 8
C  The employee hash file is called EMPLOYEES and is on unit 9
C     Note this program assumes 1 unit per character storage unit,
C                               4 units per numeric storage unit
C
C  The old and new master file names, and initial data concerning
C  current tax rates, etc. is requested from the standard input unit
C
C  Any error messages are sent to the standard output unit
C
C  Maximum number of employees
      INTEGER MAXSTF
      PARAMETER (MAXSTF=5000)
C  COMMON block declarations
      REAL TAXRTE,INSRTE,INSMAX
      COMMON /TAXINS/TAXRTE,INSRTE,INSMAX
      INTEGER RECNUM(MAXSTF)
      COMMON /HASH/RECNUM
C  Miscellaneous variables
      CHARACTER*20 OLDFIL,NEWFIL,DATA
      INTEGER STFNUM,I
      REAL HRS,MINS
C
C  Get old and new master file names and open them
      PRINT *,'Name of old master file? '
      READ '(A)',OLDFIL
      PRINT *,'Name of new master file? '
      READ '(A)',NEWFIL
      OPEN (7,FILE=OLDFIL,STATUS='OLD',ACCESS='DIRECT',RECL=56,
     *     ERR=93)
      OPEN (8,FILE=NEWFIL,ACCESS='DIRECT',RECL=56,ERR=94)
```

```
C  Open hash table file, and read hash table
       OPEN (9,FILE='EMPLOYEES',STATUS='OLD',FORM='UNFORMATTED',ERR=95)
       READ (9) RECNUM
C  Get data file name and open it
       PRINT *,'Name of this week''s data file? '
       READ '(A)',DATA
       OPEN (5,FILE=DATA,STATUS='OLD',ERR=91)
C  Open payslips file
       OPEN (6,FILE='PAYSLIPS',STATUS='NEW',ERR=92)
C  Read tax rates, etc.
       PRINT *,'Current rate of tax (%)? '
       READ *,TAXRTE
       PRINT *,'Current insurance deduction rate (%)? '
       READ *,INSRTE
       PRINT *,'Maximum gross pay for insurance? '
       READ *,INSMAX
C  Convert percentages to fractions
       TAXRTE=0.01*TAXRTE
       INSRTE=0.01*INSRTE
C  Main loop to update payroll data
       DO 10, I=1,MAXSTF
          READ (5,'(I4,2X,F3.0,1X,F2.0)') STFNUM,HRS,MINS
C  Check for end of data
          IF (STFNUM.EQ.0) GOTO 11
C  Update file and print payslip
          CALL UPDATE(STFNUM,HRS+MINS/60.0)
   10 CONTINUE
C  No terminator
       PRINT 296,MAXSTF
C  All payroll data processed - check for any unpaid employees
   11 DO 20, I=1,MAXSTF
C  Any positive elements in the hash table represent employees whose
C  records have not been updated - i.e. they were not paid this week
C  Update their records with zero hours worked
          IF (RECNUM(I).GT.0) CALL UPDATE(RECNUM(I),0.0)
   20 CONTINUE
       STOP
C  Error during file opening
   91 PRINT 291,DATA
       STOP
   92 PRINT 292
       STOP
   93 PRINT 293,OLDFIL
       STOP
   94 PRINT 294,NEWFIL
       STOP
   95 PRINT 295
  291 FORMAT(1H1,'**** Error during opening of weekly data file ',
     *       A20/1H0,'Processing terminated')
  292 FORMAT(1H1,'**** Error during opening of payslips file PAYSLIPS'/
     *       1H0,'Processing terminated')
  293 FORMAT(1H1,'**** Error during opening of old master file ',A20/
     *       1H0,'Processing terminated')
```

```
      294 FORMAT(1H1,'**** Error during opening of new master file ',A20/
          *         1H0,'Processing terminated')
      295 FORMAT(1H1,'**** Error during opening of employee hash file ',
          *         'EMPLOYEES'/1H0,'Processing terminated')
      296 FORMAT(1H1,'**** Error in weekly data'/1H ,'Maximum permitted ',
          *         'number of records (',I5,') read with no terminator'/
          *         1H0,'Some employees may not have been paid!')
          END

          SUBROUTINE UPDATE(NUMBER,HOURS)
C
C This subroutine updates an employee's master record
C and prints his payslip
C
C Dummy arguments
          INTEGER NUMBER
          REAL HOURS
C COMMON block declarations
          REAL TAXRTE,INSRTE,INSMAX
          COMMON/TAXINS/TAXRTE,INSRTE,INSMAX
C Employee master file record
          CHARACTER*20 NAME
          REAL STDHRS,HRATE,ORATE,ALLOW,CUMGRS,CUMALL,CUMTAX,CUMINS,CUMNET
C KEY is an integer function that finds an employee in the hash table
          INTEGER KEY,RECORD
          EXTERNAL KEY
C Miscellaneous variables
          REAL GROSS,TAX,WKTAX,WKINS,PAY
C Get master file record number for this employee
          RECORD=KEY(NUMBER)
C Get employee's record
          READ (7,REC=RECORD) NAME,STDHRS,HRATE,ORATE,ALLOW,CUMGRS,
          *      CUMALL,CUMTAX,CUMINS,CUMNET
C Calculate gross pay
          IF (HOURS.GT.STDHRS) THEN
            GROSS=HRATE*STDHRS+ORATE*(HOURS-STDHRS)
          ELSE
            GROSS=HRATE*HOURS
          END IF
C Calculate tax due
          CUMGRS=CUMGRS+GROSS
          CUMALL=CUMALL+ALLOW
          TAX=TAXRTE*(CUMGRS-CUMALL)
          WKTAX=TAX-CUMTAX
C Calculate insurance deduction
          IF (GROSS.GT.INSMAX) THEN
            WKINS=INSRTE*INSMAX
          ELSE
            WKINS=INSRTE*GROSS
          END IF
C Calculate nett pay
          PAY=GROSS-(WKTAX+WKINS)
C Print payslip
          WRITE (6,200) NAME,NUMBER,GROSS,WKTAX,WKINS,PAY
      200 FORMAT (1H1,A20,4X,I6/1H0,F8.2,2(5X,F8.2)/1H0,10X,F8.2)
```

```
C   Update master file
        WRITE (8,REC=RECORD) NAME,STDHRS,HRATE,ORATE,ALLOW,CUMGRS,
       *         CUMALL,TAX,CUMINS+WKINS,CUMNET+PAY
        RETURN
        END

        INTEGER FUNCTION KEY(NUMBER)
C
C   This function returns the position in a hash table of NUMBER
C
C   Dummy argument
        INTEGER NUMBER
C   Common block declaration for hash table
        INTEGER MAXSTF
        PARAMETER (MAXSTF=5000)
        INTEGER RECNUM(MAXSTF)
        COMMON /HASH/RECNUM
C   Miscellaneous variables
        INTEGER I,START
C   Calculate initial point for searching
        START=MOD(NUMBER,MAXSTF)+1
C   Search from there to end of table
        DO 10, I=START,MAXSTF
          IF (RECNUM(I).EQ.NUMBER) THEN
C   Employee found
            GOTO 50
          ELSE IF (RECNUM(I).EQ.0) THEN
C   Empty cell - therefore no entry for this employee
            GOTO 99
          END IF
  10 CONTINUE
C   Not yet found - so search rest of table
        DO 20, I=1,START-1
          IF (RECNUM(I).EQ.NUMBER) THEN
C   Employee found
            GOTO 50
          ELSE IF (RECNUM(I).EQ.0) THEN
C   Empty cell - therefore no entry for this employee
            GOTO 99
          END IF
  20 CONTINUE
C   Employee's staff number not in table - print error and stop
  99 PRINT 299,NUMBER
 299 FORMAT(1H1,'*** Error - Employee number ',I4,' not on file'/
       *       1H0,'Processing terminated')
        STOP
C   Staff number found - set entry negative and return index as KEY
  50 RECNUM(I)=-RECNUM(I)
        KEY=I
        RETURN
        END
```

Notice that the hash table search starts from the initial guess and proceeds to the end of the array. If a zero is found then it means that the employee cannot be on file. In a full hash table system, with both entry and retrieval, the employee would be entered in the table at this point. If neither the correct number nor a blank is found then the table is searched from the beginning up to the start point.

When a match is made the index to the array is kept as the record number and the entry in the table is negated. Finally, when all the data has been read, the hash table should consist of zeros and negated staff numbers. Any positive entries have not been paid and so UPDATE is called to calculate their pay (that is, a tax refund) on the basis of 0 hours worked. Since this simplified system does not add any new entries to the hash table it is not necessary to save it at the end of the run.

Since the program copies all the records from the old file (7) to the new file (8), any failure can be dealt with by re-running the complete job from the old file.

17.6 The INQUIRE statement

For most purposes the statements already described will enable a program to carry out any file operations it requires. There are, however, occasions, especially when writing a general-purpose subroutine, when it would be useful to find out, or check up on, the various details that are applicable to files (for example, whether they are formatted or connected for direct access). This can be achieved by means of a special statement that can provide any required information of this nature about a file:

```
INQUIRE (list)
```

(Note the spelling.) This statement allows the program to enquire about a file that is defined by name or that is connected to a named unit. In the first case the list (see Figure 17.9) must contain a FILE specifier and no UNIT specifier, while in the second case there must be a UNIT specifier and no FILE specifier. Any of the other specifiers may appear at most once.

Several of these specifiers (ACCESS, FORM, RECL, BLANK) are similar to those used in an OPEN statement but have the reverse effect. Thus

```
ACCESS=acc
```

will cause the character variable *acc* to be assigned the value 'SEQUENTIAL' or 'DIRECT' as appropriate. If no file is connected then *acc* becomes undefined.

Figure 17.9
Specifiers for use with
INQUIRE.

```
UNIT=u or u or FILE=fn

EXIST=lex
OPENED=lop
NUMBER=num
NAMED=lnm
NAME=fn
ACCESS=acc
SEQUENTIAL=seq
DIRECT=dir
FORM=fm
FORMATTED=fmt
UNFORMATTED=unf
RECL=len
NEXTREC=nr
BLANK=bl
ERR=s
IOSTAT=ios
```

Similarly

FORM=*fm*

causes the character variable *fm* to be assigned the value `'FORMATTED'` or
`'UNFORMATTED'`, or to become undefined;

RECL=*len*

causes the integer variable *len* to be assigned the record length of the file if
it is connected for direct access, or to become undefined otherwise; and

BLANK=*bl*

causes the character variable *bl* to be assigned the value `'ZERO'` if blanks are
to be treated as zeros and `'NULL'` if they are to be ignored; if there is no
connection, or if the file is not formatted then *bl* becomes undefined.

The SEQUENTIAL, DIRECT, FORMATTED and UNFORMATTED specifiers provide
a way of determining what is *allowed* with a file, regardless of whether it is
connected. In each case the character variable is assigned the value `'YES'`,
`'NO'` or `'UNKNOWN'`. Thus

DIRECT=*dir*

will cause the character variable *dir* to be assigned the value `'YES'` if direct
access is allowed on this file, `'NO'` if it is not allowed, and `'UNKNOWN'` if the
processor cannot determine whether it is allowed or not.

The EXIST specifier allows a program to determine if a file (or unit) exists. If it does then the logical variable *lex* is set *true*; if it does not then it is set *false*.

OPENED is somewhat similar and sets the logical variable *lop* to *true* if the specified file is connected to some unit, or to some file; otherwise it is set *false*.

NAMED also assigns a value to a logical variable; in this case *lnm* is set *true* if the file has a name, otherwise it is set *false*.

Closely related to these specifiers are NUMBER and NAME. NUMBER causes the integer variable *num* to be assigned the number of the unit currently connected to the specified file, while NAME causes the character variable *fn* to be assigned the name of the file currently connected to the specified unit. In both cases if no unit or file is connected (or in the latter case if the file has no name) then the variable becomes undefined. Thus we may write

```
      INQUIRE (FILE='MYFILE',OPENED=LOP,NUMBER=N)
      IF (LOP) THEN
C  MYFILE is opened and connected to unit N
        .
        .
        .

      ELSE
        OPEN (7,FILE='MYFILE')
      END IF
        .
        .
```

Finally the NEXTREC specifier sets the integer variable *nr* to the value *n+1*, where *n* is the record number of the last record read or written to the file if it is connected for direct access; if no records have yet been written or read then *nr* is set to 1. If the file is not connected for direct access, or if its position is indeterminate because of an error, then *nr* is undefined.

INQUIRE will normally only be used in certain specialized situations, where it can be extremely useful. One more general situation, however, could be to avoid the necessity of reading the file names in a program such as the payroll program developed in Example 17.3. For example, a cycle of three files could be used in such a way that the oldest was deleted at the end of each run. At the beginning of execution, therefore, only two of the three files will exist. INQUIRE can be used to establish which two exist and then use this knowledge to open the correct files. The following subroutine will do this:

```
      SUBROUTINE OPNFIL
C
C  This subroutine opens three files in a Grandfather, Father, Son
C  file cycle
C
C  Unit 7 is the old master file
```

```
C  Unit 8 is the new master file and does not yet exist
C  Unit 15 is not used on this run, but should be deleted at the end
C          of an error-free run
C
C  Miscellaneous variables
       INTEGER U(3),I
       LOGICAL F(3)
C  File names
       CHARACTER*20 FILE(3)
       DATA FILE/'MASTERFILE-1','MASTERFILE-2','MASTERFILE-3'/
C  Establish which files exist
       DO 10, I=1,3
          INQUIRE (FILE=FILE(I),EXIST=F(I))
    10 CONTINUE
C  Now set unit numbers
       IF (F(1).AND.F(2)) THEN
C  Files 1 and 2 exist;  3 should not
          IF (F(3)) GOTO 99
          U(1)=15
          U(2)=7
          U(3)=8
       ELSE IF (F(2).AND.F(3)) THEN
C  Files 2 and 3 exist;  1 should not
          IF (F(1)) GOTO 99
          U(2)=15
          U(3)=7
          U(1)=8
       ELSE IF (F(3).AND.F(1)) THEN
C  Files 3 and 1 exist;  2 should not
          IF (F(2)) GOTO 99
          U(3)=15
          U(1)=7
          U(2)=8
       ELSE
C  No combination of two files exists
          GOTO 99
       END IF
C  Open all three files
       DO 20, I=1,3
          OPEN (UNIT=U(I),FILE=FILE(I),ACCESS='DIRECT',RECL=56,ERR=98)
    20 CONTINUE
       RETURN
C  Error during opening
    98 PRINT 298,FILE(I)
   298 FORMAT (1H1,'**** Error during opening of ',A20/
      *         1H0,'Processing terminated')
       STOP
C  Wrong number of files exist
    99 PRINT 299,(FILE(I),F(I),I=1,3)
   299 FORMAT (1H1,'**** Invalid file combination:'//
      *         1H ,6X,'File name',5X,'Exists',/
      *       3(1H ,A20,3X,L1/),
      *         1H ,'Processing terminated')
       STOP
       END
```

Figure 17.10
Error table produced by
subroutine OPNFIL.

```
**** Invalid file combination:

        File name        Exists
MASTERFILE-1               T
MASTERFILE-2               F
MASTERFILE-3               F

Processing terminated
```

This subroutine opens all three files so that unit 8 is the one that did not previously exist, unit 7 is the more recent of the other two (in cyclic order) and unit 15 is the remaining one. At the end of the program, after a successful execution, there should be the additional statement

```
CLOSE(15,STATUS='DELETE')
```

If there are not exactly two existing files an error will be produced in the form of a truth table – see Figure 17.10. Each time the program is run the updated master file created by the last run will be used as the old master file and a new one will be created. Thus the program itself will ensure that an orderly cycle is maintained. In the event of an error all three files will remain and the programmer can delete the appropriate one. If there is no error then the oldest of the three files is deleted at the end of the program.

SUMMARY

- Additional edit descriptors may be used to override default treatment of blank characters on input or signs on output.

- Files may be internal, as well as sequential or direct access.

- An internal file is a character variable or array.

- An internal file enables the edit descriptors used in formatting to be used to convert an item in memory into another format.

- The records in a direct access file can be written or read in any order.

- A hash table is a convenient method of storing a random set of identifying names for subsequent retrieval.

- The INQUIRE statement enables a program to establish details about files at execution time.

- Fortran 77 statements introduced in Chapter 17:

Input/output statements	*read/write* (*direct access cilist*) *input list*
	for example READ (7,REC=N) A,B,C
File enquiry statement	INQUIRE (*enquiry list*)

SELF-TEST EXERCISES 17.2

1 Find out the units in which the size of a direct access record is measured on your computer system, and the number of units used for the storage of the two different types of Fortran 77 storage unit (numeric and character). Also find out if there are any restrictions on the values of record numbers for direct access files.

2 What is the length of the record written by the following statements *on your computer system*?

```
    .
    .
REAL A(10),B
INTEGER J,K,L,RECNO
DOUBLE PRECISION P,Q
COMPLEX Z1,Z2
LOGICAL FLAG(5)
CHARACTER*20 STRING
    .
    .
WRITE (7,REC=RECNO) RECNO,A,P,J,K,STRING,Z1,FLAG
    .
    .
```

3 What is a hash table? And how is it used?

4 What will be printed by the following program fragment?

```
    .
    .
CHARACTER FILNAM*20
INTEGER U
LOGICAL OPEN
    .
    .
INQUIRE (FILE=FILNAM,NUMBER=U,OPENED=OPEN)
IF (OPEN) THEN
   PRINT *,FILNAM,'(',U,')'
ELSE
   INQUIRE (UNIT=U,NAME=FILNAM,OPENED=OPEN)
   IF (OPEN) PRINT *,FILNAM,'(',U,')'
END IF
    .
    .
```

PROGRAMMING EXERCISES

17.1   Even on a computer without graphics facilities, simple plots can be produced by, for instance, printing an asterisk in the appropriate column of the screen to represent a point. Use this technique to make a plot of the function $y = \cos x$ for x taking values from 0 to 4π radians. Can you make the x-axis run across the page instead of down?

17.2   Write and test a subroutine that prints a real number X, using a field width of 8, according to the following rules:

   (i) if $X = \text{INT}(X)$ then the number should be displayed as an integer;
   (ii) otherwise if it is possible, X should be printed in fixed point format to at least three significant figures;
   (iii) otherwise X should be printed in floating-point format to as many decimal places as will fit in the space available.

17.3   Write a program that asks the user for the name of a file and then writes the alphabet, as 26 elements of a CHARACTER array, to the file. The program should check to see if the file already exists, and if it does it should inform the user and request a new name (which should also be checked in the same way).
   Test the program by running it twice with exactly the same filename supplied as input.

17.4   Write a program to calculate the values of y, where $y = e^x \sin x$, for x varying from 0 to 20 in steps of 0.5. Write the output to a file in the form of a table containing the values of x and y. Use the G format edit descriptor for your values of y.

17.5   Write a program that will act as an integer calculator. The program should read a numerical expression involving the operators +, −, * and / and ending with =, and then display the result.

*17.6   The following data was stored in a file for Exercise 10.6. If this file is no longer available then type it in again.

12.36	0.004	1.3536E12	2320.326
13.24	0.008	2.4293E15	5111.116
15.01	0.103	9.9879E11	˄3062.329
11.83	0.051	6.3195E13	8375.145
14.00	0.001	8.0369E14	1283.782

Write a program that reads each line of the file as one long character string. The program should then use an internal file to extract the four numbers from each line and store them in one row of a matrix as real numbers. Finally, the program should calculate the mean of each column of the matrix.

17.7   A census has been carried out on the population of Smalltown, during which the following data was collected:

Name	Age	Address	Economic status
S.T.Shaw	26	10, High Street	A
A.M.Jones	56	2, Largeville Road	B
C.D.Jones	54	2, Largeville Road	B
S.B.Taylor	32	7, High Street	D
P.K.Smith	72	5, Largeville Road	C
T.T.Bloggs	44	8, High Street,	E

Enter this information into a file. Write a program that reads the file and provides the user of the program with the following options:

(i) He can obtain the address of a named person.
(ii) He can obtain the age of a named person.
(iii) He can obtain the names of people with a given economic status.

17.8   Modify the program you wrote for Exercise 17.7 to allow you to add new census data to the file.

17.9   Use the file described in Exercise 17.7 as a direct access file. Write' a program that reorders the records in the datafile according to age, with the youngest first, and write the reordered data back to the same file.

17.10   Where a large database is being processed, it is often neither possible nor appropriate to read all the data from a file into the computer's memory. In these cases the data should be stored in a direct access file in such a way that the record can easily be identified and read whenever it is required. The second solution for Example 17.3 (PAYRL2) illustrated how a hash table could be used to identify the correct record quickly. However, that example did not provide the means for inserting and/or deleting entries in the hash table. Write a program which will do this. Your program should

(a) *for insertion* read the staff number and then find the first vacant position in the hash table (using the hashing method used in the previous program). If there is a vacant position, and the staff number is not already in the table (human errors can occur!), then the appropriate entry should be made in the table and the current payroll details should be read and written to the master file;

(b) *for deletion* read the staff number and find its entry in the hash table. The corresponding record in the master file can easily be deleted, but deleting the entry from the hash table is not necessarily straightforward. Remember that simply deleting it might mean that another entry which originally selected this position, and then used another because it was already in use, would then fail to be found by the hashing routine. There are several possibilities – see if you can find a satisfactory one.

17.11 Data obtained from separate runs of the same experiment are usually stored in different files. The data shown below represents the results of four experiments that each measure the length (*x*) of a support girder five times:

Experiment 1	Experiment 2	Experiment 3	Experiment 4
15.523	15.518	15.538	15.529
15.534	15.536	15.526	15.541
15.519	15.544	15.545	15.530
15.525	15.527	15.550	15.539
15.532	15.549	15.519	15.532

Type each column of data into a separate file.

Now write a program that uses a subroutine to open all four files on different unit numbers. When the user supplies a name of a file to be opened, the subroutine should check that the file is not already open. All the data should then be read by the main program, and the mean length ($\bar{x}$) calculated, together with the standard deviation from the mean length (σ) for each experiment using the formulae

$$\bar{x} = \sum_{i=1}^{N} \frac{1}{N} x_i$$

$$\sigma = \sqrt{\frac{1}{N} \sum_{i=1}^{N} (x_i - \bar{x})^2}$$

17.12 (a) Write a program to sort an unformatted direct access file containing a set of real numbers, without reading the numbers into an array.

(b) If a file of numbers were too large to fit into the memory of the computer then the program written in answer to part (a) could be used to sort it. However, in such cases, speed of sorting would be important. Write a program to sort such a file, taking this factor into account.

*17.13 The second program developed for Example 17.3 (PAYRL2) uses a master direct access file to store the employee details, and a sequential file to store the hash table which identified the record structure of the master file. In order to transfer the files to a different type of computer it is necessary to be able to convert the direct access file into a sequential file, and vice versa.

Write a program that will read the names of the three files (direct access master, sequential hash table and sequential master) and will check that they are of the correct type.

For transfer from direct access to sequential, each record of the direct access file should form a record of the sequential file, except that there is an extra integer item at the start of the sequential record containing the direct access record number.

For transfer from sequential to direct access, each record of the sequential file contains an integer item as the first item representing the direct access record number; the remainder of the record should then be copied to that record in the direct access file and the hash table recreated from the same information.

Test your program with a direct access file and hash table created by the program you wrote for Exercise 17.10.

17.14 In the card game bridge, the strength of a hand is decided by the 'point count' system:

Ace = 4 points
King = 3 points
Queen = 2 points
Jack = 1 point
Other cards count nothing.

A file contains a bridge hand, stored as follows:

AK32
QT94
83
AJ7

where the Spades are on the first line, the Hearts on the second, Diamonds on the third and Clubs on the last. The abbreviations used are A = Ace, K = King, Q = Queen, J = Jack, T = Ten and other cards stored as their face value.

A hand is worthy of an opening bid if its total point count is 12 or more. Write a program to read a hand from a file as above, evaluate the point count and decide if it is suitable for an opening bid. (Bridge experts may like to extend their program to recommend a suitable bid!)

More about numerical methods

This chapter can be omitted by those with no interest in numerical applications, or who have omitted Chapter 11.

Following on from the discussion in Chapter 11 of the bisection method for the solution of non-linear equations, the **secant method** and **Newton's method**, are introduced and shown to have significant advantages over the earlier method, although each has its own areas of weakness as well.

Gaussian elimination is next introduced as a means of solving a set of simultaneous linear equations, followed by a special case – that of a **tridiagonal system**.

The next topic discussed is the fitting of a **cubic spline** through a set of random data points, and it is shown that the problem can be reduced to a tridiagonal system. A cubic spline interpolation procedure is presented utilizing the earlier results. As an example of a quite different approach to curve-fitting, the **Ellis–McLain algorithm**, which uses only local data points, is then discussed and a Fortran 77 implementation developed.

The final numerical technique demonstrated is that of integration using **Simpson's rule**, which is shown to be particularly accurate for curves interpolated using a cubic spline technique.

18.1   Numerical methods and their limitations

In Chapter 11 basic concepts involved in numerical computation were introduced and it was emphasized that, owing to such effects as *round-off*, *conditioning*, and *stability* the choice of the numerical method to be used could substantially affect the result obtained in a particular case. It is not intended to discuss these concepts any further in this book, but it is important that the programmer should be aware of the strengths and weaknesses of different methods before deciding which one to use in a particular situation. This is particularly relevant when using a sophisticated mathematical library such as the NAG library (NAG Ltd, 1988), in which there are often a large number of subroutines that, to the uninitiated, will all appear to carry out the same type of calculation.

In Chapter 11 DOUBLE PRECISION variables were discussed as a means of improving the precision of calculations, but it was emphasized that the effect of using double precision may be quite different on different computers, even where intuition might indicate that the machines would be of comparable accuracy. This is an extremely important aspect of writing programs that are to be used by many others apart from the programmer, or even by the programmer on a number of different computers, but it is a topic that is beyond the scope of this book. It should, however, be

F90 mentioned that Fortran 90 has added facilities designed to ensure that programs can be transferred between computers without these particular problems related to precision.

Chapter 14 showed how Fortran arrays could be used to implement vectors and matrices, and demonstrated the implementation of some simple matrix operations.

Chapter 11 introduced two simple but widely used techniques in numerical programming, namely the *method of least squares* for fitting a straight line as an approximation to a set of data points and the *bisection method* for the solution of a non-linear equation.

In this chapter we shall examine other methods of solution of non-linear equations, and will also consider how to solve systems of (simultaneous) linear equations. We shall also look at more sophisticated methods of interpolation and curve-fitting in which the data does not necessarily lie on a straight line. Finally methods of integration will be briefly discussed – for example, to find the area under a curve.

It is important to emphasize, however, that most of the subprograms developed in this chapter are only examples to illustrate the basic techniques. A great deal of effort has been expended by many people over many years in refining algorithms for numerical computation, especially to deal with the difficult cases, and anyone who has a serious need in this area should use procedures from one of the established libraries and not write their own.

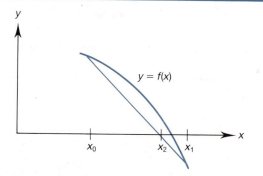

Figure 18.1
The secant method for a
bracketing interval.

18.2   The secant method for solving non-linear equations

The bisection method introduced in Section 11.5 has one major strength and one major weakness. The strength is that, because the interval is halved at each iteration, it is guaranteed to converge after a finite, and predictable, number of iterations. The weakness of the method, however, is that it is often slow to converge. One of the reasons for this is that the method does not use all the available information, since it uses only the sign of $f(x)$ at the end-points of the interval, not the value of $f(x)$ at those points. Another weakness is that, for the method to work at all, the two initial points must bracket a root. A variation of the bisection method that overcomes these weaknesses is known as the **secant method**; however, it has its own weaknesses, as we shall see.

The secant method uses the values of $f(x)$ at the two end-points of the interval to calculate the intersection of the line joining these two points with the axis, and uses the x-coordinate of this point of intersection as the end-point of the next interval (see Figures 18.1 and 18.2).

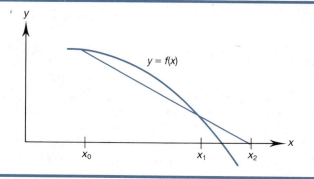

Figure 18.2
The secant method for a
non-bracketing interval.

Figure 18.3
A failure position for the
secant method.

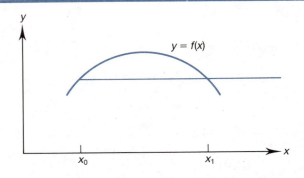

It is easy to deduce that if f_1 is the value of $f(x)$ when x has the value x_1, then:

$$x_2 = \frac{x_0 f_1 - x_1 f_0}{f_1 - f_0}$$

or:

$$x_2 = x_1 - \frac{(x_1 - x_0) f_1}{f_1 - f_0}$$

One potential problem is immediately apparent, namely the situation where f_0 and f_1 are the same, or very close to each other. This corresponds to the position shown in Figure 18.3, and clearly will cause the method to fail, since the line joining the two end-points is parallel or almost parallel to the x-axis.

Although less obvious intuitively than the situation shown in Figure 18.3, there are other situations in which the secant method may not converge, and for which another method may be better. It is thus imperative that the conditional DO loop used to control the iteration should have a sensible maximum iteration count, so that another method can be tried in the unlikely event that the secant method will not produce a solution.

The only remaining problem is the determination of the form of convergence criterion to be used. In the bisection method we used the size of the interval, which we showed to be related to the difference between the approximation to the root and its true value. However, the secant method does not necessarily lead to an interval size that tends to zero, since when it is close to a root one end-point will move ever closer to the root, while the other one does not move. The appropriate criterion in this case is therefore the difference between two successive estimates of the value of the root.

EXAMPLE 18.1

Write a program to find a root of the equation $f(x) = 0$ using the secant method. The program should use an external function to define the equation, and the user should input the accuracy required and the x-coordinates of two points within the range in which roots are to be sought that can be used as starting points for the interpolation.

This is a very similar problem to that in Example 11.2, which used the bisection method; since the method itself is very similar, the structure plan and the subsequent program will bear a strong resemblance to those developed in Example 11.2.

The main program will be essentially the same as in the earlier example and so we shall not bother with it here. One improvement that we can make, however, is to pass the function F as an argument, as described in Section 16.2. The structure plan for the subroutine might be as follows:

SECANT(F,X0,X1,T,ROOT,COUNT)

1 Repeat MAX times
  1.1 Calculate F0 and F1, the values of F(X0) and F(X1)
  1.2 If $|F0-F1|<e$, where e is a very small number, then exit with COUNT set to -1
  1.3 Calculate new end-point (X2) of interval,
    where $X2 = X1-(X1-X0)*F1/(F1-F0)$
  1.4 If $|X2-X1|<T$ then exit with root=X2
  1.5 Set X0=X1 and X1=X2

2 Set COUNT to number of iterations to indicate failure to converge

The program can now be written, and is very similar to the program in Example 11.2.

```
      PROGRAM ROOT
C
C  This program calculates a root of the equation F(X)=0 by use of the
C  secant method.
C
C  The function F(X) is supplied as an external function
      REAL F
      EXTERNAL F
C  Local variables
      REAL X0,X1,TOLER,ROOT
      INTEGER COUNT
C
```

```
C   Read range and tolerance
        PRINT *,'Type two values for X to use as the initial interval: '
        READ *,X0,X1
        PRINT *,'Type minimum difference for successive approximations: '
        READ *,TOLER
C   Call SECANT to find a root
        CALL SECANT(F,X0,X1,TOLER,ROOT,COUNT)
C   Check to see if a root was found
        IF (COUNT.EQ.0) THEN
C   Yes.  Print it
          PRINT 100,ROOT,F(ROOT)
C   No root was found.  Establish why, and print error message
        ELSE IF (COUNT.LT.0) THEN
C   Two points with almost the same y-coordinate
          PRINT 101,X0,F(X0),X1,F(X1)
        ELSE
C   MAX iterations without convergence
          PRINT 102,COUNT,X0,F(X0),X1,F(X1)
        END IF
        STOP
  100 FORMAT('A root was found at X =',F10.5,' (where Y =',F10.5,')')
  101 FORMAT('Further iteration not possible.  Last two points were'/
     *         '(',F10.5,',',F10.5,') and (',F10.5,',',F10.5,')')
  102 FORMAT(I5,' iterations have been carried out without reaching an'/
     *         'acceptable estimate.  The last two points were'/
     *         '(',F10.5,',',F10.5,') and (',F10.5,',',F10.5,')')
        END

        SUBROUTINE SECANT(F,X0,X1,T,ROOT,COUNT)
C
C   This subroutine attempts to find a root of the equation Y=F(X)
C   using the secant method.  Two initial values of X are supplied as
C   arguments, together with an acceptable tolerance for the result.
C
C   Dummy arguments
        EXTERNAL F
        REAL F,X0,X1,T,ROOT
        INTEGER COUNT
C   Parameters to control non-convergence
        INTEGER MAX
        REAL TINY
        PARAMETER (MAX=100,TINY=1E-6)
C   Local variables
        REAL F0,F1,DX,X2
        INTEGER I
C
C   Set up values of function at initial end-points
        F0=F(X0)
        F1=F(X1)
C   Loop until root found
        DO 10, I=1,MAX
C   Is this an acceptable basis for another iteration?
          IF (ABS(F1-F0).LT.TINY) THEN
C   No.  Set COUNT to -1 and return
            COUNT=-1
```

```
          RETURN
        END IF
C Yes.  Calculate next point
        DX=F1*(X1-X0)/(F1-F0)
        X2=X1-DX
C ** While testing print each estimate
        PRINT *,X2
C If iteration has converged sufficiently exit from loop
        IF (ABS(DX).LT.T) GOTO 11
C More iteration required - set new interval
        X0=X1
        X1=X2
        F0=F1
        F1=F(X1)
   10 CONTINUE
C MAX iterations without convergence.  Set COUNT to indicate failure
        COUNT=MAX
        RETURN
C A root was found.  Set COUNT to zero and return root
   11 COUNT=0
        ROOT=X2
        RETURN
        END
```

Note that, as in Example 11.2, we have included an extra PRINT statement
so that we can see each new estimate of the value of the root. Figure 18.4

(First run)

```
Type two values for X to use as the initial interval: -10,0
Type minimum difference for successive approximations: 1E-6
-9.0909469E-01
-6.0356605E-01
-5.6502097E-01
-5.6715720E-01
-5.6714332E-01
-5.6714326E-01
A root was found at X =  -0.56714 (where Y =   0.00000)
```

(Second run)

```
Type two values for X to use as the initial interval: 0,10
Type minimum difference for successive approximations: 1E-6
-4.5394897E-04
-9.0737140E-04
-5.0017523E-01
-5.5964893E-01
-5.6705147E-01
-5.6714314E-01
-5.6714326E-01
A root was found at X =  -0.56714 (where Y =   0.00000)
```

Figure 18.4
The solution of $x+e^x=0$
using SECANT.

Figure 18.5
A comparison of the
secant and bisection
iterations.

Estimates made by SECANT		Estimates made by BISECT	
(1)	−4.684781	(1)	0.0000000E+00
(2)	−4.398349	(2)	−5.000000
(3)	−5.8700084E−02	(3)	−2.500000
(4)	−7.8683245E−01	(4)	−1.2500000
(5)	−5.8827733E−01	(5)	−6.2500000E−01
(6)	−5.6633424E−01	(6)	−3.1250000E−01
(7)	−5.6714636E−01	(7)	−4.6875000E−01
(8)	−5.6714332E−01	(8)	−5.4687500E−01
(9)	−5.6714326E−01	(9)	−5.8593750E−01
		(10)	−5.6640625E−01
		(11)	−5.7617187E−01
		(12)	−5.7128906E−01
		(13)	−5.6884765E−01
		(14)	−5.6762695E−01
		(15)	−5.6701660E−01
		(16)	−5.6732177E−01
		(17)	−5.6716918E−01
		(18)	−5.6709289E−01
		(19)	−5.6713104E−01
		(20)	−5.6715011E−01
		(21)	−5.6714057E−01

shows the result of running this program twice, using different initial intervals; the same function subprogram defines the equation to be solved as was used in Example 11.2:

```
REAL FUNCTION F(X)
REAL X
F=X+EXP(X)
RETURN
END
```

It is interesting to examine the actual iterations carried out in these two cases. Figure 18.5 shows the successive estimates produced by BISECT and SECANT using the same initial interval: it can be seen very clearly that the secant method is much more efficient in this case than the bisection method, which frequently moves away from the root in the latter stages because of its inability to recognize that one of its end-points is very close to the root.

18.3   Newton's method for solving non-linear equations

Although the secant method usually provides a faster convergence than does the simple bisection method it is still not using all the available information. **Newton's method**, sometimes known as the **Newton–Raphson method**, uses the first derivative, or gradient, of the curve to help find the next approximation. Figure 18.6 shows how, given the gradient at a point x_i, it is easy to deduce a new estimate for the root.

From Figure 18.6 we can readily see that

$$x_{i+1} = OB$$

$$= OA - AB$$

$$= x_i \quad - AB$$

$$= x_i \quad - \frac{AC}{\tan \alpha}$$

$$= x_i \quad - \frac{f(x_i)}{f'(x_i)}$$

where $f'(x_i)$ is the gradient of the curve at the point C $(x_i, f(x_i))$, which is equal to $\tan \alpha$.

This formula is known as **Newton's iteration**, and is the basis for Newton's method of approximation to a root.

It is clear that the approach will be very similar to the secant method, except that only one point is needed to estimate the next one *as long as the first derivative of* f(x) *is available*. There will be situations in which the first derivative is not available, or would be very time-consuming to calculate, and in these situations Newton's method is not an appropriate

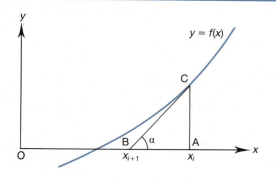

Figure 18.6
Newton's method of approximation.

one to choose. However, in many cases the derivative is readily available, and in these situations Newton's method will usually converge very rapidly. It should also be noted that this method will have the same problem that the secant method has in progressing beyond an estimate that lies on a point of the curve where the gradient is 0, or very close to it.

EXAMPLE 18.2

Write a program to find a root of the equation $f(x) = 0$ using Newton's method. The program should use external functions to define the equation and its first derivative, and the user should input the accuracy required and the x-coordinate of a point that can be used as the starting point for the interpolation.

Since Newton's method is very similar to the secant method, the structure plan and subsequent program will be based on those used in Example 18.1.

Our structure plan for the subroutine might be as follows:

NEWTON(F,DFDX,X,T,ROOT,COUNT)

1 Repeat MAX times
   1.1 Calculate gradient at X1 (GRAD=DFDX(X1))
   1.2 If |GRAD|<e, where e is a very small number, then exit with error code set
   1.3 Set X0 to X1 and calculate FX, the value of F(X) at X0
   1.3 Calculate X1 (=X0+FX/GRAD)
   1.4 If |X1−X0|<T then exit with root=X1

2 Set error code to MAX and exit

The program can now be written, and is based on that in Example 18.1.

```
      PROGRAM ROOT
C
C  This program calculates a root of the equation F(X)=0 by use of
C  Newton's method.
C
C  The function F(X) is supplied as an external function
C  The external function DFDX(X) returns the first derivative of F(X)
C
C  External functions
      REAL F,DFDX
      EXTERNAL F,DFDX
```

```
C  Local variables
       REAL X,TOLER,ROOT
       INTEGER COUNT
C
C  Read initial estimate and tolerance
       PRINT *,'Type a value to use as the initial approximation: '
       READ *,X
       PRINT *,'Type minimum difference for successive approximations: '
       READ *,TOLER
C  Call NEWTON to find a root
       CALL NEWTON(F,DFDX,X,TOLER,ROOT,COUNT)
C  Check to see if a root was found
       IF (COUNT.EQ.0) THEN
C  Yes.  Print it
          PRINT 100,ROOT,F(ROOT)
C  No root was found.  Establish why, and print error message
       ELSE IF (COUNT.LT.0) THEN
C  Gradient at current estimate is almost zero
          PRINT 101,X,F(X)
       ELSE
C  MAX iterations without convergence
          PRINT 102,COUNT,ROOT,F(ROOT),X,F(X)
       END IF
       STOP
  100 FORMAT('A root was found at X =',F10.5,' (where Y =',F10.5,')')
  101 FORMAT('Further iteration not possible.  Last approximation was'/
     *         '(',F10.5,',',F10.5,')')
  102 FORMAT(I5,' iterations have been carried out without reaching an'/
     *        'acceptable estimate.  The last two points were'/
     *         '(',F10.5,',',F10.5,') and (',F10.5,',',F10.5,')')
       END


       SUBROUTINE NEWTON(F,DFDX,X1,T,ROOT,COUNT)
C
C  This subroutine attempts to find a root of the equation Y=F(X)
C  using Newton's method.  An initial value of X is supplied as an
C  argument, together with an acceptable tolerance for the result.
C
C  The function DFDX(X) is the first derivative of F(X)
C
C  Dummy arguments
       EXTERNAL F,DFDX
       REAL F,DFDX,X1,T,ROOT
       INTEGER COUNT
C  Parameters to control non-convergence
       INTEGER MAX
       REAL TINY
       PARAMETER (MAX=100,TINY=1E-6)
C  Local variables
       REAL X0,F0,F1,GRAD,DX
       INTEGER I
C
C  Loop until root found
       DO 10, I=1,MAX
```

```
C   Obtain gradient at X1
        GRAD=DFDX(X1)
C   Is this an acceptable basis for another iteration?
        IF (ABS(GRAD).LT.TINY) THEN
C   No.  Set COUNT=-1 and return
          COUNT=-1
          RETURN
        END IF
C   Yes.  Calculate next point
        X0=X1
        F0=F(X0)
        DX=F0/GRAD
        X1=X0-DX
C   ** While testing print each estimate
        PRINT *,X1
C   If iteration has converged sufficiently exit from loop
        IF (ABS(DX).LT.T) GOTO 11
C   More iteration required
      10 CONTINUE
C   MAX iterations without convergence - return COUNT as MAX
C   and last two estimates as X1 and ROOT
        COUNT=MAX
        ROOT=X0
        RETURN
C   A root was found. Set COUNT to zero and return root
      11 COUNT=0
        ROOT=X1
        RETURN
        END
```

As with the earlier programs, we have included an extra PRINT statement to show the progress of the iteration. Figure 18.7 shows the result of running the program with three different starting-points, using the same external function F as in the earlier cases. The derivative function DFDX is extremely simple to write in this case:

```
      REAL FUNCTION DFDX(X)
      REAL X
      DFDX=1+EXP(X)
      RETURN
      END
```

It will be noticed that, although using a value of -10.0 or 0.0 as the initial value produced extremely fast convergence (five and four iterations respectively), using $+10.0$ produced a relatively slow convergence that required 14 iterations. A moment's thought about the shape of the function will make the reason for this difference quite clear: for x greater than 2 or 3 the curve is almost parallel to the y-axis, with the result that Newton's iteration does not work very well. Once again, this emphasizes the importance of thinking about the method to be used *and* the range of values in which it should be used.

| Initial value: 10.0 | | −10.0 | | 0.0 | |
| Tolerance: 1E-6 | | 1E-6 | | 1E-6 | |

Figure 18.7
Three solutions of
$x+e^x=0$ using NEWTON.

(1)	8.999592
(2)	7.998604
(3)	6.996254
(4)	5.990771
(5)	4.978316
(6)	3.951110
(7)	2.895422
(8)	1.7961388
(9)	6.8283092E-01
(10)	-2.1071767E-01
(11)	-5.4181391E-01
(12)	-5.6702631E-01
(13)	-5.6714326E-01
(14)	-5.6714326E-01

(1)	-4.9972534E-04
(2)	-5.0012487E-01
(3)	-5.6631410E-01
(4)	-5.6714314E-01
(5)	-5.6714326E-01

(1)	-5.0000000E-01
(2)	-5.6631100E-01
(3)	-5.6714314E-01
(4)	-5.6714326E-01

Root: at X=-0.56714   Root: at X=-0.56714   Root: at X=-0.56714

18.4 Solution of simultaneous linear equations by Gaussian elimination

Another type of equation that it is frequently required to solve can be written

$$ax = b$$

where a is an $n \times n$ matrix and x and b are n-dimensional vectors. This represents the set of n simultaneous equations

$$a_{11}x_1 + a_{12}x_2 + \ldots + a_{1n}x_n = b_1$$
$$a_{21}x_1 + a_{22}x_2 + \ldots + a_{2n}x_n = b_2$$
$$\vdots$$
$$a_{n1}x_1 + a_{n2}x_2 + \ldots + a_{nn}x_n = b_n$$

There are a number of methods for solving such a set of n simultaneous equations, but the most generally used is based on **Gaussian elimination**. This is a technique to convert them into a new set of n equations in the following form:

$$c_{11}x_1 + c_{12}x_2 + \ldots + c_{1n}x_n = d_1$$
$$c_{22}x_2 + \ldots + c_{2n}x_n = d_2$$
$$.$$
$$.$$
$$c_{nn}x_n = d_n$$

Having done this the solution comes very easily. Clearly

$$x_n = \frac{d_n}{c_{nn}}$$

and then, by *back-substitution*, we can deduce that

$$x_{n-1} = \frac{d_{n-1} - c_{n-1,n}x_n}{c_{n-1,n-1}}$$

In general, therefore, we can write

$$x_i = \frac{d_i - c_{i,i+1}x_{i+1} - \ldots - c_{in}x_n}{c_{ii}}$$

Before examining how we convert our original set of equations $ax = b$ into this new set $cx = d$, where d is an **upper triangular matrix**, we must state three basic rules that apply to any set of simultaneous linear equations. These are that the solution of the set of equations $ax = b$ is unchanged by any of the following operations:

- the multiplication of one equation by any non-zero constant;
- the addition (or subtraction) of any multiple of one equation to (or from) another;
- interchanging the order of two equations.

Let us now consider our original system of equations. We wish to eliminate x_1 from the second and subsequent equations. Clearly we can do this by subtracting multiples of the first equation from each of the others in turn. During this process the first equation is called the **pivotal equation**, and its first coefficient a_{11} is called the **pivot**. To eliminate x_1 from the second equation we must subtract a_{21}/a_{11} times the first equation from it; to eliminate x_1 from the third equation we must subtract a_{31}/a_{11} times the first equation; and so on. The multiplying factors a_{21}/a_{11}, a_{31}/a_{11}, and so on, are referred to as the **multipliers**.

Once this process has been carried out for all the equations, we will have a new set of equations in which only the first contains x_1. The process can now be repeated on the last $n - 1$ equations to eliminate x_2 from all but the pivotal equation, and so on. After a number of such eliminations have been carried out we shall have a set of equations in the following form:

$$
\begin{aligned}
a_{11}x_1 + a_{12}x_2 + \ldots &\qquad \ldots + a_{1n}x_n &= b_1 \\
p_{22}x_2 + \ldots &\qquad \ldots + p_{2n}x_n &= q_2 \\
&\ldots \\
&\ldots \\
p_{ii}x_i + \ldots + p_{in}x_n &= q_i \\
p_{i+1,i}x_i + \ldots + p_{i+1,n}x_n &= q_{i+1} \\
&\ldots \\
p_{ni}x_i + \ldots + p_{nn}x_n &= q_n
\end{aligned}
$$

In order to eliminate x_i from rows $i+1$ to n we must calculate the appropriate multiplier and then use it on equation i to eliminate x_i from the remaining equations. The multiplier, m_{ki}, for equation k is clearly p_{ki}/p_{ii}, which leads to a new set of coefficients defined as follows:

$$
\begin{aligned}
p_{kj} &= p_{kj} - m_{ki}p_{ij} \\
q_k &= q_k - m_{ki}q_i
\end{aligned}
$$

This process is Gaussian elimination. We would appear now to have enough information to write a program to solve a set of simultaneous equations in this way. However, there are two more matters that should concern us. The first is that, before embarking on the elimination process, we should check that there is a unique solution to the set of equations. Basic linear algebra theory tells us that this will be so if the **determinant** of the matrix a is non-zero. We should ideally, therefore, incorporate such a check in any subroutine that we write to solve a set of simultaneous linear equations.

The second matter is more serious, and concerns our old friends precision and round-off. Clearly, if the pivot at some stage of the elimination is 0 then our calculations will fail. However, we can deal with this problem by utilizing the rule that allows us to interchange two equations. If we simply look down the **pivotal column** until we find a non-zero coefficient and then interchange the two rows (or equations) we shall solve this problem.

A moment's thought, however, should indicate that a very similar problem will arise if the pivot is very small compared to other coefficients in the pivotal column, owing to round-off and other numerical inaccuracies associated with dividing a large number by a small one. Such a situation will lead to a large multiplier and the inaccuracies will be magnified for the next stage of the elimination. We can minimize this problem by choosing as the pivot the coefficient in the pivotal row that has the largest absolute value, so that the multipliers are as small as possible. This process is known as **partial pivoting**, and is essential in any implementation of Gaussian elimination.

EXAMPLE 18.3

Write a program to read the coefficients of a set of simultaneous linear equations, and to solve the equations using Gaussian elimination.

We have already discussed all the necessary theory apart from the calculation of the determinant of the matrix of coefficients. Although this appears to be a simple calculation, given that the definition of the determinant of the matrix a is:

$$a_{11}a_{22}\ldots a_{nn} + a_{12}a_{23}\ldots a_{n-1,n}a_{n1} + \ldots + a_{1n}a_{21}\ldots a_{n,n-1}$$
$$- a_{11}a_{n2}\ldots a_{n-1,n} - a_{12}a_{n3}\ldots a_{n-1,n}a_{n,1} - \ldots - a_{1n}a_{21}\ldots a_{n,n-1}$$

it is one that can easily lead to numerical problems, owing to the well-known difficulty of subtracting large numbers from each other to leave a relatively small answer. In order to simplify the program we shall omit this check from our solution to the problem, and assume that the set of equations does have a unique solution. It should, perhaps, be noted here that if it does not then at some stage of the elimination we will find that the maximum pivot in a pivotal column is 0, indicating that this row has already been eliminated. A check for this situation could be incorporated as a less efficient alternative to the initial check, but in this example it will not be.

We can therefore produce a structure plan for the program.

---

1 Read number of equations (N) and their coefficients (A and B)

2 Convert A to upper triangular form – GAUSS

3 Solve new system by back-substitution – BACK

4 Print results

GAUSS(A,N,B)

1 Repeat for I from 1 to N−1
  1.1 Set PIVOT to A(I,I), and PROW=I
  1.2 Repeat for J from I+1 to N
    1.2.1 If $|A(J,I)|>|PIVOT|$ then
      1.2.1.1 Set PIVOT=A(J,I)
      1.2.1.2 Set PROW=J

1.3 If PROW>I then interchange rows PROW and I
1.4 Repeat for J from I+1 to N
    1.4.1 Calculate multiplier M for this row
    1.4.2 Set A(J,I)=0
    1.4.2 Set A(J,K)=A(J,K)−M*A(I,K) for K=I+1,N
    1.4.3 Set B(J)=B(J)−M*A(I)

BACK(A,N,B,X)

1 Set X(N)=B(N)/A(NN)

2 Repeat for I from N−1 to 1
2.1 $X(I)=\dfrac{B(I)-A(I,I+1)X(I+1)-\ ...\ -A(I,N)X(N)}{A(I,I)}$

We can now write the program.

```
      PROGRAM SIMEQN
C
C  This program solves a set of simultaneous equations by Gaussian
C  elimination to create an upper triangular system, followed by
C  back-substitution to obtain the solution
C
C  Maximum number of equations in set
      INTEGER MAXEQN
      PARAMETER (MAXEQN=20)
C  Local variables
      REAL A(MAXEQN,MAXEQN),B(MAXEQN),X(MAXEQN)
      INTEGER N,I,J
C
C  Read number of equations
      PRINT *,'How many equations? '
      READ *,N
C  Check if allowed
      IF (N.GT.MAXEQN) THEN
        PRINT *,'Maximum allowed is ',MAXEQN
        STOP
      END IF
C  Read equations one by one (row-wise)
      PRINT *,'Type coefficients of each equation in turn'
      DO 10, I=1,N
        PRINT 100,I
  100 FORMAT('Equation ',I2,': ')
        READ *,(A(I,J),J=1,N),B(I)
   10 CONTINUE
C  Use Gaussian elimination to triangulate the equations
      CALL GAUSS(A,MAXEQN,N,B)
C  Solve new set by back-substitution
      CALL BACK(A,MAXEQN,N,B,X)
```

```
C  Print results
       PRINT 101,(I,X(I),I=1,N)
   101 FORMAT(/'The solution of the supplied set of equations is:'//
      *         ('x(',I2,') = ',F10.5/))
       STOP
       END


       SUBROUTINE GAUSS(A,MAX,N,B)
C
C  This subroutine triangulates a set of N equations Ax=B
C  using Gaussian elimination.  No checks are made as to whether
C  there is a unique solution.
C
C  Dummy arguments
       INTEGER MAX,N
       REAL A(MAX,MAX),B(N)
C  Local variables
       REAL PIVOT,ABSP,MULT,TEMP
       INTEGER PROW,I,J,K
C
C  Eliminate one element from each row in turn
       DO 40, I=1,N
C  Set initial values for PIVOT and PROW
         PIVOT=A(I,I)
         ABSP=ABS(PIVOT)
         PROW=I
C  Look for a larger potential pivot
         DO 10, J=I+1,N
           IF (ABS(A(J,I)).GT.ABSP) THEN
             PIVOT=A(J,I)
             ABSP=ABS(PIVOT)
             PROW=J
           END IF
   10    CONTINUE
C  Was a larger pivot found ?
         IF (PROW.GT.I) THEN
C  Yes.  Interchange coefficients
           DO 20, J=I,N
             TEMP=A(I,J)
             A(I,J)=A(PROW,J)
             A(PROW,J)=TEMP
   20      CONTINUE
           TEMP=B(I)
           B(I)=B(PROW)
           B(PROW)=TEMP
         END IF
C  Eliminate coefficients of X(I) from rows I+1 to N
         DO 30, J=I+1,N
           MULT=A(J,I)/PIVOT
           A(J,I)=0.0
           DO 25, K=I+1,N
             A(J,K)=A(J,K)-MULT*A(I,K)
   25      CONTINUE
           B(J)=B(J)-MULT*B(I)
```

```
   30   CONTINUE
   40 CONTINUE
C  Elimination now completed
      RETURN
      END

      SUBROUTINE BACK(A,MAX,N,B,X)
C
C  This subroutine solves an upper triangular system of simultaneous
C  equations by back-substitution
C
C  Dummy arguments
      INTEGER MAX,N
      REAL A(MAX,MAX),B(N),X(N)
C  Local variables
      REAL QUOT
      INTEGER I,J
C
C  Calculate X(N)
      X(N)=B(N)/A(N,N)
C  Now calculate remaining values in reverse order
      DO 20, I=N-1,1,-1
         QUOT=B(I)
         DO 10, J=I+1,N
           QUOT=QUOT-A(I,J)*X(J)
   10    CONTINUE
         X(I)=QUOT/A(I,I)
   20 CONTINUE
C  Solution completed
      RETURN
      END
```

One point that should be made about this program concerns the inter-changing of the rows during the elimination process. While physical interchange is acceptable for small systems of equations, it would be far too

---

```
How many equations? 5
Type coefficients of each equation in turn
Equation 1: 4,2,-2.5,4,1,-0.1
Equation 2: 3,-1,0.5,0,5,1.5
Equation 3: 1.5,2.5,3,-1,5,3
Equation 4: 1,2,-1,2,-1,0.1
Equation 5: 5,3,3,2,10,4

The solution of the supplied set of equations is:

x( 1) =    3.00000
x( 2) =   -1.00000
x( 3) =    4.00000
x( 4) =    0.50000
x( 5) =   -2.10000
```

Figure 18.8
The solution of a set of equations using SIMEQN.

Figure 18.9
The result of Gaussian
elimination by GAUSS.

$$a_{i1}x_1 \quad + \quad a_{i2}x_2 \quad + \quad a_{i3}x_3 \quad + \quad a_{i4}x_4 \quad + \quad a_{i5}x_5 \quad = \quad b_i$$

(as input to GAUSS)

4.0	2.0	-2.5	4.0	1.0	-0.1
3.0	-1.0	0.5	0.0	5.0	1.5
1.5	2.5	3.0	-1.0	5.0	3.0
1.0	2.0	-1.0	2.0	-1.0	0.1
5.0	3.0	3.0	2.0	10.0	4.0

(as output by GAUSS)

5.0	3.0	3.0	2.0	10.0	4.0
	-2.8	-1.3	-1.2	-1.0	-0.9
		-4.71429	2.57143	-6.85714	-3.17143
			-1.54545	-0.54545	0.37273
				-0.14706	0.30882

(as solved by BACK)

x(1) = 3.0, x(2) =-1.0, x(3) = 4.0, x(4) = 0.5, x(5) =-2.1

time-consuming for larger systems. The problem is similar to the one that
we met in Example 14.3 when sorting the contents of a set of related arrays,
and the solution is similar to the one used there. It is very much more
efficient not to move the rows themselves but instead to move *pointers* to
the rows. It is left as an exercise for the reader to make this change to the
above GAUSS subroutine.

Figure 18.8 shows the result of running the program with a set of
five simultaneous equations, while Figure 18.9 shows both the original set
of equations and the upper triangular set produced by GAUSS for input to
BACK. The latter was created by a modified version of the above program.

Finally, it should be pointed out that there are many situations in
which an *iterative* method is more appropriate than an analytic method
such as Gaussian elimination. In particular, iterative methods are more
appropriate for large systems where many of the coefficients are zero, that
is, where the coefficients form a sparse matrix. Such systems typically arise
when solving problems that involve partial differential equations. Two of
the best-known iterative methods are *Jacobi's method* and the *Gauss–Seidel
method*. We shall not dwell on these methods here, however, with one
exception. The interested reader can find a description of these methods in
any good numerical analysis text; converting either to a Fortran subroutine
is a good exercise.

18.5   Solving a tridiagonal system of equations

One form of sparse system that is particularly important is known as a **tridiagonal system**, for reasons that become obvious on examination:

$$
\begin{aligned}
a_{11}x_1 + a_{12}x_2 &= b_1 \\
a_{21}x_1 + a_{22}x_2 + a_{23}x_3 &= b_2 \\
a_{32}x_2 + a_{33}x_3 + a_{34}x_4 &= b_3 \\
&\cdots \\
a_{n-1,n-2}x_{n-2} + a_{n-1,n-1}x_{n-1} + a_{n-1,n}x_n &= b_n \\
a_{n,n-1}x_{n-1} + a_{n,n}x_n &= b_n
\end{aligned}
$$

Systems of equations of this type occur frequently in the solution of partial differential equations, and are also found in cubic and bicubic curve-fitting, as we shall see in Section 18.6. In order to emphasize the form of such a system it is common practice to use a different terminology for the coefficients, namely:

$$
\begin{aligned}
d_1x_1 + c_1x_2 &= b_1 \\
a_2x_1 + d_2x_2 + c_2x_3 &= b_2 \\
a_3x_2 + d_3x_3 + c_3x_4 &= b_3 \\
&\cdots \\
a_{n-1}x_{n-2} + d_{n-1}x_{n-1} + c_{n-1}x_n &= b_{n-1} \\
a_nx_{n-1} + d_nx_n &= b_n
\end{aligned}
$$

Clearly the computation involved in solving a system of this nature should be much simpler than in the general case, since in each column there is only one element to be eliminated. Furthermore, and this is another reason why a different terminology has been used, considerable savings can be made in storage requirements by storing only these tridiagonal coefficients (as three one-dimensional arrays) and ignoring the zero elements that occupy the remainder of the matrix of coefficients.

An exhaustive account of the mathematics involved in deriving a solution method will not be given here, as it is similar to that used in the previous section when discussing Gaussian elimination, except that we only need to subtract the pivotal equation from the equation immediately below it in order to transform the original set of equations into a new, upper triangular set:

$$
\begin{aligned}
D_1x_1 + c_1x_2 &= B_1 \\
D_2x_2 + c_2x_3 &= B_2 \\
D_3x_3 + c_3x_4 &= B_3 \\
&\cdots \\
D_{n-1}x_{n-1} + c_{n-1}x_n &= B_{n-1} \\
D_nx_n &= B_n
\end{aligned}
$$

Figure 18.10
A subroutine to solve a
tridiagonal system of
equations.

```
                    SUBROUTINE DIAG3(A,D,C,B,X,LOWER,UPPER,FAILED)
C
C This subroutine solves a tridiagonal system of equations of the form
C   A(I)X(I-1) + D(I)X(I) + C(I)X(I+1) = B(I) for I=LOWER to UPPER
C returning the solution in the array X.
C The logical argument FAILED is set TRUE if the solution fails
C
C Dummy arguments
      INTEGER LOWER,UPPER
      REAL A(LOWER:UPPER),D(LOWER:UPPER),C(LOWER:UPPER),B(LOWER:UPPER),
     *     X(LOWER:UPPER)
      LOGICAL FAILED
C Parameter for use in comparisons with zero, or close to zero
      PARAMETER (TINY=1E-9)
C Local variables
      REAL MULT
      INTEGER I
C
C Set FAILED to FALSE (on the assumption that all will be well!)
      FAILED=.FALSE.
C Eliminate X(I) from I+1th row
      DO 10, I=LOWER,UPPER-1
C Check that pivotal coefficient is non-zero
        IF (ABS(D(I)).GT.TINY) THEN
C Yes.  Eliminate A(I+1) from this equation
          MULT=A(I+1)/D(I)
          A(I+1)=0.0
          D(I+1)=D(I+1)-MULT*C(I)
          B(I+1)=B(I+1)-MULT*B(I)
        ELSE
C D(I) is zero.  Set failure flag and exit
          FAILED=.TRUE.
          RETURN
        END IF
   10 CONTINUE
C System is now upper triangular
C First check that final equation is not singular
      IF (D(UPPER).GT.TINY) THEN
C OK.  So solve final equation
        X(UPPER)=B(UPPER)/D(UPPER)
C Now solve remainder by back-substitution
        DO 20, I=UPPER-1,LOWER,-1
          X(I)=(B(I)-C(I)*X(I+1))/D(I)
   20   CONTINUE
      ELSE
C D(UPPER) is zero.  Set failure flag
        FAILED=.TRUE.
      END IF
      RETURN
      END
```

We can readily see that the c_i coefficients are unaltered by the transformation, and that

$$D_1 = d_1$$

and

$$B_1 = b_1$$

Furthermore, when processing the $i+1$th equation in order to eliminate x_i, a multiplier m_i will be used which is equal to a_{i+1}/D_i to give a new equation:

$$D_{i+1}x_{i+1} + c_{i+1}x_{i+2} = B_{i+1}$$

where

$$D_{i+1} = d_{i+1} - m_i c_i$$

and

$$B_{i+1} = b_{i+1} - m_i b_i$$

A Fortran implementation of this method is shown in Figure 18.10: it should be noted that no pivoting is necessary for this class of equations and any attempt to use it would destroy the tridiagonal nature of the system. Notice that we have passed both the lower and upper bounds of the five arrays as arguments to this subroutine, not their size alone, as in our other related subroutines. The reason for this is that, as was mentioned earlier, such tridiagonal systems frequently occur when solving other types of equations, and in these situations we frequently wish to process only part of a set of coefficients. We shall use this subroutine as part of our method for curve-fitting in the next section, when we shall see how this extension is necessary.

18.6 Fitting a curve to a set of data points using a cubic spline

We have considered the solution of equations of various types at some length, because this is a very common requirement in scientific programming. However, another important application is the fitting of an algebraic equation to a set of (usually) experimental data, with a view to using this equation to predict further results. In Chapter 11 we considered the simple case in which it was believed that the data satisfied a linear relationship. The more general case will now be briefly examined.

Figure 18.11
A cubic spline.

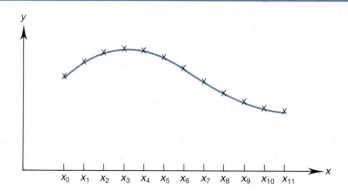

As usual in numerical analysis, there are a number of different methods for fitting a curve to a set of discrete data points; however, by far the best known and the most widely used are methods based on **cubic splines**. A spline was an instrument once used by draughtsmen to enable them to draw a smooth curve through a set of points. It consisted of a flexible wooden (or sometimes metal) strip constrained (by pins) to pass through the data points. Because the spline would take up the shape that minimized its potential energy the resulting curve was smooth.

The cubic spline is the mathematical equivalent of the draughtsman's physical instrument and enables the construction of a smooth curve that passes through all the data points. Furthermore, as a measure of its smoothness, its first and second derivatives are continuous everywhere within the range of the data points.

A cubic spline actually consists of a set of cubic polynomials, one for each pair of data points, as shown in Figure 18.11. These polynomials are chosen so that they obey the following criteria:

- In each interval $[x_i, x_{i+1}]$, $i = 0, \ldots, n-1$, the spline consists of a cubic polynomial $s_i(x)$.

- The spline passes through each data point and so:

  $s_i(x_i) = y_i$ for $i = 0, \ldots, n$

- At each of the points where two subintervals join the first and second derivatives must be continuous, and so:

  $s_{i-1}(x_i) = s_i(x_i)$
  $s'_{i-1}(x_i) = s'_i(x_i)$
  $s''_{i-1}(x_i) = s''_i(x_i)$ for $i = 1, \ldots, n-1$

For fairly obvious reasons, round-off errors will be minimized if we express the cubic polynomials as functions of $(x-x_i)$ rather than as functions of x, with the result that we shall require to find the coefficients of the equations

$$s_i(x) = a_i(x-x_i)^3 + b_i(x-x_i)^2 + c_i(x-x_i) + d_i \text{ for } i = 0, \ldots , n-1$$

Differentiating this equation twice gives us the two derivatives

$$s'_i(x) = 3a_i(x-x_i)^2 + 2b_i(x-x_i) + c_i$$
$$s''_i(x) = 6a_i(x-x_i) + 2b_i$$

If we now set

$$\sigma_0 = s''_0(x_0)$$
$$\sigma_i = s''_{i-1}(x_i) = s''_i(x_i) \text{ for } i = 1, \ldots , n-1$$
$$\sigma_n = s''_{n-1}(x_n)$$

and define the sizes of the intervals between data points to be h_i, so that

$$h_i = (x_{i+1}-x_i) \text{ for } i = 0, \ldots , n-1$$

then we can derive a new set of equations

$$\sigma_{i-1}h_{i-1} + 2\sigma_i(h_{i-1}+h_i) + \sigma_{i+1}h_{i+1} = \frac{6}{h_i}(y_{i+1}-y_i) - \frac{6}{h_{i-1}}(y_i-y_{i-1})$$

$$\text{for } i = 1, \ldots , n-1$$

This set of $n-1$ equations has $n+1$ variables, and so we need two more equations to be able to calculate a unique solution and hence a unique cubic interpolating function. This is achieved by applying some form of constraint to the spline at the end-points x_0 and x_n. This is desirable in any case since these two points are less constrained than the rest of the system. There are a number of possibilities, of which some common ones are:

- Force the second derivative of the spline to be 0 at the end-points:

$$\sigma_0 = \sigma_n = 0$$

- Force the third derivative of the spline to be continuous at the points adjacent to the end-points. This means that

$$a_0 = a_1 \text{ and } a_{n-1} = a_n$$

which leads to the two further equations

$$\sigma_0 h_1 - \sigma_1(h_0 + h_1) + \sigma_2 h_0 = 0$$
$$\sigma_{n-2} h_{n-1} - \sigma_{n-1}(h_{n-2} + h_{n-1}) + \sigma_n h_{n-2} = 0$$

● Force the first derivative (the gradient) at the end-points to be the same as that of the true curve $y = f(x)$; this assumes that further information is available about the gradient of this curve at these points. Thus

$$s'(x_0) = f'_0 \text{ and } s'(x_n) = f'_n$$

which leads to two further equations in σ_0 and σ_1, and in σ_{n-1} and σ_n, respectively.

Different treatments of the end-points will be appropriate for different situations, but it will be noticed by the observant reader that whichever one we choose we shall have a tridiagonal system. In the first case the system has $n-1$ equations in $n-1$ unknowns, since σ_0 and σ_n are no longer unknown, while the last case has n equations in n unknowns. The second case also has n equations in n unknowns, but is not strictly tridiagonal; however, it is a trivial task to convert it to tridiagonal form.

We shall not continue in detail with the derivation of a program to calculate the coefficients of the set of cubic polynomials required to interpolate a cubic spline through a given set of data points. A subroutine to calculate the values of the coefficients a_i, b_i, c_i and d_i using the first of the criteria for treatment of endpoints ($\sigma_0 = \sigma_n = 0$) will be found in Figure 18.12.

This subroutine uses the subroutine DIAG3, which was shown in Figure 18.10, to solve the system of equations in σ_i. Note that, because DIAG3 will be using only those elements of the arrays with coefficients from 1 to N-1, it must be called with array *elements* as the actual arguments, as discussed in Section 14.2. If the call had taken the form

```
CALL DIAG3(A,D,C,B,SIGMA,1,N-1,FAILED)
```

then DIAG3 would have used the first N-1 elements of each array (those with subscripts from 0 to N-2) and considered them to have subscripts from 1 to N-1. On return from the subroutine, therefore, the coefficients of the interpolating polynomials would be in the wrong places.

The subroutine SPLINE can be used by any program that requires a set of spline coefficients to fit a particular set of data, and which can then use these coefficients to create a mathematical model of the curve to use in whatever way is appropriate. The following program illustrates its use to fit a spline through 18 unevenly spaced points in the range $-3 < x < 3$ that

```
      SUBROUTINE SPLINE(X,Y,N,SIGMA,H,A,B,C,D)
C
C This subroutine calculates the coefficients A, B, C, D of the cubic
C polynomials that form a cubic spline through the set of N+1 points
C (X(I),Y(I), I=0,N)
C The second derivative of the spline is set to zero at the end-points
C
C The arrays SIGMA and H are working arrays whose size depends on N
C
C Dummy arguments
      INTEGER N
      REAL X(0:N),Y(0:N),SIGMA(0:N),H(0:N-1),
     *     A(0:N-1),B(0:N-1),C(0:N-1),D(0:N-1)
C Local variables
      INTEGER I
      LOGICAL FAILED
C Calculate values for H
      DO 10, I=0,N-1
         H(I)=X(I+1)-X(I)
10 CONTINUE
C Store coefficients of tridiagonal equations for sigma in A, B, C, D
      DO 20, I=1,N-1
         A(I)=H(I-1)
         D(I)=2.0*(H(I-1)+H(I))
         C(I)=H(I+1)
         B(I)=6.0*(Y(I+1)-Y(I))/H(I) - 6.0*(Y(I)-Y(I-1))/H(I-1)
20 CONTINUE
C Adjust values at end-points
      A(1)=0.0
      C(N-1)=0.0
C Use DIAG3 to solve the equations for SIGMA(I)
      CALL DIAG3(A(1),D(1),C(1),B(1),SIGMA(1),1,N-1,FAILED)
C It is not necessary to check FAILED since we know that the system
C of equations is properly formed.
C Now calculate the coefficients of the interpolating polynomials
C and store in A, B, C and D
      SIGMA(0)=0.0
      SIGMA(N)=0.0
      DO 30, I=0,N-1
         A(I)=(SIGMA(I+1)-SIGMA(I))/(6.0*H(I))
         B(I)=0.5*SIGMA(I)
         C(I)=(Y(I+1)-Y(I))/H(I) - (SIGMA(I+1)+2.0*SIGMA(I))*H(I)/6.0
         D(I)=Y(I)
30 CONTINUE
      RETURN
      END
```

Figure 18.12
A cubic spline
interpolation subroutine.

lie on the curve $y = e^{-x^2/2}$, and to then print out the values of the interpolated and actual functions at a series of intermediate values. The result of running this program is shown in Figure 18.13.

Figure 18.13
Test results from
SPLINE for $y = e^{-x^2/2}$.

x	exp(-0.5x**2)	Spline value
-2.80	0.019841	0.020045
-2.40	0.056135	0.055742
-2.00	0.135335	0.135567
-1.60	0.278037	0.278197
-1.20	0.486752	0.485973
-0.80	0.726149	0.726407
-0.40	0.923116	0.923759
0.00	1.000000	0.999746
0.40	0.923116	0.923061
0.80	0.726149	0.726284
1.20	0.486752	0.486363
1.60	0.278037	0.278037
2.00	0.135335	0.135706
2.40	0.056135	0.056135
2.80	0.019841	0.020719

```
      PROGRAM SPTEST
C
C  This program tests the spline subroutine SPLINE
C
C  Maximum coefficient for data points
      INTEGER N
      PARAMETER (N=17)
C  Defining external function
      REAL F
      EXTERNAL F
C  Local variables
      INTEGER I,J
      REAL X(0:N),Y(0:N),SIGMA(0:N),H(0:N),
     *    A(0:N-1),B(0:N-1),C(0:N-1),D(0:N-1),YZ,Z,ZJ
C  Test values for X
      DATA X/-2.95, -2.6, -2.1, -1.8, -1.4, -1.0,-0.75, -0.3,-0.05,
     *        0.2,  0.55, 0.9, 1.25, 1.6,  1.7, 2.1,   2.4, 3.0/
C
C  Calculate Y-coordinates corresponding to data values of X
      DO 10, I=0,N
         Y(I)=F(X(I))
   10 CONTINUE
C  Call SPLINE to fit a set of N polynomials
      CALL SPLINE(X,Y,N,SIGMA,H,A,B,C,D)
C  Now compare interpolated values with true ones
      PRINT 100
  100 FORMAT(9X,'x      exp(-0.5x**2)   Spline value'/)
      DO 20,I=0,14
C  Calculate Z
      Z=-2.8 + 0.4*I
C  Find which interval Z lies in
      DO 15,J=0,N-1
         IF (X(J).LE.Z .AND. Z.LE.X(J+1)) GOTO 16
```

```
    15   CONTINUE
C  It should not be possible to complete the loop!
C  Calculate S(Z) using coefficients for X(J)<=X<=X(J+1)
    16   ZJ=Z-X(J)
         YZ=A(J)*ZJ**3 + B(J)*ZJ**2 +C(J)*ZJ + D(J)
C  Print comparative results
           PRINT 101,Z,F(Z),YZ
   101 FORMAT(6X,F6.2,2F15.6)
    20 CONTINUE
C  All done
         STOP
         END

         REAL FUNCTION F(X)
         REAL X
         F=EXP(-0.5*X*X)
         RETURN
         END
```

The spline method of fitting polynomials through a set of data points has been presented as a two-dimensional problem; however, it is equally applicable in three dimensions: for example, to calculate the equation of a surface, $z = f(x,y)$, through a set of points whose heights above some base plane have been measured on a rectangular grid. The normal method in this case is first to interpolate the rows of data in the x direction, keeping y fixed, and then to interpolate between the resulting sets of four coefficients in the y direction, keeping x fixed. The resulting **bicubic patches** exhibit the same continuity with adjacent patches at their common boundaries as do the two-dimensional cubic spline polynomials at their common points. Such **bicubic spline interpolation** is therefore often used to create mathematical models of surfaces, using, for example, data obtained by remote sensing devices such as satellites or oceanic depth sounders; these mathematical models of the surface can then be used by a drawing program that plots a contour map or a graphical representation of the surface as viewed from any angle.

One final point relating to cubic splines should be made. We have assumed throughout the discussion that the spline polynomials must pass through *all* the data points. However, just as in the case where a linear fit is expected, when the data is the result of experiment it is likely that there may be small errors in that data. In these situations, therefore, we may require the spline to be a good fit to the data, but not necessarily to pass through all the data points. This involves a somewhat more complex mathematical treatment, and it is not intended to go into the matter here. It is sufficient to emphasize that some form of least-squares approximation is normally used so that data points that will produce significant perturbations in the polynomial will have less effect than those that lie on a smoothly fitting spline.

18.7 Curve-fitting using only local data by the Ellis–McLain method

The method of fitting a cubic spline to data described in the previous section is very effective but suffers from one major disadvantage in certain situations. This is that the spline depends upon *all* the data points, and if one data point is moved then *all* the interpolating polynomials must be recalculated. In some situations, such as a large three-dimensional system or one that is being processed interactively, the storage and/or processing overhead involved in recalculating the complete system of equations because *one* point has been moved may be unacceptable. Several variations of the basic spline concept have been developed to deal with this problem by using only *local data*. One such method was developed by the author and a colleague, primarily for use in bicubic interpolation of three-dimensional surfaces in order that other programs could use this mathematical model to produce contour maps and graphical representations of the surface.

All local methods have to relax some of the constraints normally applied to cubic splines, owing to the smaller amount of data available for use in calculating the coefficients of each polynomial. In the **Ellis–McLain method** (Ellis and McLain, 1977) the value of the function $f(x)$ and its first derivative are continuous at all points, but the second derivative is not so constrained. However, it does lead to relatively small discontinuities in the second derivatives at the data points compared with many other methods, as well as giving a good fit to a wide variety of mathematical functions.

The method operates in two phases. The first phase of the interpolation finds, for each data point (x_i, y_i), the cubic polynomial that passes through the three points (x_{i-1}, y_{i-1}), (x_i, y_i) and (x_{i+1}, y_{i+1}) and which gives a least-squares fit to the two neighbouring points (x_{i-2}, y_{i-2}) and (x_{i+2}, y_{i+2}). In the least-squares fitting these two points are weighted in proportion to the inverse squares of their distances from their neighbours x_{i-1} and x_{i+1}, respectively, in order to take account of variations in the spacing of the data. The gradient, or first derivative, g_i, of this cubic at its central point (x_i, y_i) is then calculated and saved for phase 2. At the first two and last two points a slight modification is required, and here a cubic is fitted exactly through the first and last four points.

The second phase then constructs a series of approximating polynomials $f_i(x)$ such that

$$f_i(x_i) = y_i$$
$$f_i(x_{i+1}) = y_{i+1}$$
$$f'_i(x_i) = g_i$$
$$f'_i(x_{i+1}) = g_{i+1}$$

```
         SUBROUTINE GRADS(X,Y,GRAD,LOWER,UPPER)
C
C  This subroutine fits cubics to the points at X(I-1), X(I)
C  and X(I+1), with a weighted least-squares fit to X(I-2) and X(I+2).
C  It then stores the gradients at X(I) in the array GRAD
C
C  Dummy arguments
         INTEGER LOWER,UPPER
         REAL X(LOWER:UPPER),Y(LOWER:UPPER),GRAD(LOWER:UPPER)
C  Local variables
         INTEGER I,ILESS2,ILESS1,IPLUS1,IPLUS2
         REAL X0,X1,X2,X3,X4,Y2,PROD1,PROD2,NUM,DENOM,G,COEFF2,XDIFF,
     *       XPROD,WEIGHT
C
C  Fit cubics at each data point and store gradient
         DO 10, I=LOWER,UPPER
C  Establish which points are to be used for this interpolation
         IF (I.GT.LOWER) THEN
            ILESS1=I-1
         ELSE
C  We shall use an exact fit through the first four points for I=LOWER
            ILESS1=I+3
         END IF
         IF (I.LT.UPPER) THEN
            IPLUS1=I+1
         ELSE
C  We shall use an exact fit through the last four points for I=UPPER
            IPLUS1=I-3
         END IF
C  X1 etc. are used for clarity and also to avoid repeated subscript
C  calculation
         X2=X(I)
         Y2=Y(I)
         X1=X(ILESS1)-X2
         X3=X(IPLUS1)-X2
C  First fit a quadratic through X1, X2 AND X3
         PROD1=X3*(Y(ILESS1)-Y2)
         PROD2=X1*(Y(IPLUS1)-Y2)
         DENOM=X1*X3*(X(ILESS1)-X(IPLUS1))
         G=(X1*PROD2-X3*PROD1)/DENOM
         COEFF2=(PROD1-PROD2)/DENOM
C  If X0 exists find its contribution to the cubic adjustment
         IF (I.GT.LOWER+1) THEN
            ILESS2=I-2
            X0=X(ILESS2)-X2
            XDIFF=X(ILESS2)-X(ILESS1)
            XPROD=X0*XDIFF*(X(ILESS2)-X(IPLUS1))
            WEIGHT=XPROD/(XDIFF*XDIFF)
            NUM=WEIGHT*(Y(ILESS2)-Y2-X0*(G+X0*COEFF2))
            DENOM=WEIGHT*XPROD
         ELSE
            NUM=0.0
            DENOM=0.0
         END IF
```

Figure 18.14
Subroutine GRADS for
use in Ellis–McLain
curve fitting.

```
C  If X4 exists find its contribution to the cubic adjustment
         IF (I.LT.UPPER-1) THEN
            IPLUS2=I+2
            X4=X(IPLUS2)-X2
            XDIFF=X(IPLUS2)-X(IPLUS1)
            XPROD=X4*XDIFF*(X(IPLUS2)-X(ILESS1))
            WEIGHT=XPROD/(XDIFF*XDIFF)
            NUM=NUM+WEIGHT*(Y(IPLUS2)-Y2-X4*(G+X4*COEFF2))
            DENOM=DENOM+WEIGHT*XPROD
         END IF
C  Store gradient at X2
         GRAD(I)=G+NUM*X1*X3/DENOM2
   10 CONTINUE
C  All gradients calculated
      RETURN
      END
```

Figures 18.14 and 18.15 show a Fortran implementation of these two phases in the form of two subroutines, GRADS and COEFFS. These subroutines could be tested with a program similar to the one used to test the cubic spline subroutine. Such a program can be created simply by altering the call to the procedure SPLINE so that it calls GRADS:

```
CALL GRADS(X,Y,GRAD,0,N)
```

Figure 18.15
Subroutine COEFFS for use in Ellis–McLain curve fitting.

```
      SUBROUTINE COEFFS(X,Y,GRAD,LOWER,UPPER,I,A,B,C,D)
C
C  This subroutine calculates the coefficients of the cubic
C      y = a(x-x(i))**3 + b(x-x(i))**2 + c(x-x(i)) + d
C  which has values Y(I), Y(I+1) and gradients GRAD(I), GRAD(I+1)
C  at X(I), X(I+1)
C  This cubic is valid in the range X(I) <= X <= X(I+1) as part of an
C  Ellis-McLain fitted curve
C
C  Dummy arguments
      INTEGER LOWER,UPPER,I
      REAL X(LOWER:UPPER),Y(LOWER:UPPER),GRAD(LOWER:UPPER),A,B,C,D
C  Local variables
      REAL H,DY
C
C  Calculate coefficients
      D=Y(I)
      H=X(I+1)-X(I)
      DY=Y(I+1)-Y(I)
      C=GRAD(I)
      B=(3.0*DY-H*(2.0*C+GRAD(I+1)))/(H*H)
      A=(H*(C+GRAD(I+1))-2.0*DY)/H**3
C  All done
      RETURN
      END
```

x	True value	Ellis–McLain	Spline
−2.80	0.019 841	0.019 927	0.020 045
−2.40	0.056 135	0.056 058	0.055 742
−2.00	0.135 335	0.135 373	0.135 567
−1.60	0.278 037	0.278 243	0.278 197
−1.20	0.486 752	0.486 915	0.485 973
−0.80	0.726 149	0.726 206	0.726 407
−0.40	0.923 116	0.922 938	0.923 759
0.00	1.000 000	1.000 049	0.999 746
0.40	0.923 116	0.922 901	0.923 061
0.80	0.726 149	0.726 065	0.726 284
1.20	0.486 752	0.486 903	0.486 363
1.60	0.278 037	0.278 037	0.278 037
2.00	0.135 335	0.135 347	0.135 706
2.40	0.056 135	0.056 135	0.056 135
2.80	0.019 841	0.019 918	0.020 719

Figure 18.16
A comparison of GRADS/ COEFFS and SPLINE for $y = e^{-x^2/2}$.

and by replacing the two lines that calculate the interpolated value by the following:

```
C  Call COEFFS to get coefficients for this interval
   16    CALL COEFFS(X,Y,GRAD,0,N,J,A,B,C,D)
C  Calculate F(Z) using coefficients for X(J)≤X≤X(J+1)
         ZJ=Z-X(J)
         YZ=A*ZJ**3 + B*ZJ**2 +C*ZJ + D
```

Figure 18.16 shows a comparison of the results produced by this method and by the spline method, with the same data used earlier in testing SPLINE. Both provide a good fit to the data, and have continuous first derivatives. This method, however, does not have a continuous second derivative, although the discontinuities are generally very small. For the situations where reliance on local data only is important, this is usually an acceptable compromise.

In normal use the subroutine GRADS is called first to calculate the required gradients at each data point, and then COEFFS is called to calculate the coefficients of the interpolating polynomials

$$f_i(x) = a_i(x-x_i)^3 + b_i(x-x_i)^2 + c_i(x-x_i) + d_i$$

in any required interval $x_i \leqslant x \leqslant x_{i+1}$. GRADS does not need to be called again as long as the data remains unchanged, thus avoiding unnecessary repetition of calculation. If it is subsequently required to alter one of the points, say (x_k, y_k), then it will be necessary to call GRADS once more to recalculate the gradients for $i = k-2, k-1, k, k+1$ and $k+2$ since these are the only points affected by the point (x_k, y_k). Once this has been done,

COEFFS is used, as before, to recalculate the coefficients for any required interval.

18.8   Integration of a function using Simpson's rule

The final numerical technique to be considered is the **integration** of a function $y = f(x)$. This is a very common requirement, particularly in physics and engineering, and is a problem that lends itself to a surprisingly simple solution. The reason lies in the geometric interpretation of a definite integral.

As Figure 18.17 shows, the integral of a function is interpreted as the area under the curve represented by that function. This leads us to a very simple method of evaluating the integral.

Firstly, we note that if we divide the range $a \leqslant x \leqslant b$ into n equal segments we can approximate the function by a series of straight lines, as shown in Figure 18.18, and we can then easily calculate the required area as the sum of the areas of the $n-1$ trapezoids.

This approach is known as the **trapezoidal method** of integration; however, since a linear interpolation is not very accurate in general, the trapezoidal method is not of much practical use. It does, however, lead us to a method that is considerably more accurate and *is* widely used.

Let us consider that part of the curve shown in Figure 18.18 that is bounded by $x_{i-2} \leqslant x \leqslant x_i$. We know that there is a unique quadratic interpolation polynomial $y = q(x)$ that passes through these three points, as shown in Figure 18.19. Although a quadratic polynomial is not usually appropriate for curve-fitting of the nature of that discussed in the previous two sections, it is ideal for this purpose, since its geometry leads us to expect that the error in the area bounded by $x_{i-2} \leqslant x \leqslant x_{i-1}$ will largely be compensated for by the error in the next area bounded by $x_{i-1} \leqslant x \leqslant x_i$.

Figure 18.17
The geometric representation of
$$\int_a^b f(x)dx.$$

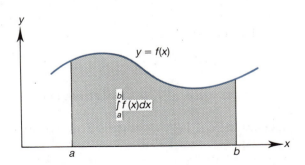

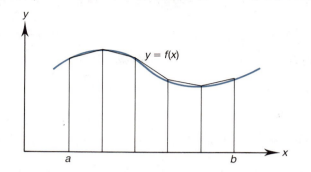

Figure 18.18
The trapezoidal method
of integration.

This approximating quadratic can easily be derived, leading to the following approximation:

$$\int_{x_{i-2}}^{x_i} f(x)\mathrm{d}x \approx \int_{x_{i-2}}^{x_i} q(x)\mathrm{d}x$$

$$= \int_{x_{i-2}}^{x_i} \left[\frac{(x-x_{i-1})(x-x_i)}{(x_{i-2}-x_{i-1})(x_{i-2}-x_i)} f_{i-2} + \frac{(x-x_{i-2})(x-x_i)}{(x_{i-1}-x_{i-2})(x_{i-1}-x_i)} f_{i-2} \right.$$

$$\left. + \frac{(x-x_{i-2})(x-x_{i-1})}{(x_i-x_{i-2})(x_i-x_{i-1})} f_{i-2} \right] \mathrm{d}x$$

$$= \frac{h}{3} (f_{i-2} + 4f_{i-1} + f_i)$$

where h $(= x_i - x_{i-1} = x_{i-1} - x_{i-2} = (x_n - x_0)/n)$ is the size of each interval in x, and $f_i = f(x_i)$.

This formula is known as **Simpson's rule**. Since, *as long as n is even*, we can clearly approximate to the area under the whole curve, $x_0 \leqslant x \leqslant x_n$,

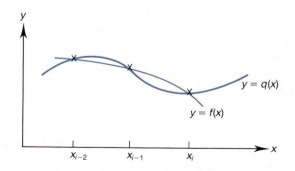

Figure 18.19
Quadratic interpolation
for $x_{i-2} \leqslant x \leqslant x_i$.

Figure 18.20
A function to perform
integration by Simpson's
rule.

```
      REAL FUNCTION SIMPSN(F,A,B,N)
C
C This function calculates the integral of the external function F(X)
C between X=A and X=B using Simpson's rule with N intervals.
C N must be even
C
C Dummy arguments
      INTEGER N
      REAL F,A,B
      EXTERNAL F
C Local variables
      INTEGER I
      REAL X,H,SUMEVN,SUMODD
C
C Calculate size of each interval
      H=(B-A)/N
C Accumulate sums of odd and even terms
      X=A+H
      SUMODD=F(X)
      SUMEVN=0.0
      DO 10, I=2,N-2,2
        X=X+H
        SUMEVN=SUMEVN+F(X)
        X=X+H
        SUMODD=SUMODD+F(X)
   10 CONTINUE
C Calculate approximation to integral
      SIMPSN=(F(A)+4.0*SUMODD+2.0*SUMEVN+F(B))*H/3.0
      RETURN
      END
```

by summing the areas of the pairs of sub-intervals we can deduce that the formula for the complete integral is

$$\int_{x_0}^{x_n} f(x)\mathrm{d}x \approx \frac{h}{3} \left(f_0 + 4f_1 + 2f_2 + 4f_3 + \dots + 2f_{n-2} + 4f_{n-1} + f_n \right)$$

which is known as the *composite form* of Simpson's rule.

An interesting aspect of Simpson's rule is that it is more accurate than might be expected: it can be shown that it provides an exact solution for cubic polynomials, which is one degree higher than one would intuitively expect of a quadratic interpolation. This is obviously of particular interest if the function being integrated has been created by a cubic spline technique as described in Sections 18.6 and 18.7, since the integration of such a curve will not add any further errors, other than those introduced by round-off, and so on.

Since definite integration produces a single numerical answer, Simpson's rule is normally implemented as a function rather than a subroutine. Figure 18.20 shows a Fortran function that will integrate the function $y=f(x)$ for a given range of x by use of Simpson's rule.

SELF-TEST EXERCISES 18.1

1   What are the advantages and disadvantages of each of the three methods introduced for solving non-linear equations (bisection method, secant method and Newton's method)?

2   What is partial pivoting? And why is it important in Gaussian elimination?

3   What is the major difference between a cubic spline curve-fitting algorithm and one using local data? What are the advantages of each method?

4   Why is Simpson's rule a particularly appropriate method for finding the area under a curve that has been fitted to a set of experimentally derived data points using a cubic spline fitting method?

PROGRAMMING EXERCISES

This chapter has presented sample programs for a number of the most common numerical problems. However, the choice of the best method for the numerical solution of mathematical problems is far from easy in many cases, and you are advised to use one of the major numerical libraries (such as the NAG Library (NAG Ltd, 1988)) wherever possible.

Most of the following examples use the procedures developed in this chapter as a means of experimenting with their accuracy and usefulness. However, the opportunity is also taken to introduce several further techniques. For more details concerning these, and other numerical methods you should consult an appropriate numerical analysis text.

18.1   In Exercise 11.5 you wrote a program to solve the following equations, using the bisection method to find those roots which lie in the range $-10 \leqslant x \leqslant 10$. Modify your program, if necessary, to print the number of iterations taken and use it to find the roots again, saving the roots and the number of iterations in a file.

    (a) $10x^3 - x^2 - 39x + 72$
    (b) $20x^3 - 52x^2 - 17x + 24$
    (c) $5x^3 - x^2 - 8x + 16$
    (d) $10x^4 + 13x^3 - 19x^2 + 8x + 48$
    (e) $x^4 + 2x^3 - 23x^2 - 24x + 144$
    (f) $9x^4 - 42x^3 - 1040x^2 + 5082x - 5929$

Now replace the subroutine that uses the bisection method by one that uses the secant method and run the program again, taking care that you do not overwrite the results saved in a file by the previous program. Finally, repeat the process using Newton's method.

Now write another program to list the three sets of results in a form suitable for comparing the effectiveness of the three methods.

18.2 Use the programs you wrote for Exercise 18.1 to produce a similar comparison for the following functions:

    (a) $\sin(3x + \pi/4)$
    (b) $\sin 3x \cos x$
    (c) $\sin 5x + 5 \cos x$
    (d) $2 - e^{\sin x}$
    (e) $\tan(x + \pi/6)$
    (f) $\sin(e^{x/3})$

*18.3 Use the Gaussian elimination method, described in Section 18.4, to solve the following systems of simultaneous linear equations:

    (a)
$$\begin{aligned} 2x + 3y + z &= 4 \\ x - 2y - z &= 3 \\ -2x + y + 3z &= 4 \end{aligned}$$

    (b)
$$\begin{aligned} 2x + y - z &= 1 \\ 4x - y - 3z &= -3 \\ x + 3y + z &= 4 \end{aligned}$$

    (c)
$$\begin{aligned} -2x - y + 4z &= 4 \\ x + 2y - 2z &= 1 \\ 3x + 4y - 6z &= -1 \end{aligned}$$

    (d)
$$\begin{aligned} x - 2y - z + w &= 3 \\ 3x + y + z - 2w &= 3 \\ -2x - 3y + 2z - w &= 4 \\ x + y - z + w &= 0 \end{aligned}$$

    (e)
$$\begin{aligned} x + t &= 1 \\ 2y - z &= 5 \\ 2x - w &= 1 \\ 2z + w &= -3 \\ y - 2t &= 3 \end{aligned}$$

How did your program deal with systems (c) and (e)?

18.4 Use the Gaussian elimination method, described in Section 18.4, to solve the following system of simultaneous linear equations:

$$\begin{aligned} 10x + 7y + 8z + 7w &= 32 \\ 7x + 5y + 6z + 5w &= 23 \\ 8x + 6y + 10z + 9w &= 33 \\ 7x + 5y + 9z + 10w &= 31 \end{aligned}$$

If the coefficients had been obtained by experimental means, or as the result of some earlier calculation, there could be some slight errors in them. In order to test the effect of this, change the coefficients on the right-hand side of the equations by one in the fourth significant figure (about 0.03%) to 32.01, 22.99, 32.99, and 31.01 and run the program again to find a new solution. Did the result surprise you?

Now change the same coefficients by one in the third significant figure to 32.1, 22.9, 32.9, and 31.1 and run it again.

This example (which is due to T.S. Wilson) illustrates the problem of ill-conditioned systems, first mentioned in Chapter 11.

18.5 In Section 18.4 it was mentioned that iterative methods were often more suitable than Gaussian elimination for the solution of simultaneous equations, especially when many of the coefficients are zero. One of the best-known iterative methods is the Gauss–Seidel method, which can be summarized as follows.

In the discussion in Section 18.4 we mainly considered the set of simultaneous equations in their algebraic form

$$a_{11}x_1 + a_{12}x_2 + \ldots + a_{1n}x_n = b_1$$
$$a_{21}x_1 + a_{22}x_2 + \ldots + a_{2n}x_n = b_2$$
$$.$$
$$.$$
$$.$$
$$a_{n1}x_1 + a_{n2}x_2 + \ldots + a_{nn}x_n = b_n$$

although we first introduced them in their matrix form

$$ax = b$$

where a is an $n \times n$ matrix and x and b are n-dimensional vectors. In this discussion only matrix notation will be used. Furthermore, it is not intended to examine the mathematics of this method here, but simply to present the result. A good numerical analysis text can be referred to for the details, if required.

We now define a new n-dimensional vector c, where

$$c_i = \frac{bi}{a_{ii}} \qquad \text{for all } i$$

and a new $n \times n$ matrix d, where

$$d_{ii} = 0 \qquad \text{for all } i$$
$$d_{ij} = \frac{-a_{ij}}{a_{ii}} \qquad \text{for all } i, j \text{ where } i \neq j$$

The Gauss–Seidel iteration is then specified by

$$x_i(m) = \Sigma(d_{ij}*x_j(m)) + \Sigma(d_{ij}*x_j(m-1)) + c_i$$

where $x_i(m)$ represents the mth iteration of x_i. A suitable convergence criterion will be the third type described in Section 11.5, namely that the difference between successive approximations should be less than a small value. This can be expressed in this context as

$$|x_i(m)-x_i(m-1)| < e \qquad \text{for all } i$$

Write a subroutine to implement the Gauss–Seidel method, and modify your existing program for the solution of simultaneous equations (or the one in Section 18.4) to use this subroutine. Use this new program to solve the five systems of simultaneous equations given in Exercise 18.3.

Which method proved to be most suitable for each system?

18.6 A solid shape is formed by rotating the curve $y = f(x)$ about the x-axis. The volume of such a shape is

$$A = \int_a^b \pi f(x)^2 dx$$

where a and b are the start and end of the curve. Write a subroutine that accepts a function name $f(x)$ and the limits a and b as its input, and returns the volume of the corresponding solid shape by evaluating the above integral. Use Simpson's rule for integration.

Confirm that for $f(x)=\sqrt{x}$, $a=1$ and $b=3$, the volume contained is 4π units.

18.7 Write a program, or programs, to perform the following actions:

(a) Calculate a set of values of $f(x)$, for x within a specified range (for example, from $x = -10$ to $x = +10$ in steps of 0.5), and tabulate these.

(b) Use these tabulated values to interpolate a set of splines, or other approximating curves, through these points.

(c) Use Simpson's rule to find the definite integral of the original function between two specified values of x, and also of the interpolated curves between the same values.

(d) Display the difference between the two integrals as one measure of the goodness of fit.

Test your program(s) on the following functions:

(i) x^2
(ii) $x^2 + 3x - 5$
(iii) x^3

(iv) $2x^3 - 3x^2 - 6x + 4$

(v) x^4

(vi) $3x^4 + 5x^3 - 2x^2 + 7x - 9$

(vii) $\sin 2x$

(viii) $\sin(x/2 + \pi/3)\cos x$

(ix) $e^{-x^2/2}$

18.8   Exercises 11.13 and 11.14 showed how the Newton quotient could be used to calculate the first derivative of a function, but also showed how the choice of h in the formula for the quotient

$$f'(x) = \frac{f(x+h) - f(x)}{h}$$

where h is small, was critical to the accuracy of the calculation. Euler's method for the solution of first-order differential equations of the form

$$\frac{dy}{dx} = g(x,y)$$

where $y = f(x)$, uses the Newton quotient to replace the differential on the left-hand side of the equation:

$$\frac{f(x+h) - f(x)}{h} = g(x,y)$$

or

$$f(x+h) = f(x) + hg(x,y)$$

If we know the value of $f(x)$ for some initial value of x (for example $x = 0$) then we can calculate the value at $x + h$, and so on. However, our experience in Exercises 11.13 and 11.14 might lead us to suppose that the choice of h will be critical, and this supposition is normally correct.

Use Euler's method in a program to solve the following problem. It is well known that in a vacuum a steel ball and a feather will fall at the same speed under the influence of gravity. However, in practice there is always some air resistance which leads to the steel ball hitting the ground first. This retarding force is normally assumed to be proportional to the square of the velocity, leading to the following equation (from Newton's second law):

$$ma = mg - cv^2$$

where m is the mass of the ball, a is its downward acceleration, g is the acceleration due to gravity, v is the velocity of the ball, and c is some constant. This, in turn, leads us to the first-order differential equation

$$\frac{dv}{dt} = a = g - kv^2$$

where $k = c/m$.

Assuming that for a steel ball of mass 1 kg the value of k is 0.001, write a program to tabulate the downward velocity of a 1 kg steel ball dropped from a stationary hot-air balloon at a great height, and hence calculate the terminal velocity of the ball (that is, the maximum speed that can be attained, which will be achieved when the retarding force due to air resistance equals the accelerating force due to gravity).

Run your program for a range of values for h to determine what is the best value (that is, the time interval between 'samplings' in this case).

18.9 Use the program you wrote for Exercise 18.8 to find the terminal velocity of a man jumping from the balloon. Assume his mass to be 100 kg and k to be 0.004.

When he has reached his terminal velocity he opens a parachute, with the result that k becomes 0.3. Modify your program to find how this affects his speed. (*Hint*: you may need to alter h again.)

*18.10 Radioactive elements decay into other elements at a rate given by the equation

$$\frac{dm}{dt} = -rm$$

where m is the mass of the original material still present at time t, and r is a constant property of the element known as the decay rate.

Analytical solution of this equation leads, among other things, to the conclusion that the mass of the original material is reduced by one half in a time T, known as the half-life of the substance, where $T = (\log_e 0.5)/r$ ($\approx 0.693/r$).

Use Euler's method to calculate the mass remaining, over a period of 500 years, of an initial 10 kg radioactive substance whose half-life is 200 years. Experiment with different values of h, starting with $h = 20$ years.

18.11 In your program for Exercise 18.10 you calculated the change in mass of an element due to radioactive decay. In general, the amount of this mass lost in energy is infinitesimal compared with that converted into another element, and can be ignored. It is simple, therefore, to calculate the mass of the new element, given the initial mass present, after a given time. However, in many cases, this new element itself decays into a third element. In this situation, clearly, a pair of simultaneous differential equations are required to describe the process. An example of this process is the decay of strontium-92 (with a half-life of about 162 minutes) into yttrium-92 (with a half-life of about 327 minutes), which in turn decays into zirconium.

Write a program which will use Euler's method to calculate how many atoms there will be of each element at 15-minute intervals over a 10-hour period, assuming that there were 10^{20} atoms of pure strontium-92 at the start of the experiment.

Run your program again using time intervals of 5, 10 and 20 minutes.

18.12 The Gaussian elimination technique, which was described in Section 18.4 as a method for the solution of simultaneous linear equations, can also be used to invert a matrix. The method is as follows.

A square matrix A is invertible if there exists a matrix $\overline{A}$ which satisfies the equation

$$A \times \overline{A} = I$$

where I is the identity matrix (that is, $I(i,j) = 0$ if $i \neq j$, $I(i,j) = 1$ if $i = j$).

The technique of using Gaussian elimination to calculate the inverse matrix $\overline{A}$, or to establish that no inverse exists, is best illustrated by an example. Suppose that we wish to find the inverse of the matrix

$$A = \begin{bmatrix} 1 & 2 & 1 \\ 3 & 1 & -2 \\ -1 & 2 & 1 \end{bmatrix}$$

The first step is to construct a new matrix B equal to $A|I$:

$$B = \begin{bmatrix} 1 & 2 & 1 & | & 1 & 0 & 0 \\ 3 & 1 & -2 & | & 0 & 1 & 0 \\ -1 & 2 & 1 & | & 0 & 0 & 1 \end{bmatrix}$$

We now apply a slight variation of Gaussian elimination so that the left-hand three columns (those corresponding to the original matrix A) become the identity matrix. The transformed matrix B will now take the following form:

$$B = \begin{bmatrix} 1 & 0 & 0 & | & 1/2 & 0 & -1/2 \\ 0 & 1 & 0 & | & -1/10 & 1/5 & 1/2 \\ 0 & 0 & 1 & | & 7/10 & -2/5 & -1/2 \end{bmatrix}$$

and the right-hand half now contains the inverse of A. If the Gaussian elimination fails (for example, because one of the rows becomes filled with zeros) then the matrix A is not invertible.

Write a program that will read a square matrix of a size specified by the user (up to a defined limit), and will use Gaussian elimination to calculate the inverse of the matrix. If the matrix is not invertible a message to this effect should be printed.

Your program should use the matrix multiplication subroutine written in Chapter 14 (or a similar one written by you) to confirm that the product of the original matrix and the calculated inverse matrix is, indeed, the identity matrix.

18.13 Use Newton's method to calculate the following values:

(a) the square root of 5,
(b) the cube root of 7,
(c) the seventh root of 2000.

Obsolete and little-used features of Fortran 77

19

The committee that produced the Standard for Fortran 77, like its successor committee, which has produced Fortran 90, was extremely reluctant to remove anything from the language for fear of making existing programs no longer valid. As a result Fortran 77 contains a number of features that should not normally be used, but are in the language to provide compatibility with earlier versions. This chapter contains brief details of some of these features, which the reader may come across in programs written by other people. *You should not normally ever use any of these features in new programs.*

19.1 Some obsolete control statements

The block IF (and in some situations the logical IF) provide a powerful decision-making capability, and one that can be used while still retaining a good overall structure for the program. Fortran 77, however, also contains statements or blocks of statements whose use encourages badly structured programs, leading to errors of several types. They are included within the Fortran 77 language purely for compatibility with earlier versions of Fortran and, with one exception discussed in Section 8.2, *they should never be used*.

They all have one thing in common, namely the identification of one or more statements by means of a statement label, followed by the transfer of control to that statement (or one of those statements), depending upon some condition. Potentially this may lead to a total breakdown of any ordered structure, and, at the very least, a partial breakdown is inevitable. It makes their use dangerous, and since they provide no capability that does not already exist there is, in the author's view, no reason to use them. Nevertheless they will be mentioned, briefly, for the sake of completeness.

The *first* is another type of IF statement: the **arithmetic** IF. It allows a three-way choice, depending on the value of an *arithmetic* expression. It takes the form

```
IF (arithmetic expression) label1, label2, label3
```

and causes control to be transferred to the statement labelled *label1* if the value of the arithmetic expression is negative, to the one labelled *label2* if it is zero, and to the one labelled *label3* if it is positive.

The *second* allows for a multi-way decision based on the value of an integer expression, and takes the form

```
GOTO (label1, label2, ..., labeln), integer expression
```

This is called a **computed** GOTO and causes control to be transferred to the statement labelled *label1* if the value of the integer expression is 1, to the statement labelled *label2* if it is 2, and so on. If the value of the integer

Figure 19.1
Counting sexes using a
block IF.

```
      DO 5, I=1,N
        IF (ISEX.EQ.0) THEN
           NF=NF+1
        ELSE
           NM=NM+1
        END IF
5     CONTINUE
```

```
      DO 5, I=1,N
        IF (ISEX) 4,3,4
   3    NF=NF+1
        GOTO 5
   4    NM=NM+1
   5 CONTINUE
```

Figure 19.2
Counting sexes using an
arithmetic IF.

expression is negative or 0, or if it is greater than the number of labels specified, then the computed GOTO has no effect and the next statement is obeyed.

The *third* is the worst of all and is known as an **assigned** GOTO. It will not be described at all.

Because of the lack of any structure in these statements, a *fourth* type is required to sort things out again, although it can be very valuable in its own right in certain situations. This statement is the **unconditional** GOTO, which we have already met as an essential part of a conditional DO loop, and simply transfers control to a specified statement:

GOTO *label*

To see why it is needed in these other situations, consider a variation of Example 7.4 in which we merely require the number of men and the number of women to be counted. Using a block IF the DO loop would be as shown in Figure 19.1, while corresponding loops for an arithmetic IF and a computed GOTO are given in Figures 19.2 and 19.3. Since the block IF has assumed that any non-zero code represents a male, the same assumption has been made for the other two versions.

A glance shows that even for this very simple problem all sense of structure has been lost in the arithmetic IF and computed GOTO versions. In both it has been necessary to include an unconditional GOTO to avoid counting each individual as both male *and* female! In the case of the computed GOTO it has been necessary to reverse the order of the updating statements so that the (unexpected) cases in which ISEX has some value other than 0 or 1 are dealt with correctly.

```
      DO 5, I=1,N
        GOTO (4,3),ISEX+1
   3    NM=NM+1
        GOTO 5
   4    NF=NF+1
   5 CONTINUE
```

Figure 19.3
Counting sexes using a
computed GOTO.

19.2   The alternate RETURN

In Chapter 16 it was mentioned, briefly, that it was possible to use an asterisk (*) as a dummy argument in association with a special form of actual argument that allows alternative places for the subroutine to return to. These are specified in the list of actual arguments by writing *label*, where *label* is a statement label in the same program unit as the CALL statement. In the subroutine an extended form of the RETURN statement is used in which the word RETURN is followed by an integer expression:

> RETURN *intexp*

If the value of the expression *intexp* when the RETURN is obeyed is 1, then a return is made to the statement labelled with the actual argument label that corresponds to the first asterisk dummy argument; if it is 2 a return is made to the second, and so on. If the value of the expression is less than 1 or greater than the number of asterisks in the dummy argument list, then a normal RETURN is made to the statement following the CALL statement.

Figure 19.4
Alternate RETURN from a
subroutine.

```
PROGRAM MAIN
REAL X,Y
INTEGER N
      .
CALL ALTRET(*10,X,Y,*20,*99,N)
5 .....
      .
10 .....
      .
20 .....
      .
99 .....
      .
END

SUBROUTINE ALTRET(*,A,B,*,*,N)
REAL A,B
INTEGER N,J
      . .
RETURN J
      .
END
```

```
        PROGRAM MAIN
        REAL X,Y
        INTEGER N
          .
          .
          .
        CALL ALTRET(X,Y,N,IRET)
        GOTO (10,20,99),IRET
    5 .....
          .
          .
   10 .....
          .
          .
   20 .....
          .
          .
   99 .....
          .
          .
        END

        SUBROUTINE ALTRET(A,B,N,J)
        REAL A,B
        INTEGER N,J
          .
          .
        RETURN
          .
          .
        END
```

Figure 19.5
An equally bad
alternative to the method
of RETURN shown in
Figure 19.4.

Figure 19.4 illustrates this process. It can be seen that if J has the value 1 then a return will be made to the statement labelled 10, if it is 2 the return will be to label 20, and if it is 3 execution will continue from label 99. If J is less than 1 or greater than 3 then execution will continue from the next statement, the one labelled 5.

In fact, the use of this facility is normally to be deplored. It serves no particularly useful purpose since exactly the same effect can be obtained with a greater degree of flexibility by returning the value of J through an additional argument:

```
        SUBROUTINE ALTRET (A,B,N,J)
```

thus allowing the calling program to preserve a good, well-planned structure. The alternate return is essentially the same as returning the value J and using it in a computed GOTO (see Figure 19.5), and is not recommended for precisely the reasons that were given in Section 19.1, when the reader was advised against using that statement.

19.3   DO **loops with real** DO **variables**

The DO variable is normally used to cause the loop to be obeyed a fixed number of times and it is therefore usually appropriate for it to be an integer; indeed in earlier versions of Fortran it *had* to be an integer. Fortran 77, however, allows the use of a real variable for this purpose if so desired, which may seem to be useful in certain circumstances. For example, consider the situation postulated in Section 5.1, in which a table of equivalent temperatures between two limits is required:

> **1**   Repeat for each Celsius temperature from 0 to 100 in steps of 5
> **1.1** Calculate Fahrenheit equivalent
> **1.2** Print both temperatures

At first sight this would seem to be quite straightforward, and ideal for the use of a DO statement of the form

```
DO 20, C=0,100,5
```

However, it is not so simple as it appears! Remember that an integer is a whole number and is always held exactly. A real number may contain a fractional part and is stored to a fixed degree of accuracy. It has been emphasized that it is never safe to assume that it is held *exactly* – rather, it is an *approximation*. Consider how the trip count is calculated.

First, the three expressions are evaluated and if necessary converted to the same type as the DO variable. In this case, therefore, *m1*, *m2* and *m3* will have the values 0.0, 100.0 and 5.0 respectively. The trip count is then calculated, using the formula

$$\text{MAX}\left(0, \text{INT}\left(\frac{m2-m1+m3}{m3}\right)\right)$$

This is where the problem lies, for since *m1*, *m2* and *m3* are all real values the expression $(m2-m1+m3)/m3$ will be calculated using real arithmetic. The result will therefore be an *approximation*, albeit a very accurate one. However, whereas *we* should expect a value of exactly 21 from this evaluation, the computer might produce a value of 21.000001 or 20.999999. For most purposes this does not matter, but in this case it does, because the next thing that happens is that the integer equivalent is produced. If the value was 21.000001 the value 21 will result, but if it was 20.999999 the truncation process will lead to a trip count of 20!

Using a real DO variable is therefore intrinsically dangerous and not to be recommended. It is always preferable to use an integer DO variable for what is, after all, a counting operation.

19.4   The P scale factor edit descriptor

In Chapter 17 the P edit descriptor, which is used to provide a *scale factor* for numeric input or output, was briefly mentioned. This is written kP, and on input, as long as the input data does not contain an exponent, it has the same effect as would an exponent of $-k$ following the data. Thus if an input record contains the three numbers 17.5, 2410 and 9.3E6, the statements

```
      READ (*,111) X,Y,Z
  111 FORMAT (3P,3F10.2)
```

will cause the variables X, Y and Z to take the values 0.0175, 0.0241 and 9 300 000.0. Let us examine this in detail.

The first number read is 17.5 and the scale factor therefore causes this to be multiplied by 10^{-3}, with the result that 0.0175 is stored in X. The next number is 2410, which (assuming that it is at the right of the input field) will therefore have a decimal point implied before the last two digits; the resulting value of 24.1 becomes 0.0241 after the scale factor of 10^{-3} has been applied. The third number is 9.3E6: since an exponent is specified, the scale factor does not apply and this is the value stored.

On output with F editing a similar process operates, but in reverse: thus the number output is the internal value multiplied by 10^k.

When a scale factor is used for output with D or E editing, however, it does not affect the value output, but only its representation. In this case the exponent is reduced by k and the mantissa (the preceding real part) is multiplied by 10^k.

When a scale factor is used for output with a G edit descriptor it has no effect when F formatting is being used. When E formatting is in operation it has the same effect as for E editing.

Figure 19.6 shows the effect of this, and it can be seen very clearly that the 3P scale factor causes the values in the first column (printed using an F12.4 edit descriptor) to be multiplied by 1000 (10^3). The values output in the remaining columns (printed using E12.4 and G12.4 descriptors) are not changed – only their format is.

The P edit descriptor is, at best, a confusing feature of Fortran 77 and it is easy to obtain erroneous results through its use. It is not recommended.

Figure 19.6
An example of the effect
of a scale factor on
output.

```
      PROGRAM FIG196
      REAL X,Y
      X=147.903
      Y=0.0147903
      PRINT 201,X,X,X,Y,Y,Y
  201 FORMAT(1H ,3P,F12.4,E12.4,G12.4)
      STOP
      END
```

(output)
```
 147903.0000   147.90E+00    147.9
     14.7903   147.90E-04  147.90E-04
```

19.5 The IMPLICIT statement

In the absence of any declaration a variable is assumed to be integer if the initial letter of its name begins with one of the six letters I-N, and real otherwise. Such undeclared variables are said to have an *implicit type* (implied, that is, by the initial letters of their name).

We can, however, alter this state of affairs by defining a new set of implicit types by means of a further specification statement

IMPLICIT *type1* (*list1*), *type2* (*list2*), . . .

where *type1*, . . . are types of variables (for example, INTEGER, COMPLEX, CHARACTER*len) and *list1*, . . . define the initial letters that are to imply the corresponding type. The list of initial letters consists of a list of one or more letters and/or ranges of letters denoted by the first and last letters of the range separated by a minus sign (for example, P-T).

Thus the statement

IMPLICIT DOUBLE PRECISION(A-H), LOGICAL(L)

will cause all undeclared variables starting with A, B, C, D, E, F, G or H to be double precision variables, all those starting with L to be logical, and, of course, those starting with I, J, K, M or N to be integer. All remaining undeclared variables (starting with letters in the range O-Z) will be real.

Because the IMPLICIT statement defines default conditions it must appear *before* any other specification statements. We have already said that it can be dangerous to rely on implicit typing of variables using the default specification; but it is far more dangerous to rely on some other form of implicit typing, since it is easy to forget that some of the normal defaults are not being used. Thus, for example, it would be very easy to write a statement such as

```
DO 10, L=N1,N2
```

despite having already defined all variables beginning with L to be logical by means of an IMPLICIT statement such as the one above. This error would, presumably, be detected by the compiler and could be corrected by including the declaration

```
INTEGER L
```

at the start of the program (after the IMPLICIT statement!). However, two statements such as

```
A = SQRT(X+Y)
Z = (A+Y)*P
```

would, with the same IMPLICIT statement, lead to a double precision version of $\sqrt{X + Y}$ being stored in A, which in turn would cause the expression in the second statement to be evaluated using double precision arithmetic before the result was stored in Z as a real value. In this case nothing would cause any error, and the correct answer would be obtained. However, no extra accuracy would be gained through the (inadvertent) use of double precision since all the values being used have been calculated using single precision arithmetic; the only effect will be a (marginal) amount of wasted time!

It is strongly recommended that the IMPLICIT statement never be used, and that variables should always be explicitly declared.

19.6 The ENTRY statement

Sometimes it might be useful to combine two or more subroutines into a single subroutine, or two or more functions into a single function, in order to take advantage of a large amount of common code. We can define additional entry points to a subprogram by means of the ENTRY statement, which takes the form

```
ENTRY ename(arg1,arg2,....)
```

An ENTRY statement may appear anywhere after the initial SUBROUTINE or FUNCTION statement, except between a block IF statement and its corresponding END IF or between a DO statement and the terminal statement of the loop it controls. If the ENTRY statement is in a subroutine then *ename* is the name of a subroutine, but if it appears in a function then *ename* is also the name of a function. In the latter case any type declaration for *ename* must take place in an ordinary type specification statement, and the variable called *ename* must not appear (other than in a type specification statement) before the ENTRY statement. The dummy arguments specified in the ENTRY statement must not appear in any statements before the ENTRY statement unless they are also dummy arguments in the initial SUBROUTINE or FUNCTION statement of the subprogram, or in another ENTRY statement that precedes this one.

The subroutine or function defined by the ENTRY statement can be used by any other program unit in the normal way and, when it is called, execution will start at the first executable statement after the ENTRY. Thus in the following example the subroutine TRANS expects the angles THETA and PHI to be in radians (as required by the intrinsic functions SIN, COS, and so on), while DTRANS expects them in degrees and carries out an appropriate conversion.

```
      SUBROUTINE TRANS(X,Y,Z,THETA,PHI,U,V)
      PARAMETER (PI=3.1415926536)
      T = THETA
      P = PHI
      GOTO 1
C   DTRANS entry has THETA and PHI in degrees
      ENTRY DTRANS(X,Y,Z,THETA,PHI,U,V,)
      T = THETA*PI/180.0
      P = PHI*PI/180.0
    1       .
              .
              .
      END
```

Notice that this is frequently, as here, a situation that requires the use of a GOTO statement to avoid some initial statements associated with the ENTRY. It would be possible to avoid this by writing

```
      SUBROUTINE DTRANS(X,Y,Z,THETA,PHI,U,V)
      PARAMETER (PI=3.1415926536)
      THETA = THETA*PI/180:0
      PHI = PHI*PI/180.0
C   TRANS entry has THETA and PHI in radians
      ENTRY TRANS(X,Y,Z,THETA,PHI,U,V)
              .
              .
              .
      END
```

However, in this case the actual arguments corresponding to THETA and PHI will always be in radians on exit from the subroutine, even if they were in degrees on entry!

In this example both subroutines have the same number and type of arguments (which in fact even have the same names), but this need not necessarily be so. Figure 19.7 shows a function that has three other entries. The four resulting functions have specifications as follows:

MEAN(A,N)	returns the average of the N values in the array A, ignoring any outside the range -10^{30} to $+10^{30}$
MEANLO(A,N,AMAX)	as for MEAN but also ignoring any numbers greater than AMAX
MEANHI(A,N,AMIN)	as for MEAN but also ignoring any numbers less than AMIN
MEANMD(A,N,AMIN,AMAX)	returns the average of those of the N numbers in the array A that lie between AMIN and AMAX, inclusive

Figure 19.7
A multi-entried function.

```
      REAL FUNCTION MEANMD(A,N,XMIN,XMAX)
C
C This function, together with three further functions accessed as
C entries to the main function, calculates the mean values of
C various elements of an array
C
C Function declarations
      REAL MEANLO,MEANHI,MEAN
C Dummy arguments
      INTEGER N
      REAL A(N),XMIN,XMAX
C Local variables
      REAL AMIN,AMAX,SUM
      INTEGER NUM
C
C MEANMD calculates the average value of A(I),
C where XMIN <= A(I) <= XMAX, for I=1 to N
C
C Set AMIN and AMAX to limits
C
      AMIN=XMIN
      AMAX=XMAX
      GOTO 1
C
      ENTRY MEANLO(A,N,XMAX)
C
C MEANLO calculates the average value of A(I),
C where A(I) <= XMAX, for I=1 to N
C
C Set AMIN to a very large negative number
C
      AMIN=-1E30
      AMAX=XMAX
      GOTO 1
```

```
C
      ENTRY MEANHI(A,N,XMIN)
C
C MEANHI calculates the average value of A(I),
C where A(I) >= XMIN, for I=1 to N
C
C Set AMAX to a very large positive number
C
      AMIN=XMIN
      AMAX=1E30
      GOTO 1
C
      ENTRY MEAN(A,N)
C
C MEAN calculates the average value of A(I), for I=1 to N
C
C Set both AMIN and AMAX to very large values
C
      AMIN=-1E30
      AMAX=1E30
C
C Common section for all four functions
C Limits have been set - so calculate average
C
    1 SUM=0.0
      NUM=0
      DO 10, I=1,N
        IF (A(I).GE.AMIN .AND. A(I).LE.AMAX) THEN
           SUM=SUM+A(I)
           NUM=NUM+1
        END IF
   10 CONTINUE
C Calculate average and store in all four return variables
      MEAN=SUM/NUM
      MEANLO=MEAN
      MEANHI=MEAN
      MEANMD=MEAN
      RETURN
      END
```

The method used is to call the dummy arguments that specify the limits (if any) XMIN and XMAX, and to use two local variables AMIN and AMAX. If one, or both, of the limits is supplied then AMIN or AMAX, as appropriate, is set to the value, or values, supplied. If one, or both, of the limits is not supplied then AMIN or AMAX, as appropriate, is set to a very large positive or negative number (for example, $+10^{30}$ or -10^{30}). The four functions then follow a common path and find the average of all the numbers that lie between AMIN and AMAX. Once this has been done all four function names are set to the average, since it is not known at this stage which was used for the entry.

This highlights another problem with what is intrinsically a less than satisfactory concept. As a general rule it is far better to write two or more separate procedures than to attempt to combine them using the ENTRY facility.

Looking to the Future

PART

III

An outline of the next standard Fortran language: Fortran 90

20

The draft Fortran 90 standard was sent out for a first international review in the autumn of 1987. Following the receipt of over 500 responses from Fortran programmers throughout the world the draft standard was extensively revised in an attempt to satisfy as large a proportion of this comment as possible. A second draft standard was then sent out for a further international review, which ended in January 1990. Following this review, the final form of the language was determined in March of that year. This chapter gives an overview of the main extensions to Fortran 77 contained in Fortran 90 (there are no deletions). There are also a number of Fortran 90 programs, procedures and modules that will, it is to be hoped, illustrate the likely style of Fortran programs in the mid 1990s and beyond as Fortran 90 compilers start to become widely available.

20.1   The status of Fortran 90

During the period from around 1980 until 1989 a great deal of work was done to produce a new revised Standard Fortran to replace Fortran 77. The detailed technical work involved in this revision was carried out by X3J3, the American National Standards Institute's Fortran Committee, with overall supervision from ISO–IEC JTC1/SC22/WG5, the International Standards Organization's Fortran Working Group. Thus, unlike the 1966 and 1978 Standards, which were developed as American Standards initially and were subsequently ratified internationally, this new Standard started life as a draft International Standard as well as a draft American Standard. This joint 'ownership' of the working draft has been of considerable benefit since it has allowed, and encouraged, international participation in the development of the revised Standard from the outset. However, it has also led to considerable tensions, not least because of the different procedural systems and the different perceptions of what Fortran should be in the 21st century between workers on opposite sides of the Atlantic.

Fortunately all those involved, at whatever level, have the same goal – to see Fortran remain as the main language for scientific and technological programming well into the next century. Despite times when it appeared that there was no possibility of international agreement on what the new Standard should contain, with the related likelihood of *two* new Standards (one for the United States, and one for most of the rest of the world), intensive efforts during 1988 and 1989 ensured that by March 1990 both committees had agreed on a final draft Standard. It was also agreed that the informal name of this language should be Fortran 90. Although the new Standard had not been formally ratified by the time of publication of this book, this was expected to take place in late 1990 or early 1991.

The next section of this chapter contains a brief summary of the main changes to Fortran that will result from the adoption of Fortran 90. As mentioned in the Introduction to this book, Fortran 90 contains all of Fortran 77 and the changes will, therefore, all be additions to the language.

The remaining sections of this chapter consist of several Fortran 90 programs and program fragments, chosen to illustrate how the new features will affect programming style. These are, for obvious reasons, the only programs in this book that have not been compiled and run on a computer. It is possible that there may be some changes in the draft Standard before it is finally ratified, and some of these programs may turn out not to be valid Fortran 90 programs when that time comes. It is, however, extremely unlikely that there will be any major changes, and the only changes in these example programs that might be needed in order that they can be compiled and run by a Fortran 90 system will probably be minor syntactic ones.

20.2   The major changes incorporated in Fortran 90

The major extensions to Fortran 77 that are included in Fortran 90 are:

(1)   an alternative source form that is not constrained by the old card-oriented fixed columnar layout;

(2)   facilities for modular data and procedure definitions, thus providing a powerful and safe form of data and procedure encapsulation;

(3)   user-defined data types, derived from one or more of the six intrinsic data types;

(4)   facilities for whole-array operations;

(5)   facilities for pointers, thus permitting the creation and manipulation of dynamic data structures;

(6)   improved facilities for numerical computation, including the availability of parameterized intrinsic numeric types;

(7)   parameterized non-numeric intrinsic data types, allowing a Fortran processor to support more than one character set simultaneously.

Other important changes include the provision of additional control constructs (CASE...END CASE, DO...END DO, DO WHILE *condition* ...), recursion in procedures, dynamically allocatable arrays, additional input/output facilities, many more intrinsic procedures, trailing comments, and the concept of language evolution, involving the removal at some future time of features of an earlier Standard that have fallen into disuse and are no longer required.

The seven major areas are briefly discussed in the remainder of this section, while examples of both major and minor changes will be found in the remainder of the chapter.

New source form

In an age when almost all programs are typed directly into the computer, the old fixed-form layout of Fortran programs, designed to take advantage of certain aspects of punched cards, has long been obsolete. While this source form remains in Fortran 90 (as does every feature of Fortran 77), an alternative syntax is introduced that has no reserved columns, allows multiple statements on a line, allows trailing comments, and makes blanks significant (thus, P R O G R A M is not allowed as an alternative for PROGRAM, neither is MY WORD as an alternative for MYWORD – although MY_WORD is an acceptable identifier).

In addition, both old and new source forms in Fortran 90 allow lower-case characters to be used as an alternative to upper-case, add a number of new characters to the Fortran Character Set, and allow identifiers to be up to 31 characters long (instead of only six).

Thus it would be possible to write a short procedure to calculate the sum of some of the elements of an array in the following two ways:

```
      REAL FUNCTION PRTSUM(A,N,FIRST,LAST)
C
C  This function is coded in the old source form.
C  It sums the elements of the array A from A(FIRST) to A(LAST)
C
C  Dummy arguments
      INTEGER N,FIRST,LAST
      REAL A(N)
C  Local variables
      INTEGER I
      REAL SUM
C
C  Initialize sum
      SUM=0.0
C  Loop to accumulate sum
      DO 10, I=FIRST,LAST
        SUM=SUM+A(I)
   10 CONTINUE
C  Return sum of required elements
      PRTSUM=SUM
      RETURN
      END


REAL FUNCTION Partial_Sum(a,n,first,last)

!  This function is coded in the new source form.
!  It sums the elements of the array a from a(first) to a(last)

   INTEGER n,first,last;  REAL a(n) ! Dummy arguments
   INTEGER I;  REAL sum            ! Local variables

   sum=0.0                         ! Initialize sum
   DO 10, I=first,last             ! Loop to accumulate sum
     sum=sum+a(I)
10    CONTINUE                     ! End of loop
   Partial_Sum=sum;  RETURN        ! Return sum of required elements
END FUNCTION Partial_Sum
```

Modules

Fortran 77 provides only one way of obtaining some form of global access to data – through COMMON blocks. This is somewhat restrictive and depends totally on the ability of the programmer to specify exactly how the data is to be arranged in the computer's memory. Not only is this an undesirably low-level approach in an era of increasingly high-level software concepts, but on newer types of computer architecture it may be impossible to achieve without considerable loss of efficiency. The **module** provides a solution for this problem, and a great deal more.

A Fortran 90 module is a new form of program unit, consisting essentially of a set of declarations and/or a set of **module procedures**, which are grouped together under a single (global) name. However, whereas in Fortran 77 declarations relate only to data objects, in Fortran 90 it is possible to declare new data types (see below), new operators, the interface with an (external) procedure, or the user-defined generic name for a set of procedures. A module thus provides the means for **encapsulating** a set of related type, data object, interface or procedure declarations and making them all available to any procedure that requires them, simply by reference to the module name in a USE **statement**. Furthermore, some of the items in a module may be specified to be **private**, in which case any procedure using the module does *not* have access to them. This concept of **data hiding** is very important in developing secure and portable software libraries.

Thus at one extreme a module may simply be used as a more secure and, possibly, more efficient way of providing globally accessible variables; at the other, it can provide sophisticated encapsulation and data hiding, which make possible a number of new approaches to Fortran programming. An example of the simple 'COMMON block replacement' use is the following module:

```
MODULE Common_Demo
     REAL a,b(50),c(10,10)
     INTEGER first,last
     CHARACTER string*20
END MODULE Common_Demo
```

The declarations in this module can be made available to any procedure that wishes to use them by the inclusion of the statement

```
    USE Common-Demo
```

In Fortran 77 the same could be achieved by including the following five statements in each procedure:

```
REAL A,B(50),C(10,10)
INTEGER FIRST,LAST
COMMON/NUMBLK/A,B(50),C(10,10),FIRST,LAST
CHARACTER STRING*20
COMMON/CHRBLK/STRING
```

More sophisticated use of modules will be found in the examples in Sections 20.5 and 20.6.

Derived data types

Most modern programming languages now allow the programmer to define his own data types. Fortran 77 and Fortran 90 both contain six (intrinsic) data types – REAL, INTEGER, DOUBLE PRECISION, COMPLEX, LOGICAL and CHARACTER – and Fortran 90 allows the programmer to define new data types derived from any combination of these. Thus, for example, a program that was concerned with two-dimensional geometry might contain definitions of new data types called Point, Line and Circle, which could be defined as follows:

```
TYPE Point
   REAL x,y          ! x and y are the coordinates of the point
END TYPE Point

TYPE Line
   REAL a,b,c        ! a, b and c are the coefficients of the
                     ! equation of the line:  ax + by + c = 0
END TYPE Line

TYPE Circle
   TYPE (Point) c    ! c is the centre of the circle
   REAL r            ! r is the radius of the circle
END TYPE Circle
```

Notice, incidentally, the syntax of the declaration of a variable having a derived type in the definition of the type Circle.

An object of a derived type can be dealt with as a whole, or its individual elements may be accessed directly:

```
TYPE (Point) p1,p2
p1 = Point(1.5,2.5)    ! p1 is the point (1.5,2.5)
p2%x = 1.5             ! p2 has an x-coordinate of 1.5
p2%y = 2.5             ! p2 has a y-coordinate of 2.5
                       ! p1 and p2 refer to points having the
                       ! same coordinates
```

In practice, the ability to define one's own data types is of little use unless one can also define operators for use in expressions involving objects of these types, and can make the type definition globally available so that derived type objects may be used as arguments to procedures. Fortran 90 allows both the definition of new operator symbols and the **overloading** of the intrinsic operators to allow them to be used with new data types. The inclusion of the type definitions and operator definitions in a module means that they can be made available to any procedure requiring them.

Array operations

Although computation involving large arrays has been an important part of scientific computing since the very earliest days of Fortran programming, it has been necessary to process arrays element by element in almost all situations. Fortran 90 at last overcomes this weakness.

In Fortran 90 all arithmetic, logical and character operations and intrinsic functions are extended to operate on array-valued operands, which may be whole arrays or array sections (subarrays). These new facilities include whole, partial and masked array assignment, array-valued constants, expressions and functions (both intrinsic and external), and the addition of new intrinsic functions to perform various array-related operations.

Thus, given the array declarations

```
REAL A(10,20),B(10,20),C(10,20),D(20)
```

the following Fortran 77 code

```
      DO 50, J=1,20
        DO 50, I=1,10
          A(I,J)=B(I,J)+C(I,J)
50    CONTINUE
      DO 60, J=1,20
        D(J)=0.0
        DO 60, I=1,10
          D(J)=D(J)+A(I,J)
60    CONTINUE
```

would be replaced by the two statements

```
      A=B+C
      D=SUM(A,2)
```

where the second argument in the reference to SUM specifies the dimension along which the summation is to take place. (SUM(A) would have delivered a scalar value, being the sum of *all* the elements of the array A.)

Pointers

Despite the increased power of arrays in Fortran 90, many applications require a different form of data structure, such as a linked list or a tree. Such data structures can be created only by use of a **pointer** mechanism. The inclusion of a pointer facility in Fortran 90 also has one further benefit, in that it makes possible the provision of a **dynamic array** capability – something that Fortran programmers have wanted for many years.

A pointer is not a data entity but an **attribute** of some data entity, and must be declared using a new form of declaration, more comprehensive than was possible in Fortran 77. Thus the statement

```
TYPE (Node), POINTER :: head, current, tail
```

declares three objects (`head`, `current` and `tail`), which are pointers to objects of a (user-defined) derived type `Node`.

Similarly, the statement

```
REAL, DIMENSION (:,:), POINTER :: in, out
```

declares two objects (`in` and `out`) that are pointers to real two-dimensional arrays.

Section 20.6 shows an example of the use of pointers to build an ordered binary tree.

Numerical computation

Most Fortran programs have a substantial computational element, and yet the facilities available for computation have not changed since the very first Fortran system: they are REAL, DOUBLE PRECISION, COMPLEX and INTEGER. Fortran 90 introduces the concept of **parameterized data types**, which allow more than two levels of precision, if the processor can support them, and enables a program to specify the precision required in a portable way. Thus

```
REAL (KIND=4) x
```

or

```
REAL (4) x
```

specifies that x is a *real* variable with a **kind type parameter** of 4, while

```
COMPLEX (KIND=8) q
```

or

```
COMPLEX (8) q
```

specifies that q is a *complex* variable with a kind type parameter of 8 – that is, each of its components is a *real* variable with a kind type parameter of 8.

The new intrinsic function SELECTED_REAL_KIND allows the user to specify the required precision, and the function will return the smallest value of the kind type parameter that will provide that precision. Thus the following declarations will ensure that the compiler will always use data types with at least 10 decimal digits of precision and an exponent range from 10^{-50} to 10^{50}:

```
INTEGER my_real
PARAMETER (my_real=SELECTED_REAL_KIND(10,50))
REAL (my_real) a,b,c
COMPLEX (my_real) p,q,r
```

A similar parameterization capability exists for integers.

Parameterized non-numeric data types

A similar parameterization capability also applies to logical and character data types. In the case of logical variables its primary purpose is to allow the processor to provide an alternative form of *logical* variable that occupies less than a full numeric storage unit – possibly only a single bit. This could be particularly important when using logical arrays as *masks* in array operations.

The parameterization of character data types serves a different and very important function: namely, enabling the use of character data appropriate to languages other than English and, in particular, Chinese, Japanese, and other Eastern languages whose characters are too numerous to be represented in a single (8-bit) byte.

For example, the following program extract is intended to be run on a processor which supports the character sets used in Chinese, Hungarian, Punjabi, Russian and Spanish, as well as English. The integer constants Chinese, Hungarian, Punjabi, Russian and Spanish are assumed to have been give appropriate kind-parameter values in a PARAMETER statement.

```
CHARACTER (Chinese)   Maggie_C*10, Name_C*6    ! Hanzi characters
CHARACTER (Hungarian) Maggie_H*30, Name_H*20   ! Hungarian letters
CHARACTER (Punjabi)   Maggie_P*30, Name_P*20   ! Gurmurki characters
CHARACTER (Russian)   Maggie_H*30, Name_R*20   ! Cyrillic letters
CHARACTER (Spanish)   Maggie_S*30, Name_S*20   ! Spanish letters
DATA Maggie_C, Maggie_H, Maggie_P, Maggie_R, Maggie_S   &
   / Chinese_'没有她什么都作不了'                          &
     Hungarian_'Őnélküle, nem csinálhatom'              &
     Punjabi_'ਉਸਦੇ ਬਿਨ ਦੂਦ ਨਹੀ ਤੇ ਸਕਦਾ'                  &
     Russian_' БЕЗ НЕЁ НИЧТО НЕ ВОЗМОЖНО '               &
     Spanish_'Sin ella, nada es posible' /
```

```
                    .
                    .
                    .
        SELECT CASE (Language)         ! "Language" is the KIND-parameter
                                       ! value for the required language
        CASE (Chinese)
          PRINT *,Chinese_'你叫什么名子';  READ '(A)',Name_C
        CASE (Hungarian)
          PRINT *,Hungarian_'Hogy hívják?';  READ '(A)',Name_H
        CASE Punjabi
          PRINT *,Punjabi_'ਤੁਹਾਡਾ ਨਾਂ ਕੀ ਹੈ ?';  READ '(A)',Name_P
        CASE (Russian)
          PRINT *,Russian_' КАК ВАС ЗОВУТ ?';  READ '(A)',Name_R
        CASE (Spanish)
          PRINT *,Spanish_'¿Cómo te llamas?';  READ '(A)',Name_S
        CASE DEFAULT
          PRINT *,'What is your name?';  READ '(A)',Name
        END SELECT
```

20.3   New forms of loops

The following program is a Fortran 90 version of the program written in
Example 8.1.

```
PROGRAM Point_plot

!  This program plots a cross at each of a set of data points,
!  and surrounds negatively coded ones with a circle.
!  The data is terminated by a point with a zero code.

        INTEGER n
        REAL x,y,width,radius    ! width is the width of each cross
                                 ! radius is the radius of the surrounding
                                 ! circle
        PARAMETER (width=0.25,radius=0.5*width)

        CALL Initialize_plotting
        DO                             ! Start of loop
          READ *,x,y,n                 ! Read next set of data
          CALL PlotCross(x,y,width)
          IF (n<0) CALL PlotCircle(x,y,radius)
          IF (n==0) EXIT               ! End if zero code
        END DO
        CALL Terminate_plotting
        STOP
END Point_plot
```

Note that the EXIT statement eliminates the need for the GOTO statement as a means of leaving a loop. Note also that the operators <, <=, >, >=, == and /= are alternatives in Fortran 90 for .LT., .LE., .GT., .GE., .EQ. and .NE.

Although not really necessary, since the EXIT statement (and a related CYCLE statement) is all that is necessary to deal with any situation, Fortran 90 has also added a DO...WHILE construct. Using this feature, the loop in the above program could be rewritten as follows:

```
n=1                            ! Initialize code
DO WHILE (n/=0)                ! Loop while code is non-zero
  READ *,x,y,n                 ! Read next set of data
  CALL PlotCross(x,y,width)
  IF (n<0) CALL PlotCircle(x,y,radius)
END DO
```

Fortran 90 has also eliminated the need for a label on the terminating statement of a DO loop, together with the need to remember which statements may not be terminating statements:

```
PROGRAM Tables

! A program to print multiplication tables from 2 to 12 times

    INTEGER I,J
    DO I=2,12
      PRINT *,' '
      PRINT *,I,' times table'
      DO J=1,12
        PRINT *,I,' times',J,' is',I*J
      END DO
    END DO
    STOP
END Tables
```

20.4   Vectors, matrices and array operations

In Section 14.4 subroutines were developed to carry out the main vector and matrix operations:

MATADD(A,B,C,N,M)   which adds the two N by M matrices stored in A and B, returning the result in C;

DOTPRD(A,B,AB,N)   which forms the scalar product of the two vectors A and B, of dimension N, returning the result in AB;

MATMLT(X,Y,Z,P,N,Q)   which forms the matrix product of the two matrices X and Y, where X is of dimension P*N and Y of dimension N*Q, returning the result in the P*Q matrix Z.

In Fortran 90 all these operations are defined within the language. The following program demonstrates their use, together with some of the other features added to Fortran 90 to facilitate array processing.

```
PROGRAM Matrix_demo

    REAL, DIMENSION(5)       :: a,b
    REAL, DIMENSION(5,10)    :: d,e,f,g
    REAL                     :: ab,x(2,5),y(5,9),z(2,9)
    INTEGER                  :: I

    a=(/1.0,2.0,3.0,4.0,5.0/)        ! assign to the whole of the vector a
                                     ! using an array constructor
    b=(/6.0,7.0,8.0,9.0,10.0/)
    ab=DOTPRODUCT(a,b)               ! assign the scalar product of the
                                     ! vectors a and b using the intrinsic
                                     ! function DOTPRODUCT

    DO I=1,10,2                      ! set up the array d by assigning
      d(:,I)=a                       ! the vector a to the odd-numbered
                                     ! rows of the array d, and the
      d(:,I+1)=b                     ! vector b to the even-numbered rows
    END DO
    e=SPREAD(a,1,10)                 ! create a matrix from 10 rows of a
    f=d+e                            ! matrix addition
    g=d-e                            ! matrix subtraction

    x(1,:)=a                         ! assign a to the first column of x
    x(2,:)=b                         ! assign b to the second column
    y=f(:,1:9)                       ! assign a suitable size section of
                                     ! the array f to y
    z=MATMUL(x,y)                    ! assign the matrix product of x and
                                     ! y to z by use of the intrinsic
                                     ! function MATMUL

    STOP
END PROGRAM Matrix_demo
```

20.5   Dynamic arrays

In Fortran 77 it is often necessary to declare arrays of a considerably larger size than are normally required, and then to input, or otherwise ascertain, the maximum size for this run of the program and use only part of the array. Fortran 90 provides a genuine dynamic array capability to deal with this problem, as illustrated in the following program fragment:

```
SUBROUTINE Work(a,b,c)       ! a, b and c are arrays whose size is only
                             ! determined during execution
    REAL, ALLOCATABLE, DIMENSION (:,:) :: a,b,c
    INTEGER :: n,m
```

```
       .
       .
       .
! At this point during the execution of the subroutine it is necessary
! to establish the required size of the arrays a, b and c
      READ *,n,m
      ALLOCATE (a(n,m), b(n,m), c(n,2*m))
! The arrays may now be used freely
       .
       .
       .
      DEALLOCATE (a,b,c)        ! the arrays have now ceased to exist
       .
       .
       .
END SUBROUTINE Work
```

20.6   Part of a geometry module

The following code shows part of a geometry module that defines several
new data types together with a number of operators that can be used in
expressions involving geometric objects.

```
MODULE Geometry

     TYPE Point
        REAL x,y               ! x and y are the coordinates of the point
     END TYPE Point

     TYPE Line
        REAL a,b,c             ! a, b and c are the coefficients of the
                               ! equation of the line:  ax + by + c = 0
     END TYPE Line

     TYPE Circle
        TYPE (Point) c         ! c is the centre of the circle
        REAL r                 ! r is the radius of the circle
     END TYPE Circle

     INTERFACE OPERATOR (.TO.)
        TYPE (Line) FUNCTION Join(point1,point2)
           TYPE (Point), INTENT(IN) :: point1,point2
        END FUNCTION Join
     END INTERFACE

     INTERFACE OPERATOR (*)
        TYPE (Point) FUNCTION Intersect(line1,line2)
           TYPE (Line), INTENT(IN) :: line1,line2
        END FUNCTION Intersect
     END INTERFACE
```

```
            PRIVATE Join,Intersect ! This prevents the names of the
                                   ! procedures being accessible outside
                                   ! the module
       .
       .
       .
CONTAINS

       TYPE (Line) FUNCTION Join(point1,point2)
! This function calculates the equation of the line between two points

           TYPE (Point), INTENT(IN) :: point1,point2  ! Dummy arguments

! The equation of the line joining the points (x1,y1) and (x2,y2) is
! (y1-y2)x - (x1-x2)y + x1y2 - x2y1 = 0
           Join%a = point1%y - point2%y
           Join%b = point2%x - point1%x
           Join%c = point1%x*point2%y - point2%x*point1%y
           RETURN
       END FUNCTION Join

       TYPE (Point) FUNCTION Intersect(line1,line2)
! This function calculates the coordinates of the point of intersection
! of two lines.
! If the lines do not intersect it returns a point at infinity.

           TYPE (Line), INTENT(IN) :: line1,line2    ! Dummy arguments
           REAL small,denom                          ! Local variables
           PARAMETER (small=1E-10)

           denom=line1%a*line2*b - line2%a*line1%b
           IF (denom<small) THEN           ! Test for parallel lines
              Intersect%x = HUGE(denom)    ! Set x and y coordinates to
              Intersect%y = HUGE(denom)    ! largest possible value
           ELSE
              Intersect%x = (line1%b*line2%c - line2%b*line1%c) / denom
              Intersect%y = (line1%c*line2%a - line2%c*line1%a) / denom
           END IF
           RETURN
       END FUNCTION Intersect
       .
       .
       .
END MODULE Geometry
```

If a procedure needed to use these geometric types and operators then it could do so in the following way:

```
SUBROUTINE Geometry_demo

    USE Geometry
    TYPE (Point) pt1,pt2,pt3
    TYPE (Line) ln1,ln2,ln3
```

```
      .
      .
      .
ln3 = pt1.TO.pt2      ! using the user-defined operator .TO.
                      ! to calculate the line joining two points
pt3 = ln1*ln2         ! using the overloaded intrinsic operator *
                      ! to calculate the intersection of two lines
      .
      .
      .
END SUBROUTINE Geometry_demo
```

In this example the two functions `Join` and `Intersect` are not accessible outside the module, although the operators they define are. If the PRIVATE statement was omitted from the module the function names would also be public, and it would be possible to write

```
ln3 = Join(pt1,pt2)
pt3 = Intersect(ln1,ln2)
```

20.7   Tree-sorted golf tournament scores

Example 14.3 demonstrated a straight selection sort in the context of the accumulation and printing of the results of a golf tournament. The following program shows a totally different approach to this problem, in which the scores are entered in a binary tree that is then 'walked through' in order to print the results in the correct order.

The module `Golf` defines two derived data types. The first of these is a simple record containing the name, four-round scores and total of a player in the tournament. The other defines, in a recursive manner, a binary tree into which the player details will be inserted as they are input by the user. The module also defines two recursive subroutines, one to insert a player in the correct place in the tree, and the other to print the entries in the tree in the correct order. As written, the latter procedure does not print the finishing position explicitly, but this would be easy to achieve if required.

The use of recursive data structures and recursive procedures provides an extremely elegant method of processing data. It is worth pointing out that the sorting of players having the same total score into alphabetic order is almost trivially easy.

The main program now consists of little more than the input of the names and scores and a call to the print procedure. It should be emphasized that, among other things, this method is totally dynamic and will cater equally easily for any number of players.

```
MODULE Golf

    TYPE Golfer
      CHARACTER*20 :: name
      INTEGER      :: round(4),total
    END TYPE Golfer

    TYPE Score_tree
      TYPE (Golfer)                :: player
      TYPE (Score_tree), POINTER :: left,right  ! Recursive definition
    END TYPE Score_tree

CONTAINS

    RECURSIVE SUBROUTINE Insert_player(player,scoreboard)

      TYPE (Golfer)                :: player
      TYPE (Score_tree), POINTER :: scoreboard

      IF (.NOT. ASSOCIATED(scoreboard)) THEN
        ALLOCATE (scoreboard)            ! (sub)tree is empty, so
        NULLIFY (scoreboard%left)        ! enter player at root
        NULLIFY (scoreboard%right)

                                         ! otherwise insert player
                                         ! in the correct subtree
      ELSE IF ( (player%total < scoreboard%player%total) .OR.        &
              ( (player%total == scoreboard%player%total) .AND.      &
                (player%name < scoreboard%player%name) ) ) THEN
        CALL Insert_player(player,scoreboard%left)
      ELSE
        CALL Insert_player(player,scoreboard%right)
      END IF
      RETURN
    END SUBROUTINE Insert_player

    RECURSIVE SUBROUTINE Print_scores(scoreboard)

      TYPE (Score_tree), POINTER :: scoreboard

      IF (ASSOCIATED(scoreboard)) THEN
        CALL Print_scores(scoreboard%left)
        PRINT "(T5,A,3X,3(I3,','),I3,' Total: ',I4)",    &
              scoreboard%player%name,                    &
              (scoreboard%player%round(I),I=1,4),        &
              scoreboard%player%total
        CALL Print_scores(scoreboard%right)
      END IF
      RETURN
    END SUBROUTINE Print_scores

END MODULE Golf
```

```
PROGRAM Golf_Tournament

! This program prints the details of the players taking part
! in a golf tournament in the order of their final scores

      USE Golf
      TYPE (Golfer)      :: player
      TYPE (Score_tree)  :: results

      NULLIFY (results)          ! Ensure that results tree is empty

! Read players' names and scores
      PRINT *,'Type scores as follows:'
      PRINT *,'--------Name-------- R1 R2 R3 R4'
      PRINT *,'A name typed as "End of data" terminates data input'
      DO
        READ '(A20,4(1X,I2))',player%name,(player%round(I),I=1,4)
        IF (player%name == 'End of data') EXIT   ! Check if end of data
        player%total = SUM(player%round)          ! Calculate total
        CALL Insert_player(player,results)        ! Insert into tree
      END DO

! All players now in tree, so print results in order
      CALL Print_scores(results)
      STOP

END PROGRAM Golf_Tournament
```

Afterword – Seven golden rules

This book has attempted to teach both the techniques of Fortran 77 programming and an approach to designing programs. This approach can be summarized in the *Seven Golden Rules of Programming*:

(1) *Always plan ahead*
     It is invariably a mistake to start to write a program without having first drawn up a program design plan that shows the structure of the program and the various levels of detail.

(2) *Develop in stages*
     In a program of any size it is essential to tackle a part of the program at a time, so that the scale and scope of each new part of the program is of manageable proportions.

(3) *Modularize*
     The use of subroutines, or groups of subroutines, that can be written and tested independently is a major factor in the successful development of large programs, and is closely related to the phased development of the programs.

(4) *Keep it simple*
     A complicated program is usually both inefficient and error-prone. Fortran 77 contains features that can greatly simplify complex program structures; modularization can also usually be of assistance here.

(5) *Test thoroughly*
     Always test your programs thoroughly at every stage, and try to cater for as many situations (both correct and incorrect) as possible. The best method, if it can be arranged, is to ask a

colleague to provide some test data, given only the specification of what the program (or module) is supposed to do.

(6)   *Document all programs*
There is nothing worse than returning to an undocumented program after an absence of any significant time. Most programs can be adequately documented by the use of meaningful names, and by the inclusion of plenty of comments. A program only has to be written once but it will be read many times, so effort expended on self-documenting comments will be more than repaid later.

(7)   *Enjoy your programming*
Writing computer programs, and getting them to work correctly, are challenging and intellectually stimulating activities. They should also be enjoyable. There is an enormous satisfaction to be obtained from getting a well-designed program to perform the activities that it is supposed to perform. It is not always easy, but it should be fun!

Appendix A
Intrinsic functions

The Fortran 77 language contains a considerable number of built-in functions, formally known as **intrinsic functions**. These are automatically available to any program that requires them and do not need to be declared, or otherwise identified, other than by means of a function reference.

Most of these functions have a **generic name**, which avoids the necessity of a different name for the same function with different arguments (for example, SIN will return the sine of its argument, which may be real, double precision, or complex, with the function result being of the same type).

In addition to their generic names these functions also have **specific names**, which are not normally needed in Fortran 77 but are still available for compatibility with earlier versions of Fortran, which did not support generic names. For example, earlier versions of Fortran had three sine functions, called SIN, DSIN and CSIN and corresponding to the three cases referred to above.

There are also a smaller number of intrinsic functions that do not have any generic capability and can take only a single type of argument.

Table A.1 shows the names of all intrinsic functions, together with the types of their arguments and results, and a brief definition of their function. The types of arguments allowed are indicated by the following symbols:

- *i*   integer
- *r*   real
- *c*   character
- *d*   double precision
- *x*   complex

In the case of generic functions, which can accept arguments of more than one type, the acceptable types are combined, so that, for example, ird means that the argument may be integer, real, or double precision. The name and specification of each generic function are immediately followed by the indented corresponding specific function names, from which the behaviour of the generic function can be deduced.

Table A.1   Intrinsic functions.

Name and arguments	Result type	Definition
ABS($irdx$)		
IABS(i)	integer	absolute value: $\lvert i \rvert$
ABS(r)	real	absolute value: $\lvert r \rvert$
DABS(d)	double	absolute value: $\lvert d \rvert$
CABS(x)	real	$\sqrt{(\mathrm{REAL}(x)^2 + \mathrm{AIMAG}(x)^2)}$
ACOS(rd)		
ACOS(r)	real	arccos(r)
DACOS(d)	double	arccos(d)
AIMAG(x)	real	imaginary part of x
AINT(rd)		
AINT(r)	real	truncation: REAL(INT(r))
DINT(d)	double	truncation: DBLE(INT(d))
AMAX0($i1,i2,\ldots$)	real	REAL(MAX($i1,i2,\ldots$))
AMIN0($i1,i2,\ldots$)	real	REAL(MIN($i1,i2,\ldots$))
ANINT(rd)		
ANINT(r)	real	rounding to nearest whole number: REAL(INT(r+0.5)) if $r\geqslant0$ REAL(INT(r−0.5)) if $r<0$
DNINT(d)	double	rounding to nearest whole number: DBLE(INT(d+0.5)) if $d>0$ DBLE(INT(d−0.5)) if $d<0$
ASIN(rd)		
ASIN(r)	real	arcsin(r)
DASIN(d)	double	arcsin(d)
ATAN(rd)		
ATAN(r)	real	arctan(r)
DATAN(d)	double	arctan(d)
ATAN2($rd1,rd2$)		
ATAN2($r1,r2$)	real	arctan($r1/r2$)
DATAN2($d1,d2$)	double	arctan($d1/d2$)
CHAR(i)	character	processor-dependent character equivalent of i
CMPLX(ird)	complex	complex number: (REAL(ird),0)
CMPLX(x)	complex	x
CMPLX($ird1,ird2$)		
CMPLX($r1,r2$)	complex	(REAL($r1$),REAL($r2$))
CONJG(x)	complex	complex conjugate: (REAL(x),−AIMAG(x))

Table A.1   (contd).

Name and arguments	Result type	Definition
COS(rdx)		
COS(r)	real	$\cos(r)$
DCOS(d)	double	$\cos(d)$
CCOS(x)	complex	$\cos(x)$
COSH(rd)		
COSH(r)	real	$\cosh(r)$
DCOSH(d)	double	$\cosh(d)$
DBLE($irdx$)		
DBLE(r)	double	double precision equivalent of r
DIM($ird1$,$ird2$)		
IDIM($i1$,$i2$)	integer	positive difference: MAX($i1-i2$,0)
DIM($r1$,$r2$)	real	positive difference: MAX($r1-r2$,0)
DDIM($d1$,$d2$)	double	positive difference: MAX($d1-d2$,0)
DPROD($r1$,$r2$)	double	double precision product $r1*r2$
EXP(rdx)		
EXP(r)	real	e^r
DEXP(d)	double	e^d
CEXP(x)	complex	e^x
ICHAR(c)	integer	processor-dependent integer equivalent of the single character c
INDEX($c1$,$c2$)	integer	if $c2$ is contained within $c1$ then the result is the position of the first character of $c2$ in $c1$; otherwise the result is 0
INT($irdx$)		
INT(r)	integer	integer equivalent of r
IFIX(r)	integer	integer equivalent of r
IDINT(d)	integer	integer equivalent of d
LEN(c)	integer	length of c
LGE($c1$,$c2$)	logical	true if $c1=c2$ or if $c1$ follows $c2$ in the lexical collating sequence; otherwise false
LGT($c1$,$c2$)	logical	true if $c1$ follows $c2$ in the lexical collating sequence; otherwise false
LLE($c1$,$c2$)	logical	true if $c1=c2$ or if $c1$ precedes $c2$ in the lexical collating sequence; otherwise false
LLT($c1$,$c2$)	logical	true if $c1$ precedes $c2$ in the lexical collating sequence; otherwise false
LOG(rdx)		
ALOG(r)	real	natural logarithm: $\log_e r$
DLOG(d)	double	natural logarithm: $\log_e d$
CLOG(x)	complex	natural logarithm: $\log_e x$
LOG10(rd)		
ALOG10(r)	real	common logarithm: $\log_{10} r$
DLOG10(d)	double	common logarithm: $\log_{10} d$
MAX($ird1$,$ird2$,...)		
MAX0($i1$,$i2$,...)	integer	largest value of $i1$, $i2$, ...

Table A.1   (contd).

Name and arguments	Result type	Definition
AMAX1($r1$,$r2$,...)	real	largest value of $r1$, $r2$, ...
DMAX1($d1$,$d2$,...)	double	largest value of $d1$, $d2$, ...
MAX1($r1$,$r2$,...)	integer	INT(MAX($r1$,$r2$,...))
MIN($ird1$,$ird2$,...)		
MIN0($i1$,$i2$,...)	integer	smallest value of $i1$, $i2$, ...
AMIN1($r1$,$r2$,...)	real	smallest value of $r1$, $r2$, ...
DMIN1($d1$,$d2$,...)	double	smallest value of $d1$, $d2$, ...
MIN1($r1$,$r2$,...)	integer	INT(MIN($r1$,$r2$,...))
MOD($ird1$,$ird2$)		
MOD($i1$,$i2$)	integer	remainder: $i1$ − INT($i1/i2$)*$i2$
AMOD($r1$,$r2$)	real	remainder: $r1$ − INT($r1/r2$)*$r2$
DMOD($d1$,$d2$)	double	remainder: $d1$ − INT($d1/d2$)*$d2$
NINT(rd)		
NINT(r)	integer	rounding to nearest integer: INT($r+0.5$) if $r \geqslant 0$, INT($r-0.5$) if $r<0$
IDNINT(d)	integer	rounding to nearest integer: INT($d+0.5$) if $d \geqslant 0$, INT($d-0.5$) if $d<0$
REAL(ird)		
REAL(i)	real	real equivalent of i
FLOAT(i)	real	real equivalent of i
SNGL(d)	real	real equivalent of d
REAL(x)	real	real part of x
SIGN($ird1$,$ird2$)		
ISIGN($i1$,$i2$)	integer	transfer of sign: $\|il\|$ if $i2>0$, $-\|i1\|$ if $i2<0$
SIGN($r1$,$r2$)	real	transfer of sign: $\|r1\|$ if $r2>0$, $-\|r1\|$ if $r2<0$
DSIGN($d1$,$d2$)	double	transfer of sign: $\|d1\|$ if $d2>0$, $-\|d1\|$ if $d2<0$
SIN(rdx)		
SIN(r)	real	$\sin(r)$
DSIN(d)	double	$\sin(d)$
CSIN(x)	complex	$\sin(x)$
SINH(rd)		
SINH(r)	real	$\sinh(r)$
DSINH(d)	double	$\sinh(d)$
SQRT(rdx)		
SQRT(r)	real	$\sqrt{r}$
DSQRT(d)	double	$\sqrt{d}$
CSQRT(x)	complex	$\sqrt{x}$
TAN(rd)		
TAN(r)	real	$\tan(r)$
DTAN(d)	double	$\tan(d)$
TANH(rd)		
TANH(r)	real	$\tanh(r)$
DTANH(d)	double	$\tanh(d)$

Appendix B
A summary of
Fortran 77 statements

This appendix is provided to give a complete summary of the Fortran 77 statements introduced in this book. It is in the style of the summaries at the end of each chapter, but with all statements of the same type grouped together. The first column indicates the purpose of the statement, the second describes its syntax, while the third column indicates the chapter in which the statement is described.

Description	Syntax	Chapter
Initial statements	PROGRAM *name*	2
	SUBROUTINE *name(dummy argument list)*	4
	SUBROUTINE *name*	4
	FUNCTION *name(dummy argument list)*	4
	FUNCTION *name( )*	4
	type FUNCTION *name(dummy argument list)*	4
	type FUNCTION *name( )*	4
	BLOCK DATA *name*	15
	BLOCK DATA	15
Type declarations	REAL *list of names*	3
	INTEGER *list of names*	3
	CHARACTER *list of names*	12
	CHARACTER**length list of names*	12
	CHARACTER *name1*len1, name2*len2, . . .*	12
	CHARACTER**length name1*len1, name2, . . .*	12
	LOGICAL *list of names*	13
	DOUBLE PRECISION *list of names*	11, 13
	COMPLEX *list of names*	11, 13
	EXTERNAL *procedure name*	16
	INTRINSIC *intrinsic procedure name*	16

Description	Syntax	Chapter
Array declarations	*type name* (*declarator*) , ...	6
	type name (*declarator1* , *declarator2* , ...)	14
	CHARACTER *name1* (*declarator list*) *len1* , ...	12
	DIMENSION *name* (*declarator list*) , ...	6
Constant declaration	PARAMETER (*name=constant-expression*)	3
COMMON block declaration	COMMON /*name*/ *list of local names*	15
	COMMON // *list of local names*	15
	COMMON *list of local names*	15
Saving local variables	SAVE *list of variable names*	4
	SAVE	4
Saving COMMON blocks	SAVE /*common block name*/	15
Sharing storage	EQUIVALENCE (*name1* , *name2* , ...)	15
Statement function definition	*name* (*dummy argument list*) = *expression*	16
Initial value specification	DATA *list of names*/*list of values*/	3
	DATA *array name*/*list of values*/	6
	DATA *list of array-elements*/*list of values*/	6
	DATA (*name* (*int*) , *int=e1* , *e2* , *e3*)/*list of values*/	6
Assignment statement	*name* = *expression*	2, 3
Arithmetic expression	*arith-expr arithmetic-operator arith-expr*	3
	where *arith-expr* is an arithmetic variable,	
	arithmetic array element,	
	arithmetic constant,	
	or arithmetic expression	
Character substring specification	*name* (*first pos* : *last pos*)	12
	name (*first pos* :)	12
	name (: *last pos*)	12
Character expression	*char-expr* // *char-expr*	12
	where *char-expr* is a character variable,	
	character array element,	
	character constant,	
	character substring,	
	or character expression	
Relational expression	*arith-expr relational-operator arith-expr*	7
	char-expr relational-operator char-expr	12
Logical expression	*log-expr logical-operator log-expr*	7
	.NOT. *log-expr*	
	where *log-expr* is a logical variable,	
	logical array element,	
	logical constant,	
	relational expression,	
	or logical expression	
Function reference	*function name* (*actual argument list*)	4
	function name ( )	4
Subroutine call	CALL *subroutine name* (*actual argument list*)	4
	CALL *subroutine name*	4

Description	Syntax	Chapter
DO statement	DO *label*, *int var=expr1*,*expr2*,*expr3*	5
	DO *label*, *int var=expr1*,*expr2*	5
CONTINUE statement	CONTINUE	5
DO loop structure	DO *label*, *int-var=expr1*,*expr2*	5
	.	
	.	
	Fortran statements	
	.	
	.	
	label CONTINUE	
Block IF structure	IF (*logical-expression*) THEN	7
	Block of Fortran statements	
	ELSE IF (*logical-expression*) THEN	
	Block of Fortran statements	
	ELSE IF (*logical-expression*) THEN	
	.	
	.	
	ELSE	
	Block of Fortran statements	
	END IF	
Logical IF statement	IF (*logical-expression*) *Fortran statement*	7
Unconditional GOTO statement	GOTO *label*	8
DO ... WHILE loop structure	*label1* IF (.NOT. *condition*) GOTO *label2*	8
	Block of Fortran statements	
	GOTO *label1*	
	label2 *next statement*	
REPEAT ... UNTIL loop structure	*label1* *first statement*	8
	Block of Fortran statements	
	IF (.NOT. *condition*) GOTO *label1*	
	next statement	
Conditional DO loop structure	DO *label1*, *var=1,n*	8
	.	
	IF (*logical-expression*) GOTO *label2*	
	.	
	IF (*logical-expression*) GOTO *label2*	
	.	
	label1 CONTINUE	
	label2 *next statement*	
Input statements	READ *, *input list*	2, 9
	READ *label*, *input list*	9
	READ *format*, *input list*	9
	READ (*control information list*) *input list*	9
Output statements	PRINT *, *output list*	2, 9
	PRINT *label*, *output list*	9

Description	Syntax	Chapter
	PRINT *format, output list*	9
	WRITE (*control information list*) *output list*	9
Input and output of arrays	READ *, *array-name*	6
	PRINT *, (*array-name*(*int*), *int=e1,e2,e3*)	6
FORMAT statement	FORMAT (*list of edit descriptors*)	9
Embedded format	' (*list of edit descriptors*) '	9
File termination statement	ENDFILE *unit number*	10
	ENDFILE (*auxiliary information list*)	10
File connection statement	OPEN (*auxiliary information list*)	10
File disconnection statement	CLOSE (*auxiliary information list*)	10
File positioning statements	BACKSPACE *unit-number*	10
	BACKSPACE (*auxiliary information list*)	10
	REWIND *unit-number*	10
	REWIND (*auxiliary information list*)	10
File enquiry statement	INQUIRE (*enquiry list*)	17
RETURN statement	RETURN	4
STOP statement	STOP	2
END statement	END	2

Appendix C
Statement order in
Fortran 77

We can identify 11 major types of statement in Fortran 77 and, as we have seen when introducing the various individual statements, there are certain restrictions on the order of statements of different types within a single program unit. The eleven major types are as follows:

(a) Initial statements
    PROGRAM
    FUNCTION
    SUBROUTINE
    BLOCK DATA
(b) Comment lines
(c) IMPLICIT statements
(d) PARAMETER statements
(e) Other specification statements
    INTEGER
    REAL
    DOUBLE PRECISION
    COMPLEX
    CHARACTER
    LOGICAL
    DIMENSION
    COMMON
    EQUIVALENCE
    EXTERNAL
    INTRINSIC
    SAVE
(f) DATA statements

(g) Statement function definition statements
(h) ENTRY statements
(i) FORMAT statements
(j) Executable statements
(k) END statements

The first line of a program unit must be an initial statement (a). A PROGRAM statement may appear only as the first line of the main program unit and indicates the starting point of the complete program.

The last line of a program unit must be an END statement (k).

Within any program unit in which they are allowed the following ordering rules apply:

(1)   Any PARAMETER statements (d) must precede any DATA statements (f), statement function definition statements (g) or executable statements (j), and must follow any IMPLICIT (c) or other specification statements (e) that define the type of a symbolic constant name defined in a particular PARAMETER statement.

(2)   Any IMPLICIT statements (c) must precede all other specification statements (e).

(3)   All specification statements (c,d,e) must precede all DATA statements (f), statement function definition statements (g) and executable statements (j).

(4)   DATA statements (f) may appear anywhere after the specification statements (c,d,e).

(5)   Any statement function definition statements (g) must precede all executable statements (j).

(6)   FORMAT statements (i) and comment lines (b) may appear anywhere.

(7)   ENTRY statements (h) may appear anywhere except between a block IF statement and the corresponding END IF statement, and between a DO statement and the terminal statement of the DO loop that it controls.

These rules are shown pictorially in Figure C.1, in which the horizontal lines separate groups of statements that cannot be mixed, and the vertical lines indicate groups of statements between which mixing can occur.

Comment lines	PROGRAM, FUNCTION, SUBROUTINE or BLOCK DATA statements			
	FORMAT and ENTRY statements	PARAMETER statements	IMPLICIT statements
			Other specification statements
		DATA statements	Statement function statements
			Executable statements
END statement				

Figure C.1
Statement ordering within a program unit.

Appendix D
Two common character codes

Character information that is to be stored in the memory of a computer must first be converted into a coded form. This coded form will almost always consist of 7 or 8 **bits** (0s or 1s), giving a total of 128 or 256 possible characters; however, some computer systems designed for use in Asian markets may also provide a coded form using 16 bits to provide a total of 65 536 characters.

Each character will, as we saw in Chapter 12, be stored in a single **character storage unit**. The compiler writer is free to choose whatever size of character storage unit he wishes, as long as it will hold one character, but typically it will consist of 8 bits, commonly referred to as a **byte**.

The actual coding system does not matter for most purposes, although it may affect the range of characters available. However, a program that contains extensive character manipulation may cause problems when transferred to another computer that uses a different character code. Most of the problems concerned with the ordering of characters can be avoided by the use of the LGT, LGE, LLE and LLT intrinsic functions for character comparisons (see Section 12.7), since these will always compare characters according to their order in the ASCII code. This code is given in the following section.

D.1 The ASCII code

The ASCII code was originally an American standard code, but also forms the basis for the widely used international standard coding system known as ISO 646. Unfortunately, this code allows certain character codes to be used for specific national characters (for example, Å or ö), which can cause

Figure D.1
The ASCII (or ISO 646)
character set.

	0	1	2	3	4	5	6	7
0			sp	0	@	P	`	p
1			!	1	A	Q	a	q
2			"	2	B	R	b	r
3			#	3	C	S	c	s
4			$	4	D	T	d	t
5			%	5	E	U	e	u
6			&	6	F	V	f	v
7			'	7	G	W	g	w
8			(	8	H	X	h	x
9			)	9	I	Y	i	y
10			*	:	J	Z	j	z
11			+	;	K	[	k	{
12			,	<	L	\	l	|
13			–	=	M	]	m	}
14			.	>	N	^	n	~
15			/	?	O	_	o	

Notes: (1) *sp* indicates the space, or blank, character.
(2) Character position 2/3 (#) may sometimes be represented as £.
(3) Character position 2/4 ($) may sometimes be represented as ¤.
(4) Character positions 4/0, 5/11, 5/12, 5/13, 5/14, 6/0, 7/11, 7/12, 7/13 and 7/14 are reserved for national use and may appear quite differently in different countries.

problems when programs are moved from one country to another. These character positions are shown shaded in Figure D.1.

The ASCII (or ISO 646) code is a 7-bit code, giving a total of 128 possible characters. The first 32 codes (0–31) and the last (127) are used for special non-printing **control codes** and are left blank in the table. The table itself is laid out in a *hexadecimal* fashion, as is conventional for such code tables, corresponding to the actual pattern of bits in the character storage unit. The order of the characters in this representation runs from the top to the bottom of each column, and then from the top to the bottom of the next column to the right. To find the decimal value corresponding to a particular character you should multiply the column number by 16 and then add the row number; thus A corresponds to 65 ($4 \times 16 + 1$) and } to 125 ($7 \times 16 + 13$).

D.2   The EBCDIC code

The EBCDIC (Extended Binary-Coded Decimal Interchange Code) was originally developed by IBM to provide more character representations than were possible with a 7-bit code. It is widely used on IBM computers (but not on IBM PCs!), but not by many other manufacturers. Neverthe-

	0	1	2	3	4	5	6	7	8	9	10	11	12	13	14	15
0					sp	&	–									0
1						/			a	j	~		A	J		1
2									b	k	s		B	K	S	2
3									c	l	t		C	L	T	3
4									d	m	u		D	M	U	4
5									e	n	v		E	N	V	5
6									f	o	w		F	O	W	6
7									g	p	x		G	P	X	7
8									h	q	y		H	Q	Y	8
9								`	i	r	z		I	R	Z	9
10						!										
11					.	$	,	#								
12						*	%	@								
13					(	)	_	'								
14					+	;	>	=								
15							?	"								

Figure D.2
The EBCDIC character set.

Note: *sp* indicates the space, or blank, character.

less, its use by IBM means that it is one of the most widely used character codes at the present time.

It is an 8-bit code, and can thus represent 256 characters. Although not all the possible character positions are used, and a number are reserved for control codes, the much larger number of available codes means that there is no need for duplicate use of the same code, as is done with ISO 646. The EBCDIC code is shown in Figure D.2, which is laid out in a hexadecimal manner similar to that used in Figure D.1.

Glossary

Note that the number in parentheses following most items in this glossary refers to the section of the book where more detailed information may be found. Further details of italicized words can be found elsewhere in the glossary.

actual argument   The argument used in a subroutine call, or a function reference, to pass information to the procedure or to receive results from it. (4.2)

adjustable array declaration   The declaration of a *dummy array argument* in which one or more of the *dimension declarators* contains a variable, which must either also be a dummy argument or appear in a COMMON *block* in the same subprogram. (6.4)

adjustable dimension   A *dimension declarator* for a *dummy array* in which one or more of the values is a variable, which must either also be a dummy argument or appear in a COMMON *block* in the same subprogram. (6.4)

analysis   The process of breaking a problem down into manageable subproblems. (4.4)

argument   A variable or other entity used to pass information to or from a subprogram. (4.1)

arithmetic IF   An obsolete form of IF statement that provides a three-way *branch* dependent on the sign of an integer variable. (19.1)

arithmetic unit   That part of the *CPU* that carries out arithmetic and other types of operation on items of data. (1.2)

array   A set of related items of the same type that are referred to by the same collective name. (6.1)

array declarator   An array name followed by a *dimension declarator* in parentheses. (6.2).

array element   A single item from the set of items that make up an array, identified by means of an integer *subscript* that follows the array name in parentheses. (6.1)

array operations   Operations that treat an array as a single object (in Fortran 90). (20.2)

array subscript   The value of the subscript expression that follows an array name in parentheses in order to identify a particular element of the array. (6.1)

ASCII   American National Standard Code for Information Interchange (ANSI X3.4 1977) – a widely used internal character coding set; also known as ISO 646 (International Reference Version). (12.4)

assembly language   A form of programming specific to a particular computer, which (usually) utilizes a symbolic form of the electronic instructions in the computer's circuitry. (1.1)

assigned GOTO   An obsolete form of statement for providing multi-way *branches*. (19.1)

assignment   The action of storing the value of an *expression* in a variable or array element. (2.1)

assignment statement   A Fortran statement that causes the value of an *expression* to be assigned to a variable or array element. (2.1)

assumed-size array declaration   The declaration of a *dummy array argument* in which the last *dimension declarator* is represented by an asterisk, indicating that the subprogram may assume that the actual array *argument* is large enough. (6.4)

assumed-size dimension   A *dimension declarator* (which must be the last) for a *dummy array* in which the value is represented by an asterisk, indicating that the subprogram may assume that the actual array *argument* is large enough. (6.4)

attribute   Qualifying information about a variable, array or other entity in Fortran 90. (20.2)

back-substitution   The procedure in which, during a *Gaussian elimination*, the solution for one variable is substituted into another equation in order to obtain a solution for another variable. (18.4)

backing store   That part of a computer system (usually magnetic) on which information is stored permanently for subsequent use; usually it consists of some combination of *magnetic tapes* and *magnetic disks*. (10.1)

backing store device   A piece of equipment by means of which information is transmitted between a computer and its *backing store*; typically a magnetic tape drive or a magnetic disk drive. (10.1)

batch processing   A mode of using a computer in which programs are run under the control of the *operating system* without any intervention by the user. (2.3)

bicubic patch   A three-dimensional equivalent of a section of a *cubic spline*, used for surface interpolation. (18.6)

bicubic spline interpolation   The process of calculating a *bicubic patch*. (18.6)

binary digit   A 0 or a 1, as used in binary arithmetic notation. (1.1)

bisection method   An *iterative method* for finding the roots of a polynomial equation; compare with secant method and Newton's method. (11.5)

bit   A *binary digit*. (1.1)

blank COMMON   A COMMON *block* that has no name; there may only be one blank COMMON block in a program. (15.4)

block   A sequence of one or more Fortran statements whose execution is controlled by a *block* IF *statement*, an ELSE IF *statement*, or an ELSE *statement*. (7.3)

block data program unit   A special form of program unit that contains no executable statements and is used to give initial values to variables and/or arrays in COMMON *blocks*. (15.5)

block IF **statement**   The form of IF statement in which a *logical expression* is used to determine whether or not a *block* of statements is obeyed. (7.1)

block IF **structure**   A program structure in which the execution of one or more *blocks* of statements is controlled by a *block* IF *statement*. (7.1)

bottom-up development   The process of developing a program by writing and testing individual procedures, or groups of procedures, and then bringing them together to form the complete program (compare with top-down analysis). (Intermission)

branch   A *transfer of control* within a single program unit. (8.2)

breakpoints   Points in a program at which it will stop when running under the control of a *debugger* to enable the programmer to investigate the current state of any required aspect of the program and its data. (Intermission)

bug   An error in a program. (Intermission)

byte   A unit of physical memory that is directly addressable and holds a single character; normally consisting of eight *bits*. (10.2)

calling program   The program unit from which a subroutine is called or a function referenced. (4.3)

central processing unit   The part of a computer that carries out the main processing of data. (1.2)

character   The Fortran data type used for storing characters and character strings. (2.1)

character function   A function whose result is of character type. (12.9)

character storage unit   The type of memory location used for the storage of a single character value. (12.1)

character string   A character constant (or a sequence of characters). (2.1)

character variable   A variable that consists of one or more *character storage units* and may contain one or more characters. (12.1)

collating sequence   The order in which a set of characters is sorted when required. (12.4)

comment   A line of a program that contains explanatory information for the programmer or other human reader, but which is ignored by the compiler; in Fortran it is identified by having a c or * in the first character position of the line. (2.1)

COMMON **block**   An area of the memory accessible to more than one subprogram for the storage of variables and/or arrays. (15.2)

compilation   The process carried out by a compiler in which a high-level language is converted into machine code. (1.1)

compilation error   An error in a program that is detected by the *compiler*. (2.4)

compiler A computer program that translates a program written in a high-level programming language, such as Fortran, into the machine code of the computer. (1.1)

complex arithmetic The form of arithmetic used with *complex numbers*. (11.6)

complex number A number consisting of a *real part* and an *imaginary part* and obeying the rules of *complex arithmetic*; it is represented by a pair of real numbers, corresponding to the real and imaginary parts. (11.6, 13.4)

computed GOTO An obsolete form of statement that provides a multi-way *branch* dependent on the value of an integer variable. (19.1)

concatenation The process of joining two character strings. (12.2)

concatenation operator An operator that combines two character strings to form a single character string. (12.2)

conditional DO **loop** A generalized form of *program loop*, in which a DO *statement* controls the maximum number of iterations, while one or more *logical* IF *statements* control the expected exit from the loop. (8.4)

conditional loop A *program loop* whose repetition is controlled by testing for whether some condition has occurred. (8.1)

conditioning A measure of the sensitivity of a numerical process to changes in the values of its parameters. (11.3)

connection The process of relating a specified input or output unit to a specified file, prior to carrying out input or output on the file. (10.4)

constant A memory location whose contents are unchanged throughout the execution of a program. (1.2)

continuation line The second or subsequent line of a Fortran statement; it is identified by having the first five character positions empty, with a character other than a blank or a zero in column 6. (2.1)

control code A non-printing coding in a coded character set which is intended to cause some action to take place on a specific type of hardware – for example, a new line on a printer. (Appendix D)

control information list A list of *specifiers* used in a READ or WRITE statement. (9.3)

control unit That part of the *CPU* that fetches instructions, decodes them, and initiates appropriate action. (1.2)

convergence The process by which an *iterative method* approaches the true solution. (11.5)

convergence criteria The criteria for determining when to terminate an iterative process. (11.5)

counting loop A *program loop* whose repetition is controlled by counting how many times it has been obeyed; compare with DO loop. (8.1)

CPU The *central processing unit* of a computer. (1.2)

creation See file creation.

cubic spline A set of cubic polynomials that together constitute an interpolating function which passes through all of a set of data points, and has continuous first and second derivatives at each of these points. (18.6)

cubic spline interpolation The process of calculating a *cubic spline* as an interpolated curve through a set of data points. (18.6)

cylinder A set of corresponding *tracks* on the parallel surfaces of a multi-surface *magnetic disk*. (17.5)

data Information to be processed by a computer program. (1.2)

data hiding Making some items in a Fortran 90 *module* inaccessible to a user of that module. (20.2)

database A collection of variables and arrays containing information that is used by a number of different subprograms. (15.3)

debugger A special program that allows a Fortran program to be run under its control so that various special aids for debugging, such as *dumps*, *breakpoints* and *single stepping*, may be used by the programmer. (Intermission)

debugging The process of establishing the cause of program errors and correcting the program to eliminate them. (Intermission)

deletion See file deletion.

derived data type A user-defined data type in Fortran 90, which can be used to supplement the *intrinsic data types*. (20.2)

determinant A function of the elements of a square matrix; it must be non-zero if the set of simultaneous linear equations whose coefficients make up the matrix are to have a unique solution. (18.4)

diagnostic Information provided by a compiler, or during the execution of a program, to inform the programmer of errors. (1.1)

dimension declarator The specification of the maximum value of the subscript of an array, and possibly also the minimum value. (6.2)

direct access device A *file storage device* that can access any file, or part of a file, directly; usually some form of *magnetic disk*. (17.5)

direct access file A form of file in which each record is written to a specified part of the file, so that the records may be written and read in any order. (10.1)

disconnection The process of cancelling the *connection* between an input or output unit and a file, which is carried out by the CLOSE statement. (10.4)

DO loop A *program loop* controlled by a DO *statement*. (5.2)

DO statement A statement that controls a DO *loop* by defining the *terminal statement* of the loop, the DO *variable*, the initial and final values of the DO variable, and the increment to be used. (5.2)

DO variable The variable used to control the number of iterations in a DO *loop*. (5.2)

DO ... WHILE loop A form of *conditional loop* that does not exist in Fortran, but can readily be simulated using *logical* IF and GOTO *statements*. (8.1)

double precision a method of storing real values that uses two *numeric storage units* for each value instead of one in order to provide approximately twice as many significant digits of accuracy. (11.2, 13.4)

dummy argument The argument used in a procedure definition that represents the *actual argument* in the procedure. (4.2)

dummy array A dummy argument that is an array. (6.4)

dummy procedure A dummy argument that is a procedure. (16.2)

dump The output produced by printing the values of program variables as an aid to *debugging*. (Intermission)

dyadic operator   An operator that is placed between its two operands. (3.2)

dynamic array   An array whose size need not be determined until execution; available in Fortran 90 but not in Fortran 77. (20.5)

edit descriptor   An item in a *format* that specifies the conversion between internal (computer) and external (human-readable) forms. (9.5)

editor   A program used to create and edit text files, including program files. (2.4)

Ellis–McLain algorithm   A method of fitting a curve to a set of data points that uses only local data points for each part of the curve. (18.7)

ELSE IF **statement**   Part of a *block* IF *structure* in which a *logical expression* is used to determine whether or not a *block* of statements is obeyed, if the preceding *block* IF *statement* did not lead to its block being obeyed. (7.1)

ELSE **statement**   The statement that precedes the final block of statements in a *block* IF *structure*, which are obeyed if neither the preceding *block* IF *statement* nor any of the preceding ELSE IF *statements* led to their blocks being obeyed. (7.1)

embedded format   A format expressed as a character expression and incorporated in an input/output statement. (9.8)

encapsulation   The grouping together of a set of related type, data object, interface or procedure declarations in a Fortran 90 *module*. (20.2)

endfile record   A special type of record that can occur only as the last record of a file and is written by an ENDFILE statement. (10.3)

end-of-file condition   A condition set when an *endfile record* is read, and which can be detected by an end-of-file or IOSTAT specifier in a READ statement. (10.3)

end-of-file record   See endfile record.

end-of-file specifier   A specifier that specifies the *label* of the statement from which processing is to continue if the statement in which it occurs encounters an *endfile record* or otherwise sets an *end-of-file condition*. (9.3)

error flag   A logical variable used to record the occurrence of an error or errors in order to make a decision about the form of further processing later in the program. (13.0)

error specifier   A specifier that specifies the *label* of the statement from which processing is to continue if an error occurs in the execution of the input/output statement containing the error specifier. (9.3)

execution   The process of obeying the instructions that make up a program. (2.1)

existence   See file existence.

exponent   (a) The power of 10 to which the *mantissa* of a real constant expressed in *exponent form* must be raised to give the required value. (2.1)
(b) The power of 2 to which the *mantissa* of a *floating-point* number must be raised to give the required value. (2.1)

exponent form   A means of expressing a real constant by means of an *exponent* and a *mantissa*. (2.1)

expression   A sequence of *operands* separated by operators, which can be evaluated to a single value. (3.1)

external file   A file that is stored on some external medium, normally the computer's *file store*. (10.1)

external function   A function subprogram that is not an *intrinsic function*. (4.2)

external function program unit   An *external function*. (4.3)

fail-safe structure   A program structure in which an error will not lead to a catastrophic failure – for example, a *conditional* DO *loop*. (8.4)

false   One of the two *logical values*; the opposite of *true*. (7.2)

field width   The number of character positions occupied by an item of input data or required for the representation of an output item. (9.5)

file   (a) A set of *records*. (10.1)
(b) A single unit of program or data that is held on some external medium outside the memory of the computer. (1.2)

file creation   The process by which a file that did not previously exist is made to exist. See also *file existence*. (10.4)

file deletion   The process by which *file existence* is terminated; this need not necessarily involve the physical removal of the file from the computer system, although it usually does. (10.4)

file existence   The state in which a file is available for access by a program. (10.4)

file storage device   A *peripheral device* on which part of the *file store* is held; typically a magnetic tape drive or a magnetic disk drive. (10.1)

file store   The set of all files that are kept in a computer's *backing store*. (10.1)

floating point   A method of storing numbers as a *mantissa* and an *exponent*. (2.2)

format   A sequence of *edit descriptors* that determine the interpretation of a line, or *record*, of input data, or the form of representation of an output record. (9.5)

format specification   A sequence of *edit descriptors* enclosed in parentheses that define the format of a *record* or set of records. (9.8)

format specifier   A specifier that specifies the *format* to be used. (9.3)

formatted data   See formatted record.

formatted input/output statement   An input/output statement that includes a *format specifier*. (10.2)

formatted record   A record consisting of a sequence of characters selected from those that can be represented by the processor being used, and which has been written by a *formatted output statement*, by a *list-directed output* statement, or by some means other than a Fortran program (for example, by being typed at a keyboard). (10.2)

Fortran (*Formula translation*)   The first generally available high-level programming language, designed by International Business Machines (IBM) and the language most widely used for scientific and technological purposes. (1.3)

Fortran 77   The current standard version of Fortran, which provided a number of improvements over the earlier version(s). (1.3)

Fortran 90   The next standard version of Fortran, which will provide major enhancements to the language. (20.2)

Fortran Character Set   The 49 characters that may be used to write a Fortran program. (12.1)

function   A subprogram that returns a single result (the 'value' of the function). (4.1)

function reference   The use of a function name in place of a variable to generate a *transfer of control* to the function, in order to carry out some action and return a value. (4.2)

function value   The value that is returned by a function. (4.5)

Gaussian elimination   A method for the solution of a set of simultaneous linear equations. (18.4)

Gauss–Seidel method   An iterative method for the solution of a system of simultaneous linear equations. (18.5)

general-purpose language   A programming language intended for use in a wide variety of different problem areas. (1.3)

generic function   An *intrinsic function* that can be called with different types of arguments, returning corresponding types of results. (4.1)

generic name   The name of a generic function. (4.1)

global data   See global storage.

global storage   Variables and arrays stored in a COMMON *block*. (15.2)

goodness of fit   A measure of how closely an interpolating polynomial passes through the original data points. (11.4)

GOTO statement   See unconditional GOTO statement.

gradient   The first derivative of the equation of a curve. (18.3)

grandfather–father–son   A safety system used when updating files in which the oldest of a three-file cycle is used for the latest update. (17.6)

hash table   An array into which data is entered in a semi-random order by use of a *hashing* technique. (17.5)

hashing   A technique used to create a *hash table*, in which the array element in which an item is to be stored is determined by converting some feature of the item, such as a related name, into an integer in a given range (namely, the size of the hash table). (17.5)

hexadecimal   A system of counting to base 16; it is particularly convenient on a binary computer, especially one that uses a *byte* as its primary storage unit, since each hexadecimal number consists of four *bits*, and two such numbers define the contents of a byte. (Appendix D)

high-level language   A form of programming a computer that uses English-like words to express the operations required of the computer. (1.1)

identifier   The symbolic name of a variable, array, constant, COMMON block or program unit; it consists of a letter followed by up to five further letters or digits. (2.1)

ill-conditioned process   A numerical process that is highly sensitive to changes in the values of its parameters. (11.3)

imaginary part   One of the two numbers that make up a *complex number*. (11.6)

implicit type   The determination of the type of a variable by the initial letter of its name. (3.2)

implied DO list   A shorthand notation for a list of array elements in an input/output list, or in a DATA statement, in which an *implied DO variable* is used to specify elements of an array (or arrays) whose subscript(s) depend on the implied DO variable. (6.5)

implied DO variable   An integer variable that is used in a construct identical to that in a DO statement to control the values of the subscripts of the array(s) specified in an *implied DO list*. (6.5)

incremental development   The process of developing, and testing, a program in stages. See also bottom-up development. (Intermission)

independent compilation   The concept by which every subprogram in a Fortran program can be compiled without the need for the compiler to be aware of any details about any other subprograms. (7.4)

infinite loop   A *program loop* whose terminating condition never occurs, and which therefore never terminates. (8.3)

information engineering   The scientific discipline of using computers to solve problems and to process information. (Preface)

input device   A piece of equipment by means of which a computer receives information from the outside world, such as a keyboard, a card reader or a paper tape reader. (1.2)

input list   The list of variable, array and/or array element names in a READ statement into which data is to be read. (2.1)

input unit   An *input device* or a *backing store device* which is being used for input. (9.3)

integer   The data type used in Fortran for the storage of whole numbers. (2.1)

integration   The mathematical technique of calculating the area under a curve; the reverse of differentiation. (18.8)

interactive processing   A mode of using a computer in which each user controls the execution of his/her program from a terminal, with input coming from the keyboard and output going to the screen. (2.3)

interface   The specification of the name and arguments of a procedure, or the primary procedure in a *module*. (4.8)

internal file   A character array or variable that can be processed as though it were an *external file* by the normal Fortran formatted READ and WRITE statements. (17.4)

intrinsic data type   One of the six data types in Fortran: integer, real, double precision, complex, logical and character. (13.1)

intrinsic function   A function provided as part of the Fortran language – for example, SIN, ABS, MAX. (4.1)

IOSTAT specifier   A specifier that stores a value in an integer variable to indicate the success, or otherwise, of an input/output operation. (17.1)

iterative method   A method of calculating a solution to a problem by successive approximations that converge to the solution. (11.5)

Jacobi's method   An iterative method for the solution of a system of simultaneous linear equations. (18.5)

JCL   See job control language.

job control language   A form of programming language used to instruct the *operating system* how to execute a particular program or sequence of programs. (2.3)

kind type parameter   The parameter used in a *parameterized data type* in Fortran 90. (20.2)

label   See statement label.

last record   The most recently written record in a *sequential file*. (10.5)

length   (a) The number of character storage units in a character variable. (12.2)

(b) The number of characters in a formatted input or output record. (10.2)

(c) The number of processor-defined units, normally *bytes* or *words*, in an unformatted input or output record. (10.2)

library   See subroutine library.

linked list   A data structure in which each element identifies its successor by some form of *pointer*; readily created in Fortran 90 by use of pointers, but not in Fortran 77. (20.2)

list-directed format   The *format* used during *list-directed input* or *output*, determined by the processor by reference to the input or output list; it is represented in an input/output statement by an asterisk. (9.2)

list-directed input   A special type of formatted input in which the format used for the interpretation of the data is selected by the processor according to the type of the items in the *input list*. (2.1)

list-directed output   A special type of formatted output in which the format used for the display of the results is selected by the processor according to the type of the items in the *output list*, and their magnitude. (2.1)

local data   The data points that define a section of an interpolating cubic curve, and those immediately adjacent to them. (18.7)

local storage   Variables and arrays that are declared locally within a subprogram. (15.1)

local variable   A variable declared in a program unit and that is not in a COMMON block. (4.6)

locality of variables   The concept that the variables declared in a program unit are known only to that program unit. (4.6)

logical expression   An expression containing one or more logical variables, logical operators, or relational operators, and which has one of the two logical values *true* or *false*. (7.2)

logical function   A function whose result is of logical type. (13.3)

logical IF statement   A statement in which the value of a logical expression determines whether the rest of the statement is obeyed. (7.4)

logical operator   An operator consisting of two, three or four letters enclosed between full stops, which is used to combine two or more logical values. (7.5)

logical value   One of the two values *true* or *false*. (7.2)

loop   See program loop.

machine code   The sequence of binary digits that causes the electronic circuitry of a computer to perform a specified operation. (1.1)

machine language   Often used as an alternative expression for *machine code* or *assembly language*.

magnetic disk   A form of file storage medium in which data is recorded in circular *tracks* on the surface of a rapidly rotating disk coated with some form of magnetic material. (17.5)

magnetic tape   A form of file storage medium in which data is recorded sequentially along the length of a tape coated with some form of magnetic material. (10.1)

main program   See main program unit.

main program unit   A program unit that starts with a PROGRAM statement; it is where the program will start executing. (4.3)

mantissa   (a) The significant digits of a number in *exponent form*, which when multiplied by 10 a given number of times will result in the required value. (2.1)
(b) The significant *bits* of a number in *floating-point* form, which when multiplied by 2 a given number of times will result in the required value. (2.1)

mask   A logical array used to control certain types of *array operations* in Fortran 90. (20.2)

matrix   The mathematical term for a two-dimensional array. (14.4)

memory   The electronic circuits that enable a computer to store information for subsequent use. (1.1)

method of least squares   A method of data-fitting in which the sum of the squares of the *residuals* is minimized. (11.4)

microcomputer   A small, yet powerful, computer whose processor and memory are contained in a small box capable of being placed on an office desk. (1.2)

mixed-mode expression   An arithmetic expression in which all the operands are not of the same type. (3.2)

modular program development   A method of programming in which different parts of the program are developed and tested independently, before being brought together to form the complete program. (4.8)

module   (a) A self-contained part of a program, consisting of one or more subprograms, which can be written and tested independently of the rest of the program. (4.8)
(b) A new construct in Fortran 90 that provides for global access to data and other entities. (20.2)

module procedure   A procedure contained within a *module* in Fortran 90. (20.2)

monadic operator   An operator that is placed before its single operand. (3.2)

multi-dimensional array An array that has more than one, and less than eight, *subscripts*. (14.1)

multiplier The amount by which each equation is multiplied during *Gaussian elimination*. (18.4)

multiprogramming A method of utilizing the speed of a computer's central processor so that it can appear to be executing several programs at once, when it is actually giving each program a small slice of its time in turn. (2.3)

NAG library A widely used library of subroutines for the solution of an extremely large range of numerical problems. (18.1)

named COMMON block A COMMON *block* which has a name. (15.3)

named constant See symbolic constant.

nested block IF structure A program structure in which one *block IF structure* is wholly contained within one of the blocks of another block IF structure. (7.3)

new source form A new free-format way of writing Fortran programs that will be introduced in Fortran 90. (20.2)

Newton's method An *iterative method* for finding the roots of a polynomial equation; compare with bisection method and secant method. (18.3)

Newton–Raphson method Another name for *Newton's method*. (18.3)

non-executable statement A statement that provides additional information (for example, a format or a type declaration statement), but is not capable of being executed so as to cause some action to occur. (9.5)

normalized floating-point form The form of *floating-point* representation used by most computers, in which the most significant *bit* of the exponent is 1. (11.1)

numeric storage unit The type of memory location used for storage of integer, real, double precision, complex and logical values. (12.1)

numerical methods Computational approaches to the solution of numerical problems. (11.1)

octal A system of counting to base 8 that is particularly convenient on a binary computer, since each octal number consists of three *bits*. (1.1)

open specifiers The specifiers used in an OPEN statement. (10.4)

operand An object (such as variable, array element or constant) that is operated upon by an operator to produce a result value. (3.2)

operating system A program that controls the operation of a computer system, including the loading and execution of programs and the storage and retrieval of information in files. (2.3)

output device A piece of equipment by means of which a computer communicates with the outside world, such as a display, a printer or a graph plotter. (1.2)

output list The list of variables, arrays, array elements and/or constants in a WRITE or PRINT statement whose values are to be output. (2.1)

output unit An *output device*, or a *backing store device* that is used for output. (9.4)

overflow An error condition arising from an attempt to store a value too large for the storage location specified; typically caused by an attempt to divide by 0, or by an extremely small number. (7.5)

overloading   The use of intrinsic operators with new data types in Fortran 90. (20.2)

parameterized data type   A new concept in Fortran 90, whereby more than one variant of the *intrinsic data types* is available. (20.2)

partial pivoting   An essential technique in a *Gaussian elimination* to ensure that the *multipliers* at each stage are as small as possible. (18.4)

peripheral device   An *input device*, an *output device* or a *backing store device*. (9.3)

peripheral unit   An *input* or *output unit*. (9.3)

pigeon sort   An extremely fast method of sorting the elements of an array. (14.3)

pivot   The first coefficient of the *pivotal equation*. (18.4)

pivotal column   The column of the matrix of coefficients of a set of simultaneous linear equations that lies below the *pivot*. (18.4)

pivotal equation   The equation from which multiples of all the other equations are subtracted during *Gaussian elimination*. (18.4)

pivotal row   The row of the matrix of coefficients of a set of simultaneous linear equations that contains the *pivot*. (18.4)

pointer   (a) An integer variable that represents the subscript to an array, and can therefore be used to point to a particular part of the array. (14.3)

(b) A mechanism in Fortran 90 that allows the creation of *dynamic arrays*, *linked lists*, *trees*, and other complex data structures. (20.2)

preconnected unit   An *input* or *output unit* that is automatically connected to the program and does not require an OPEN statement; typically the *standard input* and *output units*. (9.3)

printer   (a) An *output device* that prints the output from the computer on paper.

(b) An output device that is assumed by the Fortran processor to require a *printer control character* as the first character of each line of output. (9.6)

printer control character   The first character of each line, or record, sent to a *printer*, which is not printed but is used to determine the vertical movement of the paper before printing of the rest of the line takes place. (9.6)

private   A means of specifying that items in a Fortran 90 *module* that are not to be accessible to a user of that module. (20.2)

procedure   A self-contained part of a program that carries out a defined task – either a *subroutine* or a *function*. (4.1)

procedure library   Another term for a *subroutine library*. (14.4)

program   A sequence of instructions to a computer. (1.1)

program loop   A section of code that is repeated. (5.2)

program unit   A self-contained section of a Fortran program that begins with an initial statement (PROGRAM, SUBROUTINE, FUNCTION or BLOCK DATA) and ends with an END statement. (4.3)

quicksort   A very fast method of sorting the elements of an array. (14.3)

railroad normal form   A graphical method of describing the syntax of Fortran 77, used in the defining Standard. (Appendix B)

random access device   Another name for a *direct access device*. (17.5)

range of a DO **loop**.   The statements from a DO statement to the terminal statement of the corresponding loop. (5.3)

real   The data type used in Fortran for the storage of numbers that may have fractional parts, and which are stored using a *floating-point* representation. (2.1)

real part   One of the two numbers that make up a *complex number*. (11.6)

real-time operation   A computer application that controls, or reacts to, external activities at the time that those activities are happening. (17.5)

record   A defined sequence of characters, or of values. (10.1)

record number   The index number of a record in a *direct access file*. (17.5)

register   A special part of the memory, usually capable of higher speeds of storage and retrieval than the rest of the memory, which is used for arithmetic and other key operations. (11.1)

relational expression   A *logical expression* in which two operands are compared by a *relational operator* to give a logical value for the expression. (7.2)

relational operator   An operator consisting of two letters enclosed between full stops, which compares two values of the same numeric or character type and returns either the value *true* or the value *false*. (7.2)

repeat count   A number placed before an *edit descriptor*, or a group of edit descriptors enclosed in parentheses, which defines how many times the descriptor, or group of descriptors, is to be repeated. (9.5)

REPEAT ... UNTIL loop   A form of *conditional loop* that does not exist in Fortran, but can readily be simulated using *logical* IF and GOTO *statements*. (8.3)

residual   The difference between data value y and a value y' calculated when attempting to fit a polynomial to a set of data points. (11.4)

residual sum   The sum of the squares of the *residuals*. (11.4)

return   The transfer of control from a subprogram back to the program unit that called it (or referenced it in the case of a function). (4.2)

return variable   A pseudo-variable in an *external function*, having the same name as the function itself, whose value on leaving the function is returned as the value of the function. (4.2)

round-off error   The cumulative error that occurs during *floating-point* arithmetic operations. (11.1)

secant method   An *iterative method* for finding the roots of a polynomial equation; compare with bisection method and Newton's method. (18.2)

semantic error   An error in the logic of a program; normally not detectable until the program is executed, if then. (2.4)

sequential file   A form of file in which each record is written after the previously written record, so that the normal way of reading the records is in the same order as they were written. (10.1)

Simpson's rule   A formula used as the basis of a method of integration that gives an exact answer for polynomials of degree 3 or less. (18.8)

single stepping   Pausing after the execution of each statement when running under the control of a *debugger* to enable the programmer to investigate the current state of any required aspect of the program and its data. (Intermission)

specific name   The name of a *generic function* corresponding to its use with a particular type of argument(s); retained in Fortran 77 only for compatibility with earlier versions of Fortran that did not include *generic names*. (Appendix A)

specifier   An item in a *control information list* that provides additional information for the input/output statement in which it appears. (9.3)

stability   A measure of the sensitivity of a numerical process to small changes in its data, including *round-off errors*. (11.3)

stable process   A numerical process in which small changes in the data, including *round-off errors*, lead to only small changes in its solution. (11.3)

standard input unit   The unit that will be available by default for input: for example, the keyboard in an interactive system or on a microcomputer. (2.1)

standard output unit   The unit that will be available by default for output: for example, the screen on a microcomputer or an interactive system, or the computer's printer in a batch system. (2.1)

statement function   A function that can be expressed in a single line and is local to the subprogram in which it is declared. (16.3)

statement label   A whole number in the range 1 to 99 999 that is written in columns 1–5 of the first line of a statement to identify it. (5.2)

stepwise refinement   The method of producing a program by *top-down analysis*. (4.4)

stored-program computer   The formal name for a computer that is capable of obeying different programs (which it stores in its memory). (1.1)

straight selection sorting algorithm   A simple, and moderately efficient, method of sorting the elements of an array. (14.3)

structure plan   An English-language aid to good program design; used throughout this book. (4.4)

subprogram   A self-contained part of a Fortran program; a *subroutine*, a *function*, or a *block data subprogram*. (4.1)

subprogram program unit   A program unit that is a *subprogram*. (4.3)

subroutine   A subprogram that may return results only through its arguments. (4.1)

subroutine library   A collection of *procedures*, usually all for use in a particular application area, which avoid the programmer having to write his own procedures. (4.3)

subscript   See array subscript.

subscript expression An integer expression whose value is used as an *array subscript*. (6.1)

substring Part of a *character string*. (12.2)

symbolic constant A constant that has been given a symbolic name in a PARAMETER statement. (3.7)

symbolic name A name chosen by the programmer to identify a variable, array, constant, COMMON block or program unit, which must consist of a letter followed by up to five further letters or digits; see also *identifier*. (2.1)

syntactic error An error in the syntax of a program statement or construct; normally detected by the *compiler*. (2.4)

terminal statement The last statement of a DO *loop*; usually a CONTINUE statement. (5.2)

time-sharing A method of utilizing the speed of a computer's central processor in an *interactive processing* system, in which each user is given a small slice of the processor's time in turn. (2.3)

top-down analysis The process of analysing a problem by starting with the major steps, and successively refining each one until the individual steps are all readily soluble. Compare with bottom-up development. (4.4)

track A circular band on the surface of a *magnetic disk* on which information is recorded; a single surface will contain many tracks. (17.5)

transfer of control The interruption of the normal sequential execution of Fortran statements as a result of obeying a CALL to a subroutine, a *function reference*, or a GOTO statement. (4.5)

translation The process of converting a high-level program into machine code; see also compilation. (1.1)

trapezoidal method A simple, but not very accurate, method of *integration*. (18.8)

tree A form of data structure in which each element (or node) points to other nodes, thus creating a flexible and dynamic structure; readily created in Fortran 90 using *pointers*, but not available in Fortran 77. (20.7)

tridiagonal system A system of simultaneous linear equations in which only those elements in the matrix of coefficients that are on the diagonal or immediately above or below it are non-zero. (18.5)

trip count The number of times that a DO *loop* is to be obeyed; it is calculated from the initial, final, and increment values supplied in the DO statement *before* execution of the loop commences. (5.2)

true One of the two *logical values*; the opposite of *false*. (7.2)

truncation (a) The process in which the fractional part of a number is discarded before the number is assigned to an integer variable. (3.4)

(b) The process in which excess characters are removed from the right-hand end of a character string before it is assigned to a character variable of a shorter length. (12.2)

type specification A statement that specifies (or declares) the type of the variable(s), array(s) or function(s) in the list that is part of the statement. (3.2)

unconditional GOTO **statement** A statement that causes the next statement to be obeyed to be the one with the *statement label* specified in the GOTO statement. (8.2)

undefined value The value of a variable when it has not been assigned, or otherwise given, a value, or when it has lost its previous value – for example, following a return from a subprogram without appearing in a SAVE statement. (4.7)

undefined variable A variable that is inaccessible – for example, after a return from the procedure in which it is declared. (4.7)

underflow An error condition in which a number is too small to be distinguished from 0 in the *floating-point* representation being used; most computers will not report this form of error, and will store the number as 0. (11.1)

unformatted data See unformatted record.

unformatted input/output statement An input/output statement that does not contain a *format specifier*. (10.2)

unformatted record A record, consisting of a sequence of values (in a processor-dependent form), that is, essentially, a copy of some part or parts of the memory; it can be produced only by an *unformatted output statement*. (10.2)

unit specifier A specifier that specifies the unit on which input or output is to occur. (9.3)

unstable process A numerical process in which small changes in the data, including *round-off errors*, lead to large changes in its solution. (11.3)

upper triangular matrix A square matrix in which all the elements to the right of, and above, the diagonal are 0. (18.4)

USE **statement** The statement in Fortran 90 that accesses a *module*. (20.2)

variable A memory location whose contents may be changed when required. (1.2)

variable declaration The declaration of the type of a variable in a *type specification* statement. (3.3)

variable name The name used in a program to identify a memory location used for the storage of variable information. (2.1)

vector The mathematical term for a one-dimensional *array*. (14.4)

well-conditioned process A numerical process that is relatively insensitive to changes in the values of its parameters. (11.3)

word A unit of physical memory that is directly addressable; may consist, for example, of 16, 24, 32, 48, 60 or other numbers of *bits*. (10.2)

Bibliography

ANSI (1966). *American National Standard Programming Language FORTRAN.* (*ANSI X3.9–1966*). New York: American National Standards Institute

ANSI (1978). *American National Standard Programming Language FORTRAN.* (*ANSI X3.9–1978*). New York: American National Standards Institute

Atkinson L.V., Harley P.J., and Hudson J.D. (1989). *Numerical Methods with Fortran 77: A Practical Introduction.* Wokingham: Addison-Wesley

Ellis T.M.R. and McLain D.H. (1977). Algorithm 514 – A new method of cubic curve fitting using local data. *ACM Trans. Math. Softw.* **3**, 175–8

Hopkins T. and Phillips C. (1988). *Numerical Methods in Practice: Using the NAG Library.* Wokingham: Addison-Wesley

NAG Ltd. (1988). *The NAG Fortran Library Manual – Mark 13.* Oxford: Numerical Algorithms Group

Ralston A. and Rabinowitz P. (1978). *A first Course in Numerical Analysis* 2nd edn. New York: McGraw-Hill

SPSS Inc. (1988). *SPSS-X User's Guide* 3rd edn. Chicago: SPSS Inc.

Answers to self-test exercises

SELF-TEST EXERCISES 2.1 (page 32)

1 cc = character constant, ic = integer constant, rc = real constant. A number indicates that this is not a valid constant for the reason shown.

ic	rc	cc	ic	1
2	2	cc	rc	rc
3	rc	2	ic	rc
2	rc	rc	ic	4
rc	5	6	cc	7

1:    A character constant cannot be prefixed by a minus sign.
2:    A character string must be enclosed between apostrophes.
3:    This is an arithmetic expression, not a constant.
4:    Quotation marks (") cannot be used instead of apostrophes (').
5:    The exponent must be an integer.
6:    An apostrophe in a string must be represented by two consecutive apostrophes.
7:    The space between the apostrophes makes this into two adjacent character constants, which is illegal.

2   A number in the following table indicates that this is not a valid Fortran name for the reason shown.

OK	1	OK	OK	2
OK	3	OK	2	OK
4	5	OK	3&6	6

1:    Lower-case letters are not allowed in Standard Fortran 77 as part of a name, although many implementations will allow this.
2:    More than six characters (seven in this case); however, many implementations will allow longer names.
3:    First character of a name must be alphabetic.
4:    Illegal character in the name (–).
5:    Illegal character in the name (.).
6:    Illegal character in the name ($).

3   The results will be as follows, although probably with rather more decimal places, leading to the display spilling over onto two lines:

0.900   8.000   76.000   1.230   2.000   345.600   9.800   4.560   7.000

(Remember that a / in the input data terminates the reading process at that point.)

4   An integer is an exact binary representation of a whole number.

    A floating-point number is a representation of a number consisting of a fractional mantissa and an integer exponent.

    A real number is a binary floating-point approximation to a decimal number.

5   123 000   0.000 012 3   10 000 000   0.000 000 001

6   The compiler will probably find at least 13 errors, although there are really only seven. The errors that a compiler might find are shown in italic:

Line 1:   *Program name is too long* (TEST116).
Line 3:   *Unterminated character constant.*
            This is because the terminating apostrophe falls in column 73! (Count the characters if you aren't sure.)
Line 6:   *Illegal character; name too long; unterminated character constant;* and so on.
            The error is simply one of typing: the letter I in the word PRINT was typed as the digit 1. This led the compiler to think that PR1NT was the start of a variable name on the left of an assignment statement, but one that had an illegal character (*) as its sixth character and was too long as well. On the right of the equals sign in this supposed assignment there is a single apostrophe, leading to a further error as there is no matching terminating apostrophe! One error like this can often give rise to several quite different errors in the compiler's eyes.
Line 12:   *Variable name is too long* (AMINUSB).
Line 13:   *Variable name is too long* (AMINUSB).
Line 15:   *Missing separator; name too long; illegal character; missing separator; unterminated character constant;* and so on!
            Once again one error has given rise to several spurious ones. The *real* error is the use of only one apostrophe in the phrase What's. This will cause the compiler to terminate the character string at this point. The following s should then (in the compiler's eyes) be separated from this character string by a comma. Furthermore, it will treat the remainder of the character string (s the sum of your three numbers?) as a variable name, leading to further errors. Finally the terminating apostrophe will appear to the compiler as the start of a new character constant (with no comma to separate it from what came before!), but there is no matching terminating apostrophe.

Line 17:   *Missing separator.*
The second part of the output list is continued on line 18, but there is no comma after the last item on line 17.

Note that the variable spacing on different lines is irrelevant. Except in character constants, spaces in columns 7–72 of programs are ignored.

SELF-TEST EXERCISES 3.1 (page 59)

1
```
      -31    44     20.5  21.0
      0.0   -4.0    3     21
      6561   256.0
```

2
```
      4.833333
      4.833333
      5.000000
     17.833333
```

3
```
     The results are as follows:
     A=      3.000000 B=      2.000000 C=      3.000000
     D=    100.000000 E=    103.000000 F=    352.000000
     I=      3 J=      4 K=      5
     L=    104 M=    108 N=    358
```

SELF-TEST EXERCISES 4.1 (page 87)

1
```
     25
     24
     36
     70
```

If you didn't get these values, remember that X retains its value between calls and that the dummy argument N, which in this example always corresponds to the actual argument N1, is used to return a new value to the main program, which is then used in the next call.

2
```
     25
      8
      2
      0
```

This is essentially the same program as in the previous exercise, but using an integer function instead of a subroutine. However, since the result of the function is printed and not stored, the value of N1 is never changed. If the result had been stored before printing by a set of statements of the form

```
N1=UPDATE(N1,N2)
PRINT *,N1
```

then the results would have been identical to those in the previous exercise.

3

(a)

```
      SUBROUTINE ERROR(N)
      INTEGER N
```

(b)

```
      REAL FUNCTION CUBRT(X)
      REAL X
```

(c)

```
      SUBROUTINE QUAD(A,B,C,N,X1,X2)
      REAL A,B,C,X1,X2
C  N is used to return the number of real roots (0, 1 or 2)
C  The roots are returned in X1 and X2
      INTEGER N
```

(d)

```
      INTEGER FUNCTION FACTOR(N)
      INTEGER N
C  The function returns the lowest factor found between 2 and N
C  (actually between 2 and √N, since there cannot be any greater
C   than √N)
C  If there are no factors in this range then the number is a
C  prime number and the function returns zero.
```

(e) There is an intrinsic function (SQRT) to do this!

(f)

```
      INTEGER FUNCTION GETNUM
```

   or

```
      SUBROUTINE GETNUM(N)
      INTEGER N
```

In this instance it is not clear whether a function (with no arguments) or a subroutine is preferable. The choice would depend very much on the way that the procedure was likely to be used. In general the function would probably be more appropriate, but if the number was nearly always going to be stored by the calling program then the subroutine would be better.

SELF-TEST EXERCISES 5.1 (page 108)

1   (a)   11
        (b)   6
        (c)   3
        (d)   0
        (e)   17
        (f)   1

2   10   2   2   8   0   0

Since L is greater than M and K is positive, the second loop, which terminates on the statement labelled 30, is never obeyed. The two innermost loops are never obeyed either, therefore. The outermost loop (DO 40, I=2,4,8 after evaluation of J, K and L) is obeyed only once, but I is set to the value it would have had on the next pass.

3   10   -2   9   9   64   0

This program is identical to that in test 2 except that K is set to -I, thus causing the second loop to count down (DO 30, J=8,0,-2). On the first pass through this loop the third loop is obeyed once, but on subsequent passes it is not obeyed at all as N is less than L.

SELF-TEST EXERCISES 6.1 (page 118)

1   (a)   An array is a set of related 'variables' of the same type that are referred to by the same (collective) name. Each individual 'variable' in an array is called an array element, and is identified by following the array name by an integer expression, enclosed in parentheses.
       (b)   A dimension declarator can take either of two forms: *n* or *m:n*, the first form being a shorthand form of *1:n*, where *n* and *m* are both constants. An array declarator is the name of an array followed by a dimension declarator enclosed in parentheses – for example, KEY(0:20).
       (c)   The subscript expression must be an integer expression. There are no further constraints upon it.

2
(a)
```
        INTEGER GAMNUM
        PARAMETER (GAMNUM=50)
        INTEGER GAMBWK(GAMNUM),ADDICT(GAMNUM)
        REAL PAY(GAMNUM),LOSSWK(GAMNUM),MAXWIN(GAMNUM),MAXLOS(GAMNUM)
```
(b)
```
        INTEGER MAXEXP
        PARAMETER (MAXEXP=30)
        REAL WEIGHT(MAXEXP),HEIGHT(MAXEXP)
        INTEGER NBLOWS(MAXEXP)
```
(c)
```
        INTEGER NPTS
        PARAMETER (NPTS=500)
        REAL X(NPTS),Y(NPTS),Z(NPTS)
```
(d)
```
        INTEGER T6AM(366),TNOON(366),T6PM(366),TMIDNT(366),
     *          TEMP(-11:31)
```

In the last case it is assumed that, if the temperature is $n°$, 1 will be added to the count stored in TEMP(n). Days on which the temperature is below $-10°$ are counted in TEMP(-11), while those that are hotter than 30° are counted in TEMP(31).

3   The references to D(I) in lines 6 and 8 were probably meant to refer to an array called D; however, as far as the compiler is concerned there is no error, since both references could have been to a function called D. If there is no function called D then there will be an error during execution *but not before*. If D was meant to be an array then it must be declared with the others.

Line 7 contains a reference to K2(I) that will cause an error at execution time, since I will take values from 1 to 20 while the permitted range of subscripts for K2 is from 10 to 50. Either the declaration must be changed, or the subscript expression must be altered to ensure that it takes only permitted values.

Line 11 will cause an execution error on the first pass: it will be interpreted as K2(10)=C(-20)-A(0), where A has a permitted range of subscripts from 1 to 50. Either the declaration must be changed, or the subscript expression must be altered to ensure that it takes only permitted values.

Line 12 will cause an error during compilation, since K3 has not been declared as an array, and a function reference is not permitted on the left of the assignment operator. Even if this is corrected by declaring K3 correctly, there will be an execution error, since the permitted range of subscripts for B is not suitable. Either the declaration must be changed, or the subscript expression must be altered to ensure that it takes only permitted values.

Finally, the PRINT statement on line 15 will cause an error during compilation, since, unlike the case with the array D in the similar PRINT statement on line 8, the compiler will already have decided that K3 must be an array at line 12 and will reject the statement since K3 has not been declared.

SELF-TEST EXERCISES 6.2 (page 128)

1 An adjustable array declaration is a declaration of a dummy array argument, where the dimensional information is also a dummy argument:

```
SUBROUTINE TEST1A(A,B,M,N)
REAL A(M:N),B(N)
```

An assumed-size array declaration uses an asterisk as the dimension declarator of a dummy array argument, on the assumption that the actual array argument is at least as large as will be required:

```
SUBROUTINE TEST1B(P,Q)
REAL P(*),Q(*)
```

2 I is 11, the value it would have had on the next pass through the loop. J is 21, the value it would have taken if one more item had been read. Note that it is only in a DATA statement than an implied DO variable is different from a variable of the same name.

3
```
INTEGER MONTH(12)
DATA MONTH /31,28,31,30,31,30,31,31,30,31,30,31/
```

4
```
INTEGER LEAP(1988:2020)
DATA (LEAP(I),LEAP(I+1),LEAP(I+2),I=1989,2017,4)/24*0/
DATA (LEAP(I),I=1988,2020,4)/9*1/
```

5
(a)
```
      INTEGER MAXINS
      PARAMETER (MAXINS=50)
      INTEGER NUMINS,SCORE(MAXINS)
      .
      .
      .
      READ *,NUMINS,(SCORE(I),I=1,NUMINS)
```
(b)
```
      INTEGER MAXRDG
      PARAMETER (MAXRDG=100)
      INTEGER NUMRDG
      REAL SG1(MAXRDG),SG2(MAXRDG),SG3(MAXRDG),TIME(MAXRDG)
      .
      .
      .
      READ *,NUMRDG
      IF (NUMRDG.LE.MAXRDG) THEN
        READ *,(TIME(I),SG1(I),SG2(I),SG3(I),I=1,NUMRDG)
      ELSE
        PRINT *,'Too many readings'
      END IF
```

SELF-TEST EXERCISES 7.1 (page 155)

1   A relational operator has two numeric operands and delivers a logical result. A logical operator has two logical operands and delivers a logical result.

2   (a)   False.
        (b)   True.
        (c)   True.
        (d)   It is not possible to predict whether the result will be true or false when comparing real expressions that are mathematically equal.
        (e)   True.
        (f)   False.
        (g)   True.
        (h)   True.

3
```
      2 is even
      3 is divisible by 3
      4 is even
      5 is divisible by 5
      6 is even
      8 is even
      9 is divisible by 3
     10 is even
     12 is even
     14 is even
     15 is divisible by 3
     16 is even
     18 is even
```

```
20 is even
21 is divisible by 3
22 is even
24 is even
25 is divisible by 5
```

4

```
 2 is even
 3 is divisible by 3
 4 is even
 5 is divisible by 5
 6 is even
 6 is divisible by 3
 8 is even
 9 is divisible by 3
10 is even
10 is divisible by 5
12 is even
12 is divisible by 3
14 is even
15 is divisible by 3
15 is divisible by 5
16 is even
18 is even
18 is divisible by 3
20 is even
20 is divisible by 5
21 is divisible by 3
22 is even
24 is even
24 is divisible by 3
25 is divisible by 5
```

SELF-TEST EXERCISES 8.1 (page 174)

1 A DO ... WHILE loop need not be obeyed at all (if the condition is false at the start of the loop). A REPEAT ... UNTIL loop will always be obeyed at least once.

2 A GOTO is required to exit from a DO loop before the iteration count has expired.

If a simulated DO ... WHILE or REPEAT ... UNTIL loop is not being controlled by a DO statement, then a GOTO is required to return to the start of the loop, and another is required to exit from the loop.

3 (a) Since the number of iterations is known in advance a DO loop is appropriate:

```
      DO 10, I=1,50
         READ *,A(I),B(I),C(I)
   10 CONTINUE
```

(b)   Again, the number of iterations is known and so a `DO` loop is appropriate:

```
      READ *,NSETS
      DO 10, I=1,NSETS
         READ *,X(I),Y(I),Z(I)
  10 CONTINUE
```

(c)   In this case the number of cases is not known until the last one is input. A conditional `DO` loop is most appropriate here, to avoid reading too much data for the size of the arrays:

```
      DO 10, I=1,MAX
         READ *,X(I),Y(I),Z(I)
         IF (X(I).EQ.TERM) GOTO 11
  10 CONTINUE
      PRINT *,MAX,' records read.  No room for more!'
      STOP
  11 PRINT *,I-1,' records read.  Processing continues.'
```

4

---

1   Read tolerance value (EPSLON)

2   Initialize result variable (X)

3   Repeat the following up to 1000 times
  3.1 Calculate next term (DX)
  3.2 Add DX to X
  3.3 If DX<EPSLON then exit from loop (to step 5)

4   Print error message (no convergence) and stop

5   Print value of X

SELF-TEST EXERCISES 9.1 (page 204)

2   ♦♦♦♦♦6789 minus 4567 is 2222♦♦♦♦234.50 minus 12.34 is 222.160

3
(a)
```
  100 FORMAT (3(F4.2,4X))
      READ 100,A,B,C
```
(b)
```
  110 FORMAT (3(I2,1X,I2,5X))
      READ 110,IFT,IINS,JFT,JINS,KFT,KINS
```
(c)
```
  200 FORMAT (5X,2(F5.2,' * '),F5.2,' (',F8.2,' cubic feet)')
      PRINT 200,AFT,BFT,CFT,AFT*BFT*CFT
```

SELF-TEST EXERCISES 9.2 (page 212)

2

```
     FORMAT (1H1//20X,'ANNUAL REPORT OF HACKIT & DEBUG INC.'//
1           24X,'Year ending 15th March 19',I2///
2           15X,'Total income from sales',17X,'$',F10.2/
3           15X,'Total income from fraud',17X,'$',F10.2//
4           15X,'Total income for year',19X,'$',F10.2///
5           15X,'Software development expenses',11X,'$',F10.2/
6           15X,'Software purchase costs',17X,'$',F10.2/
7           15X,'Lawyer"s fee',28X,'$',F10.2/
8           15X,'Fines imposed by various courts',9X,'$',F10.2//
9           15X,'Total expenses for year',17X,'$',F10.2//
X           15X,'NETT OPERATING PROFIT FOR YEAR',10X,'$',F10.2)
```

3

```
◆◆◆◆◆I has the value    4
     J has the value    9
     Their product is 36

I divided by J is 0.4444

          The value of pi is  3.1416
          and the area of a circle of radius 4 is 50.2656
```

4   (a)
```
◆◆◆0.11  0.22  0.33
   0.444  0.556 0.7 0.8  0.889 1.0 1.1
   1.222 1.3 1.4  1.556 1.7 1.8
   1.889 2.0 2.1  2.222 2.3 2.4
   2.556 2.7 2.8
```

5   (b)   The printed result is identical to that in the previous case, except that everything will be printed one space to the left.

SELF-TEST EXERCISES 10.1 (page 238)

2   An unformatted record is a sequence of values in the processor's internal form, as stored in its memory. A formatted record is a sequence of characters that are a representation of an internal set of values for use by humans or by another processor.

Formatted input should be used when human-produced data is being input from an external device such as a keyboard, or from a formatted file produced on a computer. Formatted output should be used to output results for human interpretation to an external device such as a screen or a printer, or for use by another computer.

Unformatted input and output should be used when information is being stored in a file for subsequent use by the same computer, or by one that is sufficiently similar to be able to interpret the unformatted information correctly.

3   The length of the formatted record produced by the first statement is measured in characters. The length of the unformatted record produced by the second statement is measured in some processor-defined units. It is not possible, therefore, to give a general answer to the question, although there will be an answer for any given computer system.

4   27   32   37   42   47   49

(At which point the program will fail because it will have tried to read beyond the last record of the file.)

If you are not sure about this one, write down the records as they are written, and you will realize that when the file is rewound there are only 23 records in it. The first 10 of these are read and ignored, and then the final loop reads two records each time, printing only the second. There aren't enough records left to do this 10 times!

SELF-TEST EXERCISES 11.1 (page 261)

1   Overflow occurs when an arithmetic calculation results in a positive floating-point exponent that is too large to be stored in the specified type of variable (or, in the case of integer calculations, in a value too large to store in an integer variable). It is always fatal. Underflow occurs when an arithmetic calculation results in a negative floating-point exponent too large to be stored in the specified type of variable – in other words, in a value too small to be distinguished from 0. It is never fatal, and is frequently not even detected.

2   (a) $(a+b)\times(a-b)$ is preferable because it results in smaller intermediate numbers, and there is also less chance of round-off errors affecting the subtraction.

(b) $(a-b)/c$ is preferable because, if a and b are nearly equal, the second alternative is much more susceptible to round-off error.

(c)   There is no major difference in this case, although it is probably marginally preferable to carry out only a single division.

(d)   Wherever possible it is preferable to add numbers in order of increasing magnitude, so $a+b+c+d+e$ is the best order.

(e) $a/b-c/d$ is preferable unless either b or d is very small, in which case the round-off error induced in the division might be greater than the round-off errors that will occur in the denominator of the more complex alternative.

3   A stable process is one in which small changes in the data, including round-off errors, lead to only small changes in the result. An unstable process is one in which such small changes can lead to large changes. The effect of round-off is included in the definition of stability, and it follows that a stable process is relatively unaffected by round-off errors, while an unstable process may be drastically affected by them.

4   A well-conditioned process is one that is relatively insensitive to changes in the values of its parameters, while an ill-conditioned process is highly sensitive. It follows that a well-conditioned process will not be seriously affected by round-off errors; an ill-conditioned process *will* be, and, as a result, may be of no real use at all.

5   A DOUBLE PRECISION variable uses two numeric storage locations in order to allow approximately twice as much storage for the mantissa as in a REAL variable, thus storing numbers to much greater precision.

6   There will be no significant difference because, although the calculation (X–Y) in the second program is carried out using DOUBLE PRECISION variables, the values read used the same format (F10.4) in both cases. The values of X and Y are therefore both accurate to only four decimal places at best. On any computer single precision is quite sufficient for this and no extra precision will be obtained by using DOUBLE PRECISION.

SELF-TEST EXERCISES 11.2 (page 283)

1   The value of the iterated approximation should be within a specified tolerance of the true value.
     Two successive values of the iterated approximation should be within a specified tolerance of each other.
     A given function of the iterated approximation should be within a specified tolerance of the same function of the true value.

2   The residual is the difference between the value calculated using the approximating equation and the true value. The residual sum is the sum of the squares of the residuals for a given set of pairs of values.

3   The residual sum gives a measure of the goodness of fit in a least-squares approximation because it measures how far the approximated points are from the true points, regardless of whether they are above or below the true value.

4   The bisection method assumes that the two initial points are chosen so that one, and only one, root lies between them. Establishing that these two constraints apply can be difficult by purely analytical means!

5

(1.000,2.000)	(3.000,4.000)	5.000
(4.000,6.000)	(−2.000,−2.000)	(6.000,2.000)
(5.000,10.000)	(15.000,20.000)	(0.440,0.080)
(0.200,0.400)	(1.000,−2.000)	(1.000,2.000)

SELF-TEST EXERCISES 12.1 (page 308)

1   Forms◆

2   ranois

3   If the standard output unit is a printer then:

```
The actor is a daring man
```

will be printed at the top of a new page. Otherwise

```
1The actor is a daring man
```

will be printed on the next line.

4   (a)   Processor-dependent. Fortran 77 does not define the relationship between upper- and lower-case letters.
        (b)   Processor-dependent. See (a).
        (c)   Processor-dependent. Since P and Q are of unequal length, the shorter (P) is extended with a blank before the comparison takes place. The first difference is in the eighth character, where P has a blank and Q has a full stop; however, Fortran 77 does not define the collating position of punctuation characters.
        (d)   True. In the ASCII code upper-case collates before lower-case.
        (e)   False. See (d).
        (f)   True. Since P and Q are of unequal length, the shorter (P) is extended with a blank before the comparison takes place. In the ASCII code a blank collates before a full stop.

SELF-TEST EXERCISES 12.2 (page 330)

1   The subroutine finds the length, N, of its second argument (C2) and then copies it, character by character, into the argument supplied as its first argument, thus splitting the N-character string into N single characters.

2   TEST1 will fail if the first array argument (C1) is not large enough to hold the N characters in C1. This can be checked by making C1 an adjustable array instead of an assumed-size one:

```
      SUBROUTINE TEST1(C1,N1,C2)

      CHARACTER C1(N1),C2*(*)
      INTEGER I,N2
      N2=LEN(C2)
      IF (N2.LE.N1) THEN
         DO 5, I=1,N2
    5       C1(I)=C2(I:I)
         RETURN
      ELSE
C  Take appropriate error action
         .
         .
         .
      END IF
      RETURN
      END
```

3   This function is the inverse of the earlier subroutine (TEST1), and copies the N characters stored in the N elements of the dummy array C into successive positions of a single string, which is returned as the value of the function.

4   The function TEST3 will fail to work correctly if its length as declared in the procedure in which it is referenced is less than N. This can be checked by use of the LEN function:

```
      CHARACTER*(*) FUNCTION TEST3(C,N)
      CHARACTER C(N)
      INTEGER I,N,NT
      NT=LEN(TEST3)
      IF (NT.GE.N) THEN
        DO 5, I=1,N
    5     TEST3(I:I)=C(I)
          RETURN
      ELSE
C Take appropriate error action
          .
          .
          .
      END IF
      RETURN
      END
```

5   An embedded format stored in a character array is treated as a concatenation of *all* the elements of the array.

SELF-TEST EXERCISES 13.1 (page 346)

1   REAL, DOUBLE PRECISION, COMPLEX, INTEGER, LOGICAL and CHARACTER.

```
      REAL A
      DOUBLE PRECISION P
      COMPLEX Z
      INTEGER K
      LOGICAL FLG
      CHARACTER*20 NAME
      PARAMETER (A=2.5E7, P=2.5D7, Z=(1.5,2.5), K=17, FLG=.TRUE.,
     *           NAME='Miles Ellis')
```

2   The function reads N numbers from the unformatted file connected to unit U, one number per record, and returns the value .TRUE. if all the numbers have the same sign and .FALSE. otherwise.

3
```
      CHARACTER*4 FUNCTION FUNCTION TEST3(U,N)
      INTEGER U,N,I,POS,NEG
      REAL X
      POS=0
      NEG=0
      DO 5, I=1,N
        READ (U) X
```

```
     IF (X.GT.0.0) POS=POS+1
     IF (X.LT.0.0) NEG=NEG+1
   5 CONTINUE
     IF (POS.GT.0 .AND. NEG.GT.0) THEN
       TEST3='DIFF'
     ELSE
       TEST3='SAME'
     END IF
     RETURN
     END
```

SELF-TEST EXERCISES 14.1 (page 376)

1   (a)   TEST1(5,5,1,1)
         (b)   TEST1(5,2,3,3)
         (c)   There is no 1252nd element, as the array has only 1024 elements.
         (d)   481. TEST1(6,5,4,3) is the 742nd element and TEST1(4,3,2,1) is the
260th element.
Note that if an array X is declared with dimensions of *d1*, *d2* and *d3* then $X(i,j,k)$
is element number $i+(j-1)*d1+(k-1)*d1*d2$.

2   The only restriction is that the variables used to specify the dimensions
of the adjustable dummy array argument must themselves be dummy arguments
(or appear in a COMMON block in the same procedure – see Chapter 15).

3   Only the *last* dimension may be specified by an asterisk. We can see why
this is so by examining the formula shown in the answer to 1(d) above, which
shows that all the actual dimensions other than the last one are needed to work
out which memory location corresponds to a particular array element.

4   The following statements will print the contents of TEST4 as 12 rows of 15
numbers:

```
     PRINT 200,TEST4
 200 FORMAT(15F5.1)
```

because the order of storage of the elements is TEST4(1,1), TEST4(2,1),...,
TEST4(15,1),TEST4(1,2),...
        To print the array as 15 rows of 12 numbers a nested implied-DO is
required:

```
     PRINT 201,((TEST4(I,J),J=1,12),I=1,15)
 201 FORMAT(12F5.1)
```

SELF-TEST EXERCISES 15.1 (page 400)

1   X(1) will cause an error if it is accessed because it corresponds to K1(1)
in the subroutine TEST1A, where it was assigned an integer value (1). This will
not be a valid floating-point number and so any attempt to use the value of X(1)
will cause an error.
        Y(1,1) will also cause an error if accessed. In this case the array Y

corresponds to the double precision array D, and so the element Y(1,1) is the same location in memory as the first half of D(1). It will not, therefore, be a valid floating-point number and any attempt to use it will cause an error.

Y(2,15) is the same location as the second half of D(15) and will cause an error in the same way as will any element of Y.

Z(1,1) has the value 1.0, since the first half of Z corresponds to the complex array Q, and a complex variable (or array element) consists of two real variables in adjacent memory locations. Z(1,1) is therefore the same as the real part of Q(1).

Z(2,5) has the value −5.0, since it is the same as the imaginary part of Q(5).

Z(1,8) will cause an error if accessed, since the second half of Z occupies the same location as does the first half of the integer array K2 in the subroutine TEST1A, where it was assigned the integer value 10 (2×5), which is not a valid floating-point number.

M1(1) has the value 22 (2×11), since M1 occupies the same locations as the second half of K2 and the first five elements of K3, both of which are also integer arrays.

M1(6) is undefined from the information supplied since K2(16), which occupies the same location, was not given any value by TEST1A.

M1(15) has the value 15 (3×5)

M2(1) has the value 18 (3×6)

M2(15) is undefined from the information supplied, since K3(20), which occupies the same location, was not given any value by TEST1A.

2

(a)

```
      INTEGER MAXCST
      PARAMETER (MAXCST=1000)
      CHARACTER*30 NAME(MAXCST)
      COMMON /CSTNAM/NAME
      INTEGER ACCNUM(MAXCST),NSALES(MAXCST)
      REAL LIMIT(MAXCST),OWING(MAXCST),OVERDU(MAXCST)
      COMMON /CSTDET/ACCNUM,LIMIT,OWING,OVERDU,NSALES
```

Note that the names must be kept in a different COMMON block from the numeric data.

(b)

```
      INTEGER NCLASS,NEXAMS,MAXPUP
      PARAMETER (NCLASS=4,NEXAMS=7,MAXPUP=40)
      CHARACTER*30 PUPIL(MAXPUP,NCLASS),
     *   GRADE*1(MAXPUP,NEXAMS,NCLASS)
      COMMON /PUPNAM/PUPIL
      INTEGER MARK(MAXPUP,NEXAMS,NCLASS)
      REAL AVMARK(MAXPUP,NCLASS)
      LOGICAL PASS(MAXPUP,NEXAMS,NCLASS)
      COMMON /MARKS/MARK,AVMARK,PASS
```

Note the ordering of the subscripts, which is designed to aid efficiency. Typically, a problem of this nature would include one or more loops of the form:

```
        Repeat for each class
           Repeat for each exam
              Repeat for each pupil
                    .
                    .
                    .
```

By ensuring that the outermost loop controls the last subscript and the innermost loop controls the first subscript, the order in which the array elements are accessed will be the same as the order in which they are stored in memory. This can often lead to significant improvements in processing efficiency.

(c)
```
      INTEGER NPTS,MAX
      PARAMETER (NPTS=20,MAX=10)
      CHARACTER*30 NAME(MAX)
      COMMON /ASTRO/NAME
      REAL TEMP(NPTS,MAX),SWEAT(NPTS,MAX),MUSCLE(NPTS,MAX),
    * BRAIN(NPTS,MAX)
      INTEGER BLDPRS(2,NPTS,MAX),PULSE(NPTS,MAX),BREATH(NPTS,MAX),
    * TIME(NPTS,MAX)
      COMMON /ASTDAT/TEMP,SWEAT,BLDPRS,PULSE,BREATH,MUSCLE,BRAIN,
    * TIME
```

In the absence of any more detailed knowledge, the above assumes that temperature, 'dampness', expansion/contraction of muscles and brain activity are measured by some real quantity, and that blood pressure, pulse, rate of breathing and the time into the experiment are integer quantities. Since blood pressure is normally expressed as two numbers, provision has been made for this.

Note also that, although the question referred to 'an astronaut', the assumption has been made that the program will actually be used to process data relating to several astronauts.

SELF-TEST EXERCISES 16.1 (page 416)

1 An EXTERNAL statement is required in order to declare the names of any external procedures that are used in a subprogram and which have the same name as an intrinsic procedure, and to declare the names of any external procedures that appear as actual arguments in procedure calls.

It is also required to declare any dummy procedure arguments that cannot be identified as procedures from their context. (Although not mandatory, it is good practice always to declare such dummy procedures as EXTERNAL, to improve human comprehension.)

2 An INTRINSIC statement is required in order to declare any intrinsic procedures that appear as actual arguments in procedure calls.

3   A statement function consists of a single assignment statement and is available only within the subprogram in which it is declared.

It is really a form of shorthand, and will be expanded by the compiler when it is referenced, rather than causing a transfer of control. If there are many references to a function (typically an arithmetic one) that can be expressed as a single assignment statement, then it will usually be more efficient to write it as a statement function.

SELF-TEST EXERCISES 17.1 (page 436)

2   If your computer treats blanks in numeric fields on preconnected units as *nulls* then the values read should be:

(a)   I=1, J=23, K=56, X=0.12, Y=0.679
(b)   I=1, J=230, K=560, X=12.0, Y=6.709
(c)   I=1, J=23, K=56, X=0.12, Y=0.679
(d)   P=12.356, Q=12.679
(e)   P=12305.6, Q=120006.7
(f)   P=12.356, Q=12.679

If your computer treats blanks in numeric fields on preconnected units as *zeros* then the values read should be:

(a)   I=1, J=230, K=560, X=12.0, Y=6.709
(b)   I=1, J=230, K=560, X=12.0, Y=6.709
(c)   I=1, J=23, K=56, X=0.12, Y=0.679
(d)   P=12305.6, Q=120006.7
(e)   P=12305.6, Q=120006.7
(f)   P=12.356, Q=12.679

3   An internal file that is a character variable of length 100 is treated as a single record of length 100 (characters).

An internal file that is a character array having five elements, each of length 20, is treated as consisting of five records, each of length 20 (characters).

4

```
◆One    One    One    One    One    One    One    One    One    One
 One    Two    Three  Four   Five   Six    Seven  Eight  Nine   Ten
 One    Two    Three  Four   Five   Six    Seven  Eight  Nine   Ten
```

The rather surprising result of the first loop is due to the way an array is treated as an internal file. Although each element of the array is treated as a separate record of the file, a READ on an internal file always starts at the beginning of the file. Thus in the first loop the statement

```
READ (LINE1,100) LINE2(I)
```

causes each successive read to start at the beginning of the file and to read the first five characters (One◆◆).

The READ statement in the second loop, however, specifies a single element of the array LINE1 as the internal file:

```
READ (LINE1(I),100) LINE2(I)
```

and so each READ in the loop starts at the beginning of a new record.

SELF-TEST EXERCISES 17.2 (page 456)

2   Note that integer, real and logical values will all occupy the same space in a direct access record, and that double precision and complex values will require exactly twice as much, since all of these are specified in terms of numeric storage units.

On a great many computers a numeric storage unit occupies four bytes, a character storage unit occupies one byte, and the length of direct-access records is measured in bytes. In the example, the record will have a length of 22 numeric storage units and 20 character storage units. On computers such as those mentioned the record will, therefore, probably have a length of 98 bytes.

You can use the INQUIRE statement to establish the exact length of the record on your system.

3   A hash table is a table in which data is entered in a random order in such a way that it can be quickly found again. In its simplest form, some appropriate algorithm is used to convert the value to be stored into an integer key in exactly the same range as the subscripts of the table. This key is then used to identify the first place in which to look, and if this place is full (on entry) or contains the wrong value (on retrieval) then a further algorithm defines where to look next (for example, the next element).

A hash table normally consists of several 'columns', in either a single array or several related ones, with one 'column' containing the identifying data (for example, a name) and the other columns containing additional data that can be extracted once the correct subscript has been found.

4   If the file whose name is stored in FILNAM has already been opened, the program will print its name followed by the number of the unit it is connected to.

If the file has not been opened, the program will print the name of the file that has already been opened on unit U, if any.

SELF-TEST EXERCISES 18.1 (page 499)

1   The bisection method will always converge to a solution, but suffers from the disadvantages that convergence is often rather slow, that the initial points chosen *must* bracket a root, and that if this initial interval contains more than one root, only one will be found.

The secant method does not require that the initial points bracket a root, and will converge more quickly than the bisection method. However, in some cases the secant method will not converge at all.

Newton's method requires only a single initial point, and will generally converge even more quickly than the secant method; however, it requires the first derivative to be available at all points, which may be a major disadvantage in some cases.

2   Partial pivoting is the process of choosing as the pivot at each stage of the elimination the coefficient in the pivotal row that has the largest absolute value. This is essential, in order to make the multipliers as small as possible and, hence, to minimize the effect of round-off errors.

3   A cubic spline uses all the data points that are available in the interpolation for every segment of the curve, whereas a local method uses only those immediately adjacent to the segment for which the interpolation is being carried out. This means that if a single data point is moved a cubic spline interpolation must recalculate the equations of *every* segment, whereas a local method will need to recalculate only the segments including that point and, possibly, those immediately adjacent to them.

      A local method therefore has considerable benefits in an interactive system, where points may be moved and redrawn curves required quickly. However, a local method is not able to guarantee continuity of, for example, the second derivative of the curve and will therefore produce an interpolation that is, in some sense, less smooth.

4   Simpson's rule provides an *exact* solution for the area under a cubic polynomial curve. It thus adds no further errors to the interpolation when used to find the area under a cubic spline fitted to a set of experimental data points.

Answers to selected programming exercises

Note that all the sample solutions shown have program names of the form PXn m, where n.m is the number of the exercise. Blanks are not significant, and so all these names will be of six characters or less.

In some cases, especially where the program may be long, a structure plan is provided as a guide to writing a suitable solution.

2.6

```
      PROGRAM PX2 6
C  This program reads 10 numbers and prints their sum
      PRINT *,'Please type 10 numbers'
      READ *,X1,X2,X3,X4,X5,X6,X7,X8,X9,X10
      SUM = X1+X2+X3+X4+X5+X6+X7+X8+X9+X10
      PRINT *,'The sum of these numbers is ',SUM
      STOP
      END
```

If you tried running your program with the 10 numbers suggested you will almost certainly not have obtained the true mathematical answer of -1.00001 because the ninth data item (3951.44899) cannot be stored to the necessary accuracy of nine significant figures.

2.9

```
      PROGRAM PX2 9
C  This program reads four integers and prints the difference between
C  the sum of the first pair and the sum of the second pair
      PRINT *,'Please type four whole numbers'
      READ *,I,J,K,L
      IPLUSJ = I+J
      KPLUSL = K+L
      NDIFF = IPLUSJ-KPLUSL
      PRINT *,'The difference between the sums of the first and second',
     *        ' pairs is ',NDIFF
      STOP
      END
```

3.5

```
      PROGRAM PX3 5
C  This program reads up to 20 exam marks and prints their average.
C  The program uses a / in the data to terminate input.
C
C  Variable declaration
      INTEGER NMARKS
      REAL M1,M2,M3,M4,M5,M6,M7,M8,M9,M10,M11,M12,M13,M14,M15,M16,M17,
     *     M18,M19,M20,AVMARK
C  Initialize marks to zero
      DATA M1,M2,M3,M4,M5,M6,M7,M8,M9,M10,M11,M12,M13,M14,M15,M16,M17,
     *      M18,M19,M20/20*0/
C  Read marks
      PRINT *,'How many marks are there (1-20)? '
      READ *,NMARKS
      PRINT *,'Type ',NMARKS,' marks, separated by commas'
      PRINT *,'The last mark must be followed by /'
      READ *,M1,M2,M3,M4,M5,M6,M7,M8,M9,M10,M11,M12,M13,M14,M15,M16,M17,
     *      M18,M19,M20
C  Calculate the average mark
C
C  Those input variables into which no data was read will still be zero
C  and so including them in the sum will not alter the result
      AVMARK = (M1+M2+M3+M4+M5+M6+M7+M8+M9+M10+M11+M12+M13+M14+M15+M16+
     *              M17+M18+M19+M20)/NMARKS
C  Print average
      PRINT *,'The average mark is ',AVMARK
      STOP
      END
```

3.13

```
      PROGRAM PX3 13
C  This program breaks down a pay packet into the minimum number of
C  notes and coins.
C
C  Variable declarations
      REAL PAY
      INTEGER PENCE,TWENTY,TEN,FIVE,ONE,P50,P20,P10,P5,P2,P1
C  Read amount to be paid
      PRINT *,'Please give total pay in pounds and decimal pounds'
      READ *,PAY
C  Convert to pence, adding 0.5 pence to avoid rounding errors
      PENCE=100.0*PAY+0.5
C  Remove £5.40 to allow one £5 note and 40p in coins
      PENCE=PENCE-540
C  Calculate number of £20 notes and set PENCE to what is left
      TWENTY=PENCE/2000
      PENCE=PENCE-2000*TWENTY
C  Calculate number of £10 notes and set PENCE to what is left
      TEN=PENCE/1000
      PENCE=PENCE-1000*TEN
C  Calculate number of £5 notes and set PENCE to what is left
      FIVE=PENCE/500
      PENCE=PENCE-500*FIVE
```

```
C  Add the £5 already taken out
      FIVE=FIVE+1
C  Return the 40 pence already removed to the remaining pence
      PENCE=PENCE+40
C  Calculate number of £1 coins and set PENCE to what is left
      ONE=PENCE/100
      PENCE=PENCE-100*ONE
C  Calculate number of 50 pence coins and set PENCE to what is left
      P50=PENCE/50
      PENCE=PENCE-50*P50
C  Calculate number of 20 pence coins and set PENCE to what is left
      P20=PENCE/20
      PENCE=PENCE-20*P20
C  Calculate number of 10 pence coins and set PENCE to what is left
      P10=PENCE/10
      PENCE=PENCE-10*P10
C  Calculate number of 5 pence coins and set PENCE to what is left
      P5=PENCE/5
      PENCE=PENCE-5*P5
C  Calculate number of 2 pence coins and set P1 to what is left
      P2=PENCE/2
      P1=PENCE-2*P2
C  Print cash breakdown
      PRINT *,'Total pay is: £',PAY
      PRINT *,'This will require ',TWENTY,' £20 notes,'
      PRINT *,'                   ',TEN,' £10 notes,'
      PRINT *,'                   ',FIVE,' £5 notes,'
      PRINT *,'                   ',ONE,' £1 coins,'
      PRINT *,'                   ',P50,' 50p coins,'
      PRINT *,'                   ',P20,' 20p coins,'
      PRINT *,'                   ',P10,' 10p coins,'
      PRINT *,'                   ',P5,' 5p coins,'
      PRINT *,'                   ',P2,' 2p coins,'
      PRINT *,'                   ',P1,' 1p coins,'
      STOP
      END
```

4.5   A suitable structure plan might be as follows:

> 1 Get data for this customer – INPUT
>
> 2 Calculate interest due, total outstanding and minimum payment – PAYMNT
>
> 3 Print statement – BILL

> INPUT(OLD,PAID,BOUGHT,RATE)
>
> 1 Read data

PAYMNT(OLD,PAID,BOUGHT,RATE,INTRST,NEW,MINSUM)

1 Calculate interest due (OLD*RATE/100)

2 Calculate new sum outstanding

3 Calculate minimum sum due

BILL(OLD,PAID,BOUGHT,INTRST,NEW,MINSUM)

1 Print statement in an appropriate format

4.7

```
      PROGRAM PX4 7
C  This program calculates the cost of building a wall
C
C  Variable declarations
      REAL LENGTH,HEIGHT,BLEN,BDPTH,BHT,BCOST,MCOST,VOL1,VOL2,VOL
      INTEGER NBRCKS,NROWS
C  Get details of wall, bricks and mortar
      CALL INPUT(LENGTH,HEIGHT,BLEN,BDPTH,BHT,BCOST,MCOST)
C  Calculate number of bricks per row, and number of rows
      CALL BRICKS(LENGTH,HEIGHT,BLEN,BHT,NBRCKS,NROWS)
C  Calculate volume of mortar
C  There are NBRCKS-1 gaps per row to be filled with mortar
      VOL1=NROWS*(NBRCKS-1)*BHT*BDPTH*0.5
C  There are NROWS-1 rows to have mortar on top of them
      VOL2=(NROWS-1)*(NBRCKS*BLEN+(NBRCKS-1)*0.5)*BDPTH*0.5
      VOL=VOL1+VOL2
C  Print results
      CALL COST(NROWS,NBRCKS,BCOST,VOL,MCOST)
      STOP
      END

      SUBROUTINE INPUT(LEN,HT,BLEN,BDPTH,BHT,BCOST,MCOST)
C  This subroutine reads the data for a particular wall and combination
C  of building materials
C
C  Dummy arguments
      REAL LEN,HT,BLEN,BDPTH,BHT,BCOST,MCOST
C  Local variables
      REAL FT,INS,D1,D2,D3
C
C  Read size of wall
      PRINT *,'How high is the wall in feet and inches? '
      READ *,FT,INS
      HT=12.0*FT+INS
      PRINT *,'How long is the wall in feet and inches? '
      READ *,FT,INS
      LEN=12.0*FT+INS
```

```
C  Read size of bricks
      PRINT *,'What are the dimensions of the bricks? '
      READ *,D1,D2,D3
C  Longest dimension is the length, shortest the height
      BLEN=MAX(D1,D2,D3)
      BHT=MIN(D1,D2,D3)
C  Depth is the other one!
      BDPTH=D1+D2+D3-BLEN-BHT
C  Get costs
      PRINT *,'What is the cost of one brick? '
      READ *,BCOST
      PRINT *,'What is the cost of the mortar per cubic foot? '
      READ *,MCOST
C  Convert to cost per cubic inch
      MCOST=MCOST/12.0**3
C  All data now read and converted as necessary
      RETURN
      END


      SUBROUTINE BRICKS(LEN,HT,BLEN,BHT,NBRCKS,NROWS)
C  This subroutine calculates the number of bricks per row,
C  and the number of rows of rows, needed to build a wall
C
C  Dummy arguments
      REAL LEN,HT,BLEN,BHT
      INTEGER NBRCKS,NROWS
C
C  Calculate the number of rows of bricks
C  Each row is BHT+0.5 inches high (including mortar) except the top one
C  Assume that the wall is HT+0.5*BHT inches high (to allow for it not
C  being an exact number of rows) and the bricks BHT+0.5 inches high
      NROWS=(HT+0.5*BHT)/(BHT+0.5)
C  Calculate number of bricks per row using a similar assumption
      NBRCKS=(LEN+0.5*BLEN)/(BLEN+0.5)
      RETURN
      END


      SUBROUTINE COST(NROWS,NBRCKS,BCOST,VOL,MCOST)
C  This subroutine calculates and prints the cost of the materials
C
C  Dummy arguments
      INTEGER NROWS,NBRCKS
      REAL BCOST,VOL,MCOST
C
C  Local variables
      INTEGER BRICKS
      REAL BPRICE,MPRICE
C
C  Calculate total number of bricks and their cost and print details
      BRICKS=NROWS*NBRCKS
      BPRICE=BCOST*BRICKS
      PRINT *,'The wall will require ',BRICKS,' bricks, ',
     *           'which will cost ',BPRICE
C  Calculate and print cost of mortar
      MPRICE=VOL*MCOST
```

```
          PRINT *,'It will require ',VOL/12.0**3,' cubic feet of mortar, ',
     *               'at a cost of ',MPRICE
C  Print total cost
          PRINT *,'Total cost (excluding labour) will be ',BPRICE+MPRICE
          STOP
          END
```

4.8

```
          PROGRAM PX4 8
C  This program breaks down a pay packet into the minimum number of
C  notes and coins.
C
C  Variable declarations
          REAL PAY
          INTEGER PENCE,NUMBER
C  Read amount to be paid
          CALL INPUT(PAY)
C  Convert to pence, adding 0.5 pence to avoid rounding errors
          PENCE=100.0*PAY+0.5
C  Remove £5.40 to allow one £5 note and 40p in coins
          PENCE=PENCE-540
C  Print cash breakdown
          PRINT *,'Total pay is: £',PAY
          PRINT *,'This will require ',NUMBER(PENCE,2000),' £20 notes,'
          PRINT *,'                  ',NUMBER(PENCE,1000),' £10 notes,'
C  Include the £5 note already taken out
          PRINT *,'                  ',NUMBER(PENCE,500)+1,' £5 notes,'
C  Return the 40 pence already removed to the remaining pence
          PENCE=PENCE+40
          PRINT *,'                  ',NUMBER(PENCE,100),' £1 coins,'
          PRINT *,'                  ',NUMBER(PENCE,50),' 50p coins,'
          PRINT *,'                  ',NUMBER(PENCE,20),' 20p coins,'
          PRINT *,'                  ',NUMBER(PENCE,10),' 10p coins,'
          PRINT *,'                  ',NUMBER(PENCE,5),' 5p coins,'
          PRINT *,'                  ',NUMBER(PENCE,2),' 2p coins,'
          PRINT *,'                  ',PENCE,' 1p coins,'
          STOP
          END


          SUBROUTINE INPUT(PAY)
C  This subroutine returns the total pay for this person
C
C  Dummy argument
          REAL PAY
C
          PRINT *,'Please type pay in pounds and decimal pounds (pence)'
          READ *,PAY
          RETURN
          END


          INTEGER FUNCTION NUMBER(TOTAL,COIN)
C  This function calculates the maximum number of coins (or notes) of
C  the specified value which can be used to make up the total sum
```

```
C
C Dummy variables
      INTEGER TOTAL,COIN
C Local variable
      INTEGER N
C Calculate number of coins (or notes) of value COIN pence in TOTAL
C pence, and set TOTAL to what is left
      N=TOTAL/COIN
      TOTAL=TOTAL-COIN*N
C Return number of coins as the value of the function
      NUMBER=N
      RETURN
      END
```

5.1

```
      PROGRAM PX5 1
C This program produces a table of squares, cubes, square roots
C and cube roots
C
C Variable declarations
      INTEGER N,NSQD,NCUBED
      REAL X,SQRTX,CBRTX
C Loop to calculate required values
      DO 10, N=1,100
         NSQD=N*N
         NCUBED=NSQD*N
         X=N
         SQRTX=SQRT(X)
C To calculate a cube root we must use logarithms
         CBRTX=EXP(LOG(X)/3.0)
C Print values
         PRINT *,N,NSQD,NCUBED,SQRTX,CBRTX
   10 CONTINUE
C
      STOP
      END
```

5.10

```
      PROGRAM PX5 10
C This program produces cricket batting statistics
C
C Variable declarations
      INTEGER I,J,NBATS,NINNGS,MAXSCR,NTOUTS,TOTAL,SCORE,X
      REAL AVRAGE
C
C Get number of players
      PRINT *,'How many batsman? '
      READ *,NBATS
C Main loop to read details and print statistics
      DO 20, I=1,NBATS
         PRINT *,'Player number ',I
         PRINT *,'How many innings? '
         READ *,NINNGS
         PRINT *,'Please type scores for this player (-ve for not out)'
```

```
C  Initialize totals etc. for this player
       MAXSCR=0
       NTOUTS=0
       TOTAL=0
       DO 10, J=1,NINNGS
         PRINT *,J,': '
         READ *,SCORE
C  Use SIGN to set X to -1 if not out, to +1 otherwise
         X=SIGN(1,SCORE)
C  Now use MIN to add 1 to NTOUTS if X=-1, and 0 otherwise
         NTOUTS=NTOUTS-MIN(X,0)
C  Now use absolute value of SCORE for remaining calculations
         SCORE=ABS(SCORE)
         MAXSCR=MAX(MAXSCR,SCORE)
         TOTAL=TOTAL+SCORE
   10    CONTINUE
C  All scores read, calculate average and print statistics
       AVRAGE=REAL(TOTAL)/(NINNGS-NTOUTS)
       PRINT *,'Player: ',I,'  Innings: ',NINNGS,'  Not Out: ',NTOUTS
       PRINT *,'Highest Score: ',MAXSCR,'  Total Runs: ',TOTAL,
     *             ' Average: ',AVRAGE
   20 CONTINUE
C
       STOP
       END
```

6.9

```
       PROGRAM PX6 9
C  This program produces a sales invoice
C
C  Variable declarations
       REAL PRICE,CTAX(9),STAX(9),PTOT,CTOT,STOT,COST
       INTEGER CODE,NITEMS,I
C  CTAX and STAX contain the city and state tax rates for the four
C  types of goods coded 1-4 and 9
       DATA CTAX/0,3*0.05,4*0,0.05/,STAX/0.03,7*0,0.03/
       DATA PTOT,CTOT,STOT/3*0/
C
C  Read purchase details
       PRINT *,'How many items are there? '
       READ *,NITEMS
       PRINT *,'Please type details of purchases as the sales code'
       PRINT *,'followed by the price'
       DO 10, I=1,NITEMS
         READ *,CODE,PRICE
C  Update totals
         PTOT=PTOT+PRICE
         CTOT=CTOT+CTAX(CODE)*PRICE
         STOT=STOT+STAX(CODE)*PRICE
   10 CONTINUE
C  Calculate total cost and print invoice details
       COST=PTOT+CTOT+STOT
       PRINT *,'Total price of goods purchased is $',PTOT
```

```
      PRINT *,'Total City tax is $',CTOT
      PRINT *,'Total State tax is $',STOT
      PRINT *,'Total amount due : $',COST
C
      STOP
      END
```

6.16

```
      PROGRAM PX6 16
C This program prints the results of some psychology tests
C
C Variable declarations
      INTEGER NUMBER,RESULT(10),PASS(10),I,J
      DATA PASS/10*0/
C
C Ask for number of volunteers
      PRINT *,'How many people carried out the tests? '
      READ *,NUMBER
C Read data
      PRINT *,'Please type each person''s results in turn'
      DO 10, I=1,NUMBER
        PRINT *,'Volunteer ',I,': '
        READ *,RESULT
C Update total pass record
        DO 5, J=1,10
           PASS(J)=PASS(J)+RESULT(J)
    5   CONTINUE
   10 CONTINUE
C Print overall statistics
      PRINT *,'The results of the tests are as follows:'
      DO 20, I=1,10
        PRINT *,'Test ',I,100.0*PASS(I)/NUMBER,'% passed'
   20 CONTINUE
C
      STOP
      END
```

7.1

```
      PROGRAM PX7 1
C This program tells the user whether a number is positive, negative,
C or zero.  Numbers within 1E-9 of zero are considered to be zero!
C
C Constant declaration    '
      REAL SMALL
      PARAMETER (SMALL=1E-9)
C Variable declaration
      REAL NUMBER
C
      PRINT *,'Please type a number '
      READ *,NUMBER
      IF (NUMBER.LT.-SMALL) THEN
       PRINT *,NUMBER,' is a negative number'
      ELSE IF (NUMBER.GT.SMALL) THEN
        PRINT *,NUMBER,' is a positive number'
```

```
          ELSE
             PRINT *,NUMBER,' is zero!'
          END IF
C
          STOP
          END
```

7.7

```
          PROGRAM PX7 7
C  This program determines whether a number is a prime by dividing
C  it by all odd numbers up to its square root
C
          INTEGER NUMBER,MAXFCT,I
          REAL RNUM,SRTNUM
C
C  Read number
          PRINT *,'Please type a number '
          READ *,NUMBER
C  Check for even number
          IF (MOD(NUMBER,2).EQ.0) THEN
             PRINT *,NUMBER,' is divisible by 2'
             STOP
          END IF
C  Odd number - so find largest possible factor
          RNUM=NUMBER
          SRTNUM=SQRT(RNUM)
          MAXFCT=SRTNUM
C  Loop to look for factors (odd numbers only)
          DO 10, I=3,MAXFCT,2
             IF (MOD(NUMBER,I).EQ.0) THEN
                PRINT *,NUMBER,' is divisible by ',I
                STOP
             END IF
   10     CONTINUE
C  No factors found - so number is a prime
          PRINT *,NUMBER,' is a prime number'
          STOP
          END
```

7.10

```
          PROGRAM PX7 10
C  This program produces examination statistics
C
C  Variable declarations
          INTEGER I,NSTUDS,N,MARK(1000:1999),TOTMK,DISTMK
          REAL SUMMKS,AVMK,DIST
C
C  Get number of students
          PRINT *,'How many students are there? '
          READ *,NSTUDS
C  Read marks and accumulate total mark
C  Mark for student N is stored in MARK(N)
          PRINT *,'Please type ',NSTUDS,' marks in the form'
```

```
      PRINT *,'Student-number (in range 1000-1999),Mark'
      TOTMK=0
      DO 10, I=1,NSTUDS
         READ *,N,MARK(N)
         TOTMK=TOTMK+MARK(N)
   10 CONTINUE
C  Calculate average mark, and mark needed for a distinction
      SUMMKS=TOTMK
      AVMK=SUMMKS/NSTUDS
      DIST=1.3*AVMK
      DISTMK=DIST+1.0
C  Print average mark and those obtaining a distinction
      PRINT *,'The average mark achieved was ',AVMK
      PRINT *,'The following obtained distinctions:'
      DO 20, I=1000,1999
         IF (MARK(I).GE.DISTMK) PRINT *,'Student ',I,'(',MARK(I),'%)'
   20 CONTINUE
C
      STOP
      END
```

8.8

```
      PROGRAM PX8 8
C  This program produces a table of sinX for X from 0 to 90 degrees
C
C  Constant declaration
      REAL PI
      PARAMETER (PI=3.1415926536)
C  Variable declarations
      INTEGER ANGLE,I
      REAL A,ASQD,SGN,TERM,SINE
C
C  Loop to produce table
      DO 20, ANGLE=0,90
C  Convert ANGLE to radians
      A=ANGLE*PI/180.0
      ASQD=A*A
C  TERM is the absolute value of the last term calculated, and SGN
C  gives its sign
C  Initialize for first term of the series
      TERM=A
      SGN=1.0
      SINE=TERM
C  Loop to calculate successive terms until they become less than 1E-6
C  or 20 terms have been calculated (which should be more than enough!)
      DO 10, I=3,41,2
         IF (TERM.LT.1E-6) GOTO 11
         TERM=TERM*ASQD/(I*(I-1))
         SGN=-SGN
         SINE=SINE+SGN*TERM
   10    CONTINUE
   11    PRINT *,ANGLE,SINE,SIN(A)
   20 CONTINUE
```

```
      C
            STOP
            END


8.10
            PROGRAM PX8 10
      C  This program prints examination statistics
      C
      C  Variable declarations
      C  MARK will contain marks
      C  RESULT will contain -1 for fail, 0 for pass, +1 for distinction
            INTEGER MARK(101:199),RESULT(101:199),SUM,DSUM,PSUM,FSUM,
           *          TOT,DTOT,PTOT,FTOT,I,NUMBER,MK1,MK2,MK3
            REAL AVRAGE,DAV,PAV,FAV
      C  Initialize totals
            DATA DSUM,PSUM,FSUM,DTOT,PTOT,FTOT/6*0/
      C
      C  Read data - maximum must be 99
            PRINT *,'Please type student number (in range 101-199),'
            PRINT *,'followed by three marks, for each student.'
            PRINT *,'Final set of marks should be followed by a dummy set'
            PRINT *,'for student number 999.'
            DO 10, I=1,99
              READ *,NUMBER,MK1,MK2,MK3
      C  Check if this is the terminator
              IF (NUMBER.EQ.999) GOTO 11
              MARK(NUMBER)=MK1+MK2+MK3
              IF (MARK(NUMBER).GT.225) THEN
                DTOT=DTOT+1
                DSUM=DSUM+MARK(NUMBER)
                RESULT(NUMBER)=1
                PRINT *,'Student ',NUMBER,' has passed with distinction'
              ELSE IF (MARK(NUMBER).LE.150) THEN
                FTOT=FTOT+1
                FSUM=FSUM+MARK(NUMBER)
                RESULT(NUMBER)=-1
                PRINT *,'Student ',NUMBER,' has failed'
              ELSE
                PTOT=PTOT+1
                PSUM=PSUM+MARK(NUMBER)
                PRINT *,'Student ',NUMBER,' has passed'
              END IF
         10 CONTINUE
      C  Calculate averages
         11 TOT=DTOT+PTOT+FTOT
            SUM=DSUM+PSUM+FSUM
            AVRAGE=SUM/(3.0*TOT)
            DAV=DSUM/(3.0*DTOT)
            PAV=PSUM/(3.0*PTOT)
            FAV=FSUM/(3.0*FTOT)
            PRINT *,'There were ',TOT,' students averaging ',AVRAGE,'%'
            PRINT *,DTOT,' passed with distinction averaging ',DAV,'%'
            PRINT *,PTOT,' passed (without distinction) averaging ',PAV,'%'
            PRINT *,FTOT,' failed, averaging ',FAV,'%'
```

```
C
      STOP
      END


9.3
      PROGRAM PX9 3
C  This program produces a multiplication square
C
C  Variable declarations
      INTEGER I,J
C
      PRINT 200,(J,J=1,12)
      DO 10, I=1,12
        PRINT 201,I,(I*J,J=1,12)
   10 CONTINUE
  200 FORMAT(1H ,4X,12I4/1H ,4X,'X')
  201 FORMAT(1H ,I2,2X,12I4)
      STOP
      END


9.10
      PROGRAM PX9 10
C  This program produces cricket batting statistics
C
C  Constant declaration
      INTEGER MXBATS
      PARAMETER (MXBATS=20)
C  Variable declarations
      INTEGER I,J,NBATS,NINNGS(MXBATS),MAXSCR(MXBATS),NTOUTS(MXBATS),
     *        TOTAL(MXBATS),SCORE,X
      REAL AVRAGE(MXBATS)
C
C  Get number of players
      PRINT *,'How many batsman? '
      READ *,NBATS
      IF (NBATS.GT.MXBATS) THEN
        PRINT *,'Too many batsman.  Only ',MXBATS,' will be accepted'
        NBATS=MXBATS
      END IF
C  Main loop to read details and print statistics
      DO 20, I=1,NBATS
        PRINT *,'Player number ',I
        PRINT *,'How many innings? '
        READ *,NINNGS(I)
        PRINT *,'Please type scores for this player (-ve for not out)'
C  Initialize totals etc. for this player
        MAXSCR(I)=0
        NTOUTS(I)=0
        TOTAL(I)=0
        DO 10, J=1,NINNGS(I)
          PRINT *,J,': '
          READ *,SCORE
          IF (SCORE.LT.0) THEN
```

```
                        NTOUTS(I)=NTOUTS(I)+1
                        SCORE=-SCORE
                     END IF
                     MAXSCR(I)=MAX(MAXSCR(I),SCORE)
                     TOTAL(I)=TOTAL(I)+SCORE
      10    CONTINUE
C  All scores read so calculate average
             AVRAGE(I)=REAL(TOTAL(I))/(NINNGS(I)-NTOUTS(I))
      20 CONTINUE
C  All players processed - so print table of averages
          PRINT 200
          DO 30, I=1,NBATS
             PRINT 201,I,NINNGS(I),NTOUTS(I),MAXSCR(I),TOTAL(I),AVRAGE(I)
      30 CONTINUE
     200 FORMAT(1H1,'Player  Innings  Not Out   Highest    Total',
          *        '            Average'/
          *         1H ,'                        Score       Runs'//)
     201 FORMAT(1H ,I4,7X,I2,7X,I2,8X,I3,6X,I4,5X,F6.2)
C
          STOP
          END


10.2
          PROGRAM PX10 2
C  This program reads and writes numbers using files
C
C  Variable declarations
          INTEGER N(10),I
C
C  Input and output filenames are included in the program
C  Here they are called DATAFILE and RESULTS
C  DATA must already exist (obviously!), but RESULTS must not exist
C  The numbers in DATAFILE are assumed to be occupying some part of
C  the first 10 character positions of the line
C
C  Open files
          OPEN (3,FILE='DATAFILE',STATUS='OLD',FORM='FORMATTED',ERR=901)
          OPEN (4,FILE='RESULTS',STATUS='NEW',FORM='FORMATTED',ERR=902)
C  Read data from DATAFILE
          READ (3,101) N
     101 FORMAT (I10)
C  Write it in the reverse order to RESULTS
          WRITE (4,101) (N(I),I=10,1,-1)
C
          STOP
C  Error during file opening
     901 PRINT *,'Error when opening DATAFILE'
          STOP
     902 PRINT *,'Error when opening RESULTS'
          STOP
          END
```

10.11   A suitable structure plan might be as follows:

---

1   Open data files

2   Read current balances for each account into arrays ACCNT and BALNCE

3   Repeat
   3.1 Read account number from keyboard
   3.2 If account number = 0 then exit
   3.3 Get index of this account in master arrays – FIND
   3.4 If index = 0 then
        3.4.1 Add one to number of accounts
        3.4.2 Store account number and zero balance in next cell of master arrays
   3.5 Print statement – STMNT
   3.6 Set account number negative in master array to indicate that a statement has been produced for this account

4   Process any outstanding transactions for accounts for which statements have not been produced – UPDATE

5   Save master arrays in updated master file

INTEGER FUNCTION FIND(NUMBER,ACCNT,N)

1   Repeat for I from 1 to N
   1.1 If ABS(ACCNT(I))=NUMBER then return I as function value

2   Return zero to indicate that this account number is not in ACCNT

STMNT(ACCNUM,BAL)

1   Print statement heading showing account number ACCNUM and previous balance BAL

2   Rewind transaction file

3   Repeat
   3.1 Read next record
   3.2 If end of file then exit
   3.3 If account number from file = ACCNUM then
        3.3.1 If cheque number is not zero then
             3.3.1.1 Subtract cheque amount from BAL
             3.3.1.2 Print debit transaction details
             otherwise
             3.3.1.3 Add deposit amount to BAL
             3.3.1.4 Print credit transaction details

4   Print final balance, and so on

> ### UPDATE(ACCNT,BALNCE,N)
>
> **1** Rewind transaction file
>
> **2** Repeat
>   **2.1** Read next record
>   **2.2** If end of file then exit
>   **2.3** Get index of this account number in master arrays – FIND
>   **2.4** If index = 0 then
>   **2.4.1** Add one to number of accounts
>   **2.4.2** Store account number and zero balance in next cell of master arrays.
>   **2.5** If account number > 0 (that is, no statement produced) then
>   **2.5.1** If cheque number is not zero then
>   **2.5.1.1** Subtract cheque amount from BAL
>   otherwise
>   **2.5.1.3** Add deposit amount to BAL

The following is an example of the subroutine UPDATE, written according to the above structure plan:

```
      SUBROUTINE UPDATE(ACCNT,BALNCE,N)
C  This subroutine processes any transactions remaining for accounts
C  for which statements have not been produced
C
C  Dummy arguments
      INTEGER N,ACCNT(N)
      REAL BALNCE(N)
C
C  Local variables
      INTEGER I,ACCNUM,CHQNUM,DAY,MONTH,YEAR
      REAL AMOUNT
C  Function declaration
      INTEGER FIND
C
C  ACCNT(I) is negative if account details have been updated
C  Rewind transaction file and then search for relevant entries
      REWIND 3
   10 READ (3,301,END=20) ACCNUM,DAY,MONTH,YEAR,CHQNUM,AMOUNT
  301 FORMAT(I8,3X,I2,1X,I2,1X,I2,3X,I6,3X,F10.2)
      I=FIND(ACCNUM,ACCNT,N)
      IF (I.EQ.0) THEN
C  New account
         N=N+1
         I=N
         ACCNT(I)=ACCNUM
         BALNCE(I)=0
      END IF
      IF (ACCNT(I).GT.0) THEN
        IF (CHQNUM.NE.0) THEN
```

```
C  Debit transaction
            AMOUNT=-AMOUNT
            BALNCE(I)=BALNCE(I)+AMOUNT
         ELSE
C  Credit transaction
            BALNCE(I)=BALNCE(I)+AMOUNT
         END IF
       END IF
     GOTO 10
C  All transactions processed
  20 RETURN
     END
```

11.5

(a)   All three roots lie in the specified range, at $x = -3.0$, $x = 1.5$ and $x = 1.6$.
If your initial tabulation did not give changes of sign between, for example, $x = 1$
and $x = 2$ then you should have noticed that the values of x were falling as x
increased from 0 to 1, but increasing as it increased from 2 to 3, indicating a
minimum somewhere in this area.

(b)   The three roots are at $x = -0.5$, $x = 1.5$ and $x = 1.6$.

(c)   The three roots are at $x = -4.0$, $x = 0.2$ and $x = 4.0$.

(d)   The four roots are at $x = -4.0$, $x = -1.5$, $x = 0.2$ and $x = 4.0$.

(e)   The four roots are at $x = -4.0$ (twice) and $x = 3.0$ (twice). Your program
probably didn't find these, because the value of the polynomial *never* falls below
zero. However, examination of the tabulation should have indicated what was
happening (that is, that there were two minimums) and more detailed tabulation
should have solved the equation.

(f)   There are only two roots in the specified range, both at $x = 2.33333$. If
your program did not find them, see the comments in (e) above.

11.13

```
     PROGRAM PX11 13
C  This program calculates the first derivative of the function F(X)
C  which is provided as an external function
C
C  Variable declarations
     INTEGER I
     REAL H,X,DF
C  Function declaration
     REAL F
C
C  Get value of X at which derivative is required
     PRINT *,'What is the value of X? '
     READ *,X
C  Loop to calculate the derivative using the Newton quotient
C  for different values of H
     H=1.0
     PRINT 100
 100 FORMAT(10X,'H',20X,'DF/DX')
     DO 10, I=1,15
       DF=(F(X+H)-F(X))/H
```

```
                PRINT 101,H,DF
                H=0.1*H
          10 CONTINUE
         101 FORMAT(5X,F20.15,F15.10)
                STOP
                END


                REAL FUNCTION F(X)
      C
      C  Dummy argument
                REAL X
      C
                F=X*X - 3.0*X +2
                RETURN
                END
```

Using the above program we find that the result is relatively accurate for H taking values between 0.01 and 0.000 01, but that for smaller values of H the result is close to zero! Modifying the program leads to the conclusion that, in this case, the optimum value of H is around 0.000 25.

12.1

```
          PROGRAM PX12 1
      C  This program prints the Fortran character set and the internal
      C  representation of each character
      C
      C  Variable declarations
            INTEGER I
            CHARACTER CH1,CH2,FCHSET*49
            DATA FCHSET/'ABCDEFGHIJKLMNOPQRSTUVWXYZ0123456789 =+-*/(),.$":'/
      C
      C  Print column headings
            PRINT 100
       100 FORMAT(1H1,10X,'The Fortran Character Set'//
           *       1H ,'Character',4X,'Code',11X,'Character',4X,'Code'//)
      C  Loop to print table
            DO 10, I=1,23
               CH1=FCHSET(I:I)
               CH2=FCHSET(I+26:I+26)
               PRINT 101,CH1,ICHAR(CH1),CH2,ICHAR(CH2)
        10 CONTINUE
            DO 20, I=24,26
               CH1=FCHSET(I:I)
               PRINT 101,CH1,ICHAR(CH1)
        20 CONTINUE
       101 FORMAT(1H ,4X,A1,8X,I3,16X,A1,8X,I3)
      C
            STOP
            END
```

12.14   A suitable structure plan might be as follows:

---

1   Read data from file into appropriate arrays – INPUT

2   Print title

3   Repeat for each church member
   3.1 Print personal details – LIST

INPUT(FIRST,FAMILY,SEX,AGE,STATUS,NMAX,NUMBER)

1   Get name of data file and open it

2   Repeat for I from 1 to NMAX
   2.1 Read next record
   2.2 If end of file then exit from loop
   2.3 Find first space in name
   2.4 Store substring of name before space in FIRST(I), and substring after space in FAMILY(I)
   2.5 Store 'Male' or 'Female', as appropriate, in SEX(I)
   2.6 Store age in AGE(I)
   2.7 Store 'Single', and so on, as appropriate, in STATUS(I)

3   Store number of records (people) in NUMBER

LIST(N,FAMILY,FIRST,STATUS,SEX,AGE)

1   Establish exact length of the character arguments FAMILY, FIRST, STATUS and SEX

2   Modify output format to reflect size of record number and of age

3   Print record in required format

The following is a suitable implementation of the above structure plan for the subroutine LIST:

```
      SUBROUTINE LIST(N,FAMILY,FIRST,STATUS,SEX,AGE)
C  This subroutine prints personal details in the required format
C
C  Dummy arguments
      INTEGER N,AGE
      CHARACTER*(*) FAMILY,FIRST,STATUS,SEX
```

```
      C   Constant declarations
              CHARACTER*6 THREE,TWO,ONE,NONE
              CHARACTER*2 I1,I2,I3,I4
              PARAMETER (THREE=',"000"',TWO=',"00"',ONE=',"0"',NONE=' ')
              PARAMETER (I1='I1',I2='I2',I3='I3',I4='I4')
      C   Local variables
              INTEGER LFAMLY,LFIRST,LSTAT,LSEX
              CHARACTER*42 FMT
              DATA FMT/'(1H ,"000",I1,2X,A,",  ",A,2X,A,1X,A,1X,I2)'/
      C
      C   Establish exact length of various character arguments
              LFAMLY=INDEX(FAMILY,' ')-1
              IF (LFAMLY.LT.0) LFAMLY=LEN(FAMILY)
              LFIRST=INDEX(FIRST,' ')-1
              IF (LFIRST.LT.0) LFIRST=LEN(FIRST)
              LSTAT=INDEX(STATUS,' ')-1
              IF (LSTAT.LT.0) LSTAT=LEN(STATUS)
              LSEX=INDEX(SEX,' ')-1
              IF (LSEX.LT.0) LSEX=LEN(SEX)
      C   Adjust format depending on size of record number and age
              IF (N.LT.10) THEN
                 FMT(5:10)=THREE
                 FMT(12:13)=I1
              ELSE IF (N.LT.100) THEN
                 FMT(5:10)=TWO
                 FMT(12:13)=I2
              ELSE IF (N.LT.1000) THEN
                 FMT(5:10)=ONE
                 FMT(12:13)=I3
              ELSE
                 FMT(5:10)=NONE
                 FMT(12:13)=I4
              END IF
              IF (AGE.LT.10) THEN
                 FMT(40:41)=I1
              ELSE IF (AGE.LT.100) THEN
                 FMT(40:41)=I2
              ELSE
                 FMT(40:41)=I3
              END IF
      C   Print record
              PRINT FMT,N,FAMILY(:LFAMLY),FIRST(:LFIRST),STATUS(:LSTAT),
           *       SEX(:LSEX),AGE
              RETURN
              END


      13.5
              PROGRAM PX13 5
      C   This program tests the logical function WITHIN
      C
      C   Variable declarations
              CHARACTER*30 STRNG1,STRNG2
              INTEGER LEN1,LEN2
```

```
C  Function declaration
      LOGICAL WITHIN
C
      PRINT *,'Please type two character strings of up to 30 characters'
      PRINT *,'1: '
      READ '(A)',STRNG1
      PRINT *,'How many relevant characters are there? '
      READ *,LEN1
      PRINT *,'2: '
      READ '(A)', STRNG2
      PRINT *,'How many relevant characters are there? '
      READ *,LEN2
C  Test to see if STRNG2 is contained within STRNG1
      IF (WITHIN(STRNG1(:LEN1),STRNG2(:LEN2))) THEN
        PRINT 101,STRNG2(:LEN2),STRNG1(:LEN1)
      ELSE
        PRINT 102,STRNG2(:LEN2),STRNG1(:LEN1)
      END IF
  101 FORMAT(1H ,'The phrase ''',A,''' is contained within ''',A,'''')
  102 FORMAT(1H ,'The phrase ''',A,''' is not contained within ''',A,
     *           '''')
      STOP
      END


      LOGICAL FUNCTION WITHIN(S1,S2)
C  This function returns the value .TRUE. is S2 is contained within S1
C  and .FALSE. otherwise
C
C  Dummy arguments
      CHARACTER*(*) S1,S2
C  The intrinsic function INDEX returns the position of the first
C  character of its second argument in the first argument, if the
C  second argument is contained within the first, and zero otherwise.
C  It can therefore be used to provide the necessary information for
C  this function to operate.
C
      WITHIN=INDEX(S1,S2).NE.0
      RETURN
      END
```

14.2

```
      PROGRAM PX14 2
C  This program is an exercise in array handling
C
C  Variable declarations
      INTEGER I,J
      CHARACTER A(4,4),B(4,4)*2
      DATA A/'A','B','C','D','E','F','G','H',
     *       'I','J','K','L','M','N','O','P'/
C
C  Loop to create new array by concatenating 'opposite' elements
      DO 10, I=1,4
        DO 5, J=1,4
          B(I,J)=A(I,J)//A(5-I,5-J)
```

```
      5   CONTINUE
     10 CONTINUE
C  Print new array
        PRINT 100,B
    100 FORMAT((20X,4(A2,2X)))
        STOP
        END
```

Note the extra pair of parentheses in the format at statement 100; these are necessary to ensure that the format repeats from the beginning and not from the repeat count before the innermost left parenthesis. An alternative would have been

```
    100 FORMAT(20X,A2,2X,A2,2X,A2,2X,A2)
```

14.14   A suitable structure plan for this program is:

---

1 Read details of previous matches from the master file – INPUT

2 Get number of matches played (N)

3 Repeat N times
 3.1 Read match result as a single character string
 3.2 Extract the names of the two teams and the number of goals each scored – EXTRCT
 3.3 Update the record for the home team – UPDATE
 3.4 Update the record for the away team – UPDATE

4 Find the leading teams and print their names – LEADRS

5 Save current records in the master file – KEEP

INPUT(TEAM,GAMES,GOALS,POINTS)

1 If these are the first set of results then
 1.1 Open a new file
 1.2 Read names of teams from the keyboard and store in the array TEAM
 1.3 Set the arrays GAMES, GOALS and POINTS to zero
 otherwise
 1.4 Open the master file
 1.5 Read the previous contents of the arrays TEAM, GAMES, GOALS and POINTS

EXTRCT(RESULT,HOME,HGOALS,AWAY,AGOALS)

1 Find first digit in RESULT – DIGIT

2 Store substring before the digit as the home team's name in HOME

3 Convert digits in RESULT to form number of goals in HGOALS until an alphabetic character is reached – ALPHA

4 Find next digit

5 Store substring before digit as away team's name in AWAY

6 Convert remaining digits to form away team's goals in AGOALS

DIGIT(CH)

1 If CH lies between '0' and '9' then
   1.1 Return value *true*
   otherwise
   1.2 Return value *false*

ALPHA(CH)

1 If CH lies between 'A' and 'Z' or between 'a' and 'z' then
   1.1 Return value *true*
   otherwise
   1.2 Return value *false*

UPDATE(TEAM,GAMES,GOALS,POINTS,NAME,FOR,AGANST)

1 Repeat for I from 1 to 20
   1.1 If NAME=TEAM(I) then
      1.1.1 Add one to number of games played, GAMES(1,I)
      1.1.2 Add FOR to number of goals scored, GOALS(1,I)
      1.1.3 Add AGANST to number of goals conceded, GOALS(2,I)
      1.1.4 If FOR>AGANST then
         1.1.4.1 Add 1 to number of games won, GAMES(2,I)
         1.1.4.2 Add 3 to number of points, POINTS(I)
         otherwise if FOR=AGANST then
         1.1.4.3 Add 1 to number of games drawn, GAMES(3,I)
         1.1.4.4 Add 1 to number of points, POINTS(I)
         otherwise
         1.1.4.5 Add 1 to number of games lost, GAMES(4,I)
      1.1.5 Exit from loop

LEADRS(TEAM,GAMES,POINTS)

1 Repeat until at least three teams have been listed
   1.1 Find maximum points obtained by any team, MAXPTS

> **1.2** Repeat for I from 1 to 20
>> **1.2.1** If POINTS(I)=MAXPTS then
>>> **1.2.1.1** Print team's name, number of games played and number of points obtained
>>> **1.2.1.2** Add one to count of teams listed
>>> **1.2.1.3** Negate POINTS(I) to ensure that this team is not listed again
>
> **2** Reset all POINTS(I) to positive values

> KEEP(TEAM,GAMES,GOALS,POINTS)
>
> **1** Rewind master file
>
> **2** Write the arrays TEAM, GAMES, GOALS and POINTS to the file
>
> **3** Close the file

15.6

```fortran
      SUBROUTINE INPUT
C This subroutine reads data from a housing survey from a file on
C unit 3 and stores it in COMMON blocks
C
C Constant declaration
      INTEGER MAXPPL
      PARAMETER (MAXPPL=100)
C COMMON block declarations
      INTEGER NAMLEN(2,MAXPPL),AGE(MAXPPL),INCOME(MAXPPL),NUMPPL
      CHARACTER NAME(2,MAXPPL),SEX(MAXPPL),STATUS(MAXPPL),HOUSE(MAXPPL)
      COMMON /CHOUSE/NAME,SEX,STATUS,HOUSE
      COMMON /NHOUSE/AGE,INCOME,NUMPPL
C Variable declarations
      INTEGER I
      CHARACTER NAMES*30
C
C Read data from file
  100 FORMAT(A30,1X,A1,1X,I3,1X,A1,1X,A1,1X,I5)
      DO 10, I=1,MAXPPL
        READ (3,100,END=11) NAMES,SEX(I),AGE(I),STATUS(I),HOUSE(I),
     *    INCOME(I)
C Split name into first name and family name
        CALL SPLIT(NAMES,NAME(1,I),NAME(2,I),NAMLEN(1,I),NAMLEN(2,I))
   10 CONTINUE
C No end of file read
      PRINT *,'No end of file read - number of records read is ',I-1
C All data read - store number of records
   11 NUMPPL=I-1
      RETURN
      END
```

This subroutine uses the subroutine SPLIT to separate the two names read from columns 1–30. The first names will be stored in the first column of NAME, while the family names will be stored in the second column. The array NAMLEN contains the lengths of the two names.

16.3

(a)
```
REAL CTEMP,F
CTEMP(F)=5.0*(F-32.0)/9.0
```

(b)
```
REAL METRIC
INTEGER FT,INS
METRIC(FT,INS)=2.54*(12*FT+INS)
```

(c)
```
LOGICAL WHOLE
REAL X
WHOLE(X)=MOD(ABS(X),1.0).LT.1E-4
```

(d)
```
LOGICAL FACTOR
REAL X,Y
FACTOR(X,Y)=MOD(MAX(ABS(X),ABS(Y)),MIN(ABS(X),ABS(Y))).LT.1E-4
```

16.7   A suitable structure plan might be as follows:

> **1** Ask whether encrypting or decrypting is required
>
> **2** If encrypting then
> **2.1** Read keyword
> **2.2** Input message, encrypt it, and print or store the encrypted message – ENCODE
> otherwise
> **2.3** Input encrypted message, decrypt it, and print or store the decrypted message – DECODE

> ENCODE(KEY)
>
> **1** Convert KEY to corresponding integers (KMOD(1:KEYLEN))
>
> **2** Calculate length of keyword (KEYLEN) and number of blocks of the encrypted message that will fit on one line
>
> **3** Read message to be encrypted – INPUT
>
> **4** Repeat for each line of the input message
> **4.1** Repeat for each character in the line
> **4.1.1** Ignore second and subsequent consecutive spaces
> **4.1.2** Convert alphabetic characters to corresponding integers between 1 and 26, and spaces to zero – CHRPOS
> **4.1.3** Add appropriate modifier from KMOD
> **4.1.4** If integer is greater than 26, subtract 26

4.1.5 Store corresponding letter in next encrypted position – POSCHR

4.1.6 Update character, block and line counts for encrypted message, as appropriate

5 If necessary add extra characters to complete the last block of encrypted characters

6 Print or store the encrypted message – OUTPUT

DECODE

1 Read message to be decrypted – INPUT

2 Extract the first block. This is the keyword, KEY, of length KEYLEN

3 Convert KEY to corresponding integers (KMOD(1:KEYLEN))

4 Calculate number of blocks of the encrypted message that will fit on one line

5 Repeat for each line of the input message
  5.1 Repeat for each character
    5.1.1 Ignore spaces between blocks
    5.1.2 Convert characters to corresponding integers between 1 and 26 – CHRPOS
    5.1.3 Subtract appropriate modifier from KMOD
    5.1.4 If integer is less than 0, add 26
    5.1.5 Store corresponding letter (or space if integer was zero) in the next position of the decrypted message – POSCHR
    5.1.6 Update character, block and line counts, as appropriate

6 Print or store the decrypted message – OUTPUT

INPUT, OUTPUT, and the functions for use in character–integer conversions (CHRPOS and POSCHR) are much simpler, and are left to the reader.

16.14 The first message can be decoded by the program written for Exercise 16.7, and reads as follows:

```
MODIFY THE PROGRAM YOU WROTE FOR EXERCISE SIXTEEN POINT SEVEN SO THAT
INSTEAD OF USING THE KEYWORD FOR ENCODING AND DECODING EACH BLOCK IT IS
ONLY USED FOR THE FIRST BLOCK SEMICOLON THEREAFTER THE PREVIOUS BLOCK IS
USED TO ENCODE OR DECODE THE NEXT ONE STOP
```

The second message can only be decoded by this modified program!

17.6
```
      PROGRAM PX17 6
C  This program is an exercise in the use of an internal file
C
```

```
C  Variable declarations
      REAL X(4,5)
      INTEGER I,J,N1,N2,WIDTH,START(4),END(4)
      CHARACTER LINE*80,FORM*25,DIGIT(0:9)
      DATA FORM/'(F20.0,F20.0,F20.0,F20.0)'/
      DATA DIGIT/'0','1','2','3','4','5','6','7','8','9'/
C
C  Open input file
      OPEN (3,FILE='DATAFILE')
C  Loop to read and process each line of the file
      DO 50, I=1,5
         READ (3,'(A)') LINE
C  Loop to find the end of each number
         START(1)=1
         DO 30, J=1,4
            DO 10,N1=START(J),80
C  Find first non-space character
               IF (LINE(N1:N1).NE.' ') GOTO 11
10          CONTINUE
C  Now find next space - character after end of next number
11          DO 20,N2=N1,80
               IF (LINE(N2:N2).EQ.' ') GOTO 21
20          CONTINUE
C  Save length of this number, including preceding spaces
21          END(J)=N2-1
            IF (J.LT.4) START(J+1)=N2
30       CONTINUE
C  Build appropriate format
         DO 40, J=1,4
            N1=3+6*(J-1)
            N2=N1+1
            WIDTH=END(J)-START(J)+1
            FORM(N1:N1)=DIGIT(WIDTH/10)
            FORM(N2:N2)=DIGIT(MOD(WIDTH,10))
40       CONTINUE
C  Now read LINE as four numbers into the matrix X
         READ (LINE,FORM) (X(J,I),J=1,4)
50    CONTINUE
C  All numbers have now been read into the matrix - calculate means
      DO 60, J=1,4
         PRINT 100,J,(X(J,1)+X(J,2)+X(J,3)+X(J,4)+X(J,5))/5.0
60    CONTINUE
100   FORMAT(1H ,'The mean of the values in column ',I1,' is ',G12.7)
C
      STOP
      END
```

Note that this program first analyses the contents of the array LINE to determine the field width needed for the four numbers, and then uses Fortran I edit descriptors to extract and convert the numbers. Also note the use of a G edit descriptor for the output of the means.

17.13 A suitable structure plan is as follows:

> 1 Ask which way conversion is to go
>
> 2 If from direct access to sequential then
>   2.1 Transfer direct access master file and sequential hash table file to a formatted sequential file – DIRSEQ
>   otherwise
>   2.2 Transfer sequential file to direct access file and reconstituted hash table file – SEQDIR

> DIRSEQ
>
> 1 Get name of direct access file
>
> 2 If it does not exist or if it is possible to tell that it is incompatible (for example, not direct access, formatted, wrong record length) then fail
>
> 3 Get name of hash table file
>
> 4 If it does not exist or if it is possible to tell that it is incompatible (for example, not sequential, formatted) then fail
>
> 5 Get name of new sequential file
>
> 6 If it already exists then fail
>
> 7 Open files
>
> 8 Read hash table
>
> 9 Repeat for I from 1 to size of hash table
>   9.1 If hash table entry is not zero then
>   9.1.1 Read record I from master file
>   9.1.2 Write same record preceded by I and corresponding hash table entry to new file
>
> 10 Place end of file marker on new file

> SEQDIR
>
> 1 Get name of sequential file
>
> 2 If it does not exist or if it is possible to tell that it is incompatible (for example, not sequential, unformatted) then fail
>
> 3 Get name of new direct access file
>
> 4 If it already exists then fail
>
> 5 Get name of new hash table file
>
> 6 If it already exists then fail

7   Open files

8   Initialize hash table to zeros

9   Repeat for I from 1 to size of hash table
    9.1   Read next record from sequential file
    9.2   If end of file then exit
    9.3   Write same record without first two items (RECNO and NUMBER)
          to record RECNO of new direct access file
    9.4   Store NUMBER in cell RECNO of hash table

10 Write complete hash table to new hash table file

An example of the subroutine SEQDIR written according to this structure
follows:

```
      SUBROUTINE SEQDIR
C  This subroutine copies a sequential file to a direct access one
C
C  Constant declaration - record length of direct access master file
      INTEGER RL
      PARAMETER (RL=56)
C  Local variables
      INTEGER RLEN,I,RECNO,NUMBER
      CHARACTER AYORN,FYORN,DFILE*20,HFILE*20,SFILE*20
      LOGICAL EXISTS
C  Hash table
      INTEGER MAXSTF
      PARAMETER (MAXSTF=5000)
      INTEGER RECNUM(MAXSTF)
C  Employee record
      CHARACTER*20 NAME
      REAL STDHRS,HRATE,ORATE,ALLOW,CUMGRS,CUMALL,CUMTAX,CUMINS,CUMNET
C
C  Get names of files
      PRINT *,'What is the name of the sequential file? '
      READ '(A)',SFILE
C  Check file
      INQUIRE(FILE=SFILE,EXIST=EXISTS,SEQUENTIAL=AYORN,FORMATTED=FYORN)
      IF (EXISTS) THEN
        IF (AYORN.EQ.'NO') THEN
          PRINT *,SFILE,' is not a sequential file'
          STOP
        END IF
        IF (FYORN.EQ.'NO') THEN
          PRINT *,SFILE,' is not a formatted sequential file'
          STOP
        END IF
      ELSE
        PRINT *,SFILE,' does not exist'
        STOP
      END IF
      PRINT *,'What is the name to be given to the direct access file? '
      READ '(A)',DFILE
```

```
C   Check file
        INQUIRE(FILE=DFILE,EXIST=EXISTS)
        IF (EXISTS) THEN
          PRINT *,DFILE,' already exists'
          STOP
        END IF
        PRINT *,'What is to be the name of the related hash table file? '
        READ '(A)',HFILE
C   Check file
        INQUIRE(FILE=HFILE,EXIST=EXISTS)
        IF (EXISTS) THEN
          PRINT *,HFILE,' already exists'
          STOP
        END IF
C   Open files
        OPEN (7,FILE=DFILE,STATUS='NEW',ACCESS='DIRECT',RECL=RL)
        OPEN (8,FILE=HFILE,STATUS='NEW',FORM='UNFORMATTED')
        OPEN (9,FILE=SFILE,STATUS='OLD',FORM='FORMATTED')
C   Initialize hash table
        DO 10, I=1,MAXSTF
          RECNUM(I)=0
     10 CONTINUE
C   Copy sequential records to new direct access file
        DO 20, I=1,MAXSTF
          READ (9,900,END=21) RECNO,NUMBER,NAME,STDHRS,HRATE,ORATE,
     *           ALLOW,CUMGRS,CUMALL,CUMTAX,CUMINS,CUMNET
          WRITE (7,REC=RECNO) NAME,STDHRS,HRATE,ORATE,ALLOW,CUMGRS,
     *           CUMALL,CUMTAX,CUMINS,CUMNET
C   Insert entry into hash table
          RECNUM(RECNO)=NUMBER
     20 CONTINUE
    900 FORMAT (2I10,A20,9F15.2)
C   All records copied - now save hash table
     21 WRITE (8) recnum
C
        RETURN
        END
```

18.3

(a) $x = 3.0$ $y = -2.0$ $z = 4.0$
(b) $x = -1.0$ $y = 2.0$ $z = -1.0$
(c) $y = -2.0$ and $x = 2z - 3$.

Your program will probably have come up with actual values for x and z; the one shown in Section 18.4 produced the results $x = 1.67882$ and $z = 2.33941$ when run on my computer. However, substituting the value 2 for y in each of the three equations results in the following equations:

$$-2x + 4z = 6$$
$$x - 2z = -3$$
$$3x - 6z = -9$$

which are all the same equation, thus showing that the system of equations has no unique solution.

(d) $x = 2.0$ $y = -1.0$ $z = 4.0$ $w = 3.0$
(e) $x = 2.0$ $y = 1.0$ $z = -3.0$ $w = 3.0$ $t = -1.0$

This is a somewhat sparse system, but it should not cause any problems.

18.10

```
      PROGRAM PX18 10
C  This program uses Euler's method to solve the differential equation
C  defining the radioactive decay of an element
C
C  Variable declarations
      REAL MASS,HLFLFE,PERIOD,H,TIME,K
      INTEGER I,N
C
C  Read initial mass, half-life, simulation time, and interval (h)
      PRINT *,'What is the initial mass? '
      READ *,MASS
      PRINT *,'What is the half-life of this substance? '
      READ *,HLFLFE
      PRINT *,'How long is the simulation to cover? '
      READ *,PERIOD
      PRINT *,'What interval is to be used? '
      READ *,H
C  Euler's method leads to the equation  m(t+h)=(1+hlog(0.5)/T)m(t)
C  where T is the half-life of the substance, or
C  m(t+h)=km(t), where k=1+hlog(0.5)/T
      K=1.0+(H*LOG(0.5))/HLFLFE
C  Use this equation in a loop to calculate and print remaining mass
      PRINT 100
      TIME=0
      PRINT 101,TIME,MASS
C  Calculate number of iterations required
      N=PERIOD/H+0.5
      DO 10, I=1,N
         TIME=TIME+H
         MASS=K*MASS
         PRINT 101,TIME,MASS
   10 CONTINUE
  100 FORMAT(10X,'Time  Mass Remaining')
  101 FORMAT(10X,F5.1,5X,F7.3)
C
      STOP
      END
```

Using the above program we can compare the calculated values at 200 years and 400 years with the true values, which are 5 kg and 2.5 kg since the half-life is 200 years. We find that with the interval (h) set at 20 years the calculated figures are 4.88 kg and 2.38 kg, but that $h = 5$ gives 4.97 kg and 2.47 kg, while $h = 2$ gives 4.99 kg and 2.49 kg. Smaller values of h make no significant difference!

We may therefore deduce, by using $h = 2$, that after 500 years 1.76 kg will remain.

Index to programs and procedures

This book contains over 150 complete programs and procedures, all of which, apart from a few Fortran 90 examples, have been fully tested on a Research Machines Nimbus AX computer using the Prospero PC Fortran compiler. Some of these programs and procedures are purely demonstrations of a particular type of statement or programming construct and do not solve any identifiable problem. The remainder are detailed in this index.

The first part of the index lists all complete programs, while the second and third parts list all complete procedures, including those which form part of larger programs. Many of these programs and procedures are specific to the particular problem being solved, and should be treated simply as examples of how to write Fortran 77 programs, but a substantial number can be used with little or no modification in other programs. Particular examples of this latter category are those concerned with the implementation of various numerical methods.

Complete programs

Subroutines

Functions

Index

DATE DUE

MAY 0 6 1992			
DEC 1 6 1992			
2/18/93			
5-19-94			
8-21-94			

DEMCO